Development in Adolescence

Development in Adolescence

Hershel D. Thornburg

The University of Arizona

Brooks/Cole Publishing Company
Monterey, California
A Division of Wadsworth Publishing Company, Inc.

© 1975 by Wadsworth Publishing Company, Inc., Belmont, California 94002. All rights reserved. No part of this book may be reproduced, stored in a retrieval system, or transcribed, in any form or by any means—electronic, mechanical, photocopying, recording, or otherwise—without the prior written permission of the publisher: Brooks/Cole Publishing Company, Monterey, California 93940, a division of Wadsworth Publishing Company, Inc.

ISBN: 0-8185-0155-9
L.C. Catalog Card No.: 75-19936
Printed in the United States of America

10 9 8 7 6 5 4 3 2

Manuscript Editor: *Lyle York*
Production Editor: *Micky Lawler*
Interior Design: *Bernard Dix*
Cover Design: *John Edeen*
Cover Photograph: *Jim Pinckney*
Illustrations: *Robert Carlson*
Typesetting: *Holmes Composition Service, San Jose, California*
Printing & Binding: *R. R. Donnelley & Sons Co., Crawfordsville, Indiana*

Photographs on pages 6, 70, 108, 112, 160, 182, 253, 269, 301, and 418 and chapter-opening photos for Chapters 1, 3, 4, 5, 6, 7, 8, 9, 11, 12, 13, 14, and 15 by *Jim Pinckney*.

Photographs on pages 13, 46, 51, 101, 194, 224, and 431 and chapter-opening photo for Chapter 10 by *George Pearce*.

Photographs on pages 147, 157, 179, 213, 341, and 415 by *James H. Winkler*.

*To My Father,
Ellis Thornburg*

Preface

This book explores adolescent development from three perspectives: theory, research, and contemporary social forces. The third perspective represents a departure from the traditional basic text, because it is my conviction that the usual approach to adolescence fails to consider the relevant contemporary variables that affect adolescent development. The primary function of the text is to integrate a discussion of the adolescent's stabilities and changes with a treatment of modern environmental influences.

The book is designed as a basic text for the student of adolescent development at the undergraduate level. It is appropriate for courses dealing with adolescence in departments of psychology, human development and family life, nursing, home economics, education, or counseling. In short, this book is for anyone studying adolescence or dealing with adolescents on a daily basis.

The first chapter provides the reader with an orientation to the study of adolescence, placing some emphasis on the contemporary state of the field. Chapters 2, 3, and 4 provide basic historical, theoretical, and developmental information on adolescence. Chapter 5 discusses socialization, a critical aspect of adolescence. Chapters 6, 7, and 8 are devoted to the primary socialization forces interacting with adolescents—parents, peers, and the school. Chapter 9 considers the unique socialization processes faced by adolescents from disadvantaged and ethnic groups. The next four chapters discuss drug use, sexuality, and delinquency as both normal and abnormal forms of adolescent behavior. Because much behavior is motivated by the search for identity, Chapters 14 and 15 discuss various adolescent attempts to achieve self-awareness within society and the many routes, both traditional and nontraditional, that contemporary adolescents follow in their search.

Throughout the text, material accenting historical and contemporary aspects of adolescent development is set off from the main text in boxes. This book is similar in topic coverage to the newly published second edition of *Contemporary Adolescence: Readings*, because reaction to the topics included was highly favorable.

A textbook as a final product represents the cooperative efforts of the author and many others involved in the publishing process. In this respect, I am most grateful to Terry Hendrix of Brooks/Cole for his assistance in the writing project. I would especially like to thank Kenneth Russell of the University of Arizona for his criticism and guidance in the initial and later stages. I would also like to thank the other reviewers, whose suggestions were incorporated in the preparation of the final product: Frank B. W. Harper of the University of Western Ontario, John N. McCall of Southern Illinois University at Edwardsville, Elizabeth I. Mullins of Kent State University, and Dee L. Shepherd-Look of California State University, Northridge.

My dependence upon Alice Schoenberger, who typed the manuscript, made the writing-typing process a valuable interchange of ideas. In addition, I would like to thank Kathleen Ruyle, who also helped in the manuscript preparation. My final word of thanks goes to my wife, Ellen, who not only consistently supported me in my writing efforts but also provided invaluable help in the often tedious activities of preparing indexes and finding missing references.

Hershel D. Thornburg

Contents

1 Contemporary Adolescence   1

The Concept of Human Development   3
Stages of Development   4
Adolescent Developmental Tasks   4
The Development of Expressive Behavior   12

2 Adolescent Development: Philosophical and Theoretical Views   15

Early Philosophical Views of Man   16
The Beginning of a Systematic Theory of Adolescent Development   18
Theoretical Views of Adolescence   19

3 Physical and Emotional Growth   35

Physical Growth   36
Emotional Growth   53

4 Intellectual Growth   61

Early Theories of Intelligence   62
The Developing Cognitive Structure: Piaget   63
Special Characteristics of Adolescent Thought   71
Two Contemporary Theories of Intelligence   74

x   Contents

5 Developmental Socialization   79
Socialization and Culture   80
Developmental Socialization   84

6 The Adolescent in the Family   105
Structural Change within the Family   107
Family Structures and the Adolescent   110
The Adolescent's Search for Autonomy   111
Attitudes toward Home   118
One-Parent Families   135
Unwed Adolescent Mothers   139

7 Peer Relationships   143
Group Identification   144
Peers versus Parents   146
Is There an Adolescent Subculture?   151
The Generation Gap   167

8 The Adolescent and Education   175
Intellectual Developmental Needs   176
Is the School an Academic Institution?   177
Students' Attitudes toward School   181
How Parents View the Schools   190
How Teachers and Administrators View the School   191
Influences on Students' Educational Aspirations   193
Underachievement   202
Attrition   205
Curriculum Alternatives   210
Teaching Responsibility for Learning   212

9 Cultural Variations in Adolescence 217

Culture 218
Subculture 218
Counterculture 220
Crossculture 220
Culturally Different Youth in a Pluralistic Society 222
The Lower-Class Milieu 226
Puerto Ricans 227
Appalachian Whites 228
Migrant Workers 229
Indians 229
Mexican Americans 232
Blacks 236

10 The Social Use of Drugs in Adolescence 241

Drug Abuse 242
Drug Dependence 244
Drugs in Society 245
Drugs and the Social Environment 249
Alcohol 249
Nicotine 255
Barbiturates 257
Stimulants 259
Legal Drug Use 262

11 The Use of Illegal Drugs in Adolescence 265

Solvents 266
Marijuana 267
The Hallucinogens 274
The Narcotics 278
Multiple Drug Use 281
Extent of Drug Use 281
The Drug User 284
Drug Education 286

12 The Adolescent and Sex 293

Our Changing Sexual Norms 294
Dating 300
Petting 302
Premarital Sex: Attitudes 304
Premarital Sex: Behaviors 306
Permissiveness 308
Sex-Information Sources 314
Should There Be Sex Education in the Schools? 320

13 Adolescent Delinquency 331

Incidence of Delinquency 333
Official Treatment of Delinquents 335
The Roots of Delinquency 339
The Delinquent Subculture 343
Female Delinquency 356
Gang Delinquency 361
The Dropout and Delinquency 369
Preventing Delinquency 371

14 Identity Pursuits   381

The Identity Search and the Contemporary Adolescent   383
Activism   384
Alienation   390
The Counterculture   395

15 Aspirations and Self-Realizations   407

The World of Work   409
Adolescent Work Opportunities   413
Adolescent Work Motives   416
Work Opportunities for Disadvantaged Youth   423
Work Alternatives   425
Educational Aspirations   425
Women's Aspirations   431
Adolescent Marriage   433
Changing Life-Styles   436

References   439

Author Index   469

Subject Index   477

Contemporary Adolescence 1

Youth today have come to think of themselves as unique, as a generation of people who have little historical precedent, and as the unquestionable shapers of tomorrow. This viewpoint is not strictly American; it is often expressed by youth around the world. Finding themselves the focus of attention and clearly constituting a large proportion of the world's population, the youth of the 1960s attempted to change the social order by demanding reform and asserting their uniqueness. Thus, as we shall see in this chapter and throughout the text, contemporary social phenomena have a key role in the present-day conception of adolescence.

In contemporary terms, adolescence may be defined approximately as the age range of 11 to 22 years. The traditional age range of adolescence (13–18) is based more on the physiological growth and pubertal changes that occur in youth. The contemporary definition reflects increasing social as well as physical pressures on youth across a broader age span because of changing social structures. The definition might be broken down as shown in Figure 1.1.

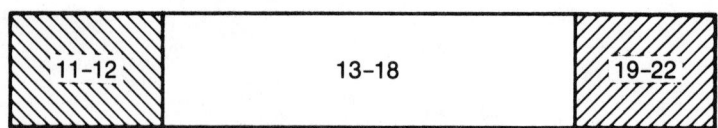

FIGURE 1.1. Traditional and contemporary age ranges for adolescence.

11–12: The contemporary view of adolescence encompasses these ages because of the involvement of youths in this age range in such behaviors as drug use, delinquency, sex, drinking, and smoking. In addition, their desire to imitate older adolescent models results from the suggestiveness of advertising and the mass media.

13–18: Although over the past 75 years the onset of puberty has gradually occurred at an earlier age (see Chapter 3), it is still appropriate to place puberty between the ages of 12 and 14 for most adolescents. Growth norms show a tapering off between 17 and 19. From a strictly physiological and biological vantage point, the age range of 13–18 still constitutes an adequate definition of adolescence.

19–22: The contemporary view of adolescence also includes this age range because of changes in social phenomena. Greater involvement among youth in post-high-school education and occupational training, and, sometimes, delay in marital plans, has delayed entrance into the adult world and caused the transition to become more ambiguous than traditionally. The exception is, of course, the youths of this age group who become employed, perhaps also married, during or after high school. For them, adolescence ends earlier.

THE CONCEPT OF HUMAN DEVELOPMENT

Yet, despite the changing social phenomena that have brought about the contemporary view of adolescence, it is important at the beginning of this book to view the study of adolescence within a larger context—the study of human development. Although adolescence is a unique, somewhat distinct period, it has its antecedents in childhood and is the forerunner of adulthood. By understanding how adolescence relates to other developmental periods, we can better understand contemporary adolescent behavior patterns.

Human development refers to the progressive growth of a living organism over time, from the simple single cell at conception to the vastly complex adult being. Development is thought to be basically biological. It not only organizes life but also differentiates structure and function. Two processes, *growth* and *maturation*, describe the structural developmental changes that occur.

Structural Development

Growth is the *quantitative* change in bodily dimensions. Such change occurs not only externally—change in body size, for example—but also internally, as in organ and brain size. The rate of an individual's growth varies; some parts of the body grow at faster rates than other parts. However, regardless of rate, physical growth is measurable. For example, the head size of a child can be measured at 3 months and then again at 6 months to determine growth. Or a child's head size could be measured at 3 months and compared to the average child's head size at that same period.

Change in an organism can also be *qualitative*, and this process is called *maturation*. Such development is internal; for example, cells become increasingly organized and inter-related, although gross bodily changes may not be observed. Growth and maturation are both physical processes and are, of necessity, related. In fact, both structural processes probably occur simultaneously in the individual. That is, while cell reproduction increases the size of the hand, the existing nerve cells interrelate with the new cells, thus changing the quality of the hand as well.

Functional Development

In development, when a person becomes aware of the physical and social environment and its benefits or dangers, he or she becomes an interacting organism. Through *development* and *learning*, ways of viewing one's life processes emerge. Now the individual not only is physical in nature but, through interaction and learning, has become emotional, intellectual, and social as well. Later we shall consider in more depth the adolescent's emotional, intellectual, and social development.

STAGES OF DEVELOPMENT

The study of human development generally views a person as moving from one stage of life to another. The individual has been studied through infancy, childhood, preadolescence, adolescence, young adulthood, and old age. Table 1.1 provides an overview of these stages of development. The age ranges shown in the figure represent the span of time in which there is a shift in emphasis within the development and learning processes. At best, specific ages to designate movement from one major concern to another are arbitrary. It would be more accurate to view growth and maturation as a continuous process, in which the phenomena of each stage would be superimposed on the continuum with the dynamics of preceding stages. The goals or tasks within a specific stage and the way each stage moves into the succeeding stage would also be shown.

For example, Willmott (1966) found that during adolescence most individuals withdraw from the mixed-age society of childhood into the single-age society of their peers, and that as they mature toward courtship and marriage they rejoin the mixed-age society as adults. The reason for the movement into strong adolescent peer groups is multifaceted. Probably the primary reason, although most adolescents are unaware of it, is that the transition from childhood to adulthood involves several dramatic changes; adolescents essentially must give up childhood, resolve identity issues, and gain some insight into what adult roles they must play.

ADOLESCENT DEVELOPMENTAL TASKS

During the different developmental stages of an individual's life, he or she must encounter and resolve major events that will influence

TABLE 1.1. Stages of human development.

Infancy

    Prenatal period   (conception to birth)
    Neonatal period   (birth to 4–6 weeks)
    Infancy   (4–6 weeks to 2 years)

Childhood

    Early childhood   (2 years to 5 years)
    Middle childhood   (6 years to 8 years)
    Late childhood   (9 years to 11 years) ⎫
                                                          ⎬ Preadolescence

Adolescence   ⎭ (9 to 13 years)

    Early adolescence   (11 years to 13 years)
    Middle adolescence   (14 years to 16 years)
    Late adolescence   (17 years to 19 years)

Young adulthood

    College-age youth   (18 years to 23 years)
    Young adulthood   (24 years to 29 years)

Adulthood

    Early adulthood   (30 years to 45 years)
    Middle adulthood   (45 years to 55 years)
    Late adulthood   (55 years to 65 years)
    Old age   (65 years and beyond)

behavior and learning. The pioneering work of Robert Havighurst in 1943 described these major events as *developmental tasks*, which occur from birth through old age. Havighurst divided his developmental stages into (1) infancy and early childhood, (2) middle childhood, (3) adolescence, (4) early adulthood, (5) middle age, and (6) late maturity. Here we will consider only the preadolescent (Thornburg, 1970c) and adolescent age ranges. (Preadolescence is the age range along the continuum between the end of childhood and the beginning of adolescence.)

In 1952 Havighurst set forth a series of ten tasks that should be accomplished during the adolescent life span.

1. Forming new and more mature relations with agemates of both sexes
2. Achieving a masculine or feminine social role
3. Accepting one's physique and using the body effectively
4. Achieving emotional independence from parents and other adults
5. Achieving assurance of economic independence
6. Selecting and preparing for an occupation
7. Preparing for marriage and family life
8. Developing intellectual skills and concepts necessary for civic competence

Growing up is a recurring theme in the adolescent's mind.

9. Acquiring a set of ethics as a guide to behavior
10. Desiring and achieving socially responsible behavior

Developmental tasks may be defined as skills, knowledge, functions, or attitudes that an individual normally acquires during a specific period of his or her life. *Physical maturation* is a necessary, although not totally sufficient, condition for resolving developmental tasks. In adolescence, for example, renewed sexual energies set the condition and need for forming new and more mature relationships with agemates of both sexes (Task 1). *Cultural expectations* also set for the individual a series of developmental tasks. For example, striving for economic independence and learning socially responsible behaviors are culturally determined needs. A third force, *personal values,* also establishes conditions for necessary developmental tasks. Acquiring a set of ethics as a guide to behavior (Task 9) and selecting and preparing for an occupation (Task 6) illustrate personal motives for task accomplishment.

Most tasks, including those with a strong biological basis, are affected by social approval or disapproval. Furthermore, society determines to some extent the timetable an adolescent must use to work out different tasks. Post-World War II industrial and technological changes, a shift from rural to urban living, and ongoing social changes cause us to view these tasks somewhat differently than we would have viewed them at the time that Havighurst initiated his theory (Thornburg, 1970a). Havighurst has also attested to the changes that have occurred in the past three decades in the revision of his developmental tasks, which appeared in 1972.

In his 1972 book, Havighurst set down a revised set of eight developmental tasks. In his revision, he considered particular contemporary social and cultural phenomena affecting the resolution of each task. There is an additional developmental task to which Havighurst has given little attention. We will refer to this task as developing conceptual and problem-solving skills. Figure 1.2 presents this additional task (Task 9), along with Havighurst's revised developmental tasks, and the age ranges at which they are projected to be resolved. In our text discussion, we will consider these tasks in the order in which they are usually resolved.

Task 1. Forming new and more mature relationships with age-mates of both sexes. During preadolescence, most peer relationships are formed with members of the same sex, including close friendships. The preadolescent's behavior patterns are beginning to be shaped by peers. The behavior patterns exhibited are often what the preadolescent thinks the group expects (Gordon, 1962).

Initially, peer development in adolescence occurs among isolated same-sex cliques. Dunphy (1963) suggests that this same-sex group represents the persistence of the preadolescent gang into the adolescent period. As these youths move into junior high school, their peer associations become more heterosexual, although on a more limited basis than during middle adolescence. They often enter cautiously into heterosexual interaction, generally within the security of group settings where members of the same sex are present (Thornburg, 1970a).

Heterosexual involvements are instrumental in learning proper sex roles, a development that is crucial to our consideration of acceptable adolescent social behaviors. By high school, almost all boys and girls are socializing with the opposite sex. Havighurst (1972) notes that from the age of 12 or 13 on most adolescents are involved in social experimentation, and that at ages 14 to 16 there is a movement toward more intimate and less group companionship.

Task 2. Achieving a masculine or feminine social role. Social phenomena have caused the traditional wife-and-mother role to give way to a great extent to the alternative roles now available to the female. With increasing acceptance of female aggressiveness, greater educational opportunities for women, the accelerated movement of females into the occupational world, greater sexual freedom, liberalized abortion laws, contraceptives, and an attitude that all members of the family should share in housework, today's adolescent female has more choices available than her counterpart of earlier generations.

Adolescent males are not thrown into so ambiguous a role dilemma, since most social and occupational positions are still allocated to men. The tendency to stereotype occupations by sex gives most adolescent males aspirational advantages over adolescent females. Havighurst (1972) suggests, however, that the woman's entrance into the occupational world has caused the man's role to be more broadly defined.

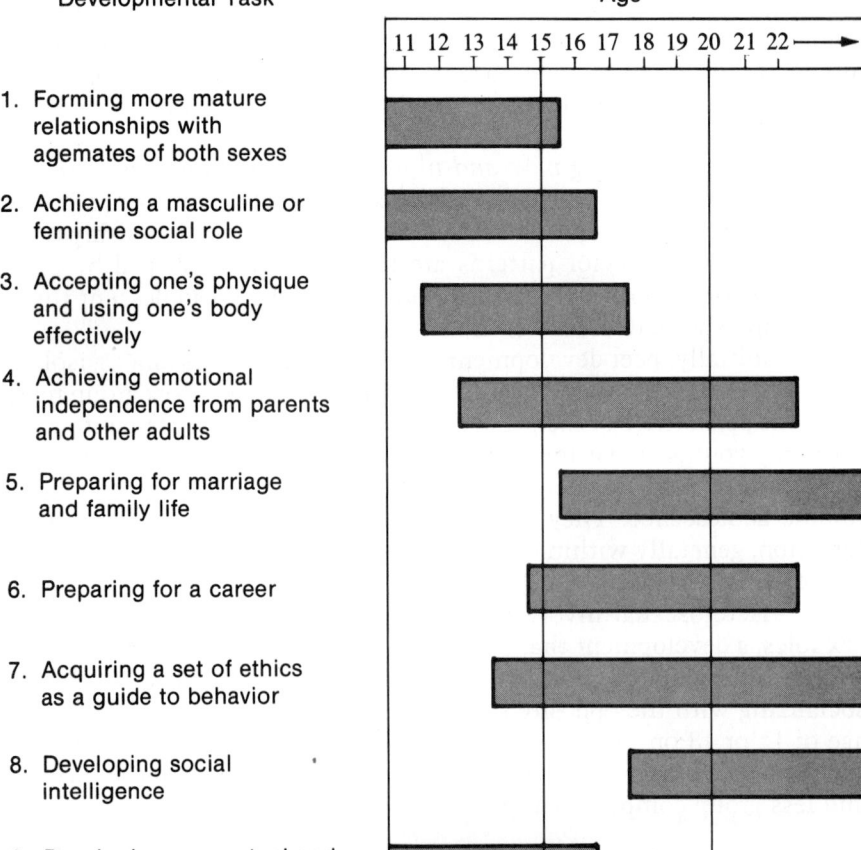

FIGURE 1.2. Havighurst's developmental tasks and the age range at which they are generally resolved.

Task 9. Confirming concepts and learning problem-solving skills. During the period of adolescence, the individual's intellectual capacity completes its development. Throughout his or her elementary school experiences, the child develops simple concepts of logic and reasoning. These concepts come about through assigning meaning to things within the environment. With the help of concrete props, the child learns to deduce and to solve problems. With the later acquisition of more varied concepts and with an increase in ability to solve problems, the preadolescent (around age 11) develops the facility to perform mental operations abstractly, without the help of concrete props.

By the time the individual reaches adolescence, he or she acquires the language skills necessary to think abstractly. The adolescent also learns to think reflectively, to hypothesize, and to solve complex problems. At the same time, the adolescent expands his or her knowledge in particular subject areas and applies academic skills to everyday experiences. By 16 or 17, the adolescent has developed, through maturation, all of the components for thinking. He or she now has the capacity for adult thought in elementary form.

Task 3. Accepting one's physique and using the body effectively. Havighurst describes this task as to "become proud, or at least tolerant, of one's body; to use and protect one's body effectively and with personal satisfaction" (1972, p. 51). A major problem for adolescents during this period is learning how to channel sexual energy and drive into socially acceptable behaviors. This problem is often compounded by the adolescent's criticism of his or her physical appearance, early maturation, parental overprotectiveness, and in some cases religious influence.

Many attitudes toward one's body derive from comparison of oneself with others. Adolescents are particularly concerned with height, weight, complexion, size of hips and breasts in females, and size of genitals and muscles in males (Angelino & Mech, 1955a). These anxieties are accentuated by society's emphasis on early maturation and physical attractiveness. The closer an adolescent's body fits the cultural stereotype, the greater is his or her reinforcement and the less anxiety he or she feels. As adolescents begin to accept themselves for what they are, anxiety about personal appearance is reduced and elements of personal pride begin to appear.

Task 4. Achieving emotional independence from parents and other adults. Achieving independence has always been difficult for American adolescents. As they develop peer relationships, they exercise behavioral independence; but in so doing they often run into conflicts with parents and the adult world. Such conflicts are often generated by the adolescent's need to relinquish childhood ties with parents and to find sufficient independent behaviors that are not overpowering. Physical maturation causes the adolescent to want fewer controls and inhibitions from parents. Increased social skills learned through peer interaction facilitate self-reliance and create a degree of emotional as well as behavioral independence. Yet, occasionally, rapid and drastic behavioral change only intensifies adolescent conflict. Therefore, although youths should learn to throw off their habits of dependency on adults, the goal is often best accomplished with a degree of parental guidance.

Task 5. Preparing for marriage and family life. Adolescents experience physical and emotional attraction to the opposite sex. As attachments become deeper, attitudes toward sexual involvement, marital commitments, and child rearing emerge. Common interests, similar tastes, comparable ideologies, and effective communication broaden the adolescent's awareness and may allow for the emergence of a realistic attitude toward marriage.

Three Cheers for the Girl Scouts!

The Girl Scout Council in Philadelphia has been under severe criticism recently from parents who object to a new merit badge called "To Be a Woman." To earn the badge, Scouts must visit an abortion clinic. One irate parent's reaction was "If a girl needs this sex information, she has violated the Girl Scout pledge to be clean in thought, word, and deed."

The individual's attitude toward the sexual encounter is only one phase of learning the total sex role. No single code of sexual morality or behavior exists today. The results of contemporary attitudes toward sex are the diverse expressions of adolescent sexuality. Societal pressure for adolescent male sexual involvement seems to be greater than for female involvement (Reiss, 1967). With the gradual decline of the double standard, however, this discrepancy may disappear (Smigel & Seiden, 1968). However, for the adolescent male, premarital intercourse tends to increase self-esteem, because he sees this act as a "conquest in which he has fulfilled a goal and has enhanced his own narcissism" (Fink, 1970, p. 46). It may well be that, in both the male and the female, adolescent sexual activity is precipitated more by societal expectations and personal fantasies than by personal needs.

Task 6. Selecting and preparing for an occupation. To a considerable extent, both industrialization and automation are related to occupational opportunity. They have made the tasks of achieving assurance of economic independence and selecting and preparing for an occupation more difficult in our society. Automation has reduced the number of unskilled and semiskilled jobs, thus eliminating many opportunities for meaningful work experiences for youth.

Havighurst (1972) believes that the effects of a highly productive economy and a decreasing job market have (1) decreased the ethical value of work and preparation for an occupation, (2) made economic independence nearly impossible for the vast majority of young people under 18, and (3) made a career more difficult to plan and to prepare for. The developmental task of selecting an occupation or a career is increasingly becoming a challenge for adolescent females. Many jobs once awarded only to males are now given to qualified females. Yet two factors make the task more complex for females than for males: many occupations are still not accessible to them, so they must discern which choices are most realistic; and their choices may be tentative, depending on when and whom they marry.

Occupational mobility, job obsolescence, and stricter job requirements therefore point out the importance of making adolescents aware of the changing occupational world. Indeed, perhaps the most successful career prototype is the adolescent who acquires transferable occupational skills.

Task 7. Acquiring a set of ethics as a guide to behavior. An individual's value system begins to form through the social-psychological influences of the family. Throughout childhood the individual is educated into the parental value system. During adolescence the individual's values are tested by experiences outside the family. Although adolescents may become disenchanted with the beliefs of their parents and society, they must either accept such values or find alternatives. Thus the adolescent accepts some parental values, rejects others, and modifies still others. Gradually the adolescent develops a personal value system and a philosophy of life. Using this personal value system, the adolescent learns to resolve ambiguities and to accept himself as an individual.

Since the 1940s, there has been a decrease in religious interest in America. Individuals have developed new ethical codes and practices that do not center around any religious dogma. Although recent research indicates an increasing concern for religion today among the general population (Thornburg, 1969c, 1971d), many adolescents consider traditional religions meaningless and can find no help within their framework. For these reasons, many young people have adopted Eastern religions in order to find new understanding of life and fulfill their religion needs. Through parents, peers, religion, philosophy, and ideals, a value hierarchy emerges in the adolescent and serves as a guide for subsequent adult behavior.

Task 8. Developing a social intelligence. Because the learning of social and civic skills generally follows the learning of academic skills, this task is usually not accomplished before late adolescence. Young people acquire civic intelligence through an understanding of what society gives to them and, in turn, of what they may give to society. However, not all individuals are capable of achieving this understanding to the same degree.

In today's complex society, the social order often becomes confused, and civic responsibility frequently is lost in the apparent inconsistencies of our political structure. As a result, today's youth must learn new coping skills. One such skill includes the ability to tolerate ambiguity. Not all things are black or white; not every question can be answered. A second skill is the ability to delay gratification (Hollister, 1966). To take a responsible role in the social and political system, adolescents must understand that some things take time. A third social skill is the ability to tolerate seemingly insoluble problems within our society, such as civil rights and international conflict. The individual's ability to cope with such problems can strengthen his or her personal frame of reference.

THE DEVELOPMENT OF EXPRESSIVE BEHAVIOR

Throughout the ages, humans have adapted to the changing environment. Today's adolescent finds a social order somewhat removed from

---

The succession principle

The succession principle in biology asserts that in the natural evolution of communities or habitats, the distribution of species changes in response to the evolving demands of the settings and its surrounding environment, leading in time to progressive changes in the structure of the society and the flow of energy. In the present context, the concept of succession stresses the time perspective in viewing the evolution of schools as they respond and adapt to surrounding social, technological, and demographic changes. Such a perspective includes two aspects: (a) an historical awareness of those past events and personalities which shape current norms, policies, and student characteristics; and (b) an anticipatory problem-solving perspective which is future- and planning-oriented. It suggests the continuous scanning of the environment to assess potential problems and identify potential opportunities. For example, a legislated change in the racial composition of the school serves as a current reminder that the lack of a planning orientation can signal turmoil and increased polarization in the school culture. The succession principle helps to find the means by which the social environment assesses and copes with the impact of its changing surroundings.*

---

*From E. J. Trickett and D. M. Todd, "The High School Culture: An Ecological Perspective," *Theory into Practice,* 1972, *11*(1), 30.

Contemporary Adolescence 13

the natural order and more aligned with the perceived needs of humans. Although critical changes occur in today's adolescent, they are not unlike those changes that occurred in previous generations. The difference lies within our society and the adolescent's interaction with it. "A man, viewed as a behaving system, is quite simple. The apparent complexity of his behavior over time is largely a reflection of the complexity of the environment in which he finds himself" (Simon, 1969, p. 23).

The past 15 years have brought about dramatic changes in expressive behavior in some adolescents. This behavior has been expressed through involvement in drugs, delinquency, crime, sex, ecology, civil rights, politics, foreign affairs, and education. The 1960s brought into sharp focus the vulnerability of youth to social, economic, and political

Contrary to the popular idea, adolescent energies are not always misused.

forces. Adolescents have been influenced by society and the media as well as by peers in their behavioral patterns. In 1960, 60 million Elvis Presley records alone were sold, a figure far surpassed later by the number of Beatles recordings sold. The advent of the "new morality" in the middle 1960s led to more open sexual expression among youth. In 1964, student activism moved into its overt rebellion stage, beginning with the Free Speech Movement at the University of California, Berkeley. The Timothy Leary cults also sprang up in Greenwich Village during the mid-1960s. Political and international concerns became more openly manifest with the Vietnam protests and draft evasion. This new behavioral style of adolescents resulted largely from their inability to understand the complex sociocultural milieu of the period and their attempts to resolve both personal and social issues, which had taken on an urgency for them.

This chapter has oriented you to some of the broadly defined social changes that have occurred in our society as well as basic developmental resolutions that today's youth must encounter. It is not meant to present an exhaustive view of contemporary social phenomena; we will look more closely at such phenomena in the following chapters.

To consider contemporary social phenomena as the defining characteristic of adolescent behavior would be somewhat inaccurate. It would negate the concept of human development. In looking at adolescent behavior, we must consider two factors. First, whatever the total adolescent is, he does not occur in a vacuum. We must consider his childhood antecedents as well as his contemporary circumstances. Second, the social changes that have occurred since World War II also have historical roots, which we will examine throughout the book.

Adolescent Development: Philosophical and Theoretical Views 2

Before the birth of the modern study of adolescent psychology, theories of adolescent development were not clearly distinguished from theories of child development. Because these theories were often based on philosophical and theological views of mankind, it might be useful to our later study of adolescent developmental theories to consider briefly some of these positions now.

EARLY PHILOSOPHICAL VIEWS OF MAN

Scientific theories of human development provide partial explanations of various physiological and maturational processes affecting individual growth. Theories before 1900 commonly based their hypotheses on personal experiences, philosophical thought, or religious beliefs. In this sense, they are seen as prescientific explanations of development. The child was viewed as the eventual adult, and little differentiation was made between one developmental stage and the next. Growth was viewed as continuous quantitative—not qualitative—change.

Greek Philosophy

Plato's writings provide the basis for the early Greek philosophy of the nature of man. Plato thought that education was meaningful if it provided experiences for children before they reached the age of reason, adolescence. Each child was to be recognized for his individual differences and each child guided into those areas for which he seemed most suited. Plato expressed concern for the importance of training children early so that they would easily adjust to adult life and their role in an occupation.

Plato saw man as having two distinct aspects—body and soul; but in considering the nature of man Plato emphasized the soul, which he viewed as having three distinct components. The first component was man's desires and appetites. In essence, this element was the instinctual part of man, which left alone would not only seek gratification but serve to make man unwise and foolhardy. Plato envisioned the second component of the soul to be characterized by *temperance, endurance,* and *conviction.* Finally, Plato saw the third element of the soul to be *rationality,* which he described as the supernatural, immortal part of man. For Plato, reason was the real soul of man, and it freed the soul from the body, the ultimate goal in man's striving. In Plato's view, this aspect of man was the last to emerge developmentally. Nevertheless, the basis for eventual rational thought was found in one's childhood training, which guided and fulfilled individual aptitudes.

Predeterminism

Some 300 years after the time of Christ, the doctrine of *innate sin* (or original sin) was the dominant view of the nature of man in the Western world. According to this view, the child was born with the tendency to sin and possessed, by nature, moral weaknesses and desires to do wrong. To overcome this innate sin—embodied in the flesh—it was believed that man must be redeemed, that he must learn to communicate with God so that his soul could be transformed to immortal worthiness. Until the time of the philosopher Jean Jacques Rousseau, this viewpoint went unchallenged. Rousseau, however, claimed that man was innately good and that he learned to do wrong from his environment.

Then, in the seventeenth century, the philosopher John Locke refuted both doctrines—of innate sin and innate good—by proposing that at birth the mind was a blank slate. He believed that the mind contained no inherent thought but was highly impressionable and susceptible to environmental influences. Although he did not view man as being predisposed to any specific behavior, Locke, like Plato, saw the ultimate of man's striving to be the emergence of rationality. He strongly believed that man should deny himself his emotional desires and follow reason.

In the nineteenth century, Jean Lamarck, a French zoologist, placed renewed emphasis on Locke's position. Lamarck believed that man was devoid of innate tendencies at birth. Perhaps the most striking aspect of his theory was that, whereas he believed that an individual learned traits through environmental influence, he also maintained that the individual genetically transmitted those traits to offspring. This view, known as *predeterminism*, made environment the crucial variable in determining the nature of man, while allowing for some genetic trait transmission from generation to generation.

Preformationism

According to the theory of *preformation*, man's tendencies and characteristics exist at birth. The original proponent of preformationism was Tertullian, a second-century Christian who advanced the doctrine of innate sin. Preformationism was a widespread philosophy during the periods of Renaissance and Reformation, exemplified in the doctrines of John Calvin. All behavioral determinants were thought to be predestined, and therefore qualitatively the child and the eventual adult would be the same. The child was not considered distinctive as a child but was instead perceived as a miniature adult. Development thus was thought to be simply a matter of quantitative growth. This position is reflected in the art of the pre-Renaissance period, in which we see youngsters dressed as miniature adults rather than in children's clothes.

Evolution

Since the publication of Charles Darwin's *Origin of Species* (1859) and later his *The Descent of Man* (1871), the theoretical questions about the nature of man and the seemingly unquenchable thirst for understanding human development thrust us into a new age of scientific exploration. Darwin has been referred to as the most vital single force in establishing child psychology as a scientific discipline (Mussen, Conger, & Kagan, 1974).

According to Darwin's theory, "Biological life is continuous, from a single cell organism, through numerous, more complex stages to the ultimate human mind and body" (Muuss, 1968, p. 31). Darwin advocated a *phylogenetic* position—that is, the evolution of a genetically related species or race—by searching for evidences of man in animal life.[1] Darwin believed that there was a natural biological selection process. To survive, Darwin said, man had to be an adaptive organism. Since environments in the world differed, variations in man emerged and were inherited by offspring.

Of necessity, Darwin rejected earlier, unscientific theories. "The notion of innate ideas or innate sin was a highly popularized concept of human development until Darwin's writings, and even later among those who completely rejected Darwin's evolution theories" (Thornburg, 1973b, p. 2). In many respects Darwin's work provided the transition from the unscientific to the scientific study of man, by regarding man as a biological species within the natural order. In contrast, most pre-Darwinian philosophical and theological positions were based upon a dichotomy between man and the rest of nature. Without question, his theory was the immediate forerunner to the concepts of adolescent psychology advanced by G. Stanley Hall.

THE BEGINNING OF A SYSTEMATIC THEORY OF ADOLESCENT DEVELOPMENT

The modern movement of adolescent development is thought to have begun with G. Stanley Hall's work on adolescence. His classic book on adolescence, written in 1904, presents what is probably the first systematic theory of this developmental period in the world (Ross, 1972). Several conceptions were forerunners to Hall's theory:

---

[1] In contrast to Darwin's theory, Locke's position reflected *ontogeny*—the development of an individual organism. Lamarck's theory considered both phylogeny and ontogeny. Supporting Locke's environmental position, Lamarck's view attests to ontogeny. However, his view that learned traits can be genetically transmitted to offspring attests to phylogeny.

1. Plato's ideas on the components of man's soul share some parallels with Hall's views. Like Plato, who conceived man's desires and appetites as an instinctual part of the soul, Hall envisioned the basic part of man as instinctual. Furthermore, he saw this basic aspect of humans as characteristic of children's early behavior. In addition, Plato's idea of rationality as the last aspect of man to emerge is similar to Hall's conception. Hall viewed civilized man as the final phase of development—a point reached after 25 years of age.
2. In his book *Emile* Rousseau referred to the critical events of puberty, its subsequent sexual urges, and an impending period of emotional conflict.
3. Some 100 years before Hall, Lamarck advanced his theory of acquired characteristics. This idea that traits learned by one generation can be passed on to the next appealed to Hall. Like Lamarck, he recognized that, although man is basically biological, environmental forces are sometimes persuasive in man's development.
4. Accepting the theories of Darwin, Hall extended Darwin's idea of evolution in his theory of *recapitulation*, which maintains that the human growth period is a re-enactment of the history of mankind (Alissi, 1972).
5. Ernst Haeckel, a contemporary of Darwin, supported Darwin's position by advancing a biogenetic law that essentially states that complex living forms descend from simple ones. Thus, ontogeny (the individual's development) is a brief and rapid repetition of phylogeny (the evolution of a species) (Haeckel, 1879). Later, Hall endorsed this position.

The child-study movement, which began in 1882, proposed to collect data on children and adolescents as part of renewed scientific interest in man's nature. Hall promoted the movement and, during this period, worked out most of the structural divisions between child and adolescent development. In fact, it has been suggested that Hall's 1904 book was the highlight of the entire child-study movement (Ross, 1972).

THEORETICAL VIEWS OF ADOLESCENCE

Recapitulation Theory: G. Stanley Hall

It is indeed accurate to say that Hall made the first significant distinction between childhood and adolescence. The backbone of his theory was the idea that man re-enacts, or relives, each major stage in the evolution of mankind. Based on Darwinism, this genetic viewpoint contended that the "experiential history of mankind becomes a part of the genetic constitution of the individual" (Beller, 1973, p. 103). Hall saw infancy as a recapitulation of the prehistoric stage and childhood as a re-enactment of the cave-dwelling stage (Alissi, 1972). In fact, Hall viewed the child as considerably more ancient than the man. Because he viewed the child as a half-anthropoid ancestor of man (1909), in effect, he considered the adolescent to be the transition between the ancestral child and the emergent man. To Hall, however, the period of adolescence was not merely a transitional stage; it was also a necessary evolutionary stage during which man became a more complete organism. In this vein, Hall wrote that adolescence was the "bud and promise for the race" (1904, p. 50).

Hall agreed with anthropologist Lewis Henry Morgan's three stages of mankind. From 8 to 12 years of age, Morgan believed that the child is in a savage stage characterized by instinct. He maintained that, from 12 to 25, the individual is in the barbarian stage, the time during which the emotions begin emerging. This stage corresponds to the period

It's hard to imagine that these miniature-adult clothing styles were popular in the early twentieth century.

Hall calls adolescence. Finally, from age 25 on, man has reached the point of being civilized—a view comparable to our idea of rational man today.[2]

Storm and stress. In his discussion of the adolescent period, Hall's biogenetic view gave way to the idea of social and environmental forces more than it did in any other stage. He referred to these forces as *Sturm und Drang* (storm and stress) and described adolescence as a period of inevitable emotional conflict and contradictions. In effect, he maintained that as the demands for socialization increase society places less emphasis on physical growth and more emphasis on social, emotional, and cognitive growth. While the adolescent is coping with the culmination of physical and mental growth, the socialization process is making conflicting demands. The disharmony between the developing adolescent and society creates the inevitable storm and stress.

Eventually, psychoanalytic writers came to view Hall's idea of storm and stress as somewhat simplistic, although they did not deny its existence. Furthermore, Margaret Mead's (1928) study of the Samoan culture cast doubt on the inevitability of storm and stress for all adolescents, indicating that it is culturally rather than biologically bound. Nevertheless, Hall's contention that social and emotional experiences are instrumental in thrusting the adolescent toward maturity is a basic postulate with which few theorists disagree.

Intellectual growth. Hall saw corollaries between the child's way of thinking and primitive thinking, but he viewed the adolescent's mentality as a form of individual expression. Although Hall advocated drill and memorization for the child, he believed that these forms of rote learning must give way to experiential learning, gained through the adolescent's new interests and desires for freedom. "There is an outburst of growth that needs a large part of the total kinetic energy of the body. There is a new interest in adolescents, a passion to be treated as an equal by one's elders, to make plans for the future, a new sensitiveness to adult praise or blame" (Hall, 1904, p. 453). Hall felt that the adolescent keenly responded to his environment and should be given the latitude to explore it and to express himself. He also believed that the mind was still in a state of plasticity, a factor that could cause the mind to grow in leaps and

---

[2]It is interesting to speculate that the social stress on human development runs almost in reverse to Morgan's and Hall's descriptions of man's development. Within our society development of rational or intellectual man is given high priority. Emotional man is slow to develop, and instinctual man finds few avenues of legitimate expression. These discrepancies might lead us to hypothesize that today's youth live in an intensified storm-and-stress period.

bounds on the one hand and to become fatigued and reluctant to learn on the other.

Many of Hall's contemporaries felt that he had overstated the saltatory way in which the adolescent developed. His emphasis on adolescence caused him to ignore child development and to advocate that adolescents may be even more instrumental than adults in precipitating social reform. As a result, Hall was sharply criticized and never given the prestige that so often comes to an innovative theorist.

Biological Theory: Arnold Gesell

The idea that biological determinants are a major shaping force in adolescent development was advanced by Arnold Gesell as a result of his longitudinal study of the developing human from birth to age 16. Gesell was one of Hall's students, and he accepted much of Hall's theory. However, he placed more emphasis than did Hall on the observable behaviors of the child and adolescent and on the role of environmental variables in adolescent development. Gesell believed that the pattern of human growth followed certain laws of maturation and did not, in fact, follow the theory of evolution of the human race (phylogeny) and the idea of individual development of the child (ontogeny). He felt that through maturation and positive or negative environmental factors an individual learns how to adjust, and thus that behavior is a form of conscious rather than unconscious growth.

Gesell described adolescence as a period of rapid and intense physical growth in which the changes occurring in the body are so profound that they involve all aspects of the organism (1956). For the most part, Gesell's theory is normative; that is, through observation he concluded that certain behaviors at certain points in maturation characterized most adolescents.

Age groups. In his study of human development, Gesell found particular characteristics in the age range between 10 and 16 that he applied to his ideas on adolescence as a whole. According to Gesell, the 10-year-old is in a developmental stage of equilibrium. Marking the consummation of several years of childhood growth—both physical and mental—this year seems to be an interlude period. Dominant characteristics of this age are stability, good family adjustment, confidence, and educational assimilation.

In Gesell's view, the 11-year-old is in a year of transition. A youth of this age becomes quarrelsome and argumentative, often rebellious. Questions about the family arise, extreme moods appear, and traces of individuality are observed. In short, this is a period of disequilibrium, a factor Gesell attributed to impending biological changes.

Gesell describes the 12-year-old as "predisposed to be positive and enthusiastic rather than negative and reticent" (1956, p. 105). The peer group takes on increasing importance. The 12-year-old is more objective, less self-centered, and less argumentative than he or she was in the transition stage. A growing concern for social recognition is noticed.

As the adolescent reaches 13, according to Gesell, he or she tends to withdraw from the family and to become introspective. Corollary to changes in body structure and chemistry are greater insecurity and anxiety in regard to self. The 13-year-old distinctly views him- or herself as an adolescent, having abandoned childlike behaviors.

According to Gesell, the 14-year-old is more outward and enthusiastic than younger adolescents. Friendships are tremendously expanded as the adolescent of this age seeks peers who will support his or her ego ideals. The 14-year-old is more idealistic, often to the extent of worshiping movie stars and sports figures. At this age, the adolescent becomes interested in being accepted by others—in whether he or she has "personality."

Gesell characterizes the 15-year-old as outgrowing parental control and attempting to break away from it, as well as from the control of other authority figures and institutions such as the school. This pursuit of autonomy results from the adolescent's insatiable need for independence. Self-awareness, perception, and feelings grow. Although he or she is often quiet and withdrawn during these periods of trying to break away from control, the adolescent is vulnerable to feelings of anger, hostility, and violence.

Finally, Gesell describes the 16-year-old, the prototype of the preadult (Muuss, 1968), as displaying greater social adjustment and emotional control than he or she did at a younger age. With the search for independence virtually completed, self-confidence replaces rebellion, and serious thoughts of the future—that is, educational plans, occupational aspirations, and marriage—begin to appear.

In his descriptions of these age groups, Gesell presents normative data on what thoughts, feelings, and behaviors are prevalent at each age. He also suggests decisive differences in the calmness or the storminess of growth at each age. He maintains that movements from equilibrium to disequilibrium to equilibrium are the maturational states that cause the adolescent to grow. In retrospect, Gesell's description of these transitions from year to year is comparable to Hall's position on storm and stress.

Psychoanalytic Theory: Sigmund Freud

Like Gesell, Sigmund Freud agreed with Hall that human development is biological. Freud maintained that such development is marked by a series of stages, which are biologically universal to humans. In his description of these stages, Freud places more emphasis on the first decade of life than on later years, contending that to a great extent the individual's development through adolescence to adulthood has its roots in the successful or unsuccessful resolution of childhood developmental stages. Freud believed that these stages originated in the sexual instinct, which he called the *id*. (Freud's concept of the id is a striking parallel to Plato's idea of desires and appetites as the instinctual part of man.) Further, he believed that this sexual instinct was the primary factor in determining whether the individual's personality development would be normal. In addition to the id, Freud postulated the *ego* and the *superego*. The ego is the rational, civilized, reality-oriented part of man. Since it possesses a perceptual quality, it may control or modify instinctual urges. The ego also has coping mechanisms for dealing with the environment. The superego, commonly referred to as the conscience, may assist the ego by defining socially acceptable attitudes and behaviors.

Freud constructed five stages of development ranging from birth to late adolescence (see Table 2.1). Let's take a look at these psychosexual stages and consider their relationship to adolescent development.

Oral stage. During this stage, the mouth is the primary erogenous zone. The child generally experiences pleasure by stimulating the lips and tongue—the sucking response—during feeding periods and especially by coming into physical contact with the mother. Any interference with the feeding (sucking) process, Freud believed, leads to fear and anxiety or frustration. If the sucking needs are satisfied, the child feels secure. "The infant's feeding experience is presumed to have not only short-term effects of relative satisfaction or frustration, but long-term consequences as well. Excessive gratification of oral impulses, too intense frustration, or a combination of the two will lead to oral fixation" (Ferguson, 1970, p. 55). The orally dissatisfied baby may in his later adolescent behaviors be distrusting and insecure, according to Freud.

Anal stage. By the age of 18 months to 2 years, the child becomes aware of the gratification associated with defecation. The child learns to experience gratification by eliminating or withholding feces. Elimination activity is an automatic (reflexive) process for the young child. During the anal stage, the child physiologically matures enough to be able to control the anal sphincter, thus withholding feces at will.

With the beginning of toilet training, the child learns to regulate his or her reflexive impulses. In so doing, the child not only begins to feel autonomous but is often interested in the feces. The child does not see them as disgusting or as having an intolerable odor; only through interac-

TABLE 2.1. The psychosexual stages.

Stages	Age
Oral ⎫	0 to 1 year
Anal ⎬ Pregenital	2 to 3 years
Phallic ⎭	4 to 5 years
Latency	6 to 12 years
Genital	13 to 18 years and beyond

tion with adults does the child learn these reactions. "Social reinforcement often accompanies successful toilet training. Mothers, and sometimes entire families, encourage an infant in this respect often with extrinsic rewards. The ability to use the toilet allows the child to receive the approval of parents and avoid shame which often accompanies unsuccessful toilet experiences" (Thornburg, 1973d, p. 25). Baldwin (1968) points out that in some homes a child who wets his pants or bed is publicly ridiculed, inducing feelings of shame in the child. Horrocks (1969) asserts that if a child's exploratory interests are inhibited by toilet training that is too strict, the child may revert to the more dependent oral stage and will not achieve autonomy at this stage.

Phallic stage. This stage, which begins between ages 3 and 4, is characterized by erotic stimulation of the penis for the boy and of the clitoris (the erectile organ of the vulva corresponding to the male penis) for the girl. The child's sexual feelings are expressed by handling his or her own genitals and by playfully exploring the bodies of other children. This behavior is basically curiosity, and it is a forerunner to the development of the so-called Oedipus complex.

The *Oedipus complex* in the male child, which usually manifests itself by the age of 4, is the outcome of two inner struggles.[3] First, boys begin to form associations between themselves and their mothers to gratify libidinal (basic biological) urges. Second, boys often show hostility and aggression toward their fathers, whom they view as competitors, thus thwarting libidinal gratification. Since such strong libidinal attachment goes to the parent of the opposite sex, the child may indicate a desire to possess the opposite-sex parent exclusively and to dispense with the presence of the same-sex parent.

Freud believed that the Oedipal complex produces anxieties in the boy that give rise to the *castration complex*. The boy imagines that his father (the rival) will cut off his penis. To begin with, the boy assumes

---

[3]Freud saw storm and stress as a result of inner conflict, basically unconscious, that can motivate behavior. Thus Freud extended Hall's storm-and-stress theory.

that everyone has a penis, and then he notices that girls do not have one. This assumption and finding, combined with the awareness that appendages such as fingers and toes can be severed, intensify the boy's fears. Because the father is generally perceived as a powerful figure, the boy may abandon his desired love object, the mother, and begin to identify more strongly with his father. When this identification occurs, the Oedipal conflict begins to resolve itself.

The Oedipal situation for the girl is more obscure because the girl's feelings must be transferred from her mother, her symbiotic love object, to her father. During the Oedipal period, the boy continues to love his mother; but the girl, comparing her genital area with male genitals and viewing such organs as a source of pleasure, develops *penis envy*. This envy results in hostility and resentment toward the mother. Consequently the girl turns to the father who possesses the penis, and views him as her suitable love object. Because the girl does not experience castration fears, she does not have the same repressive motives as the boy, and she may continue her attachment to her father indefinitely.

Freud's contention that the Oedipus complex is a universal human behavior has been equivocally accepted. Some anthropological evidence suggests that this phenomenon is more culturally than biologically bound. Malinowski's studies (1927, 1961) in the Trobriand Islands reveal no evidence of father-son rivalry—primarily, he felt, because of the islanders' comparatively primitive culture. Nevertheless, the Oedipal complex is still a basic part of Freudian theory.

Latency stage. Around 6 to 7 years of age, children begin to incorporate social mores beyond toilet training and to learn the prohibitions against oral, anal, and genital stimulation. The curbing of such feelings usually thrusts them into the latency period, a time during which the libido is not active and its energy is transferred to more socially acceptable behavior. Clearly, the *ego*, which mediates the demands of the id and of reality, is a more dominant feature than the id during this period. Grinder (1973) suggests that this sexually dormant period allows the cognitive powers to develop. Blos (1961) indicates that the processes of judgment, logic, and empathy stabilize during this period, and that growth in physical stature permits greater independence and opportunity for environmental mastery.

Some Freudian proponents believe that this latency period extends into adolescence, usually until around age 12. But today's sociocultural milieu may possibly facilitate sexual arousal prior to physiological puberty. Therefore, the latency period may no longer extend across a six- to seven-year period.

Genital stage. During puberty (ages 13 to 18), there is a reawakening of libidinal interests in the individual. Sexuality is now in its final form; and the adolescent, with new sexual urges, looks for sources of gratification outside the home and entertains thoughts about reproduction. Muuss (1968) suggests that pubescent sexuality manifests itself in three ways: (1) through external stimulation of the erogenous zones, (2) through internal tension and a physiological need to release sexual products (a condition not present in childhood sexuality), and (3) through psychological "sexual excitation," which may be influenced by the former two manifestations of sexuality.

The renewal of sexual energy comes from physiological maturity. The genital organs mature, the endocrine system produces high concentrations of sex hormones, and the sexual exploration of one's own genitals (masturbation) or the genitals of a member of the same or opposite sex arouses much stronger sexual feelings than in any stage prior to puberty (Thornburg, 1973a).

Freud stressed that the first five to six years of life are crucial in establishing character traits that become permanent by adolescence. How well the adolescent meets and successfully resolves crises is directly related to how successful the individual was in resolving childhood developmental crises. The adolescent girl, for example, often has difficulty breaking ties with her mother, a situation that represents a pull toward an earlier dependent state. To avoid this problem, there is often a resurgence of Oedipal feelings toward the father (Deutsch, 1944). How successfully the childhood Oedipal situation was resolved determines how well the adolescent Oedipal resurgence will be met.

Psychoanalytic Theory: Erik Erikson

Since Freud's original theory was advanced, several variations have emerged. Erikson's (1950, 1959, 1963, 1965, 1968), based on findings in cultural anthropology, is one of the more exaggerated variations. Ego development became the central issue in his theory, whereas instinct was central to Freud's. Erikson outlines eight stages of man, based on the *epigenetic* principle of psychosocial development. Epigenesis suggests that new systems evolve and change with time, and that these new qualities are structural changes that have not appeared earlier—a concept contradictory to that of preformation, discussed above. Erikson believes that normal human development occurs at a regular rate and sequence, and that during each stage of development the individual is endowed with instinctual urges in different bodily zones. This idea of sequence of development is similar to Freud's view of the psychosexual stages. (Erikson also stresses that interaction the individual might experience within the social and physical environment is affected by the inherent psychosexual functions of the bodily zones.) The first five stages in Erikson's theory correspond to the stages Freud hypothesized. However, because of his interest in the vicissitudes of personality throughout a human's life cycle, Erikson advanced three additional stages. Table 2.2 summarizes all of Erikson's stages of human development. Now let's take a closer look at two of these stages—*puberty and adolescence* and *young adulthood.*

TABLE 2.2. Eight stages of human development.

Chronological age	Developmental periods	Psychosexual quality
0–1	Oral sensory	Trust versus mistrust
2–3	Muscular-anal	Autonomy versus shame, doubt
4–5	Locomotor-genital	Initiative versus guilt
6–12	Latency	Industry versus inferiority
13–18	Puberty and adolescence	Identity versus role diffusion
19–25	Young adulthood	Intimacy versus isolation
26–40	Adulthood	Generativity versus stagnation
41 plus	Maturity	Integrity versus disgust, despair

Adapted from E. H. Erikson, *Childhood and Society*, New York: W. W. Norton, 1963. From *Adolescent Development* by H. D. Thornburg. Copyright 1973 by W. C. Brown Company. Reprinted by permission.

Puberty and adolescence: Identity versus role diffusion. Erikson sees puberty as a time when youth question the continuities and regularities on which they had relied earlier, a time when they consciously seek their own identities. Identity may be defined as "the establishment and re-establishment of sameness with one's previous experiences and a conscious attempt to make the future a part of one's personal life span" (Muuss, 1968, p. 50). Adolescents must contend with three major factors in identity striving. First, they must accommodate sexual maturation and its accompanying urges. Second, they must contend with physical growth. Height, weight, body hair, sex organs, facial blemishes, and overall appearance are all part of this growth. Third, they must actively seek some understanding of their eventual functions as adults in society. Erikson believes that adolescents reach this understanding by selecting occupational goals and moving toward realization of these goals. Some role diffusion exists when adolescents who are consciously striving for occupational opportunity are thwarted in their attempts to attain it. Their ego identities are also diffused by their tendency to maintain folk heroes as substitute identities because of their inability to cope effectively with their own ego needs. Erikson also places much stress on the availability of positive, unambiguous cultural models as a way to facilitate identity resolution.

Identity formation meets its crisis in adolescence (Erikson, 1965). If adolescents are oriented toward middle-class standards, the socialization process and need for identity are thought to be more easily managed, especially since such youth have working definitions of success and future goals. However, with adolescent socialization becoming more ambiguous than it was in the past, these resolutions appear to be more confusing to the adolescent today. Certainly, the primary forms of identity resolution, as Erikson sees them, stretch beyond the traditional age range of adolescence into young adulthood.

Young adulthood: Intimacy versus isolation. This stage follows adolescence and describes the psychosocial pursuits characteristic of the early 20s. During this stage the individual strives for intimacy, and identity seems to be a prerequisite to intimacy. The late adolescent or young adult normally is ready to pursue social as well as sexual intimacy with another person. Erikson believes that individuals are most capable of realizing intimacy if they can merge their own identities with that of other individuals without loss of personal identity. He feels that an intimate relationship requires self-discipline and ethical strength. Furthermore, he thinks that the search for intimacy is more complicated than the ego-identity search of the 13- to 18-year-old. In the ego-identity search, the "love affairs through which the adolescent passes contribute to the development of the ego as one identification succeeds another, and the adolescent is aided in defining and revising his own definition of his ego" (Harsch & Schrickel, 1950, p. 216). In the intimacy search, one's own identity becomes involved with the identity of another person. Erikson sees isolation occurring if a person's ego identity is too weak to sustain the uncertainties of intimacy. Such a person may be unable to meet the demands of intimacy that seem too unreasonable and too restrictive of personal freedom.

Cultural Theories: Margaret Mead and Ruth Benedict

The first real challenge to Hall's storm-and-stress hypothesis came from Margaret Mead, a cultural anthropologist who studied adolescent behavior in Samoa and New Guinea. Finding that some primitive cultures had no stressful periods comparable to those experienced by American youth, Mead concluded that stress was determined more by cultural factors than by biological ones. Ruth Benedict's research (1950) later supported Mead's contentions that storm and stress is not universal.

It is easier to understand the anthropological view if adolescence is considered to be the "period of development in human beings that begins when the individual feels that adult privileges are due him which are not being accorded him, and that ends when the full power and social status of the adult are accorded to the individual by his society" (Sieg, 1971, p. 338).

To some extent, this definition negates the theories of developmental stages, which in essence is what Mead and Benedict did. The anthropological definition of adolescence denies the universality of particular adolescent traits and behaviors. Being a culturebound phenomenon, age does not become a relevant factor either. Most anthropologists contend that the patterns of different cultures determine whether development occurs continuously or in stages. Because they believe that there are distinct cultural variations in adolescent development and different rates of change within each culture, they can find no evidence of universality.

It is not that Mead really denied the biological nature of man but that she ignored it. Her research pointed to specific transitional events within the primitive cultures, such as puberty rites, that allow the children within it to know exactly where they stand in relation to adult status and social acceptance. For example, Mead discussed in detail the Arapesh of New Guinea, a culture in which the adolescent is relatively free from difficulty. She described these children of 7 or 8 as happy, confident children who experience no upheaval or shame and exhibit no aggression toward others (1939). The Arapesh boy is initiated into adult status at age 13 by puberty rites and becomes engaged to an Arapesh girl 7 or 8 years old. The girl lives in the home of her husband-to-be. As the boy matures and learns to assume sole responsibility for being the provider, and as the girl moves toward puberty, the transition occurs from big brother or little sister to betrothed. Mead (1935) reported no disturbances among boys or girls in this culture.

Benedict (1954) also views growth as a continuous process—not simply a continuous process during adolescence but a process begun at birth. Mead also found relatively continuous growth in the Samoan child. Growth from childhood to adulthood varies from culture to culture, and the process is especially complicated in America. Muuss (1968) contrasts the continuity or discontinuity of growth in American and Samoan cultures:

> The pattern by which the child obtains independence varies from one culture to another. In some cultures, such as the American, the difference between a child and an adult is emphasized sharply by social and legal institutions. The change from one mode of interpersonal relationship to another creates discontinuity in the growth process.
> One example of this discontinuity in our society is the emphasis on the sexless nature of the child (or, since Freud, we should say on the

social restrictions of sex expression in the child) as contrasted with adult sexual activities. The child never, or rarely, sees childbirth, sexual intercourse, and death; pregnancy is camouflaged, evacuation veiled with prudery, breastfeeding hidden, and girls menstruate the first time without knowing what it is all about.

Samoan youth has an opportunity to see birth and death near home and many have seen a partly developed fetus, the opening of dead bodies, and occasional glimpses of sexual activities. Sex life is not repressed or inhibited by society, but is considered natural and pleasurable. Perversion, homosexuality, promiscuity, and other sexual activities, which because of their social and moral stigma divert emotional development toward neuroses in American society or which may result in unsatisfactory marriage, are relatively harmless in Samoa; they are considered "simply play" and are without moral stigma. In Samoan society, most experiences follow a relatively gradual, continuous line of development without severe interruptions, interferences, or restrictions [1968, pp. 70–71].*

Anthropologists see the continuous growth process as a cultural phenomenon, with each person reacting to the social expectancies of the culture. The more clearly these expectancies are defined, the less ambiguous is the adolescent period and the less stressful is growing up for the adolescent. The intensity of adolescent experiences thus depends upon societal attitudes and upon the length of time the individual spends in transition.

Psychological Theory: Eduard Spranger

In 1928, psychologist Eduard Spranger developed a theory of adolescence that represented a significant departure from Hall's position. Spranger viewed adolescence as a transition period from childhood to physiological maturity—the stage during which the adolescent's undeveloped and undifferentiated mental structure and psyche reach full maturity. He advocated that the adolescent years are essentially psychological and cannot be explained by physiological states. Further, he maintained that during this period the adolescent establishes a hierarchy of values.

In 1955, Spranger set forth three basic tenets of adolescence that, to some extent, resolve the controversy that generated out of Hall's and Mead's positions:

1. Adolescent development is a form of rebirth in which the person sees himself as another person when he reaches maturity. It is a storm-and-stress period.

*From *Theories of Adolescence* (2nd ed.) by R. E. Muuss. Copyright 1968 by Random House, Inc. Reprinted by permission.

2. A second pattern of development is a slow, gradual growth process in which the adolescent acquires cultural values and ideas common within the society.
3. The adolescent may grow through active participation. A youth consciously improves himself, overcoming disturbances and crises by his own energetic and goal-directed efforts. Self-control and self-discipline characterize such behaviors [Thornburg, 1973a, p. 3].

Spranger is one of a few psychological theorists who focused solely on puberty and adolescence. Furthermore, he never generalized his ideas to any culture other than his own, the German. He seemed to care little about deviant adolescent behaviors. Rather, he concerned himself with the normal adolescent's ideals, values, and goals.

Sociological Theory: Kingsley Davis

In reaction to Hall's recapitulation theory and other theories dealing primarily with biological man, several authors began advancing theories that related development to social phenomena. Adolescence is the phase of development in which social development lags noticeably behind physical and mental development. "In terms of growth, strength, fecundity, and mental capacity, full maturity tends to be attained only a short time after puberty; but socially, the adolescent still has a long way to go, in most cases, before full status is reached" (Davis, 1944, p. 8). Sociologist Kingsley Davis believes that social maturity comes at middle or even old age rather than at adolescence, a structure that creates a socially subordinate role for the adolescent. Davis contends that four sociological factors influence adolescent development—occupational placement, reproductive control, authoritarian organization, and cultural acquisition.

Occupational placement. Occupational selection may be by ascription or by choice. If selection is by choice, Davis suggests that the earlier the individual decides on an occupation the more intensive his training can be. Yet the later the decision the more accurately the occupation may represent the individual's abilities and interests. In complex societies such as those of the Western world, the choice of an occupation becomes associated with social recognition and approval. If the standards for occupational selection are raised, the status of the adolescent is necessarily lower because the adolescent finds him- or herself at the bottom of the ladder. The more competitive the occupational market is, the greater is the stress on the adolescent to make appropriate choices.

Reproductive control. "In its determination of the adolescent status, every society must somehow recognize the fact that the reproductive capacity first appears at the inception of adolescence. One crucial question is whether the adolescent shall be permitted to gratify his sexual desires through normal heterosexual intercourse or whether such gratification must be postponed" (Davis, 1944, p. 12). It is striking that, in American society, premarital chastity is strongly encouraged and, at the same time, postponement of marriage until after puberty is taken for granted. Freedom of marital choice in American society also encourages striking competition between the sexes. Stress arises in the adolescent from the gap between physical maturation, with its concomitant sexual desires, and the prevailing societal ideals of chastity and postponement. For the adolescent male, this stress may be further complicated by the competitive occupational struggle as well as by the competition involved in courtship and dating.

Authoritarian organization. In America, compared with other countries (especially Far Eastern countries), youths tend to think that getting a job, moving out of the home, or getting married entitles them to unequivocal independence. Because in function this independence may not occur readily, conflict often arises. In other countries—such as India, China, and Japan—such parental authority was never expected to be totally relinquished; therefore, little conflict occurred.

E. K. Beller (1973) observes that one sociological determinant of conflict between parental authority and the adolescent is the rate of social change. He feels that the more rapidly the society changes, the greater will be the difference in cultural content that the generations experience at the same developmental point. This factor, combined with the younger generation's difficulty in obtaining emancipation, creates stress and anxiety in the adolescent.

Cultural acquisition. To inculcate cultural values in children and youth, American society has set up school systems. But school environments are often structured factually and abstractly and may not equip the student with the skills necessary to handle concrete problems in everyday life. Davis suggests that, in addition to academic and social school functions, the adolescent should be given some meaningful activity outside the school that helps him relate these functions to his extracurricular life. For example, if a boy or girl takes woodworking in high school, this learning experience will prove especially valuable if he or she also gets a part-time job after school working as a carpenter's helper.

In applying these various philosophies and theories to our study of adolescence, we should consider three questions: Does it broaden our understanding of today's adolescent? Are certain theoretical statements still clearly relevant to today's youths? And has any early theory system been extended or modified through the years by other theorists and researchers?

One limitation in the study of adolescence has been that most theories are extensions of child-study theory, as is the case with Freud's and Gesell's hypotheses. On the other hand, Erikson's extension of Freud's work clearly gives credence to the developmental nature of adolescence. In addition, developmental tasks—as discussed in Chapter 1—specify designated goals or behaviors that are time-bound to adolescence.

The more perspectives through which we view the adolescent experience, the more complete will be our conceptualization of the adolescent. We can better understand the adolescent period if we draw on history and theory as they pertain to the contemporary interaction process that adolescents encounter.

Physical and Emotional Growth 3

Since the beginning of our century, the study of adolescence has included an examination of the basic developmental processes of physical and emotional growth. Traditionally oriented texts have devoted considerable attention to these aspects of adolescent development.

This chapter presents important and relevant materials concerning the physical and emotional development of the adolescent in a somewhat more condensed form than in a traditional text. The information cited here is basically noncontroversial and is accepted by most theorists. This is not the case regarding the material on interaction and behavioral processes discussed in Chapters 5 through 15. Specifically, this chapter will trace the history of knowledge about physical and emotional growth in adolescence, how they affect the individual adolescent, and their relevance to the contemporary study of adolescence.

PHYSICAL GROWTH

The adolescent's physical growth can be determined in several ways. One index is *morphological age,* which gives normative data on height and weight. Another is the emergence of *secondary sex characteristics,* which includes breast and primary-sex-organ development. Still other indications of physical development are *skeletal growth* and *glandular changes.* These physiological changes indicate that the individual is approaching puberty. The movement into puberty is characterized by the same growth sequence in all individuals, although the *rates* of growth vary from individual to individual.

Pubertal Events

The series of physical changes that the adolescent undergoes stretches across a continuum from prepuberty to postpuberty, with puberty representing the midpoint. The events of puberty have been divided into three phases: prepuberty, pubescence, and puberty. These phases involve the emergence of secondary sex characteristics and the ability to carry on reproductive functions.

1. *Prepuberty:* this phase begins with the onset of secondary sex characteristics, which includes the production of sex-specific hormones and

the emergence of observable physical differences between males and females. Kestenberg points out that "menarche and first seminal emissions are not to be taken as evidence of puberty. First menstruations are anovulatory and first emissions do not contain mature spermatozoa" (1967, p. 428).
2. *Pubescence:* in this phase, sex cells proliferate, and the emergence of secondary sex characteristics nears completion. According to Meredith (1967), female pubescence includes increases in the size of the breasts, ovaries, uterus, and hips, and onset of menstruation. In boys, increases in the size of the penis, testes, and scrotum occur.
3. *Puberty:* in this phase, ovulation and discharge of mature spermatozoa begin to occur, and reproduction is possible (Wilkins, 1965).

Prepubertal physical changes and anxieties in the female. The time of least growth in girls is from age 9 to age 10. From age 10 on, the girl typically begins a growth spurt that reaches its peak at around age 12. A sharp decline in growth follows this spurt, with height and body-proportion changes occurring more slowly (Meredith, 1939; Tanner, 1962). Table 3.1 indicates that internal changes in girls begin around age 7 and that external changes begin around age 10. Although the uterus and ovaries have already begun to develop, the girl's external genitalia grow more slowly than the boy's. Characteristic external changes in girls are gain in weight, increase in height, development of breasts, and increase in hip size and in pigmentation of hair (Bryan & Greenberg, 1952; Frisch & Revelle, 1970; Shuttleworth, 1937).

The 10- to 11-year-old girl experiences breast budding and enlargement, with full development commonly experienced within three years. During the eleventh to twelfth year, genital growth becomes accelerated, and the bony pelvis begins to remold. In addition, there are evidences of vaginal secretions, gonadotropin (a gonad-stimulating hormone) in the urine, and cyclic estrogen secretions. Pubic hair continues to grow, and around age 13 axillary hair begins to appear (Reynolds & Wines, 1948). Each change is a prelude to the most dramatic prepubertal physiological change, *menarche,* the initiation of menstruation.

Zeller (1952) holds that as the girl moves toward menarche she develops a special psychic function called *virginity,* which morphologically is invested in the hymen, the protective membrane of the vagina. Kestenberg (1967) feels that, because of this psychic function, internal vaginal sensations and secretions may create emotional trauma for the girl. Although she is sufficiently prepared to contend with external growth changes, she is confused by these internal sensations and tries to deny them or cover them up.

TABLE 3.1. Stages of sexual differentiation.

Age	Boys	Girls
3–7	Infantile characteristics. Very small amounts of estrogen and 17-ketosteroids in urine.	
7–8	Excretion of estrogens and 17-ketosteroids increases.	Ovarian follicles advance. Uterus growth.
9–10	Low gonadotropin and testicular androgens in urine.	Growth of bony pelvis. Budding of nipples.
10–11	Growth of testicles and penis.	*Prepuberty.* Pubic hair. Budding of breasts. Estrogen excretion accelerated.
11–12	Prostatic activity.	Remolding of the bony pelvis. Vaginal secretion, pH changes, cornification, and glycogenization. Accelerated growth of external and internal genitals. Gonadotropins appear in urine. Estrogen excretion accelerated, and cyclic.
12–13	*Prepuberty.* Pubic hair. Marked increase of gonadotropin.	Pigmentation of nipples. Mammae filling in.
13–14	Active spermatogonia. Rapid growth of penis and testicles. Subareolar node on nipples.	Axillary hair. Menarche.
14–15	Axillary hair. Down on upper lip. Voice changes. Great increase in testicular androgens.	*Puberty.* Earliest normal pregnancies. Pregnanediol excretion in luteal phase. Great increase in estrogen excretion. Increase in 17-ketosteroids.
15–16	*Puberty.* Mature spermatozoa. Marked testosterone rise.	Acne. Deepening of voice.
16–17	Facial and body hair. Acne.	Arrest of skeletal growth. Ovulatory cycles stabilize.
21	Arrest of skeletal growth. Increase of 17-ketosteroids and testosterone.	

Adapted from Talbot et al. (1952) and Wilkins (1965). From "Phases of Adolescence: Part III; Puberty, Differentiation, and Consolidation" by J. S. Kestenberg, *Journal of the American Academy of Child Psychiatry,* 1968, 7(1), 113. Copyright 1968 American Academy of Child Psychiatry. Reprinted by permission of the author and of the editor of the *Journal.*

Prepubertal physical changes and anxieties in the male. Boys usually experience their growth spurt some 12 to 18 months after girls. This spurt is characterized by change in height, enlargement of the testes and penis, appearance of pubic hair, seminal emissions, and involuntary erections by age 12 (Asayama, 1957). Evidences of pubic hair and an increase in gonadotropin by age 13 nearly complete the growth spurt, which begins tapering off by age 14 (Tanner, 1962).

Initial involuntary ejaculations may produce anxiety in the adolescent boy. He may consciously manipulate his penis (masturbate) to activate genital sensations and to gain control over his sexual urges. His external genitalia are his primary developmental interest (Freud, 1924). As he strives to regulate his sexual urges, he begins to see himself in a new social sex role. Kestenberg (1967) believes that this emerging sex role creates two conflicting fears in the boy and these anxieties may cause him to doubt his masculine potential. The adolescent boy fears that suppression of masturbation and storage of semen, which he believes is in the testicles, will burst these organs. He also fears that excessive ejaculation will deplete the testicles of semen and lead to infertility and impotence. Adolescent boys also commonly fear having an erection in public.

Puberty. Puberty, as we have seen, is the period during which the adolescent matures sexually. In medical terms, it is the period marked by the ripening of the ova in the female and the sperm in the male. But we would be distorting the importance of this period in the adolescent's development if we thought of puberty only as a period of developing reproductive capabilities. For pubertal growth also involves glandular changes and growth in body size. Table 3.2 summarizes the changes that occur during pubescence.

Glandular changes. The *pituitary gland* produces two hormones that facilitate puberty. The *growth* hormone determines the increase in body size, especially height and extensions of the trunk. The *gonadotropin* hormone facilitates sexual maturation, especially through

TABLE 3.2. Changes during adolescence by sex.

Girls	*Boys*
Growth in pubic hair	Growth in pubic hair
Growth of hair under arms	Growth of hair under arms
Light growth of hair on face	Heavy growth of hair on face
Light growth of hair on body	Heavy growth of hair on body
Slight growth of larynx	Considerable growth of larynx
Moderate lowering of voice	Considerable lowering of voice
Eruption of second molars	Eruption of second molars
Slight thickening of muscles	Considerable thickening of muscles
Widening of hips	Widening of shoulders
Increase in perspiration	Increase in perspiration
Development of breasts	Slight temporary development of breasts around nipples
No change in hairline	Receding hairline at temples
Menstrual cycle	Involuntary ejaculations
No change in neck size	Enlargement of neck
Growth of ovaries and uterus	Growth of penis and testicles

From *The Young Adult: Identity and Awareness* by G. D. Winter and E. M. Nuss. Copyright © 1969 by Scott, Foresman and Company. Reprinted by permission of the publisher.

interaction with the *gonads* and the other endocrine glands that play an active role in bringing about pubertal changes.

The female gonads are the *ovaries* and the male gonads the *testes*. As the gonads develop, so do germ cells and other glands that affect the development of genitalia and of other secondary sex characteristics. As the gonadal sex hormones reach a high level in the body, the gonadotropin hormones being slowing the growth hormones until growth of the sex organs is eventually arrested. This relationship between sex hormones and growth hormones allows the sex organs to develop beyond their childhood size, but it stops the process before they enlarge to abnormal proportions (Scheinfeld, 1971).

Growth in body size. The growth spurt in height and weight actually begins in preadolescence and continues into the first two to three years of adolescence (Thornburg, 1974d). Height and weight are the two adolescent-growth determinants that can be measured. Growth in height typically follows a regular pattern. An increase in height is an earlier indication of pubertal changes than is a gain in weight (Frisch & Revelle, 1970). Height changes differ for boys and girls. Figures 3.1 and 3.2 illustrate the variance in peak growth years between the sexes (Tanner, 1962).

Weight gain usually results from bone and muscle growth. As the bones grow, they become heavier. By adolescence, bone weight constitutes approximately one-sixth of the total body weight. Muscle growth also contributes significantly to body weight; pronounced growth in muscle tissue occurs from age 12 to 15 for girls and from age 15 to 17 for boys (Heald, Daugela, & Brunschyber, 1963). At maturity, muscles contribute almost 50 percent of a person's total body weight.

Postpuberty. With the arrest of skeletal growth, the adolescent advances into the postpubertal stage. Research indicates that 50 percent of 17-year-old boys have reached postpuberty—a percentage increased to 83 for 21-year-olds (Talbot et al., 1952). At this stage, the male takes on adultlike facial features and body shape. Facial blemishes subside, and pigmented facial hair is noticeable. There is also an increase in heterosexual activity such as petting and intercourse.

Skeletal growth usually stops about two years earlier in the female. She takes on adultlike behaviors at this earlier age as well. By around age 19, a regular ovulatory cycle has been established. This cycle occurs not only because of changes in the pituitary glands and ovaries but because of changes in body temperature, blood pressure, pulse, respiration, weight, and vitamin use (Southam & Gonzaga, 1965).

Variances in physical development. Differences in physical development between boys and girls have become evident through research.

Physical and Emotional Growth   41

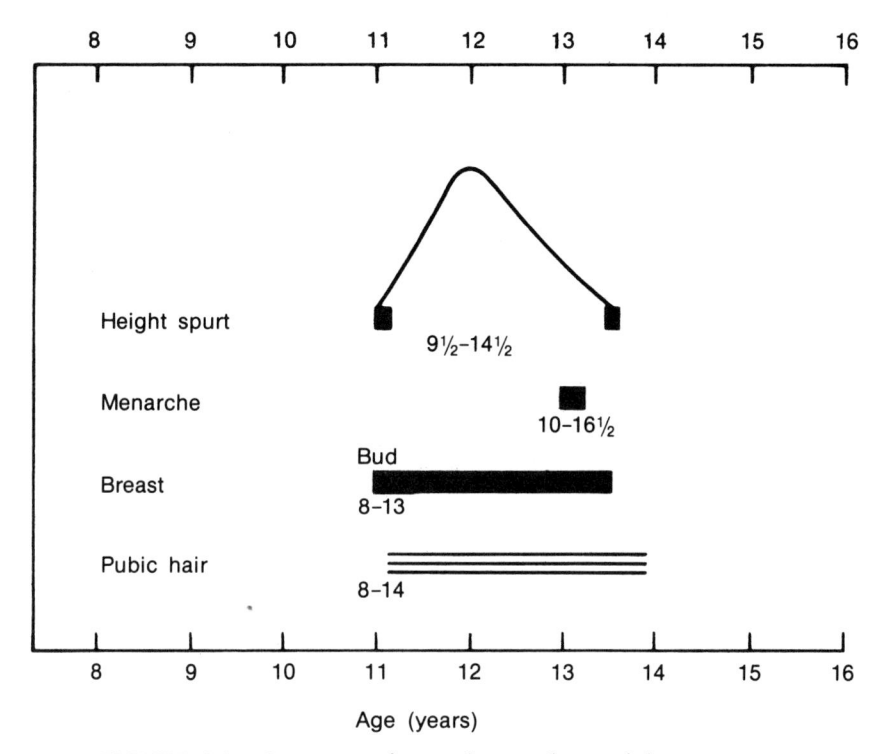

FIGURE 3.1. Sequence of growth in girls at adolescence. An average girl is represented. The range of ages within which some of the events may occur is given by the figures placed directly below them. From *Growth at Adolescence*, 2nd ed., by J. M. Tanner. Copyright © 1962 by Blackwell Scientific Publications Ltd., Oxford. Reprinted by permission.

So far in our discussion, we have considered only normative data. The information tells us the *average* physical and sexual development for males or females in a particular age group. Individuals who vary from these established norms have often been categorized as *early maturing* or *late maturing*. Because differences in development exist between males and females, let's consider early- and late-maturing girls and boys separately.

    Early maturation in girls. For the early-maturing girl, the most noticeable physical change is breast development, which is often accompanied by early menarche. The girl who has early breast development is confronted with social situations that increase her sexual anxieties. Stolz and Stolz (1944) found that these girls were embarrassed by their conspicuousness, bigness, tallness, and complexion, and by the fact that they were already menstruating. The early-maturing girl who is attractive may be envied by her female peers for her "grown-up" look. Similarly, she may be ignored by her male agemates. Because of her age, she does not have the emotional background to deal adequately with her anxieties. In researching preadolescents, Faust (1960) found that although more prestige is afforded the early-maturing junior high girl than the normal maturer, for the most part this standing works to her disadvantage. In many cases the early-maturing girl is vulnerable to sexual enticements and tends to date more frequently than her normal- or late-maturing counterparts (McCandless, 1970).

Sometimes the early-maturing girl is looked on with disdain. She may acquire an unfavorable reputation because of her early physical development and often-accompanying precocious sexual interests. Rogers

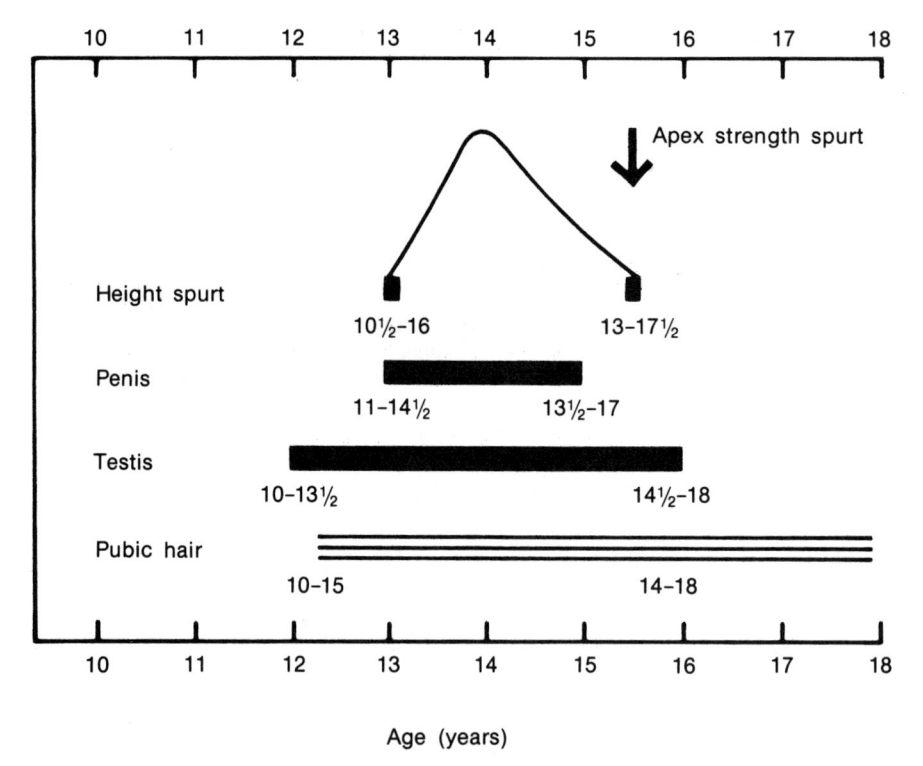

FIGURE 3.2. Sequence of growth in boys at adolescence. An average boy is represented. The range of ages within which each event charted may begin and end is given by the figures placed directly below its start and finish. From *Growth at Adolescence*, 2nd ed., by J. M. Tanner. Copyright © 1962 by Blackwell Scientific Publications Ltd., Oxford. Reprinted by permission.

(1972a) believes that this attitude toward the early-maturing girl may be changing for two reasons. First, all girls mature more rapidly now, so that the early maturer is less conspicuous than she was in the past; second, with greater female assertiveness than previously, the taller, "grown-up" figure has become more acceptable. Perhaps the greatest problem facing the early-maturing girl is the physical precociousness that prematurely catapults her into heterosexual contacts. In effect, these associations shorten the adolescent growth period needed for subsequent adult maturity.

Early maturation in boys. The discrepancy between physical changes and societal expectations may prove advantageous for the early-maturing boy. Research evidence indicates that early-maturing boys are larger for their age, more athletic, and more heterosexual, and that they possess more leadership abilities (Latham, 1951; Tanner, 1961). Kinsey describes early maturers as the "more alert, energetic, vivacious, spontaneous, physically active, socially extrovert, and/or aggressive individuals in the population" (1948, p. 325).

Eichorn (1963) found that boys' early physical maturation brought about adultlike behaviors. However, as Rogers (1972a) points out, the continued pressure for the early maturer to excel may throw him into situations with which he cannot effectively cope.

Late maturation in girls. Because the late-maturing girl is not so socially and sexually aggressive as the early-maturing girl, the late maturer may in fact be popular with her peers and sometimes selected for leadership roles. Because success in heterosexual interests is closely connected with physical growth and appearance, this girl is not thrown into the mature social role so early as her normal- or early-maturing counterpart. The slow-maturing girl is generally on a par with the normal-maturing boy, since she still has the advantage of early growth patterns; that is, she is slow in developing her overall body size and proportions. The late-maturing girl's primary anxiety may result from her lack of physical strength for competitive athletics (Mussen & Jones, 1957).

Late maturation in boys. Slow physical development is most noticeable in the late-maturing boy. Not only does he mature more slowly than his male peers, but he also develops more slowly than the late-maturing girl. Since there is considerable emphasis on genital and muscle growth among boys, he is often embarrassed to undress around other boys. His feelings of inferiority are also compounded by girls' greater interest in early-maturing boys.

The late-maturing boy has difficulty competing athletically. Viewing his underdeveloped body as the primary reason for physical ineptness, the boy may become self-conscious and withdrawn. His classmates frequently reject him socially and rarely choose him for leadership roles. To avoid rejection, the late-maturing boy may revert to childish behaviors, such as attention-getting devices (Jones & Bayley, 1950). This immaturity has been known to persist well beyond adolescence and even sometimes into middle adulthood (Jones, 1957). Even though he is no longer physically different, the late maturer tends to remain more immature socially and sexually than do early and normal maturers.

Adolescent Growth Factors

Many adolescents do not understand the growth and endocrine changes that go on during adolescence. Certain food elements are essential for growth; for example, calcium is necessary for proper development of the skeletal system and protein for tissue growth. Because physical growth is not self-sustaining, the adolescent must become aware of the importance of a wholesome diet (Daniel, 1970).

Nutritional deficiency. Often an adolescent becomes finicky about the foods he eats. Sometimes a high-calorie diet still has nutritional deficiencies, especially if the diet includes large amounts of carbohydrates and sugar. Typically, high caloric intake leads to obesity, low energy levels, heart disorder, hyponutrition, and susceptibility to disease. Several studies have indicated the other extreme—that adolescents may not have an adequate caloric intake; such a deficiency can result in an inadequate metabolism of protein and calcium, thus delaying growth and reducing activity (Daniel, 1970). Poor nutritional patterns not only create deficiencies during adolescence but, as Rogers (1972b) points out, are instrumental in establishing eating habits and attitudes that persist throughout the lifetime and are frequently passed on to the next generation.

Malnutrition may occur in an adolescent who looks reasonably healthy. It may result from excessive intakes of starchy foods and too little protein. Nutritional deficiencies may cause delay in the growth spurt, thus delaying puberty (Adams, 1972). Frisch and Revelle (1969) studied adolescent male and female growth patterns in seven Latin American and seven Asian countries. They found that, in countries where the daily per capita intake exceeded 2300 calories, the maximum adolescent growth spurt in boys occurred around age 13 and in girls around age 12.3. In countries where the daily caloric intake was less than 2300 calories, the spurt maximized around 15.5 years for boys and 13.5 years for girls.

Obesity. Obesity occurs when the caloric intake exceeds growth and energy requirements. It is due sometimes to environmental influences and in some cases to heredity. Wolff (1966) found that obesity is more likely to occur in a child if a parent overeats than if the parent eats moderately. It is difficult to know what constitutes an excessive caloric intake for an adolescent. A highly active adolescent may eat considerably greater amounts of food than an inactive adolescent, because the active person expends more energy each day. If the daily caloric intake exceeds the energy output, fatty tissue will accumulate. The best way to regulate excessive caloric intake and fat accumulation is to increase one's activity level and to eat greater amounts of food containing calcium and protein and smaller amounts of those containing carbohydrates and fats.

Few adolescents understand the nature of obesity or the necessary corrective measures. Obesity is usually symptomatic of some underlying emotional problem, which can also delay puberty. Adams (1972) cites a clinical case of a 15½-year-old obese girl who had many complex emotional problems. After psychiatric treatment the patient persisted in obese behaviors, expressing much hostility toward the psychiatrist. Finally, through hospital confinement and caloric-intake control, at 16 the girl began responding with weight loss and menstruation. Additional psychotherapy over the next two years allowed her to move forward and eventually live a well-adjusted adult life.

Fatigue. The sources of adolescent fatigue are well known. Puberty generally causes a resurgence of energy. As the body grows and moves through endocrine changes, the adolescent expends more energy than he or she takes in. In addition, the adolescent's activities often extend into what has heretofore been sleep time. Lack of adequate rest can cause general fatigue. It is not uncommon for many young adolescents to rest when they come home from school or after some strenuous activity. Sometimes fatigue can be attributed to emotional stress. An adolescent may sleep well beyond the demands of his body as a means of escaping or avoiding problems.

Poor health. Systemic ill health and personal neglect both interfere with adolescent growth. A primary cause of poor health is disease. Typical adolescent diseases are tuberculosis, diabetes mellitus, kidney infections, and mononucleosis. In addition, an adolescent may suffer from anemia, gastrointestinal disorders, and collagen disorders (Adams, 1972; Pickle, 1967). One disease source is endocrinopathology, which involves hormonal deficiencies. Such deficiencies will affect the adolescent's growth patterns, frequently causing thyroid and ovarian disorders. Some endocrinopathological problems are caused by chromosomal aberrations. For example, Turner's syndrome is a deterioration of chromosomes through heredity. This condition usually causes ovarian disorders.

Exercise is instrumental in physical development. Opportunities for exercise—in school and out, organized or spontaneous—help adolescents understand the importance of their bodies to their total lives.

A female suffering from this disease is short in stature and does not reach puberty. Other chromosomal variations also affect growth, and in turn behavior, in the developing adolescent. Ferdon (1971) has summarized these basic patterns, shown in Table 3.3.

Another disease source is inappropriate care of the body. For example, fatigue resulting from a generally run-down condition serves as a catalyst for mononucleosis. Simple neglect is also a source of disease. For instance, failure to brush the teeth allows bacteria to organize in the mouth. An acid condition develops that eventually causes breakdown of

TABLE 3.3. Basic patterns of sex-chromosome complements.

Pattern	Phenotype
XX	Normal female
XO	Turner's syndrome (short stature, never reaches puberty)
XXX or XXXX	Normal-appearing female but infertile
XY	Normal male
XXY or XXXY	Klinefelter's syndrome (often feminine characteristics)
XYY or XYYY	Normal-appearing male with facial acne, often unusually tall and of below-average intelligence

From "Chromosomal Abnormalities and Antisocial Behavior" by N. M. Ferdon, *Journal of Genetic Psychology*, 1971, *118*, 282. Copyright 1971 The Journal Press. Reprinted by permission.

calcium in the teeth. High sugar and carbohydrate intake, a consumption problem quite common to adolescents—in combination with poor oral hygiene—is the primary contributor to tooth decay in adolescents.

Disregard of systemic health and personal neglect are both factors that can interfere with adolescent growth. The interaction of the two is cyclic and may continue until long-lasting or undeterminable deleterious effects occur. The concept of good adolescent health is not something one should expect an adolescent to derive on his own. Parents and professionally trained adults in the health sciences must help instill the operative concept of body care and management.

Skin blemishes. Acne, which affects about 85 percent of all teen-agers (Grinder, 1973), is the single most disturbing skin blemish for adolescents. Although acne has been erroneously attributed to masturbation in the male and menstruation in the female, acne is a normal developmental occurrence (Hurlock, 1973). It derives from an imbalance of hormones in the body. Oil glands become more active, and the oily skin produces blackheads or pimples. Once the surrounding skin tissue becomes sufficiently irritated, the oily sacs erupt, causing acne. Because of the stress on beauty in our culture, the acne condition, although common among adolescents, takes on negative connotations and causes poor self-images.

Accidents. Accidents are the greatest single cause of death among adolescent boys, especially among those 15 to 19. For the 15-to-24 age range, the 1960 accident rate was 56 deaths per 100,000 adolescents, 38 of whom were motor vehicle victims (*Trends*, 1961). Their increased physical growth and strength cause adolescents to take on a daring attitude; they often exercise their physical capabilities but fail to exhibit

Most youths consult their physician less often than once a year when they have medical-care problems, and many never do so because they don't get sick. Surprisingly, many use the services of pseudomedical men.

Identification of Health Problems. "Which are the health problems you have and would like to have solved?"

Health problems	Respondents with health problems*		
	Total and percent (n=1346)	Male (n=738)	Female (n=608)
Nervousness	393 29.2%	177 24.0%	216 35.0%
Dental problems	366 27.2%	205 27.8%	161 26.5%
Menstrual problems	135 10.0%	—	135 22.4%
Acne	246 18.3%	170 23.0%	76 12.5%
Health worries	121 9.0%	61 8.3%	60 10.9%
Headaches	120 8.9%	52 7.0%	68 11.2%
Obesity	79 5.9%	38 5.1%	41 6.7%
Venereal disease	10 0.7%	5 0.7%	5 0.8%
Other	104 7.7%	59 8.0%	45 7.4%

*Absolute and percent distribution by sex.
From "A Survey of Health Problems, Practices, and Needs of Youths" by J. J. Sternlieb and L. Munan, *Pediatrics*, 1972, 49(2), 180.

comparable emotional strength and good judgment. Swimming accidents and drug overdoses resulting in death are also common among youth but less common than automobile accidents.

There are, of course, considerably more injuries than deaths among adolescents. High school athletics are likely to lead to injury, especially the contact sports. Head injuries are the most serious problem. They commonly result in loss of consciousness or orientation. Because there is an urgency for the "high school hero" to get back into the game, it is quite common to do a first-aid job on a boy and throw him back into action. Recurrences of head injuries may cause perceptual difficulties or recurring loss of consciousness well into adult life. A second major injury area is within the cartilage tissue, usually in the knee. Knee locking and leg buckling may tear cartilage to an irreparable degree or damage ligaments. These injuries may require surgery. The total injuries in high school football alone exceed .75 million annually.

Self-perceived unacceptable physical features. Perceptual discrepancies often occur in the adolescent. His own perception of his body type may be translated into self-image. In turn, his self-image may affect the way the adolescent perceives others' perceptions of him.

Frazier and Lisonbee (1950) conducted a study of adolescent body images among 580 tenth-grade boys and girls. Analysis of their data reveals two major concerns: (1) unattractive physical features or defects that cause anxiety and (2) physical features that are perceived as unacceptable to the individual.

Some physical features that concern adolescents are scars, moles, birthmarks, protruding chin, large ears, big feet, uneven teeth, long nose, skinny neck, receding chin, and thin face (see Table 3.4). In reality, these self-perceived physical limitations may be no drawback or limitation at all. The task of accepting one's physique (Havighurst, 1972) is without question a perceived emotional state that compounds resolving the task of self-acceptance. Again, this concern generally stems from comparing oneself with others. Such concerns are nevertheless temporary, and with increased emotional and rational maturity they may be overcome. Rarely do such concerns become an over-riding fear in the adolescent (Angelino, Dollins, & Mech, 1956; Croake, 1967, 1971).

Social Concerns Related to Physical Growth

As their bodies change, adolescents become more conscious of their appearance and their acceptability to others. They consistently compare themselves with agemates and judge themselves by the norms of acceptability set by society. Our society provides social reinforcement for attractive, mature adolescents who take on adult characteristics early in their physical and social development. Unfortunately, adolescents who are unattractive or slow in developing receive no comparable reinforcement. Body ideals are taught and perpetuated through the media and advertising and through the general attitudes held by parents and peers (Schonfeld, 1964)—ideals to which youths are exposed well before adolescence. Adolescents who do not see themselves as meeting society's expectations develop anxieties or express discontent with themselves.

Girls are generally more concerned about their appearance than are boys. They are thrust into this area of concern earlier because they mature more rapidly than boys. For example, the 13-year-old girl is much

TABLE 3.4. Items of self-description checked by 10 percent or more of 580 tenth-grade boys and girls, with amount of expressed concern.

Boys

Item of description	Percent checking	Percent of concern
Blackheads or pimples	57	51
Lack of beard	34	2
Heavy eyebrows	27	1
Scars, birthmarks, moles	20	13
Irregular teeth	17	39
Heavy lips	14	5
Protruding chin	13	6
Ears stick out	13	6
Oily skin	12	27
Freckles	12	—
Heavy beard	11	13
Glasses	11	23
Dark skin	10	4
Receding chin	10	4
Gaps in teeth	10	26
Too long nose	10	8
Too thin face	10	15
Too large ears	10	8

Girls

Item of description	Percent checking	Percent of concern
Blackheads or pimples	57	82
Heavy eyebrows	24	11
Freckles	23	24
Oily skin	22	52
Scars, birthmarks, moles	22	30
Glasses	21	31
High forehead	19	8
Too round face	19	21
Too homely	18	42
Dry skin	16	43
Irregular teeth	16	42
Thin lips	15	13
Low forehead	13	3
Too long nose	11	23
Too big nose	11	44
Receding chin	10	13
Odd-shaped nose	10	23

From "Adolescent Concerns with Physique" by A. Frazier and L. K. Lisonbee, *School Review*, 1950, 58, 397-405. Copyright 1950 University of Chicago Press. Reprinted by permission.

This young girl is losing her childhood facial features and is rapidly moving toward adolescence.

closer to approximating adult stature than is the 13-year-old boy (Dwyer & Mayer, 1969; Havighurst, 1972). Girls also perceive their bodies to be more closely related to their subsequent dating and marriage roles (Fisher, 1964; Kurtz, 1969). In addition, girls are thrown into the social behaviors of using cosmetics and selecting clothing that will accentuate their physical features—a behavior strongly suggested and reinforced by our society.

Body image. Schilder (1935) describes body image as an individual's perception of his or her own body. This definition implies that the way an individual views his or her body depends on psychological and sociological factors. Schonfeld (1964) suggests four factors that determine an individual's body image:

1. Subjective perceptions stemming from actual sensory experiences, particularly visual and tactile, that have developed since infancy.

2. Internalized psychological factors arising from personal emotional experiences.
3. Sociological factors relating to the way parents and society react to the individual and the way the individual interprets these reactions.
4. Attitudinal factors based on experiences, comparisons, and identifications with bodies of other persons.

Body type. The most extensive work on body build (somatotype) was done by Sheldon (1940, 1942). Sheldon believed in a continuum of body types rather than in discrete categories. However, he did believe that most people could be described as one of three body types that fell on the continuum. He referred to these three types as *endomorphic, mesomorphic,* and *ectomorphic.* Sheldon believed that basic body type is determined in embryo. Three germinal layers of embryo—the endoderm, mesoderm, and ectoderm—reproduce body tissue. The layer that reproduces the fastest remains dominant throughout the individual's critical growth periods.

The *endoderm* is the inner layer of cells. From these cells the digestive and respiratory tracts develop. An endomorph is characterized by a short, flabby build that results from a predominant abdominal section. There is an underdevelopment of the bones and muscles. Sheldon's work was not so much an attempt to classify body builds as to identify the personality or temperament that characterized each type. The endomorph likes to eat, likes bodily comforts, and is sociable (Hilgard et al., 1971). The *mesoderm* is the middle layer of cells, from which the muscles and bones grow. The mesomorph is strong, muscular, well proportioned, and generally equipped for strenuous physical demands (Hall & Lindzey, 1957). The mesomorph is energetic and likes exercise. Because he tends to gain a great deal of social reinforcement, he is often assertive, socially oriented, boastful, uninhibited, and self-assured (Hassan, 1967; Sanford, Adkins, Miller, & Cobb, 1943). The *ectoderm* is the outer layer of cells from which the skin and nervous system develop. The body-surface area, brain, and central nervous system are more predominant in the ectomorph than in the endomorph or the mesomorph. Later maturers are commonly ectomorphs, who are characterized by tall, lanky physiques. The ectomorph is highly sensitive and is often plagued with worries and fears. Such an individual frequently withdraws because of a fear of interaction. Research by Sanford and his associates (1943) on the structured personality (characterized by orderliness, self-sufficiency, quiet dignity, cooperativeness, and strong conscience) indicates that more ectomorphs than either endomorphs or mesomorphs fit this personality description.

Most researchers hypothesize that society's ideal is most like the mesomorph (muscular). The greater the deviation from this body type, the greater the anxiety and concern over appearance. More research has been done with males than with females. Studies among males have indicated that the mesomorphic male is regarded as most attractive and the extreme endomorphic male as the least attractive (Calden, 1959). Research by Lerner and his associates (Lerner, Schroeder, Rewitzer, & Weinstock, 1972) among adolescent males clearly showed a strong positive attitude toward the mesomorph stereotype and an unfavorable attitude toward the endomorph and ectomorph stereotypes. Similarly, Staffieri (1967) found that mesomorphic boys received more peer approval, and Felker (1968) found they had better self-conceptions, than males of the other two body types. According to Calden (1959), females rated the mesomorphic male as most attractive and the extreme endomorphic male as most repulsive.

Research further indicates that these stereotypes exist prior to adolescence. Staffieri (1972) investigated 60 females, 30 ages 7 to 9 and 30 ages 10 and 11. He presented each subject with three silhouettes representing the endomorphic, mesomorphic, and ectomorphic body types. He also presented each subject with a list of 38 adjectives to use in describing these body types. Results of the study show that all of the adjectives assigned to the endomorph were unfavorable. In all, 40 girls preferred the mesomorphic silhouette, and 20 preferred the ectomorphic silhouette. None chose the endomorphic profile. Age seemed to have no significant effect on choice of silhouette.

EMOTIONAL GROWTH

As we saw in Chapter 2, G. Stanley Hall's emphasis on storm and stress focuses primarily on the emotional needs of the adolescent. Emotions generate from the *affective* state of the individual—that is, the complex feeling state within an individual. Although emotions derive from the affective component of the mind, they may encompass cognitive and psychomotor components of the mind as well. Stresses in the adolescent's life may involve any part or combination of the mind's components, since the interaction of some components creates stress on some occasions and alleviates it on others.

Emotion, like physical and intellectual skills, has its roots in childhood. An individual is predisposed to certain emotional feelings through learning. An *attitude*, for example, is an emotional predisposition that prompts a person to act in some way toward another person, object, or ideal. Attitudes may be learned by pairing attitude stimuli to attitude responses. Attitude stimuli may include *concrete objects*, such as an automobile or a motorcycle; *persons*, such as a boyfriend, a girlfriend, or a parent; a *group of people,* such as a minority group or politicians; *social institutions,* such as the school; *values,* such as fidelity, integrity, or morality; and *social issues,* such as war, civil rights, or ecology (Loree, 1970).

Emotionality in an adolescent generally involves all components of the mind, although in varying degrees.

1. *Interests:* These behaviors occur when an individual is free to choose. For an adolescent, interests include things that occupy his or her attention—things that the individual might spend time, money, and energy on. Because interest objects are so diverse, interest may be thought strictly to involve a "feeling" (affective) state (Thornburg, 1973e).
2. *Appreciations:* These behaviors occur when an individual chooses an activity based on his feelings toward it and his understanding (cognition) of it. An adolescent may listen to acid rock, not just because of an interest in this type of music, but because of an understanding of the meaning communicated through the lyrics. Appreciations, then, may be considered to involve both a "feeling" and a "thinking" state.
3. *Attitudes:* These behaviors involve positive or negative dispositions toward environmental objects. An adolescent who hates a particular subject in school has a negative attitude toward that subject. This attitude often causes the adolescent to underachieve or even to generalize his negative attitude to the school itself. On the other hand, an adolescent who has a positive attitude toward politics is likely to become actively involved in political activities. Attitudes include "feeling," "thinking," and "behavioral" components.
4. *Values:* These behaviors may best be described as the consistent expression of attitudes to the point of internalization. Inconsistency between values and behaviors occurs during adolescence, since youths are testing values to see if they want to maintain them in their adult life. Although attitudes and values have the same components, values are persistent, often characterizing behavior.

Emotionality may become intense during adolescence. Disturbing thoughts may go through the adolescent's mind. Stress in the environment may become so intense that the adolescent may entertain the idea of escaping to drugs, committing suicide, or withdrawing into loneliness. Fear of being unacceptable to others often causes emotional panic. Such panic may result in unpredictable or undesirable behavior on the part of the adolescent. Social stimuli may overload the mind to the point that the adolescent thinks his or her "head is going to explode." Traumas such as rape or pregnancy are difficult to deal with and may leave the adolescent with emotional scars well beyond adolescence.

These types of emotional experiences may lead to the confusions and disillusionments featured in the storm-and-stress hypothesis of adolescent emotional development.

In today's social milieu, it is common for adolescents to act out emotionally against authority. This rebellion against authority is evidenced by use of tobacco, alcohol, and drugs, by high delinquency rates, by defiance of parents, by diverse behaviors counter to the main culture, and by activist movements among youths. Erikson (1963) holds that attainment of ego-identity is the crucial task of adolescence. Technological advances and continued education have caused many youths to delay employment and marriage (Rosenmayr, 1972), thus compounding the identity crisis. Antisocial behavior may be an attempt to find identity, an alternative action for youth who have been otherwise thwarted in their identity search.

Emotional Manifestations

Fear. Some childhood fears carry over into adolescence, and other, new fears are created in adolescence. Fears usually generate from natural phenomena, social relationships, and unknowns.

In childhood, fear comes from events within the environment that overpower the child, creating insecurity. In adolescence, fear primarily involves the uncertainties of being an adolescent. Most adolescent fears are perceptual or imaginary. They pose less of a real threat than do childhood fears. However, there is a basic difference in adolescent fears. When something is very important to adolescents, they are sometimes hesitant to express their views because of the fear that they may lose what is of value to them. For example, some adolescents who consider religion an important part of their lives are often hesitant to discuss the subject openly because they anticipate ridicule from peers.

Since the experiences of adolescents are often diversified, they sometimes find themselves without the necessary skills to cope with new experiences. Unless they are decisively self-confident, adolescents may demonstrate uncertainty. To alleviate their skepticism, they may become affiliated with others who provide a source of security (Zimbardo & Formica, 1963).

Croake and Knox (1971) investigated the fears of 212 ninth-grade students living in the southeastern United States. Table 3.5 summarizes their findings. In general, they found that girls had more fears than boys. This finding has also been reported in the research of Angelino and Shedd (1953), Russell and Sarason (1965), and Croake (1967). In addition, Croake and Knox's 1971 study showed that adolescents from lower socioeconomic classes have more fears than middle-class youth, espe-

TABLE 3.5. Categorical percentage of fears by sex and socioeconomic level.

Category	Sex Male	Sex Female	Socioeconomic level Upper	Socioeconomic level Lower	Total sample
Animals	9.04	10.55	10.22	9.73	9.79
Future	10.97	8.62	9.88	9.79	9.79
Supernatural phenomena	8.39	9.68	9.45	8.93	9.03
Natural phenomena	6.62	10.87	7.11	11.40	8.74
Personal appearance	8.47	9.17	9.23	8.68	8.82
Personal relations	10.56	10.56	11.06	10.30	10.56
School	10.37	10.05	10.86	10.64	10.21
Home	11.71	10.21	10.40	9.67	10.95
Safety	8.77	8.46	8.52	9.02	8.61
Political	13.02	12.35	13.24	12.32	12.68

From "A Second Look at Adolescent Fears" by J. W. Croake and F. H. Knox, *Adolescence*, 1971, 6(23), 279-284. Copyright 1971 Libra Publishers, Inc. Reprinted by permission.

cially fears related to their families (Angelino et al., 1956; Croake, 1967). Fears about politics, family life, and personal relationships seemed most dominant. Boys indicated stronger fear tendencies regarding the future than girls, who were more likely to fear natural phenomena and animals.

Showing adolescents the discrepancy between real and imaginary states helps reduce their fear. Worry comes primarily from imaginary situations; although it may contain elements of real fear, these are usually exaggerated. One way in which adolescents can reduce both fears and worries is by discussing them openly.

Anxiety. This general emotional state arises from continued apprehensions. Adolescents may experience anxiety while learning to play their new sex roles (Horrocks, 1969). They may also experience anxiety within their family structure, especially if they view one parent as punitive or threatening. In addition, they may experience anxiety within the school setting: from too intense study, from achievement-related tests (Scharf, 1964; Spielberger, 1966), or from social situations.

Research has shown that attempts to cover up self-perceived weaknesses or dissatisfactions cause anxiety because of the fear that others will find out the truth. Irritability, uneasiness, depression, unhappiness, and sudden shifts in mood are symptomatic of underlying anxiety states. Prolonged educational or occupational pursuits, as well as excessive preoccupations with personal success or failure, sanity, or sex, perpetuate anxiety, even to the point of emotional or mental disorder (Gallemore & Wilson, 1972).

Since anxiety is more deeply ingrained in the personality than fear, it is not so easily reduced or alleviated. It may be helpful to adolescents suffering from anxiety to (1) increase instances of behavioral situations that result in positive feelings, (2) accumulate intellectual information on an anxiety-producing subject, thus changing their perceptions (Anderson, 1973), and (3) work on gradually defining their ego-identity throughout adolescence.

Guilt. Guilt results primarily when an internal conflict exists between the values that an individual holds and the behaviors he or she expresses. Since value-behavior inconsistency is highly prominent throughout adolescence, more guilt potential exists (Thornburg, 1973c). Early parental and social teachings are sources of adolescent guilt. Religious teachings also place behaviors on a right-wrong continuum. The more socialized a deviant adolescent is, the stronger his or her guilt feelings are.

Two considerations are basic to our discussion of value-behavior incongruity. The young child is primarily socialized through interaction with parents. Throughout the first few years of life, the child takes on parental values rather than generating his or her own. Most childhood behaviors, as well, conform to parental expectations. Therefore values influence behaviors, and, when discrepancy occurs, so does guilt. However, as the child moves toward adolescence, behaviors begin to influence values. When a behavior is repeatedly expressed, the adolescent may subsequently align his or her values accordingly. Many youths engage in behaviors that, because of their value discrepancy, initially produce guilt. But eventually such behaviors become part of their belief system (Thornburg, 1973c).

This incongruity can also be explained by Festinger's theory of *cognitive dissonance* (1957). *Dissonance* is the state of discord produced when two incompatible situations confront an individual. The attempt to modify or eliminate one of the factors represents the search for *consonance*. Festinger believes that the adolescent will actively try to reduce dissonance, thus seeking consonance, and purposely avoid situations in which dissonance will increase. That is, the adolescent may disband some behaviors or modify some values in order to restore value-behavior consonance.

For illustration purposes, let's say that an adolescent opposes the smoking of marijuana. *Consonant* with this belief is the fact that his parents and legal sanctions also oppose the use of marijuana. *Dissonant* to his belief is the fact that other important individuals, his immediate peer group, support its use. If the adolescent begins smoking marijuana, dissonance exists. Its continued use may, however, cause the adolescent to shift values. Thus marijuana use would become consonant, and disuse would become dissonant. This ongoing conflict creates states of guilt. These states can be alleviated only by abandoning a behavior or modifying one's values.

Love and affection. Love, infatuation, and sex each represent an emotional state involving different degrees of feeling. Love involves strong feelings toward other individuals induced by sympathetic understanding, ties of friendship, or affection for the opposite sex. Infatuation involves affectional feelings that have a false base. Sex involves strong physical desires toward another person.

As an emotion, love has special meaning to the adolescent. Up to this time, the adolescent has directed affection toward parents, siblings, close relatives, and friends. Pleasant associations have caused the adolescent to maintain these feelings. Now love seems to be more totally encompassing. The adolescent falls in love or wants to give love or wants to make love. The love emotions are more intense, and they usually extend themselves to some selected member of the opposite sex.

Sometimes the adolescent experiences infatuation rather than love. Because the individual is so attracted to or enthralled with another individual, he believes he is experiencing love. Consider the 13-year-old girl "falling in love" with a 17-year-old boy. Many adolescents have difficulty distinguishing between infatuation and love. The primary difference is discrimination. In love, the individual begins to show concern for another individual. In infatuation, the individual often uses another individual for personal satisfaction; his concerns are more superficial and may be detrimental.

Sexual desire may also become confused with love. Initially, the individual is physically attracted to another individual. As an association persists, regardless of the original reason for its initiation, the demand for emotional involvement usually increases. The superficiality of sex and infatuation may begin to show as the demand for reciprocal affection increases. The more legitimate the feelings between two individuals, the more evident they are in behavioral interchange (Keislar, 1961).

Happiness. Youth today seem to approach life somewhat more seriously than youth in the past. Today's adolescents tend to abandon frivolousness and thrill-seeking behaviors for more "relevant" experiences (Erikson, 1967). But, in so doing, adolescents frequently fail to recognize the simple pleasures of growing up. Happiness and seriousness are not mutually exclusive, however. Table 3.6 summarizes the major causes of happiness for the adolescent.

Perhaps adolescents are happiest when they are aware of their

TABLE 3.6. Causes of happiness in adolescence.

Good adjustment to a situation
Capacities and training that enable an adolescent to "fit" into a situation will lead to self-satisfaction, which is essential to happiness.
Feelings of superiority
Success in activities highly valued by the social group leads to ego inflation and feelings of superiority. These are especially satisfying to the adolescent, who is typically plagued by uncertainty, insecurity, and self-doubt.
Release of pent-up emotional energy
Laughing, exercise, and many other overt expressions release pent-up emotional energy, and lead to a general feeling of well-being.
Perception of comic elements in a situation
The ability to perceive humor in embarrassing situations involving others leads to feelings of superiority which are ego-inflating. Perceiving humor in situations in which oneself is involved may also be satisfying, but the adolescent is usually unable to feel anything but embarrassment.

From *Adolescent Development*, 4th ed., by E. B. Hurlock. Copyright 1973 by McGraw-Hill Book Company. Reprinted by permission.

environment (home, school, or any other place) and are able to adjust to it. Often adolescents turn to their peers as a source of happiness, although in doing so they may well be avoiding the unpleasantness of other situations (O'Connell, 1960; Thompson & Gardner, 1969). For example, peers may encourage a particular behavior that an adolescent enjoys, such as smoking marijuana, whereas parents may disapprove of the behavior. Thus peers are perceived as a group that lends happiness to the specific behavior, and the discussion of marijuana use with parents is viewed as unpleasant.

Building Emotional Skills

In the process of emotional growth, adolescents should gain some control over their feelings. If they can see the humor in one situation and the seriousness in another, they are learning adaptive skills. They can better realize a sense of well-being and contentment when they obtain some balance of emotions.

One way to help adolescents build emotional skills is to allow them to express their feelings without guilt or shame. Too often an adolescent's emotionality is interpreted in light of social expectations. Of course, emotional expressions should not always be subject to social control, but adolescents do need to learn when they can or cannot express themselves freely. Unfortunately, no one has really defined acceptable or unacceptable emotional limits. Adolescents must intuitively discern these limits for themselves. Too much control may damage or suppress psychological well-being, creating "automaton behavior."

Reflecting on behaviors and exploring alternatives. Acceptance of the adolescent's emotional feelings is important. If adults can learn to acknowledge adolescent emotions, then youths can allow themselves to experience a wider range of emotionality as well as to reflect on their behaviors. Once adolescents feel accepted and can reflect on their behaviors, they can look at alternative emotions and behaviors. For example, suppose an adolescent boy is "unmistakably" in love with a girl classmate. Suddenly the girl loses interest in him and begins dating another boy. The trauma for the boy in love is very emotional. Because he can see no real reason why the girl should abandon him, he begins to have doubts about himself. If he can be led to see that the girl may have decided to stop seeing him for other reasons, the boy may seek out the approval of other girls without fears of inadequacy or rejection. Or he may come to realize that the girl only rejected aspects of him, not his total being.

Developing coping skills. In the process of emotional growth, adolescents should gain some control over their feelings. Several controlled emotional expressions are identifiable. One such expression is *change in mood.* Moods are dispersed emotional states in which the emotion gradually loses its intensity and is overcome (Zuk, 1956). A second controlled expression is *escape,* which usually comes about by fantasizing, daydreaming, watching television, going to the movies, or withdrawing to one's room. By escaping adolescents can release feelings without fear of social disapproval. Another controlled emotional expression is *displacement.* To avoid social disapproval, adolescents commonly transfer their emotional feelings to another person. Humor is one way of displacing emotions. The subtle transfer of stress or guilt from oneself to another person is also a form of displacement. These forms of emotional alternatives provide the adolescent with increased emotional skills, thus opening up the possibility of greater emotional responsibility and maturity with age and experience (Garai, 1970).

Whereas G. Stanley Hall placed almost total emphasis on the physical and emotional nature of the adolescent, the contemporary theorist is more inclined to think of social and cultural factors as the primary determinants of adolescent behavior. The balance lies in recognizing that many of the physical and emotional skills and problems that emerge from the maturation process are affected by the culture in which one lives and the social influences under which one was reared. This interaction, of course, is similar to the interaction of heredity and environment, which results in the phenomenon of intelligence—the subject of the next chapter.

Intellectual Growth 4

The concept *intelligence* has been defined in many ways. For example, intelligence has been referred to as (1) the ability to do abstract thinking or, more precisely, (2) the ability to judge, comprehend, and reason; and it has been designated as (3) the ability to adapt to the environment or, more precisely, (4) the total ability of an individual to act purposefully and rationally in his environment. Adolescent intelligence has been defined specifically as "a general capacity for processing information and for utilizing abstract symbols in the solution of abstract problems" (Ausubel & Ausubel, 1966, p. 412).

Throughout this discussion I will refer to intelligence as an ability that is *developmental*, having its roots in genetic transmission and culminating its growth during adolescence. Intellectual development is considered to be tied to two basic processes—the interaction of heredity and environment and the increased mental capacity that occurs throughout the growth of the individual. Heredity establishes the limits of intelligence, but, as Ferguson (1956) has pointed out, the culture determines which intellectual abilities will be developed. Some people, because of their genetic endowment, have a greater capacity for intellectual skills than other people. However, a nonstimulating environment might prevent adequate development of intellectual potential, and a favorable environment might enhance this development.

EARLY THEORIES OF INTELLIGENCE

Single-Factor Theory: Lewis Terman

Early psychologists thought that intelligence was *monogenetic*—based on a single general *(g)* factor that is inherited. This aspect of intelligence was thought to develop as the individual matured. In 1916, Lewis Terman expanded this theory of intelligence. The general factor *g*, Terman believed, represented the individual's ability to verbalize and to think abstractly. Two things may be said in support of Terman's ideas. First, because most existing intelligence tests are highly verbal in content, the assessment of intelligence is affected by the individual's verbal facility. Second, because the school places great emphasis on learning to think abstractly, verbal facility is commonly viewed as an important intellectual component. In addition, most adolescent intelligence is characterized by skill in abstract reasoning, hypothesis making, and problem solving, each of which is related to verbal ability. The disadvantage to Terman's simple concept of intelligence as a g factor is that, since intelligence tests measure g, and g includes the verbal abilities required for test taking, we end up defining intelligence as "what the intelligence tests measure."

Two-Factor Theory: Charles Spearman

Another theory, advanced by Charles Spearman in 1927, enlarged upon Terman's theory to account for variations in intelligence. Spearman (1927) postulated that there were two factors of intelligence, both of which were inherited. He maintained that all intellectual activities have in common the g factor. Spearman defined the g factor as the dominant intelligence factor that determines the variety and complexity of intellectual tasks a person can do. Spearman's second factor, called s, overlaps with the g factor. The s factor also exists in each intellectual act. In contrast to the g factor, however, the s factor varies from one type of intellectual activity to another. The specific s abilities that Spearman discussed were logical, mathematical, mechanical, attentive, and creative (Spearman & Jones, 1950). For example, an adolescent who has average general ability but is exceptionally strong in science is high in s factor. With these two factors, Spearman was able to account for variations in intelligence.

THE DEVELOPING COGNITIVE STRUCTURE: PIAGET

Jean Piaget's writings (1950, 1952, 1960) reflect an interest in intelligence different from that of the preceding theoretical approaches. Piaget's primary interest is in *cognitive growth*, the course of development of intellectual functioning. His theory of cognitive growth has probably spawned more research in the past 15 years than any other single intelligence theory.

Piaget offers several definitions of intelligence, all couched in somewhat general terms. For example, "Intelligence is a particular instance of biological adaptation" (1952) reflects his training as a biologist. In another source (1950), he defines intelligence as a "form of equilibrium toward which all the structures ... tend." Still another definition (1950) states that intelligence is a "system of living and acting operations." In these three definitions, Piaget presents his concept of intelligence as a biological adaptation, involving mental activity, in which the person seeks equilibrium within his environment.

Piaget's framework hypothesizes that all species inherit two "invariate functions"—*adaptation* and *organization*—that determine the manner in which any organism behaves and develops intellectually. Organization is a hereditary property that allows the organism to come to terms with its environment through either physical or psychological mechanisms. Piaget contends that, although the individual does not inherit particular intellectual reactions, he does inherit the tendency to organize his intellectual processes.

Physical structures—breathing apparatus, the circulatory system, temperature regulators—interact and are coordinated into an efficiently organized system. Psychologically, organization involves the interaction of the organism's sensory and cerebral structures in responding to the environment—in other words, the integration of external events into coherent psychological structures.

All organisms engage in adaptation, an inherent tendency to modify behavior in response to their environment. The ways in which adaptation occurs vary from species to species, from individual to individual within a species, and from one developmental stage to the next within an individual. An example of the last type of adaptation is the newborn infant, uncomfortable in wet diapers, who seeks to adapt (to get his mother or father to relieve his discomfort) by crying. At a later stage, he may use nonverbal gestures; still later, words may be involved in his adaptation to the environment.

Adaptation consists of two complementary processes: *assimilation* and *accommodation.* Assimilation refers to the organism's incorporation of external reality into its already existing psychological structures. Accommodation is the process by which the organism's psychological structures are modified to adapt to specific aspects of its environment.

As humans organize their behaviors and thoughts and adapt to the environment, they create in the process certain new psychological structures, which Piaget terms *schemata* (plural of *schema*). The schemata represent a kind of conceptual framework into which incoming environmental stimuli (inputs) must fit if the individual is to perceive and act on these stimuli. Although the processes of adaptation and organization are invariant, these schemata, or conceptual structures, are variant; that is, they change as a result of the person's experience. In other words, through his experiences with his environment, a child constantly creates new schemata in order to continue the innate processes of organization and adaptation to the environment.

The person's first schemata are exemplified by the reflexes of the newborn infant. As the infant interacts with the environment, certain ready-made schemata that already exist (reflexes) begin to vary with circumstances and experience. For example, the "sucking schema" of the newborn may be observed when any kind of object is placed near the infant's mouth. However, as he becomes experienced in nursing, the infant begins to differentiate objects, some of which will bring on the sucking response and some of which will not. Thus a new, more discriminatory schema replaces the original ready-made schema of sucking. This process can be termed *intellectual development*.

Stages of Intellectual Development

Piaget hypothesizes that humans develop through adaptation over a series of defined maturational *periods* and subperiods, or *phases*. The periods and phases of interest here are (1) the *sensorimotor period* (0–2 years); (2) the *preoperational period* (2–7 years), with phases of (a) *preconceptual thought* (2–4 years) and (b) *intuitive thought* (4–7 years); (3) the *concrete-operations period* (7–11 years) and (4) the *formal-operations period* (11–15 years). Although Piaget has attached ages to each period, experiments by him and others have shown these age boundaries to be flexible. However, the developmental progression itself remains invariant.

Sensorimotor period (0–2 years). At this stage, mental activity involves primarily the coordination of simple motor responses to incoming sensations. The first four months of an infant's life are characterized by changes in the ready-made reflexive schemata and coordination of these schemata into higher-order schemata. For example, the child develops the "looking schema," the "reaching schema," and the "grasping schema." When a child finds an object in his environment that he can see, reach, and grasp at the same time, coordination of the schemata is taking place. The later stages of the sensorimotor period are characterized by the development of trial-and-error experimentation—exploring the problem of which of several responses is most effective in obtaining the goal object (Thornburg, 1973e). During these months the child forms an idea of the permanence of objects. After 18 months the child begins to show evidence of foresight, or contemplation prior to action.

Preoperational period (2–7 years). The phase of *preconceptual thought* (2–4 years) is the growth phase characterized by the child's acquisition of the capacity to form mental symbols representing absent things or events. This ability frees the child from the need always to have something in front of him in order to think about it. Mental symbols, in

Piaget's terminology, are *signifiers*. The child attaches meaning to symbols by assimilating them into the schemata that he already has available; for this reason, these signifiers have a unique meaning to each individual child.

During this phase the child begins using language. At first, words are closely related to objects and people in his immediate environment. Toward the end of this stage, words may be used to signify absent things. The child also can pretend that one thing is another; thus imaginative play begins.

Intuitive thought (4–7 years) is the growth phase characterized by the child's ability to enter into socialized behavior. The child can also group objects into classes by attributes, but he can attend to only one dimension at a time. For example, if a ball of clay is made into a pancake shape, he is likely to say that there is less clay in the pancake than in the ball because it is so thin. He has not yet fully developed the principle of *conservation*, which states that no changes occur in quantity of matter even though the matter may change in size, shape, or orientation.

Concrete-operations period (7–11 years). The age span included in this period is roughly equivalent to the time that the child is in elementary school. The most obvious change during this period is the child's ability to use written words and numbers. During the preceding stages, the spoken word came to symbolize people, experiences, and concrete objects. Now the written word or number possesses the same potential.

During the concrete-operations period, the child also learns relational and combinational procedures whereby he is able to classify, order, and group objects. For example, he is able to perform additive, subtractive, repetitive, and equalitive functions. These abilities contrast with his abilities of the preceding stages, when his attempts to systematize were incomplete and characterized by irreversibility of thought, transductive reasoning (seeing relationships between the particular and the particular), and egocentric thinking.

As an illustration of the movement from the preoperational to the operational period, consider that we have presented a child with identical beakers, A and B, both filled to the same height with a liquid (see Figure 4.1). Asked if the quantities of liquid are equal, the child agrees that they are. The liquid from one of the beakers is then poured into a differently shaped beaker, C. Asked if beakers A and C are equal, the preoperational child will answer "no." The child at the preoperational stage can focus on only *one* aspect of the situation, either the height of the liquid in container C in relation to the height of the liquid in container A or the breadth of the liquid in container C in relation to the breadth of the liquid in

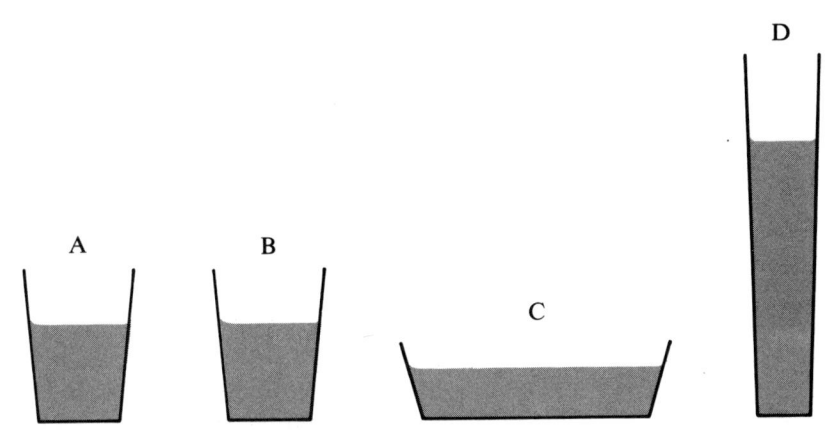

FIGURE 4.1. Conservation of continuous quantities. From *Piaget's Theory of Intellectual Development* by H. Ginsburg and S. Opper. Copyright © 1969 Prentice-Hall, Inc. Reprinted by permission.

container A. If he focuses (*centers*) on the height, he will say that A has more liquid; if he centers on the breadth, he will say that C has more liquid. If the procedure is reversed by pouring the liquid from C back into B, the child will then judge the two amounts of liquid as being equal. And if a fourth beaker, D, of still another shape, is introduced and the liquid from B poured into it, the child will again judge that their quantities are unequal.

The child at the operational level has the ability to *decenter*—that is, to focus on more than one property at a time. Therefore he is able to judge equality between any combinations, A and B, A and C, or A and D. The child recognizes that transforming the shape of the liquid does nothing to the quantity.

During the concrete-operational stage, the child learns to master logical operations using concrete objects as referents. The child begins to think according to some logical model of reasoning. Around age 7 or 8, he becomes able to *conserve*, or to realize that some things remain the same in quantity although they may change in size, shape, form, color, or orientation. Conservation of mass tends to be the first conservation principle acquired, followed by conservation of weight and volume (Muuss, 1967).

The learning of conservation principles leads directly to an understanding of *reversibility*. Piaget defined reversibility as "the permanent possibility of returning to the starting point of the operation in question" (Inhelder & Piaget, 1958, p. 272). This ability to retrace one's intellectual behavior, or to see that an idea can be expressed differently and thus reversed, is also a significant step in the growth process. The ability to do reversible intellectual operations is basic to the process of carrying on logical deductions, a crucial factor in adolescent hypothesizing. The behavioral criterion for the existence of the reversible operation is the ability to conserve (Piaget, 1966).

During the concrete-operations period the child also acquires the ability to do *class-inclusion* and *serial-ordering* operations. Class inclusion refers to the ability to see something in two relationships, as an entity in itself and as a part of something. The ability to hold several pieces of information in memory and to reverse the thinking process allows for the emergence of classification, or category, systems. Learning that all balls are part of the general category "balls" while also seeing that each individual ball is whole in itself is an example of class inclusion.

Seriation (ordering) occurs when an individual can impose some structure and order on things about him—for example, rank groups from large to small. During the concrete-operations period, the child is able to order concrete objects on a hierarchy such as tall to short in height, light to heavy in weight, or large to small in groups. The critical limitation of this ability at this stage is that all objects must be presented concretely. The child cannot engage in abstract mental ordering until the formal-operations period.

Muuss (1967, 1975) summarizes the four concrete-operational groupings advanced by Piaget as follows:

1. *Combinativity.* Two or more classes may be combined into one larger, more comprehensive class of the same grouping. All men and all women—all adults. Logical relationships such as A is larger than B and B is larger than C may be combined into a new statement that A is larger than C. The ability to combine subclasses into supraclasses is essential to the understanding of a hierarchy of classifications.
2. *Reversibility.* Every operation is reversible. Every mathematical operation has an opposite that reverses it. Supraclasses can be taken apart so that the effect of combining subclasses is reversed. All adults, except all women—all men. Motor actions are reversed by retracing the steps. The degree of reversibility of the child's thought processes is an important indication of the child's cognitive development.
3. *Associativity.* The child whose operations are associative can reach a goal in various ways; he can make detours in thought, but the results obtained by these different routes remain the same. For example, $(3 + 6) + 4 = 13$, and $6 + (3 + 4) = 13$. Another illustration is: All females and all males = all people, or all boys and men plus all girls and women = all people.
4. *Identity or nullifiability.* An operation which is combined with its opposite becomes nullified. Illustrations of nullifiability in thought are: $3 - 3 = 0$, $5x \div 5 = x$, all Americans except those who are

Americans equals no one. I drive one mile west and I drive one mile east = I am where I started [Muuss, 1967, pp. 298–299; 1975].*

Transition between concrete operations and formal operations. There is no clear-cut transition of intellectual functioning between the concrete-operations stage and the formal-operations stage. Ausubel and Ausubel (1966) feel that, upon entering adolescence, the child is still somewhat dependent intellectually on the concrete-operations stage, primarily in the sense that he provides himself with concrete props in order to do abstract thinking. They suggest three determinants of the transition:

1. The developing individual gradually acquires a working vocabulary of transactional or mediating terms that makes possible the more efficient juxtaposition and combination of different relatable abstractions into potentially meaningful propositions.
2. He can relate these later propositions more readily to cognitive structure and hence render them more meaningful in view of his growing fund of stable, higher-order concepts and principles encompassed by and made available within that structure. A sufficient body of abstract ideas that are clear and stable is obviously necessary before he can hope efficiently to manipulate relationships between them so as to develop meaningful general propositions.
3. It seems reasonable to suppose that after many years of practice in meaningful understanding and manipulating relationships with the aid of concrete-empirical props, he gradually develops greater facility in performing these operations, so that eventually he can perform the same operations just as effectively *without* relying on props [Ausubel & Ausubel, 1966, p. 408].

Formal-operations period (11–15 years). This period is typified by the transition from thoughts about reality to thoughts about possibility. Before acting on a problem confronting him, the adolescent analyzes the situation and suggests hypotheses on the possible outcomes. He is also able to devise experiments to test these hypotheses, so that he can reach a conclusion on the basis of these experiments. The child at the previous stage, concrete operations, can reason and hypothesize about current and concrete experience, but it is only during the formal-operations period that he becomes capable of understanding and directly manipulating relationships between abstractions. The adolescent no longer needs to base his reasoning on concrete or current experiences. The thoughts of the adolescent involve second-order constructs (operating on operations), abstract ideas, and understandings based on previously

*From *Theories of Adolescence* (3rd ed.) by R. E. Muuss. Copyright 1975 by Random House, Inc. Reprinted by permission.

established verbal abstractions. Reality becomes secondary to possibility, and the form of the argument becomes as evident as the content.

Abstract thinking is the basic characteristic of this developmental period. The adolescent can now carry on hypothetical and combinatorial operations. Reflective thinking is another major characteristic of this stage, as is the ability to synthesize, a combinatorial operation. It is generally thought that between ages 15 and 17 the adolescent reaches his full intellectual growth potential and has a capacity similar to that of the adult (Inhelder & Piaget, 1958; Phillips, 1969).

Inhelder and Piaget (1958) refer to two distinct stages within the formal-operations period. Stage III-A, which encompasses ages 11 to 13, is somewhat reflective of the transition between concrete operations and formal operations. During the process of moving out of preadolescence and into adolescence, the individual's cognitive structure is still growing.

The school provides opportunities for active use and continued development of intellectual skills.

However, movement away from the use of concrete or environmental props occurs in the forms of experimentation, hypothesis making, and synthesis and analysis of cognitive materials; also, exploratory ideas begin to dominate the adolescent's thinking. These developments are characteristic of the 14-to-15 age range, the III-B period designated by Inhelder and Piaget. It is important to remember, as Elkind (1971) points out, that the basis for designating two distinct stages for the formal-operations period of adolescence lies in the fact that there are two distinct periods of time during which the mind goes through a state of reorganization and disequilibrium. The first stage (III-A) is characterized by transition, and the second stage (III-B) represents the final restructuring of the mind before it realizes its full growth potential. Intellectual processes in the III-B stage are definitely more abstract, more reflective, and include more self-generated thought about thoughts.

SPECIAL CHARACTERISTICS OF ADOLESCENT THOUGHT

Differentiation of mental abilities. Elkind points to the fact that one characteristic of adolescent mental growth is the differentiation of mental abilities. "Whereas mental growth during childhood is relatively even, during adolescence some mental abilities are more developed than others, depending upon the individual" (1971, pp. 122–123). This differentiation is often reinforced by the secondary-school system, which offers adolescents the opportunity to explore their own special-interest areas, whereas in primary education a core of academic subjects is taught to every individual.

Motivation. A variety of factors enter into the actual realization of mental abilities within high school. One's own motivation is a strong determinant of one's intellectual expressions. For example, if a high school boy doesn't like English, he may perform in such a manner that he is evaluated as somewhat unintelligent. What could be happening in this particular instance, however, is that he not only dislikes English but fails to see any relevance in it, and is more interested in investing his intellectual energies in peer-sanctioned behaviors. Thus adolescent peer groups may be a deterrent to the adolescent's realization of intellectual functioning while in high school. Another deterrent may be the fact that most adolescents view their high school as a social rather than as an academic institution (Braham, 1965; Coleman, 1961; Friesen, 1968). We will explore these topics more thoroughly in Chapter 8.

Problem solving. Perhaps the optimal intellectual-functioning level and the most important learning achievement facing adolescents is the ability to do effective problem solving, since most of adult thought consists of acting on or reacting to problem situations within the environment. Although children can effect some problem-solving behavior through appropriate environmental props, an individual begins to use effectively his abstract problem-solving abilities only in adolescence. The fact that the adolescent can raise questions and generate hypotheses indicates that his abstract-reasoning ability has become more developed, and the development of this ability becomes indicative of how well he will function as an adult. When encountering a problem-solving situation, the adolescent can distinguish between the facts and the hypotheses surrounding the situation. He can then systematically go about synthesizing and evaluating information presented to him to determine its accuracy, validity, and relevance to the problem he is encountering. The more this type of thinking dominates the adolescent's behavioral expressions, the further he has moved into the formal-operations stage.

Adolescent egocentrism. Up to this point, I have characterized adolescent thought as consisting of reflective thinking, abstract thinking, and the movement from thoughts about reality to thoughts about possibility. Elkind (1967) proposes that the adolescent's primary intellectual task is the *conquest of thought,* a task he resolves upon completing the three processes discussed here. Elkind observes that, in the process of fulfilling this task, the adolescent develops *egocentrism* by around age 14. This egocentrism emerges as a result of the adolescent's ability to conceptualize the thoughts of others as well as his own thoughts. The adolescent may extend this new perception of the thoughts of others to the belief that others are preoccupied with his appearance and behavior, a belief that constitutes egocentrism. Egocentrism is also characterized by an inability to separate the real from the unreal.

Elkind identifies two mental configurations that characterize adolescent egocentrism: the imaginary audience and the personal fable. The *imaginary audience* is the adolescent's belief that he is the center of attention. It causes him much self-consciousness, since he perceives his audience as sometimes admiring and sometimes critical. The adolescent will do things to please his audience, often becoming self-critical if he feels he has failed to do so. The girl who is a cheerleader, the boy at a school dance, and the "egghead" in science class all see themselves as the focus of attention.

The *personal fable* is an untrue story that an adolescent tells himself and wants to believe. According to the fable he creates, the adolescent may regard himself as unique, invulnerable, or even immortal.

The adolescent who thinks he will live forever, the girl who has had intercourse several times but believes that only others can get pregnant, and the boy who is hooked on heroin but says he can quit when he wants to all illustrate this phenomenon. Some adolescents have feelings of a special relationship with God not enjoyed by anyone else (Long et al., 1967).

Most accounts of egocentrism come from clinical evidence or from adolescent autobiographies or diaries. For example, the presentation of oneself as truly unique and as the center of attention—manifestations of both the personal fable and the imaginary audience—may be seen in the following example. An adolescent boy of 14 related the following dream:

> I dreamt that one afternoon I walked out onto our portal headed for the swimming pool when I observed under the decked porch bleachers with some 2000 spectators sitting and waiting for me to swim. I was so taken back by this event that I decided to favor them by walking on the water. My repeated success in performing such a feat brought the audience to its feet, then its knees in admiration and homage.

As the adolescent moves toward the culmination of his intellectual development, his egocentric focus passes. The imaginary-audience phenomenon is often dispelled by interaction with others. The adolescent comes to realize that others are equally concerned with themselves and do not focus on him as much as he had previously thought. A factor enabling the adolescent to gradually overcome the personal fable is his or her growing interest in the opposite sex (Elkind, 1967). A very good point regarding one's personal fable, a phenomenon that characterizes many adolescents and adults in our society, has been made by Looft:

> It seems entirely possible that an individual may continue to entertain personal-fable notions throughout his fantasy life. That is, through the course of social interaction the person not only discovers that his personal experiences are not necessarily unique, but he also learns that it is socially undesirable to express such notions of uniqueness to others. Thus, his personal fable may go "underground," but in an altered form; intellectually he now understands the fallacy of his theory of uniqueness, but affectively he continues to derive enjoyment from it in his imaginational life [Looft, 1971, p. 490].

It is important to point out that the imaginary audience and the personal fable are primarily cognitive distortions that are a natural result of adolescent growth (Thornburg, 1973a). These behaviors do not indicate that the individual who sees himself as the focus of attention has an ego problem, or that the personal fable is an indication of neurosis or psychosis. Nevertheless, as Looft (1971) has pointed out, it is possible for the developing adolescent to attach affective meaning to his egocentric experiences. If such emotional meaning is gratifying, it may persist beyond the age at which we would expect it to disappear. The adolescent usually breaks away from his egocentric focus around 16 or 17, when he becomes capable of differentiating the real from the unreal.

TWO CONTEMPORARY THEORIES OF INTELLIGENCE

Multifactor Theory: J. P. Guilford

The most elaborate theory of intelligence has been advanced by J. P. Guilford, who maintained that three dimensions of intelligence exist: the *contents of thought*, the *operations of thought*, and the *products of thought*. These three dimensions are not inherited, according to Guilford, but environmentally determined. Each of these dimensions, Guilford believed, is broken into subcategories, which inter-relate to make 120 factors comprising intelligence. Approximately 80 of these factors had been identified at the time Guilford expounded this theory (1966).

Guilford described three dimensions of intelligence, shown in Figure 4.2. The *operations* category involves the different ways in which an individual operates intellectually. The intellectual act itself is an operation consisting of the interaction of the *content* and the *product*. Content of thought is the material involved in thinking. Product of thought refers to the internal complexity of the material. For example, if an adolescent were learning a science formula, his mental processes would involve symbolic thought in content and thoughts about relationships between the symbols in product, since a formula combines symbols into a relationship.

To show the diversity of intellectual functioning, let's consider the interaction of contents and products in the operation category *cognition*. This intellectual operation may best be described as comprehension or inductive reasoning. Comprehending cognitive *units* involves understanding word structures and word meanings. Placing objects or ideas into *classes* according to their common properties is an activity instrumental in concept learning. Comprehending *relationships* involves recognizing the relationships among objects, ideas, or concepts. Comprehending *systems* involves seeing several components in some kind of organized total structure. Making *transformations* involves rendering information from one form to another, such as taking data in a line graph and transforming them into a bar graph. Guilford described transformations as "changes, revision, redefinitions, or modifications, by which any product of information in one state goes over into another state" (1959, p. 64). Finally, comprehending *implications* involves perceiving different courses of action and eventually selecting the most appropriate one.

Guilford describes the contents of thought as the materials involved in thinking. He proposes four kinds of content. First, *figural content* represents concrete objects, the things that we perceive through the senses. This content level is the young child's method of dealing with spatial concepts. The second kind of content is *symbolic*; it includes letters, symbols, digits, or signs that have no real significance in themselves but have meanings attached to them. The third kind of content, *semantic*, is used in verbal thinking and verbal communication. For example, the word "football" has meanings attached to it that enable the

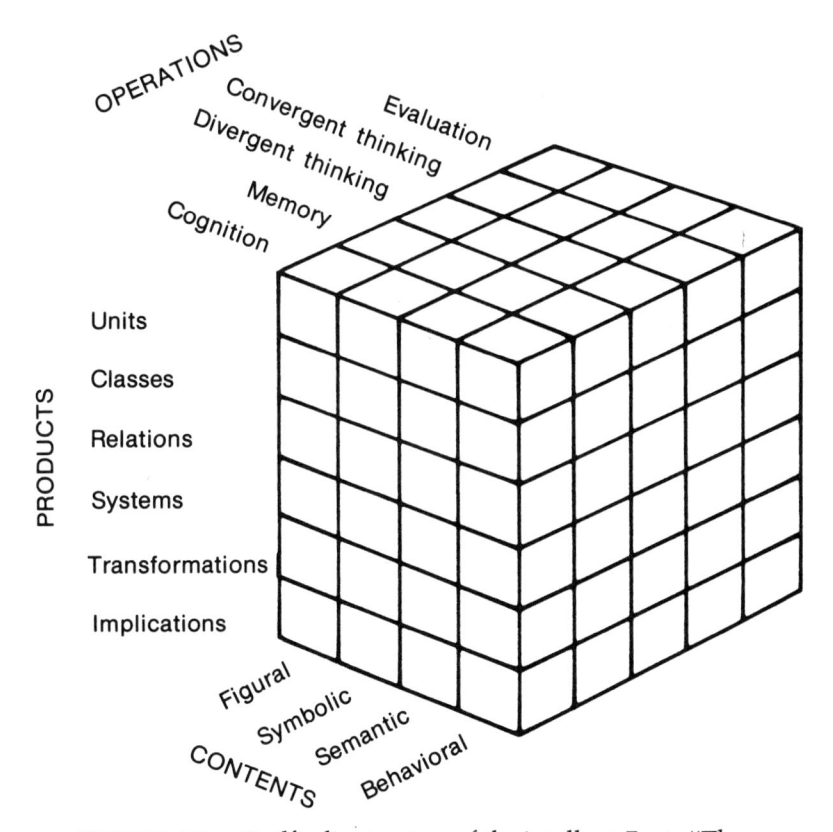

FIGURE 4.2. Guilford's structure of the intellect. From "Three Faces of Intellect" by J. P. Guilford, *American Psychologist*, 1959, 14, 469-479. Copyright 1959 by the American Psychological Association. Reprinted by permission.

76   Chapter 4

adolescent to visualize the figural referent, just as the abstract word "morality" has meanings that allow a group of adolescents to converse about the concept. The fourth kind of content is *behavioral*; it consists of essentially nonverbal communications that are used in social interactions. Behavioral content can be illustrated by the actions that would cause an adolescent boy to say "The new girl I met says she likes me, but I know she doesn't."

Theory of Mental-Ability Levels: Arthur Jensen

Arthur Jensen (1969) also hypothesizes two different levels of intellectual functioning.[1] Jensen's research began with his examination of the reasons for the rather limited effects of compensatory-education programs, such as Head Start and Higher Horizons, aimed at improving the educational success of lower-socioeconomic-class (culturally different) children. The primary purpose of these compensatory programs, as determined from evaluation studies, was the improvement of the IQ of these children; but tests administered to the children after a period of involvement with these programs showed little average IQ gain, and follow-up studies have shown that most of the gains made were not maintained through the first year of the children's regular schooling (U.S. Commission on Civil Rights, 1967).

The basic premise upon which these compensatory programs were based was that the lower IQ of the culturally different child was due to a lack of preschool environmental stimulation, and that a change in the child's environment to one more like the middle-class environment would increase his IQ. Therefore, most of these programs were aimed at

---

[1] A great deal of controversy concerning the relative influences of heredity and environment on the intellectual nature of the individual has arisen since the appearance of Arthur Jensen's article entitled "How Much Can We Boost IQ and Scholastic Achievement?" in a 1969 issue of the *Harvard Educational Review*. Jensen's view that intelligence is primarily genetic and his opinion that special education has only a minimal influence on increasing intelligence have evoked violent and ongoing positive and negative reactions. Some papers that discuss the pros and cons of the Jensen report are: (1) L. G. Humphreys and H. P. Dachler, "Jensen's Theory of Intelligence"; A. R. Jensen, "Jensen's Theory of Intelligence: A reply"; and L. G. Humpreys and H. P. Dachler, "Jensen's Theory of Intelligence: A Rebuttal." All of these appear in *Journal of Educational Psychology*, December 1969. (2) S. Scarr-Salapatek, "Race, Social Class, and IQ," *Science*, December 24, 1971. (3) W. Shockley, "Dysgenics, Geneticity, Raceology: Challenges to the Intellectual Responsibility of Educators"; N. L. Gage, "IQ, Heritability, Race Differences, and Educational Research." Both of these appear in *Phi Delta Kappan*, January 1972. (4) W. Shockley, "A Debate Challenge: Geneticity Is 80% for White Identical Twins' IQ's"; A. R. Jensen, "The Causes of Twin Differences in IQ: A Reply to Gage"; and N. L. Gage, "The Causes of Race Differences in IQ: Replies to Shockley, Page, and Jensen." All of these appear in *Phi Delta Kappan*, March, 1972. (5) R. Hernstein, "IQ," *The Atlantic*, 1971, 228.

broadening the experiential backgrounds of these children by bringing them into direct contact with those experiences considered "normal" for the preschool child in the middle-class home. Jensen rejects this environmental-deprivation hypothesis as the cause of different intellectual-ability levels among the various socioeconomic and racial groups and proposes, instead, that one's level of intellectual ability is primarily a function of *heredity*. He acknowledges environment as a factor but terms it a *threshold variable*, in the belief that if the environment is not *severely* restricted, changes in the environment will not make an appreciable difference in IQ. If the environment is severely restricted—for example, in cases in which children have been maltreated by being shut in a room with no environmental stimulation—changes in the environment will make a significant difference in the level of intellectual functioning. Therefore, according to Jensen, the primary variance factor in different mental abilities is heredity.

How much *learning* ability is hereditary? Jensen hypothesizes (1969) that there are two levels of learning ability. *Level I, associative ability*, involves the registration of stimulus inputs in the neural mechanism, the consolidation of these inputs, and the formation of associations, with very little internal transformation of these inputs as they are emitted in the form of responses. Digit memory, serial rote learning, and paired-associate learning are included in this level of intellectual ability. *Level II, conceptual ability*, involves the *self-initiated* substantial transformation and elaboration of the stimulus input before a response is emitted. Concept learning and problem solving are examples of this kind of ability, which is most truly measured by tests that are relatively "culture free" (that is, that do not require knowledge of a particular culture) and high in the g factor of overall intellectual functioning.

On tests that measure level I abilities and are, by definition, relatively "culture free," Jensen and his coworkers (1969) found that lower-class children, regardless of ethnic and racial origins, did no worse than environmentally "privileged" middle-class children. But on less culture-free tests measuring level II abilities, the lower-class children scored lower than the middle-class children. Jensen concludes from this research that the two kinds of abilities, associative and conceptual, are necessary components of intellectual functioning; through further research, he has developed the hypothesis that level I associative ability is a necessary but not sufficient requisite for the conceptual ability of level II. That is, he believes that high performance on level II tasks depends upon better than average ability in level I, but that the reverse does not hold true. This hypothesis and the test results from his research also suggest to Jensen that level I associative ability is distributed more or less evenly among all socioeconomic classes, but that level II conceptual ability is lower among lower socioeconomic classes than among middle socioeconomic classes, as a result of hereditary factors.

Jensen avers that the reason lower-class children do less well in school than middle-class children is that the schools tend to emphasize those skills connected with conceptual activities (level II abilities). He pleads that the schools recognize different types of learning abilities among different groups and provide different methods of instruction that will capitalize on the existing abilities of each learner. He believes that we can provide equal education for all children only when we have recognized these differences and modified our instructional procedures to account for them.

Although psychologists are clearly not in agreement on what intelligence is or on all of the variables that affect intellectual functioning, the various theories do account for most adolescent intellectual behaviors. These behaviors might be better understood within the concept of several intelligences rather than that of intelligence. If adolescents do possess different figural and semantic operational abilities or different degrees of g, these variations will affect the nature of adolescent interaction with peers and adults. These differences may be most noticeable in a school environment. If a teacher's *modus operandi* is aligned with the Jensen hypothesis, the methods of instruction may be varied so that no adolescent is placed at a learning disadvantage.

Adolescents realize their intellectual potential through both hereditary abilities and environmental stimulation. Piaget's contribution to our understanding of the developmental nature of intelligence is invaluable to an understanding of adolescent thinking processes. The developmental unfolding of abstract reasoning results in highly flexible problem-solving abilities, the highest realization of intellectual potential in the adolescent.

Developmental Socialization 5

Just as intelligence is often defined as an individual's means of using mental processes to adapt to his environment, socialization is the process by which an individual learns and adapts to the ways, ideas, beliefs, and values of his particular culture. Both are developmental processes. Since to a young child society consists largely of his family, the first values he learns are those of his parents. However, socialization is a lifelong process; as the child moves into preadolescence and adolescence, other sources—such as siblings, peers, his school, his church, and the mass media—become influential in the socialization process. These alternative influences encourage the adolescent to question and adopt values and behaviors that often exclude or conflict with those of his home. Through the resolution of the resultant value and behavior conflicts and the processes of social maturation and social integration, the individual moves into the developmental stage called adulthood.

SOCIALIZATION AND CULTURE

The manner in which an individual is socialized depends upon the culture in which he or she lives. The particular society determines what goals, values, and behaviors are acceptable in the individual. The more a child's parents accept their society's expectations, the more likely they are to teach the child such values as normative. As the child becomes an adolescent, however, he may challenge these normative values and behaviors if they seem to have become incongruous with his immediate social environment, which has now expanded to include peers and adults other than his family.

McNeil (1969) has conceptualized the socialization process as shown in Figure 5.1. This overview presents the major ways in which an individual is socialized. Through socializing agents, individual responses to the environment emerge as personality traits, which in essence regulate behavior and determine the values and behaviors the individual will retain in adulthood. Bloom (1964) suggests that most personality traits are formed during childhood, although the behaviors in which they manifest themselves continue to be learned during adolescence.

A classic study of socialization in adolescence was reported by Hollingshead in *Elmtown's Youth* (1949). He defined adolescent socialization as "the period in the life of a person when the society in which he functions ceases to regard him (male or female) as a child and does not

THE RAW MATERIAL	→WILL BE SOCIALIZED ALONG THESE DIMENSIONS	→IN DYNAMIC INTER-ACTION WITH THESE AGENTS AND FORCES OF SOCIALIZATION	→LIMITED BY THESE INDIVIDUAL CHARACTERISTICS	→TO FORM THESE LIFE THEMES AND SYSTEMS OF BEHAVIOR	→WHICH WILL FORM THE ADULT
the newborn biological organism with physical needs and inherited characteristics	emotional social cognitive perceptual intellectual behavioral expressive	*Agents* parents siblings peers relatives teachers *Cultural forces* social class religion race school community mass media voluntary groups	age sex development rate stage constitution intelligence	oral anal sexual aggressive achievement affiliation self-esteem	traits character personality role preference goals
	WHILE SELECTIVELY ACQUIRING skills knowledge attitudes values motives habits beliefs needs interests ideals				

FIGURE 5.1. The process and components of socialization. From *Human Socialization* by E. B. McNeil. Copyright © 1969 by Wadsworth Publishing Company, Inc. Reprinted by permission of the publisher, Brooks/Cole Publishing Company, Monterey, California.

accord to him full adult status, roles, and functions" (p. 6). Hollingshead believed that adolescence should not be considered to be marked by a specific point in time, such as puberty, because the nature, form, content, and duration of the adolescent's developmental process vary among social classes and cultures. North America's sociocultural milieu is so complex today that Hollingshead's concept of the relativity and flexibility of adolescent socialization bears even greater significance now than when he first advanced it.

Hollingshead's research supported the idea that adolescent behavior is transitional behavior, dependent both upon the particular society and, more specifically, upon the position the individual holds within his social environment. The adolescent's behavior is mediated by home and neighborhood influences; "the effects of differential learning in the home and the neighborhood during the childhood years are the basic conditioning factors which give rise to the highly significant differences in social behaviors observed among the adolescents in the different [social] classes" (Hollingshead, 1949, p. 441).

In effect, all socialization is learned through the continuous process of social reinforcement and punishment (Davis, 1944). One mechanism created by our environment that determines much of our behavior at any age level is *socialized anxiety*, the anticipation or fear of punishment if one does not behave according to social expectations. This anxiety functions as the main force motivating an individual to adapt to societal demands. Although individuals differ, they must adapt generally to these demands, since no society is open enough to accommodate the individual's every need. The potential for socialized anxiety increases for the adolescent as he begins to experience perceptual incongruities between what he learned from his parents and what he sees actually happening in society, and he commonly experiences disorganization, inhibitions, or guilt.

Social-Class Variation in Adolescent Socialization

The concept of socialized anxiety is most applicable to middle-class youth because, more than lower-class youth, they are eligible for the primary tangible rewards offered by society for acceptable behavior. Davis (1944) contended that socialized anxiety is derived from social-class position. This idea is still supported in the more contemporary research of sociologists like Elder (1970) and Katz (1967). Davis expressed the lower-class dilemma as follows:

> In order to understand the prestige motivation of individuals of middle status, one must remember the severe social and biological punishments

associated with low status. The anxiety which middle-status people learn is effective, first because it involves the threat of loss of present status, and secondly because it leads, as the individual may plainly see in "successful" persons, to the rewards of power, of social prestige, and of security for one's children.

Now, it is a difficult task to socialize in the middle-class way of behavior those great masses of low-status children. To the upper-middle-class child, who learns and climbs fast, the prestige rewards appear certain and relatively near. Our society cannot hope to educate the great masses of lower-class people in any really effective manner until it has *real* rewards to offer them for learning the necessary anxiety [Davis, 1944, pp. 213–214].

Elder (1970) discusses this social-class barrier in relation to attempts by black Americans to ascend the social ladder. He cites two beliefs held by black parents that tend to intensify achievement frustration and racial consciousness among the young. First is the idea that black youth must put forth extraordinary effort, relative to their white peers, in order to overcome racial barriers and achieve a "good" life. Second is the assumption that money and material goods are effective reinforcers of desirable behaviors. Among parents who are economically limited, money and goods may be viewed as symbols of success and as desirable rewards for fulfilling standard societal expectations. Katz (1967) found that material rewards do have positive reinforcing influence on the behavior of lower-class youth. Coleman and his associates (1966), however, felt that a fatalistic view was held by disadvantaged youth. "It appears that children from advantaged groups assume the environment will respond if they are able to affect it; children from disadvantaged groups do not make this assumption, but in many cases assume that nothing they do can affect the environment—it will give benefits or withhold them but not as a consequence of their own action" (Coleman, Mood, Campbell, et al., 1966, p. 321).

Elder's research among high-school-age black males (1970) cites a great deal of evidence that supports Coleman's assertion. These black youths perceived themselves as disadvantaged because of racial oppression, social discrepancies in the school environment, some of their parents' values that they had adopted, distorted aspirational levels, and poor self-concepts. These findings also support Havighurst's conclusion (1970) that for the adolescent the nature of the reward/punishment system is a matter of the approval or disapproval of the larger community—in many cases, the peer group. Engaging in dangerous or high-risk exploits, sex, and drug taking are the adolescent's means of gaining status among peers. As Havighurst has suggested, external rewards have positive-reinforcement value for disadvantaged youths. But because these rewards seldom come to them, society—and especially the schools as an arm of society—must frequently and systematically provide reinforcement to lower-class youths in order to effectively socialize them.

DEVELOPMENTAL SOCIALIZATION

As you can see from the preceding discussion, the study of the nature of human behavior has taken on a new sociological emphasis due to the increased complexity of our environment and the wide range of potential responses to it. Social development begins at the moment a child becomes able to interact knowingly with his environment, and it continues throughout adulthood. As the individual grows and society changes, the individual must develop adaptive skills. Table 5.1 presents a conceptual model of the nature of human socialization and provides a framework for discussing the individual's concomitant learning of values and behaviors throughout his lifetime.

In the following section, we will examine in detail the developmental stages of socialization. Below are some major points outlining our discussion:

1. The family is the locus of the child's initial social learning.
2. The dominant influence in the child's socialization throughout the first eight years of life is the family; some responsibility is delegated to the school.
3. Education in morality and values begins quite early and becomes a major aspect of the socialization process. Kohlberg's moral stages (1971) will be used here to illustrate the developmental nature of moral learning.
4. Throughout childhood there is a high degree of consistency between values and behavior.
5. In preadolescence the child experiences new social influences from peers, which facilitate transition to a more advanced moral level and cause him to experience a growing discrepancy between values and behavior.
6. Social maturation and ego-identity resolution become the primary tasks of adolescence. They are characterized by alternative social learnings and by much inconsistency between values and behavior. They often manifest themselves as follows:
    a. Values control behavior; therefore behavioral inconsistencies produce guilt, anxiety, shame, and so on.
    b. Behavior affects values; therefore behavioral inconsistencies cause change in values.
    c. These two discrepancies are essential to the processes of the adolescent's emancipation and value formation.

TABLE 5.1. Developmental socialization: A conceptual model.

Operation	Social-learning acquisition	Social-learning confirmation	Social maturation	Social integration	Social identity
Stage	Early and middle childhood	Preadolescence	Adolescence	Late adolescence and young adulthood	Adulthood
Age range	Birth–8	9–13	14–18	19–23	24 on
Task	Acquisition of social behaviors	Learned behaviors confirmed and solidified	Alternative social learning	Synthesis of self-social ideas	Finding one's social role
Primary influence	Parental	Parent/peer	Peers	Peer/society	Society
Peer influence	Minimal	Loosely defined	Strong	Strong	Loosely defined
Stage transfer	Facilitates →	Solidifies ←	Breaks away ← Facilitates →	Facilitates →	Interrelates ←

From *Child Development* by H. D. Thornburg. Copyright 1973 by William C. Brown Company, Publishers, Dubuque, Iowa. Reprinted by permission.

7. During young adulthood the need to integrate oneself into the larger society becomes paramount. This integration is facilitated by the full development of moral values and by movement in the direction of consistency between values and behaviors.
8. Adult socialization is characterized by the identification of one's social role and by a minimization of value-behavior discrepancies.

Now, referring to Table 5.1, let's examine in detail the stages in socialization.

Social-Learning Acquisition

This period, childhood, typically encompasses the age range of birth to 8 years. Because during infancy the child's primary source of gratification is his family, especially his mother (Gordon, 1972), he places much importance on adult affiliation. During the preschool period the child extends his interest to others to some degree, but he does not reduce

Operation	Social-learning acquisition
Stage	Early and middle childhood
Age range	Birth–8
Task	Acquisition of social behaviors
Primary influence	Parental
Peer influence	Minimal
Stage transfer	Facilitates ⟶

his interaction with his family. It is during this time that the parents explain many objects and ideas to the child. By the time the child has moved through the preschool years, whether he has been in nursery school or not, the parental influence is still quite thorough and effective and still dominates the child's social behavior (Clausen, 1966). During childhood some interaction with peers goes on, but such influence is thought to be minimal. Outside influences in the primary grades in school tend to reflect and reinforce parental and societal values in the child rather than present alternatives. One's friendships at this time are usually loosely defined and confined to one's own sex. These friendships are limited in their resourcefulness as alternative learning models, since primary school children are not yet experientially socialized but are still largely influenced by their parents' teachings. Since the child's primary grades in school are characterized by core learning, academics take precedence over social teachings. When formal social learning in school does occur, the child tends to use his parents rather than his teachers as reference points (Hawkes, Burchinal, & Gardner, 1957).

Identification. To be adequately socialized, a person must be capable of developing emotional attachments to others and must be able to adopt the norms and values of his culture. One of the most important early avenues of socialization is *identification*, the process by which an individual acquires the characteristics and values of a role model because he wishes to be like the model in some respects.

Surprisingly, it may not be necessary for an individual to identify with his species before he can further identify with particular individuals. Some interesting research with animals has given rise to the concept of *primary socialization*, or species identification. For example, a dog that has been raised with cats, or even with birds, will prefer their social companionship to that of other dogs, although it will display fondling and courting behavior toward its own species (Kuo, 1960). Similar conclusions have been derived from research on *imprinting*, a long-lasting form of early social attachment. Research on a number of species reveals that isolated young develop strong and lasting attachments to certain animals or objects to which they are exposed immediately after birth. Later these animals prefer to associate with the object with which they were imprinted and even are sexually indifferent to members of their own species. Hess (1959) found that a gosling exposed to a man within a few hours after its birth preferred the company of the man to the company of other geese later in its life. These findings have led to the speculation that there is a certain time period during which the presence or absence of a particular kind of environmental stimulus has the most influence on development. Puppies, for example, appear to go through a critical period for social attachment. "From 3 to 7 weeks the puppy is in an extremely interesting stage in which its sense organs and cerebral cortex are not yet completely developed but in which it has extremely sensitive emotional reactions and is capable of making associations. This is the time when primary socialization normally takes place and during which it is easier for a dog owner to establish a strong social bond" (Scott, 1958, pp. 51–52).

Higher mammals also appear to go through such critical periods for socialization. Rhesus monkeys kept apart from other monkeys during their early months tend to neither associate nor mate with other members of their species later in life. Such critical periods may also exist in the human infant, possibly during the postneonatal period (from 6 to 8 weeks after birth through the first year of life), when fear of strangers begins to develop and the child reacts to separation from his mother (Schaffer & Emerson, 1964). Furthermore, there is some evidence that psychopaths who appear unable to develop deep emotional attachments and who tend to disregard the opinions and feelings of others have experienced early deprivation of parental love and care (Smith, 1966).

Perhaps more relevant to human infants is the phenomenon that Mussen, Conger, and Kagan (1974) describe as *separation anxiety*. Between 10 and 18 months of age, the infant begins to fear that his mother is abandoning him when he sees the mother leave the house. The infant has built a strong bond with the mother, since she is usually the one adult who consistently interacts with him. The closer the attachment of mother and infant, the greater the anxiety. Mussen, Conger, and Kagan (1974) describe three conditions under which separation anxiety may occur: (1) separation from the mother, (2) disruption of the infant's habitual responses to the mother, and (3) inability to make the relevant response that brings his mother to him. Separation anxiety is apparently developmental in nature; it disappears around 18 months of age. All of this evidence supports the contention that feelings of nurturance and warmth are crucial to children throughout the first two years of life. Children's perception of acceptance or rejection from people in their environment allows deep-rooted feelings of security or estrangement to develop.

Imitation. After his first two years, a child becomes capable of imitative responses. Moving toward his third year, he clearly begins to learn by directly imitating models within his environment. *Imitation* describes attempts by the child to imitate aspects of the model's behavior and assumes a desire on the part of the child to be like the model; it is a concrete evidence of the identification process. Imitation continues throughout childhood and is often strongly evidenced in the adolescent.

Modeling is a term used by Bandura (1969) and others (Sears, 1953; Vernon, 1972) to conceptualize the process whereby a child acquires new behavior patterns, or modifies already existing ones, as a result of *observational learning*—the process of watching others engage in some behavior and copying their acts. Observational learning is generally contrasted to *stimulus-response learning*, in which a person acquires new behavioral patterns by emitting responses that are strengthened, weakened, or shaped by natural or socially arranged consequences. For example, Bijou and Baer (1961) and Elkind (1971) show how young children learn language through shaping of their response behaviors. The importance of differential reinforcement in shaping human behavior has also been well documented in this literature.

If a person changed his behavior only as a result of experiencing the consequences of his own acts, it is likely that much of our behavior would never be learned. For example, a child can learn directly from experience, such as from sticking his finger into an electrical outlet; the child is not likely to repeat the experiment. On the other hand, a parent's warning about electrical outlets can also be learned vicariously, and it is not necessary for the child to experience the outcome directly in order to get a feeling for the consequences (Thornburg, 1973e). For example, if one twin emits a behavior (such as sticking his finger into an electrical outlet) that evokes sharp disapproval, possibly even punishment, and the other twin observes this interaction, the vicarious aspect of the situation might cause the second twin to avoid emitting the behavior that evoked such parental disapproval toward the first twin.

Research on modeling has been extensive. Work by Bandura and his associates (Bandura & Huston, 1961; Bandura, Ross, & Ross, 1963) has shown that modeling may be carried out through imitating a person, a film, a cartoon, or any other object that can be imitated. The most common operative modeling stimuli for postinfant humans are verbal statements or physical actions. Through verbal modeling, the child learns to interact with spoken words or written symbols (Thornburg, 1973e).

Parental nurturance. Let's take modeling as a source of identification one step further. Research supports the theory that warm, positive parent-child relationships produce the strongest identification and also enable the child to successfully identify with his parent of the same sex. In one study (Mussen & Rutherford, 1963), kindergarten boys who revealed high- and low-masculinity behaviors in their play activities were asked to make up stories for the experimenter. The boys who were rated high in masculinity told more stories involving father nurturance than did the boys showing less masculinity. Similarly, in doll play, highly feminine girls were more likely to portray the role of the mother as nurturant than girls low in femininity. Of additional interest in this study was the fact that the fathers of the highly masculine boys were rated as no more masculine than the fathers of the boys low in masculinity, and the girls high in femininity did not have mothers who were unusually feminine in their behavior. These results suggest that the degree of masculinity or femininity displayed by the child's model is less important to the child's successful sex-role identification than a supportive relationship with the child, which apparently facilitates the child's adoption of the role of the same-sex parent.

Theories of identification. One theory of identification (Mowrer, 1960) suggests that it is rewarding to the child to behave like the parent because he thereby reminds himself of the loved parent or to some extent reproduces actions that, when made by the parent, give him pleasure. The idea that a person imitates another in order to recreate the pleasure produced by the presence of the loved one accounts not only for why the imitated response is rewarding to the child but also for a reverse type of imitative behavior, in which the parent imitates the child. Parents frequently copy a child's acts that they consider endearing, such as a child's way of talking or walking. The replication of such acts appears to be both pleasurable to the parents and reinforcing to the child.

Another theory (Kagan, 1958) is that a child may identify with parents in order to get control of the means of gratification that his parents control, such as mastery of the environment or love from the other parent. The child interprets his likeness to the model as a source of gratification. One experiment (Bandura et al., 1963) appears to support this theory. The experimenters set up several experimental groups and devised two conditions for them. Each experimental group consisted of a male adult, a female adult, and a child. One of the adults acted as controller of resources (food and play materials). In one condition, these resources were dispensed to the other adult while the child observed. In the other condition, the child was the sole recipient of the objects. The results indicated that, whether or not the child was the recipient of the incentive objects, he was more likely to imitate the adult controlling the resources than the other adult. Bandura and his associates concluded that the child imitates models who control desirable resources.

Identification may serve to reduce anxiety. Freud first introduced this theory in his discussion of the way in which a boy resolves his Oedipus complex. The male child begins to identify with his father at the age of 5 or 6 in order to reduce his apprehension that the father will attack him as a rival for the affections of the mother. This process, known as "identification with the aggressor," was hypothesized to relieve anxiety by enabling the boy to see himself as similar to the oppressor rather than as the oppressed.

According to Freud, identification also involves the incorporation of parental standards and values. The previously amoral child begins to guide himself as external authorities previously guided him. Self-observation, conscience, and the formulation of ideals develop as differentiated functions of the ego, forming a new mental organization known as the *superego*, which enforces adherence to prescriptions and proscriptions by means of condemnation and the inculcation of guilt.

Identification generally facilitates the crucial socialization process in the developing child. A child may have several motives for imitating his parents and wanting to be like them. He may find it enjoyable to act as they do, or he may attempt to reduce his anxiety by strongly identifying with the dominant parent. The child adopts parental sex roles, moral rules, and values in the process of identification. Identification provides a direction for growth, an affinity with one's species, a capacity for emotional relationships with others, and a sense of individual identity, each of which is realized over time and in the process of development.

Moral development. Research on values and conscience development in the child has been going on for some time; the definitive work is Jean Piaget's *The Moral Judgment of the Child* (1948). As a developmental psychologist, Piaget interpreted intellectual and moral growth as corresponding. Two primary ideas dominate his thinking, and several studies done since are somewhat supportive of them: (1) early in a child's experiences (such as preschool age) the child interprets the observable consequences of his behavior and bases his value judgments on this external evidence, and (2) as the child moves toward 9 to 11 years of age he begins to *cognize*—that is, internalize the rightness and wrongness of things.

Aronfreed (1968) outlines four characteristics of the child's moral development, basing his ideas on Piaget's works:

1. The young child at first judges the severity of transgressions with respect to their visible damage or harm. As the child becomes older, its judgments become more sensitive to the transgressor.
2. Younger children tend toward the perception of "imminent justice"—the perception that punishment is impersonally ordained in the very performance of a transgression. The older child becomes more perceptive of how punishment follows from principles which take into account the consequences of a transgression for other people.
3. The young child judges the appropriateness of punishment by its severity rather than by its relevance to transgression. Younger children seem to perceive that the expiation of a transgression is proportionate to the magnitude of external retribution. The older child is more likely to recommend that the transgressor make restitution or that punishment be tailored to have reciprocity with the transgression.
4. The child first interprets rules as having a fixed or absolute legitimacy that is given by external authority. Gradually, the child comes to see that the application of rules may be relative to people and situations, and that rules are established and maintained through reciprocal social agreements [Aronfreed, 1968, p. 258].*

If evidence from Piaget's research is accurate, it is appropriate to conceptualize the nature of moral growth as developmental. Kohlberg (1971) has enlarged upon Piaget's system, as you can see from the following extract:†

I. Preconventional Level
At this level the child is responsive to cultural rules and labels of good and bad, right or wrong, but interprets these labels in terms of either the physical or the hedonistic consequences of action

---

*From *Conduct and Conscience* by J. Aronfreed. Copyright 1968 by Academic Press, Inc. Reprinted by permission.
†From *Zygon* by L. Kohlberg. Copyright 1971 University of Chicago Press. Reprinted by permission.

(punishment, reward, exchange of favors) or in terms of the physical power of those who enunciate the rules and labels. The level is divided into the following two stages:

Stage 1. The Punishment and Obedience Orientation. The physical consequences of action determine its goodness or badness regardless of the human meaning or value of these consequences. Avoidance of punishment and unquestioning deference to power are valued in their own right, not in terms of respect for an underlying moral order supported by punishment and authority (the latter being stage 4).

Stage 2. The Instrumental Relativist Orientation. Right action consists of that which instrumentally satisfies one's own needs and occasionally the needs of others. Human relations are viewed in terms like those of the marketplace. Elements of fairness, of reciprocity, and equal sharing are present, but they are always interpreted in a physical, pragmatic way. Reciprocity is a matter of "you scratch my back and I'll scratch yours," not of loyalty, gratitude, or justice.

II. Conventional Level

At this level, maintaining the expectations of the individual's family, group, or nation is perceived as valuable in its own right, regardless of immediate and obvious consequences. The attitude is not only one of conformity to personal expectations and social order, but of loyalty to it, of actively maintaining, supporting, and justifying the order and of identifying with the persons or group involved in it. At this level, there are the following two stages:

Stage 3. The Interpersonal Concordance or "Good Boy-Nice Girl" Orientation. Good behavior is that which pleases or helps others and is approved by them. There is much conformity to stereotypical images of what is majority or "natural" behavior. Behavior is frequently judged by intention—"he means well" becomes important for the first time. One earns approval by being "nice."

Stage 4. The "Law-and-Order" Orientation. There is orientation toward authority, fixed rules, and the maintenance of the social order. Right behavior consists of doing one's duty, showing respect for authority, and maintaining the given social order for its own sake.

III. Postconventional, Autonomous, or Principled Level

At this level, there is a clear effort to define moral values and principles which have validity and application apart from the authority of the groups or persons holding these principles and apart from the individual's own identification with these groups. This level again has two stages:

Stage 5. The Social-Contract Legalistic Orientation. This level generally has utilitarian overtones. Right action tends to be defined in terms of general individual rights and in terms of standards which have been critically examined and agreed upon by the whole society. There is a clear awareness of the relativism of personal values and opinions and a corresponding emphasis upon procedural rules for reaching consensus. Aside from what is constitutionally and democratically agreed upon, the right is a matter of personal "values" and "opinion." The result is an emphasis upon the "legal point of view," but with an emphasis upon the possibility of changing law in terms of rational considerations of social utility (rather than freezing it in terms of stage 4, "law and order"). Outside the legal realm, free agreement and contract is the binding element of obligation. This is the "official" morality of the American government and Constitution.

Stage 6. The Universal Ethical-Principle Orientation. Right is defined by the decision of conscience in accord with self-chosen ethical principles appealing to logical comprehensiveness, universality, and consistency. These principles are abstract and ethical (the Golden Rule, the categorical imperative); they are not concrete moral rules like the Ten Commandments. At heart, these are universal principles of justice, of the reciprocity and equality of the human rights, and of respect for the dignity of human beings as individual persons.

Kohlberg feels that each of his moral stages is prerequisite to each successive stage. He does not see any formal moralizing by the child before age 4, the *preconventional* level, during which time the child is generally well behaved and responsive to cultural labels of good and bad (1972). The direct relations to a child's behavior by his parents or other significant individuals determine to a considerable extent whether the child will retain the behavior. He tends to do what he wants to do and then wait for physical consequences, such as punishment or reward. He interprets punishment as "bad" and reward as "good," abandoning punishing or stressful situations in deference to authority (1971). In this stage, the child obeys rules essentially in order to avoid punishment. Kohlberg sees stage 1—*the punishment and obedience orientation*—as beginning to dominate the child's thinking around age 7 (Piaget's concrete-operations stage). By that age, early parental influences are well established in the child, and he has had some exposure to formal schooling.

The combination of parental influence and a limited concept of morality causes the 1- to 8-year-old to be highly consistent in his behavior and values (see Table 5.2). The basic concepts of right and wrong are usually taught in the process of the parents' attempts to develop appropriate behaviors within the child. If a child's behavior brings parental approval he feels more secure and therefore is likely to repeat a behavior that is not only acceptable to his parents but also instrumental in satisfying his own needs or feelings. The strength of these early parental influences is also often carried into preadolescence (Petrich & Chadderdon, 1969).

Social-Learning Confirmation

The age range of 9 to 13, described by many as late childhood, will be designated here as preadolescence. During this period, social behaviors

TABLE 5.2. From consistency through inconsistency to consistency.

Primary influences	Consistency range	Stage	
Parents	Behavior ⟵⟶ Values	Childhood (1–8)	Consistency
Parents/ peers	Behavior ⟵ — ⟶ Values	Preadolescence (9–13)	Toward inconsistency
Peers	Behavior ⟵ – – ⟶ Values	Adolescence (14–19)	Inconsistency
Peers/ society	Behavior ⟵ — ⟶ Values	Young adult- hood (20–26)	Toward consistency
Society	Behavior ⟵⟶ Values	Adulthood (27 on)	Consistency

From "Behavior and Values: Consistency or Inconsistency" by H. D. Thornburg, *Adolescence*, 1973, 8(32), 513-520. Copyright 1973 Libra Publishers, Inc. Reprinted by permission.

learned from parents are confirmed. At the same time, parental influences begin giving way to peer influences, and the peer group becomes a stronger socializing force with which the preadolescent must contend.

How is the period of social-learning confirmation distinguished from the earlier period of social-learning acquisition? Basically, the individual is now most concerned about finding out whether those things he has been taught are important. The child is now more inquisitive and assertive by nature. Through his own curiosity, he is able to test and determine the validity of ideas presented to him. This new ability is facilitated by two factors. First, preadolescents are more outgoing than children (Elkind, 1966). Their desire to be popular with friends causes them to associate with others of similar interests or values. In these associations, they will experience some variance from early parental teachings. The feasibility of the alternatives presented to the child and the satisfaction he experiences from acting on them will determine whether he dismisses earlier teachings or whether earlier teachings prove plausible and thus become more solidified. This interaction with peers begins challenging parental interaction as the primary socialization influence on the child (Slater, 1962) and, during the closing stages of preadolescence, the influence of peers becomes markedly visible (Levitt & Edwards, 1970).

Operation	Social-learning confirmation
Stage	Preadolescence
Age range	9–13
Task	Learned behaviors confirmed and solidified
Primary influence	Parent/peer
Peer influence	Loosely defined
Stage transfer	Solidifies ↑

Second, during preadolescence there is a relaxing of the consistency between behaviors and values that characterized early childhood (see Table 5.2). This motion toward inconsistency is not fully realized, however, until the child reaches adolescence.

The second stage in Kohlberg's moral-development scheme begins around age 9 and covers a two-year age span. This stage, *the instrumental relativist orientation*, involves conforming in order to obtain rewards and doing favors if someone does a favor in return. Consciousness of fairness, equality, and reciprocity appears. Preadolescents do not yet value the friendship of others for itself or expect loyalty or gratitude; rather, preadolescents "use" each other, in the vernacular sense, in order to satisfy their own needs.

During preadolescence, a shift occurs from Kohlberg's *preconventional* morality level to his *conventional* morality level. That is, as the preadolescent begins to develop formal thinking processes, he becomes more socially and morally conforming as he begins to conceptualize that good behavior is that which pleases or helps others and is approved by others. This movement toward conventional morality is spurred by the preadolescent's increasing need for peer approval.

The confirmation of early social and moral learning is evidenced around ages 8 and 9. Children expect others to act toward them the way they have been taught to act. But by age 10 or 11 this closely knit behavior-value structure begins to break down, as the preadolescent asserts himself as a more social being (Elkind, 1971; Thornburg, 1973c). His values and behavior become diversified and increasingly unpredictable, for several reasons: (1) the family as an influential unit is being severely challenged, (2) the preadolescent is increasingly concerned with the socialization process in school, (3) peer approval is taking on importance for him, and (4) physical growth and development patterns are causing him to view himself in a new light.

Social Maturation

Now let's examine the period of social maturation called adolescence. The ideas, beliefs, and values of one's culture become increasingly important over the course of one's development. To the adolescent, understanding and interpreting social and cultural phenomena are distinctly important as skills in adjusting to his society. The highly dominant influence the family had in his childhood years has given way to other influences, although some parental values are still strongly entrenched; the process that began during preadolescence of reconsidering parental teachings in light of some distinctly different peer behaviors culminates in adolescence. In essence, a great part of adolescent socialization consists of *moving from predominant parental influence to predominant peer influence.*

The individual strives for *social maturation* during adolescence —that is, for satisfactory interaction with and adjustment to his environment. Enrollment in a junior or senior high school brings the adolescent in contact with a diverse group of peers, and new friendships generally emerge. Same-sex peer groups drawn from school are more integral and permanent than the tenuous ones formed in earlier developmental stages. These strong same-sex peer friendships provide the adolescent with the security needed to begin establishing cross-sex peer attachments (Sherif & Sherif, 1964). Membership in peer groups is symbolic of acceptance, which results in confidence for the maturing adolescent.

Operation	*Social maturation*
Stage	Adolescence
Age range	14–18
Task	Alternative social learning
Primary influence	Peers
Peer influence	Strong
Stage transfer	Breaks away ← Facilitates →

Thus, attempts to mature socially are usually best facilitated by strong peer affiliations, instrumental in helping the adolescent break away from earlier stages of development and, toward the end of adolescence, facilitating movement into young adulthood. Adolescents have strong affiliative needs, for several reasons. First, affiliation is helpful in the *emancipation* process. Although some emancipation from parents begins in preadolescence, distinct behavioral and emotional breaks are more likely to occur during adolescence. Affiliation with one's friends who are also striving for emancipation provides incentive for movement toward independence from childhood ties.

Group affiliation also tends to spur *competition*. It is sometimes difficult to separate the real value of competition from its damaging effects, because our society demands so many attainments for achieving success that many individuals compete in an unwholesome way in order to achieve it. In addition, adolescent competition is often exploited because its raw energies have proven profitable to segments of our society. However, a wholesome, seemingly natural competition occurs among youth that aids the social-maturation process.

Conformity also plays a role in helping the adolescent become more mature. Much emphasis is placed today on being oneself, on being individualistic. At the same time, one of the strongest reasons for group affiliation is conformity. Many peer affiliations are based on values or behaviors that demand total participation by the member in order to maintain his status within the group.

The adolescent's strong urge toward *heterosexual attachments* is also a factor in social maturation. The sexual-maturation process gives the youth desires and energies that he simply did not have before. Earlier heterosexual relationships often take the form of group social interaction of both sexes, moving later into smaller heterosexual clique behavior (Dunphy, 1963), dating, or sexual intimacy.

Finally, one more avenue to social maturation is *achievement*. If an individual is able to perform satisfactorily in relation to a socially defined standard of excellence, set by his peers or by his school, or in competition, this performance facilitates maturity. The resulting social reinforcement also enhances his feelings of competence and self-determination. Such achievement-success tends to foster independence in males. Female adolescents seem to gain greater social approval through developing interpersonal skills (Douvan & Adelson, 1966). Some variance in these peer social-reinforcement patterns may appear as sex-role attitudes change, although no distinct alternative reinforcement pattern has yet clearly emerged.

Moral development. It is during adolescence that the final three stages of Kohlberg's moral-development model occur. At this point, the individual's intellectual development allows the mind to logically comprehend morality and value concepts as well as rational processes (Elkind, 1971). During early adolescence (13–14), a type of morality emerges that Kohlberg identified as stage 4, *the "law-and-order" orientation*. Many adolescents experience moral conflict during this stage. Their strong peer associations, experiences of alternative social learning, strivings for emancipation, and experimentation with diverse behavioral expressions offer many challenges to their concepts of law and order. The adolescent's conflict during this stage stems from the confrontation between these challenges, on the one hand, and, on the other, his attitude toward authority as absolute and his inability to see any relativism in the concepts of obedience and disobedience. He feels a strong need to conform to his social order as well as to maintain, support, and justify it (Kohlberg, 1969).

Kohlberg's stage 5 is described as *the social-contract legalistic orientation*. The adolescent now defines appropriate action in terms of general individual rights in balance with standards that have been critically examined and agreed upon by the whole society. Kohlberg (1971) has illustrated that the 15- to 16-year-old would consider life to be a universal human right, but would also believe that society has the right to confine an individual for life if he has committed a grave crime against society.

Kohlberg sees more relativism in stage 5 than in earlier stages. For example, regarding rules, Kohlberg contends that this stage of morality is characterized by "an emphasis upon the legal point of view, but with an emphasis upon the possibility of changing law in terms of rational considerations of social utility, rather than freezing it in the terms of stage 4 (more absolute), law and order" (1971, p. 1067).

Kohlberg's stage 6 is *the universal ethical-principle orientation*. During this stage, "right" is "defined by the decision of conscience in accord with self-chosen ethical principles appealing to logical comprehensiveness, universality, and consistency" (1972, p. 297). This description of the acquisition of abstract moral rules is similar to my designation of one adolescent developmental task as that of *acquiring a set of ethics as a guide to behavior* (see Chapter 1). In function, however, it is a goal that is seldom fully met by the adolescent and perhaps never met by many individuals. In order to develop abstract ethical principles, one must have the ability to think abstractly and must have some awareness of *social intelligence*—coping skills that enable the individual to deal effectively with human situations, both in and out of school. Respect, trust, fidelity, human rights, dignity, and honesty are some abstract words that may translate an emergent moral-value system into some type of ethical guide to behavior. Not all people can behaviorally execute these intellectual concepts, and many never gain a social intelligence comparable to their academic intelligence.

Behavior-value discrepancies. It was stated earlier that behavioral autonomy and emotional autonomy are more likely to be realized by the adolescent than is value autonomy. However, this statement does not minimize the importance of value autonomy or the fact that many youths strive for it.

As youths move out of preadolescence into adolescence, discrepancies between their behavior and their values become more evident. This period may be characterized as one of inconsistency between what one does and what one believes. This inconsistency is a natural outgrowth of the adolescent's needs to emancipate himself and to determine a value system for himself. The adolescent may perceive these goals as requiring rejection of most of the parental and societal values he has learned, or he may perceive little discrepancy between these goals and the values he has learned. Some factors involved here are the relative strength of parental values within the adolescent's value system, the strength of influence of his peers, the degree to which parental values differ from peer values, and the degree to which both of these differ from societal values. The adolescent is clearly quite involved with peers, especially in the behavioral realm. Many peer values seem to him to be legitimate alternatives to existing values (Thornburg, 1973a).

The arrows in Table 5.1 show that each socialization stage has an effect on the subsequent developmental stage. This transfer effect is decisive during the social-maturation period. First, as the adolescent moves from parental involvement toward strong peer involvement, the transfer effect helps him break away from earlier infantile patterns of behavior. In addition, it will subsequently facilitate the development of more mature adolescent relationships, not only with his peers but with parents and society as well.

Two considerations are essential to a discussion of the value-behavior discrepancies that may result from these transitions. First, values influence behavior. If values influence behavior but are also disregarded, guilt may result. Guilt is more likely to occur if parental or religious influences have been a decisive determinant of one's values. If the individual's personality constructs have become closed or restricted, this system of constructs will be unable to tolerate a wide range of different behaviors. Guilt, remorse, anxiety, frustration, and shame may characterize the affective state of the behaver who deviates from his established values.

Second, behavior affects values. It is possible that behavioral inconsistencies, after repeated incidents of the same behavior, will produce a value shift. Many youths engage in behaviors that initially, because of value discrepancy, produce guilt, only to find eventually that these behaviors have become part of their value system. This phenomenon was explained by Festinger (1957) in his theory of cognitive dissonance. His theory states that when a person has inconsistent cognitions about himself or his environment, he is placed in a state of dissonance. Because dissonance creates tension, the individual is motivated to eliminate the feeling. In the adolescent, this motivation may either make him change his behaviors in order to bring them in line with his values or make him change his values in order to bring them in line with his behaviors.

The effect that behavior may have on values is exemplified by the case of adolescent premarital sexual involvement. Let's assume that an individual upholds the standard that premarital sex is "off limits." However, he observes that premarital sex is common among his peers. Therefore he engages in the experience, rationalizing to himself that it is not so wrong after all. His continued persistence in premarital sex behavior causes his perceptual inconsistencies to dissipate, and the end result is that he has aligned his values with his behavior.

During adolescence maximum value inconsistencies occur, facilitated by the dominant peer influence. In fact, peer groups often form on the basis of common value structures as well as that of common behaviors (Thornburg, 1971c). Peer groups may adhere to differing values or behaviors that are (1) characteristic of youth but different from those of the whole society or (2) different from those of most youth *and* different from those of the whole society. Considering the myriad beliefs and behaviors found among youth, both possibilities are certainly plausible.

Social Integration

During the stages referred to as late adolescence and young adulthood, the process of social growth is reaching completion (Dunphy, 1963). *Social integration* now becomes the primary developmental function. Most of the adolescent's basic developmental tasks have been worked through, his functioning capacity is becoming stronger, and the highly important peer influences characteristic of adolescence are breaking down in favor of a growing societal influence on the adolescent's social

Operation	Social integration
Stage	Late adolescence and young adulthood
Age range	19–23
Task	Synthesis of self-social ideas
Primary influence	Peer/society
Peer influence	Strong
Stage transfer	Facilitates $\longrightarrow$

integration. That is, upon entering young adulthood (ages 19–23), most individuals carry with them the values and behaviors characteristic of adolescence. If the young adult delays entrance into the larger society by remaining in an educational setting, for example, peer influences may continue to prevail over societal influences, delaying his social integration. However, if the young adult is beginning to find his way in the world, as is the case among noncollege youth, society becomes the prevailing influence, and social integration begins (Thornburg, 1971c).

The young adult's values have been affected by parents, peers, and society in varying degrees. The degree of conservatism or liberalism of his ideas, for example, is a reflection of the values he has learned throughout his lifetime.

Research among young adults, using Kohlberg's moral stages, confirms that they show a wide range of individual concepts of morality. Haan and her associates (1968) researched different kinds of moral attitudes among youth, relating their actions to their attained level of moral judgment. They found that young people whose attitudes toward

Values are an outcome of socialization. This young girl values her relationship with nature.

societal and institutional goals were somewhat traditional held a moral concept similar to Kohlberg's stage 4, *the "law-and-order" orientation.* Political activists who were heavily involved in the Free Speech Movement of 1964 fell at *the social-contract legalistic* or *universal ethical-principle* level of morality, stages 5 and 6. They were more inclined than the first group to think in terms of moral relativism or self-created ethical systems. In contrast, Peace Corps volunteers, although action oriented, fell more often at stage 4 than at either stage 5 or stage 6. It appears that the moral level an individual attains may depend upon (1) the individual's ability to conceptualize and thus comprehend his total environment and (2) the consistency of the value models within his environment and their degree of liberalism or conservatism.

As has been demonstrated, adolescence is a time of considerable inconsistency between values and behaviors. Young adulthood can be characterized as the period in which the movement back toward consistency begins (see Table 5.2). The inconsistencies experienced during adolescence are instrumental in helping the person sort out his values, which may have been derived from any or all of these: parents, school, society, peers, and religion. The person's experiences in comparing these different value sources are helpful to him in restoring some value-behavior consistency. However, it would be premature, if not impossible, for anyone to assert that his values and behaviors are totally consistent. Residual effects from adolescence still characterize many behaviors in this developmental stage. The social-integration period is, however, a dynamic period of time in which the emerging adult moves toward more consistent behaviors and values.

Social Identity

The age range that constitutes adulthood varies according to the theoretical model being discussed. Erikson (1963) described adulthood as 26–40, designating maturity as the stage beyond 40. Gordon (1972) extends young adulthood to 29, refers to the ages 30–44 as early maturity, and designates beyond 45 as full maturity. In Table 5.1, adulthood is

Operation	Social identity
Stage	Adulthood
Age range	24 on
Task	Finding one's social role
Primary influence	Society
Peer influence	Loosely defined
Stage transfer	Interrelates ↑

described as age 24 on. As interest in life-span psychology increases, undoubtedly further research will provide better defined subcategories conceptualizing the developmental nature of the adult. However, since my emphasis here is on the changing socialization experience, I would say that adulthood occurs when an individual has successfully integrated himself or herself into the society and has accepted a defined social role and an orientation toward future roles. Adulthood entails a high degree of stability and identification with the society—the ability to see oneself and society as inter-related without becoming so absorbed by one's social role that one loses one's personal identity.

By the time an individual reaches adulthood, he has discovered that he can function more effectively when he is experiencing a minimal amount of internal conflict. Although it is probably impossible to reach perfect consistency between values and behavior, a working level of consistency can be attained. When the social-integration and social-maturation processes are realized, the individual returns to the high degree of consistency he had experienced in childhood. Of course, the child exhibits value-behavior consistency because he knows little more than that which is directly taught him. Neither his maturation process nor his experience has taught him to challenge what he learns. For the adult, the reverse is true; he has had every opportunity to challenge both his basic beliefs and his actions. Therefore, the intermediate developmental stages of experience—the intellectual, emotional, and behavioral pursuits characteristic of preadolescence, adolescence, and young adulthood—serve as learning experiences that eventually produce the behavior-value consistency of adulthood.

The Adolescent in the Family 6

As you saw in Chapter 5, the family assumes almost total responsibility for the socialization of the young child. Because the family is the child's basic source of information, chief supplier of needs, and primary interpreter of acceptable social behaviors, the child commonly adopts the attitudes and values of his parents.

How does the adolescent differ from the younger child with respect to family relationships? First, the direct influence of the family lessens as the adolescent engages in more interaction with his peers, actively strives for independence, and gains some self-assurance regarding his ability to provide for himself. Because the transition from childhood to adolescence is not easily made, there may be some difficult moments for both the parents and the adolescent, stemming from the adolescent's turning to sources outside the home for much teaching, counsel, and interaction. With very few exceptions, peers are the most frequent source.

Second, the difficulties of the adolescent period, which seem to increase throughout early and middle adolescence, are compounded by changes within the adolescent himself. Many adolescents feel that they are young adults now and no longer need parental control or guidance. Nevertheless, some ambivalence occurs between their striving for independence and their occasional desire to retain the security of earlier-childhood dependency. Another source of ambivalence is the adolescent's disorganized energies. Since most of his goals are not yet well defined, his behaviors are often impulsive, in contrast to the constructive channeling of energy that parents usually advocate. His stress on individuality and demands for immediate gratification are often emotionally generated and may negate the logic imposed by parents. Thus much parent-adolescent conflict arises from the clash among the adolescent's (1) retention of earlier-childhood dependencies, (2) need for parental approval, and (3) personal striving for independence.

Today's adolescents can easily find socialization sources outside the home. In the process, they often begin to view the home skeptically, generally seeing it as more restrictive and punitive than other sources of social interaction. The adolescent has strong biological drives, which must be expressed in some manner. Emotionally, he may be extremely sensitive, interpreting most experiences egocentrically in his search for ego-identity. Socially, he finds approval among his friends to be more important than parental approval. As a result, he may give little consideration to the home or to individual members within it.

Many parents interpret these new forms of adolescent behavior as rejection of the home. Others conclude that they no longer have any effective influence on their adolescent's behavior. Consequently, some parents become more authoritarian when their children become adolescents in order to assure themselves that their authority and importance are still recognized. In some instances, this parental stance may be valid. At the same time, in other instances it would be more helpful for parents to be sensitive and responsive at the adolescent's need level than to expect the adolescent always to respond and conform to their need level.

If parents want their adolescent to be an integral part of the family, they should look for ways to help the adolescent share his behavioral and emotional experiences with his family. They should also keep in mind the fact that peer influences on behavior, which may seem to cause an adolescent to abandon parental values, are indicative more of normal growth than of parental neglect. Parents should show a willingness to let their adolescents exercise behavioral alternatives—in effect, help promote the parent-adolescent relationship rather than try to maintain the parent-child relationship. The adolescent's striving for independence means that he or she is becoming a more complete being. At the same time, many youths feel a need and desire for parental interaction, and they still want to feel that they are part of family life.

STRUCTURAL CHANGE WITHIN THE FAMILY

Because of social-class and regional differences in people, the range of family social behaviors is extremely varied. With the increased urbanization and increased technology of the past two or three decades, not only has the society undergone much change, but the family has shown evidence of structural change as well. Now more than two-thirds of the total U.S. population are city dwellers, and more than half of the families move at least once every five years (Sebald, 1968).

Accelerated social change has also caused today's parents and their adolescents to grow up in decisively different worlds. The fact that the two generations have had such different environmental experiences often causes a breakdown in communication and understanding popularly known as the "generation gap." Because their societal frames of reference are so different, it is often difficult for parent and adolescent to conceptualize some goal or value in the same manner. The frustration experienced by both is often dramatically expressed, and thus more conflict often is apparent than in reality exists.

In some cases, changes in social values have lagged behind changes in social behaviors. For example, our technological society emphasizes the role of the responsible male provider, yet advancing technology has made gainful and meaningful employment more difficult to obtain. The ever-present possibility of a father's unemployment holds

Greater mobility across socioeconomic and racial lines has caused many variations in the traditional family's structure, although not necessarily in its functions.

psychological hazards for the family and especially for the male adolescent, who has been taught to view himself as a potential provider. Families of semiskilled and unskilled workers are particularly affected by the threat of unemployment.

The lack of employment opportunities for today's youths is not accidental. Automation has created a demand for technical skills that young people must spend considerable time acquiring before they become eligible to enter the work force (Cole & Hall, 1970). Adolescents who cannot meet these increasing educational and training requirements face the threats of uncertain employment and prolongation of their dependence on the family (Thornburg, 1971c). This pattern is borne out in the comparative study of youth from the ages of 16 to 21 in 1960 and 1970 done by Havighurst and his associates (Havighurst, Graham, & Eberly, 1972). Table 6.1 summarizes their statistics, attesting to the unavailability of work among today's youth. Although the percentage of high school dropouts is gradually declining, the percentage of unemployed out-of-school youth is increasing.

The increase in the number of working mothers has also influenced change in family structure, which we will explore in more detail later in this chapter. The 1970 U.S. Census showed that 42.2 percent of the labor force were women 16 years of age or older. Of those, 63.9 percent were married. Movement of women out of the home and into educational, occupational, or community endeavors has caused all family members to reconsider the role of the mother. Mead (1971) asserts that societal pressure toward both marriage and child-rearing for women has lessened, a factor that undoubtedly will affect the adolescent girl in her goal orientation and decision-making, and the adolescent boy in his attitude toward females. This change in society's idea of the woman's role has also had the effect of moving the predominant family structure increasingly away from the patriarchal pattern and toward the democratic pattern.

These societal changes of the last few years have also brought about a gradual decline in adult authority. Concomitant with the new emphasis on individuality and self-expression among youth is the attitude that parents no longer hold authority simply by virtue of being parents. Today's adolescent feels more inclined to talk back, to defy their

TABLE 6.1. Changing status of youth: 1960–1970.

	Ages: 16–21	1960	1970	Percentage shift over 10 years
Out of school	White male	40.4	38.0	− 6
	Nonwhite male	52.9	44.1	−17
	Nonwhite female	58.1	49.7	−14
	White female	52.0	45.3	−13
Unemployed (as percent of labor force)	White male	9.9	12.0	+21
	Nonwhite male	15.3	24.9	+63
	Nonwhite female	17.3	31.7	+83
	White female	7.8	13.4	+72
Not in labor force	White male	42.1	38.4	− 9
	Nonwhite male	49.5	51.0	+ 3
	Nonwhite female	69.9	59.6	−15
	White female	61.8	50.6	−18
	Ages: 14–19			
Married	White male	3.1	2.8	−10
	Nonwhite male	4.3	1.6	−63
	Nonwhite female	12.1	8.7	−28
	White female	13.3	9.6	−28

From "American Youth in the Mid-Seventies" by R. L. Havighurst, R. A. Graham, and D. Eberly, *National Association of Secondary School Principals Bulletin*, 1972, 56(357), 2. Reprinted by permission.

> The number of working mothers with children in this country is soaring. More than 57 percent of all women with children aged 6 to 17 worked during 1972. Some of the pressures bringing mothers to the labor market are divorce, falling birth rates, boredom, and simple economic necessity, the last the most important and frequent pressure.
>
> As an increasing number of American mothers seek and obtain employment, the need for increased and improved child day-care centers grows more acute.
>
> From *Parade* Intelligence Report (June 2, 1974).

authority when he feels that his parents are wrong, or to believe that no one, including parents, has the right to *tell* him what to do, how to feel, or what to aspire to in life. Therefore, in order to gain respect from their adolescent children, today's parents must *demonstrate* respect for their children and regard for their wishes and must *show* individual qualities and strengths that their adolescents can admire.

For the adolescent growing up in our society before the 1960s, his home, his peer group, and other structured experiences such as school, church, Boy Scouts and Girl Scouts, 4-H clubs, and so on were his authority sources. With the 1960s came an ambiguous, elusive fourth authority source that we might call individualism. It reflected a growing discontent and dissonance with traditional authority. As the level of dissonance became higher, youths began to isolate themselves from authority sources. The adolescent now thought of himself as capable of choosing for himself rather than submissive to the influences of authority. He turned to music, literature, activism, drugs, and sex as avenues of individualistic expression. The skepticism and capriciousness with which the family was viewed bred alienation, which resulted in anxiety. Self-enhancement was to come through exercising individuality and resolving the identity crisis described by Erikson (see Chapter 2). Adolescents are never free from authority, however. Rather, they may find more leeway for expressions of individuality in new authority sources. Therefore most youth, rather than seek to overthrow all authority, select the authority they choose to listen to. In the contemporary individualistic society, parental authority rarely emerges as their primary authority choice.

FAMILY STRUCTURES AND THE ADOLESCENT

What are some of the types of parental authority operating in today's family? Which best encourages adolescent development? The most comprehensive categorization of family structures was originally devised by Elder in 1962:

1. *Autocratic.* In this structure, the adolescent is not allowed to express his opinions or to have any say in decisions affecting him.
2. *Authoritarian.* Although the adolescent may contribute to the discussion of problems, he must yield to the parents' final decision.
3. *Democratic.* The adolescent actively interacts with his parents in making decisions, although final approval must come from the parents.
4. *Equalitarian.* All family members have equal opportunity to discuss family matters. The distinction between generations does not prevail.
5. *Permissive.* The adolescent is given responsibility for decision making greater than that assumed by his parents.
6. *Laissez-faire.* The adolescent may choose to accept or disregard parental desires in family decisions.
7. *Ignoring.* The parents do not engage in decision making with the adolescent; rather, he is allowed to "do his own thing" without question.

Since one of the purposes of parental socialization is to prepare the adolescent to make important decisions, in theory the democratic and equalitarian structures should best facilitate the emergence of decision-making skills. In contrast, the autocratic and ignoring structures should foster no such skills. Research has confirmed these ideas and has also shown that the home of the democratic type best promotes achievement (Bowerman & Elder, 1964). This research, conducted among a male sample, found the tendency to achieve to be much stronger among adolescents from democratic homes than among those from autocratic homes. Rosen (1962) did similar research on paternal authority and subsequent adolescent self-reliance. He found that highly authoritarian fathers did not encourage independence, self-reliance, or achievement.

THE ADOLESCENT'S SEARCH FOR AUTONOMY

The active goal of the adolescent is to break the infantile ties that he developed and enjoyed during his earlier stages of development. As these ties are broken, some alternative relationship must take their place. At this point, the adolescent's desire for an autonomous relationship with parents can be a source of misunderstanding, but parent-adolescent interaction can, alternatively, be an effective basis for growth throughout adolescence. An adolescent-adult relationship can be built on the adolescent's new abilities, behaviors, and interests rather than on his past needs. Unfortunately, this relationship does not occur among many adolescents and parents.

Adolescents often are unable to break their early emotional bonds with parents logically or objectively. They may become rebellious, emotional, or hypercritical in order to persuade their parents that they are different now and must be independent. Such behavior has the potential to breed alienation, antiparental attitudes, and the beginning of the highly popularized concept of the generation gap.

Although it is true that independence is difficult to obtain within some family structures, it may not be necessary for the adolescent to openly defy or rebel against parents in order to gain independence. It is equally important for the parents to see that the adolescent is becoming a distinct individual and that earlier ties should be replaced by a more mature parent-adolescent relationship. Both adolescents and parents need

Doing things together as a family remains important to most adolescents, who continue to gain strength from the family even while they actively strive for autonomy.

to remember that gaining independence from one's parents is actually a normal developmental process. Researchers (Douvan & Adelson, 1966) have determined that there are three essential goals that youths must strive for in the course of this process: (1) behavioral autonomy, (2) emotional autonomy, and (3) value autonomy.

Behavioral Autonomy

Behavioral autonomy is the type of autonomy sought earliest by the adolescent. Today's youth desire to be behaviorally expressive quite early in life and, even though society today permits many behaviors, some of these behaviors may still be unacceptable to parents. Parents may view adolescents as rebellious, and adolescents may see parents as old-fashioned. Because many adolescent behaviors acceptable today were unacceptable in their parents when they were adolescents, the two generations lack a common reference point for understanding. Is this lack an adequate basis for generational conflict? It has always been true, even in decades when the range of acceptable social behaviors was narrower, that adolescents have desired experiences beyond those their parents had when they were young.

Research by Douvan and Adelson (1966) shows that there is a decisive increase in behavioral autonomy during adolescence. Behavioral autonomy is especially sought in regard to dating, employment, economic resources, and choice of leisure-time companions. Table 6.2 shows the behavioral shift in a sample of girls from the ages of 11 to 18 and the behavioral shift in a sample of both girls and boys from the ages of 14 to 16.

The most obvious behavioral shift was in dating, although an increase occurred in all behaviors listed. Also of primary importance is the fact that there was a 24-percent jump in peer involvement and a 22-percent drop in parental interaction. Almost half of the girls sampled showed a shift between amount of time spent with parents and amount of time spent with friends.

The fact of the need for behavioral autonomy does not imply that the only type of behavioral freedom desired by the adolescent is antisocial, rebellious, and so on. In many cases, it merely implies that the 13-year-old wants to go to the high school football game by himself instead of accompanied by parents, as he was at an earlier age. Or perhaps it implies the desire to go with a group of girls to a drive-in after school rather than come directly home. Too often parents assume that certain freedoms will be used unwisely and to the detriment of their adolescents. The adolescent may very well experience behavioral situations that he cannot cognitively or emotionally accommodate before he has learned

TABLE 6.2. Indices of behavioral autonomy for girls at 11 and 18 and for boys and girls aged 14 to 16.* S=subject.

	Change in girls from 11 to 18		Girls 14 to 16 (N=822) %	Boys 14 to 16 (N=1045) %
Item	(N=206) from %	(N=148) to %		
1. S dates or goes steady	4	94	72	59
2. S has a job outside home	34	60	56	47
3. S has some independent funds	63	84	74	
4. S spends most of free time with				
a. friends	22	46	32	
b. family	68	44	56	

*The data for boys are incomplete because some questions asked in the study of girls were not included in the boys' study.
From *Adolescent Development: Readings in Research and Theory* by M. Gold and E. Douvan, p. 132, table 22. Copyright © 1969 by Allyn and Bacon, Inc., Boston. Reprinted by permission.

certain coping skills. In these cases, the parents should be willing to help the adolescent interpret his experiences. It is appropriate for parents to set definable limits on the adolescent's experiences; in fact, some youths are reassured by the fact that parents do so. It is important, however, not to exhort the adolescent to "take more initiative in doing things," while actually meaning "Take more initiative in doing the things I want you to do."

Emotional Autonomy

Emotional autonomy is defined as "the degree to which the adolescent has managed to cast off infantile ties to the family" (Douvan & Adelson, 1966, p. 130). The adolescent must give up much of his childhood dependency, learn self-control and self-reliance, and come to identify with his parents as friends or confidants rather than as models. Parents can facilitate these processes by encouraging adolescent independence. If they set up conditions for gradual emancipation, the adolescent will be able to work out his independence with minimal internal conflict or rebellion.

Gold and Douvan (1969) feel that emotional autonomy is more difficult to accomplish than behavioral autonomy. They contend that girls are particularly reluctant to abandon earlier emotional ties. The emergence of new adult-adolescent relationships indicates a degree of emotional maturity in the adolescent, since it requires casting aside the need to maintain the protective ties characteristic of childhood. Too often, emotional autonomy is thought to be attained by the adolescent only by making a complete break. In fact, however, emotional autonomy is characterized by a new relationship with parents, not by an emotional break that severs all effective communication (Thornburg, 1973a). Nevertheless, Gold and Douvan (1969) feel that behavioral autonomy satisfies the need for independence before indicators of emotional autonomy, such as detachment, appear—usually later in adolescence. The research of Westley and Elkin (1957), Bowerman and Elder (1962), and Douvan and Adelson (1966; see Table 6.3) gives supportive evidence for such a delay.

Although there are indications in Table 6.3 of some emotional growth, the evidence is still overwhelming that the typical adolescent girl (11 to 18) is family oriented and compliant. In areas such as employment, parent-peer conflicts, and confidant relationships, the parent emerges as the primary source to which she turns.

It should also be noted that it is within the area of emotional autonomy that pathological conditions most often arise. Many adolescents enjoy the security found in their childhood ties so much that they never want to let them go completely and therefore never become emotionally autonomous. In the Douvan and Adelson study (1966), only about one-third of both the boys and the girls transferred their emotions to sources outside the home. On the parents' part, some invest so much emotional energy in a child that they are very reluctant to relinquish the parent-child relationship. Adolescents and parents alike must work to promote a balance between severing earlier emotional relationships and developing more mature emotional relationships.

Value Autonomy

It is not really clear how much value autonomy an adolescent attains. This type of autonomy, being the most complex, generally develops in late adolescence or young adulthood, after major decisions on educational goals, occupational plans, and marriage have been encountered and a workable degree of self-identity attained.

In some cases, the adolescent's value system and that of his parents are so similar that the parents' values will be perpetuated by the adolescent as his value pattern in adulthood. This lack of value conflict is especially common among parents and adolescents who hold to middle-class and working-class values. Typically, however, adolescents think that accepting parental values will put them out of step with their peers. If peer values are adopted, parental conflict may arise. In addition, the adolescent must consider a third value source, his society. Through the

TABLE 6.3. Indices of emotional autonomy for girls at 11 and 18 and for boys and girls aged 14 to 16. S=subject.

Item	Change in girls from 11 to 18 (N=206) from %	(N=148) to %	Girls 14 to 16 (N=822) %	Boys 14 to 16 (N=1045) %
1. S thinks friendship can be as close as family relationship	53	71	61	42
2. S disagrees with parents about:				
a. Ideas	12	46	34	
b. More than one issue out of six	54	59	56	
3. S would take advice of friends on more than one issue out of six				29
4. S chooses adult ideal				
a. outside the family	22	48	38	36
b. within the family	66	52	55	45
5. Projective: Response to request from lonely mother to give up good job and return to home town				
a. reject request	8	26	18	
b. comply, conditionally comply	78	59	66	
6. Projective: Response to parental restriction				
a. accept, reassure parents	51	38	36	
7. Projective: Response to conflict between parent-peer pressure				
a. parent oriented	78	61	63	
8. S chooses as confidant				
a. friend	5	33	26	
b. one, both parents	67	36	45	
9. Part in rule making				
a. S has some part	45	64	58	
10. Attitude toward parental rules				
a. Right, good, fair	47	56	56	

From *Adolescent Development: Readings in Research and Theory* by M. Gold and E. Douvan, p. 132, table 22. Copyright © 1969 by Allyn and Bacon, Inc., Boston. Reprinted by permission.

internal struggle with these varied value sources, the adolescent moves toward value autonomy.

In the last few years, such writers as Aronfreed (1968), Hoffman (1964, 1967), Kohlberg (1964), and Piaget (1948) have attempted to designate the family as the primary value source for the adolescent. One study, by Hoffman (1967), analyzed the behaviors of some 450 preadolescents (all 12-year-olds) to determine the effects that parental behaviors had on the internalization of moral values. He cited three basic ways in which the family asserted its influence:

1. *Power assertion.* This category includes physical punishment, the deprivation of material objects or privileges, and the direct application of force, or the threat of any of these.
2. *Love withdrawal.* This category includes techniques whereby the parent more or less openly withdraws love by ignoring the child, turning his back on the child, refusing to speak to him, explicitly stating that he dislikes him, or isolating him.
3. *Guilt induction regarding parents.* This mode of influence appeals to the child's guilt potential by referring to the consequences of the child's action for the parent.

Hoffman and Saltzstein (1967) found that power assertion was the least effective means of promoting the development of moral standards and the internalization of controls, primarily because power assertion elicits hostility in the child and also provides him with a model (the parent) for outwardly expressing hostility.

In contrast, the researchers found that guilt induction was the most effective way of teaching moral standards:

> Induction not only avoids the deleterious effects of power assertion, but also is the technique most likely to optimally motivate the child to focus his attention on the harm done others as the salient aspect of his transgressions, and thus to help integrate his capacity for empathy with the knowledge of the human consequences of his own behavior.

The third technique, love withdrawal,

> stands midway between the other two techniques in promoting internalization. It provides a more controlled form of aggression by the parent than power assertion, but less than induction. It employs the affectionate relationship between child and parent perhaps to a greater degree than the other two techniques, but in a way more likely than they to produce a disruptive anxiety response in the child. However, it falls short of induction in effectiveness by not including the cognitive material needed to heighten the child's awareness of wrongdoing and facilitate his learning to generalize accurately to other relevant situations, mainly by failing to capitalize on his capacity for empathy [Hoffman & Saltzstein, 1967, p. 54].

In summary, the following points can be made about adolescent striving for autonomy. First, in striving for independence, it is not necessary to sever all emotional feelings for one's parents. Second, to achieve autonomy, it is necessary for some adolescents to maintain a certain emotional distance from their parents. Third, for many adolescents, movement toward autonomy may proceed one step at a time—gradually instead of in erratic, sudden spurts. Fourth, we must not overlook the fact that some adolescents can realize identity-striving only by making distinct emotional breaks. Finally, although desires for autonomy appear in all adolescents, some find maintaining the status quo with their parents to be the most satisfying interpersonal relationship.

ATTITUDES TOWARD HOME

Positive parental interaction is an important factor in the adolescent's development of positive attitudes toward the home. Although adolescent-peer interaction is as crucial as or even more crucial to the adolescent than adolescent-adult interaction, the adolescent may still have effective interpersonal relations with his or her parents. Some observers have been quick to attribute strained home relationships to the "generation gap." This label refers to a concept more arbitrary than factual, especially if one looks at some of the major studies that have focused on parent-adolescent conflict.

For example, Meissner (1965) reports on his study of 1278 high school boys in the eastern United States, in which he examined their perception of and interaction with parents. He found a distinct difference between attitudes toward the father and attitudes toward the mother. Thirty-five percent of the students felt that their fathers were cold or indifferent, whereas only 13 percent thought so of their mothers. Fifty-one percent thought that their fathers were more or less old-fashioned, and 41 percent regarded their mothers that way. Only 39 percent thought that their fathers understood their difficulties, whereas 54 percent thought that their mothers did. Thirteen percent saw their fathers as "nervous," and 30 percent perceived their mothers as "nervous."

The typical adolescent attitude that emerges decidedly favors the mother over the father. Although this configuration may or may not run counter to the presumed identification of the male child with the father, it does indicate that typical perceptions of parents influence the course of child development. Apparently the father becomes fixed in the role of agent of parental authority and restriction, whereas the mother is perceived as more responsive to emotional needs for sympathy, acceptance, and understanding. Moreover, these trends in the data, although not always significant, suggest that the foregoing perceptions become more dominant as the adolescent moves from the freshman year to the senior year of high school.

In general, the attitudes toward parents tapped by Meissner's questions were positive. The majority thought of their parents as not overprotective or overly concerned about them (62 percent) or overly strict (85 percent). Most (74 percent) felt proud of their parents and liked to have them meet their friends.

Meissner's study also analyzed positive and negative parent-child interaction. The younger boys felt that they had adequate social opportunity and freedom, and they generally accepted parental authority and guidance. However, the older boys studied expressed dissatisfaction with home life, with the imposition of parental ideas, and with the level of parental understanding of their problems and behaviors. Their dissatisfaction increased as they grew older. Because of their increasing skills and diversifying social participation, the senior boys felt that they should be treated as more mature people. The parents' failure to do so caused their dissatisfaction. However, Meissner suggests that this dissatisfaction may also stem from the adolescents' growing ability to deviate from parentally influenced patterns, an essential part of development toward mature and independent functioning.

It is interesting that Meissner's positive results are similar to those found by Moore and Holtzman (1965), who studied the attitudes of 13,000 high school students toward their parents. They found that (1) 73 percent of the students valued their parents highly and felt that they should be responsible for them throughout their parents' lives, (2) 75 percent disagreed with the proposition that parents should sacrifice everything for their children, (3) 80 percent felt that the two parents should share family responsibilities equally, and (4) approximately 75 percent felt no urgency about getting married and leaving home. Therefore, available research indicates that positive parent-child interaction is widespread.

In a cross-cultural study, Kandel and Lesser (1969) examined the nature of parent-adolescent interactions in the United States and Denmark, the degree of adolescent independence experienced in both countries, and the correlation between family structure and the degree of adolescent independence. The sample consisted of 2327 American and 1552 Danish adolescents. The researchers found (see Table 6.4) that the authoritarian pattern of decision making was not only the most frequently observed in the United States but was three times as prevalent here as it was in Denmark. The democratic family structure was decisively the most common pattern in Denmark. Paternal authoritarianism was more dominant in both countries than maternal authoritarianism, as Elder (1962) had demonstrated before in studying the American family structure.

Other data in Table 6.4 indicate varying degrees of adolescent

TABLE 6.4. Adolescents' perceptions of patterns of interaction with mother and father, by country.

Family pattern	Interaction with mother United States	Interaction with mother Denmark	Interaction with father United States	Interaction with father Denmark	Cross-cultural differences* Mother	Cross-cultural differences* Father
Parental authority						
Authoritarian	43	15	53	31	.001	.001
Democratic	40	61	29	48		
Permissive	17	24	18	21		
Total N	(983)	(950)	(955)	(936)		
Communication						
Percent of adolescents						
Who feel that parent "always" explains her (his) decisions	30	43	21	33	.001	.001
Total N	(973)	(937)	(954)	(930)		
Who talk over "most" or "all" their problems with parent	41	52	23	26	.001	.001
Total N	(970)	(946)	(952)	(938)		
Reliance						
Percent of adolescents						
Who depend "very much" or "quite a bit" on parent for advice and guidance	59	54	43	50	.05	.05
Total N	(825)	(852)	(827)	(846)		
Affective relations						
Closeness to parent						
Extremely close	33	22	21	19	.001	.001
Quite close	30	35	29	36		
Moderately close	26	30	27	31		
Not close	11	13	23	14		
Total N	(967)	(944)	(935)	(936)		
Percent of adolescents						
Who enjoy doing "many" things with parent	35	35	34	43	not significant	.001
Total N	(971)	(941)	(953)	(941)		
Modeling						
Wanting to be like parent in						
Most ways	42	30	36	36	.001	.001
Many ways	21	40	21	38		
Few ways	37	30	43	26		
Total N	(968)	(941)	(937)	(935)		

*Significance of differences *between* countries for each pattern, as measured by Chi-square.

From "Parent-Adolescent Relationships and Adolescent Independence in the United States and Denmark" by D. B. Kandel and G. S. Lesser, *Journal of Marriage and the Family,* 1969, 31(2), 351. Copyright 1969 by National Council on Family Relations. Reprinted by permission.

acceptance of their parental-interaction patterns. For example, regarding interaction with the mother, 59 percent of the U.S. sample depended heavily on her guidance, 89 percent felt some degree of closeness to her, 63 percent found themselves wanting to be like their mother in many or most ways, and 35 percent enjoyed doing things with her. Although percentages for these interactions with the father were not so high, nevertheless a large number of respondents indicated consistent interaction with their fathers. These lower percentages for adolescent-interaction probably stem from the adolescent's perception that the father is more authoritarian and difficult to talk with about problems. In a comparison of the two countries, in almost all of the described categories the adolescent-parent relationship among the Danish families was significantly more interactive than among the American families, a finding probably due to the characteristic differences in styles of family decision making between the countries.

Kandel and Lesser summarized their results as follows:

> An inescapable conclusion from these results is that in the United States, parents treat their adolescents as children longer than in Denmark. Danish adolescents are expected to be self-governing; American adolescents are not. One can speculate about conditions in the two countries which lead to these differences in family structure. For example, children in the United States remain in school longer than in Denmark. They are not expected to make adult decisions as quickly as the Danes. Yet, at the same time American children have more money and experience greater pressure to spend in adult ways than the Danes. Having delayed the adulthood training—that is, teaching the children self-discipline—the parents are faced in the United States with adolescents who are in fact more dependent on them psychologically yet have the greater economic opportunity to do things independently. We would suggest that children in the United States are subject to a delayed socialization pattern, both in terms of autonomy from parent control as an adolescent and perhaps discipline as an earlier child. We would speculate that, as young children, Danes are subject to stronger discipline than the Americans. If this were indeed true, the discipline exercised at an early age would create a child who as an adolescent is far more disciplined and one to whom, as a consequence, the parent can afford to give freedom [Kandel & Lesser, 1969, p. 358].*

C. L. Stone (1963) discussed the relationship between the degree of parental understanding and the number of activities that an adolescent shares with his parents. Figure 6.1 is an adaptation of Stone's data. As you can see in the figure, the more the adolescent perceived that the parents

---

*From "Parent-Adolescent Relationships and Adolescent Independence in the United States and Denmark" by D. B. Kandel and G. S. Lesser, *Journal of Marriage and the Family*, 1969, 31(2), 358. Copyright 1969 by National Council on Family Relations. Reprinted by permission.

Frequency of doing things for fun with family

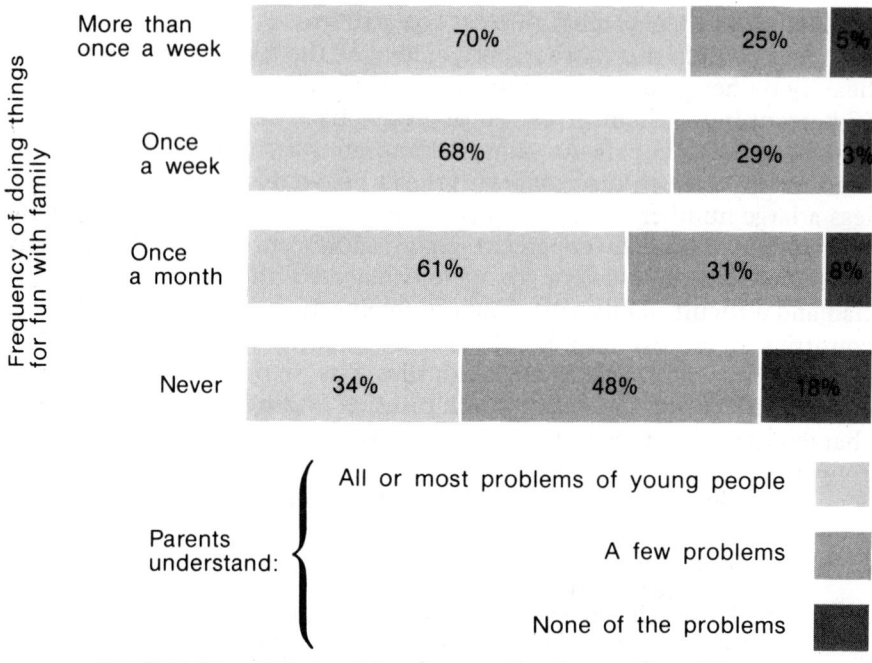

	All or most problems	A few problems	None of the problems
More than once a week	70%	25%	5%
Once a week	68%	29%	3%
Once a month	61%	31%	8%
Never	34%	48%	18%

Parents understand:
- All or most problems of young people
- A few problems
- None of the problems

FIGURE 6.1. Relationship of parental understanding of young people's problems and the frequency with which the adolescent does things for fun with the family. From "Family Recreation: A Family Dilemma" by C. L. Stone, *Family Life Coordinator*, 1963, *12*, 85-87. Copyright © 1963 The E. C. Brown Foundation. Reprinted by permission of The E. C. Brown Foundation, Portland, Oregon.

understood his problems, the greater was the incidence of their doing enjoyable family things together. For instance, 70 percent of the youths who thought that their parents understood their problems also reported doing things with their parents more than once a week.

The complications of parent-adolescent interaction are compounded by the adolescent's strivings for autonomy, by the increasing importance of his peer group, and by changing social influences. Because of rapid social change, many contemporary adolescent experiences fall outside the range of parental understanding (Friedenberg, 1969; Schaimberg, 1969). Furthermore, the adolescent may feel that his parents do not try to understand his problems (Rallings, 1969). Both parents and adolescents bear responsibility for increasing their communication, although parents may have to initiate new activities and new forms of communication. It remains important to remember, as Horrocks (1969) has suggested, that the home is both status-defining and experience-defining for the adolescent.

> Tragedy can be overcome!
> I experienced a very tragic childhood because my father terrorized and beat me all the time. He wanted me to be a child prodigy and achieve goals he himself was unable to achieve. I was not allowed to play with other children and didn't have the common childhood toys around the home. Instead, my time was spent practicing the piano and studying my school subjects. After several years of this I decided at age 12 that I couldn't stand it any more, so I took an entire bottle of aspirin in a suicide attempt. Obviously I did not succeed, but I did get a rather severe beating from my father once I returned home from the hospital.
> My life, when I was 13, took a turn for the better when my father died. He had been placed in a mental institution, but he escaped, came home, broke into the house, and shot my mother seven times. In less than an hour he turned the gun on himself and committed suicide. My three younger sisters and I were placed in foster homes while my mother was recovering from her gunshot wounds.
> Some six months after the tragedy our family came back together, but because my mother was disabled I had to get a job to help support the family. I decided to get my butt in gear and make something of myself, and I did. I finished high school, completed college, and now have an excellent job. Better still, I have an optimistic outlook on life. My future is promising, and I am extremely glad that my tragic childhood did not turn me into a criminal or a bum, as many people had predicted for me.

Parental Roles

Both parents play important roles in adolescent socialization. As an outcome of societal differentiation and reinforcement, mothers and fathers tend to play distinctively different roles. Traditionally, the father is more concerned about economic goals and the mother about emotionally meaningful behaviors such as interpersonal relationships and child rearing. Larson and Myerhoff (1965) see the father as *positional, formal,* and *rational* in his interaction with the adolescent. The father's positional role parallels his occupational role in our industrial society; that is, he passes on to the adolescent the concepts of work, responsibility, and goal orientation. The mother is thought to be more *personal, expressive,* and *emotional.* That is, she is more concerned about her adolescent as a person and about the effectiveness of his interpersonal relationships. Both forms of parental involvement facilitate the adolescent's awareness of his social environment and his acquisition of social and sex roles.

The father's role. Adolescents most commonly perceive the father as formal, reality oriented, and authoritarian. The positional role of the father is designed to prepare a son or daughter for impending adult roles. The middle-class father views the successful adult male as showing initiative and as highly responsible, aggressive, competent, and competitive. In addition, the male is emotionally stable and capable of exercising self-restraint, since such values characterize the middle-class occupations. The father tries to socialize his son to this standard. The father's concern for his daughter is generally not so intense, since he views her impending role as that of wife and mother. Occupational careers in which she might show interest are viewed as temporary, usually modifiable by marriage or by her husband's career.

These are traditional views, of course, which are being modified to some extent in present-day society. Awareness is growing that the ways in which a parent views a child's sex role are implicitly tied to the way in which the parent views his or her own role within the family structure. For example, Larson (1974) found the following attitudes in a study involving 464 fathers and 536 mothers. Both husbands and wives felt that it was the father's responsibility to do odd repair jobs and chores such as taking out garbage and mowing the lawn. In contrast, both felt that it was primarily the mother's responsibility to attend to child care, housework, and meals.

There is inconsistency in the data regarding the nature of the father's influence on the adolescent. One study (Hoffman & Saltzstein, 1967) indicates that the father's role is minimal in teaching morality and values; another study (Peterson, Becker, Hellmer, Shoemaker, & Quay, 1968) asserts that the father may be more influential than the mother in shaping attitudes. Moore and Holtzman (1965) found that adolescents saw their mothers as less authoritarian than their fathers, and that, if the mother was too permissive, the father tended to tone down her permissiveness somewhat. Research over the years has always shown adolescent-mother relationships to be stronger than adolescent-father relationships, although extensive research by Douvan and Adelson (1966) revealed that 25 percent of the girls they studied had experienced open conflict with their mothers. The father's role is important, however, in that it allows the adolescent to see the world through ideals, attitudes, and experiences different from those of the mother. In addition, the father commonly teaches moral standards by direct instruction in their cognitive content as well as through his disciplinary techniques.

Rogers (1972b) contends that the father now stands in a dual position. An emerging group of youth see the father as gentle and benign, whereas some adolescents continue to perceive him as autocratic within his private kingdom.

The mother's role. Adolescents do seem to feel that their mother is the more responsive and empathic of the two parents. This feeling probably carries over from their birth and early rearing, when strong emotional attachments were made. This strong attachment causes the adolescent to turn most often to Mother for counsel or favors; it is also one reason that, later, emotional autonomy is so difficult to accomplish.

The traditional wife-and-mother role continues to be vitally important for most women today (Holm, 1970), although from women's increasing aggressiveness, greater sexual freedom, greater education, wider choice of employment, and greater tendency to make housework everyone's responsibility, one gets the impression that the traditional wife-and-mother role has been abandoned. Certainly today's society provides more role alternatives for women than ever before in our history, but a large number of females still prefer the wife-and-mother role.

The mother's role may very well change as the female's role in the larger society changes. Mothers are working outside the home in increasing numbers, and this factor will obviously affect their behavior within the home. It is not imperative to choose one role over the other, since a complementary combination role can be and is being worked out by many women today.

At the turn of the twentieth century, the family structure was primarily patriarchal and the male was the provider of the family's needs. The female was economically dependent upon and generally subservient to the male. With the increase in industrialization and the critical shortage of male workers during World War II, the female found entrance into the occupational world easier than before. The concomitant shift in family structure allowed more democratic interaction patterns to develop. The movement was toward complementary family roles; men and women were regarded as equal, although emphasis on their basic differences remained. Masculinity still meant activity, strength, dominance, and emotional restraint. In contrast, femininity was believed to be characterized by passivity, sentiment, weakness, and submission. The more contemporary movement toward equality is based on the concept of complementary human roles rather than on the masculine/feminine or dominance/submission arrangement. One does not deny the basic differences between the sexes; one only sees them as secondary to the total human being. A new, more flexible human role has been created, in which the same occupational and social opportunities are open to men and women both inside and outside the family (Linner, 1971).

Potential barriers to the new woman's role. There are at least three identifiable barriers within our society that prohibit many women from realizing their potential. The first barrier is *discrimination*. The most obvious discrimination against women has been in employment. The majority of employed women are working in the less advantaged professional and clerical fields, semiskilled jobs, service jobs, and so on. Holm (1970) points out that women's involvement in the more advantaged professional and technical areas has actually been declining. Today 39 percent of these workers are women, whereas in 1940 45 percent were women. Mead (1971) observes that, after World War II, high female employment in these advantaged jobs was diminished by the public plea for women to give up their jobs for the sake of our fighting men, who were returning home as the war ended.

Mead believes that the occupational world again opened up to women in the 1960s because the country was in need of cheap labor. "We were very short of cheap labor so we told them they needed to be fulfilled" (1971, p. 55). A woman was told that it is very unrewarding to stay at home, and that once she has her children she must fulfill herself by moving out into the society.

At least 60 percent of the working mothers in the United States *must* work in order to keep up with the spiraling economy. "Fulfilled" or not, many of these women fall within range of Mead's description, since

---

Proposed revision of sex-discrimination guidelines from The Federal Register, *December 27, 1973.*

> Sec. 60–20.2(c) An employer shall not require preemployment information from job applicants of one sex which it does not require of job applicants of the other sex. Such information includes, but is not limited to, inquiries concerning anticipated temporary disability, child care problems, and marital status. . . .
>
> Sec. 60–20.3(c) The employer shall not make any distinction based upon sex in employment opportunities, wages, hours, or other conditions of employment. Nor shall the employer make a distinction based upon sex in the granting of fringe benefits, including medical, hospital, accident, life insurance, pension and retirement benefits, profit sharing and bonus plans, credit union benefits, leave and other terms and conditions of employment. *Proposed Alternative (A):* It shall not be an excuse that the cost to the employer of such benefits is greater with respect to one sex than the other. *Proposed Alternative (B):* In the area of employer contributions for insurance, pensions, welfare programs and other similar "fringe benefits," the employer will not be considered to have violated these guidelines if his contributions are the same for men and women or if the resulting benefits are equal.

they have limited education and work in low-paying, low-prestige jobs.

If one compares incomes of men and women, one finds not only a wide disparity in earnings but a gap that is still widening (U.S. Department of Labor, 1970). This disparity is due in some measure to unequal pay for equal work (despite recent legislation—see box) but mostly to the fact that women are more likely to be employed in low-skilled and low-paying jobs. Men still have the greater opportunity in our society to obtain professional and other high-paying jobs (Fuchs, 1974).

Furthermore, the "fringe" benefits of employment show an even greater disparity than does pay in many cases. Women are less likely to hold occupations characterized by on-the-job training, health-care and retirement benefits.

Interpreting the gap between men's and women's earnings

Much has been made of the rather puzzling observation that the ratio of earnings of all women to those of all men has declined during the past 20 years. This observation refers to annual earnings, or the earnings of full-time, year-round workers who are not necessarily representative of the total. But average hours and weeks worked during the year fell for women relative to men from 1949 to 1969. If annual wages and salaries are divided by total hours worked during the year, the result is a much modified decline in the hourly wage of women relative to the hourly wage of men.

An additional factor which would produce a relative decline in women's earnings is the relative decline in their general educational level and their labor market experience during the period. In 1950, women in the labor force had on the average more schooling than men did: but this advantage was eliminated by 1970. Since education has an effect on earnings—both men's and women's earnings increase with education—it is important to take these changes into account. An approximate adjustment for educational level increases the differential in 1949 and 1959, because women in the labor force then had more education than men. After the educational adjustment, the differential shows little change from 1949 to 1969.

What has not been accounted for is the experience differential between men and women. . . . this difference seems to be the most important factor causing a divergence in hourly earnings. But since the labor force participation of women, particularly married women, was increasing rapidly during the period, it is very likely that the constant flow of entrants into the labor force resulted in a decline in the average experience of women in the labor force during the 20 years.

The foregoing suggests that if we could compare women and men with a given amount of experience and education the ratio of women's hourly earnings to men's might well show an increase over the 20 years—a narrowing in the gap.*

*From *The Economic Report of the President*, Council of Economic Advisers, 1974.

A second barrier is the *sex-typing* of occupations. Our society perpetuates the idea that some occupations are better suited for men and others for women. The proportion of female doctors or male nurses is small. Ships hire stewards; airlines hire stewardesses. Most businesses are run by men, and men hold most high political offices. Have you ever seen a male dental hygienist or a female butler? The fallacy in these occupational stereotypes lies in the fact that the few people who have dared to cross sex-stereotype boundaries have proven themselves to be quite competent, both in the job itself and in overcoming these built-in occupational prejudices.

The fact that many women are given menial tasks to do today that once were done by men is an indication that these jobs were actually more exploitative than too physically demanding for women. In Russia, dock workers are women, as are most carpenters and bricklayers. Why are American women "too weak" to unload ships? Similarly, in Russia, most physicians are women. Why are American women "too emotional" to be physicians? Additional occupational stereotypes are:

1. Women can't work for women.
2. Women can't supervise because they are too emotional.
3. Women are job-oriented while men are career-oriented.
4. Men and women can't travel together as a business-professional team.
5. Women are more patient and better than men at routine, repetitive jobs.
6. It doesn't pay to train and promote women because of high absenteeism and turnover rate [Holm, 1970, pp. 9–10].

Pollock (1971) stresses the mythological aspects of advertising and their debilitating effects on the self-fulfillment of women:

> The fantasy purveyors in advertising understand the potential of the myth, and manipulate it in its least rational manifestations. In their work, our norms of health, our God-given truths, are metamorphosed into a stream of injunctions. Women are told repeatedly that they will be valueless, lonely, unhappy, unless they emulate the slim, glamorous, young model in the ads; they are told that, like the dumb housewife of another kind of ad, they will find security, fulfillment, even ecstasy in sinks and sheets that are whiter than white. Advertisements geared to men tacitly or overtly promise adoring and available women as the reward for purchase [1971, p. 722].

A third barrier to women's self-fulfillment is their *personal limitations*. It is difficult to overcome well-taught, consistently reinforced notions that women are not so capable in the occupational, economic, and social worlds as men. Probably one of the most significant barriers to

Increasing evidence continues to dispel the notion that men are superior to women in aptitude. The following table shows, in fact, that perhaps the reverse is true. Whatever happened to sex stereotyping?

Comparisons of the performance of men and women in selected aptitude areas.

Aptitude	Group with higher average performance
U.S. EMPLOYMENT SERVICE	
Numerical reasoning	—
Spatial reasoning	Male
Form perception	Female
Clerical perception	Female
Motor coordination	Female
Finger dexterity	Female
Manual dexterity	—
HUMAN ENGINEERING LABORATORY	
Abstract visualization	Female
Analytical reasoning	—
Eyedness	—
Finger dexterity	Female
Foresight	—
Grip	Male
Graphoria (accounting aptitude)	Female
Ideaphoria (flow of ideas in verbal pursuits)	Female
Inductive reasoning	—
Memory for design	—
Number memory	—
Observation	Female
Objective personality	—
Pitch discrimination	—
Rhythm memory	—
Silograms (word association)	Female
Structural visualization	Male
Subjective personality	—
Timbre discrimination	—
Tonal memory	—
Tweezer dexterity	—
Vocabulary (English)	—

NOTE: Dashes indicate no significant difference. Although the differences shown are statistically significant, in most cases they would be of little practical significance. To illustrate, USES research has found spatial reasoning to be important for many of the skilled trades. But the level required exceeds an employed worker average for only one trade. Studies of seniors in high schools throughout the country showed that 67 percent of the boys and 62 percent of the girls equal or exceed this average. This means that more than half the girls have at least the minimum amount of spatial reasoning needed for most skilled trades.

From "Sex Stereotyping: Its Decline in the Skilled Trades" by J. N. Hedges and S. E. Bemis, *Monthly Labor Review*, 1974, 97(5), 19.

women's greater participation in these areas lies in their lack of self-confidence and their own reservations about their capability to make decisions as effectively as men. Although many women find the home too physically and socially restrictive, the age-old idea that the woman's place is in the home is difficult to overcome.

Blue-collar wives

The Social Research, Inc., of Chicago reports that some changes are beginning to occur among 40 million women who constitute what has been thought to be the most stable group in American society. Among the more significant changes in attitude found by the Social Research study are:

1. A shift in career values. Almost a third say they would not choose homemaking as a career if they were 15 years old.
2. A new desire for independence. Eight years ago, close to half of the women queried thought that a personal second car was just a luxury; today, the same number see it as a necessity.
3. A desire for fewer children. In 1965, most blue-collar wives thought four children were an ideal family. In 1973, 71 percent in their early twenties say they plan to have two children, one, or none.
4. A new interest in community and jobs. The blue-collar wife is expressing a marked interest in the larger world, no longer confining herself to domestic matters.*

*From "No More Starch for Blue-Collar Wives," MS. Gazette, *MS. Magazine*, February 1974.

Many women sincerely believe that they must play a subordinate role in society. They are intimidated by their view of men as the dominant group. In addition, their experience has been that men usually put them down severely, stereotyping or labeling them in order to reinforce female dependency and male superiority. Dominant groups also tend to determine both philosophical and moral cultural stigmas. If the female continues to perceive herself as weaker, she will indeed have little control over society's attitudes. The more that women—individually and collectively—decisively contribute to the social, political, economic, and occupational systems, the easier it will be for each woman to realize her potential.

The new woman's role and the adolescent girl. To attain equality with men in the society, young women must be better prepared emotionally, educationally, and occupationally to enter the larger society. Holm (1970) suggests that the American family raises girls in the Cinderella image—to go to school, meet Prince Charming, marry, rear children, and live happily ever after. This dream, of course, is not commonly realized in American society today. Now, more women are employed (3.2 million make more money annually than their husbands, according to the 1970 U.S. Census), fewer women feel obliged to marry or to maintain a marriage they view as unsuccessful, women see more alternatives to childbearing and child rearing, and there is more sexual precociousness among adolescent girls than ever before.

Therefore, adolescent girls need to be taught greater self-awareness, the relevance of educational training to subsequent adult functioning, a self-concept freer of sex-role emphasis, and a confidence that they have talent and may involve themselves in activities that have been considered male oriented. If a mother feels powerless, or if a family structure is paternally autocratic, feelings of inferiority are usually experienced by the female children, and the coping skills they learn are limited. If family relationships are based on male supremacy, both male and female children will gain a limited understanding of themselves as total individuals. Offering the adolescent girl a variety of learning and experiential situations will allow her to gain a broader concept of self, so that she will be able to gain respect and self-esteem through avenues other than getting a man and rearing a family.

Working Mothers: The Adolescent's Response

With the resurgent movement of women into the occupational world, considerable research has been focused on the effects of maternal employment on children and adolescents. The results of research in this area are conflicting. Various studies show the effects precipitating negative personality traits, positive personality traits, or no noticeable changes one way or the other. What are some of the reasons for these contradictions?

In any research, we strive for a random sample so that our results can be generalized to the larger population. In addition, we try to control all variables that may affect the outcome of the research in some way. Two problems encountered in researching working mothers are that we often cannot (1) obtain a random sample or (2) effectively control important variables. Such considerations as how much a mother works, how long she has worked, whether she works voluntarily or involuntarily, whether she likes her work, how old her children were when she went to work, whether she is head of the household or an economically contributing member, and what her attitudes are about working, child rearing, family sharing, and so on will affect the outcome of any study. We must also attempt to control variables such as socioeconomic status, educational level, occupational level, age, family size, place of residence, and ethnic background. The complexity of these variables may make studies seem to support one another when upon analysis they do not, or seem to be in open conflict when upon analysis they are not. Keeping these limiting conditions in mind, let's examine some general findings on the effects of working mothers on children.

Essig and Morgan (1945), on comparing 500 daughters of working and nonworking mothers, found that girls whose mothers did not work were better adjusted in the area of family life and expressed strong feelings of love toward their mothers. In contrast, there was a noticeable lack of love, understanding, and interest between many of the working mothers and their daughters. Glueck and Glueck (1957) found greater emotional conflict in delinquent boys of working mothers than in boys of nonworking mothers. Similarly, Rouman (1956) found evidence that both male and female adolescents with working mothers lacked self-reliance and social skills and had tendencies to withdraw.

All of these studies were done before the 1960s, the decade during which women moved into several roles alternative to that of homemaker. Several studies done during and since the 1960s have obtained more positive results. Perhaps this decade of social change set a new basis for considering the emotional and personality traits of contemporary adolescents. For example, Yarrow (1961; Yarrow, Scott, Deleeuw, & Heinig, 1962) studied working and nonworking mothers according to their satisfaction or dissatisfaction with their roles. His sample consisted of intact families matched for number, age, and sex of children and for the mother's age and education. He found few differences between the working mothers and the nonworking mothers in their warmth, sensitivity, and ability to satisfy the child emotionally. *Dissatisfied* nonworking mothers were actually less adequate in mothering and less confident about their child-rearing ability than the working mothers. He did find some evidences of more overt rebellion among children of working mothers. In contrast, Roy (1961) found no noticeable effects on adolescents' behavior as a result of the mother's working.

Other researchers have found that whether or not the mother works does not have so crucial an effect on the child's personality characteristics as does the quality of the maternal role she plays. For example, McCord and his associates (McCord, McCord, & Thurber, 1963) investigated lower-class adolescent sons of working mothers. If the mother-son relationship was stable, the fact that the mother worked had no debilitating effects on the boy. However, if the family interaction was unstable, the mother's employment was interpreted as rejection by the son.

Douvan and Adelson (1966) found that girls whose mothers worked part time were better adjusted than girls whose mothers worked full time. They concluded that when a mother works full time, she is unable to meet the emotional needs of her daughter, a situation that may cause the daughter to seek relationships outside the home prematurely to fulfill her needs. Nye (1952) reported similar effects in his study of part-time and full-time working mothers. A more recent study by Nelson (1971) found that girls with nonworking mothers had better adjustment scores (as measured by the Minnesota Counseling Inventory) than girls whose mothers worked either full time or part time. Nelson also found that, in contrast, boys whose mothers worked full time had better personality adjustment than those whose mothers worked part time or not at all.

Two apparent trends emerge from an examination of the reactions of adolescents to the idea of the working mother. First, the reactions usually range from mild acceptance to strong rejection of the idea. Second, adolescents show a tendency to stereotype job opportunities and to disapprove of the working mother's holding what they regard as "a man's job."

Entwistle and Greenberger (1972) studied the attitudes held by 270 boys and 305 girls in ninth grade in Maryland about the woman's work role. The data were broken down into IQ, race, and socioeconomic classifications for comparison.

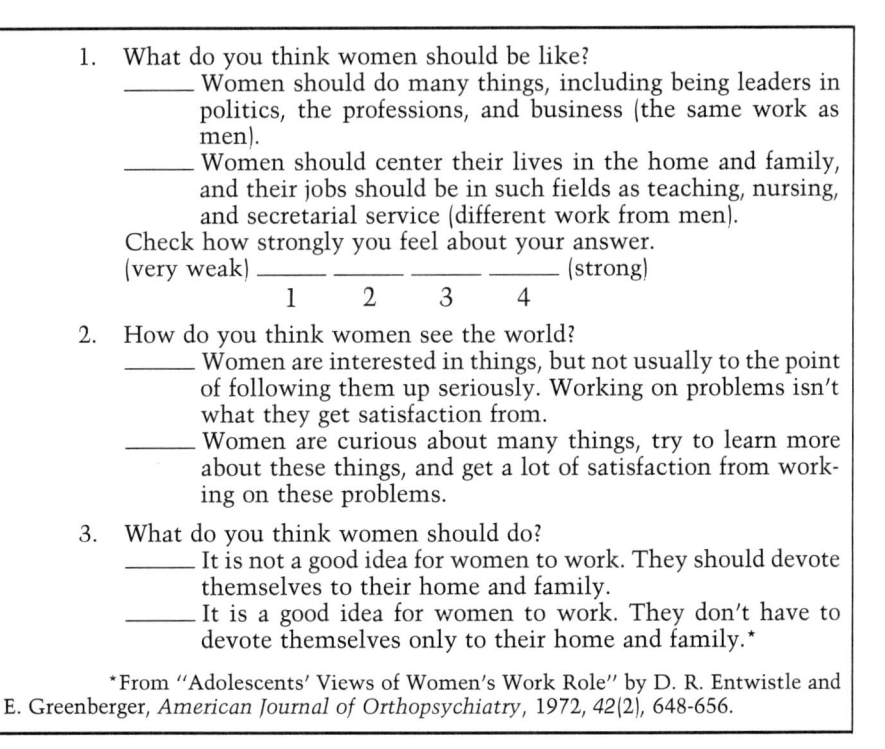

---

1. What do you think women should be like?
   _____ Women should do many things, including being leaders in politics, the professions, and business (the same work as men).
   _____ Women should center their lives in the home and family, and their jobs should be in such fields as teaching, nursing, and secretarial service (different work from men).
   Check how strongly you feel about your answer.
   (very weak) _____ _____ _____ _____ (strong)
              1   2   3   4

2. How do you think women see the world?
   _____ Women are interested in things, but not usually to the point of following them up seriously. Working on problems isn't what they get satisfaction from.
   _____ Women are curious about many things, try to learn more about these things, and get a lot of satisfaction from working on these problems.

3. What do you think women should do?
   _____ It is not a good idea for women to work. They should devote themselves to their home and family.
   _____ It is a good idea for women to work. They don't have to devote themselves only to their home and family.*

*From "Adolescents' Views of Women's Work Role" by D. R. Entwistle and E. Greenberger, *American Journal of Orthopsychiatry*, 1972, 42(2), 648-656.

The material in the box presents the researchers' questions. The results of their study indicate a marked difference in opinion between boys and girls about women's roles; boys tended to hold more conservative opinions. Some general trends emerge if subgroup differences are temporarily ignored. Both sexes were decidedly against the idea of women's holding men's jobs (Question 1). Both sexes reacted positively to Question 2 (how women see the world); boys were slightly positive and girls were strongly positive. On Question 3 (whether women should work), most of the girls were mildly positive and the boys were consistently negative.

As a group, the black boys studied appeared more liberal in their attitudes toward women than the white boys, but this stance may stem from a social-class-related willingness for women to work (shared by whites of the same socioeconomic class) that reflects the need in high-poverty areas for women to work in order to maintain family subsistence. The favorable attitudes of blacks toward women's holding jobs may also be a direct consequence of their having been socialized in families with female heads or in families that needed two wage earners to maintain subsistence. Work expectations for female blacks were not coupled with a desire to see women in positions of leadership, even though blacks generally were a little more favorable toward this idea than whites.

The most liberal views on women's holding men's jobs were expressed by high-IQ blue-collar white students of both sexes, but the boys' scores in this category still indicated opposition. White-collar white boys were even more conservative on this issue, considerably more so than white-collar white girls. High-IQ white girls, who are most upwardly mobile occupationally, experience potential negative peer-group pressure by males, both because boys are much more traditional in their views of women's working and because boys may feel threatened by these girls' direct competition for their jobs. The jobs in question are in politics, the professions, and business—the presumed vocational targets of high-IQ white white-collar males. It has already been noted that, in this study, blue-collar boys of high IQ expressed a slightly more liberal view than white-collar boys toward women's holding "men's" jobs, but perhaps they were being so liberal because the jobs listed were somewhat unrealistic in terms of the vocational aspirations of blue-collar students. For them to imagine a woman holding such a job might not have been so personally threatening.

A study by Frye and Dietz (1973) also investigated high school students' attitudes toward working women (see Table 6.5). These investigators selected 197 students in Tennessee, including 69 sophomores, 64 juniors, and 64 seniors. Their data revealed that boys held a more traditional position than girls about the changing female sex role. For exam-

TABLE 6.5. Percent of males and females agreeing with stereotype statements on women's role.

Statement	Males (N=123)	Females (N=74)
The most important work for a woman is that of wife and mother.	87	61
A career should be more important to a man than to a woman.	65	47
Affectionate, motherly, housewifely women are more admired by men than are career girls.	59	41
Women are happiest when they work for men rather than for other women.	81	64
Competing with men tends to make a woman less feminine.	67	42
Women should not work outside the home except in cases of financial necessity.	56	20
Men generally like women who are not too intelligent or competitive on the job.	50	43
Men are happier when they work for other men rather than for women.	70	73

From "Attitudes of High School Students Toward Traditional Views of Women Workers" by V. H. Frye and S. L. Dietz, *Journal of the Student Personnel Association for Teacher Education*, 1973, 11(3), 102–108. Copyright © 1973 American Personnel and Guidance Association. Reprinted by permission.

ple, 87 percent of the boys felt that the most important work for a woman was that of wife and mother. There was moderate male acceptance of the mother's working if it was an economic necessity. On both points there was considerable disagreement on the part of the girls, whose attitude toward working mothers was consistently more liberal than the boys'.

Frye and Dietz also asked these high school students to sex-type 20 common occupations. Analysis of these data indicates that both male and female adolescents are traditional in their sex-typing of occupations. When these youths become adults, their attitudes are likely to limit career choices for women—a factor that was suggested earlier in this chapter as a major limitation to the female's achievement of equality within the society.

ONE-PARENT FAMILIES

Popular opinion holds that children and adolescents who come from broken homes, especially those broken through divorce or separation, have severe problems in development and adjustment. Before discussing at length research findings on broken homes, let's look at the practical side of the situation. The primary responsibilities of providing for the physical, emotional, and social needs of children are best met by both parents. One-parent families create a distortion of the family unit, and the task of taking upon oneself total responsibility for child rearing is more than many individuals can cope with effectively. In addition, problems may arise from the parent's engaging in new sexual patterns and from changes in the economic structure of the family.

The national divorce rate exceeds 40 percent today. In several states more than half of the couples married eventually obtain a divorce. In spite of the increasing prevalence of divorce, one of the most difficult problems facing single parents, especially females, comes from the attitudes of society toward divorced people. A high degree of isolation and discrimination is often felt by these individuals within mainstream society; the prevailing social philosophy infers some pathological condition or moral failure on the part of divorced people. Their children and adolescents also commonly feel the brunt of this social stigma.

One has only to read the popular literature or turn on the television to see the immoral motives of the divorced man or the menacing threat to the taxpayer's dollar of the divorced woman. Advice columns advocate "saving the marriage for the sake of the children." Yet at some point we must view divorce with a greater degree of realism. Although it is generally asserted that two individuals at the time of marriage make a lifetime commitment to each other, it is often the case that the commitment cannot be kept. Is it better to physically separate and go through the necessary readjustive processes, or should a couple keep their home physically intact, although it is emotionally broken, for the sake of their children? There is increasing evidence that children may be better off living in a one-parent family structure, where parent and child can make the necessary adjustments, than remaining in a family structure characterized by fighting, hostility, cruelty, or bitterness. The social-emotional adjustment of children is usually better in the long run in a physically broken home than in a physically intact, emotionally broken home.

The research done by Goode (1956) yielded three distinct feelings on the part of divorced women. First, they had a strong tendency to worry about the effects of divorce on their children. Second, after remarriage, these women thought that their children's lives had improved as a result of the original divorce. Finally, whether they remarried or not, most women believed that their children experienced better lives than they would have if the unsatisfactory marriage had been continued. Other research by Nye (1957) and Landis (1960) found that children from broken homes had fewer psychosomatic illnesses and experienced less delinquent behavior and better emotional adjustment than did children from emotionally strained unbroken homes.

Thomes (1968) was concerned with the effects of paternal absence on children from 9 to 11. Her subjects were 47 children whose parents were divorced or separated and 37 children from intact families. Their parents were matched by age, education, and economic status (low), and all were white. She questioned the children individually at home concerning themselves and their aspirations and their ideas about parental duties, the makeup of the family, and their relationships with other children.

Although both groups of children indicated "father" less often than "mother" as the person who performed parental duties such as discipline, only four children from the broken homes failed to include "father" in their description of a "home." About one-third of the children in both groups said that they would go to their fathers first with a problem. Hostility toward the father was comparable in both groups. When asked what they wanted most for the family, only six children from the broken homes said "a father." Children in both groups scored alike in describing themselves and what they would like to be.

Thomes suggests two reasons why the absence of the father seemed to have so little effect on the children: (1) their age and (2) the length of time the fathers had been gone. The child from 9 to 11, she maintains, is in a period of "relative quiescence in personality development," and, since the absent fathers had been away from home for at least two years, the children had already experienced the immediate period of adjustment following the father's departure.

Burchinal (1964) compared the characteristics of adolescents from unbroken, broken, and reconstituted families. In his study, unbroken families were defined as those with both biological parents present. Reconstituted families were of three types: mothers and stepfathers, fathers and stepmothers, and divorced parents who had both remarried.

Burchinal found no significant differences in emerging personality characteristics or social relationships between adolescents from broken or reconstituted homes and those from unbroken homes. Although he did find the immediate effects of divorce to be emotionally distressing, he contended that adolescents whose parents were divorced recovered psychologically within a short time period, a finding later corroborated by Thomes' research, discussed above. Of the many social variables researched, only four appeared to be significantly different among certain family types (see Table 6.6). For example, boys from the three types of families were asked how many of their schoolmates they liked. Their responses fell into three distinct patterns. The first pattern, a group consisting of (1) boys from unbroken families and (2) boys who lived with their mothers only, seldom reported having three or fewer friends at school, and these two groups reported having four or more friends with almost equal frequency. The second pattern, a group consisting of (1) boys

TABLE 6.6. Responses of the adolescents to social-relationship items having significant differences by the family types.

Sex of respondent and school-relationship question	Unbroken families		Mothers only		Mothers and stepfathers		Both parents remarried		Fathers and stepmothers		Total	
	Number	percent	Number	percent	Number	percent	Number	percent	Number	percent	Number	percent
Girls												
How well do you like school?												
Very well	217	34.3	31	38.8	21	35.6	12	33.3	5	35.8	286	34.8
Pretty well	350	55.4	36	45.0	31	52.5	14	38.9	8	57.1	439	53.5
Not very well and not at all	65	10.3	13	16.2	7	11.9	10	27.8	1	7.1	97	11.7
Total	632	100.0	80	100.0	59	100.0	36	100.0	14	100.0	821	100.0
$X^2 = 15.87$, $df = 8$, $P < .05$												
Teachers give more attention to others.												
Much or somewhat more	238	38.0	34	42.5	34	58.6	20	55.6	3	21.4	329	40.4
Hardly ever or not at all	389	62.0	46	57.5	24	41.4	16	44.4	11	78.6	486	59.6
Total	627	100.0	80	100.0	58	100.0	36	100.0	14	100.0	815	100.0
$X^2 = 15.90$, $df = 4$, $P < .05$.												
Teachers harder on you than others.												
Much or somewhat more	102	16.1	17	21.2	20	33.9	5	13.9	1	7.1	145	17.7
Hardly ever or not at all	530	83.9	63	78.8	39	66.1	31	86.1	13	92.9	676	82.3
Total	632	100.0	80	100.0	59	100.0	36	100.0	14	100.0	821	100.0
$X^2 = 14.69$, $df = 4$, $P < .05$.												
Boys												
How many of your schoolmates do you like?												
One to three	68	9.5	9	12.2	9	18.0	7	15.2	6	23.1	99	10.9
Four	295	41.3	33	44.6	13	26.0	12	26.1	12	46.1	365	40.1
Five or more	351	49.2	32	43.2	28	56.0	27	58.7	8	30.8	446	49.0
Total	714	100.0	74	100.0	50	100.0	46	100.0	26	100.0	910	100.0
$X^2 = 17.06$, $df = 8$, $P < .05$.												

From "Characteristics of Adolescents from Unbroken, Broken, and Reconstituted Families," by L. J. Burchinal, *Journal of Marriage and the Family*, 1964, 26, 49. Copyright 1964 by National Council on Family Relations. Reprinted by permission.

whose mothers had remarried and (2) those whose biological parents had both remarried, reported having four or fewer friends least frequently among the patterns and reported having five or more friends most frequently among the patterns. The third pattern, a group consisting of boys whose fathers had remarried, reported having the fewest friends at school. The only pattern emerging clearly from this comparison was that boys living with their fathers and stepmothers had the fewest friends.

Clear interpretation of the girls' responses was more difficult. The only consistent result was the more favorable responses of girls living with their fathers and stepmothers, suggesting that these girls had more positive attitudes toward school and maintained better relationships with teachers than did the other girls studied. However, the girls from unbroken homes did not uniformly display more favorable attitudes toward school than the girls from other types of homes, although the girls from unbroken homes were absent less frequently.

Douvan and Adelson (1966) found results that conflicted with Burchinal's. They concluded that there are noticeable differences between boys reared by their mothers and boys from other family patterns. Their data indicated that masculine development is impeded in the maternally dominated home, an observation also found in the research of Biller (1970) and Hetherington (1965). Boys reared by their mothers find it difficult to accept authority, and many of their behaviors are characterized by overassertiveness and pseudomasculinity. Douvan and Adelson found that, in addition, these boys are typically loners with few, if any, close friends. However, their research found that the maternally dominated home had no comparable harmful effects on the adolescent girl.

UNWED ADOLESCENT MOTHERS

In 1966, more than 72,000 unmarried teen-age girls gave birth to children. It is estimated that in the latter half of the 1970s the total will reach 80,000. This figure constitutes approximately 41 percent of all projected out-of-wedlock births, although the average unwed mother is not a teen-ager. In 1963, the average age was 22. However, the tendency toward earlier sexual involvements is gradually moving the average age toward the teen-age years; approximately two percent of all unwed mothers are now younger than 15 (U.S. Census, 1970).

Studies show that the rates of illegitimate births are increasing most rapidly in urbanized areas, especially among nonwhite adolescent girls (*Illegitimacy*, 1965; Sauber & Rubenstein, 1965). In New York City the majority of unwed mothers are between 20 and 24, and about 30 percent are teen-agers.

140   Chapter 6

> A female 16½ years old sought psychological counseling in a private center. At the initial interview, she gave the impression of feeling helpless and guilty about having a saline abortion at 20 weeks' gestation.
>
> She lived in the East with her mother and brother, who was one year older than she. Her parents had divorced when she was 9 years old. She had been going with her boyfriend for three years; he was 19. She felt acceptance from his parents, and the two anticipated marriage when she completed high school in 1975. Her mother, however, disapproved of the relationship.
>
> Just prior to her pregnancy the couple had run off together, but they returned because they were concerned about the boy's parents. The young girl was elated about her pregnancy. She believed this situation would develop into their having to get married. When she informed her mother of her condition, the mother became outraged and immediately sent her daughter to the West to be with her father, who had remarried and whom she had not seen for five years.
>
> Counseling sessions revealed that she desired to have the baby and that, once she knew that marriage to her boyfriend was impossible, she desired to put the baby up for adoption. She said that she had had the abortion to satisfy her mother and felt very guilty because of it. She strongly believed that life starts at conception and that her 20-week fetus had been alive. After the abortion, she experienced an abrupt change in her interpersonal relationships; depression became the rule more than the exception.
>
> What factors went into this girl's total behavior? How could she be helped to deal with her guilt? How would you respond to her belief that she had killed a person?

There is considerable discrepancy in the data on whether these teen-age girls choose to keep their child or give it up for adoption. In the New York City study conducted by Sauber and Rubenstein (1965), 80 percent of the 333 mothers interviewed chose to keep their babies. Two-thirds of this group were nonwhite. In contrast, Friedman's study of a New England maternity home for white girls (1966) found that, although they showed some reluctance, 80 percent wanted to give up their babies for adoption. The social-class and ethnic differences between the adolescent girls of these two studies may account for this difference in results.

The adolescent girl has a need to complete her own development. Not all of the major developmental tasks, as described in Chapter 1, have yet been resolved. That autonomy has not yet been achieved is attested to by the new dependency the girl often develops on her mother once the baby is born. Her unresolved ego-identity often makes it impossible for her to build a permanent relationship with a partner. Her commitment to work and responsibility is not totally conceptualized, although the new child may help precipitate this development. Finally, her values and ethical commitments are still in their intermediate stages. It is unlikely that the child will help much to facilitate their development. The extent to which the child interferes with the adolescent mother's achievement of her developmental tasks may have some bearing on her effectiveness as a mother.

> My decision to marry, at age 16, was the decision I thought would change my life. At the time, I thought all my basic desires would be met: group and male acceptance, independence from my mother, and the identity of being a wife and, hopefully, a mother. Well, in truth, the outcome was that (1) I never felt or experienced any sense of worth, esteem, or identity through our married friends, my husband, or my child; and (2) I was still dependent not only on my mother but on my husband as well.
>
> I decided to divorce my husband, went back home, and found that I was essentially right where I had been when I left home the first time to get married. Not only did I have *me* to bring up, but I had a dependent child to raise, and I was right back in the waiting arms of the mother I was so anxious to be free of. I am 20 now, and I don't know what I'm going to do.

Perhaps one of the most significant limitations an adolescent mother experiences is a basic lack of understanding of how to care for a baby and what to expect from the mother-child relationship. De Lissovoy (1973) did longitudinal research with 48 married adolescent parents to determine their understanding of child care. Developmental norms, which tell us when we can expect certain behaviors from a child, can give mothers some degree of understanding in how to nurture the baby toward various expressive behaviors and motor skills. The teen-age parents studied by de Lissovoy were totally unaware of when certain types of behaviors could occur, always expecting them well in advance of their actual occurrence. De Lissovoy noted that most teen-age parents found caring for their children to be a trying experience. Special training programs or child-welfare clinics may be necessary to help both married and unmarried teen-age parents understand themselves, their baby, and their new interpersonal roles.

The comments that have been made here on the adolescent in the family have attempted to clarify some of the confusion surrounding the role of the family in the adolescent's life. In summary: Most adolescents find the home to be a satisfying place, have respect for their parents, and feel no sense of urgency to leave home. However, because the father is generally considered to be the more authoritarian parent, he will probably be the person against whom the adolescent will rebel the most. The mother is considered to be more empathic, understanding, and emotional, instilling lasting values of love and affection. The changing role of the mother may have some effect on the manner in which adolescents develop, although at this point research evidence is inconclusive, contradictory, and limited. The same is true of the research on broken homes, but most studies indicate that broken homes may not cause severe personality problems any more often than other types of family structures, especially as the broken family unit becomes more prevalent and accepted as an alternative within our society.

Peer Relationships 7

As was suggested by the socialization model presented in Chapter 5, adolescence is a period of time during which the active goal for the individual is *social maturation*. Presumably, this maturation is facilitated by increased social experiences and greater involvement with peers. Dominant peer influence promotes alternative social learning; that is, it helps an adolescent break away from childhood behavioral patterns and facilitates his learning of more diverse social behaviors. There is common agreement among researchers that the adolescent goes to his peers in order to work out value conflicts and to help himself adjust to maturational changes.

In this chapter, we will examine reasons behind the movement toward group identification in adolescence, the comparative influences of parents and peers on adolescents, and two theoretical questions that are widely debated among social scientists: whether an adolescent subculture exists, and whether a true "generation gap" exists between adolescents and their parents.

GROUP IDENTIFICATION

The idea has been advanced that group interaction, such as membership in cliques or crowds, is necessary for social maturation. During adolescence most individuals become members of a heterosexual group that helps them define their roles. Dunphy (1963), who has outlined five stages of group development in adolescence, found that around 80 percent of all youth held some type of group membership (see Figure 7.1). The remaining 20 percent were studied by Burlingame (1967) and Lerman (1967), who found that some youth do not get involved with a group even when offered the opportunity to do so. Grinder (1969) has defined this noninvolvement as *solitariness*, maintaining that some youth attain social maturation as loners.

Dunphy's Stage 1, the precrowd stage, is more characteristic of the preadolescent than of the adolescent. Preadolescent groups are typically unisexual in composition, and their interaction is generally focused on sex-typed activities (Ausubel, 1954). Movement into adolescence causes cross-sex cliques and crowds[1] to form, usually among school or

---

[1]Dunphy defines a clique as a group of associates ranging in number from 3 to 9, with a mean membership of 6.2. In contrast, a crowd's average size is 20.2; its range, 15 to 30. Further analysis reveals that a crowd is essentially an association of cliques.

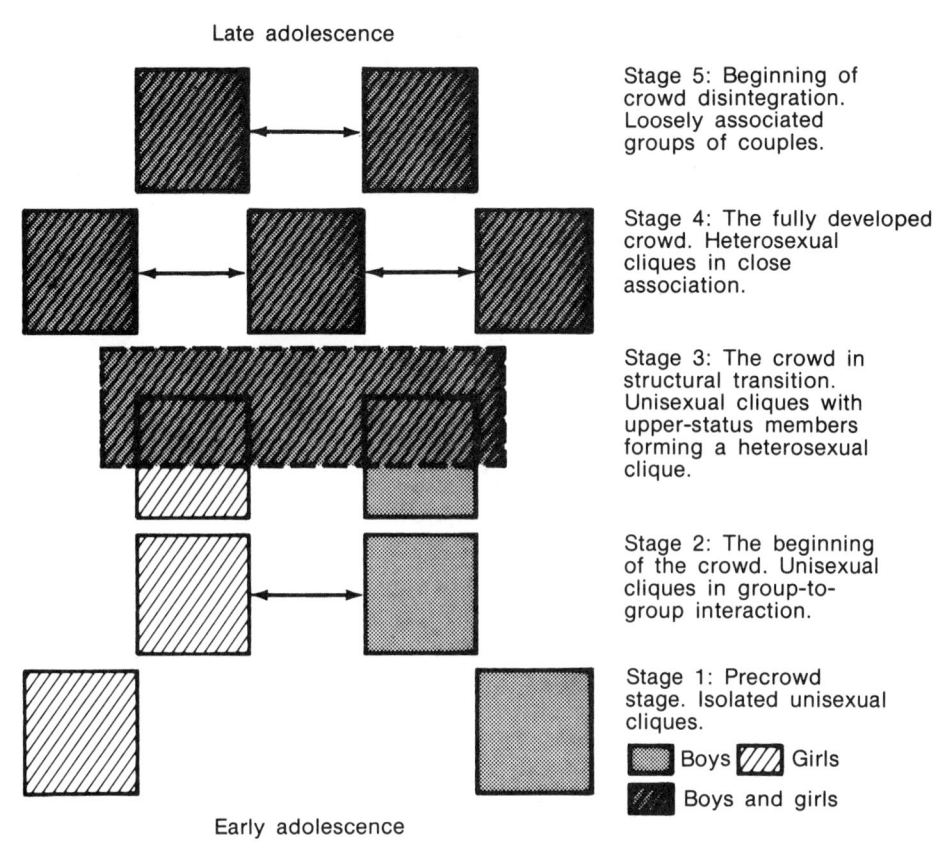

FIGURE 7.1. Stages of group development in adolescence. From "The Social Structure of Urban Adolescent Peer Groups" by D. C. Dunphy, *Sociometry*, 1963, 26, 236. Copyright 1963 by the American Sociological Association. Reprinted by permission.

neighborhood friends. These groups represent the first peer-group associations that offer rewarding social behaviors alternative to those of the family (Grinder, 1969). Stage 2 in Dunphy's model, "unisexual cliques in group-to-group interaction," represents the first true peer group, since the members are of similar age and the cliques' interactions have reciprocal acceptability—that is, boys now find girls acceptable, and vice versa.

Stage 3 sees the formation of heterosexual cliques. According to Dunphy, upper-status members of the unisexual cliques begin to engage in individual heterosexual interaction such as dating. Dunphy has described the movement into Stage 3 and the transitions into Stages 4 and 5 as follows:

Those adolescents who belong to these emergent heterosexual groups still maintain a membership role in their unisexual clique, so that they possess dual membership in two intersecting cliques. This initiates an extensive transformation of group structure by which there takes place a reorganization of unisexual cliques and the reformation of their membership into heterosexual cliques (Stage 4). While the cliques persist as small intimate groups, their membership now comprises both sexes. Stage 5 sees the slow disintegration of the crowd and the formation of cliques consisting of couples who are going steady or engaged. Thus there is a progressive development of group structure from predominantly unisexual to heterosexual groups [Dunphy, 1963, p. 235].

There are several reasons why group identification is so important to developing adolescents. First, it helps them in the process of emancipation. Although Bandura (1964) suggests that emancipation from parents is more or less completed, rather than initiated, at adolescence, most writers believe that the process continues throughout adolescence and is aided by peer association.

Second, group identification spurs competition. Healthy competition can be an aid to social maturation. However, today's society demands so many attainments in exchange for conferring success upon an individual that the struggle may result in unhealthy competition and may affect the individual's overall life-style. Some degree of natural competitiveness seems to be inherent in the adolescent growth process.

Third, group identification promotes heterosexual attachments. In the early stages, adolescents usually identify with same-sex groups; as they mature, they band into heterosexual groups, as we have seen in Dunphy's model. By 14 or 15, adolescents are comfortable around members of the opposite sex and participate in social activities with them. Many are even dating regularly. Dating represents the highest stage of group development, for at this point the crowd disintegrates into loosely associated groups of couples.

Finally, group identification promotes conformity. Adolescent group conformity may be linked to common values, or it may stem from a need for acceptance, a fear of rejection, or a desire to escape loneliness. Like adults, adolescents manifest conformity in small social units or reference groups, which vary in activities, sentiments, and behavioral norms.

PEERS VERSUS PARENTS

Several studies indicate, despite all these reasons for peer-group identification, that throughout adolescence parents continue to have the major impact (Aberle & Naegele, 1952; Bordua, 1960; Campbell, 1969;

The desire to be the center of attention is part of the normal developmental process. Peer groups often facilitate this need.

Douvan & Adelson, 1966; Ellis & Lane, 1963; Kahl, 1953; Kandel & Lesser, 1969; Myerhoff & Larson, 1965; Rehberg & Westby, 1967; Sewell & Shah, 1968; Simpson, 1962; Slocum & Stone, 1963; Straus, 1962). These studies maintain that parents have stronger influence on aspirations than peers—for example, on educational and occupational plans.

A second body of literature states the contrary—that adolescents are minimally influenced by their parents. These studies (Bowerman & Kinch, 1959; Coleman, 1961; Duncan et al., 1968; Haller & Butterworth, 1960; Herriott, 1963; Krauss, 1964; McDill & Coleman, 1965; Musgrove, 1966; Rosen, 1964) show that adolescents tend to follow peers, to the point of rejecting the parents' wishes, in order to conform.

It is likely that high school youths will be influenced by the reference group they perceive as most helpful to their process of identity resolution, since the social-maturation process requires the active breaking of childhood ties, the definition of identity, and the formulation of future plans (Thornburg, 1971c). However, in their search for identity youths often face the dilemma of which group—peers or parents—to model in establishing behavior patterns. They fear that too-strong peer associations will bring about parental disapproval; at the same time, if they disregard peer influence in order to gain parental approval, they may receive strong disapproval from peers. As a result, the adolescent is likely to use both groups for reference, playing each situation "by ear" (Larson, 1972). In each case, the adolescent's perceived needs strongly influence his choice. Floyd and South (1972) have conceptualized this dilemma (see Figure 7.2).

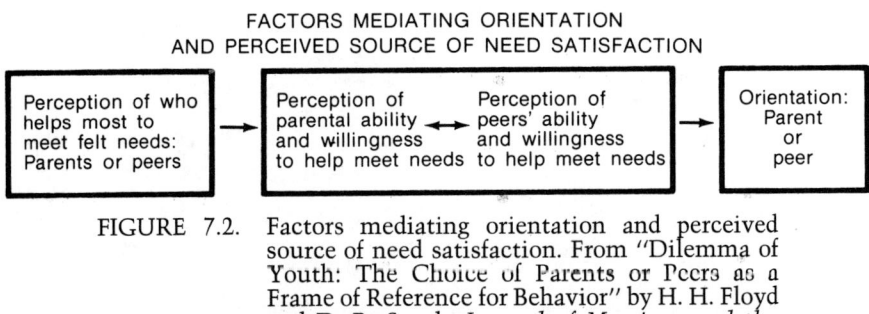

FACTORS MEDIATING ORIENTATION
AND PERCEIVED SOURCE OF NEED SATISFACTION

| Perception of who helps most to meet felt needs: Parents or peers | → | Perception of parental ability and willingness to help meet needs ↔ Perception of peers' ability and willingness to help meet needs | → | Orientation: Parent or peer |

FIGURE 7.2. Factors mediating orientation and perceived source of need satisfaction. From "Dilemma of Youth: The Choice of Parents or Peers as a Frame of Reference for Behavior" by H. H. Floyd and D. R. South, *Journal of Marriage and the Family*, 1972, 34(4), 633. Copyright 1972 by National Council on Family Relations. Reprinted by permission.

The extensive research of Coleman (1961) has been used as a basic reference to validate the concept of adolescent peer solidarity. Coleman asked each of his subjects which of these things would make him the most unhappy: (1) if his parents did not like what he did, (2) if his (favorite) teacher did not like what he did, or (3) if his best friend did not like what he did. Coleman's evidence is that 43 percent of the high school students in his sample felt that it would be worse to earn disapproval from a friend than to earn parental disapproval. His conclusion was challenged, however, by the research of Epperson (1964), who declared that an adolescent has multiple loyalties, and that the acceptance of one's peers does not always necessitate the disapproval of one's parents. Asking a question comparable to Coleman's, Epperson found that only 20 percent of his sample chose more often to incur parental disfavor. Table 7.1 compares the disparate results of the Coleman and Epperson studies. Coleman found much more concern with peer acceptance and much less concern with parental acceptance than did Epperson.

Brittain (1963; 1967/68; 1969) has suggested in his research that parents and peers tend to influence adolescents in separate but overlap-

TABLE 7.1. Epperson data contrasted with Coleman data.

| | Boys | | Girls | |
Evaluating agent	Epperson* %	Coleman** %	Epperson* %	Coleman** %
Parent	80.4	53.8	80.5	52.9
Teacher	3.6	3.5	1.2	2.7
Best friend	15.8	42.7	18.1	43.4
Number of cases (excluding nonresponses)	82	3621	77	3894

*This sample, drawn from a comprehensive high school of 2200 in a medium size city (pop. 60,000), is approximately 50% 10th graders, 42% 11th graders, and 8% 12th graders.
**This sample includes students from all ten of Coleman's schools, representing small-town, rural, city and suburban high schools with enrollments ranging from 150 to 1950.
From "A Reassessment of Indices of Parental Influence in the Adolescent Society" by D. C. Epperson, *American Sociological Review*, 1964, 29, 95. Copyright 1964 by the American Sociological Association. Reprinted by permission.

ping behavioral domains. He contends that certain types of choices are peer compliant and other types parent compliant. From his 1963 research he concluded that peer-compliant choices generally had to do with status and identity needs within the peer group. In contrast, status within the larger society was more parentally guided than peer guided. Regarding the adolescent's susceptibility to influence on his educational plans, Kandel and Lesser (1969) strongly support Brittain's hypothesis that parents are more influential in choice areas perceived as more difficult and important. They found that as many as 85 percent of the middle-class adolescents they studied and 82 percent of the lower-class adolescents were directly influenced by parents in making educational plans. Therefore Kandel and Lesser, along with Brittain, conclude that parents have a stronger influence than peers on the adolescent's life goals.

Although more recent research, by Larson (1972), is in general agreement with the research just reported, two distinct variations arise in Larson's conclusions. First, Larson questions whether all adolescent choices of action must be peer or parent compliant; that is, perhaps a situational dilemma does not always demand commitment to one reference group or the other. To illustrate this point, Larson created seven situational dilemmas in which some 1500 high school students were to respond indicating either peer or parent compliance. For example:*

> You have been invited to a party which you want very much to go to. Your best friends have decided to go and are urging you to go, too. They

*From "The Influence of Parents and Peers During Adolescence: The Situation Hypothesis Revisited" by L. E. Larson, *Journal of Marriage and the Family*, 1972, 34(1), 69. Copyright 1972 by National Council on Family Relations. Reprinted by permission.

will be very unhappy if you don't go. Your parents, however, do not approve of the party and are urging you not to go. Your parents will be very unhappy if you do go. What would you do?

1. ( ) Go to the party
2. ( ) Stay home

Suppose the situation above is reversed. Your parents are urging you to go to the party. However, your best friends have *not* been invited and are urging you not to go. You really don't want to go to the party. Your parents will be very unhappy if you don't go; your best friends will be very unhappy if you do go. What would you do?

1. ( ) Go to the party
2. ( ) Stay home

The responses showed that the *content* of the particular situation was more important to these students in the choice of a course of action than the pressure of parents or peers by itself; that is, the answer was often "It depends."

Second, although Brittain had found that current status and identity needs were better met by peer compliance, Larson did not find this to be the case. Rather, he found some trend toward parental compliance. Larson summarized his findings by stating that the youth he studied were:

1. Well aware of future statuses and roles, the significance of decisions involving situational issues, and have achieved a reasoned sense of independence.
2. Able to sort out content alternatives into levels of priority assigning lesser significance to issues of temporal importance, and
3. Prepared to give credence and compliance to the pressures of parents and peers when they are realistic [Larson, 1972, p. 73].

The problem of parent or peer choices has been put in a developmental perspective by Floyd and South (1972). They contend that age is a factor in determining reference choice. In effect, their study indicates that with social maturation there is a gradual shift from parent compliance to peer compliance. Their findings may be summarized as follows.

First, there were significant differences in orientation among the classifications by age-grade level and sex of the respondents. It was found that, for both males and females, peer orientation increased with an increase in their age-grade level until the tenth grade, at which point there was a leveling off (males) or a reduction (females) in peer orientation. Further, it was revealed that, although both sexes experienced an increase in peer orientation, females tended to reach their peak in degree of peer orientation at an earlier age-grade level than did males.

These findings might be explained by several perspectives on the question of why youth become more peer oriented with increasing age and why the sexes differ in regard to this trend. Komorovsky's (1950) position that males are encouraged to become emancipated earlier and are allowed more independence and privacy in their personal affairs than are females reflects the view that youths have a natural inclination to reject parents in favor of peers that will prevail if obstacles to this tendency are removed. This assumption could account for the slightly higher incidence and degree of male peer orientation at the sixth-grade level, but it does not adequately account for the greater incidence and degree of female peer orientation at the seventh, eighth, and subsequent grade levels.

Perhaps the movement away from parental orientation is not merely a matter of "releasing the brakes" but also the result of a "push" from the adult world and/or a "pull" from peers. It may be that, before reaching the sixth grade, males are even more peer oriented relative to females than research indicates, although Floyd and South's (1972) study and the results reported by Bowerman and Kinch (1959) show that females apparently were more peer oriented than males within a year or two after sixth grade.

The earlier physical maturation of females is a convenient explanation for the findings in question, but it can be accepted only insofar as physical maturation is viewed as stimulating changes in interpersonal relationships. It is likely that the onset of puberty raises questions, doubts, and fears, and that it provokes needs in youth to which members of the adult world, especially parents, are unable, unwilling, or not permitted by convention to respond. The problems of puberty, of course, occur in both males and females, but they occur earlier in females. The inability of parents to meet youthful needs at this stage of life must make other youths with similar needs and experiences appear especially attractive.

Some research (Bowerman & Kinch, 1959) shows that an adolescent feels emotional distance from parents, and that he is more likely to form strong emotional attachments to his peers. However, as Elder (1972) has pointed out, even when the adolescent feels that he has parental support, preference for one value source or the other may vary with the issue or the situation. Parental influence is greatest in areas in which parents have expertise and knowledge, such as future plans (Brittain, 1963; Kandel & Lesser, 1969), whereas peer influence dominates decisions about the here and now. It is likely that Epperson's (1964) contention is most accurate—that, indeed, adolescents have multiple loyalties.

IS THERE AN ADOLESCENT SUBCULTURE?

There has been considerable disagreement on whether there is such a thing as an adolescent subculture. Those who contend that the adolescent subculture is a myth cite the fact that youths' values are only temporarily different from their parents'. They contend that a distinct subculture must be characterized by a longer-term value difference. On the other side of the argument are those who contend that an adolescent subculture does exist because a subculture is based on common social groupings, language, behavior, and ideologies.

In order to provide a more definitive frame of reference for the ensuing discussion of this debate, I've made the following hypotheses (Thornburg, 1973a):

1. Adolescent youth do engage in distinctive patterns of behavior, many of which are quite different from those of adults; therefore we can contend that a *behavioral adolescent subculture* exists.
2. Adolescent youth do hold identifiable values in common with their parents; therefore we can contend that a *value adolescent subculture* does not exist.
3. Research indicates that college youth may be an exception to the second statement, since they show not only behavior but also value differences from their parents in many cases.

The Behavioral Subculture

As Eisenstadt (1956) has pointed out, a radical social-psychological transition between childhood and adulthood takes place in industrial societies. This transition enables the adolescent to try out new roles and form new relationships. Every child must eventually leave his family unit and associate with his peers. He must also earn status within his peer group if he is to develop socially and resolve his ego-identity problems. People, things, situations, associations, and events can symbolize the status an adolescent has achieved, and they thus enable adolescents to assign status and rank to one another. Examples of common status-defining criteria among adolescents are speech, clothes, physical appearance, money, ownership of certain status objects, and choice of meeting places.

Speech. One of the strongest arguments for the existence of an adolescent subculture is the distinctiveness of their language and communication systems. The nature of adolescent speech, like that of all people, is affected by socioeconomic class and group affiliation; like that of all subcultures, it is distinguished by cultural idioms and an emphasis on certain topics of interest. The nature of an adolescent's speech identifies the motives, values, roles, and rules that allow his behaviors to be understood and accepted by peers.

To the speaker who wants to maintain acceptance and identity with the right group, words become crucial symbols. In a middle-class high school that draws on a cross-section of the population, you will find many different types of expressions. The more conservative student will use common parental language, with some dabbling in the more general adolescent vocabulary with terms such as "far out," "right on," and "uptight." Many general slang terms such as "hassle," "heavy," "getting it on," "punch-out," and "bitching" may be adopted by all subgroups. The antisocial adolescent, often attached to a hippie or drug-using group, uses such expressions more often. Rural adolescents also have their own set of terms, and of considerable importance to their group identification is the twang in their voice. The athletes' jargon is equally clearly identifiable.

Clothes. Clothes are very important symbols by which all individuals, and adolescents especially, evaluate one another. It is important to wear the "in thing" in order to give evidence of belonging to a peer group and behaving in line with its norms. Research (Ryan, 1966) shows that girls place emphasis on clothes as a symbol of social status, whereas boys more often see clothes as an expression of individuality and autonomy. Similarly, if an adolescent is socially conscious, always seeking to increase his status, he is much more aware of clothing than if he does not especially desire social mobility (Anspach, 1961).

Adolescents wear sex-appropriate and group-appropriate clothes. They know that inappropriate clothes are unacceptable, and they attempt to wear what is right for the social occasion. They are also very style conscious, keeping up with the latest fashion, whether or not this fashion demands neatness. The "unisex" trend in clothing has provided the adolescent great latitude in dressing. In essence, the purpose of wearing either stylish or antistylish clothes is to gain some attention, especially as the adolescent becomes interested in the other sex (Ostermeier, 1967).

Physical appearance. Although it may seem absurd or unfair to adults, adolescents have an uncanny ability to find certain facial features—a nose that is too big, eyebrows that are too light or too heavy, a chin that protrudes, ears that are too large—unacceptable. Weight, body proportions, and early or late maturation are important criteria for peer social acceptance. Acne is potentially traumatizing. Use of facial creams, cosmetics, and special treatments and visits to the dermatologist all attest to the importance the adolescent places on his complexion.

Money. Money helps establish status with peers by providing the means to obtain material objects that confer status. It also buys privileges, mobility, and independence for many youth.

> *Related by a college student to the author:*
>
> Have you ever heard of Bell's palsy? Well, I hadn't until it struck me! I think I shall remember it as the most traumatizing experience I had as an adolescent. One day, when I was 16 and in my junior year of high school, it hit me—right out of the clear blue sky!
>
> Bell's palsy affects the neck and facial nerves, and for almost five months the left side of my face was paralyzed. The right side functioned normally, and you can imagine what I looked like with half of my mouth paralyzed and the other half working like crazy.
>
> The first week after I was affected I stayed home from school, not wanting to see or be around any of my friends. But then boredom, plus the realization that I couldn't hide myself forever, put an end to my staying home. I decided to go back to school and begin adjusting to a problem that I was stuck with.
>
> After a while everyone at school got used to me, and things were not so bad. However, I don't think I ever got used to being stared at in public. It made me extremely self-conscious, and I perceived myself as being unacceptable to others. It was a difficult thing to adjust to.
>
> In time I recovered about 95-percent use of the left side of my face, but even today I can feel traces of Bell's palsy. Most people who know me today would never suspect that I had ever been paralyzed. But I know. Besides, I take terrible pictures!

Bernard (1961) views the teen-age culture as a product of affluence. She presents an array of statistics supporting the common-sense deduction that, as bands played or singers sang, and as adolescents tuned in radios, attended concerts, and bought records, a culture of common

> According to a survey conducted by the Gilbert Youth Research group in June 1974, the 41 million youth in the United States are record-conscious. In fact, young people between 14 and 25 years of age buy 80 percent of the records sold in the United States. Incidentally, that buying power comes to an astonishing 35 billion dollars yearly.
>
> A few more statistics from the Gilbert report are that 90 percent of our youth read magazines, 84 percent watch TV, 93 percent listen to the radio, and 85 percent read the newspaper. This exposure makes them consumers and they are shrewd buyers—not so gullible as the middle-aged businessman may think they are. In fact, they are rather persistent in looking for discounts, and they take a dim view of being "ripped off."

tastes and preferences emerged. She characterizes the adolescent society as a leisure class with money to spend on material items—clothes, cosmetics, records, and cars. The adolescent culture also has a literature of its own, the teen-age magazines. Hurlock (1973) gives a summary presentation of what money symbolizes to the adolescent:

Socioeconomic Status
Having money readily available at all times, being able to spend money on luxuries and treats for one's friends, and being able to take friends for a ride in one's car—all symbolize high status.

Identification with the Leading Crowd
Creating the impression of affluence by always having spending money implies that the adolescent belongs to the leading crowd, which normally is relatively well-to-do.

Sex Appropriateness
Sex appropriateness is shown (1) by how the adolescent gets his spending money and (2) by how he spends it. Earning part of one's spending money at afterschool jobs in stores, factories, or offices is regarded as masculine; relying on an allowance supplemented by baby-sitting jobs is considered feminine. Spending money for sports and dates is regarded as masculine; spending for clothes and beauty aids is regarded as feminine.

Independence
Whether the adolescent's money comes from an allowance or from earnings, it symbolizes his autonomy. The person who has money is seen as a person who can demand what he wants, can come and go as he pleases, and can buy what he wants without interference [Hurlock, 1973, p. 177].*

Status objects. Much status carries over to the adolescent from his parents' status. The value of their home, their neighborhood, the number and make of cars, the swimming pool, the number of telephones and televisions, the jewelry worn, and the church attended all constitute parents' status value. Boys and girls alike enjoy fixing up their rooms with the "in things" that give them greater peer status.

The adolescent girl may strive for status by having many clothes and cosmetics, being socially prominent in her school and community, living on the right street, having slumber or pool parties, or attaching herself to a male who has status. She may enjoy driving but is also often interested in being a passenger in the right make of car. She thrives upon her parents' affluence, since she is primarily a consumer (Packard, 1961).

One of the strongest status symbols for a boy is driving, then owning, his own car. Coleman (1961) found that between the freshman and senior years there was a 50-percent increase in car ownership. This

*From *Adolescent Development*, 4th ed., by E. B. Hurlock. Copyright 1973 by McGraw-Hill Book Company. Reprinted by permission.

increase is probably due to more boys' becoming of driving age and finding part-time employment as they grow older, enabling them to own a car.

Elder (1972) contends that, with the increase in society's mobility, youth have been taught the automobile's value in meeting transportation needs, achieving freedom of movement, and symbolizing the driver as a particular kind of person. Driver training is available in most high schools and is even required in some. Elder found that 40 percent of high school seniors are car owners, and considerably more have access to a car.

Meeting places. Elder (1972) has stressed the emergence as a social setting for youth of the drive-in, available because of the car. The frequency of going to a drive-in among adolescents in the greater San Francisco area is reported in Table 7.2. Elder theorizes that the drive-in gives an adolescent a chance to perform before an audience of peers. In addition, a majority of the boys he questioned felt it to be a good place to meet girls. After school, after athletic events, and on weekends seemed to be highly popular times to frequent the drive-in.

There is little doubt about the status attached to the drive-in. Elder suggests three identifying characteristics of regular adolescent drive-in customers: "greater preoccupation with cars, more involvement in heterosexual activity, and a stronger desire for social independence and adult leisure privileges" (1972, p. 282). Elder further hypothesized that there would be social and interest differences between adolescent boys

TABLE 7.2. Drive-in patronage among American boys and girls, by grade level.

Frequency* of drive-in patronage	Attendance at drive-in by sex (percentages)					
	Grade level of boys**			Grade level of girls***		
	7–8	9–10	11–12	7–8	9–10	11–12
Frequently	13	22	30	10	11	26
Occasionally	49	47	45	49	44	40
Never	38	31	25	41	45	34
Total	100	100	100	100	100	100
	(435)	(486)	(425)	(180)	(198)	(185)

*"Frequent" patronage refers to those who attended a drive-in eating establishment at least once each week. The "occasional" category includes all youth who attended less frequently.
**$\gamma = 0.22$.
***$\gamma = 0.16$.

From "The Social Context of Youth Groups" by G. H. Elder, Jr., *International Social Science Journal*, 1972, 24(2), 280. Copyright © Unesco 1972. Reprinted by permission of Unesco.

Social behavior, whether pro- or anti-, is the dominant theme of most peer groups. Youth tend to designate certain areas of town or certain activities as distinctly theirs.

who patronize drive-ins and those who don't. Table 7.3 reports many of his findings. It is clear, from a comparison of percentages, that there is greater interest in cars and in heterosexual interactions, and lower school achievement, among those who make the drive-in an integral part of their social lives.

Three Types of Peer Groups

Three distinct groups can be identified among today's adolescents: (1) high school youths, (2) noncollege youths, and (3) college youths. These groups differ in their intellectual functions, their social environments, and their attitudes and values (Thornburg, 1971c).

TABLE 7.3. Social differences between adolescent boys who patronized drive-ins and other youth, by grade in school.

| | Percentage of adolescent boys by grade-level and drive-in patronage ||||
| | Grades 7–8 || Grades 9–12 ||
Social variables	Regulars* Min. N = 50	Others Min. N = 154	Regulars* Min. N = 210	Others Min. N = 233
Interest in car				
Car is very important	68	49	84	60
Rides around in car: four or more hours per week	29	19	50	17
Owns car	—	—	34	10
Heterosexual interest				
Engaged in social dating	54	14	88	43
Dates at least once a week	32	5	47	12
Contact with parents and peers				
Talks with parents: four or more hours per week	21	20	29	23
Often discusses future with father	20	25	31	29
Talks with friends: four or more hours per week	27	28	61	45
Status vis-à-vis school and authority				
Poor grades: self-reported C or lower	52	38	38	28
Truant last year	40	24	65	28
Drinks beer, wine, or liquor away from home	19	6	55	18

*The "regulars" are boys who patronized the drive-in at least once a week; "others" refers to boys who never visited a drive-in.
From "The Social Context of Youth Groups" by G. H. Elder, Jr., *International Social Science Journal*, 1972, 24(2), 283. Copyright © Unesco 1972. Reprinted by permission of Unesco.

High school youth. Most high school students are occupied with breaking childhood emotional bonds, developing friendships, participating in high school activities, and considering their future. Parental, school, and peer influences are all obviously instrumental in these processes. Several studies have reported that high school students are primarily concerned about their immediate school environment, especially the social aspects of it. Although many high school students engage in student activism, drug taking, and sexual experimentation, they commonly do so more out of conformity than for the sake of individuality. Often such behaviors facilitate acceptance by another individual, a clique, or a gang. The popular students in high school are highly social, and many students identify strongly with the school's athletes or cheerleaders (Coleman, 1961).

Coleman found that the adolescent's high school world was, in fact, basically social. In studying ten high schools, ranging in size from fewer than 100 to more than 2000 students and representing both rural and urban communities, Coleman found that social life was more valued by youth than was the academic life of the high school. Cars, music, and television were all considered more important than homework. Being an athlete gave boys a distinct advantage. For those who were not athletic, association with the popular students was important.

It is likely that these individuals, still in the process of social maturation, are more involved in resolving developmental tasks (Havighurst, 1972; Thornburg, 1970a) than they are in integrating themselves socially or in preparing to tackle the problems of our society and the world. The degree to which adolescents are successful in resolving the different issues they encounter, and the strength of the influence of the peer group in the resolution process, will largely determine how much their values will be modified and will help them determine whether they will (1) drop out of high school, (2) graduate from high school but move directly into the occupational world, or (3) delay occupational involvement by gaining more education in college.

Among today's high school students, a 30- to 35-percent dropout rate exists, highly concentrated in the inner cities and among minority youth. These dropouts constitute the group most marginal to the society, since they are often uneducated and unemployed. Few legitimate uses of their energies can be made. Such marginal youth are often delinquent and gang oriented.

The streets are the geographical setting for many nonschool youth. Researchers have examined street culture in their study of gangs, deviancy, and delinquency. In the course of these investigations a number of concepts and propositions have been offered regarding this segment of adolescent society. Much research (Short & Strodtbeck, 1965) has been goaded by conflicts between proponents of the continuity theory of adolescent delinquency (Miller, 1958) and the proponents of the theory of the delinquent subculture as a function of the inability to attain commonly held social goals (Cloward & Ohlin, 1960; Cohen, 1955). Miller's theory can be applied only to gang behavior among lower-socioeconomic-class adolescents. He believes that the strong cohesiveness of such gangs arises because their focal concerns and values are conducive to law-violating behavior; gang members are constantly concerned about the makeup of the gang and each member's continued allegiance to it. Cloward and Ohlin and Cohen, in contrast, believe that lower-class gangs arise because lower-class life does not prepare the individual adolescent to compete for status in a society dominated by middle-class standards for acceptance and achievement. These adolescents' adjustment problem is directly proportional to the middle-class influences with which they interact. Both of these theories will be discussed in greater detail in Chapter 13.

Sherif and Sherif (1966) were interested in determining degrees of

Peer behavior is typically informal.

conformity and deviation among non-high-school youth. Through a multitude of findings, they argued strongly that the peer group is exceedingly important to its members and that parents and adults usually do not have a clear idea of the causes of youth's behavior in areas of "immorality": drinking, sexual behavior, vandalism, and theft.

The idiosyncratic nature of the delinquent peer group is reflected in the Sherifs' discussion of the preferences of a group of second- and third-generation Mexican-American boys from a poor neighborhood in a southwestern city: "Besides liking sports, the boys all watched games on television. They greatly preferred rock and roll to popular Mexican music, hot dogs and hamburgers to tortillas and beans, modern dance steps to traditional ones, Hollywood movies to Mexican films" (Sherif & Sherif, 1966, p. 26). The members of this gang wore their hair long, in contrast to another in the city, which had norms for clean-cut appearance.

Increasing evidence generally supports the proposition that, as **aggregates** of individuals interact and become groups, differentiation of status, leadership, and effective initiative occurs. Sherif and Sherif (1964) caution that, even though adolescents will often state "We have no leader—we just hang around informally together," observers have reliably identified specific individuals who have leadership roles. These observers argue, as did Short and Strodtbeck (1965), that shifts in "system requirements" often produce shifts in leadership from the incumbent leader to an individual with alternative skills. The latter investigators also theorized that much delinquent behavior results from the precarious position of the gang leader who has few resources with which to maintain his group's esteem.

Common problems certainly exist among high-school-age youth, whether they are enrolled students or dropouts. The social-maturation process is complicated by school variables, peer affiliations, social class, normality or lack of it, and parental interaction. In addition, these youth must contend with an ever-changing social environment.

Noncollege youth. About 75 percent of American youths do not attend college. Approximately half of these youths drop out of high school; the other half seek employment upon completing high school. During the last 15 years, American society has focused to such an extent on alienation and activism among college youth that this large block of noncollege youth has gone relatively unnoticed. Significantly, however, it is among noncollege individuals that the least adolescent-parent value discrepancy exists. Those writers who contend that the existence of an adolescent subculture demands a value difference between adolescent and parent, and therefore that there is no such subculture, will find support for their contention here. There is generally little discrepancy between the values held by noncollege youth and the values held by their parents.

The somewhat extensive analysis of youth undertaken by CBS News in 1969, cited earlier in this chapter, reveals several interesting differences between noncollege adolescents and college students and some similarly interesting unanimities between noncollege youth and adults in our society. The survey inquired into the views of 2881 noncollege youth and 723 college youth. In addition, more than 300 parents of youths of each group were included in the study.

There were some interesting and relevant findings from the survey. First of all, noncollege youth tend to be traditionally oriented. They perpetuate parental value systems more often than their college counterparts. Second, there is a high degree of unanimity among noncollege youth, their parents, and college youths' parents. Third, in some areas of opinion, there is high consistency between noncollege and college youths. Finally, the most noticeable value differences among the four groups surveyed were seen in the college youths. Thus they are most representative of the "generation gap," although 66 percent of the college youths in the survey thought that the concept of the generation gap is exaggerated in our society (*Generations Apart*, 1969).

In order to understand the similarities and differences among the groups studied, let's analyze the differences among the responses to the following summary statements. The numbers represent the percentages agreeing with the statements.

1. Statements representing traditional values in America

Statement: Hard work will always pay off.

| NCY[2] | 79 | CY | 56 |
| NCY parents | 85 | CY parents | 76 |

Statement: Everyone should save as much as he can regularly and not have to lean on family and friends the minute he runs into financial problems.

| NCY | 88 | CY | 76 |
| NCY parents | 98 | CY parents | 90 |

Statement: Compromise is essential for progress.

| NCY | 88 | CY | 80 |
| NCY parents | 85 | CY parents | 82 |

Statement: Belonging to some organized religion is important in a person's life.

| NCY | 82 | CY | 42 |
| NCY parents | 91 | CY parents | 81 |

Statement: Competition encourages excellence.

| NCY | 82 | CY | 72 |
| NCY parents | 91 | CY parents | 84 |

Although our society has always maintained and perpetuated many social norms and policies, the society has also always undergone change. These two groups of youth were asked what types of changes they would like to see in our society. Two different trends emerge. There is a set of changes that both noncollege and college youth would like to see. There is another set in which considerable discrepancy exists between the opinions of the two groups.

2. Which of the following changes would you welcome in our society?

More emphasis on technological improvement

| NCY | 63 | CY | 56 |

[2]NCY stands for noncollege youth; CY stands for college youth.

More emphasis on personal responsibility
NCY   87   CY   84
More emphasis on friendliness and neighborliness
NCY   94   CY   92
More sexual freedom
NCY   22   CY   43
More acceptance of other people's peculiarities
NCY   60   CY   80
More respect for authority
NCY   86   CY   59
Less emphasis on money
NCY   54   CY   72
More emphasis on law and order
NCY   81   CY   57
More emphasis on self-expression
NCY   70   CY   84
More vigorous protests by blacks and other minority groups
NCY   9   CY   23

These statistics reveal that noncollege youth in the 17–23 age group hold strong traditional values. The CBS study found that noncollege youth were similarly traditional about changing social issues—premarital sex, homosexuality, abortion, and extramarital sex. In each case the college youth were considerably more tolerant and open-minded about these increasing social behaviors.

3. Questions concerning acceptance of social restraints

Question: Is having an abortion morally wrong?
NCY   64   CY   36
NCY parents   66   CY parents   50

Question: Are relations between consenting homosexuals morally wrong?
NCY   72   CY   42
NCY parents   79   CY parents   63

Noncollege youths viewed the world of work in more concrete terms than did college youths. The security of the job, its income, and its prestige were essential considerations. Although some also expressed concern about the meaningfulness of the job and the opportunity it offered them to make some type of social contribution, these concerns were more strongly felt by college youths.

4. Which of the following considerations will have a relatively strong influence on your choice of career?

Your family	NCY	36	CY	31
The money you can earn	NCY	49	CY	41
The prestige of your job	NCY	20	CY	23
The security of the job	NCY	46	CY	42
The ability to express yourself	NCY	43	CY	66
The challenge of the job	NCY	47	CY	71
The opportunity the job offers to make a meaningful contribution	NCY	56	CY	76

American social structure has been basically middle-class throughout its history. Middle-class standards and values for the individual have always included the ability to provide for oneself and one's family. This attitude has been transferred to the social order as well. Nevertheless, the 1960s brought to our society many challenges to our social and political policies at home and our involvements abroad. The following questions in the CBS survey examine opinions in the area of international involvements.

5. Which of the following values do you think are worth fighting a war for?

Keeping a commitment				
NCY	28	CY	14	
Containing the Communists				
NCY	69	CY	43	
Maintaining our position of power in the world				
NCY	51	CY	25	
Protecting allies				
NCY	50	CY	38	
Counteracting aggression				
NCY	67	CY	56	

The questions and answers presented here are only representative of the areas examined in the study. In summary, the following characteristics emerged from this comparison of noncollege youth and college youth. The noncollege youth were (1) more traditional, (2) more religious, (3) more concerned with law and order, (4) more respectful of authority, (5) more work oriented, (6) more money oriented, (7) more conforming, (8) less sexually permissive, (9) less drug oriented, and (1) less activism oriented (*Generations Apart*, 1969).

College youth. Throughout our previous discussion the implication has been that college youth constitute a type of young people different from either high school or noncollege youth. Having resolved basic developmental tasks during high school and acquired a sense of the value of more education and self-understanding, these individuals have extended their growth period by remaining in a learning environment for an additional two or more years. As a result, they present many challenges to the society and its mores and policies. They have, in fact, attempted to move away significantly from traditional positions toward more progressive ones. For instance, as Carry (1968) has pointed out, they no longer hold to the traditional view that every rule, right or wrong, must be obeyed, or that modern youth "never had it so good." In fact, many youth feel that some of our laws and processes supposedly protecting youth actually discriminate against them.

College youth are not, however, protesting or working to make changes or innovations on their own. They too have strong peer affiliations. There are several bases for their affiliations. One is common living accommodations. A group of boys or girls living in a particular dorm may find strong peer friendships within the dorm, since it actually constitutes their home-away-from-home. Greek houses are even more distinct social groups. Sororities and fraternities place much emphasis on companionship and on the allegiance of members to one another. Thus their social-reinforcement system is strong (Baur, 1967).

A second basis for peer affiliation is the college major being pursued. Many youths who are in fine arts, for example, find most of their peer affiliations among other fine-arts students. Their friendships are based on a common goal and common ideologies.

A third basis for peer-group affiliation among college youth is membership in one of the four distinct subcultures defined by Gottlieb and Hodgkins (1963). Their groups were: (1) the *academic* subgroup, composed of students who want a good education and are willing to study for it; (2) the *consumer-vocational* subgroup, composed of those students focusing on their vocational careers; (3) the *nonconformist* subgroup, who concentrate on social issues and use the university as an avenue for political expression; and (4) the *collegiate*, or *social*, subgroup, who are mainly interested in social and athletic activities.

Lewis (1969) added that students of these four types vary in their degree of and interest in intellectualism. His research was based on the proposition that intellectualism is a set of attitudes and includes the

TABLE 7.4. Intellectual ferment (percentage agreeing).

Academic subculture (N = 98)	Collegiate subculture (N = 68)	Nonconformist subculture (N = 128)	Consumer-vocational subculture (N = 107)
A. Most important reason for being in college: to obtain a degree			
15.3	33.8	14.8	48.6
B. Would like to get most out of college: education, knowledge, and understanding			
53.1	35.3	40.6	21.5
C. Intellectual values: would definitely seek information about an examination from others who had already taken it			
12.2	39.7	22.7	33.6
D. Leisure-time activity: intellectual and/or musical pursuits			
74.5	39.7	100.0	51.4

From "The Value of College to Different Subcultures" by L. S. Lewis, *School Review*, 1966, 77, 34. Copyright 1966 University of Chicago Press. Reprinted by permission.

belief that a college education is a means of cultivating the ability to use the mind in making life experiences more meaningful. Table 7.4 provides Lewis's comparative statistics.

Part A of the table indicates that a very small percentage of those in the academic and nonconformist subcultures are in college simply to obtain a degree, that about one-third of the collegiate subculture are there to do so, and that almost half of the consumer-vocational subculture are there to do so. On the other hand, Part B indicates that only 21.5 percent of the consumer-vocational subculture are chiefly interested in education, knowledge, and understanding, whereas those in the academic subculture are more strongly oriented in this direction. Lewis believes that it would not be an overstatement to say that those in the consumer-vocational subculture have almost no intellectual goals, whereas those in the academic subculture have the clearest intellectual goals.

Part C tries to ascertain degree of intellectualism, as the investigators define it, by asking the four groups whether or not they would attempt to obtain information on an exam from others who had already taken it—a form of cheating. Many of the consumer-vocational group, along with those of the collegiate group, showed a nonintellectual attitude—namely, that they would definitely seek information about an examination from others who had already taken it. A large majority of those in the academic and nonconformist subcultures, particularly the former, indicated an attitude that is more intellectual—namely, that they would not seek this information. Almost three times as many persons in the consumer-vocational subculture as in the academic subculture said that they would seek information about an exam.

Part D shows that those in the nonconformist and academic subcultures engage in activities more closely associated with intellectual matters than those engaged in by members of the consumer-vocational and collegiate subcultures. All of those questioned in the nonconformist subculture, and 75 percent in the academic subculture, indicated that they engage in intellectual and/or musical leisure-time pursuits; about 50 percent in the consumer-vocational subculture and about 40 percent in the collegiate subculture do so.

Whatever the basis for peer association on the university campus, the significant factor is that such associations exist and are quite important to university students. Although opportunities for individuality exist on a university campus, affiliation is still an important need and an active pursuit for most college youth, as it is for high school and noncollege youth. They are extending their social-maturation process and continuing to use peer associations to help in the social-integration process.

THE GENERATION GAP

A popular idea emerged in the 1960s that there were highly significant differences between parents and adolescents. Primarily through the mass media, people learned that there was a "generation gap." This notion became a handle easily gripped by those who wanted to pit adults against youth, and vice versa. The archetype of youth offered by the media was the student activist, who many concluded was at extreme odds with the older generation.

With time, behavioral scientists began to wonder if there really was such a thing as a generation gap, or if the behaviors they were observing were superficial signs of nonconformity that told a great deal about youth's discontent with society but considerably less about generational differences. Earlier in this chapter, the position was asserted that generational differences have been overstressed, since evidence does not show wide discrepancies between parent and adolescent viewpoints. The following statements outline my position on the generation-gap issue.

1. If what we mean by "generation gap" is that there are points of disagreement between parent and adolescent, then we must recognize that there are numerous historical accounts of such problems; thus the generation gap is neither new nor unique to today's youth.

2. If what we mean is that adolescents behave differently from their parents, this fact should come as no surprise, since social forces governing adolescents and parents are distinctly different, and there is recognized discrepancy between the adolescent's own values and his behaviors.
3. If we are inferring a value difference between parents and adolescents, research supports this contention only among some segments of college youth.
4. If we contend that the generation gap has little to do with value discrepancy, but that today's youth are enacting their values in nonapproved ways rather than using the traditional ways of their parents, then a gap may well exist.
5. If we contend that today's youth have difficulty coping with social, economic, and political issues, we may more accurately describe the phenomenon as a "fitting-into-society" gap, one that seems to be more difficult to bridge for college youth than for noncollege youth.

Some of the most definitive work on generational conflict has been done by Bengtson (1970). He has analyzed three distinct positions on the existence or nonexistence of a generation gap, which will be discussed to some extent here.

The Great-Gap Position

Advocates of this position contend that there are great differences between youths and parents in their values, in their acceptance of social institutions, and in their acceptance of authority and nationalism. The yearning for social revolution that characterized many adolescents from 1964 to 1969 is often used to illustrate this position. American youth were indeed dedicated to making our society different, although the thought of being subdued by the Establishment haunted many.

Various "gap" characteristics have been advanced by Angel (1968) and Chickering (1967). Angel stated that differing values, affluence, education, and communication were the forces pulling apart the age groups in our society. Chickering posited that the gap appeared when the "war babies" came of age, and that the four factors that created the new youth environment were Oedipal childhood, widespread communications, increased affluence, and The Bomb. The most crucial factor was mass communications, for the postwar child was surrounded by advertising and television. This worldwide information source available to American youth enhanced their awareness of social and political contradictions and gave them license to become social critics. As Chickering stated it, "The media made hypocrites, squares, finks, and fnerds of the world's big shots, and made hippies and swingers of us little boys" (1967, p. 605).

Two well-known proponents of the great-gap position are Margaret Mead and Edgar Friedenberg. Mead's contentions (1970) are quite comparable to Angel's and Chickering's; she too emphasizes the different environmental experiences our contemporary youth have had since childhood. Generational discontinuity exists because parent and adolescent operate from different reference points. Friedenberg (1969) feels that youth are not rebelling against parents but abandoning them. He believes that, because adults have failed to listen to and understand their adolescents, the result has been alienation. Bengtson has analyzed this position thus: "Regardless of the many roots of generational differences, the *Great Gap* position emphasizes that there are basic and, in some sense, irreconcilable differences in behavioral predispositions between age groups in American society, and the force of these differences is resulting in rapid cultural transformation" (1970, p. 18).

The Gap-Is-an-Illusion Position

Another viewpoint states that there may be some gap between parent and adolescent but that it is not so great as the media have led us to believe. Bengtson (1970) feels that, although there are inevitable behavioral differences between parents and youths, the continuities and solidarity between them take precedence over the differences. This point has been demonstrated in several research studies.

The comparative data from the CBS News survey reported earlier, for example (*Generations Apart*, 1969), revealed little discrepancy between youth and their parents, especially among noncollege youth. Most youth thought that the idea of a generation gap was exaggerated, 57 percent stated that they enjoyed their parents very much, and only 18 percent said unequivocally that communication problems were their parents' fault. Research by Lerner and his associates (Lerner, Schroeder, Rewitzer, & Weinstock, 1972) also demonstrates little generation gap among noncollege youth, although research by Weinstock and Lerner (1972) does show a gap among college youth.

Let's look at another example. Greater sexual permissiveness has been cited as an area of generational conflict. But the evidence, as summarized by Smigel and Seiden (1968), clearly demonstrates that generational differences in sexual behavior were strong only up to World War I. The researchers stated:

> Most of the studies of sex completed after Kinsey's main works appeared have been limited to collecting statistics on attitudes. The most extensive of these studies, for which data were collected through 1963, was conducted by Ira Reiss (1967), on sexual permissiveness. Reiss's findings point to a coming together of sexual practices, and, for the young at least, of attitudes about sex. He found definite movement away from

the orthodox double standard toward a standard of permissiveness with affection.

The earlier studies of Kinsey and Terman point up important differences in sexual behavior between the generation of women born before 1900 and the generation born in the following decade. Kinsey found that 73.4 percent of women born before 1900 had had no premarital intercourse, but among those born between 1900 and 1909, only 48.7 percent had been virgins at marriage. The figures for those born in the 1920–1929 generation are the same—48.8 percent (Reiss, 1961). Terman's findings are essentially in agreement. The statistics for both the Kinsey and the Terman studies referred to here are for women of all ages, and not just for college women (Davis, 1929). Terman found that 74 percent of the females born between 1890 and 1899 had had no premarital intercourse, whereas among those born between 1900 and 1909, the percentage of virgin brides had dropped to 51.2. His figures reveal that this trend also held for men: of those interviewees born between 1890 and 1899, 41.9 percent had had no premarital coitus, whereas of the interviewees born in the next generation, 32.6 percent had had no such premarital experience (Terman, 1938; Kinsey, 1948). Clearly, the major change in sex practices occurred in the generation born in the decade 1900–1909, which came to sexual maturity during or immediately after World War I, a period characterized by marked social change and innovation [Smigel & Seiden, 1968, p. 7].*

The CBS survey *(Generations Apart,* 1969) found some differences of opinion among college youth, noncollege youth, and their parents regarding premarital sex. The figures stand for percentages answering yes.

Question: Are premarital sexual relations morally wrong?
| NCY | 57 | CY | 34 |
| NCY parents | 88 | CY parents | 74 |

The discrepancies are not so great on the issue of extramarital sex.

Question: Are extramarital sexual relations morally wrong?
| NCY | 77 | CY | 77 |
| NCY parents | 92 | CY parents | 90 |

It may very well be that the greater liberalization of attitudes toward premarital sex among college youth is affected by their ideological environment, and that the discrepancy arises from the fact that premari-

---

*From "The Decline and Fall of the Double Standard" by E. O. Smigel and S. Seiden in Volume 376 of *The Annals* of The American Academy of Political and Social Science. Copyright © 1968 by The American Academy of Political and Social Science. Reprinted by permission.

tal sex is common within their behavioral realm, whereas extramarital sex is a possible future behavior. In the sexual realm, adolescents may well feel the compulsion to "do their own thing," but this attitude is not truly representative of a generation gap.

The Selective-Continuity-and-Difference Position

This position incorporates salient aspects of the two just discussed. There is a continuity between parental values and adolescent values, based on the fact that they are comparable and on the fact that, as the adolescent becomes an adult, the existing value differences progressively disappear. The factors accounting for the differences are the changing social order and the interaction of the adolescent with the new environment, which gives rise to new behaviors. This definition of the generation gap reminds us of the earlier discussion of adolescent subcultures, in which a behavioral subculture was seen to exist, but minimal support for a value subculture emerged. In many cases, adolescents are exercising parental values but, because they are living in a new environment, these values take behavioral forms different from those of the parents.

Bengtson has broken down generational differences into components to show the interaction effects among them (see Figure 7.3). Here he discusses six possible ways in which generational differences can be expressed:

> Type A: *Social revolution.* There are substantial differences between age groups; the differences are induced by primarily structural factors, such as age-status inequities or adherence to an outmoded ethic. Major social change will be the result as youth move into adulthood, permanently imprinted by the inequities they have experienced (Friedenberg, 1969; Mead, 1970; Seeley, 1969; Mannheim, 1952).
> Type B: *Normal rebellion.* There are substantial differences between age groups in norms, values, and behaviors; but these differences are primarily due to maturational factors. When children grow up and assume adult responsibilities, the great differences will disappear. Social change, therefore, will be minor, and the rebellion largely individual (Bettelheim, 1965; Reiss, 1967; Davis, 1940).
> Type C: *Social evolution.* There are major differences between age groups in some areas, and major continuity in others. Behaviors and norms are different, while values are not. The normative differences and the acting out lead to new styles of life and thus social change. A selective gap between generations will result in major changes on issues, such as sexual mores, racism, and the like, but the changes will be gradual and selective, rather than sudden and revolutionary, because the value system is transmitted more or less continuously (Keniston, 1965; Block et al., 1970).

Type D: *Nothing really new.* There are major differences in some areas because of normative contrasts, but continuity in others because the value system that youth will assume in adulthood is constant: responsibility, protection of home and family, necessary materialism. For example, youth become less permissive of premarital sex as they themselves become parents (Adelson, 1970; Bell, 1966).

Type E: *Social change, but not by generations.* There is great change evident in our society, but the change is not led primarily by generational conflict. All three generations are going through the social change, and to identify it with age group differences is to ignore the real ideological bases. Also, one must be aware of historical constancy in age group differences: there have always been certain differences, but today's are no greater and to call them a gap is a misnomer. The change is structure wide (Feuer, 1969; Adelson, 1970).

Type F: *Solidarity will prevail over tangential differences.* There are some apparent differences between children and their parents over largely peripheral issues that have to do with maturational factors. Despite such inevitable disagreements there is overwhelming solidarity between generations in most families; there is a basic, permanent, and constant solidarity between generations that will continue to develop (Campbell, 1969; Douvan & Adelson, 1966; Walsh, 1970) [Bengtson, 1970, pp. 26–27].*

Summarizing our discussion on the generation gap, we should not lose sight of the normal developmental nature of the adolescent, the changing environment, the environmental discrepancy between the adolescent's time and his parents', and the effects that adolescent-society and adolescent-parent interactions have on his subsequent behavioral and value expressions. Conger (1972) has aptly defined five factors, crucial to understanding generational differences, that are commonly overlooked. They are:

1. Many current pronouncements about this gap are based on faulty analysis and inappropriate conclusions. They derive largely from comparing nonrepresentative samples of adults with equally nonrepresentative samples of young people (Conger, 1971; Scammon & Wattenberg, 1970). The mass media, and a number of social scientists as well, have tended to picture adolescents, whether favorably or unfavorably, in terms of the manifest characteristics of visible, controversial, sometimes highly articulate minorities: high school and junior high school activists, minority group militants, hippies and teeny boppers, even, at times, hard-drug users and delinquents (Feigelson, 1970; Fort, 1969; Gerzon, 1970; Roszak, 1969; Yablonsky, 1968).
2. Popular stereotypes also confuse and confound comparisons between adults and adolescents generally with those between individual par-

*This excerpt from "The Generation Gap: A Review and Typology of Social-Psychological Perspectives," by V. L. Bengtson, is reprinted from *Youth & Society,* 2(1), Sept. 1970, by permission of the publisher, Sage Publications, Inc.

TABLE 7.5. Nature and effect of generational difference.

		Structural factors; permanent change	Developmental factors; temporary change
Extent of generational difference	1. "Great gap"	A. Social revolution	B. Normal rebellion
	2. "Selective gap"	C. Social evolution	D. Nothing really new
	3. "Illusory gap"	E. Social change, but not by generations	F. Solidarity will prevail

This excerpt from "The Generation Gap: A Review and Typology of Social-Psychological Perspectives" by Vern L. Bengtson is reprinted from *Youth & Society*, 2(1), Sept. 1970, 26, by permission of the publisher, Sage Publications, Inc.

ents and their adolescent sons and daughters, despite the fact that these may differ significantly. In one recent study (Harris, 1971), two-thirds of adolescents 15 years of age and older replied yes to the question, "Do your parents approve of your values and ideals?" but a majority of them responded negatively to the question, "Do they approve of the way your generation expresses their ideals?" Adolescents also tended to be more critical, generally in rather stereotyped terms, of the older generation as a whole than of their own parents (Gallup & Davis, 1969; Harris, 1971; *Generations Apart*, 1969).

3. There is also a widespread tendency to confuse generational differences that may indeed be new, either in kind or in magnitude, with those that have traditionally separated parents and children—if for no other reason than that successive generations occupy differing positions in the life cycle (Conger, 1971). The adolescent who is just becoming aware of the insistent stirring of sexual impulses will inevitably differ from the middle-aged adult who perceives his urgency waning. Adolescents need ways to consume their energy; adults look for ways to conserve it. Young people are concerned about where they are going; adults are concerned about where they have been. Adults, having personally experienced the many partial victories and defeats and the inevitable compromises of living, tend to be tempered in their enthusiasms, and cautious in their moral judgments. Young people, in contrast, tend to be impatient, impulsive, and given at times to imperious moral judgments that allow little room for shades of gray. They are more likely to move rapidly from profound joy to despair.

4. Even some of the more sophisticated formulations of generational conflict (Davis, 1940; Keniston, 1971) have underemphasized the potential of parents, as well as adolescents, to change with changing times. It has recently been observed, although systematic data are lacking, that adults who are currently the parents of adolescents are more likely to be sympathetic and understanding, not only toward their own children, but toward adolescents generally. At any rate, it is clear that many of today's parents have undertaken an "agonizing

reappraisal" of a number of their own attitudes and beliefs in the face of social change—not infrequently as a consequence of exposure to the concerns of their own adolescent sons and daughters (Conger, 1971).
5. Finally, there is a widespread tendency to overlook the possibility that parents and adolescents may be able to differ in some of their values and modes of behavior, and still remain capable of mutual understanding and respect [Conger, 1972, pp. 209–212].*

The set of emergent values generated by adolescents is commonly called the youth culture. This concept implies that youths have become alienated from mainstream society, have developed their own culture, and, in order to make their feelings known, have acquired allegiances to liberal, sometimes radical, points of view. Peer-group solidarity has seemed to prevail over parental solidarity, creating what is often called a generation gap. It would be well to remember that, although ideally adolescence is the time in which the young make decisions about themselves, they often find it difficult to do so in a changing society. In the process of identity searching, some seek out adults, but many make attachments with other adolescents, who are also seeking answers amidst change, violence, and affluence. High school youth, high school dropouts, noncollege youth, and college youth alike seek out friends and philosophies that best accommodate their needs. Some will become alienated, some will find their place in society, and some will continue to allude to the generation gap (Thornburg, 1971c).

*Excerpted from "A World They Never Knew: The Family and Social Change" by J. J. Conger. In J. Kagan and R. Coles (Eds.), *Twelve to Sixteen: Early Adolescence.* Copyright 1972 W. W. Norton & Company, Inc. Reprinted by permission.

The Adolescent and Education 8

In the previous chapter, we focused on the adolescent as a social being. One of the more significant social institutions within which adolescents interact is the school. Here they meet with friends and carry on both academic and social pursuits. Since more youths are in school today than in previous decades, and because few attractive alternatives to school are available to high-school-age youths, the adolescent's social world and his school are fairly inseparable. In this chapter, we will explore how both the adolescent's developmental intellectual needs and his social needs are fulfilled by the school.

INTELLECTUAL DEVELOPMENTAL NEEDS

As you saw in Chapter 3, the adolescent is capable of highly conceptual and abstract mental functioning in school. The movement into adolescent thought is not strictly developmental; the mind learns some entirely new skills and becomes able to relate more components, giving the adolescent a more varied mental ability than he had before. For example, as we saw in Chapter 4, he acquires the ability to *decenter*. A limitation characteristic of middle-childhood thinking is the ability to focus on only one aspect or property of a situation. With decentering, the individual's attention can encompass two or more dimensions or aspects of a stimulus event simultaneously (Looft, 1971). Decentering enables the components of logic and reasoning to become firmly established in the mind.

There are two other learning processes that the adolescent is intellectually ready to acquire and that the teacher should be aware of in order to increase instructional effectiveness. First, the adolescent has well-developed *conceptual skills*. His increased abstract-thinking ability allows him to learn elaborate concepts. This does not mean that concrete-empirical props are no longer useful to the adolescent thinker (Ausubel & Ausubel, 1966), but it does mean that their importance has diminished. The distinct advantages to instructing at the adolescent's conceptual level are that he will (1) understand as he learns rather than use rote or repetition methods, (2) generate his own thoughts about the instructional material as well as learn from the teacher, (3) have self-motivation and self-reinforcement systems available that facilitate better learning, and (4) gain meaning from materials that makes them relevant to him (Thornburg, 1973a).

The second learning process that the adolescent is ready to acquire is *problem solving*. It is thought that problem solving represents the most highly integrated use of intellectual skills known (Bruner, 1966; Gagné, 1974). In essence, problem solving is the application of various concepts to academic and environmental situations. Therefore, the adolescent has the ability not only to conceptualize extensively but to apply his concepts to real or simulated experiences. Maslow (1943) believes that the adolescent has both highly developed thinking skills and an intrinsic desire to relate to the world in order to understand himself better. The effective teacher will bring the present and anticipated worlds of the adolescent into the classroom, teaching the adolescent to see the perceptual world from more than one viewpoint. Thus the teacher may even precipitate perceptual change in the learner as the adolescent incorporates new ideas into his cognitive structure. In addition, by thus bridging the critical gap between classroom learning and environmental experience, the teacher can give the adolescent some measure of self-understanding and confidence.

The position has been established that the adolescent is a highly capable learner and is willing to accept challenges to integrate what he learns in the academic setting with what he sees in his real world. Nevertheless, many adolescents underachieve, hold negative attitudes toward school, or drop out either functionally or physically. This problem may stem from one or more of the following situations: (1) the adolescent's social world is more important to him than his academic one, (2) he is not challenged to work at his intellectual-skill level, (3) he is unmotivated because he sees the school as an academically sterile environment, or (4) his curriculum is outdated and clearly irrelevant to his world. Let's examine these situations one at a time.

IS THE SCHOOL AN ACADEMIC INSTITUTION?

Adolescents have three identifiable sources of functioning: (1) instincts, which have gained increased strength due to maturational and pubertal events; (2) emotions, which have become more intense due to ambivalence between independence of and dependence on parents; and (3) cognitive abilities, which have moved from the concrete to the abstract level. In addition to these three (sometimes conflicting) sources of functioning, adolescents must interact with a complex social environment. Influential aspects of their environment are parents, peers, teachers, and the media. The cumulative effects of these interaction sources and the conflicts among them may confuse adolescents' thinking, adding to their emotional vulnerability, one factor that may cause adolescents to be more concerned with social behavior than with academic behavior.

Strong statements have been made since 1960 declaring that our schools are decisively more social than academic. One of the main supporters of this position has been James Coleman, who sees adolescents forming well-defined subcultures that exclude the adult world. For this reason, according to Coleman, peer-group social behaviors are more important for the adolescent than his teachers and academic studies. Coleman's work shows that most adolescents regard the school as a primarily social environment (1961).

Changes in the social role of adolescence within society have led Coleman (1965) to delineate five changes instrumental in encouraging today's adolescent to view the school as a social environment. First, Coleman suggests that adolescents now become socially sophisticated earlier than adolescents of previous generations, and, as a result, tend away from unquestioned obedience and awe of adults. Second, the social system of the high school has become the adolescent's social environment. Third, the school has been set apart as a social system because of the decreasing need for adolescent participation in the adult world. The fourth change cited by Coleman is the emergence of commercial entertainment designed especially for the adolescent. Finally, Coleman suggests that compulsory school attendance motivates students away from learning and toward "getting by"—a philosophy by which teacher and student alike become satisfied with fulfilling formal requirements rather than engage in real teaching and learning.

Coleman conducted an extensive study (1961) among ten rural and urban high schools ranging in enrollments from 100 to 2000, in towns ranging in size from fewer than 1000 to more than 1 million. This in-depth exploration of the high school world covered all aspects of the adolescent's own society—his unique symbols and language as well as his special interests and activities.

When Coleman asked what it took to get into the leading crowd at school, most adolescents replied that academic success was not highly important. "It takes athletic prowess, knowing how to dance, owning a car, having a good reputation, or liking parties, and often not being a prude (for girls) or a sissy (for boys). Good grades and intelligence are mentioned, but not very often, and not so often as any of the other items" (Coleman, 1965, p. 19).

> In *every* school the boy named as best athlete and the boy named as most popular with the girls were far more often mentioned as members of the leading crowd, and as someone "to be like," than was the boy named the best student. And the girl named as best dressed, and the one

A great deal of nonacademic learning occurs in the school halls, on the grounds, and at athletic events.

named as most popular with boys, were in every school far more often mentioned as being in the leading crowd and as someone "to be like," than was the girl named as the best student [Coleman, 1960, p. 344].

Only 31 percent of the boys wanted to be remembered as brilliant students, compared with 45 percent who wanted to be remembered as athletic stars. Among the girls, only 28 percent wanted to be remembered as brilliant students, whereas 72 percent wanted to be remembered as most popular or as leaders in activities (Coleman, 1961).

Coleman's major conclusion was that the American high schools actually encourage adolescents to divert their energies and abilities into athletics and social activities. Some teachers stress with individual adolescents the need to concentrate their efforts in academic pursuits, but neither the teachers nor the intellectually inclined students are socially reinforced for such behavior. Rather, most high schools create mediocre learning environments and actively reinforce teachers and adolescents for being part of the social milieu. How many academic classes are dismissed to hold a pep rally for the football game? Have you ever heard of a pep rally for students entering the National Merit Scholarship contest? Since peer reinforcement, a strong social force, combines with the school's

TABLE 8.1. Percentages of students giving selected criteria as important for being a "big wheel" in their high school, by sex.

Criteria	Boys N = 142	Girls N = 178
Personal qualities $P < .001$	60.6	89.3
Material possessions $P = N.S.$	49.3	55.1
Activities-athletics $P < .02$	35.9	23.6
Academic achievement $P = N.S.$	21.8	25.8
"Right" friends $P = N.S.$	17.6	10.1

From "High School Student Perceptions of Prestige Criteria" by E. E. Snyder, Adolescence, 1972, 6(25), 132. Copyright 1972 by Libra Publishers, Inc. Reprinted by permission.

social reinforcement, no wonder few adolescents view their school experiences in academic terms.

Other studies support Coleman's contentions. Cawelti (1968) asked the same questions as Coleman of a group of students in a suburban high school that sends most of its graduates to college. They too wanted to be remembered first for popularity with others (54 percent), second for leadership in activities (28 percent), and third for academic achievement (18 percent).

In another study, Snyder (1972) questioned 320 high school juniors and found that they placed much stress on personal qualities, material possessions, and social activities. The relative percentages of their interests are shown in Table 8.1. In Snyder's study, girls placed more emphasis on personal qualities than did boys, whereas boys placed more emphasis on athletics than did girls.

Friesen (1968) conducted a comparable survey in Canada, where he investigated the academic-athletic-popularity syndrome among 15,000 students in 19 Canadian high schools. He asked his subjects whether they preferred to be remembered for academic achievement, athletics, or popularity. He had begun his research with the hypothesis that Canadian adolescent society has developed a hierarchy of values in the order of athletics > popularity > academics, similar to the hierarchy demonstrated by Coleman's U.S. sample. However, his results showed that this hypothesis must be rejected. The commonly accepted position that adolescent boys value athletics, and girls social success, much more than academic achievement is not tenable among Canadian students in light of Friesen's evidence.

Friesen asked his sample to rank these three values according to how "enduring" they considered them to be in their lives. The pattern for boys emerged in the order of

>   academics > athletics > popularity.

For girls, the order was

>   academics > popularity > athletics.

When asked to rank them in order of most satisfying in school, boys ranked them

>   academics > popularity > athletics.

Girls ranked them

>   popularity > academics > athletics.

When the subjects were asked which value was of greatest importance for the future, academic achievement was chosen overwhelmingly by both boys and girls. The order was

>   academics > popularity > athletics.

Friesen's data indicate that satisfaction of the adolescents' immediate needs within the high school environment was achieved through athletics and popularity. This finding is comparable to Coleman's, although Friesen found fewer Canadian students dependent upon athletics and popularity than Coleman found among American students. Regarding enduring values—that is, those things important now and in one's future—the Canadian students placed much stronger emphasis on academics than on the other areas. We can't say that this finding conflicts with Coleman's, however, since the Coleman study did not pose questions in exactly the same way. What does seem to be a fair comparative appraisal of the two studies is that the Canadian students tended to place less emphasis on athletics and popularity than the American students and somewhat more emphasis on academics. Nevertheless, *prima facie* evidence supports the idea that both Canadian and American high schools are strongly influential social environments.

STUDENTS' ATTITUDES TOWARD SCHOOL

Now let's discuss some of the many problems that stem from students' lack of interest in school as an academic institution. Charges of outdated curricula, lack of active student participation in policy making, and unconcerned teachers reflect the growing negative attitudes of some students. These attitudes often result in underachievement, political activism, behavior problems, or attrition—dropping out of school. Students also display much apathy within the high school, directing their energies toward peer and social involvement rather than toward academic excellence. This apathy arises in great part from the students' perceptions of

Informal classroom environments can be created by arranging seating in a circle, in which everyone can have direct eye contact. Youth view the informal classroom as a positive learning climate.

their own (1) normlessness, (2) powerlessness, and (3) meaninglessness within the school environment.

Normlessness gives rise to socially unapproved behaviors that adolescents believe necessary for achieving certain goals (Hoy, 1972). The high school student who feels social distance often engages in behaviors on the basis of their potential effectiveness in promoting change, irrespective of school or societal norms. Thus students have injected into their school environment the idea that one is justified in "getting ahead by any means." This philosophy is reinforced to some extent by teachers' similar disengagement from the teaching process—that is, simply going through the motions of teaching without showing real interest or motivation in their own academic subjects. In his research on attitudinal climates in several high schools, Hoy (1972) found that this disengagement factor among teachers was a significant contributor to student alienation. Students, too, come to view school as a game, the rules of which they can break if breaking them is an effective means to an end.

Powerlessness is the expectation on the part of an adolescent in the school environment that he can do little to influence or assert control over his own affairs (Hartley & Hoy, 1972). Rather, he believes he is being manipulated by teachers and administrators. He sees no effective way of registering discontent with school policies or activities.

The other perceptual disadvantage students may feel in school is *meaninglessness*. The relevance to actual life situations of what is occurring in the school environment is an important variable here. If the adolescent feels that what he is learning is unrelated to his future-goal expectations, or if he gains neither intrinsic nor extrinsic reward from the teaching-learning situation, feelings of meaninglessness appear. These feelings may result from the teacher's failure to adapt teaching to the students, from his domination of the classroom, or from his failure to help students assess and resolve value conflicts.

Feelings of meaninglessness, normlessness, and powerlessness all attest to *alienation*, an attitudinal state that the student may avoid if he has the opportunity to make a recognizable contribution to his school and classroom environments.

A poll conducted by *Life* magazine in 1969 among 2500 students in 100 high schools indicates that students are seeking greater participation in the policy-making processes of their schools. Tables 8.2 and 8.3 reflect student opinions, as well as contrasting parent and teacher opinions, on their involvement in policy making. The results of this poll and others attest to the fact that the school must consider ways to be more open to student input, a consideration strongly supported by Hoy's (1972) and Hartley and Hoy's (1972) research.

A statewide survey ("High School Students," 1970) was con-

TABLE 8.2. Student participation in policy making.

	Students	Parents	Teachers
Want more	58%	20%	35%
Want less	2	11	4
About same	39	65	60
Not sure	1	4	1

ducted in Ohio among 1100 students randomly selected from grades 10 through 12 in 74 different high schools, polling students on their values and on how they would improve their schools. Traditional value systems were revealed by most students. A primary value cited was the desire to achieve happiness in life through understanding and communicating with people. The most common answer given by these students to questions on how they would improve the Ohio schools was "Better communication." Students want more communication with their school administration, and, if they don't get it, they often open their own channels by demonstrating. The need for greater communication between administration and students, between faculty and students, and even among students themselves is evidenced in these respondents' answers to nearly all school-related questions.

Of the students questioned, 90 percent felt that they should be involved in curriculum planning, 72 percent felt that they should have a hand in disciplinary problems, and 64 percent viewed dress and conduct rules as a joint student-administration decision. There was evidence, however, that students are not seeking to take over the running of the schools. An overwhelming majority (85 percent) disagreed with the statement "The average student in our school would do better if students could run the schools." They wanted only to be involved in decision making that affects them—not to make the actual decisions—according to the report.

About 66 percent of all the students were satisfied with their curricula and 52 percent with their teachers. About 66 percent agreed that

TABLE 8.3. Importance of student participation in policy making.

	Students	Parents	Teachers
Very important	54%	25%	30%
Somewhat important	34	38	39
Not very important	11	33	31
Not sure	1	4	—

The *LIFE* Poll by Louis Harris and Associates, Inc., for *LIFE* Magazine. Copyright © 1969, Time, Inc. Reprinted with permission.

"the teachers are trying to do their best," although agreement was higher among students in nonpublic schools and much lower (50 percent) among black students. Students were split fairly evenly among agreement, disagreement, and indecision on whether school was helpful to them in meeting the problems of real life.

"Communicate with the students" and "Make the courses more interesting and exciting" are the key phrases emerging from the massive number of data collected in this study. Communication was stressed both as the outstanding quality of a good teacher and as one of the major suggestions for how teachers could do a better job. When asked what makes a good teacher, nearly half named "ability to communicate with the students, open-mindedness." Only about 25 percent answered "knowledge of subject matter and wisdom," and all other qualities received less mention.

> In my freshman year in high school, I had an algebra teacher who was very intelligent and had excellent rapport with the students. One day he made the chalk squeak on the blackboard, and half of the students complained that it bothered them. He immediately stopped his discussion and explained that there was no reason for that sound to bother anyone. He said that the irritation was a result of conditioning and that, if people didn't think about it, it wouldn't bother them. He then announced that he was going to scratch the board with his fingernails, telling the students that their discomfort was really unfounded.
>
> He scratched the board with his fingernails and, within five or ten minutes, had effectively persuaded almost the whole class that they were not bothered by the sound. By rationally explaining and demonstrating a process, this teacher gave everyone a positive experience. It was rewarding to overcome the discomfort that the sound had always caused before.

Students were split 50-50 on whether the more valuable ability in a teacher is to teach a specific subject or to give guidance in thinking. College-preparatory students favored the teaching of the subject more than did those in other curricula, however. These results are highly similar to those found by the *Life* survey on issues involving teachers and administrators. Students showed comparatively affirmative attitudes on these issues, as is indicated in Table 8.4.

Furthermore, other research indicates that students like school more than they dislike it. A longitudinal comparison of data from the annual Purdue Opinion Poll suggests that there was some decline in highly positive attitudes toward school, but no overall decline in general

TABLE 8.4. The bright side of high school.

	Students (%)	Parents (%)	Teachers (%)
Rate teachers good to excellent	81	78	87
Think class schedule is satisfactory	80	—	69
Feel teachers are genuinely concerned with helping students learn things useful later on	76	76	90
Rate principal good to excellent	73	79	—
Believe teachers can feel free to depart from subject matter to talk about things students are interested in	70	72	92
Do not feel teachers make passing college tests main purpose of education	68	67	85
Do not feel teachers concerned more with tests than with what students learn	68	65	82
Rate school administration good to excellent	67	76	75
Rate facilities good to excellent	66	76	65
Feel grade system is fair	65	62	69
Think teachers have freedom to express own ideas and opinions	64	63	74
Rate high school good to excellent	81	71	79

The *LIFE* Poll by Louis Harris and Associates, Inc., for *LIFE* Magazine. Copyright © 1969, Time, Inc. Reprinted with permission.

interest, during the decades of the 1950s and 1960s. Leidy and Starry (1967) discovered these trends by comparing student responses from polls taken in 1953, 1958, 1965, and 1967. Looking at the data in Table 8.5, you can see that students generally feel good about their school experiences.

Critics of the public schools, such as Charles Silberman (1970), contend that research results such as those just discussed do not necessarily support the position that the schools are highly relevant, meaningful, and supportive of the students' identity struggle. Silberman is inclined to believe, rather, that the schools are tragically effective in persuading students to pursue their education within the bounds of established policy. The results of this successful persuasion are lack of interest or motivation, underachievement, and willingness to accept the status quo. Silberman describes the total process as "education for docility." As Conger has described it, "Too often, it appears, they overemphasize order, discipline, and conformity at the expense of self-expression, intellectual curiosity, creativity, and the development of a humane, sensitive human being who is concerned with values, capable of self-reliance and independent judgment, and able and willing to learn for himself" (1973, p. 322).

TABLE 8.5. Taking everything into consideration, how do you feel about school?

	1953	1958	1965	1967
I like it very much	32%	27%	21%	16%
I like it most of the time	43%	46%	51%	57%
I don't like it very much	23%	24%	24%	25%
I dislike it	2%	3%	2%	2%

From "The American Adolescent: A Bewildering Amalgam" by T. R. Leidy and A. R. Starry, *NEA Journal*, 1967, 9. Copyright 1967 National Education Association. Reprinted by permission.

Sex Differences in Attitudes

Berk and her associates (Berk, Rose, & Stewart, 1970) analyzed data for 565 boys and girls in grades 4 and 5, the preadolescent age range. The questions they asked of the students were eventually sorted into ten attitudinal areas. They found in every case (see Table 8.6) that girls had more favorable attitudes toward school than boys. In fact, five of the scales showed highly significant differences. Regarding general attitude toward school, girls were decisively more positive than boys and, in addition, more positive toward specific classes. Girls also indicated a more

TABLE 8.6. Comparison of attitude-scale scores according to sex.

	Boys		Girls		Uni-variate
Attitude scale	M	SD	M	SD	F[a]
Attitude toward school	3.33	1.59	4.04	1.45	32.96**
Relationship with teacher	3.16	1.73	3.83	1.42	24.87**
Self-image	11.44	3.60	11.04	3.37	2.46
Attitude toward class	11.30	3.95	12.21	3.57	8.96*
Social adjustment	2.93	1.23	2.95	1.22	.02
Anxiety	3.56	1.66	3.70	1.54	.84
Importance of doing well	8.20	1.68	8.81	1.51	19.19**
Conforming vs. nonconforming pupil	2.75	1.14	3.18	1.26	18.00**
Other image of class	2.89	1.37	2.95	1.41	.05
Interest in school work	2.83	1.52	3.03	1.50	2.95

Note: 12 cases with missing data were deleted from the analysis. For boys, $N = 260$; for girls, $N = 293$.
[a] $df = 1/546$.
*$p < .002$.
**$p < .0001$.
From "Attitudes of English and American Children toward Their School Experience" by L. E. Berk, M. H. Rose, and D. Stewart, *Journal of Educational Psychology*, 1970, 61, 36. Copyright 1970 by the American Psychological Association. Reprinted by permission.

favorable relationship with the teacher. The study also showed that girls felt more strongly than boys about the importance of doing well, and this difference may have contributed to the fact that they also were stronger in conformity than boys. The results of this study on sex differences are in line with several other studies (Fitt, 1956; Jersild & Tasch, 1949; Tenenbaum, 1940; Yamamoto, Thomas, & Karns, 1969) that found girls to be more positive toward school than boys, although these studies did not test the same attitudes.

Analyzing their data according to socioeconomic status, Berk and her associates (Berk et al., 1970) found only one of the factors listed in Table 8.6 to be significant. High-socioeconomic-status students expressed less anxiety than low-socioeconomic-status students. This is an interesting finding, considering that anxiety was not one of the significant differences when the responses were analyzed according to sex. It may well indicate that there are interpersonal relationships within most school environments that affect the lower-class students more negatively than the middle- or upper-class students.

Cheating

One of the adverse effects of either alienation or apathy among students is that students often follow the path of least resistance by cheating. This behavioral phenomenon is not new; it is probably as old as tests, and research since the pioneer study by Hartshorne and May in 1928 has revealed high incidences of cheating. A more recent study by Schab (1968) indicated that more than 90 percent of high school students admit to having cheated in school at various times. When asked how much cheating was currently going on, boys and girls closely agreed in estimating that 97 to 99 percent of their peers had cheated at some time or cheated regularly. Adams reported 92 percent in his study of cheating in 1960.

Schab conducted a second study (1969) in Georgia with 835 boys and 794 girls attending 22 different secondary schools. When asked to estimate the amount of cheating occurring in their schools, the girls in the Georgia sampling appeared more pessimistic than the boys: the girls believed that more than half of the students cheated three-fourths of the time or more, whereas the boys estimated that more than half of the students cheated only half of the time or less. The difference between the mean of the estimates made by the male subjects and the mean of those made by the female students was found to be statistically significant at well beyond chance level. This difference did not appear, however, when the responses to the question of who does more cheating were tabulated. Both sexes agreed (by a proportion of three or four boys to one girl) that boys did more of it than girls, and that poor students did more of it than good ones.

Schab was interested in the ways these students handled many school-oriented behaviors. When the students were asked to admit or disavow participation in 12 different antisocial behaviors, some differences between the sexes were observed. About equal percentages of boys and girls admitted giving help to others on tests and having forged their parents' names to excuses. A significantly larger group of boys admitted taking illegal aids into examinations and using them. More boys than girls turned in work done by others, depended on their parents to do their schoolwork, engaged in plagiarism, lied about school to their parents, and forged their teachers' names. More boys also removed books from the library illegally, pretended illness in order to skip school, failed to turn in valuables found at school, and gave other students higher grades than they deserved when correcting their papers.

Several value statements regarding cheating in school and in the general society were presented to these students by Schab. Their reactions, summarized in Table 8.7, indicate differences between boys' and girls' attitudes toward cheating and dishonesty. Boys seemed more willing than girls to accept the idea of general dishonesty within school and society. When questioned on why they practiced cheating, the students

TABLE 8.7. Statements of honesty/dishonesty in American life.*

	Percent accepting	
	Boys	Girls
A cheater in school cheats on the job	71.8	71.9
Breaking a law is dishonest	80.3	82.9
A cheater in school cheats at home	43.9	46.5
Cheating is always discovered	82.3	83.9
Some teachers are dishonest	58.5	55.5
Cheaters can't be trusted	61.6	60.7
It is necessary to be dishonest at times	39.8	27.2
Cheating only hurts the cheater	78.2	84.9
Cheating is a sin	63.0	70.7
Honesty is always the best policy	80.1	84.5
Adults are more dishonest than children	32.8	26.3
Crime does not pay	87.1	90.3
Success in business demands some dishonesty	40.3	24.3
Most advertising is dishonest	48.0	42.7

*The percentages above the rule were not significantly different according to sex. Those below the rule exceeded at least the .05 level of confidence.

From "Cheating in High School: Differences between the Sexes" by F. Schab, *Journal of the National Association for Women Deans, Administrators, and Counselors,* 1969, 3(1), 41. Reprinted by permission of the National Association for Women Deans, Administrators, and Counselors and the author.

listed the fear of failure as the main cause; following were laziness, the need to satisfy parental demands for good grades, and the ease with which cheating could be accomplished. Other reasons frequently mentioned were the need to keep up with others, the difficulty of the schoolwork, and the need to get into college. These findings were confirmed once again by Schab in another study on high school cheating, reported in 1971.

HOW PARENTS VIEW THE SCHOOLS

What are parents concerned about in the schools? Research indicates that some of their common preoccupations are—in order of frequency—discipline, racial integration, school size, curriculum, financial support for the school, quality of teachers, and drugs.

A Gallup poll of 1973, authorized by *Phi Delta Kappan*, and a Harris survey of 1969, authorized by *Life* magazine, both show discipline to be the number-one concern among parents. To some extent, their involvement is generated more from concern for the parental idea of authority than from concern for the best interests of the adolescent. The Harris survey showed that 62 percent felt that discipline was more important than self-generated inquiry, a response that decisively indicates a practical, present-oriented parental attitude. Similarly, parents felt that routine homework was very important. When asked how the school should handle unruly students, 63 percent of the parents thought that it should "crack down" on them, whereas only 35 percent advocated trying to understand the adolescents' problems. An analysis of Tables 8.2–8.4 indicates that, in matters concerning school, parents are considerably more restrictive and traditional than either teachers or students.

Next to discipline, the issue of racial integration was most important. A breakdown of the Gallup poll's results indicates that approximately 4 percent of the parents thought that less integration should occur, and that another 25 percent advocated no change. These percentages are comparable to those found by the Harris survey, in which only 32 percent advocated integration. Furthermore, of the parents Harris polled, only 27 percent felt that race matters should be discussed in the classroom.

Parents also show some concern about school size and curriculum, the financial support of the school, the quality of teachers, and drugs. However, parents apparently show little positive concern about the internal workings of the school. Both the Gallup and the Harris surveys indicated that parents willingly relinquish actual decisions on rules, curriculum, and discipline to teachers and administrators. Few see any real need for change in curriculum.

HOW TEACHERS AND ADMINISTRATORS VIEW THE SCHOOL

Generally speaking, teacher attitudes tend to be more similar to those of students than to those of parents. The Gallup survey indicated their concerns in the following order of frequency: financial support for the school, discipline, racial integration, curriculum, and size of the school and classes. Teachers in the Harris survey seemed to be sympathetic with the students' desire for participation in policy making (see Tables 8.2 and 8.3), although they align themselves more with parents on rules, curriculum, and discipline. Cawelti (1968) found different results on teacher and student attitudes; 70 percent of the students he polled stated that they had no opportunity for involvement in school policy making, and another 71 percent claimed to have no freedom because of faculty control.

Principals' concerns are similar to teachers', but they focus especially upon behavioral problems. A study by Kingston and Gentry (1961) was conducted among 288 white and 132 black high school principals in Georgia. Student behaviors of most concern to them are shown in Table 8.8. Although this table reveals many contemporary concerns, the study

TABLE 8.8 Types of student behavior most frequently of concern to high school principals of Georgia.

Student behavior	Percent
Failure to do homework and other assignments	66.66
Congregating in halls and lavatories	41.19
Truancy	33.80
Smoking in school or on grounds	30.71
Impertinence and discourtesy to teachers	22.38
Cheating on homework	20.23
Cheating on tests	18.09
Destruction of school property	17.14
Stealing small items	14.28
Obscene scribbling in lavatories	12.38
Using profane or obscene language	5.00
Lying of a serious nature	4.52
Stealing (money, cars, etc.)	4.04

From "Discipline Problems and Practices in the Secondary Schools of a Southern State" by A. J. Kingston and H. W. Gentry, *National Association of Secondary School Principals Bulletin,* 1961, *45,* 33–44. Reprinted by permission.

was conducted before widespread drug use became a problem among students and therefore fails to register concern in this area. Upon analyzing their data on student problems according to grade level, Kingston and Gentry found an overwhelming percentage of problems (63 percent) among freshmen. This finding is interesting and somewhat puzzling, since research shows that freshmen had the best *attitudes* toward school, with a progressive deterioration in attitudes in grades 10, 11, and 12 (Cawelti, 1968; Thornburg, 1974c). Is it possible that there is little correlation between attitudes toward school and behavior? Seniors seemed to be more vocal in their displeasure with school. Among seniors, 69 percent felt that there was too much regimentation. In contrast, only 38 percent of the freshmen in Cawelti's study felt that the school was too regimented. Perhaps attitudes and behaviors are not related, since freshmen are more prone to act out in behavioral ways displeasing to principals, whereas the more dissatisfied seniors find less need to resort to overt behaviors.

Behavioral Norms in the Classroom

There is some evidence supporting the idea that the more a student approximates classroom behavioral norms, fits the structure created by the teacher, and achieves well, the better is his interaction with the teacher. Grimes and Allinsmith (1961) compared structured and unstructured teaching methods and tested the hypothesis that the teaching method used interacts with the student's personality characteristics to determine the student's response to instruction. Anxiety and compulsivity, for example, were found to interact with each other and with the teaching method. Results of this study showed that highly anxious or highly compulsive children taught primary reading by a structured method were superior readers by the third grade compared with children with the same characteristics taught by an unstructured approach. Compulsive children did better than less compulsive children in the structured program; compulsivity made no difference in an unstructured setting. Although variation in anxiety level made no difference in the achievement of the children in the structured situation, a high level of anxiety in unstructured settings impeded scholastic performance. Children who were judged to be both highly anxious and highly compulsive were strikingly more competent when taught by the structured method than by the unstructured method. Those who were classified as highly anxious but noncompulsive were exceptionally low in achievement in the unstructured setting.

Knafle (1972) investigated the relationship between behavior ratings and grades, hypothesizing that the higher the student's grades, the more favorably he or she would be rated by the teacher. For 441 black girls in grades 10 and 11 who attended school for at least 150 days during the school year, good behavior ratings were found to accompany good marks in all subject areas studied (commerce, English, math, foreign languages, science, and social studies), and unsatisfactory behavior ratings were found to accompany failing marks in all subject areas except foreign languages. Both male and female teachers who gave favorable behavior ratings also tended to give higher grades than teachers who gave unfavorable behavior ratings. Social-studies teachers gave the highest proportion of "excellent" behavior ratings, and English teachers gave the highest proportion of "unsatisfactory" behavior ratings.

School administrators and teachers can help a student integrate himself into his society by responding to the student's social needs. They can strengthen his self-concept and enhance his interaction potential by providing opportunities for academic success, social success, and peer and faculty acceptance. For example, Spaulding (1964) suggests that a teacher's personality and behavior can affect the social development of his or her students. Teachers who are interested in and supportive of students have a positive effect on the personalities and social behaviors of those students. Spaulding (1963) found high self-concepts among the pupils of teachers who were socially integrative or learner-supportive. Poorer self-concepts were found when teacher behavior was domineering, threatening, or sarcastic. Of course, the student himself represents a variable in measurements of this type. That is, regardless of how a teacher interacts with a class, he may have a positive effect on one child but a less positive or even a negative effect on another child.

INFLUENCES ON STUDENTS' EDUCATIONAL ASPIRATIONS

Influences on students' educational and occupational aspirations—specifically, on their decisions regarding whether to go to college and where to go to college—come from several major quarters. In this section, we will discuss the relative influences exercised by the student's family, peers, and school authorities.

The Family Nationwide surveys such as Douvan and Adelson's (1966) and Bachman's (1970) indicate that parents play a strong role in influencing their adolescent's educational and occupational aspirations. To a considerable extent, the *model* provided by the parent is the strong determinant, because the characteristics actually being transmitted are *values* that guide the person toward educational excellence and a self-enhancing occupation. Thus, an adolescent may reject his father's par-

There are occasions when teacher-directed activity dominates the classroom or the individual efforts of a student.

ticular occupational role in the process of his identity and autonomy striving, but at the same time he is unlikely to abandon the desire for educational and/or occupational training that will be potentially rewarding.

In fact, studies show that parents who promote their adolescents' aspirations also promote their autonomy and independence, although this effect is not always perceived by the adolescents themselves (Bell, 1963; Norman, 1966). Such parents also stress achievement (McClelland, 1961), promote adaptive skills (Morrow and Wilson, 1961), and show a basic respect for knowledge. The more parents indicate high aspirational levels themselves (as models), the more likely adolescents are to identify with them and adopt such attitudes.

A questionnaire designed by Stahmann and his associates (Stahmann, Hanson, & Whittlesey, 1973) was administered to a sample of high school seniors in Iowa. The questionnaire asked for the student's perceptions regarding (1) the three most important factors influencing his college choice, (2) a ranking of people as to their influences on his decision to attend or not to attend college, and (3) a ranking of sources of information about college as to their influences on his decision to attend or not to attend college.

A questionnaire was also administered to the parents of these students. The parent questionnaire elicited similar information: (1) the three most important factors influencing the student's college choice, (2) a ranking of people as to the influence they had on their son's or daughter's decision about attending college, and (3) a ranking of sources of information about colleges as to the influence they had on their son's or daughter's decision about attending college.

The parents ranked "advice of parents or other family member" as the most influential factor in their child's choice of college. Second was "cost of attending college," and third was "location of college." The students agreed with their parents and ranked "advice of parents or other family member" as the most influential factor in choice of college. Unlike their parents, the students ranked "location of college" second and "cost of attending college" third.

Parents ranked themselves as the most influential people in their son's or daughter's decision on college attendance. They ranked brothers or sisters as second in influence, followed in order by high school counselor, friends in high school (peers), friends already attending college, high school teacher, other relatives, and college recruiter.

The students agreed with their parents on the first two rankings, rating parents as most influential and brothers or sisters as next most influential. The ranking of other sources by the students, in descending order of influence, was friends in high school, friends already attending college, high school counselor, other relatives, high school teacher, and college recruiter. A primary difference between the rankings given by parents and students was that the parents saw the high school counselor as being more influential than the student's friends, either those still in high school or those attending college. The students rated the influence of their friends as greater. It is also interesting to note that both the parents and the students rated the college recruiter as the least influential person of the eight listed.

Another variable affected by parental influence is the adolescent's achievement. Morrow and Wilson (1961) studied the family interactions of 48 high- and low-achieving boys. Their results indicated that there was higher achievement orientation among boys when their families shared ideas and experiences together. The parents of the high achievers provided greater social reinforcement to their adolescents by showing trust and giving approval of behavior. This did not seem to be the case in the low-achieving boys' families. In contrast, their parents demonstrated more dominance, restrictiveness, and tendency to punish. Therefore it appears that, when an adolescent underachieves, parents are more controlling, more arbitrary, and less satisfying to the adolescent. And, in general, the more the parents promote achievement, the more likely an adolescent is to be educationally and occupationally oriented.

Peers

Considerable attention has been given to the influences of the peer group on the scholastic efforts and aspirations of the individual (Alexander & Campbell, 1964). There is little question that acceptance by peers is one of the adolescent's strongest needs. But does this need pertain chiefly to the immediate situation or to decisions that have long-term consequences as well?

Peers seem to have a strong effect on one another if there is a high degree of closeness and some reciprocity in the relationship (Alexander & Campbell, 1964; Kandel & Lesser, 1969). Theoretically, this kind of influence consists of the ability of two individuals to comparably influence one another's cognitive and affective behaviors and values (Rigsby & McDill, 1972). The idea of reciprocity has been advanced and researched by numerous individuals. Alexander and Campbell (1964) undertook to find out whether a student of a given personal-status level (defined as the degree to which he or she is accepted by peers) was more likely to plan to go to college if his best friend was going, hypothesizing that the relationship is more positive when there is reciprocity (when both friends have the same plan) than when there is none. Some of the results of their research are reported in Table 8.9.

TABLE 8.9. Percent of students who definitely expect to go to college—by personal-status level, college plans, and reciprocation of first choice.*

Personal-status level	Reciprocates		Does not reciprocate	
	Choice plans to attend	Choice doesn't plan to attend	Choice plans to attend	Choice doesn't plan to attend
I (High)	96.9 (97)	64.0 (25)	81.5 (54)	62.5 (16)
II	78.1 (73)	39.6 (48)	69.0 (58)	41.2 (34)
III	75.9 (54)	22.2 (45)	70.6 (34)	43.2 (37)
IV	53.3 (60)	24.3 (74)	53.1 (49)	20.4 (54)
V (Low)	51.0 (49)	5.3 (152)	25.5 (51)	7.0 (114)

*Numbers in parentheses in all tables are the base from which the percentage derives; e.g., in the upper left-hand cell, 96.9 percent of the 97 cases of high personal status, when the best friend reciprocates the choice and is college-bound, expect to attend college.

From "Peer Influences on Adolescent Educational Aspirations and Attainments" by C. N. Alexander, Jr., and E. Q. Campbell, *American Sociological Review*, 1964, 29, 570. Copyright 1964 by the American Sociological Association. Reprinted by permission.

In their statistical analysis, Alexander and Campbell found the average Q value (that is, interquartile range—a measure of variance) for the association between the student's college plans and his friend's to be .777 when the decision was reciprocal and .327 when it was not. The association was in the expected direction, and was much stronger, under conditions of reciprocation; therefore the data support the hypothesis that a student and his best friend tend to make similar college plans and that the similarity is greater when the decision is reciprocal.

Kandel and Lesser (1969) were also interested in the effect reciprocity has on adolescents' educational choices. Upon determining the effect of reciprocity on the decision of whether to attend college, they found that one's best friend's educational plans greatly influenced one's choice.

Rigsby and McDill (1972) investigated several dimensions of peer relationships and their effects on adolescents' aspirational choices. A sample of 20,345 students was evaluated on the four measures shown in Table 8.10. The first measure, a perceptual one, was based on student responses to the question "Of the people your own age with whom you spend most of your free time, how many plan to go to college *or* are already going to college?"

The other three measures were based on sociometric data gathered from the friends named by the respondent in answer to the question "What boys (girls) *here in school* do you go around with most often?" The second measure, shown in the second row of Table 8.10, is the actual percentage of the respondent's friends (up to four) who indicated that they intended to go to college. This measure differs from the previous one in being an actual rather than a perceived one. The third peer-group-impact measure is the percentage of the respondent's friends (up to four) who come from families in which the father has at least some college education. Finally, an average of these friends' academic values was included as a peer-impact measure. One can argue that it is really through values that peers influence each other. This variable, more than any other, seemed to measure the student's basic scholastic commitment.

Several important patterns can be seen in the results shown in Table 8.10. Perhaps the most striking is that the effects of the peer group assessed by the first two measures are more than twice as great as those assessed by the last two measures. A second result is that the *perceived* reciprocal choice of college among friends was more influential in the subject's decision than was the *actual* number of friends who went to the same college.

Rigsby and McDill concluded that close friends in this study had a strong influence on one another's educational plans, primarily (1) be-

TABLE 8.10. Independent effects of academic emulation, father's education, ability, academic values, and each of four measures of peer-group impact on college plans.

Measure of peer-group influence	Academic emulation	Father's education	Ability level	Academic values	Peer-group measure
Perceived proportion of friends with college plans	.056	.126	.090	.139	.396
Actual percentage of friends with college plans	.056	.155	.110	.151	.301
Percent of friends with highly educated fathers	.083	.175	.141	.179	.137
Friends' average academic values	.109	.202	.149	.167	.090

*Weighted effects of predictor attributes**

*The effect parameters for the predictor variables are estimated from a continuous-time, discrete-state, Markov process (Coleman, 1964). The parameters are analogous to dummy variable regression coefficients where the independent variables are dichotomies and the dependent variable is a percentage.

From "Adolescent Peer Influence Processes: Conceptualization and Measurement" by L. C. Rigsby & E. L. McDill, *Social Science Research*, 1972, *1*, 314. Copyright 1972 by Academic Press, Inc. Reprinted by permission.

cause they were highly similar in scholastic values and academic pursuits and (2) because a high degree of reciprocity (see the first two rows of Table 8.10) existed among them.

Parents or Peers?

As was suggested in Chapter 5, the adolescent is quicker to adopt his peers' behaviors than to adopt his peers' values. Therefore, parents are likely to have a stronger effect than peers regarding long-term issues and goals, which are based on values. These different modes of influence generally become more evident when the person becomes an adult than during his adolescence. As evidence we have examined has shown, it is likely that parents are more influential than peers in the adolescents' educational plans (Conger, 1973; Kandel & Lesser, 1969). Even during the height of student activism, I found that, although Vietnam, the draft, and civil rights were of real concern to college-age youths, their dominant concern was their education—a factor that points to parental influence on their long-range plans (Thornburg, 1969b, c; 1971d).

Kandel and Lesser (1969) found, however, that 57 percent of their sample had made long-range plans that were in agreement with both parents and peers. They also found that those adolescents who agreed with their parents were more likely than those who disagreed with their parents to agree with their peers. Kandel and Lesser contend that, although adolescents primarily adopt parental goals, peers tend to reinforce such goals rather than propose conflicting goals. Therefore, no polarization exists between parents and peers on issues concerning the adolescent's future.

The Coach

Recent research (Rehberg, 1969; Rehberg & Shafer, 1968; Snyder, 1972; Spreitzer & Pugh, 1973) indicates that the advice the high school coach gives his players is positively associated with the players' decision to attend college. Although empirical data are lacking, several investigators have noted the theoretical relevance of the coaching role in adolescent male socialization.

The influence of the coach in the socialization process for athletes emerges as particularly important when several dimensions of the coach-player relationship are analyzed. Since participation in high school athletics is a highly prized prestige-granting activity, the coach exercises considerable power and authority in selecting players and granting rewards and punishments. The players, in turn, voluntarily submit to the coach's control and influence. Brim (1966) has noted that the coach's selection procedure helps to assure that those who enter the sports activity will not present problems for the socialization process involved in the activity. Additional characteristics of the coach-player relationship that are likely to result in effective socialization are the high degree of participant involvement by players and coaches and the probability that their relationships will be expressive and affective (Snyder, 1972).

Snyder (1972) investigated players on 270 Ohio high school basketball teams to determine how strong an effect the coach has on the adolescent's educational plans. Of the respondents, 96 percent were juniors or seniors. When the athletes were questioned as to what person had the most influence on their subsequent educational plans, coaches ranked third in priority behind the mother (first) and the father (second), as you see in Table 8.11. When the data were controlled for the variables of father's education and occupation, they suggest that boys from the lower socioeconomic classes are more strongly influenced by coaches than boys from the middle or upper middle classes.

The coach's advice on whether to attend college and his advice on where to attend college were positively associated with the player's decisions. Advice on whether to attend college showed approximately the

TABLE 8.11. Reference persons cited by players as most important influence in their thinking about educational and/or occupational plans, by socioeconomic status of father (percentages).

Person cited as most important	Education of father			Occupation of father		
	Less than high school N = 80	High school N = 145	Some college or more N = 64	Semiskilled, unskilled N = 58	Clerical, sales, skilled, farm N = 153	Professional, executive, proprietor N = 68
Mother	33	31	23	22	35	19
Father	21	36	53	26	37	44
Coach	19	9	13	19	12	10
Classroom teacher	10	6	3	9	7	3
Girlfriend	9	6	0	7	5	3
Brother	3	5	3	7	0	9
Minister or priest	3	3	0	3	0	4
Sister	1	1	0	2	1	0
Other relative	1	0	2	2	0	1
Boyfriend	1	0	2	2	0	1

From "High School Athletes and Their Coaches: Educational Plans and Advice" by E. E. Snyder, *Sociology of Education*, 1972, 45(3), 317. Copyright 1972 by the American Sociological Association. Reprinted by permission.

same relationship to educational plans as did the player's socioeconomic background. Because the coach is providing advice about going to college, and perhaps making arrangements with colleges and college coaches for visits, he is perceived by the player as influential.

In summary, these data demonstrate moderate positive relationships between the coaches' advice and the players' decisions on college attendance. However, the two advice variables—whether to attend college and where—are not entirely independent in their effects on players' educational plans. In addition, although many players perceive their coaches as influential, this influence is actually spread over many areas other than educational plans. In Snyder's study, 70 percent of the players indicated that their coach gave them advice about personal problems. Other advice included the topics of whom to date (22 percent), how often to date (49 percent), manner of dress (73 percent), swearing (84 percent), and hair style (88 percent).

Rehberg (1969) advanced five possible explanations for the relationship between educational goals and athletic participation. Briefly, they are:

1. Athletics facilitate association with achievement-oriented peers. Popular students are (1) disproportionately middle class and (2) disproportionately college oriented, and they (3) receive higher grades than other students and (4) regard athletic competence as a crucial peer-group-membership variable (Coleman, 1961).
2. There is some transfer from athletic-achievement traits to academic achievement (Eidsmore, 1963; Strodtbeck, 1958)—that is, to the extent that athletic participation has an incremental effect on grades and educational expectations (Coleman, Mood, Campbell, et al., 1966).
3. Levels of an adolescent's aspirations and self-esteem are a function of the internalized appraisals of significant others. To the extent that competence in sports elicits positive appraisals from significant others, participation in sports may well serve to enhance the self-esteem of the adolescent participant and therefore raise his scholastic performance and educational expectations.
4. The theory of status consistency suggests that an individual is subject to pressure to behave in a congruent manner—that is, to present a consistent self (Sampson, 1963). Rehberg suggests that an athlete finds himself under pressure to present a consistent image among scholastic performance, educational goals, and athletic ability—pressure that is intensified by the athlete's greater visibility and prestige as compared with the nonathlete's.
5. Because the athlete is a more conspicuous person in school and in the community, he may receive scholastic and career counseling and en-

couragement superior in quality and quantity to that received by the nonathlete.

As we have seen, the student's attitudes toward school are influenced both positively and negatively by parents, peers, and school authorities. Now let's look at some of the problems arising from the school's failure to satisfy the adolescent's diverse needs—underachievement and attrition.

UNDERACHIEVEMENT

In its broadest sense, underachievement refers to a student's performing academically below his capability, as determined by achievement or aptitude scores and past academic records. An underachiever can be of any intellectual range. The criterion for determining underachievement is not potential but actual behavior.

Research by Kraft (1969) among 84 high school students identified five common traits among underachievers: (1) negativism, (2) inferiority feelings, (3) high anxiety, (4) boredom, and (5) overprotectedness. Boredom was reflected in lack of interest in school, lack of ambition, laziness, and "fooling around" in class. Negativism was indicated by dislike of a particular subject or dislike of a particular teacher; it was caused by being exposed to a poor teacher or by being forced into undesired curricula choices.

I took two years of Latin in high school. My teacher was an old man on the verge of outright senility. He was actually the English teacher, but since somewhere in his dim past he'd learned some Latin, the administration had him take on the few deviates who chose Latin over Spanish. Not surprisingly, he did a very poor job. Considering myself much too bright to be wasting my time under this simple old man, I gradually became more and more hostile. Frustration finally pushed me beyond decorum and I verbally insulted him in class; that is, I told him what I thought of him as a Latin teacher.

Had I stood up and shot him with a .45, I couldn't have inflicted a more grievous wound. The ensuing grief that came down on my head was considerable; it included lectures from the teacher, the principal, and my mother. However, none of these punishments deterred me from being a smart aleck in the future—on the contrary. What did keep me from harassing the old man again was that, days later, he took me out into the hall and told me how upset he was.

Other studies show that highly intelligent students show especially strong trends toward underachievement. Eisenman and Platt (1972) found 80 percent of the underachievers in their study to be intellectually gifted but to tend toward mediocrity. They speculated that this problem was caused by a lack of intellectual stimulation within the school, where achievement seemed to be based more on conformity to teachers' expectations than on success in critical thinking, self-improvement, or imagination.

In a study of 80 high school males, Propper and Clark (1970) linked underachievement with alienation. They tested these students for the five personality traits that Davids (1953) defined as the components of an alienation syndrome: pessimism, distrust, anxiety, egocentricity, and resentment. After examining each of the subjects on these dimensions, they found that low-achievers in academics could be characterized by Davids' alienation profile. The researchers concluded that deficient personality and motivational characteristics militate against the full use of one's intellectual resources in the academic environment. Their conclu-

---

A junior high school boy was referred to a psychologist, at his mother's request, because he was "flunking everything" and had become a real problem at home and at school. She saw his behavior as unmotivated and somewhat withdrawn. His typical after-school activities were playing the stereo and going for walks.

The boy's mother was very busy with social activities, bridge clubs, church, and Country Club. His father was a successful lawyer and had much interest in athletics. The boy had an older brother who excelled in athletics, made good grades in school, and aspired to be a lawyer.

In his initial interview, the boy stated that he came only at his mother's insistence. As the interview progressed, he revealed that he was not doing well in school; in fact, he had received four failing marks. He reported considerable trouble in communicating with his father, and he thought that his father hated him because he made references to his being lazy and a goof-off. The purpose of his frequent walks was to get away from his father, who always felt that he should be studying or showing interest in athletics.

What family dynamics are going on in this case?

Although the boy blames his father for his behavior, is it possible that his mother and his father are highly similar in their functions?

Is it possible that the boy suffers from a learning disability?

How critical is the need for acceptance from the boy's perspective?

Is it possible that he has misinterpreted his father's intentions? In what way?

sion is similar to Kowitz's contention that the underachiever is a "rebel against the educational regime ... [who] has chosen a path of passive non-resistance to instruction rather than one of active aggression against it" (1965, p. 473).

The problem of underachievement seems more prevalent among boys than among girls (Ford, 1957). This fact may be due to the earlier social maturation of the adolescent girl. Girls also seem to have a greater propensity for social interaction and to see more prestige value in academic achievement than boys, who typically choose athletics or automobiles as achievement symbols. Since the alternatives for channeling female energies in high school are somewhat limited, girls often direct their energies toward academics. Perhaps they are more motivated in the classroom for these reasons.

The hypothesis generated by this examination of underachievement is that the classroom environment is not challenging enough to motivate active adolescent participation in academics. The dullness of the high school classroom becomes accentuated when the adolescent compares it with the other places in which his energies may be expended within the school environment. Classroom environment shapes the motivation and behavior of the adolescent through its effects on the individual's perceptions of what is expected of him and the subsequent reinforcement for doing so (Alschuler & Irons, 1973; Litwin & Stringer, 1968). Hence the importance of a positive classroom environment.

Ways in which to organize a classroom in order to effect a facilitative learning environment have been stated by McClelland (McClelland & Alschuler, 1971). They are:

1. *Achievement.* Ability to organize clearly, feedback of results: students feel that they are graded fairly and know when they do well.
2. *Power.* Morale: students obey, feel that they belong to the class, don't cheat, and so on. Standards: the teacher holds high standards for schoolwork and classroom order.
3. *Affiliation.* Teacher warmth: the teacher provides a great deal of warmth, support, and encouragement. Togetherness: students like each other and are friendly in class.

Alschuler and Irons (1973) believe that the interaction among these factors in the classroom can positively alter the classroom environment, thus increasing motivation and learning on the part of the student, reciprocal regard between teacher and pupil, and satisfaction with the school in general. The implication of their conclusion is that effective teaching and learning involve the total environment.

ATTRITION

There are several reasons why a student may drop out of school. Dropping out is not simply the result of unsuccessful school experiences; it may have social, psychological, economic, cultural, and political causes as well. Although analysis of individual dropouts indicates failing grades and poor reading levels to be precipitators in their dropping out, broader research (Thornburg & Grinder, 1975) has shown a variety of basic reasons for leaving school—such as lack of interest in school, poor relationships with teachers or peers, negative attitudes toward school, desire to find a job, desire to get married, pregnancy, enlistment in the military, and expulsion.

Estimates place the national dropout rate at around 30 percent, and the rate exceeds 50 percent in some densely populated inner-city areas where there are large concentrations of minority youth. Although the total number of youths in school today is higher than it has ever been, the fact remains that more than 7.5 million youths dropped out of high school in the United States during the 1960s (Fitzsimmons, Cheever, Leonard, & Macunovich, 1969).

The decrease in the number of skilled and unskilled jobs available has become an even greater problem to the larger society as a result of the increase in the number of adolescent school dropouts. Available job-training programs are usually reserved for the high school graduate and therefore do not help alleviate the problem of employment for the dropout. The most viable solution seems to be that the schools become more innovative and oriented toward the individual in order to maintain their students' interest and perhaps reduce the dropout rate.

Attitudes toward School

The compulsory-attendance laws of the United States usually require students to stay in school until they complete the eighth grade or reach 16. During these elementary and junior high school years the student may develop many negative associations, and, when he eventually has some choice in the matter, he may drop out of school. Research on potential dropouts' attitudes toward school is limited. However, their attitudes are undoubtedly reflected in some of the reasons they give for leaving school. The research available tends to focus on youths from impoverished areas, who in most cases are minority youths.

Ahlstrom and Havighurst's study (1971) in Kansas City involved black and white youths from culturally disadvantaged areas who had

> Lacy (1968) devised a dropout scale that has predictive value within the public schools:
>
> The dropout scale.
>
> | Factor | Weighting | Total possible |
> |---|---|---|
> | Sex | 2 for male, 0 for female | 2 |
> | Attendance | 1 for each 5 days absent previous semester up to 40 days to nearest 5 days (2½ or more = 1). | 8 |
> | School marks | 1 for each "D" previous semester; 2 for each "E" previous semester | 8 |
> | Scholastic aptitude | Use most recent IQ score. 1 for each 5 points below 100 to nearest 5 points; subtract 1 for each 5 points above. | ±6 |
> | Reading ability | Use latest reading test grade level compared with actual grade level at time taken to nearest ½ year. 1 point for each ½ year retarded; subtract 1 for each ½ year accelerated. | ±8 |
> | Over-age for grade | 2 points for each year over-age to nearest whole year. 0 if at correct age or under-age. | 6 |
> | Course of study | 0 if academic (college prep.); 2 if non-academic (general, commercial, vocational). | 2 |
> | Total | | 40 |
>
> From "Identifying Potential High School Dropouts" by C. L. Lacy, *The School Counselor*, 1968, 16(1), 38. Reprinted by permission.
>
> For example, in a sample of 154 students, 62 were identified as potential dropouts and 92 were not. Of those identified, 26 dropped out of school and 36 did not. Of those who were not identified as dropouts, only 2 dropped out. The practical implications of such a scale may be that additional guidance may be given to potential dropouts as a deterrent to their dropping out.

been placed in a work-study program (half-day work, half-day school). In assessing their attitudes toward school, the authors found that 50 percent of the students expressed generally favorable attitudes toward school, whereas 24 percent were strongly negative. Negative attitudes were especially strong in regard to irrelevant curriculum, feelings of boredom, teachers' stress on grades, teachers' prejudice, and school restrictions.

Potential dropouts' attitudes toward school possess certain common characteristics, even though dropouts come from various minority and majority groups and from both urban and rural areas. For example, let's compare the evidence provided in the Ahlstrom and Havighurst study (1971) with that from one of my studies (Thornburg, 1971b). The same attitude-measurement instrument was used in both of these studies. The former was done in a city, primarily among blacks; the latter was done in rural Arizona, primarily among Mexican Americans and Indians. Interestingly enough, strong similarities in negative attitudes toward school were found between the two studies. Some of the comparative statistics are shown in Table 8.12.

TABLE 8.12. Attitudes toward school: A comparison.

| | Percent agreement ||
Statement	Thornburg's study (1971)	Ahlstrom and Havighurst's study (1971)
Pupils really do not learn the things in school that they want to learn.	62	60
Too much of what we have to study does not make sense.	49	47
Pupils have to keep reading and studying the same things over and over in school.	48	53
Pupils are always treated fairly in school.	63	49
Teachers expect too much of students.	58	61
School can be very boring at times.	83	86
Some pupils are always making fun of other pupils in school.	83	91
There is too much importance placed on grades in school.	74	62
Teachers always seem to like some pupils better than others.	82	74

From *School Learning and Instruction: Readings*, edited by H. D. Thornburg. Copyright © 1973 by Wadsworth Publishing Company, Inc. Reprinted by permission of the publisher, Brooks/Cole Publishing Company, Monterey, California.

Curriculum Options

Now that curriculum options are becoming of greater concern to students of all grade levels, it is imperative to present potential dropouts with innovative programs and options in order to hold them in school, moving away from the standard or traditional curriculum and preparing courses and materials more in line with the individual needs of these students. The following discussion will describe two examples of different types of programs currently in operation that are designed especially for the high-risk potential dropout.

In one study (Thornburg, 1971b), freshmen enrolled in a rural Arizona high school were placed in a special dropout-prevention project. These youths' performance was followed throughout their ninth-grade year to ascertain the effectiveness of a special team-teaching project in English and mathematics in (1) holding the students in school and (2) effecting change in their attitudes toward school.

The dropout-prevention project began during the 1968–1969 academic year, evolving out of concern shared by administrators and interested faculty about the high dropout rate occurring in the school. The program had three primary purposes: (1) to increase the rate of attendance of potential dropouts, (2) to increase their "holding power," and (3) to reduce their negative attitudes toward school.

Each year, around 45 percent of all freshmen were considered to be potential dropouts. For the study, each of the students designated as a potential dropout was placed in one of three different curriculum programs. The first group was more or less a control group. Of these youths, 165 of necessity had to be placed in the regular classroom with the regular academic students. Second, approximately 120 of these potential dropouts were placed in vocational-education programs (in this case, programs in agricultural skills for the boys and in home-economics skills for the girls). Third, around 45 students were placed in the special English-math team-teaching program mentioned above.

The commitment made to the special English and math classes by several classroom teachers served to perpetuate the program. Although it is most crucial to cultivate holding power among potential dropouts during the ninth grade, these teachers continued the program for the potential dropouts through all the high school years. The designated special curricula for each grade level were:

1. Ninth grade—English and mathematics
2. Tenth grade—English and biology
3. Eleventh grade—English and American history
4. Twelfth grade—social studies

The study clearly demonstrated that the special team-teaching program was effective in changing students' attitudes toward school and in holding students in school. When one compares the 9.3-percent dropout rate among those in the special program with the rate for the vocational students (18 percent) and the rate for the regular classroom students (12 percent), it is the lowest (Thornburg, 1974c).

Further analysis of the data indicates that this special program was especially effective in reducing the dropout rate among minority students. The majority of the potential dropouuts studied came from three minority groups: Mexican-American, Indian, and black.

Analysis of the home environments and family backgrounds of these three groups revealed the following general characteristics: (1) The majority of youth from all three ethnic groups lived with both biological parents, although the diversity of parental structures was greater among Mexican Americans and blacks than among Indians. (2) The average number of children in their homes was excessive—Mexican-American, 6.2; Indian, 5.5; black, 8.3. (3) Black and Indian fathers' education represented all levels of attainment, from fewer than six years through college. Educational attainment was much lower among the Mexican-American group; 66 percent of the fathers had less than a sixth-grade education. (4) The same trends existed among the three groups for mothers' education. (5) More than 80 percent of the fathers' occupations among all three ethnic groups fell into skilled-, semiskilled-, or unskilled-worker classifications. (6) Most mothers stayed in the home, and approximately 33 percent from each minority group held some working-class occupation.

The variable of race should not be taken lightly. Studies repeatedly indicate that members of minority groups are more likely than Anglo students to drop out of school. In addition, the history of this Arizona high school in particular reflects a much higher incidence of attrition among minority members than among Anglos. It was concluded that this program was more effective in reducing the dropout rate among minorities than was the vocationally oriented program or the regular academic program.

A second experimental program aimed at potential dropouts is being carried on in a school in Ohio ("Xenia," 1972). Storefront School is held in an old apartment house. During 1972, its enrollment consisted of 15 students from one Ohio county. During the year before the project began, these 15 "turned-off" students had established a skimpy 45-percent average attendance record in their regular high school programs before dropping out altogether. Classes at Storefront run from 9 A.M. to noon, five days a week, and students have the option in the afternoon of either going back to their home school for classes or taking an independent-study course. About the only way to graphically measure Storefront's success up to this point is to compare attendance rates. Whereas afternoon attendance at the home school has dropped off to about 45 percent, Storefront's morning classes have been drawing about 85-percent attendance.

According to Storefront's teacher, there is no such thing as a typical dropout. He divides his students into three rough categories. "One is the low-income, keep-my-mouth-shut, not-really-interested-in-anything, in-school-because-somebody-says-I-should-be kind of kid. Another type is the average kid who likes to do things when he wants to and is in trouble every once in awhile. Then we have the interested intellectual, who gets disgusted with the kids on the other end who are here because somebody said they should be.

"These are kids who know what they want to do, but they resent authority and being treated like a second-class person," the instructor points out. "One of the boys was late getting back to the high school from lunch. He had his pass and was going directly to class when he was grabbed by a school person and accused of forging the pass. It's this feeling the kids get of not being trusted, of being harassed, being watched. Their way of fighting back is just dropping out or running away from it."

At Storefront, the whole approach is different. The students are doing basically the same things that the high school students are doing, but they are doing them in a different environment. They have turned their education into what is relevant to them rather than what is relevant to the teacher or the curriculum director.

"Acceptance" seems to be the key word at Storefront. "I think this is my strength right now," the school's teacher claims. "They know I'll accept anything they do as their own action. That doesn't mean that I'll accept it as what we all have to do. And they accept me as I am. I think that's the most important thing that we've done this year—learning to accept one another at face value."

CURRICULUM ALTERNATIVES

The experiment at Storefront was an attempt to attack some of the roots of the dropout problem. It also represents one type of curriculum alternative being tested in the high schools. There is extensive literature advocating curriculum innovations and alternatives for today's high schools. The recent demands by adolescents to have their school environment made more relevant has caused concerned educators to consider changes that could be made and that would function in the students' best interests. It once was contended that the school alone was the adolescent's avenue to learning, in which he or she could receive, through textbooks and classroom lectures, the wisdom and knowledge of the past. Today, youths may very well learn as much outside the classroom as inside it. They focus on life outside the classroom as their present and future world, and therefore they often consider their time in school to be meaningless.

Curriculum alternatives are one way in which the schools can respond to students' new needs. Fantini (1973) advances five criteria that he believes must be applied in choosing legitimate curriculum alternatives. They are:

1. Alternatives must be made available to students, teachers, and parents by choice. They cannot be superimposed.
2. They cannot claim the capacity to replace existing alternatives like the standard school. Premature claims of superiority, belittling the

worth of other alternatives, tend to create a negative political climate. The option is for those students, parents, and teachers who are *attracted* to it. The existing alternatives are just as legitimate as those being proposed.
3. They must give evidence of being geared to the attainment of a comprehensive set of educational objectives, those for which the public school is accountable, and not merely selected ones. Public schools are responsible for intellectual and emotional development. This includes development of such basic skills as reading, writing, speaking, and appreciating; learning-to-learn skills such as critical thinking, planning, problem solving; talent and career development; citizenship preparation; a positive feeling of self-worth; and the like.
4. They are not designed to promote exclusivity—racial, religious, or socioeconomic. Equal access must be available.
5. They are not dependent on significant amounts of extra money to implement and do not increase the per-student expenditures beyond those of established options. The idea is to utilize existing resources differently—perhaps more effectively [Fantini, 1973, p. 445].*

Gorman (1972), in stressing innovative change, has paralleled some of Fantini's contentions. Gorman recommends that an organizational structure be flexible enough to give teachers and students the opportunity for self-stimulation and stimulation by others. As he states, "In today's high school too much teacher time and too much student time is pre-empted by classes" (p. 567). In delineating necessary innovations, Gorman (1972) recommends four specific changes:

1. The high school must increase the routes to learning. Variety must replace the monotony of five 30-pupil classes per week in every subject.
2. Resource centers or work-study laboratories must play a greater role in the student's learning. These could be presided over by teacher aides, who would be responsible for securing teacher assistance as needed.
3. However widely believed, it is pure delusion that mass education must be forever and in all ways mass managed. Every student must have under way at any given time a project, problem, or investigation that he pursues individually, one that is uniquely his. This principle asks us to go only one step farther down the trail of individualization that the conscientious teacher has long traveled through assigning individual supplementary readings, compositions, and reports.
4. Assignments on which students labor must be much more frequently self-initiated or self-imposed. In other words, the student will be pursuing his own questions, providing much of his own motivation. The

*From "Alternatives within Public Schools," by M. Fantini, *Phi Delta Kappan*, 1973, 54(7), 445. Reprinted by permission.

teacher's ingenuity will be challenged and tested as he seeks to help the student find answers to his own questions. Something new will be learned every day, something that no one in that school knew the day before.

The movement toward independent study has been one of the most common innovations, although research by Alexander and Hines (1966) found such programs operating in fewer than one percent of the secondary schools. Feeling that training in independent study is crucial in helping the learner become self-directed, Alexander and Hines describe five patterns of independent study that they have found operating in the schools.

> *Independent study privileges or option.* This is a pattern in which independent study is optional, although encouraged and facilitated by scheduled time, for a large number of students, even the entire student population.
> *Individually programmed independent study.* In this pattern each member of some designated group is guided individually (but not tutored individually, as in tutorial instruction for achieving some norm) in planning and conducting a program of independent study related to his particular learning needs. This pattern sometimes uses programmed material.
> *Job-oriented independent study.* This pattern focuses independent study, as we defined it, on preparation for a particular job, vocation or career. This preparation may range from a semi-skilled occupation to graduate-level research in an academic discipline.
> *Seminars based on independent study.* In this pattern the seminar is more than a class by this name. It is a situation wherein students engaged in independent study can come together to share their reading, projects, or research findings.
> *"Quest-type" programs for development of special aptitudes.* This pattern includes a variety of independent study activities for students who work almost completely on their own in the exploration, extension, and refinement of special talents, aptitudes, and interests not necessarily related to career choices [Alexander & Hines, 1966, pp. 111–112].*

TEACHING RESPONSIBILITY FOR LEARNING

For some students, the implementation of curriculum alternatives has provided the kind of setting they need for growth. Highly individualistic and creative students, who feel stifled by regimentation and standards imposed upon them by more traditional schools, can to a large

*From "Independent Study in Secondary Schools," by W. M. Alexander and V. A. Hines, University of Florida Cooperative Research Project No. 2969, 1966. Reprinted by permission.

Teachers often require students to make oral presentations, an activity that draws upon the person's communications and social skills as well as his academic ones.

extent assume responsibility for the pursuit of education uniquely suited to them.

For other students, an academic program in which the teacher does not tell them what to do, what to learn, or how, is not sufficient. Many of these students, who achieve well under a traditional system, have been disturbed by the removal of external rewards they have been used to receiving for their academic competence and performance. One must remember that they have spent many years learning to make the system work for them, and the replacement of that system with a more innovative, more self-directed one has caused confusion, anxiety, and some resentment. These students are probably entitled to feel that resentment; for unless we can provide these students with alternative paths to success that take into account their desires for clarity, direction, and structure, we have replaced one dogmatism with another. It may be that the student who tells us that he *wants* to be told what to do, or that he *needs* for the teacher to have clear expectations of his work, can be taught eventually to be more a collaborator with the teacher than a conformer. But perhaps he will always feel most comfortable and be most productive with a great deal of direction. If so, he should have it, without loss of dignity.

In summary, we should keep in mind the results of the studies by Cawelti (1968), Coleman (1961,1965), Friesen (1968), Leidy and Starry (1967), and others, which emphasize that the school's social environment is more important than its academic environment for most of today's high school students. Coleman has made an interesting observation about curriculum in relation to this problem:

> It is obvious that the content of the curriculum is a responsibility of the school, and that it will affect the education a child receives. It is less obvious, but no less true, that the standards and values current among the students are primarily the responsibility of the school and do affect the education a child receives. The failure to incorporate an attention to student values in a formal philosophy of education means that each high school principal is on his own. If he is perceptive and imaginative and constantly alert, he can, along with his teachers, incline these peer-group standards toward educational goals. If the principal does not take interest or action, he leaves the molding of standards to the teenagers themselves, as well as their absorption in those activities that happen to catch their attention [Coleman, 1965, p. 34].

"Those activities that happen to catch their attention" are usually social. What alternatives to maintaining a social environment do today's educators have? Howard (1966) suggests that they develop student responsibility for learning. Previous attempts to do so have been limited to organizational innovations such as flexible scheduling, extracurricular activities, and independent study. Howard proposes a basic concept, based on psychological principles, that will give the student some choices in what he will learn. Howard describes three specific subconcepts within his concept of student choice.

1. *Content options.* The student is presented with enough optional and alternative learning situations to enable him to choose the material that is most appropriate for his interests and needs.
2. *Time options.* Students will grow in their ability to assume responsibility if they have some control over how fast they learn. Allowing a student to set his own learning pace provides him with incentive to become interested in a topic and to pursue it in depth.
3. *Facility and personnel options.* Students should have some opportunity to decide where they work, what materials they need, and what faculty assistance they desire.

Howard's appeal to reject a standard curriculum and traditional methods of instruction places a great deal of responsibility on the learner.

Yet, if we consider (1) the impact that socialization in school has on today's youths, (2) the de-emphasis on the academics in lieu of social activities, and (3) the fact that one out of three students drops out of school, Howard's ideas do not seem so far advanced in our society. We need to provide our adolescents with a program that emphasizes intellectual activities. Perhaps the challenge to the school can be simply stated: "The adolescent intellect deserves more respect and greater expectations" (Johnson, 1965, p. 204).

The adolescent who has negative feelings toward his education will find it difficult to adjust to policies and behave as expected within his school system. His difficulties are often increased when the curriculum is not diversified enough to meet the range of his needs. A more diversified curriculum and increased teacher interest in students alleviate only part of the problem. Educators must promote an environment that lends itself to self-generated student thinking and responsibility. It is the school's task to stimulate the adolescent, to build his self-respect and confidence through granting him responsible freedom, and to offer him opportunities to experience satisfaction and success in his academic work.

Cultural Variations in Adolescence 9

Adolescents, like all people, live in a cultural context, and their learning and development are affected by the practices of the dominant culture, of specific subcultures, and of the recent phenomenon called the counterculture. This chapter will focus on the specific attributes of several variations on the dominant culture that exist in the United States and on how they affect adolescents.

CULTURE

Culture may be thought of as the sum total of the knowledge, beliefs, morals, customs, and ideologies acquired by a member of a society. These cultural constituents provide the basis for interactions and relationships among members of society. The types of cultural attributes most familiar to people are those overt behaviors of an individual that reveal the effects the culture has had upon him. These overt behaviors represent the internal attitudinal state of the individual.

Humans define their culture through their interactive processes. Of necessity, humans learn about their culture through association with others; therefore, it is appropriate to say that culture is socially created, not instinctively determined. Culture is socially shared as well. Individuals collect into groups or social units in order to share, and be reinforced for approximating, culturally acceptable behaviors. In order for culture to be attractive to individuals, desired goals or incentives to seek higher goals must be made available, and individuals must be rewarded for seeking them. Thus, modes of social action have come to meet individual needs. Integrating the elements of one's culture into one's personality allows the social being to emerge and function well within his social-cultural context.

SUBCULTURE

A *subculture* may be defined as a distinctive pattern of shared values, behaviors, and ideologies manifested in a style of life significantly different from that of the dominant culture and from those of other subcultures. Zurcher (1972) indicates that the label of "subculture" has been applied to such various aggregates as delinquents, suburbanites, prison inmates, blue-collar workers, hippies, poor people, and drug users. Some aspects of subculture to be dealt with in this chapter are further defined here.

Race. Some misunderstanding surrounds the term *race*; people attach social and political meaning to it, although, in its strictest sense, it refers only to biological characteristics. Common distinguishing racial features include skin pigmentation, head shape, stature, facial features, and the color, distribution, and texture of body hair (Haring, 1957). Within the three primary racial types, Caucasoid, Mongoloid, and Negroid, there are more than 30 variations.

Functionally, the implications of racial distinctiveness are determined to a considerable extent by the dictates of the society. When no distinct cultural value is placed upon race, one's racial membership is of little significance; but, since our society is race conscious (Triandis, 1971), most racial groups that vary from the dominant culture are relegated to an inferior status.

Ethnic group. MacIver and Page (1949) view *ethnic groups* as formed on the bases of real and assumed physiological traits and of national and regional group traditions. These traditions are passed on from generation to generation and may be expressed through family life-styles, language, religion, or other customs unique to the particular group. In our society, the extent of a group's ethnicity is determined by the attitudes of the dominant society as much as by the distinctiveness of the ethnic group itself. If the group attempts to approximate the dominant society, ethnicity may be reduced and acceptance increased. On the other hand, wide divergence from the primary culture may lock the divergent group into a less acceptable social position.

Minority. The term *minority* has been used to refer to those groups whose members share racial or ethnic traits divergent from the traits of the dominant group and that are consequently treated differently (Wirth, 1945). "Minority" is a term more generally applied than "race" or "ethnic group." It is also a more relative term. What constitutes a minority group in one country or region may be the dominant group in another country or region. In the United States, the dominant (majority) group has traditionally defined social norms and, in turn, assigns the degree of acceptance for each minority group. Recent years have seen the emergence of minorities vocally demanding recognition, often violating the rules and roles assigned to them by the dominant group.

Social class. *Social-class* distinctions involve the assignment of rank and privilege to some individuals and of disdain and restriction to others (Bernard, 1970). Social class is assigned to both adults and adolescents according to their associations, socioeconomic status, education, organizational memberships, use of leisure time, values, and neighborhood, and according to the quality of their personal possessions such as clothes, works of art, and jewelry.

Lower social class is assigned to most minority people in the United States, since their lives are characterized by low income, poor housing, inadequate living space, inadequate education, high unemployment rates, and feelings of powerlessness and hopelessness.

COUNTERCULTURE

Recent years have seen the emergence of the *counterculture,* a group affiliation that stands in opposition to the cultural norms and values prevalent within the dominant culture (Denhardt & Allen, 1971) or regards them as irrelevant. It has been most attractive to those youth whose values are diametrically opposed to those of the mainstream culture. Countercultures differ from subcultures in that subcultures are living units within the pluralistic society, whereas countercultures are made up of youths who, regardless of subculture membership, set themselves apart from the adult culture. If the present counterculture can be said to have a conscious purpose, it is to introduce conflict and thus precipitate social change. It is likely that counterculture affiliation in part serves the identity-striving motive so crucial to youth. Although the counterculture's importance as a social unit cannot be overlooked, its parameters are more nebulous than those of the other culture forms discussed here. Therefore, we will discuss the counterculture in detail in Chapter 13.

CROSSCULTURE

The term *crossculture* is popularly used in comparisons of youth in the United States with youth of any other country. This use of the term is often innaccurate, for *crosscultural* in its strict sense refers to a comparison of a Western culture with an Eastern culture. Studies of cultural variations among youth focus either on (1) regional differences between groups of youth who are part of the Western world—for example, differences between Australian and American youth—or on (2) crosscultural differences between youth of the Western world and youth of the Eastern world—for example, differences between young people in Thailand and young people in America.

The world's youth must be thought of as a generation exposed to certain common conditions and experiences. However, in order to analyze the motivational basis for any one group of youth's activities, we must give some thought to their social stratum, social context, and ideologies (Rosenmayr, 1972). The political and economic systems under which adolescents live and the primary ways in which they are socialized determine to a considerable extent the standard of normality for youth and the necessary adjustments youth must make in order to be acceptable to that standard (Backman & Finlay, 1973).

In 1940, Kingsley Davis delineated three reasons for generational conflict in Western societies:

1. The differences between the content of experiences for youth and that of their parents when they were young
2. The lack of clearly defined steps or cultural events indicating an increase in adolescent autonomy and a decrease in parental authority
3. The psychological and sociological differences between youth and parents—youths' imagination as opposed to parents' experience, and youths' need for independent behaviors versus parents' role as supervisor of children

Since 1940, American society has changed vastly, primarily through advanced technology and the communications media. In addition, American psychologists were not then so concerned with regional or crosscultural differences among youths as sociologists are today. Now, the mass media have brought the world's youths before us all. This change was made especially clear during the 1960s, when attempts to explain unrest among the youth of the United States compared it with the unrest among other young people around the world.

One example of the Western world's influence on Eastern youths comes from Thailand. Youth problems there possess striking similarities to those in Western countries—in particular, social protest characterized by violence and sensation. Sasidhorn (1970) suggests that this similarity is mainly due to imitation. The press, radio, television, and films constantly show Thai youths how their Western counterparts protest against society. Sasidhorn also points out that dress modes and criminal behaviors are likewise directly imitated through media exposure of the Western world.

One of the results of global communication has been that the universality of youth's behavior has become more evident during the last ten years. Most nations have become conscious of the problems youths face and cause. Consideration of youths' problems of adjustment to modern living conditions—increasing unemployment, the special problems of disadvantaged youths, the increase in delinquency, the lack of relevance of school experiences, increased political and social involvement, protests, and challenges to authority figures—reveals that the behavior of young people has more importance than at any other time in modern history (Zygulski, 1972).

CULTURALLY DIFFERENT YOUTH IN A PLURALISTIC SOCIETY

Today's adolescents find themselves caught in the web of *cultural pluralism*. Our nation is made up of several smaller units that have developed and retained a culture peculiar to themselves. At the same time that individuals need to participate in the economic and political systems of the larger society, they attempt to maintain the beliefs and behaviors unique to their subculture. In a truly pluralistic society, the person who feels divided loyalties in his attempts to conform to both cultural systems would be free to maintain full membership in his subculture and also to participate in any or all facets of the dominant culture. There is some question whether a truly pluralistic society has yet emerged in the United States.

Havighurst has suggested that minority groups, especially blacks, Chicanos, Puerto Ricans, Indians, and Southeastern Europeans, are demanding a combination of (1) the opportunities to earn money and become educated through the common economy and public-supported education and (2) the right to maintain their own cultural identity and to be respected for this identity. In this sense, he sees cultural pluralism as:

1. Mutual appreciation and understanding of the various cultures in the society
2. Cooperation of the various groups in the civic and economic institutions of the society
3. Peaceful coexistence of diverse life-styles, folkways, manners, language patterns, religious beliefs, and family structures
4. Autonomy for each subcultural group to work out its own social future, as long as it does not interfere with the same right for other groups*

*From "The American Indian: From Assimilation to Cultural Pluralism" by R. L. Havighurst, *Educational Leadership*, 1974, *31*(8), 587.

For years, the member of a subculture or minority group in the United States has been marginal to the dominant society. He or she is, as Stonequist expressed it:

posed in psychological uncertainty between two (or more) social worlds; reflecting in his soul the discords and harmonies, repulsions and attractions of these worlds, one of which is often "dominant" over the other; within which membership is implicitly if not explicitly based on birth or ancestry [Stonequist, 1937, p. 8].

Minority status has been found to intensify already existing group identity, or to actually create it, in cases when individuals rally as a result of discrimination. Because they have been forced to live in particular locations and associate with one another, members of subcultures have become communities, feeling an allegiance and a sense of responsibility to one another (Lewin, 1941; Rothman, 1962). Goldberg has viewed the individual with marginal existence in the following way:

If (1) the so-called "marginal" individual is conditioned to his existence on the borders of two cultures from birth, if (2) he shares the existence and conditioning process with a large number of individuals in his primary groups, if (3) his years of early growth, maturation, and even adulthood find him participating in institutional activities manned largely by other "marginal" individuals like himself, and finally, if (4) his marginal position results in no major blockages or frustrations of his learned expectations and desires, then he is not a true "marginal" individual in the defined sense, but is a participant member of a *marginal* culture, every bit as real and complete to him as is the nonmarginal culture to the nonmarginal man [Goldberg, 1941, p. 52].

Marginality, and the discrimination that accompanies it, stand in opposition to the myth that America is the great "melting pot" of the world. Although it is true that there are more divergent groups in America than in any other country in the world (Rose, 1964), this ideal has been an illusion for most of the ethnic groups in the United States, especially for those groups that have not been assimilated into mainstream America. For the most part, these groups have remained uneducated, undernourished, in poor health, and marginal to the society. The 1960s saw many of these groups emerge in reaction because they no longer believed in the myth and were no longer content to live by its ideology. Thus these groups created new symbols around which the young rallied with minimal interference from their parents. To a varying extent, older members of these groups are willing, along with the younger members, to express their discontent and to refuse to accept social discrimination.

Kardiner and Ovesey (1962) established a model (see Figure 9.1) showing the effects of social discrimination on the American black. This model seems applicable to other minority groups as well. Kardiner and Ovesey state that the human personality organizes itself around the need to adapt. As is illustrated in Figure 9.1, a person's self-esteem is usually

Minority adolescents sometimes face more learning difficulties in school than their Anglo peers.

low if he consistently perceives an unpleasant image of himself from the behavior of others toward him. The authors explain their diagram as follows:

> In the center of this adaptational scheme stand the low self-esteem (the self-referential part) and the aggression (the reactive part). The rest are maneuvers with these main constellations, to prevent their manifestation, to deny them and the sources from which they come, to make things look different from what they are, to replace aggressive activity which would be socially disastrous with more acceptable ingratiation and passivity. Keeping this system going means, however, being constantly ill at ease, mistrustful, and lacking in confidence.
>
> This is the adaptational range that is prescribed by the caste situation. This is, however, only a skeletal outline. Many types of elaboration are possible, particularly along projective or compensatory lines. For example, the low self-esteem can be projected as follows:

Low self-esteem = self-contempt → idealization of the white → hostility to whites

Frantic efforts to be white = unattainable

introjected white ideal → self-hatred → projected onto other Negroes = hatred of Negroes

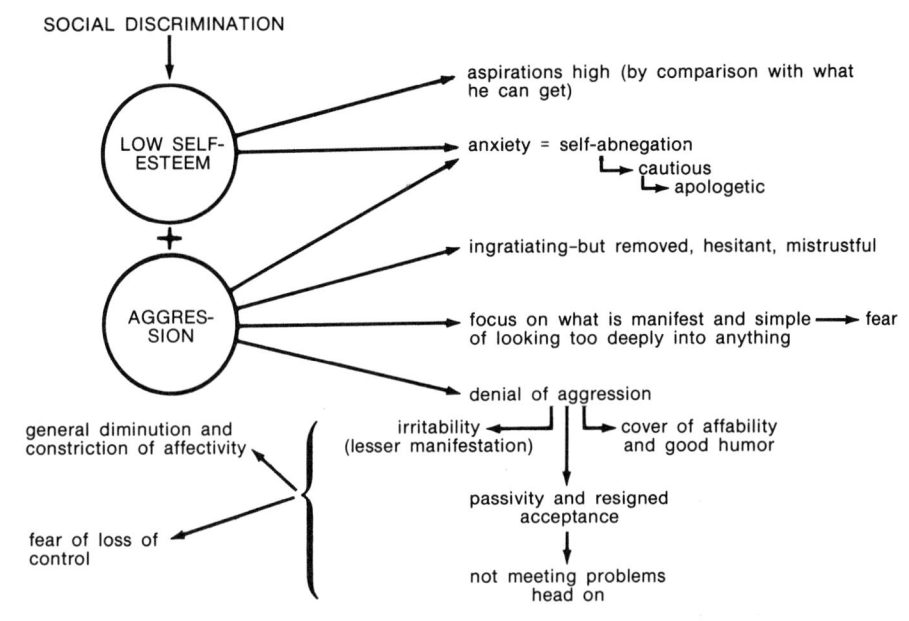

```
SOCIAL DISCRIMINATION
        │
        ▼
   ┌─────────┐ ────────► aspirations high (by comparison with what
   │  LOW SELF-│              he can get)
   │  ESTEEM  │ ────────► anxiety = self-abnegation
   └─────────┘                    └► cautious
        +                              └► apologetic
   ┌─────────┐ ────────► ingratiating-but removed, hesitant, mistrustful
   │ AGGRES- │
   │  SION   │ ────────► focus on what is manifest and simple ──► fear
   └─────────┘           of looking too deeply into anything
                 ────────► denial of aggression
```

FIGURE 9.1. The effects of social discrimination. From *Mark of Oppression* by A. Kardiner and L. Ovesey. © 1962. Reprinted by permission.

The low self-esteem can also mobilize compensations in several forms: (1) apathy, (2) hedonism, (3) living for the moment, (4) criminality.

The disposition of aggression is similarly susceptible to elaboration. The conspicuous feature of rage lies in the fact that it is an emotion that primes the organism for motor expression. Hate is an attenuated form of rage, and is the emotion toward those who inspire fear and rage. The difficult problem for those who are constantly subject to frustration is how to contain this emotion and prevent its overt expression. The chief motive for the latter is to avoid setting in motion retaliatory aggression.

The most immediate effect of rage is, therefore, to set up a fear of its consequences. Fear and rage become almost interchangeable. When the manifestations of rage are continually suppressed, ultimately the individual may cease to be aware of the emotion. In some subjects the *only* manifestation of rage may be fear.

The techniques for disposing of rage are varied. The simplest disposition is to suppress it and replace it with another emotional attitude—submission or compliance. The greater the rage, the more abject the submission. Thus, scraping and bowing, compliance and ingratiation may actually be indicators of suppressed rage and sustained hatred. Rage can be kept under control but replaced with an attenuated but sustained feeling—resentment. It may be kept under control, but ineffectively, and show itself in irritability. It may be kept under sustained control for long periods, and then become explosive. Rage may show itself in subtle forms of ingratiation for purposes of exploitation. It may finally be denied altogether (by an automatic process) and replaced by an entirely different kind of expression, like laughter, gaiety, or flippancy [Kardiner & Ovesey, 1962, pp. 77–78].*

There is no question that today's disadvantaged youth find themselves struggling to maintain identity both within their own culture and within mainstream culture. Perhaps the more successful any single minority group is in achieving some national image, the better this pluralistic role can be realized. The true realization of the "American dream" would give those living in a marginal existence freedom of choice to participate—or not to participate—in the dominant culture.

THE LOWER-CLASS MILIEU

More than 50 percent of the United States population falls into the economic category of lower class (by definition, the lowest third economically); the estimates run from 25 to 40 percent for the upper-lower class and from 15 to 25 percent for the lower-lower class (Havighurst & Neugarten, 1967). These individuals often experience feelings of oppression, disruption, powerlessness, and stress (Dodson, 1967). Many are without work and dependent upon public assistance. Their lack of economic resources means that they have little or no control over important parts of their lives. To a considerable extent, their work, housing, and economic assistance are arbitrarily administered by those who are more fortunate.

The lower class's educational achievement is also a limiting factor. There is evidence to show that lower-class youth score lower on intelligence tests and in classroom achievement, factors that may be partially caused by negative attitudes toward school and learning. Because these youth never can fully realize most of the middle-class goals, aspirations, and values placed before them, their marginality to the dominant culture is reinforced (Lever & Upham, 1968).

There are more matriarchally based homes among the lower class than among the middle class. These family units are usually extended, and thus the socialization of children is a responsibility shared by several relatives and older siblings in addition to the mother. To some extent, this structure breeds stronger family relationships than does that of middle-class homes, where the family head, often authoritarian, delineates all functions and activities of the home (Clausen, 1966).

There are also trends toward earlier sexual permissiveness and

*From *Mark of Oppression* by A. Kardiner and L. Ovesey. © 1962. Reprinted by permission.

marriages among the lower class, although the sexual encounters are more casual and less binding, and there is a high incidence of separation between parents and of abandonment by the father. Whereas for the middle class marriage and procreation in marriage are important social practices, these standards are less applicable to the economically limited lower class. Sensual orientation, demands for immediate gratification, and a pervading sense that most of what one has is tied to the immediate family circle are all factors that cause larger families and perpetuate the tradition of early marriage.

Lower-class people can be found in the ghettos of cities, in the slums of smaller towns, and in rural areas; they are concentrated in poverty pockets such as Appalachia, in the fields of labor designed for migrant workers, and in specially designated reservation areas such as those set aside by the federal government for Indians. They tend to have little feeling of personal identity, to be transient and unstable, and to perceive themselves as always subject to the will of other men or of God. The effects that such attitudes have on adolescents growing up under these circumstances will be dealt with in the following discussion of certain lower-class groups in America: Puerto Ricans, Appalachian whites, migrant workers, Indians, Mexican Americans, and blacks.

PUERTO RICANS

The Puerto Ricans are densely concentrated in several large cities. They represent about 16 percent of the population of New York City. They are of mixed racial origin and are Spanish speaking. They initially immigrated to the United States from an overcrowded and economically destitute island. However, their plight was improved little through moving into areas like New York City, where they congregated in Spanish Harlem. Their movement into the larger cities was headed by those who lived in the cities of Puerto Rico, whereas the island's rural residents tended to immigrate to the western United States.

Puerto Rican adolescents have one distinct advantage that their immigrant Mexican counterparts do not have—citizenship. Still, this advantage compensates little for their substandard housing, marginal incomes, and low-status jobs, and for the discrimination they suffer. Nevertheless, they are qualitatively different from several other groups. They are a highly literate group; more than 50 percent living in Puerto Rico know English (Rose, 1964). They are proud and have a history of avoiding federal assistance as much as they can. In Chicago, for example, most Puerto Ricans are self-supporting. Although their environments are limiting, they have good adjustive skills, making the most of their situations. These factors influence the Puerto Rican adolescent to strive for living improvements, more education, and better employment; therefore, there is continued movement among these youths to enhance themselves within their families and social environments.

APPALACHIAN WHITES

The Appalachian Mountain regions include all or part of nine states of the southeastern United States. Here millions of poor white people live; well over 1 million are unemployed. Behind its protective mountains, Appalachia has not kept pace with the rest of America, and its people have been subject to a marginal existence. More than one-third of the Appalachian people have an income of less than $3000, and about 15 percent have less than a fifth-grade education. In the 1960s, the people of Appalachia called for federal help with flood control, highway construction, and education. The first two concerns were partially met; the third was ignored (Schrag, 1971).

The mountain people are highly isolated and typically suspicious and resistant to outside help. They tend not to become involved in community affairs. Because of their subsistence living patterns, they are not education oriented; they often send their children to school only on the days when they are not needed at home.

Stevic and Uhlig (1967) have suggested several reasons for nonacceptance of change in the Appalachian area. First, as long as coal was "king," men felt little need to seek new occupational areas. Father and adolescent son went together to the coal mine because the supply of workers never quite kept up with the demand for skilled miners. Second, since a family could live fairly well under the "protection" of the coal mine owner-operator, the miner felt no need or desire to look elsewhere. The owner-operator provided housing, food, clothing, work, schools, church, and social life. Third, the mine owner may not have always wanted the miner to know about other occupational opportunities, since he needed the miner and his strong-bodied sons. He also needed the fertile women of Appalachia to bear sons and daughters to perpetuate his supply of laborers. This staggering dependency relationship, fostered by the company-store concept, accepted by the miners, and promoted by the owners, has brought about many of the present occupational problems and much hopelessness among adolescents in Appalachia.

In investigating the occupational choices most desired by 965 students in five southeastern Kentucky high schools, Stevic and Uhlig (1967) found that low-paying and low-ranking jobs were the most commonly chosen. These included the jobs of filling-station attendant, truck driver, machine operator in factory, and farm hand. In contrast, the higher-status jobs named in the study were not selected. These included the jobs of minister, county judge, owner of business, and airplane pilot. Although coal mining is indigenous to Appalachia, most adolescents preferred not to become miners. They also rejected menial jobs such as garbage collector, street sweeper, and shoe shiner, feeling that unemployment relief was more desirable. Since occupational knowledge and opportunities are quite limited in Appalachia, perhaps the desired occupational choices reported by these adolescents were realistic, although they do not approximate the typical middle-class aspiration level.

MIGRANT WORKERS

Migrant workers are represented by many different minority groups, and, because their numbers are small, they have neither roots nor leverage. Migrant workers are truly the lost minorities of America. Blacks, Mexican Americans, "wetback" Mexicans (immigrant Mexicans who do not seek citizenship), and poor whites make up most migrants. Since their work is seasonal, they move with it; they are forced to live in dilapidated housing, move their children from school to school, and neglect their health and nutrition; and they have virtually no income. They are without question the lowest paid and most poorly educated people in the United States.

Children who grow up in these homes become caught in a self-perpetuating cycle. Having minimal skills and education, they are in no position to effect change; neither do they have the motivation. However, they do have family unity. Those migrant workers who live in the United States may make even less money today than they did ten years ago, due to automation and cheap illegal labor. The extreme exploitation of wetback Mexicans in southern Texas and California is an example.

Children of migrant workers often work in the fields with their parents. They have limited educational opportunities and, when they are in a school for a short time, are faced with strong teacher and pupil biases against them. Having no viable alternatives to this situation, they withdraw from education and the world, back into their migrant environment where their energies are exploited and their talents unrealized.

INDIANS

Ralph Nader (1968) put the plight of the American Indians in perspective. He described how, in 1849, the Bureau of Indian Affairs (BIA) was established in the Department of the Interior for the purpose of improving the life of the Indian. However, under the Bureau's direction, the Indians' land shrank from 150 million to 53 million acres. The Indians became wards of the United States government in 1871; they were culturally devastated and physically abused, often to the point of death, and they became entwined in the most intricate web of bureaucratic regulations ever inflicted anywhere in this nation's history. Nader stated:

> In the meantime, the BIA has prospered, growing to its present size of approximately 16,000 employees providing services of a federal, state, and local government in one administrative bundle. Together with smaller programs in Indian health (under the Public Health Service) and antipoverty programs (in OEO), current fiscal year appropriations for Indians totaled about $60 million or an average income per reservation family of some $5600 if paid out in cash. The (actual) average family income is $1500 per annum [Nader, 1968, p. 89].

The last few years have seen an increase in militancy among Indian youth because of increasing awareness of the injustice still being done to them. The greatest militancy has occurred among Indian young people who have left their reservation areas and moved into cities like Denver, Chicago, Los Angeles, and Minneapolis. Some intertribal relationships and political and intellectual ferment occur among these urban Indian youth, who are not bound by reservation restrictions and are not so inclined to perpetuate the Indian culture that dominates reservation life. These youth are so few in number, however, that it is questionable what impact they may have in helping the cause of all American Indians.

There is still a strong adherence to the old Indian ways on most reservations. Even on reservations where young Indians have been given greater responsibilities, such as the Zuñi and Hopi, reservation policies are still tempered by the older Indians, who strive to maintain the distinctiveness of their cultures. It is on reservation land that Indians live in the poorest housing and have the poorest sanitary conditions and lowest incomes, and reservation land has minimal production potential.

Indian children and adolescents may be bused to schools off the reservation or may live in reservation boarding schools. Because the public-school structure is not very adaptive to the Indian student's needs, he learns minimal skills and is often socially isolated in that environment. Indian students have low reading levels, tend to score poorly on intelligence and achievement tests, and usually show lower levels of achievement than their Anglo counterparts. Their levels of various types of school achievement are often lower than those of other minority youth (Thornburg, 1974c).

Two-thirds of American Indians live on reservations; most of these are in the southwestern United States. Youths from these reservations are taught so well by their parents to maintain their cultural heritage and distinctiveness that they are more reluctant to move into mainstream America than are youths from other minority groups. Therefore, it is extremely important to Indian adolescents that our society become truly pluralistic; only then will their plight take an upward turn.

As is often the case, differences between Indian children and youth and their middle-class counterparts are more perceived than real. Robeck (1971) found this to be true in research comparing children on the Umatilla Indian Reservation in Oregon with white children. Like those of other Indian tribes, children on the Umatilla Indian Reservation have a higher dropout rate than white Americans, whether they attend public or reservation schools. On a national average, Indians are more disadvantaged educationally than black or Chicano children. Even when Indian children remain in school, the achievement gap between them and white children becomes greater with each successive grade. Robeck's study compares the learning potential of Indian and white children attending the same kindergarten classes and given the same opportunities to learn communication skills.

Robeck hypothesized that (1) Indian and white children would show no significant differences in their abilities to learn preprimary skills in association, conceptualization, and self-direction, and that (2) English-speaking Indian children would not show significant differences from their white classmates in listening and speaking abilities.

Umatilla and white kindergartners of Washington School in Pendleton, Oregon were taught the *KELP* (Kindergarten Evaluation of Learning Potential) items and scored on their ability to reach criterion performance at three levels: association learning, conceptualization, and creative self-direction. Mean differences between the groups were analyzed for total achievement and for levels of learning on *KELP*. English functioning was analyzed for understanding of directions, expression of ideas, language-learning potential, and nonverbal performance.

Both of Robeck's conjectures were confirmed. (1) Results showed no significant differences between the Indian and white kindergartners on school activities that required association learning, conceptualization, or creative self-direction, and no differences appeared based on teacher observation of learning potential. (2) Indian children scored significantly higher on tasks that demonstrated their understanding of the teacher's oral instructions than did the white children on the same items, and the Indian children's scores on oral understanding were higher than their scores on expressing ideas in English. A paper-and-pencil test given to all of the subjects at the end of the year (the *KELP* Summary Test Booklet) confirmed the kindergarten teacher's observations. This study suggests that environmental factors, rather than learning potential, account for much of the disparity between Indian and white children in school achievement.

MEXICAN AMERICANS

The typical family unit within the Mexican-American pluralistic culture is nuclear, and the strength of family bonds completely overshadows all other bonds in importance. The essential social unit comprises the parents, the children, and the parents' brothers and sisters. The mother's sisters are of particular significance.

In its authority structure, the Mexican-American family is highly traditional. Family authority within the nuclear unit is invested in the father, as primary breadwinner; the family structure is clearly patriarchal, with the female playing an ancillary role. This tradition characterizes the Mexican-American family as it does the Mexican family.

The structure of the mainstream American family was altered by the elimination of subordinate kinship roles in the early 1900s, leaving father, mother, and child as the components of the nuclear family. By 1930, social change had caused the family's structure to evolve from patriarchal to democratic, the role of the wife moving up in status. At the same time, there was a rapid influx in the Mexican-American population through birthrate increases and immigration. Since Mexican Americans are marginal to mainstream American culture, however, they made no attempt to adopt new family-structural roles but, rather, perpetuated the patriarchal structure within the nuclear family.

The last two or three decades have seen some movement within the Mexican-American family toward a less patriarchal structure. Many mothers are abandoning their self-effacing role for a stronger voice in the home, primarily because they are gaining greater familiarity with alternative roles and working in increasing numbers. Urbanization is another factor working to change the Mexican-American family structure; in many urban families, the restrictions placed on women and children may vary little from those placed on their Anglo counterparts. In fact, Derbyshire's (1968) studies of Mexican-American families in the Los Angeles barrios concluded that the patriarchal structure and the male strength and dominance that accompany it exist only because the female feels it best to play the subordinate role. "Females frequently verbalize dissatisfaction with their husband's and father's position in the family but give and promote family respect out of deference to his loss of status in Anglo culture" (Derbyshire, 1968, p. 77).

Patella (1971) examined the living and work patterns of some 600 families in Texas. She was unable to consistently support her hypothesis that the Mexican-American subculture is male oriented, with the father having full responsibility for supporting the family. Whereas the males examined perceived the situation thus, Patella's female sample failed to support the idea. In her sample, about one-third of the Mexican-American women were either working or looking for work—a factor that may partially explain these results. Her study reflects considerably greater female interest in working than does my study (Thornburg, 1974c), which found 20 percent of the females working. The latter study was done in rural Arizona, where work opportunities are limited. Nevertheless it still reflected a percentage much lower than the percentages of Anglo (50 percent), black (36 percent), and Indian (33 percent) working mothers found in the same study.

The Mexican-American male has some difficulty extending his dominant family role into his work role. In fact, he finds himself in a subservient role comparable to the one in which he places his wife and children. Heller (1966) believes that the socialization processes imposed by the Mexican-American father are not conducive to the development of the capacities needed within our industrialized society. She feels that the Mexican-American father stresses family ties, honor, masculinity, and immediate gratification to the exclusion of more successful (middle-class) values such as achievement and independence and the ability to defer gratification.

It is interesting to speculate how much the change in sex roles among middle-class Americans may affect Mexican-American sex roles. Two points should be considered. First, since there is no evidence that the Mexican-American male has made any inroads into mainstream America, we must conclude that his role today is still primarily a marginal one. Second, since the most significant sex-role change in middle-class American society is taking place among females, some change is also occurring among Mexican-American women, although not to the same extent. The Mexican-American woman often supplements her husband's salary today. This change affects the self-effacing role she has often played in the past. She is more decisive in financial management and other family matters. In many homes, this greater freedom exercised by the mother facilitates greater independence in the children. However, since the cultural roles for women and children in Mexican-American society are distinctly different from those in mainstream American society, it would be erroneous to assume that the changes taking place in the lives of working Mexican-American mothers are qualitatively the same as those occurring in the lives of middle-class American women in general. Their apparent greater freedom may be superficial.

In some instances, the male children of a household resent their mother's employment. Being reared in the image of his father, the adolescent boy's masculinity (*machismo*) is threatened by his mother's working. Research evidence indicates that having a working mother often causes boys to be alienated from their subcultural peers. This problem does not exist among girls, who have no *machismo* ethic to uphold. The adolescent boy's problem may be further compounded if the father is unemployed, although such a case is often viewed to be an uncontrollable circumstance and therefore poses no real threat to the father's status as head of the household.

Mexican-American Youth and Education

Although increasing numbers of Mexican-American youth are staying in school, it is still true that, in the southwestern United States, the dropout rate is higher among them than among other minority and Anglo youth. One-sixth of the school-age population in the five southwestern states is Spanish-speaking; yet the dropout rates for each grade level among this segment of the population are much higher than among non-Spanish speakers. Research in the Dallas area found the Mexican-American dropout rate between fifth grade and twelfth grade to be 79 percent (Ulibarri, 1972); a California study showed 50 percent dropping out by eighth grade and an additional 25 percent dropping out in high school (Manuel, 1965); and a rural Arizona study showed the Mexican-American high school dropout rate to exceed 50 percent (Thornburg, 1974c).

Unquestionably, one reason for this high dropout rate is the persistent failure and underachievement of Mexican-American children throughout their formal school years. Research in California found 64 percent of the Mexican-American students to be below average in reading, compared with 27 percent of the Anglos. A Civil Rights Commission Report (U.S. Commission, 1972) found that almost 50 percent of the Mexican-American students tested were performing three years below grade level. The previously mentioned Arizona study found the mean reading level of students entering high school to be at the 5.2 grade-placement level. Similarly, the Dallas study demonstrated that more than half of the Mexican-American high school graduates there read below ninth-grade level. Information on arithmetic achievement places 39 percent below grade level and, on language achievement, 56 percent below grade level. The profile on Mexican-American youths in Arizona on the Academic Promise Test, which measures math and language abilities, placed 72 percent of the 123 students below the twentieth percentile.

When Mexican-American children enter school, they are bilingual, bicultural, and often alienated from the larger society. The Civil Rights Commission Report indicates that 47 percent of Mexican-

American first graders do not speak English as well as the average Anglo first grader. The state-by-state percentages are: Arizona, 30; California, 36; Colorado, 27; New Mexico, 36; Texas, 62. Furthermore, Table 9.1, which is adapted from the Civil Rights Commission Report, indicates the extent to which these southwestern states' schools discourage the use of Spanish.

TABLE 9.1. Percentage of schools in southwestern states that discourage use of Spanish in secondary school classes.

Arizona	29.4
California	18.2
Colorado	46.4
New Mexico	32.1
Texas	66.7
Southwest	39.2

From *The Excluded Student, Report III.* U.S. Commission on Civil Rights, 1972.

The problem is further compounded by the fact that the schools are very limited in their attempts to offer bilingual education, as can be seen in Table 9.2. The commission estimated that, of the nearly 1.1 million Chicanos enrolled in school in the five states, only 29,000 were involved in bilingual programs. It is evident that public-school norms make these students appear academically inferior and, consequently, encourage them to drop out of school.

The problem cannot be resolved by the school alone; furthermore, the schools have shown little willingness to actively attack it.

TABLE 9.2. Percentage of schools offering bilingual education and the percent of Mexican-American pupils enrolled in bilingual education classes, by state.

State	Percentage of schools	Percentage of Mexican-American pupils enrolled
Arizona	0*	0*
California	8.5	1.7
Colorado	2.9	.7
New Mexico	4.7	.9
Texas	5.9	5.0
Southwest	6.5	2.7

*Less than one-half of 1 percent.
From *The Excluded Student, Report III,* U.S. Commission on Civil Rights, 1972.

Research by Anderson and Evans (1973) indicates that an increase in the amount of English spoken at home is likely to improve the child's achievement at school. Another study, by Keele (1973), found that students who were tutored by Mexican-American school aides significantly increased their reading ability.These results suggest that perhaps the most crucial variable affecting Mexican-American achievement is the extent to which Spanish is spoken in the schools, not the extent to which English is spoken in the homes. Considering the fact that more than 50 percent of the Mexican-American secondary-school students attend schools that are composed predominantly of their own ethnic group, it seems most appropriate that the curricula be designed with Mexican Americans—the *majority* group—in mind. Observation of school programs fails to reveal any school programs that are designed for Mexican Americans, regardless of their minority status or predominance within the school. Comparative research in two rural Arizona high schools, one of which had a Mexican-American enrollment of 35 percent and the other of 56 percent, indicated that these students in both schools were comparable in reading ability, intelligence, and grade placement.

Another major problem is that Mexican-American youths are commonly given fewer advantages by teachers than are their Anglo counterparts. Jackson and Cosca (1973), for example, sampled 494 classrooms (188 in Texas, 171 in California, and 135 in New Mexico) to determine the nature of classroom interaction. Specifically, the researchers were interested in determining whether or not Mexican-American and Anglo students were treated comparably in teacher-pupil interactions. In all, 12 interactions were assessed, and Jackson and Cosca point out in some detail the wide disparity in three types of interactions: (1) teachers praised and encouraged Anglos 35 percent more often than they did Mexican Americans, (2) teachers accepted 40 percent more of the Anglo students' ideas than those of the Mexican Americans, and (3) teachers directed 21 percent more of their questions to Anglos than to Mexican Americans. The researchers concluded that "The Chicanos in the Southwest not only receive less of the teaching behaviors which most facilitate learning, but many probably are confronted with the awareness that their teachers are treating them (as individuals and as an ethnic group) less favorably than their Anglo classmates" (Jackson & Cosca, 1973, p. 425). The researchers infer that such discrepancies, attributable to both teacher bias and inappropriate school programs, have negative effects on Mexican Americans' motivation, achievement, and school attitudes.

BLACKS

For years, the black man of America was the most marginal and abused in our society. Only within the last two decades has he emerged with a somewhat better position—an improvement that came from the insistent collective efforts of black leaders in America and not from whites' recognition of injustice and desire to change it. By middle-class standards, many blacks (approximately 48 percent) still live in poverty, with the majority of those living in intense rather than moderate poverty. Yet, compared with each of the subcultures just discussed, blacks are in the most advantageous economic, social, educational, and political position.

Black poverty has a unique history in our society. It has perpetuated itself through the economic and racial injustices levied on blacks through the years by whites. Black life-styles have been characterized by fear, lack of food, political injustices, poor housing, disease, and a present-oriented religion. The average black family income is about 50 percent of the average white family income.

The society of the South has felt the impact of these conditions more than that of the North or the West. Of the nation's black families living in poverty, about 73 percent reside in the South (Lever & Upham, 1968). This fact is partially attributable to the dense concentrations of blacks in the South and to the fact that more southern blacks live in rural areas (where poverty is widespread), whereas northern blacks live in cities. The social, political, and economic environments of the South still militate against the black man, another factor that contributes to his oppression.

The family structure of lower-class blacks is primarily the same as that of lower-class whites. However, in the actual process of living, the vicissitudes of the lower-class black family are greater, and it is much less stable. In fact, there are innumerable one-parent families among blacks. Families may be broken through the early death of one of the parents, divorce, abandonment, or separation. Roughly ten percent of all children in the United States live with only one parent, usually the mother, and most of these children are nonwhite. The effect of this distorted—often matriarchal—structure is that there is little opportunity for the children to develop strong affective ties to two parents. The child from a broken home in the black community is especially likely to suffer stress and anxiety rather than continuity and security, since he is constantly exposed to disruption in his environment (Beiser, 1965).

First of all, the child's needs for dependency are frustrated. The mother is a frustrating object to many black adolescents. It is not the intent of the mother to neglect or mistreat her children; on the contrary, she usually has strong maternal feelings, is excessively protective, and has every hope of being a good provider. The child's or adolescent's perception may be somewhat different. Children often relate stories of frustration, discipline, cruelty, cursing, and a general attitude that indicates that the mother hates them. The double role of full-time parent and full-time breadwinner that is forced on many black mothers undoubtedly accounts for many of her children's difficulties.

Another source of frustration for the black child is the intense sibling rivalry that develops when an older child is given the responsibility of caring for younger children. This rivalry produces much anxiety and aggression, which may result in open conflict, running away, and so on. Since the home structure is often debilitating, children may develop personality characteristics among which distrust prevails. Therefore, when thrust into the outer world, the black adolescent immediately mistrusts it, since he has often been told that there are those, primarily whites, who will work against him and make his life difficult.

Schab (1968) investigated adolescent blacks' attitudes toward home, school, and religion, hypothesizing that the discrepancies that continue to exist for blacks within American society would make their attitudes qualitatively different from those of their white counterparts. He examined the attitudes of more than 500 white and 400 black high school students in Georgia. When asked to describe their parents as strict or lenient, 26 percent of the blacks characterized them as strict, compared with 15 percent of the white students. Similarly, 26 percent of the blacks characterized them as lenient, compared with 20 percent of the whites. The remaining percentages wavered between the two polar positions.

The majority of both groups of adolescents (about 60 percent) felt obliged to tell their parents where they went and what they did. Both groups (85 percent) opposed parental interference in choice of friends. However, Schab noticed a difference in the responses related to marriage against parental wishes. Whereas 57 percent of the white students said that they would disregard parental opinion, only 35 percent of the black students said that they would rebel against such pressures.

This study also indicated differences in the forms of punishment administered by the students' parents. Removal of privileges was reported by 60 percent of the white students and by 37 percent of the black students. Punishment with household work was indicated by 20 percent of the blacks and by only 2 percent of the whites. In both groups 15 percent reported being occasionally subjected to corporal punishment. Still, 31 percent of the black students said that they were never punished, compared with only 19 percent of the whites. When asked how well they liked their homes, 75 percent of both groups responded favorably; only 1 percent chose to describe their homes as very bad.

Ghetto youths present additional problems. They are extremely poor, and they live in a densely populated environment that at best could be called a slum. In addition, their educational and value orientations do not prepare them to compete in the middle-class world. Hellenbrand (1961) described their various value orientations and beliefs as:

1. *Toughness.* The emphasis on masculinity is almost compulsive and has reactive origins.
2. *Smartness.* The ability to outsmart, con, or manipulate has great status value.
3. *Excitement.* Continuous stimulation and excitement characterize ghetto life, although conditions often alternate between boredom and drudgery and extreme danger or trouble. People often live from one crisis to another.
4. *Fate.* A common attitude is fatalism—belief that man is a pawn.
5. *Autonomy.* The mask of independence and toughness covers up strong dependency needs. Both authoritarian and nurturing behaviors seem to be connected with the individual's search for a highly restrictive environment.
6. *Submission to Nature.* The lower-class culture feels that it is best to submit to conditions as they are, since it is impossible to change things.
7. *Present-Orientation.* The lower-class culture lives for the moment.

Lower-class black boys must declare their masculinity in the most direct ways they know. These involve avoidance of women, whom they view as trying to emasculate them; scorn for middle-class standards, including the striving for academic achievement; and hatred for authority (Thompson, 1962). They quickly assume the attitude that educational and cultural pursuits are feminine concerns and therefore not for them. They regard women teachers as desexualized automatons, for whom they have either contempt or pity. Men teachers are often suspected of being not quite "right," especially white male teachers, since Negro males, especially lower-class ones, perceive white men as being somewhat feminine anyway.

The black adolescent's image was at least partially enhanced by the mergence of the black-power movements and militancy during the 1960s. These national movements gave individual black adolescents (especially males) something powerful with which to identify. The various black-power movements tried to ensure more equality and less injustice for black Americans. Groups such as the Student Nonviolent Coordinating Committee, established in Atlanta in 1960, were formed as civil-rights organizations. The Students' Afro-American Society was organized by black students enrolled in predominantly white universities. Its efforts focus primarily on demands for new curricula, black housing, black athletic coaches, more black faculty, black foreign-exchange programs, and scholarships for black students ("New Black Student," 1969).

The pursuit of civil rights shifted in focus in the mid-1960s toward gaining black power through violence. However, as student activism in general waned in the early 1970s, so did the militancy of the black movements. Yet the gains they made left an image that otherwise might never have emerged, through which today's black youths can enhance their self-identity and visualize alternative lives within mainstream America that heretofore were simply imaginable.

The future of America's minority youth is somewhat dependent upon whether or not human rights will be more openly implemented and made available to America's people. Ideally, ours is a free society in which pluralism allows equal rights and dignity to all adolescents regardless of subcultural membership. As Konopka (1973) has stated it, our society is obligated to create conditions under which human rights can be secure. Every adolescent is entitled to the rights to:

1. be himself, to think his own thoughts and to speak them, consistent with the rights of others;
2. grow and to develop his abilities to their full potential;
3. air his grievances and to see redress;
4. make mistakes without unreasonable punishment; and
5. receive justice [Konopka, 1973, p. 294].

The Social Use of Drugs in Adolescence 10

Drug use in society is not a new phenomenon. Various forms of drug use have been known around the world for centuries. Movements toward drug usage that reflected the social or political nature of their times occurred during the fall of Rome, during the Renaissance and Reformation, throughout the French Revolution and Napoleonic Wars, and following World War I (Adler, 1970). Drug use often stems from attempts to evade frustration, lessen depression, or escape from oneself. In the mid-1800s, hashish was popular; so were absinthe in the 1870s, morphine during the Civil War, cocaine after World War I, heroin during World War II, methadone immediately after it, and of course, every conceivable drug today (Adler, 1970; Baden, 1972).

A drug is a chemical that has an effect upon the body or the mind. Sometimes a drug is used as a substitute for chemicals the body may lack, such as insulin. Drugs may be used to man's advantage in fighting off infectious conditions or in stepping up or slowing down glandular activity. Technically, a drug is harmless unless it has a susceptible host. Used for specific reasons and in consultation with a physician, a drug may promote and preserve good health. This, of course, is not the way in which many adults and adolescents use drugs. Any drug can be harmful when taken in excess or when taken in combination with other drugs, or if the user is hypersensitive to the particular drug ingested. Because drugs may produce beneficial results, some individuals have concluded that they will solve any problem. This attitude often leads to misuse and overdose of drugs.

DRUG ABUSE

Any substance capable of altering the individual's mood or conscious state has abuse capability. It is appropriate to use the term "abuse" when self-medication, or self-administration of a drug, leads to psychological or physical dependence or abnormal behavior, either separately or collectively ("Dependence on Cannabis," 1967).

Ullmann and Krasner (1969) defined abuse in relation to society's expectations of proper use. The individual acts in a way that is harmful and improper to himself and that abuses the body, often creating physical addiction or psychological dependence. To most individuals, social expectations usually imply that one can ingest any amount of a drug, so long as it falls within the limits of tolerable behavior. In reality, a drug abuser commonly responds more to his physiological tolerance level than to social norms for drug use.

Since it is impossible to avoid the reactions of others to drug abuse, drug abuse necessarily involves both the social and the psychological aspects of the individual. Individual drug abuse might be symptomatic of several behaviors, such as (1) inability to integrate socially or psychologically, (2) social or personal withdrawal, and (3) weakening or destruction of an individual's physical integrity. Drug abuse may be thought of, then, as the chronic or occasional ingestion of any substance that harms the thinking, feeling, or behavioral state of the individual in a way that creates a social, physical, or psychological deficiency. These effects are dependent on the lethality and duration of the abuse as well as on the individual's internal and external reactions.

A group of physicians from the state of Massachusetts were asked for their attitudes about the relative damage from drug abuse to individuals and society. Their responses are presented in the table.

Rankings by physiological and psychological damage are for the habitual users of these products.
The rankings of hospital beds are for the relative number of general and psychiatric hospital beds directly occupied at the present time because of the use of these substances.
A ranking of one indicates most damaging substance; a ranking of seven indicates least damaging substance.

Physiological damage		Psychological damage		Damage to whole society	
Opiates	1.86	Opiates	1.74	Alcohol	1.89
Alcohol	2.60	Psychedelics	1.89	Opiates	2.31
Psychedelics	2.94	Alcohol	2.94	Psychedelics	2.97
Tobacco	3.31	Marijuana	4.11	Marijuana	4.00
Marijuana	4.91	Tobacco	5.33	Tobacco	4.11
Caffeine	5.80	Caffeine	5.61	Aspirin	6.07
Aspirin	6.12	Aspirin	6.21	Caffeine	6.08

Number of hospital beds		Dependency danger	
Alcohol	1.40	Opiates	1.26
Opiates	2.86	Alcohol	2.26
Tobacco	3.00	Tobacco	3.53
Psychedelics	3.47	Psychedelics	3.82
Marijuana	5.00	Marijuana	4.82
Caffeine	5.63	Caffeine	5.10
Aspirin	6.11	Aspirin	6.53

From "Attitudes of Medical Profession toward Drug Abuse," American Journal of Public Health, 1973, 63(12), 1037.

DRUG DEPENDENCE

Drug dependence is the state of physical or psychological need resulting from periodic or continuous use of a specific drug (Eddy, 1965). It results from taking certain drugs regularly and frequently in increasing amounts and at shorter intervals. Not everyone who takes a chemical develops a dependence on it, and degree of dependence will vary with the individual involved. Furthermore, since there are several types of drug dependence, one must be specific as to its nature—such as barbiturate dependence, morphine dependence, or amphetamine dependence.

Dependence is based on a psychological or emotional need to continue using a drug because it results in feelings of well-being or pleasure, or relief from uncomfortable tension. If an adolescent is using a drug that acts as a depressant to the central nervous system, his dependence is likely to be based on both a physical and a psychological need. Abuse of narcotics will result in both types of dependence. In contrast, abuse of marijuana or more powerful hallucinogens will cause only a psychological dependence.

When drug abuse results in dependence, the drug serves in effect as a catalyst, making the individual's inner condition more pronounced. Such dependence is not easily overcome. The Committee on Alcoholism and Drug Dependence contends that it is not possible to tell if such dependence has subsided unless the user can undergo a three-year period of abstinence (Committee on Alcoholism, 1970). The user must also be free of any other psychoactive drug, including alcohol; he must be socially functioning, and he must not suffer from a psychological disability that represents a continuation of the psychodynamics of his drug dependence. Progress toward breaking dependence is indicated when the period of abstinence grows longer, the period of relapse grows shorter, and the primary and secondary effects of drug dependence are markedly reduced.

The drugs most often abused are:

1. Narcotics, such as heroin, codeine, and morphine
2. Sedatives, such as alcohol, barbiturates, and tranquilizers
3. Stimulants, such as amphetamines
4. Hallucinogens, such as marijuana, hashish, and LSD

Habituation. Habituation is the *psychological* desire to repeat the use of a drug intermittently or continuously. Habituating drugs do not produce physical dependence or cause withdrawal symptoms when a person ceases using them. Some, however, produce a tolerance in the user, causing him to increase the dosage in order to gain the desired euphoric or behavioral effect. The development of tolerance is indicated when repeated administration of a given dosage of a drug produces a decreasing effect, and increasingly higher dosages must be taken in order to obtain the original effects (Jones, Shainberg, & Byer, 1973).

Addiction. Addiction generally implies both physical and psychological dependence on a drug. It is a state of chronic or periodic intoxication produced by the continued use of a natural or synthetic drug. Extended definitions of addiction and habituation have been stated by the World Health Organization; they are shown in Table 10.1. When a physiologically addicted abuser attempts to stop, withdrawal symptoms occur—not a consequence of habituation. The symptoms are most pronounced in narcotic and barbituate withdrawal. For example, during narcotic withdrawal, the user may experience depression, nervousness, abdominal pain, general irritability, and nausea. The tendency to repeat use of the drug is quite common, since the user is motivated to alleviate these symptoms.

DRUGS IN SOCIETY

Within our society, drug abuse is complex in both behavioral incidence and definition. Attempts to classify and objectify drug use require categorization of health, medical, moral, legal, social, and economic impacts. Of necessity, we must be concerned with the specific drugs being abused, the characteristics of the individuals who use drugs, and the social conditions that precipitate drug use or under which drug use commonly occurs.

The history of pharmacology is replete with medicines that were advocated to be the most advanced cure for different physical ills. Eventually it was found, however, that the cure-all was addicting or habituating. Modern society scoffs at witches' brews, medicine men, alchemy, and sorcery. It relies instead on the modern pharmaceutical laboratory and its researchers. Replacing the traveling medicine man, with his minstrel comedy designed to get the customer interested in a healing elixir, are neatly labeled shelves providing whatever drug for whatever cure. Representative samples of drug advertising and its marketing appeal are "For relief of insomnia, depressed mood, loss of appetite, agitation, crying, or apprehension, take . . . " and "This product helps relieve insomnia, indecisiveness, lack of interest, fatigue, anxiety, crying, hopelessness, guilt feelings, lack of esteem, negativism." In effect, haven't we just dressed up the medicine man? Hardly any old medicinal herbal concoctions claimed to cure more ills than do those legitimate drugs thus advertised.

TABLE 10.1. Definitions of addiction and habituation.

Drug addiction

Drug addiction is a state of periodic or chronic intoxication produced by the repeated consumption of a drug (natural or synthetic). Its characteristics are:
1. An overpowering desire or need (compulsion) to continue taking the drug and to obtain it by any means
2. A tendency to increase the dosage (tolerance)
3. A psychic (psychological) and generally a physical dependence on the effects of the drug
4. Abstinence syndrome produced when drug is suddenly withdrawn
5. A detrimental effect on the individual and on society

Drug habituation

Drug habituation is a condition resulting from the repeated consumption of a drug. Its characteristics are:
1. A desire (but not a compulsion) to continue taking the drug for the sense of improved well-being or effect it produces
2. Little or no tendency to increase the dosage (tolerance)
3. Some degree of psychic dependence on the effects of the drug, but absence of physical dependency and, hence, of abstinence syndrome
4. Detrimental effects, if any, primarily on the individual

From *Drugs and Alcohol* (2nd. ed.) by K. L. Jones, L. W. Shainberg, and C. O. Byer. Copyright © 1973 Harper & Row, Publishers, Inc. Reprinted by permission.

Furthermore, today's people are caught in a double bind, for social propaganda confuses as many people as it helps. For instance, consider the adolescent who is being urged by his peers to take drugs—let's say "speed." There are several problems he may encounter. First, throughout his childhood he was probably exposed to some drug use—taking cillian or mycian, an amphetamine or barbiturate, or an aspirin. Furthermore, he knows that his mother takes tranquilizers because of her anxiety tendencies, and that his overweight sister takes diet pills. Yet, conflicting social norms exist to counter these norms. Parental and societal pressure is opposed to adolescent drug use, whereas peers may reinforce it. Inasmuch as acceptance within his peer group is a crucial variable, and considering the amount of drug use (presented as legitimate) within his home environment, he engages in drug use, rationalizing that it really isn't wrong. His continued persistence in drug use will cause perceived inconsistencies to dissipate, and the end result will be the realignment of his attitude and behavior.

The picture becomes even more confused when we consider the multilateral attack on different forms of synthetic additives and drugs that are thought, with prolonged use, to have harmful effects. Let's look at some examples.

The Food and Drug Administration (FDA) has shown that rats fed a five-percent solution of saccharin developed large malignant tumors. If further tests show similar results, the use of saccharin may be banned except for diabetics. The FDA has endorsed the National Academy of Science's recommendation that adults consume no more than one gram of saccharin per day ("FDA Endorses," 1971).

Hexachlorophene (HCP), advocated as an effective and useful antibacterial agent, is nevertheless restricted to availability through prescription only. Infant deaths, damage to mucous membranes, and burned or denuded skin have resulted from its use.

Multiple-vitamin tablets with iron sold under ten different brand names were recalled by the FDA because of contamination consisting of excessive amounts of amobarbital. This drug depresses breathing and may be fatal to persons sensitive to barbiturates, particularly alcoholics and individuals with pulmonary diseases ("Contamination," 1972).

The American Academy of Allergy has recommended that aspirin, and other medications containing aspirin, be labeled with a warning that the drugs can harm some persons. Aspirin has long been recognized to cause severe asthmatic attack in some asthmatics. Research has shown that children who develop asthma after their tenth birthday are much more likely to have adverse reactions to aspirin than those who have an earlier-childhood history of asthma. Studying 1298 children over a 14-year span, Falliers found that 36 percent of the children who developed asthma after age 10 also developed a tolerance to aspirin ("Late Onset Asthma," 1972).

Acrylic glue has been found to be hazardous. Researchers at Duke University investigating the monomer component in methyl methacrylate discovered that it can depress heart and lung functions, seriously damage the lung tissue, and even, in high concentration, result in death ("Acrylic Glue," 1972).

Following reports of death of youths inhaling the vapors of some pressurized household products, the FDA has proposed warnings against misuse on product packages. Self-pressurized products using fluorocarbon propellants can injure or kill if deliberately misused. The FDA suggests that all such product labels include the warning "Do not inhale directly; deliberate inhalation of contents can cause death."

Federal authorities lifted their ban on the sale of aerosol glue March 1, 1974, after further research found that inhalation of the substance did not pose an unreasonable risk of chromosome damage ("Federal Agency," 1974).

About one percent of all elementary-school children are prescribed drugs as therapy for hyperactivity. Some research has indicated that these drugs may suppress height and weight gains. Drug dosage did not seem to alter the child's developmental pattern so much as did the duration and frequency of treatment. Up to one-third less than expected height and weight gain occurred with long-term treatment in some children.

In 1963, the Surgeon General's report warned that cigarette smoking may be hazardous to one's health, primarily by increasing risk of lung diseases and oral cancer. Since that time, the number of smokers has diminished, but a higher number of cigarettes are being consumed by users. In the United States in 1973, consumption was around 554 billion cigarettes. In 1965, 41.6 percent of the population 17 or older smoked. In 1970, the figure had dropped to 36.7 percent. The actual number of smokers dropped from 50.7 million to 48.8 million. Meanwhile, the number of smokers using over one pack of cigarettes a day increased, and the number using fewer than 15 a day decreased.

Evidence that might support cigarette use includes research indicating that smokers are less anxious than nonsmokers, and that smoking desensitizes people and raises their level of tolerance to disturbing physical sensations.

The FDA effectively persuaded the Bureau of Narcotics and Dangerous Drugs to significantly reduce the production quota of amphetamines and methamphetamines in 1973. They contended that amphetamine diet pills are of little value, that amphetamines are unsafe in injectable form, and that they have great abuse potential. Production of oral amphetamines was reduced 39 percent and that of methamphetamines 57 percent.

Maintenance treatment of patients 18 years of age and older with oral dosages of methadone as a substitute for heroin is commonly administered at some 450 drug-addiction centers in the United States. Although there is a two-year restriction on methadone maintenance because of its strong addicting powers, the FDA's decision to increase methadone use was made after consultation with the National Institute of Health, the Bureau of Narcotics and Dangerous Drugs, and the Special Action Office for Drug Abuse Prevention of the White House.

Recent research indicates the high probability that steroid drugs and protein-rich diets, commonly given to athletes to help them perform better, may form eating patterns leading to overweight after their athletic years, as well as shortening their life span. The research also found that excessive use of vitamins A and D can be toxic (Freydinger, 1973; Nelson & Gastineau, 1973).

The Washington, D.C., Medical Society has gone on record as favoring milder marijuana laws. It states "There appear to be no serious or lasting physical and mental effects from moderate or intermittent usage in healthy adults" ("Medical Group," 1974).

Edward M. Brecher and the editors of *Consumer Reports* claim that the 400-million-dollar federally funded drug-education program of the early 1970s publicized and thus actually popularized drug use. The report calls for (1) a distinction made between more and less hazardous drugs, (2) repeal of antiquated and unreasonable drug laws, (3) no publicity for prohibited drug use, (4) a total ban on alcohol and cigarette advertising, and (5) legalization of marijuana (Brecher, 1972).

DRUGS AND THE SOCIAL ENVIRONMENT

Because we are a fast-paced nation, we find it more convenient and expedient to rely on drugs to alleviate temporary physical or psychological distress than to resolve distress through introspective methods or the exercise of patience. In fact, Americans have become so used to taking drugs that they may develop a tolerance to some drugs that reduces their effectiveness in times when the need for the drug is paramount.

Prior to 1965, drug abuse was considered to be a phenomenon of the inner city and its slum areas. Crime, juvenile delinquency, and drug use were all associated with deprivation, broken homes, lack of parental guidance, and lack of opportunity to attain one's aspirational levels. Today, however, drug abuse has crossed socioeconomic lines, racial lines, social-class and geographical barriers, and religious prohibitions. The modern movement toward drug use associated with adolescents from suburbia is usually believed to result from affluence, parental permissiveness and overindulgence, boredom, and lack of insight and creative potential.

In truth, it is the number of drug outlets, such as drug stores, discount houses, and convenience markets—all of which are within walking distance of most people—that make drugs more available and thus create abuse potential. The fact that some 1 trillion pills a year are consumed by the American public attests to the fact that the drug supply is plentiful and drug use therefore more likely. Children, adolescents, and adults alike are more apt to turn to some medication or drug for relief of discomfort than to seek an alternative form of alleviation. Strong social enticements and reinforcement make us a drug-oriented society.

ALCOHOL

The use of alcohol by adults in our society has become a widely accepted and socially approved behavior. Because alcohol is legal, few think of it as a drug or consider the varied effects that it can have on the

The Gallup poll put drinking at a 35-year high in 1974.			
Year	Drinkers	1974 Audit of drinkers by groups	
1939	58%		Use alcoholic beverages
1945	67		
1946	67		
1947	63	National	68%
1948	58	Men	76
1949	58	Women	61
1950	60	Under 30 years	79
1951	59	30-49 years	75
1952	60	50 years and older	54
1956	60	$20,000 and over	88
1957	58	$15,000-19,999	78
1958	55	$10,000-14,999	64
1960	62	$7,000-9,999	58
1964	63	$5,000-6,999	57
1966	65	Under $5,000	46
1969	64	East	78
1974	68	Midwest	75
		South	51
		West	70
		Professional and business	85
		Clerical and sales	78
		Manual laborers	71
		College-trained	83
		High school	70
		Grade school	45
		Protestants	61
		Catholics	83

individual consuming it. Alcohol acts on the nervous system as a depressant. One of its first systematic actions is to depress the power of restraint; it makes some individuals appear less shy and more open, aggressive, jovial, and so on (Thornburg, 1973b). Because the person who has had too much to drink finds his emotional and psychological restraints less binding, he often behaves in a different way than when he has not had excessive quantities of alcohol.

The incidence of alcohol use among American adolescents is excessively high. In fact, more youths use alcohol than all other drugs combined. Its use among youths between 12 and 17, as indicated by a national survey taken in 1971, revealed the following statistics (Shafer, 1972). During the month in which the respondents were questioned, 23 percent had used beer, 14 percent wine, and 12 percent hard liquor; 6 percent had used beer five or more times during the month; and 5 percent had used wine, and 3 percent hard liquor, frequently.

Suchman's study in 1967 among students at a West Coast university indicated that alcohol use was prevalent in 94.1 percent of the population, with 47 percent indicating frequent use. These results are similar to Blum's (1969) in his study of high school and college youth, in which he found a 90-percent incidence of use. An Illinois college study by Levy (1973) indicated a 96.5-percent use of alcohol. A 1973 study in San Mateo, California, showed that 85 percent of all high school students reported using alcohol at least once during the school year; 53 percent indicated using it more than ten times, and 29 percent indicated using it 50 times or more. In the same study, 76 percent of the seventh and eighth graders reported using the drug at least once; 22 percent of these had used it more than 50 times (San Mateo, 1973). In a midwestern survey, Crowther and Baumer (1971) found that 57 percent of their high school sample reported alcohol use.

A 1972 study among 7288 high school students in Monroe County, New York, showed that 85 percent had tried alcohol at least once, 55.9 percent of whom were still using it, and 45 percent of whom had used it more than 15 times. Table 10.2 is adapted from the study by Yancy and his associates (Yancy, Nader, & Burnham, 1972) and gives comparative figures for the incidence of alcohol use in six different geographical areas of the United States and Canada.

Sociocultural Correlates of Adolescent Alcohol Use

By the time the adolescent graduates from high school, he or she has quite probably established a regular light to moderate drinking pattern. The proportion of adolescent drinkers varies from community to community—anywhere from 30 percent to 80 percent of the adolescent population. This variation reflects regional and ethnic subcultural differences (Maddox, 1970). Although the vast majority of adolescents are either abstainers or light to moderate drinkers, between 2 percent and 6 percent of the adolescent population are problem drinkers—drinkers for whom alcohol has come to occupy more than an incidental role in their lives.

A large number of empirical studies reviewed by Maddox (1970) showed that the majority of adolescent drinkers report that their first drinking experience occurred in their own home with parents and/or relatives present, that they see drinking as an adult behavior, and that alcoholic beverages are typically readily available around the house. Jessor, Graves, Hanson, and Jessor (1968) found that unsanctioned introduc-

TABLE 10.2. Comparison of reports of drug use by North American senior high school students.

Survey	Date	N	Alcohol, %	Marijuana, %	Amphetamines, %	Barbiturates, %	LSD, %	Heroin, %
Madison, Wisconsin	1969	800						
Ever used			87.0	36.9	9.9	Not	5.8	1.3
"Frequently"			21.0	7.8	0.6	surveyed	1.1	0.4
Utah	1969	45,997						
Ever used			Not	12.2	10.0	Not	4.9	Not
Ten times			surveyed	8.3	4.8	surveyed	2.7	surveyed
Dallas, Texas	1969	25,587						
Ever used			71.0	14.0	8.0	5.0	6.0	3.0
Ten times			35.0	6.0	2.0	1.0	1.6	1.0
Toronto, Canada	1968	4,631						
Ever used*			57.4	9.0	7.6†	4.0	5.2	1.9†
Once a month			29.8	3.1	4.5†	2.3	1.2	1.1‡
	1970	5,022						
Ever used*			69.2	23.4	12.4	4.9	10.1	4.0‡
Once a month			31.5	7.3	3.7	2.4	4.7	2.6‡
San Mateo, California	1968	13,259						
Ever used§			64.2	30.5	16.4	Not	8.9	Not
Ten times§			22.0	16.1	6.4	surveyed	3.1	surveyed
	1969	16,391						
Ever used§			71.5	37.2	20.4	Not	12.2	Not
Ten times§			29.9	22.2	8.2	surveyed	4.2	surveyed
	1970	18,175						
Ever used§			75.3	41.6	22.2	16.2	13.0	Not
Ten times			34.2	25.6	8.4	5.5	3.7	surveyed
Monroe County, New York (Present study)	1971	7,288						
Ever used			85.0	27.7	14.2	14.9	8.6	2.6
Fifteen times			45.0	13.2	3.0	3.7	2.7	0.6

*In the past six months †All "stimulants" not including "speed" ‡All "opiates" §In the past 12 months
From "Drug Use and Attitudes of High School Students" by W. S. Yancy, P. R. Nader, and K. L. Burnham, *Pediatrics*, 1972, 50(5), 743. Copyright 1972 by the American Academy of Pediatrics. Reprinted by permission.

tions to drinking and heavy consumption patterns among high-school-age children were related to the heavy drinking behavior of the adult males they observed. Summarizing the research in this area, Maddox (1970) concluded that knowledge of an adolescent's parents' drinking patterns is the single most accurate tool for predicting his or her drinking behavior. Unfortunately, however, there is a lack of systematic investigation into individual variables, which could explain the substantial number of "false positives" in the research reviewed above. (For example, personal feelings of shame over heavy parental drinking could explain why a given adolescent is an abstainer even though his parents are alcoholics.)

More recently, Jessor, Collins, and Jessor (1972) found that reinforcement for drinking, especially by peers, plays a prime role in predicting abstainer or drinker status among junior and senior high school students. Studies of college-student peer groups, specifically fraternities, have supported the theory that peer influences on adolescent attitudes toward drinking and drinking behavior are substantial. Gusfield (1970) and Rogers (1970) both found that fraternity members are more likely to

Adolescents tend to make the same use of socially accepted drugs as adults do.

be drinkers than nonfraternity members. Gusfield went one step further by showing that fraternity members with high-user parents (who would, therefore, be expected to be high users) drank no more frequently or excessively than fraternity members with low-user parents.

Although the drinking that occurs in the context of adolescent gangs may at times be an expression of rebellion and hostility, Maddox (1970) has found that this is not typically the case. In the absence of adequate data on peer influence, hypothesizing motives such as rebellion and hostility remains equivocal. Uncontrolled selective factors (both self- and group-determined) that affect fraternity or gang membership may play roles as significant as or more significant than that of group membership itself.

The evidence on the relationship between religious affiliation and drinking behavior is fairly conclusive. Maddox (1970) points out that, due to the norms concerning drinking upheld by the respective religions, the average drinker will probably be a Jew or a Catholic rather than a Protestant. Snyder (1958) found, however, using a sample of college alcohol users, that the intoxication rates for ascetic Protestants and Mormons are much higher than for Jewish students. Similarly, Skolnick (1958) found that the rate of social complications due to drinking for Jewish students who drink is much lower than the rate of social complications for student drinkers who are members of ascetic Protestant groups. Finally, Gusfield (1970) found that Protestant college students were more often high users of alcohol than were Jewish students. Thus, although fewer Protestant and Mormon than Jewish students drink, those Protestant and Mormon students who do drink are more likely to be problem drinkers than the Jewish students.

The belief is widely held that many adolescent problem drinkers drink and get drunk in order to escape from their high levels of anxiety and depression. Williams (1968) tested this idea and found that alcohol does afford problem drinkers with some relief when they are moderately intoxicated, but not when they are severely intoxicated. Although the results of his study can explain why an anxious and depressed person might drink moderately and frequently, they do not explain why an anxious and depressed individual would become a problem drinker (indulging in both excessive and frequent drinking), since relief from anxiety and depression is apparently not gained from excessive alcohol consumption.

Using the personality variables that differentiated problem drinkers from nonproblem drinkers in his 1970 study, Williams studied the personality changes that occur as a person consumes more and more alcohol. Using a male college sample, Williams found that the personality descriptions of nonproblem drinkers under the influence of alcohol closely matched the personality descriptions of problem drinkers when sober. Williams concluded that a problem drinker feels more at home in a drinking situation than a nonproblem drinker because he finds himself surrounded by people who are now just as aggressive, self-centered, and impulsive as he is. This conclusion would explain why an adolescent male with this set of personality traits might tend to drink frequently, but it does not adequately explain why he will drink excessively.

Alexander and Campbell (1967) have found that adolescent drinking represents an expression of hostility toward the norms and authority of the total society. Similarly, it may provide a means for expressing aggression against an individual who symbolizes such authority. Alexander has expressed the fear that, if drinking results from the defiance of parental authority, it may become a symbol of rebelliousness and independence, thus justifying its use among greater percentages of youth.

However, societal sanction of alcohol cannot justly or even arbitrarily draw the line between adult and adolescent use, expecting the adolescent to accept such a division. Better rationale for adult use or greater acceptance of adolescent use must emerge. In either case, the early and highly prevalent use of alcohol among our youths may throw them into a spirit of drug use that otherwise might not be so accentuated.

NICOTINE

Nicotine no longer has medical uses. Taken in tobacco, it acts variably as a depressant, a tranquilizer, or a stimulant. Because of its excessive use, tobacco is one of the most physiologically damaging substances used by man. When smoked in cigarettes, it is the primary cause of lung cancer. It also contributes to other cancers, coronary and artery diseases, and emphysema of the lungs.

Smoking may be one of the adolescent's first initiations to adultlike behaviors. Cigarettes are easily obtainable, and smoking is viewed by many children and adolescents as a relatively acceptable way of striving for independence. The frequency of cigarette use in adolescents exceeds 50 percent and ranks next to alcohol as the most common drug use among youths. However, cigarette smoking usually occurs prior to alcohol use. The combination of both behaviors in the preadolescent or early adolescent may precipitate a tendency toward continued and more diverse drug use.

The incidence of regular cigarette smoking among adolescents reached a low point in 1965 but has increased since then (Edson, 1973). Figure 10.1 shows the comparative incidence of cigarette use by boys and

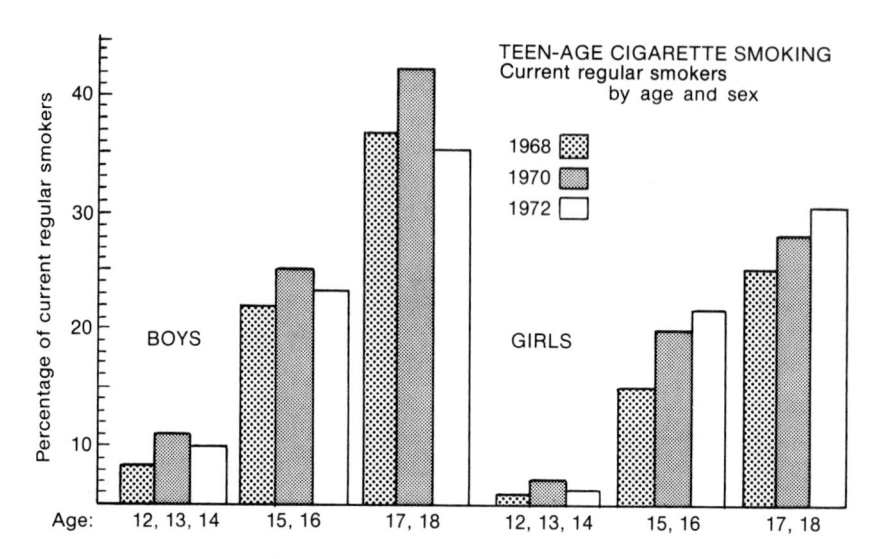

FIGURE 10.1. From "Schools Attack the Smoking Problem" by L. Edson, *American Education*, 1973, 9(1), 10. Reprinted by permission.

girls for 1968, 1970, and 1972. From 1968 to 1972, the increase in regular smoking was 4 percent for the boys and 3.5 percent for the girls, particularly girls in the 15–16 age group. About 4 million youths between 12 and 18 smoke on a regular basis. Even though some slowdown was indicated between 1970 and 1972, it is estimated that approximately 1 million youths take up smoking annually. Although most teen-agers feel that smoking is harmful, this opinion does not appear to be a sufficient motive to quit.

Adolescents smoke out of curiosity, to seek peer approval, and to exercise their emerging desire for autonomy. Adolescent smoking is probably qualitatively different from adult smoking. For example, social reasons for smoking seem to be quite common in the adolescent but uncommon in the adult (McKennell, 1970). Early adolescents report that the use of cigarettes helps them in striving for social confidence, although this particular motive seems to decline with age. McKennell (1970) observed that adults were motivated to smoke for personal rather than social reasons. They listed their primary motives to be nervousness, relaxation, solitude, food substitution, and desire to accompany an activity such as working or watching television.

It is likely that the adolescent's decision to smoke is affected by the attitudes toward smoking held by his or her parents. Several independent investigations have reported a direct relationship between the prevalence of parents' smoking and their adolescent child's smoking

(Cartwright, Martin, & Thompson, 1959; Horn, Courts, Taylor, & Solomon, 1959; Levy, 1973; Mausner & Mischler, 1967; Salber & McMahon, 1961). These results were consistent with each other and with the theoretical explanations of identification and the modeling process proposed by psychoanalytic theory and social-learning theory.

Although the use of cigarettes is often an outcome of the adolescent's growing interest in adult-like behaviors, as well as of curiosity, it is reasonable to assume that adolescent smoking is considered inappropriate by most adults. Adolescents usually experience this adult intolerance through restrictive and punitive measures—at least those adolescents who get caught. Many educational institutions have strict rules against students' smoking on the school grounds. The apprehended student is typically paddled, given detention, or suspended from school for a few days. An experimental program in Illinois evolved out of the persuasion that these ways of handling smoking behavior were ineffective. As an alternative to suspension, students were given the opportunity to attend four two-hour seminars designed to inform them on the consequences of smoking. The primary goal of these sessions was to reduce the incidence of cigarette smoking on campus (Herzog, 1970).

Using teaching materials from the Tuberculosis Institute, the American Cancer Society, and the Heart Association, the four seminar sessions focused on (1) the respiratory and circulatory systems, (2) what happens physiologically and biochemically when you smoke, (3) cancer and emphysema, and (4) the psychology of cigarette advertising. Herzog and his associates (Herzog, Sudia, & Harwood, 1970) reported that, of 198 students followed up after the course, 12 percent stopped smoking, and 85 percent significantly reduced smoking; in addition, after five months, the new nonsmokers had an increased lung capacity. Much controversy could arise over instituting such a program as a school function. However, it is important to point out that this school district, when it saw a problem in the school environment, constructively and objectively attempted to correct the situation by showing the students who were part of the problem some existing behavioral alternatives.

BARBITURATES

Sedative drugs are manufactured for the medical purposes of reducing tension and anxiety, treating certain psychosomatic disorders, and inducing sleep. Certain sedatives are used in the treatment of epilepsy. The barbiturates, made from barbituric acid, are by far the largest group of sedatives. The first sleep-producing barbiturate (Veronal) was synthesized in 1903. Today there are over 50 commercial brands on the market.

The barbiturates vary in duration of action. They range from the very fast-acting thiopental (Penthothal), which can be used as an anesthetic, to the moderately fast-acting pentobarbital (Nembutal) and secobarbital (Seconal), to the slow-acting phenobarbital (Luminal). Fast-acting barbiturates may be heavily abused. Without careful medical supervision to avoid habituation, increasing doses may be used to produce the desired effect, and physical dependence may occur.

On the street, the sedatives are called "goofballs," "sleepers," and "downers." They appear in a variety of colored capsules or tablets. Seconals are called "red devils," Nembutals "yellow jackets," Tuinals "rainbows," and Amytals "blue angels." Besides the barbiturates, other sedatives that may be abused include glutethimide (Doriden), chloral hydrate, bromides, and certain minor tranquilizers such as meprobamate (Miltown, Equanil) and chlordiazepoxide (Librium).

The principal response elicited by barbiturates is a depression of the central nervous system. They act upon the cerebral centers and interfere with the passage of impulses within the brain. They appear to affect the enzyme processes by which energy is acquired, stored in the protoplasm of the cells, and utilized. They depress brain function, and, in large doses, depress the brain centers responsible for maintaining the rhythm of respiration. The sedative effect may cause dependence. Overdoses result in extreme depression and often in coma and death. They are known to trigger suicidal tendencies. In 1970, over 3000 barbiturate suicides occurred, a figure that is close to the annual average in the United States.

There is little question that barbiturates are heavily used. According to statistics, 178 million prescriptions for mood-changing drugs were filled by U.S. pharmacies in 1967. Of these prescriptions, about 65 percent were for sedative drugs (31 percent for barbiturates and other sedatives and hypnotics, 34 percent for minor tranquilizers). Most of these prescriptions went to some 30 million adult Americans (Bates & Crowther, 1973).

Although undoubtedly the majority of these drugs are legally used for medical purposes, an unknown but large quantity of barbiturates also enters illegal channels. Recent estimates indicate that, of all the barbiturates manufactured in the United States, more than half are diverted to illicit use. A good share of the "goofballs" being distributed today on the black market are capsules that were legally manufactured but that found their way into illicit channels by theft, exportation and reimportation from a foreign country, hijacking, and indiscriminate sales to unauthorized persons.

Barbiturate Abuse

Although all barbiturates are abused, those most frequently abused are the powerful, quick-acting drugs such as pentobarbital (Nembutal), secobarbital (Seconal), amobarbital (Amytol), or combinations of these. Because the drugs are physically addicting, withdrawal effects occur when administration is stopped. Addiction to 50 or more sleeping pills a day has been reported. Those who take excessive amounts of barbiturates often go into a coma. However, in persons used to taking large doses, instead of producing drowsiness or sleep, barbiturates may produce restlessness, excitement, and even delirium—symptoms resembling the excitation of an alcoholic. Persons intoxicated with barbiturates may appear to be inebriated and may be mistaken for "drunks." Their coordination is poor, their speech is slurred, and they become irritable, confused, and unsteady of gait. Ability to accomplish skilled, precise tasks is lost. Judgment, perception, and memory are impaired. In extreme cases, disorientation, aggressive behavior, hallucinations, and paranoid delusions may develop.

When dependence is severe, sudden barbiturate withdrawal may require emergency medical treatment. The abuser gets sweaty, fearful, sleepless, and tremulous. He may suffer convulsions that occasionally lead to death. In order to help a user withdraw from barbiturate use, the amount must be gradually decreased, under medical supervision, until the need for and dependence on the drug diminish (Strack, 1968).

STIMULANTS

Stimulants, usually amphetamines, induce a transient sense of well-being, self-confidence, and alertness. They are used to combat fatigue, curb appetite, and reduce mild depression. Amphetamines have chemical properties that stimulate the actions of the central nervous system—in direct contrast to barbiturates, which slow down (depress) the actions of the central nervous system.

The stimulants include cocaine, amphetamine (Benzedrine, "bennies"), dextroamphetamine (Dexedrine, "dexies"), and methamphetamine ("speed," "crystal"). Stimulants are also known as "uppers" or "pep pills." Mild stimulants include coffee and tea, which contain caffeine. Pill stimulants are being frequently ingested yearly; Levy's college study (1973) reported a 23.9-percent use, and the high school study by Yancy and his associates (1972) reported a 14.2-percent use.

Amphetamines are used medically to curb appetite when weight reduction is necessary, relieve mild depression, and keep patients awake who are suffering from narcolepsy—a disease characterized by uncontrollable desire to sleep. Although the efficacy of amphetamines in these cases has not been questioned, controversy surrounds their use because, when taken over a long period of time, the drugs may cause dependence in the patient—particularly if he violates his physician's precautions.

In the United States, approximately one-fourth of all medical prescriptions for mood-altering drugs are for stimulants, mainly amphetamines. In addition, it is estimated that half of the legally manufactured supply of amphetamines finds its way into illegal channels for nonprescribed use. This black market is a common source of supply for habitual users. Although the exact number of amphetamine abusers is not known, the use of enormous quantities of amphetamines has drastically increased. Quantities of amphetamines are also used without supervision for weight reduction or to keep awake over prolonged periods. Concern over the extent of amphetamine use has caused the Food and Drug Administration to place greater restrictions on the number of them that can be manufactured by the pharmaceutical houses.

Users usually begin by "dropping" diet pills, either for kicks or to keep awake. However, they often develop a dependence on them. When amphetamines are abused, users take doses many times those prescribed for medical purposes. The normal dosage in a prescribed diet pill is from 5 to 15 milligrams (mg) (Smith, 1969); it is not uncommon for a "speedster" or "pill head" to take from 1000 to 5000 mg per day. Excessive dosages may result in disorganization, paranoia, or even psychosis (Johnson & Westman, 1968; Strack, 1968). Amphetamines are not usually fatal. However, they may cause the user to go through an elation-depression cycle, known as the upper-downer syndrome, which is brought on by the use of an amphetamine followed by a barbiturate. During the syndrome the user does not sleep, does not eat, and is highly excitable for a period of three to four days. When his supply runs out, or when he collapses from physical exhaustion, he may sleep for 24 to 48 hours and then awake with a ravenous appetite. A period of depression, sometimes lasting for weeks, may then follow (Smith, 1969).

To gain a maximum "high," many persons take amphetamines intravenously, although oral consumption is more frequent ("Two Doctors," 1969). Methedrine is also used to produce a high similar to that of the intravenous amphetamine (Johnson & Westman, 1968). Black-market laboratories manufacture *methamphetamine,* which, injected into the bloodstream, provides an initial euphoric flash that has been described as a whole-body orgasm. A "speedster" may repeatedly inject himself to get these sudden euphoric flashes (Smith, 1969).

Heavy amphetamine users, or "speed freaks," become physically debilitated and suffer from malnutrition. With no desire for food or sleep, they lose weight and become careless about personal hygiene. They become susceptible to infections, such as viral hepatitis, transmitted by a dirty needle. There is evidence of liver damage from high doses. Brain-cell damage has also been reported. Social and moral deterioration also occurs in heavy users. They tend to become impulsive, irritable, unreliable, and unstable. Their behavior may become assaultive and unpredictable (see box). Of all drug abusers, "speed freaks" most resemble the post-World War I cocaine user, whose behavior was largely responsible for the term "dope fiend." "Speed freaks" invariably become suspicious of those around them, and in extreme cases they suffer from paranoid delusions of being threatened or of being the object of a plot. Schizophrenia-like disturbances resulting from prolonged heavy use may last for several months after the drugs are discontinued. The depression into which heavy amphetamine abusers fall when they come down ("crash") from their high is extremely severe. Suicide has occurred during these moods. Lethargy, fatigue, muscle pains, ravenous hunger, and mental depression are the chief symptoms when the drugs are discontinued. Some scientists regard these symptoms as stimulant withdrawal, indicating a true physical dependence.

Is there a relationship between drugs and crime? Research was done on this question in Palo Alto, California, by randomly selecting 50 male adolescents who were assaultive juvenile offenders and 80 who were nonassaultive juvenile offenders. The researchers found:

> Fifty male adolescent assaultive offenders incarcerated in California were compared for drug use and criminal behavior with 80 nonassaultive offenders of similar background by utilizing semi-structured interviews and a review of official records.
>
> In 36 of the 56 assaults resulting in tissue damage, the assailant described himself as under the influence of a drug at the time of the offense. Alcohol or secobarbital, alone or in combination with other drugs, were reported in 31 of the 36 drug-related assaults including seven assaults that resulted in the death of the victim. Marihuana used alone or with other drugs was associated with six assaults; amphetamine was linked with two offenses.
>
> The study subjects overwhelmingly selected secobarbital as the drug most likely to enhance assaultive tendencies.*

*From "Drug Involvement in Criminal Assaults by Adolescents" by J. R. Tinklenberg, P. L. Murphy, P. Murphy, C. F. Darley, W. T. Roth, and B. S. Kopell, *Archives of General Psychiatry*, May 1974, 30, 685.

"Speed" can occasionally kill, from accidents resulting during paranoid delusions, through homicidal rages, or through injections of the drug mixed with contaminated substances. Death from overdose in the tolerant individual, however, is uncommon. Most frequently, the deterioration of personality, judgment, and health resulting from continued use of "speed" leaves the "speed freak" in a limbo, neither physically dead nor physically alive.

Another frequently used stimulant is cocaine. It has been known to the Peruvians and Bolivians for years; chewing coca leaves was part of their ceremonial and everyday living patterns before the Europeans' discovery of South America. In 1860 cocaine was isolated from coca for medical use, and around the turn of this century it was used for a period of time as treatment for morphine addiction.

Today, cocaine ("coke," "gold dust," "snow," "star dust") is commonly used among heroin addicts to increase the potency of heroin. Although its use has always been limited, it has become more popular since the early 1960s. As it is used in the United States, the drug is of relatively new interest compared with heroin or amphetamines; therefore, it is more commonly a drug users' supplement than a primary drug.

LEGAL DRUG USE

Although many prefer not to think of alcohol and tobacco as drugs, they nevertheless produce (or have the capacity to produce) mood and mind alterations in the user. Furthermore, barbiturates and amphetamines are commonly used prescription drugs in our society. Today's adolescent, therefore, has been exposed to all of these drug forms and to adult models who participate in the consumption of them.

There are numerous nonprescription commercial pain preparations, as well. These include aspirin, Anacin, Excedrin, Empirin, Bufferin, Alka-Seltzer, cough syrups, paregoric, etc. Research indicates that college students' use of most of the drug categories described in this chapter parallels that of the adult population (Levy, 1973). Table 10.3 indicates a high frequency of use of nonprescription and prescription pain preparations, alcohol, and tobacco. Comparatively, each of these forms seems to be more commonly used than heroin, marijuana, or the psychedelics.

Owing to the widespread and increasing use of pharmaceutical agents of all kinds, interaction among drugs is increasingly being recognized as a hazard. The high incidence of alcoholism (Weiner, 1970) and the fact that many alcoholics are not recognized as such magnify this problem. Interaction between alcohol and other drugs may contribute to accidental or suicidal deaths in individuals who have consumed barbiturates while they were inebriated (Sundby, 1967). Both acute alcohol intoxication and alcoholism may affect the dosage requirements in many clinical situations that require the use of drugs—for example, anesthetics, oral hypoglycemic agents in the treatment of diabetes, or anticonvulsants in epilepsy therapy (Forney & Hughes, 1968).

The well-known clinical interactions of ethyl alcohol and drugs appear paradoxical. Inebriated individuals, whether they are alcoholics or

TABLE 10.3. Weighted sample using drugs during lifetime, past year, and past month.*

Drug	Ever used %	Used past year %	Used past month %
Nonprescription pain preparation	93.1	91.0	71.0
Alcohol	96.5	93.6	79.0
Amphetamines	23.9	16.3	6.2
Cocaine	4.6	2.4	0.8
Heroin	1.6	1.2	0.4
Marijuana	49.3	44.2	27.3
Prescription pain preparation	66.5	39.8	12.0
Psychedelics	14.5	11.6	3.6
Psychic energizers	3.9	2.6	0.7
Sleeping pills	21.2	10.1	2.5
Tobacco	79.4	59.0	44.8
Tranquilizers	17.7	10.4	4.1

*Entries in these columns are cumulative so that % Ever used includes % Used past year, and % Used past year includes % Used past month.
From "Drug Use on Campus: Prevalence and Social Characteristics of Collegiate Drug Users on Campuses of the University of Illinois" by L. Levy, Drug Forum, 1973, 2(2), 145. Reprinted by permission.

not, display a striking sensitivity to a wide variety of drugs, including sedatives such as barbiturates. These effects of acute and chronic ethanol intoxication have been attributed, respectively, to additive and adaptive phenomena in the central nervous system (Forney & Hughes, 1968).

The assertion was made at the beginning of this chapter that drug use is a general social phenomenon, not one peculiar to the adolescent. Indeed, the adolescent may very well be encouraged to use drugs because of the prevalence with which they are used in society at large. Therefore, a great deal of adolescent drug use can be attributed to a general societal attitude toward drugs and to significant adult models for drug use of one form or another.

The Use of Illegal Drugs in Adolescence 11

In contrast to the preceding chapter, this chapter will focus on adolescents' use of drugs that are illegal and that carry strong negative social sanction. Specifically, we will discuss the use of solvents, marijuana, the hallucinogens, and the narcotics. The incidence of illegal drug use in our society is impossible to document accurately. Those statistics that do emerge are better thought of as trends, rather than facts, in the incidence of drug use. Conflicting opinion and evidence are especially troublesome in research on marijuana and the hallucinogens.

Current research tells us that acquaintance with and extensive use of marijuana are common among all segments of society, crossing all racial and socioeconomic lines and dipping down into the age range of elementary-school children. Official statistics usually cite the age range of 12 to 25 for its common use. Because marijuana is regarded by many as neither addicting nor habituating, its use is advocated by many youths and professionals. However, it becomes a potential drug problem for the immature, insecure, status-seeking adolescent.

Greater conflict and controversy surround the stronger hallucinogens, which carry strong negative sanction and are thought to entail high risk to the user. Yet the use of such drugs has been popularized by known figures in the society and through music, movies, and popular art. Scientific evidence on these drugs tends to be conflicting and, in some cases, inconclusive. This problem is due, in part, to the fact that research with human subjects on these drugs is extremely limited and no longitudinal information is available on marijuana or most hallucinogens. LSD, the most commonly researched hallucinogenic drug, has been shown to have some deleterious effects, but many drug advocates persuasively discount any scientific evidence that has been gathered at this point. The struggle between presenting objective evidence and "selling out" to established, conservative opinion makes it quite difficult to make sense of the drug world, to which adolescents so often turn and for which adults so often exhibit disgust. Let's examine what we do know, nevertheless, about the drugs most commonly used by adolescents.

SOLVENTS

Among preadolescents, drug usage commonly starts with the sniffing of solvents, more generally known as "glue sniffing." The substances typically inhaled are glue, gasoline, lighter fluids, paint thinner, cleaning fluids, and similar volatile hydrocarbons (Kaplan, 1970; Strack, 1968). The sniffing of such substances will produce a state similar to alcohol intoxication. Kaplan describes its effects as follows:

> In the first half hour or so, blurring of vision, ringing in the ears, loss of coordination, slurring of speech, and perhaps hallucinations will occur. Drunkenness is the typical symptom. A sense of floating or spinning is often experienced. Marked changes of mood can occur. After this follows a letdown period. Drowsiness, stupor, perhaps nausea, and sometimes unconsciousness are exhibited. This period is frequently blanked-out to memory after recovery [Kaplan, 1970, pp. 20-21].

Tolerance for solvent sniffing may develop, but physical dependence does not. It is highly possible for psychological dependence to develop, especially in children or young adolescents. This activity, in fact, is the preadolescent's counterpart to the use of marijuana or stimulants in the older adolescent. Intoxication is commonly achieved by placing glue in a plastic bag and taking several deep breaths to bring on a rapid exhilaration. One of the most hazardous results of glue sniffing is the suffocation that often occurs during administration. Gasoline sniffers usually inhale fumes directly.

Brozovsky and Winkler (1965) point out that glue sniffing is often carried out in the restrooms of elementary and high schools. Chapel and Taylor (1970) note that its use is so well established in some users that intoxication is enhanced by drinking wine or beer between sniffs. Therefore, the problem is common enough and potentially hazardous enough to warrant educating preadolescents regarding its nature, its effects, and its relationship to the subsequent use of additional drugs. It is also important to dispel the popular idea that glue sniffing really isn't that dangerous anyway. Reports of actual physical damage other than liver damage resulting from solvent abuse are rare, although the toxicity of these solvents for humans is widely recognized among those involved in their industrial use.

MARIJUANA

Marijuana is dried plant material from the Indian hemp plant *Cannabis sativa*. The plant grows wild in many parts of the world, including the United States, and it is frequently cultivated for its commercial value as fiber for rope and for use in bird seed. As a drug, it is known by such names as "pot," "grass," "weed," "Mary Jane," and many others.

For use as a drug, the leaves and flowering tops of the plant are dried and crushed or broken into small fragments, which are then typically rolled into thin homemade cigarettes, often called "joints." It may also be smoked in small pipes and is occasionally incorporated into food and eaten. The smoke smells like burning rope or alfalfa. Users sometimes burn incense to mask its distinctive odor.

Marijuana varies greatly in strength, depending on where it is grown, whether it is wild or cultivated specifically for smoking or eating, and which portions of the plant actually go into the drug mixture. Marijuana is also sometimes adulterated with other materials, such as marijuana seeds and stems, tea, catnip, or oregano, which reduce the strength of the resulting mixture.

Hashish ("hash") is the potent dark brown resin collected from the tops of high-quality cannabis. Because of the high concentration of this resin, it is often five or six times stronger than the usual marijuana, although the active drug ingredients are the same.

Tetrahydrocannabinol, or THC (technically, delta-9 THC), is known to be the basic active ingredient in marijuana and hashish. The amount of this chemical present determines the strength of a given sample of the drug. Although various substances called THC have been sold illegally, the high cost and the difficulty of producing THC make it very unlikely that it is actually available illicitly. To date, no samples of THC purchased on the black market have been found on chemical analysis to be THC.

Here are some facts about marijuana. (1) Usage and arrests for marijuana possession and sale are increasing. (2) Possession and sale are prohibited by law in most nations of the world; 79 countries have agreed to control the drug under a United Nations treaty. (3) Heavy marijuana use may be associated with abuse of other drugs, such as LSD, amphetamines, and barbiturates. (4) THC is a powerful mind-altering drug, like LSD. (5) Frequent heavy use of more concentrated forms of cannabis, such as hashish and dagga, or bhang, has been associated with physical, mental, and emotional deterioration.

Until recently, traffic in drugs took place only among criminal elements in our society. Since the early 1960s, however, drug sales in LSD, other hallucinogens, amphetamines, barbiturates, and especially marijuana, have rapidly increased among college and high school students who ordinarily are not involved in illegal activities. Although some youths sell marijuana only to friends, their sources are sometimes commercial sellers who traffic in other drugs. Studies of the spread of marijuana and LSD use have often shown the new user to be zealous in making converts to the new experience.

There is no quality control on illicit drugs; sometimes sellers deal in counterfeit or adulterated products, for which inexperienced users may pay high prices. Some youths have paid well to smoke grass clippings, ground leaves, oregano, catnip, parsley, or manure. The Bureau of Narcot-

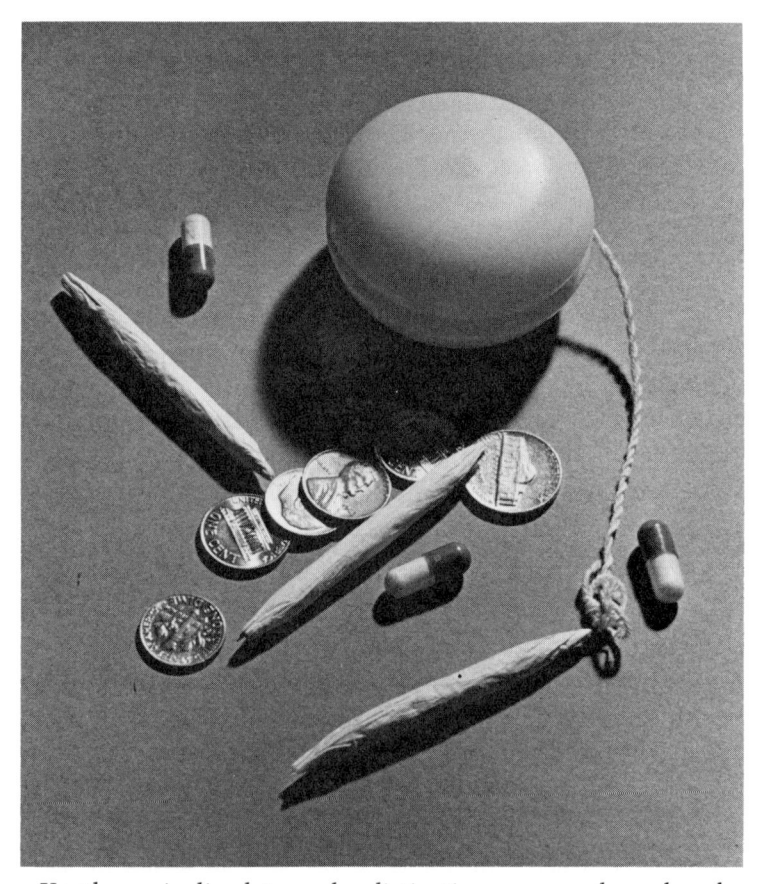

Youth are inclined to make distinctions among drugs based more on their effects on the user than on their legality. To an adolescent a joint often seems comparable to or less harmful than a beer, since its effects are rarely any more pronounced.

ics and Dangerous Drugs laboratories have found that up to 17 percent of purported marijuana specimens analyzed are not in fact cannabis.

Short-Term Effects

Some frequently reported short-term physical effects of marijuana (in low dosage) are: dilation of the blood vessels in the eye (called "conjunctival injection"), causing a bloodshot appearance; increase in heart rate; irritation of the throat; and dryness of the mouth. There are no consistent changes in blood pressure, respiratory rate, amount of force needed to effect the knee-jerk reflex, or strength of the stimuli needed for visual or auditory response. The appetite for food is often increased, and some marijuana users become drowsy. Although these changes occur, all of them are not necessarily found in every person using the drug. Contrary to popular belief, marijuana use cannot easily be determined by examining the pupils of the eye. Marijuana has sometimes been called an aphrodisiac; however, although it may increase tactile sensitivity, there is no evidence that it stimulates sexual desire or potency. Its use, like the use of alcohol, may reduce inhibitions.

Some commonly experienced short-term psychological and social responses to marijuana intoxication (in low dosage) are euphoria (a "high" or a heightened sense of well-being), a feeling of detachment and relaxation, a feeling that sensations are more intense, changes in the perceptions of distance and time, a tendency to be easily distracted, disruption of thought and speech, suggestibility, an increased sense of sociability, and hilarity.

Long-Term Effects: Dependence and Tolerance

Marijuana does not produce a dependence of the opiate type; that is, a person does not suffer physical symptoms of withdrawal upon cessation of use. Psychological dependence on marijuana, however, is common among long-term heavy users. In 1965, the World Health Organization's Expert Committee on Addiction-Producing Drugs made an official statement describing the dependence potential of cannabis products, paraphrased below.

> Drug dependence of the cannabis type is a state arising from chronic or periodic administration of cannabis. Subjective effects are (1) moderate to strong psychic dependence, based on the attainment of desired subjective effects; (2) absence of physical dependence—so that there is no characteristic abstinence syndrome when the drug is discontinued—and (3) little tendency to increase the dosage and no evidence of tolerance.

Hollister (1969) reports that two-thirds of the users in his study in Egypt expressed a wish to stop using hashish, but that their habituation to the euphoria and other effects, as well as their motive to conform to an expected social pattern, made them continue using the drug. He indicates that a similar pattern may be emerging in the United States. An individual may develop tolerance to certain drugs. Little is known about tolerance to marijuana, but more recent studies indicate that some tolerance does develop. Any tolerance is minimal, however, compared to that which can develop to the opiates, amphetamines, or barbiturates.

In the case of a drug such as marijuana, whose effects are so varied, inconsistent, and in the long term unknown, and the use of which is inextricably involved with social issues, the researcher frequently finds his data used for purposes he did not intend. As a number of commentators on the present drug scene have pointed out, the serious consequences of drug abuse affect a statistically small number of abusers. If the number of abusers of marijuana continues to increase, however, the number of persons suffering serious adverse effects will also grow.

Surveys indicate that the vast majority of users are experimenters, and that only a relatively few move on to other drugs or become heavy, chronic users, or "potheads." The 1972 report of the National Commission on Marijuana and Drug Abuse stated that there were then over 24 million marijuana users in the United States, mainly between 12 and 25 years of age. Approximately 10 percent were regular users. College students were the first large group in the general population to become interested in marijuana. In college surveys of drug use, use of marijuana has been reported more than that of any other illicit drug. In one study, the highest rates of use were found at small, progressive liberal-arts colleges that are highly selective and grant considerable independence to students. The lowest rates were found at teachers' colleges, junior colleges, community colleges, and the smaller denominational colleges. In most studies, students in the arts, social sciences, and humanities were more likely to have tried marijuana than those in scientific, professional, or vocational fields. In cases in which marijuana use was reported separately for the sexes, fewer women than men reported using it. New surveys are rapidly being reported, but the results can still be expected to provide trends rather than precise indices of use.

One possible indicator of marijuana use is the sales of cigarette papers beyond the amount used for rolling tobacco cigarettes. Enforcement statistics are also often used as indicators of illegal behavior. Although marijuana-arrest statistics are not an accurate indicator of the extent of use, arrests have increased markedly since 1960. Another factor affecting statistics is that state laws vary in their definition of marijuana; some classify it as a narcotic drug, others as a hallucinogen. And, of course, law-enforcement agencies may vary in the strictness of their enforcement of drug laws.

The United Nations World Health Organization estimates the number of marijuana users worldwide to be between 200 and 250 million people. Of users in the United States, it was estimated that fewer than 10 percent of them, or 800,000 to 1,200,000, are long-term users who devote significant amounts of time to obtaining and using marijuana. Another 2 or 3 million are estimated to use it socially, usually in a group context.

Recent surveys have revealed an increase in marijuana use. In 1969, surveys revealed an increase of 5 to 12 percent in the secondary schools of one California county district and among college students nationwide. Use in one particular school was as high as 75 percent. Recent evidence from San Mateo, California, indicates that, among both males and females in junior and senior high school, there has been a steady increase in both experimental and regular marijuana use. Table 11.1 provides comparative data for 1969, 1971, and 1973.

TABLE 11.1. Incidence of marijuana use in high school.

	Any use during year							More than 50 times during year				
	1969		1971		1973		1969		1971		1973	
Grade	M	F	M	F	M	F	M	F	M	F	M	F
Eighth	24*	22	29	26	34	32	**	**	**	**	10	8
Tenth	42	36	50	48	56	52			23	17	28	19
Twelfth	50	38	59	48	61	57			32	19	32	20

*Percentages are rounded to the nearest whole number.
**No survey was taken.
Adapted from *Surveillance of student drug use.* San Mateo, Calif.: Department of Public Health and Welfare, 1973.

In a national sample of 5050 students from 38 different colleges and universities, Gergen, Gergen, and Morse (1972) found that 36.7 percent had experience with marijuana, 11.7 percent with hallucinogens, and 8.2 percent with amphetamines. The marijuana percentage was slightly down from the 42 percent reported in a Gallup poll in December 1970.

Cross and Davis (1972) studied 178 students (91 males and 87 females), 114 of whom were volunteers from general psychology courses and 64 from advanced courses. They were administered the Rotter Incomplete Sentences Blank (Rotter & Rafferty, 1950) and an extensive questionnaire about drug use. Testing was anonymous, and the subjects were assured that the data would be used only by the investigators. The drug questionnaire asked about marijuana, LSD, amphetamines, barbiturates, narcotics, and alcohol. Since marijuana was clearly the most popular drug, and all other drugs (except alcohol) were used by only a small minority of the subjects, only the marijuana data are discussed here. One hundred, or 56 percent of the subjects, had tried marijuana at least once. Five categories of marijuana users, roughly paralleling the classifications described by Nowlis (1969), were developed. A description of each category, with the percentage of subjects included in it, follows.

Adamant nonusers (22 percent) have never considered using a drug and state that drug use should be prohibited.

Nonusers (21 percent) have seriously considered using the drug but have not actually done so. They state that marijuana use might be allowed if it were subject to proper controls.

Tasters (24 percent) use marijuana less than once a month.

Recreational users (15 percent) use marijuana from one to four times a month.

Regular users (17 percent) use marijuana more than once a week.

Attitudes toward Marijuana

The average adolescent is attracted to marijuana out of curiosity or peer pressure and out of the conviction that it is relatively harmless—in fact, less harmful than alcohol or tobacco. The relaxed, uninhibited disposition that characterizes many users is seen as a way to "be oneself" and is sought after by many users as a momentary utopia. During the four to six hours in which the drug normally influences the user, a sense of lightness and tranquility is enjoyed.

The apparent harmlessness of marijuana, as expressed by most users, has caused its proponents to advocate its legalization. They contend that prohibiting its free use only reflects the absurdity of our social and legal codes (Fort, 1968; Johnson & Westman, 1968). In fact, even a study conducted by the American Medical Association stated that it is a relatively harmless drug ("Dependence on Cannabis," 1967). However, this attitude is not reflected in its overall membership, for 85 percent of some 28,000 physicians polled in 1969 were opposed to the legalization of the drug. Their primary reason was that marijuana often leads to addiction to more dangerous drugs ("Modern Medicine Poll," 1969).

A *Psychology Today* survey (Clark & Funkhouser, 1970) conducted in 1970 among 127 medical researchers and 490 medical practitioners revealed the following attitudes about marijuana.

1. Supervised use of marijuana was rated as safe by 58 percent of the researchers, compared with 39 percent of the practitioners.
2. Twenty-eight percent of the researchers and 46 percent of the practitioners thought that marijuana held mental-health dangers.
3. Compared with alcohol, marijuana was seen as equally dangerous or less dangerous by 68 percent of the researchers and 54 percent of the practitioners.

Johnson (1972) found a more pronounced negative attitude toward marijuana. He found a 60-percent disapproval of marijuana use in a midwestern high school sample. Similarly, the Monroe County, New York, study by Yancy and his associates (1972) revealed that 44.6 percent thought that marijuana caused loss of ambition, and 48 percent felt that it led to heavier drugs. An even greater percentage (73.6) thought that it could cause psychological dependence.

The varied conclusions drawn from a myriad of research studies and position papers have led to equally varied beliefs about marijuana use, from the belief that it is extremely dangerous to the belief that it is socially beneficial. Adolescents therefore have difficulty knowing what attitude they should hold toward their use of it or toward its use by others. The setting for a person's first use of marijuana is usually a group. Occasional users of marijuana almost always use it at social affairs, seldom alone. Sometimes young people find that marijuana smoking is the key to acceptance by a group that considers itself sophisticated and daring. In groups of this kind, occasional use may develop into long-term use or involvement with other drugs, depending on the leadership and the experiences of the group. If the group includes members who are "chipping" heroin (using it at irregular intervals), there is a chance that new members of the group will be tempted to try it. If the group includes LSD users, this route is also open. The more closely a person is tied to a drug-using group, the more likely he or she is to wind up using drugs. The power of a group to encourage or discourage the behavior of its members is enormous.

THE HALLUCINOGENS

Hallucinogens (also called psychedelics) are drugs capable of eliciting changes in sensation, thinking, self-awareness, and emotion. Alterations in time and space perception, illusions, hallucinations, and delusions may be minimal or overwhelming, depending on the dosage and the drug. The results of hallucinogen ingestion are variable, and the same person experiences different reactions on different occasions.

A large number of natural and synthetic hallucinogens have been identified. LSD is the most potent and the best studied. Mescaline from the peyote cactus, psilocybin from the Mexican mushroom, morning glory seeds, DMT, STP, MDA, and others have somewhat similar effects. LSD is an odorless, colorless, tasteless drug. Dr. Albert Hofman synthesized LSD—lysergic acid diethylamide—in 1938; this acid is found in ergot, a fungus that grows on rye and wheat. Dr. Hofman discovered its ability to alter perception in 1943. Today LSD is described as a hallucinogenic agent because of the visual hallucinations reported by LSD "trippers" (Johnson & Westman, 1968; Richards, Joffe, Smith, & Spratto, 1969).

The legitimate production and use of LSD are now limited by the Federal Food and Drug Administration to carefully controlled research projects. Because of this strict control, and because its hazardous side effects are becoming widely known, the unauthorized self-administration of LSD appears to be on the decline. However, there are many, attracted by the glamor and excitement surrounding the drug, who continue to ignore, or are unaware of, the dangers involved in experimenting with LSD. Although self-administration of LSD has been popular with college and high school students, its abuse is by no means limited to the young. Adults from a wide range of social and economic backgrounds also experiment with it. The reasons for LSD abuse are varied as its users. Some are merely curious about its effects, especially its alleged ability to increase sensory awareness. Others have heard about the "consciousness-expanding" or "mind-bending" properties of LSD and hope to gain greater personal insights from its use. Still others use LSD to escape day-to-day stress. Another group, frequently users of other drugs, are drug-dependent persons.

Suchman (1968) found that only 10 percent of the college students in his West Coast study had used LSD, and that only 1.2 percent used it frequently. Levy (1973) found recent use of psychedelics among 3.6 percent of his sample. Their use was most prevalent on college campuses and in areas with a high concentration of youth such as the Haight-Ashbury in San Francisco, Greenwich Village in New York, and Sunset Boulevard in Los Angeles. The youths of these areas enjoy a sense of community and often share the experience of "turning on." For some adolescents, turning on creates a sense of oneness that is not felt at any other time; others enjoy deep religious experiences in which they feel that they are communicating with God. Yet few users report that an LSD trip makes them permanently more contemplative, aware, or "conscious." If LSD use could be defined as a syndrome, its users, who are commonly social dropouts, appear to be searching for something in their mental explorations that will give meaning to their lives.

LSD has caused its users more severe psychological damage than has any other drug (Richards et al., 1969). For many LSD users, turning on results in psychic disturbance that may continue for an extended period after the drug wears off. Psychotic behaviors have been found in users who apparently had stable emotions and personalities before using the drug ("Pop Drugs," 1969; Strack, 1968). Although the exact biochemical changes that take place within the human body when LSD is ingested are still largely a mystery, much is known about the ways in which the drug produces its effects.

Central Effects

The most readily observable effects of LSD are called "central" because of LSD's action on the central nervous system. This action is capable of producing, in turn, a wide range of physiological effects. Central effects include:

1. Stimulation of electrical activity in the brain (as reflected by activation of the electroencephalograph, the apparatus that detects and records brain waves).
2. Stimulation of that part of the brain called the reticular formation, which results in heightened sensitivity to sensory stimuli coming from the outside through the sense organs. This action causes distortion of what is perceived, leading to hallucinations and various other psychological changes.
3. Stimulation of those parts of the brain called the brainstem—the medulla and the midbrain. Stimulation of these structures causes the pupils to dilate (a common effect of LSD), the body temperature to rise, the hair to "stand on end," and the sugar content of the blood to increase. It also produces a rapid heart rate and elevated blood pressure.
4. Nausea, dizziness, headache, and sometimes loss of appetite.
5. Stimulation of certain reflexes, such as the knee jerk.
6. Decreased muscular coordination and vomiting, especially when large doses of LSD are taken. A fine tremor of the fingers and hands may occur.

Perceptual and Psychological Effects

The impact of LSD on the senses is striking. The function of perceiving, organizing, and interpreting sense impressions from outside the body as they reach the brain can be severely affected by the drug. A user may notice a sharp increase or intensification of colors and feel that they are "brighter than ever." An individual having taken LSD may first become aware of its effects by noticing that the outlines of objects have begun to waver and to appear distorted. The frame of a picture might seem to waver, for example, or a wall appear to move. If a person looks at a painting while under the influence of LSD, he may notice that the colors appear to run. Ordinary objects may suddenly appear luminous; a glow may appear around another person's head. These phenomena represent a loosening of the normal boundaries of perception.

The term "hallucinogenic" applied to LSD implies that it may cause hallucinations or false perceptions without adequate or relevant stimuli from the environment. But LSD hallucinations are rarely the true type of hallucinations seen by severely disturbed mental patients. Dr. Jerome Levine of the National Institute of Mental Health put it this way:

> Hallucinations, and by a hallucination I mean a false sensory perception without a basis in external reality, are rather rare with LSD. What are

> more common are what may be called pseudohallucinations, where the individual may see something but at the same time he also knows his perception doesn't have a basis in external reality. For example, he may see geometric forms or figures or brilliant colors, and he realizes that they really don't exist out there, but he is seeing them [Ludwig & Levine, 1965, p. 95].

In short, LSD affects a person's stability and the "hold'" he or she has on the world. It loosens, and in some cases altogether shatters, a person's firm relationship with that world.

The psychological effects produced by LSD are much less predictable and understood. Each person undergoes an individualized reaction. Even when the drug is administered for research purposes under controlled conditions, there is no way of determining which persons might suffer undesirable psychological effects. Neither is it possible to predict the results of a single experience, even in normal individuals.

The effects of most drugs depend on the dosage. Fully effective doses of LSD have been as low as 35 micrograms; dosages of ten times this amount or more are often taken, but the effects are qualitatively the same. Differences in dosages primarily affect the duration of the episode, with larger dosages producing longer durations. Of course, LSD purchased illegally carries no guarantee that the stated amount of the drug is actually present or that the drug is actually LSD. Moreover, drugs that have been manufactured or packaged illegally may include impurities that can alter the expected effects or produce adverse reactions.

The Possibility of Chromosome Damage

Several investigators have explored the possibility that LSD may cause an abnormal amount of breakage in the chromosomes of the white blood cells (Dishotsky, Loughman, Mogar, & Lipscomb, 1971; Jacobson, 1968). Chromosomes are the tiny particles in the body's cells that transmit hereditary traits from parent to offspring. If abnormal chromosomal damage occurs, birth defects in the offspring or miscarriages may result. One study (Loughman, 1967) made a statistical analysis of the number of chromosome breaks occurring in a large number of persons to whom the drug had been administered under experimental conditions. From this study, no statistically significant number of chromosome changes occurred. Some individuals did show marked changes, but one would expect such changes on the basis of human variability in reaction to drugs.

Even though statistical evaluation found no conclusive results, it was found that the drug does affect pregnant women. One ongoing study (Richards et al., 1969) of women who showed chromosome changes from

LSD taken prior to conception shows, to date, that there were 6 malformed infants among the 62 born. There were also 12 defective fetuses among 28 abortions that occurred, and, among those women who had a second child, four defective infants were born out of a total of eight.

Another study (Jacobson, 1968) involved 66 women of childbearing age who had voluntarily taken LSD from 1 to 176 times before or during pregnancy and who had exhibited definite genetic damage of the chromosomes. A sociomedical team at George Washington University in Washington, D.C., reported that there had been 35 abortions and 25 births of normal-appearing babies in these LSD users within 18 months. Four fetuses that were obtained through therapeutic or spontaneous abortions showed defects of the central nervous system so severe that normal development would have been impossible. Of the 25 apparently normal babies, 22 have shown chromosome breakage, the same type of damage found in their mothers. Four have congenital defects not considered serious—hernias, birthmarks, or scars. The babies were studied at 2 weeks, 6 weeks, 3 months, and from then on at three-month intervals.

THE NARCOTICS

The narcotics include opium, morphine, heroin, methadone, and codeine. They are depressants that have a pronounced effect on the central nervous and respiratory systems. They are primarily used to relieve pain, although there is no known medical use for heroin. They do not have anticonvulsant effects, as do the barbiturates, and they rarely impair motor coordination.

There are records of opium use as far back as 1552 B.C. It was popularly used for pleasure for centuries, and it was employed for the alleviation of many ailments in Europe and America in the 1700s and 1800s. The practice of opium smoking was introduced to the United States for the first time around 1840 by the Chinese laborers who had immigrated to California. After the Civil War, it spread eastward.

Morphine was isolated from opium in 1803 in a German laboratory. After the hypodermic syringe was brought to the United States in 1856, the subcutaneous use of morphine was widely recommended by physicians, who thought it to be nonaddictive. Soldiers fighting in the Civil War were given morphine frequently for pain. So many soldiers subsequently became addicted that it became known as "the army disease." Nevertheless, many physicians persisted in using the drug as a cure for alcoholism, in effect simply converting alcoholics into morphinists. This practice of the late nineteenth century corresponded with the development of patent medicines, which commonly used as their active ingredients opium and alcohol.

By 1890, the medical profession recognized the morphine problem and began using codeine to cure morphinism. This practice generally worked well, and very few cases of codeine addiction were reported. However, in 1898, heroin was synthesized from morphine in Germany. It was immediately pronounced to be the most useful and effective analgesic ever known to man, and it was used throughout Europe and the United States as the nonaddictive treatment for opium, morphine, and codeine addiction. Not until 1910 did the medical profession become acutely aware that heroin was highly addictive (Terry & Pellens, 1928).

Heroin use became illegal in 1914 with the passage of the Harrison Narcotic Act. One of its immediate effects was, ironically, a boost in heroin addiction. The act markedly restricted the ability of physicians and pharmacists to dispense opiates; heroin thus became the narcotic most easily available illegally, and heroin trafficking increased. Therefore the number of opium and morphine addicts decreased and the number of heroin addicts rose (Baden, 1972). Up until World War II, there were usually fewer than 50 deaths per year from narcotic abuse in the United States. During the war, the number of deaths decreased because heroin and morphine were not readily available. The morphine shortage in Germany led scientists to synthesize methadone, which was introduced to the United States after the war was over. When international trade was resumed, heroin again became accessible. By 1950, the deaths in New York City attributable to heroin had exceeded 50; they rose to 200 by 1960 and to over 1,000 by 1970. Now it is estimated that there are between 1,000 and 1,500 deaths per year in New York City alone, approximately 30 percent of which are teen-agers. An analysis of the death rate in New York City in 1969 revealed that, of the 1,106 people who died, 56 percent were black, 23 percent white, and 21 percent Puerto Rican.

Heroin is, of course, both addicting and habituating. Its physical effects are so strong that a regular pattern of its use seems necessary for survival. In the United States, approximately 2.1 million people between 12 and 25 years of age have experimented with heroin (Shafer, 1972), and it is estimated that there are over 500,000 addicts. Many youths select heroin because it produces euphoria and serenity. Given intravenously, it produces a high or "kick" almost orgasmic in nature, followed by a quiet period in which the user feels high self-esteem and self-confidence.

Heroin is the only drug in the opiate family that cannot be obtained by prescription, although codeine is commonly available in different types of syrups and pills sold over the counter. The Food and Drug Administration requires physicians who prescribe narcotics to keep a record of all narcotics dispensed. The manufacture, distribution, possession, and consumption of any narcotic are subject to stringent international, federal, and state regulations. Illicit sale is usually considered a felony, and penalties are quite severe.

Although it is difficult to determine the actual extent of heroin addiction in the United States, it has reached proportions that cause great concern regarding the drug and its use, the increase in the number of addicts, and the number who are seeking help, including adolescents. Rehabilitation programs currently operating in the United States can be divided into two groups: (1) rapid or gradual withdrawal from narcotics, voluntarily or after civil commitment; and (2) chronic, voluntary maintenance doses of oral methadone. The use of chronic administrations of narcotic oppositionists (antagonists), such as naloxone and cyclazocine, is still experimental. Most treatment programs include efforts at psychological and social rehabilitation, but the degree to which they offer group or individual psychotherapy, job and family counseling, vocational training, legal aid, and appeals to ethnic pride, group loyalty, or religious motivation is highly variable.

The results of treatment programs in the United States have not been entirely satisfactory. In the first place, many addicts are not attracted to these programs. Testifying before the Senate Subcommittee on Alcoholism and Narcotics on May 23, 1972, Dr. Jerome Jaffe, Director of the White House Special Action Office for Drug Abuse Prevention, estimated that only 50,000 to 60,000 of the nation's 250,000 to 500,000 addicts were on methadone and only 50,000 in drug-free withdrawal programs. The number who are on waiting lists for these programs is not known. Second, many addicts fail to benefit from current treatments. Some patients leave treatment; others sell the methadone intended for their treatment on the black market, abuse illicit drugs or alcohol, or relapse during or after treatment. Of course, treatment results vary with characteristics of the patients, the program, and the community, as well as with the treatment measures used.

Critics of the methadone program have stressed methadone's addictive potential and its abuse; that is, many heroin addicts being maintained by methadone also continue to use heroin, and therefore their cure is virtually impossible (Heyman, 1972). Methadone treatments can break the heroin habit, but the long-term effect of methadone maintenance is methadone addiction (Lennard, Epstein, & Rosenthal, 1972). It causes physical and psychological depression, as does heroin. However, since methadone eliminates the craving for heroin and the symptomatic discomfort of withdrawal, it has potentially greater psychological-rehabilitation benefits than does heroin maintenance.

Heroin use among youths is very low in percentage; studies report fewer than one percent as regular users (Levy, 1973; Yancy, Nader, & Burnham, 1972). In Levy's college sample, he found that only 1.6 percent had ever tried heroin, while Yancy found a 2.6-percent experimental use among high school youth. The likelihood of heroin use is greater in metropolitan areas, where it is more common and where pushers make it available in varying doses in order to appeal to a wide segment of the youth population. The number of youths "hooked" on heroin is unknown, but it is estimated to be very small.

MULTIPLE DRUG USE

One of our society's more serious drug problems is the multiple use among so many youths. One type of multiple drug use consists of using more than one drug from the same category. For example, the heroin addict may visit a methadone-treatment center but continue to use heroin as well, or the barbiturate user may take Seconal and Amytal in conjunction with each other, or the glue-sniffer may drink beer at the same time.

A second type of multiple drug user crosses drug categories. This type of abuse is seen in the person caught in the upper-downer syndrome (amphetamines and barbiturates), for example, or in the heroin user who uses cocaine to increase the effect, or in the occasional drinker who takes tranquilizers as he drinks.

Research on marijuana use and other drug-use patterns in marijuana users has revealed high incidences of other drug use. It has caused some speculation as to whether participation in the counterculture gives a person an attitudinal predisposition and susceptibility to marijuana and to more harmful drug usage. One study ("Drugs on Campus," 1971), for example, reports that, among marijuana smokers, 83 percent had also smoked tobacco, 91 percent had used amphetamines, 90 percent had tried alcohol, 82 percent had used barbiturates, 62 percent had tried LSD, and 11 percent had tried heroin.

Blum's research (1969) with college students found that 50 percent of the marijuana users had used amphetamines as well, 33 percent barbiturates, 24 percent hallucinogens, and 6 percent heroin. Solomon's study (1968) within a hippie commune showed that, among all marijuana users, 97 percent of the men and 80 percent of the women had used LSD, 70 and 52 percent methedrine, and 20 and 13 percent heroin.

EXTENT OF DRUG USE

Yancy and his associates (1972) found high incidences of drug use among high school students. Table 11.2 bears out their findings. This study, conducted in New York, showed an 85-percent use of alcohol, strikingly similar to the 84.3-percent alcohol use Suchman (1968) found

TABLE 11.2. Monroe County (New York) high school students' reported experience with drugs.

	Tried it at least once %	Tried it more than 15 times %	Still using it %	Had an unpleasant experience with it %
Alcohol	85.0	45.0	55.9	23.4
Marijuana	27.7	13.2	21.7	4.9
Barbiturates	14.9	2.9	9.2	4.7
Amphetamines	14.2	8.0	9.4	5.1
LSD	8.6	2.7	6.3	4.9
Mescaline	8.3	1.8	7.5	3.4
Glue	7.2	1.3	3.3	3.9
Opium	6.8	1.4	5.6	3.3
Cocaine	3.7	0.6	3.6	2.7
Heroin	2.6*	0.6	3.0*	3.2*

*Because of the small n for heroin users, a small number of incorrectly marked responses accounts for the discrepancies in these essentially equivalent percentages.

From "Drug Use and Attitudes of High School Students" by W. S. Yancy, P. R. Nader, and K. L. Burnham, *Pediatrics*, 1972, 50(5), 740. Copyright 1972 by the American Academy of Pediatrics. Reprinted by permission.

on the West Coast among college students. Further examination of Table 11.2 indicates an appreciable total incidence of drug use. Drug use for some began as early as the seventh grade, although most students reported beginning in the tenth or eleventh grade. After experimenting with drugs, a number of students reported no further use of the drug; and, as was the case in several other drug surveys, more boys than girls used drugs (Blum, 1969; Gossett, Lewis, & Phillips, 1971; Smart, Fejer, & White, 1970; Smith, 1970).

A 1970 readers' poll by *Psychology Today* brought 14,748 responses on the extent of drug use. Respondents were asked to report their rates of drug use. Table 11.3 is adapted from these data. Almost half of the respondents (47 percent) had tried marijuana at least once, and 18 percent had tried LSD. Coffee, tea, and aspirin were the drugs used most often (only two percent had never used them). Tobacco was used daily by 46 percent of the respondents, and 14 percent reported drinking alcohol at least once a day. Sedatives and amphetamine stimulants were used at least once a week by ten percent of the respondents. Eleven percent reported having taken opiates, such as heroin or cocaine, at least once.

Asked to rate the personal risk they felt was involved in taking each of the drugs, the respondents said that the most dangerous drugs were the opiates, LSD, and the other hallucinogens. Coffee, tea, and aspi-

> ## 56% IN HIGH SCHOOLS TRY NARCOTICS*
>
> This headline, startling to the Los Angeles community, represents a twofold problem regarding the use of drugs among adolescents. First, it points out that many youths have experimented in one form or another with drugs. Second, it sensationalizes the problem by implying that all drug use involves narcotics.
>
> In truth, the study found that 56 percent of the high school students and 31 percent of the junior high school students polled in Los Angeles tried drugs at least once during the 1973–1974 school year. But only 4 percent of the high school students used heroin or methadone (narcotics). Forty-eight percent of high school students and 20 percent of junior high school students used marijuana, the majority of them only once. More frequent drug use involved hashish, amphetamines, and barbiturates.
>
> Of the 100,000 high school students in the survey, 25 percent indicated using hashish, 23 percent amphetamines, 18 percent barbiturates, 15 percent LSD, 9 percent solvents (glue, paint thinner), 9 percent cocaine, 6 percent methamphetamine, 2 percent methadone, and 2 percent heroin. Next to marijuana (20 percent), the second most commonly used drug in junior high was solvents (8 percent).
>
> *From *The Los Angeles Times*, June 7, 1974.

rin are rated as safest. Marijuana and alcohol were rated as moderately dangerous, but both were regarded as safer than tobacco, sedatives, and amphetamines.

The regular marijuana users also tended to be tobacco smokers. About 60 percent of the respondents who used marijuana at least once a week smoked tobacco daily. But only 26 percent of the daily tobacco smokers used marijuana at least once a week, and 42 percent of the daily tobacco users had never tried marijuana. About 67 percent of those who never used tobacco had never tried marijuana. Heavy marijuana users also tended to use amphetamines, LSD, and opiates more often than persons who used marijuana infrequently or not at all. For example, 24 percent of the daily marijuana users took amphetamines once a week or more, whereas only about eight percent of the respondents who used marijuana once a month—or less often—took amphetamines that frequently.

The strongest relationship found in this study was between marijuana and LSD use. Of those who had never tried marijuana, 99 percent had never tried LSD. But 31 percent of those who used marijuana

TABLE 11.3. Extent of drug use among readers of *Psychology Today*.

	Use daily	Use weekly	Use monthly	Use yearly	Used once	Never used
Coffee or tea	77	11	6	2	2	2
Aspirin	6	24	48	18	2	2
Alcohol	14	37	28	11	4	5
Marijuana	7	13	10	5	11	53
Sedatives (tranquilizers)	6	5	11	15	26	37
Amphetamines	6	4	8	11	19	51
Tobacco	46	5	6	6	13	23
LSD	.2	1	4	5	7	82
Other hallucinogens	.2	.4	2	4	9	84
Opiates	.4	.2	1	1	8	89

Adapted from "Feedback on Drugs" by David Popoff, *Psychology Today*, 1970, 3(11), 51. Copyright © 1970 Ziff-Davis Publishing Company. Used by permission.

at least once a month had tried LSD, 58 percent of the once-a-week marijuana users had tried it, and 77 percent of the daily marijuana users had tried it. The same trend existed for the other hallucinogens.

The relationship between marijuana use and opiate use is weaker; only 14 percent of the daily marijuana users had taken opiates more than once or twice. But people who used marijuana twice a month or less frequently were no more likely than marijuana nonusers to have tried opiates.

Four out of five of all marijuana users and LSD users reported positive effects from the drugs—at least pleasant, "floaty" feelings. The more often a person used marijuana, the more positively he tended to rate his experience with the drug. This trend was similar for LSD users.

The majority of respondents (62 percent) would like marijuana to be at least as legally available as alcohol, but only nine percent wanted LSD to be that easy to get. Users of marijuana and LSD were much more in favor of making the drugs legally available than were nonusers. But even 40 percent of the people who had never tried marijuana felt that it should be at least as available as alcohol, and 33 percent thought that it should be available only for research.

THE DRUG USER

Smith (1969) has classified drug users into four categories: (1) experimental, (2) periodic or recreational, (3) compulsive, and (4) ritualistic.

The *experimental* user is characterized by curiosity and a tendency toward group conformity. Since his friends use drugs, he too wants to experience being high. Table 11.4, from the study by Yancy and his associates (1972), gives some experimental evidence on the extent of experimental use among adolescents. In all drug categories, curiosity was the strongest motivation source. Other influential motivation sources were the drug's pleasurable effects and the fact that one's friends used it.

It is likely that the experimental user is the most naïve drug user and therefore the most likely to benefit from drug education. Reports concluding that drug education promotes rather than deters drug use cite the susceptibility of this type of individual to the desire to experiment. However, exposure to drug possibilities without concomitant information on why drugs are used, legitimately and illegitimately, can create additional incentive for experimental use without instilling appropriate caution—one of the purposes of drug education.

The *periodic or recreational* user, like the experimental user, takes drugs for fun, pleasure, and excitement. However, he has gone beyond the experimental stage by becoming a regular user; he has developed some social pattern for its use, and is generally a practiced user of one specific drug rather than a multiple drug user.

The *compulsive* user has developed a physical or psychological dependence on one or more drugs. This category commonly comprises as many adults as adolescents, most of whom are seeking a euphoric state

TABLE 11.4. Monroe County (New York) high school students' reasons for beginning to use drugs.

	Curiosity %	Because it is pleasurable %	Because my friends use it %	Need to rebel %	Psychological need %
Alcohol	27.1	55.4	9.9	2.1	5.5
Marijuana	56.0	25.4	7.4	3.1	8.1
Amphetamines	62.0	12.4	5.1	4.1	16.4
Barbiturates	61.8	11.1	5.1	4.1	17.9
Glue	69.7	8.8	5.9	4.5	11.1
LSD	66.8	11.0	5.0	5.0	12.2
Mescaline	65.9	11.5	4.9	4.8	12.9
Opium	66.4	9.8	4.8	5.3	13.7
Cocaine	68.2	8.4	5.0	5.0	13.4
Heroin	66.4	7.0	4.9	6.5	15.2

From "Drug Use and Attitudes of High School Students" by W. S. Yancy, P. R. Nader, and K. L. Burnham, *Pediatrics*, 1972, 50(5), 741. Copyright 1972 by the American Academy of Pediatrics. Reprinted by permission.

that will break into the routine or boredom of their lives. The final two categories in Table 11.4 represent reasons for adolescent drug use that may be tied to some dependence. First, the need to rebel finds some outlet in drug use. Second, some adolescents express definite psychological reasons for using drugs. In the overall picture, however, the percentage of youths who express these two reasons as primary motivators for drug use are a definite minority among drug users.

The *ritualistic* user believes that drugs provide spiritual or religious experiences (Richards et al., 1969; Smith, 1969). Contrary to common belief, these users are not drug abusers. They are cultists seeking revelation through drugs. Many of them go on to spiritual practices that do not include drug use and stop taking them altogether, although they may remain in a drug-oriented society.

DRUG EDUCATION

As I mentioned above, some researchers have found indications that drug education may increase the amount of drug use instead of effectively prevent it among adolescents (for example, Brecher, 1972). If this is the case, however, the program in question must be inappropriate, for it is difficult to believe that enlightenment is a greater motivator for drug use than ignorance. Most drug-education programs focus on the legal and medical aspects of drug use, although there has been some shift in emphasis toward the user and his motives for drug use (Smith, 1969; Weissman, 1969).

Drug-abuse education has come to a point at which the effectiveness of past programs must be examined and new directions for future programs determined. Existing programs have, for the most part, developed directly from the initial attempts of alarmed educators to curb drug abuse through the presentation of brief concentrated sessions stressing the dangers of the commonly abused drugs. The apparent failure of such sessions has often been interpreted as evidence that ignorance about drugs and their effects is not a major cause of drug abuse. This suggestion, however, must carry with it the assumption that the information has been adequately presented and received. But this assumption is put in question by an examination of the numerous barriers to communication that arise between educator and student.

Drug-abuse education is most commonly carried out in secondary schools, where the immediacy of the problem and the difficulty in adjusting curricula have led to the administration of concentrated programs. These often take the form of a special event for a single day or part of a day. The general consensus on such one-day crash programs on drug abuse is that they tend only to sensationalize the topic and perhaps even encourage curious experimentation (Barty, Bethell, & Bellward, 1973; Lewis, 1969, 1970).

Lewis (1971) has suggested that a comprehensive drug-education program requires a national consensus directed toward building an antidrug movement similar to the antismoking movement. The drive against smoking in the United States has been highly effective, despite the vested commercial interests supporting smoking and their sophisticated advertising counterattack on the growing antismoking sentiment. The antismoking campaign captured the imagination of the people and won large numbers of converts, who became agents for the establishment of a new social norm. Today, many enlightened people shun cigarettes and frown on smoking. We have nothing like this national consensus in the area of drugs, largely because of the confusion between hard drugs and soft drugs. The conservative, conformist, antiyouth overtones of much marijuana criticism effectively alienate one major constituency for an anti-drug-abuse campaign—young people themselves—by creating divisiveness and suspicion.

The primary aim of a drug-education program in the secondary schools should be to provide information that helps students understand the social, medical, moral, and legal implications of drug use in *personal* terms. To accomplish this goal, drug education can be organized into two categories: topical—giving information—and dynamic—dealing with decision making (Lewis, 1969).

A significant body of information is now available for presentation in a topical manner. The justification for this approach to information dissemination is twofold: first, the subject of drugs is very much on the minds of students and, second, drug use is a matter of great concern in our society at present. Therefore, just like racism, pollution, and violence, it is a valid subject for inclusion in the curriculum.

The dynamic approach to drug education focuses on how a young person arrives at the decision to use or not to use drugs. It requires an examination of the motivational forces and situations that lead students to seek this form of experience over others. And it requires the imparting of a feeling for what drug use means in personal terms. This focus is the critical feature of the entire effort because, in the last analysis, the choice of using drugs or not using them is in the hands of the student.

Society is depending more and more on the schools to develop strategies to overcome adverse environmental influences on young people. Schools are looked upon as a shield against a host of evils, from VD to alcoholism. They have also had a growing influence on the socialization process. These are strong reasons for expecting the schools to offer preventive drug education.

Without question, other social institutions (the family, churches, community agencies) are also working to curb the drug problem. Without question, it is a social issue, not simply a school issue. Pearce (1971) holds that we must conceptualize the needs of the individual in order to effectively educate. This educational concept is a far cry from the stopgap or cookbook approaches used by so many antidrug programs. Because it recognizes the nature of the individual, it may be the only effective way of preventing drug abuse.

Vogl (1970) focused on the role that physicians, police officials, clergymen, teachers, and ex-drug addicts play in the educative process, contending that the most effective approach is through organized groups generated out of community concern about drugs. Vogl asserts that specially organized groups are often more effective in communicating with youths about the drug problem than already established groups, such as school and church. He cites instances of such special groups' effectiveness in reducing the drug problem in several communities.

Whether drug-abuse-prevention programs are based in the community or in the schools, it is important to avoid some approaches that youths perceive as unrealistic. Levin (1972) has summarized some of these stereotyped approaches or "myths."

Myth 1: Education to the dangers of drugs and familiarity with hip language are the keys to prevention. Much of the drug-abuse literature and advertising campaigns link an emphasis on the various synonyms for marijuana, heroin, amphetamines, etc., with "horror" stories of drug abuse. The assumption seems to be that if parents know what their children are talking about when they mention "ups," "downs," "bennies," "Mary Jane," etc., we will be well on the way to solving the drug problem. Familiarity with terms becomes a substitute for action.

The horror-story approach frequently distorts the most common drug realities and neglects completely the fascination of danger for people seeking excitement as an easy proving ground for their significance via distorted bravery.

Myth 2: The only way to eliminate drug abuse is to eliminate the drug culture. The self-righteous and the uptight seem to believe that the only way we can eliminate the abuse of drugs is by wiping out what they see as a drug culture and its symbols: long hair, communes, alternative life-styles, and the rejection of materialist values associated with many young people. Actually this is a self-defeating absurdity. Unless these life-styles are recognized and encouraged, we will cut off the necessary alternatives and push youth toward drugs as a way out. Increasingly, idealistic young people are becoming vigorous opponents of hard drugs, which they see as inhibiting social action for needed change.

Myth 3: Treatment of the individual drug user is the answer. Every time we take a habitual heroin addict out of the market to treat him, we remove a sponge—an individual who is absorbing enough heroin to supply a start in the habit for ten neophytes. Unless we eliminate the supply of drugs, someone else will take the user's place. If we simply take the present drug consumers out of circulation, the pusher will open up new populations. Frequently, by lowering the price temporarily, he will turn to high school kids as a market. Heroin is *never* dumped as surplus!

Myth 4: Group confrontation programs like Daytop, Synanon, and Phoenix House are really the only answer for the treatment of the addict. Although these programs have a degree of success with some individuals, their overall social significance is grossly exaggerated. They reach a small proportion of the drug-abuse population, with controversial results at high cost. In addition, they operate on assumptions and practices that must be questioned as part of an overall ideological approach to drug abuse. They are modeled after Alcoholics Anonymous in their belief that the addict, like the alcoholic, is essentially an inadequate personality who will remain an addictive personality. The Synanon approach stresses the use of enormous external pressure in a highly undemocratic and often brutal fashion, the aim being to control the addict by making him conform to group demands.

Myth 5: Rehabilitated addicts are decisive for any effective antidrug program. They are the crucial antidrug agents. There is no question that former addicts can play a role in a treatment program. Ex-addicts obviously have a lot of drug know-how, can uncover a good deal of manipulation by addicts, and can function as positive models illustrating the possibility of kicking the habit. Thus antidrug programs can profitably use some ex-addicts as part of an overall approach. However, their use should be highly selective: the ex-addicts should be used only after careful training, and for certain specific purposes with particular target groups [Levin, 1971, pp. 30–33].*

It is important to root an antidrug program in the community itself. However, although community reaction to drug use is characterized by strong feelings, no organizational framework is available that is so extensive as the school system. Assuming, therefore, that the schools presently represent the best organization for disseminating drug education to the masses of children and adolescents, two factors must be assured for the program to be successful. First, the community—from its leaders to its parents—must give strong support to the schools in setting up and implementing drug education. For example, the schools must be allowed to discuss more than the legal and medical aspects of drugs. Concern must be shown for the user and his reasons for use. The mandate of the community to the schools is to do something to help kids with the drug problem. A similar mandate was given in the mid-1960s for sex education. However, when the schools decided to act upon the mandate, the community intervened with claims that they were violating parental

*From "New Myths about Drug Programs" by T. Levin, *Social Policy*, 1971, 2(3), 30-33. Reprinted by permission.

authority and moral teachings. It remains to be seen whether the existing drug-education mandate will be carried out by the schools and supported by the community.

Second, a curriculum must be established that deals with the real world of the adolescent, has credibility for him, and presents a fair and open discussion of the drug scene. Lewis (1975) has devised several guidelines for building a drug-education curriculum. Because they meet the criteria discussed here, some are presented in brief:

1. *Assess the level of the students' sophistication about drugs.* This assessment is critical, since overestimating students' knowledge expects too much of the learners, and underestimating their knowledge causes them to lose interest in the "same old stuff."
2. *Involve students in program planning.* Inasmuch as the drug world is more real to the adolescent than to the teacher, students' input can ensure a higher degree of accuracy.
3. *Include alcohol and tobacco in the discussion.* A more legitimate approach to the total drug problem can be made if the teacher recognizes and presents the problems in our society that result from alcohol and tobacco consumption among adults and adolescents.
4. *Don't sensationalize.* The greater the exaggeration of the drug problem and the more incidents of excessive drug use cited, the more the adolescent will perceive that he is being conned.
5. *Make drug education part of an ongoing classroom experience.* The more thoroughly drug education is integrated into the existing curriculum, the more effective its potential. Some in-service training of teachers will probably be required, but one does not have to be an expert to teach about drugs. Basic information and good materials can help all classroom teachers assume a partial role in this program.
6. *Emphasize the motivational factors that affect a student's decision to use drugs.* Student discussion of *social* factors, such as peer pressure and the influence of adult drug use, is as important as a consideration of *personal* factors, such as curiosity, boredom, defiance of authority, and search for a pleasurable or aesthetic experience. A discussion of motivations should also deal with the reasons for using a drug once versus the reasons for using it repeatedly. The kinds of motivational forces that may operate in the initial decision to experiment with drugs may not be the same as those that affect chronic drug use.

The use of drugs is not in itself an irresponsible act. Medical and scientific uses serve important individual and social needs and are often essential to people's physical and psychological well-being. Furthermore, it is inappropriate to generalize the use of drugs for pleasure and other nonmedical purposes as inherently irresponsible. Some forms of drug use have come to be socially acceptable and show no long-term deleterious effects.

Irresponsibility in the use of drugs, whether in an adolescent or in an adult, occurs when it impedes the individual's integration into the social and economic system of the larger society. Inasmuch as an individual's productivity and social functioning are essential to the American value structure, it is appropriate to judge drug use in that light.

Nevertheless, social changes are continuously occurring. Perhaps America's value structure will also change with time. In times of economic crisis, people often resort to sustaining crutches available in their environment. Furthermore, the emerging leisure ethic and the search for individuality and greater meaning in a society perceived as impersonal have caused much recreational use of drugs. In reality, one's use of drugs for medical purposes or for leisure purposes does not constitute abuse unless it inhibits one's productive role in society or interferes with the basic rights of other individuals with whom one comes in contact.

The Adolescent and Sex 12

In this chapter, we will explore the implications for the adolescent of our changing sexual norms, examining the attitudes of the larger society and of adolescents in particular toward dating, petting, and premarital sex; adolescents' sex-information sources; and the question of sex education in the schools.

OUR CHANGING SEXUAL NORMS

Our social norms are changing. Greater tolerance for behaviors once considered intolerable has emerged and has brought with it more varied perspectives on the family, religion, and politics. Adults and adolescents alike are encouraged to be more individualistic. Biases that once impinged upon various racial groups and social classes and on the female sex are changing. As traditional roles assigned to such groups change, it is inevitable that the role of the individual will also change. If we accept the idea that human sexuality is influenced by the interrelationship between the individual and society, it is not surprising that sexual behaviors and attitudes have also changed.

Undeniably, change has occurred in the way we view human sexuality. It is likely that industrialism, the growth of the mass media, new ideologies and technology, and the changing role of women have stimulated such change. The recent historical trend toward freer sexual expression made its first marked appearance among those persons born between 1900 and 1910 (Kinsey, Pomeroy, & Martin, 1948; Terman et al., 1938). This group was exposed to other nations' customs as a result of World War I, to increasing industrialization, and to the days of prohibition. Beginning with Freud, let's discuss some of the primary forces that have contributed to our contemporary sexual emphasis.

Freud's Contribution to Ideas of Human Sexuality

Not until the late nineteenth century, with the teachings of Freud, did any significant changes in attitudes toward and understanding of human sexuality occur in America. Freud explained sex in natural terms rather than in the Judeo-Christian terms that had been used for centuries. Freud saw the individual as a sexual being who, from birth, matured through several stages of sexual feelings and expressions. Sexuality was a natural instinct that sought proper social expression, not a shameful urge that suddenly emerged at puberty and became legitimized only by marriage. Freud made two highly significant contributions to people's understanding of themselves sexually: he made sex something people could talk about with respect and scientific openness, and he showed sex to be not only central to the private life of the individual but also to the social life of individuals, groups, and society.

Petras (1973) sees Freud's contributions as having influenced contemporary sexual attitudes in three ways:

1. He demonstrated that there is a connection among apparently divergent and unrelated forms of sexual activity. In particular, he showed a connection between one's early-childhood experiences and one's sexual expressions (and sometimes perversions) in adulthood.
2. He demonstrated that human sexuality goes through developmental stages. Psychological stages are linked to changes in the body.
3. He showed how forms of sexual activity early in one's life can serve as a foundation for adult behavior. Often an early experience, while not important in itself, becomes important as later experiences are defined in terms of one's overall psychological framework.

The teachings of Freud were commonly misunderstood or misinterpreted, especially by those who held to strict religious standards for the regulation of sexual behavior. Freud was not an advocate of sexual freedom, license, or promiscuity. In fact, he was something of a puritan and a rationalist; he sought to bring the irrational, primitive side of human nature under the disciplined control of the ego. He appears to have been a highly moral man in the sense that sexual morality is defined by the Judeo-Christian ethic. He believed that without controls—some of which are ego generated and some of which superego generated—a person was likely to become an insensitive, sexually repressed, even distorted individual. When sex plays its proper role in the personality development of the individual, it contributes to growth, development, and socioemotional health.

Some misinterpretation of Freud may have resulted from the fact that his teachings occurred during a time when America was changing. The beginning of industrialization, the effects of World War I, and the days of prohibition were instrumental in liberalizing peoples' expressions of their sexual impulses. To some, Freud's theory was the excuse they needed, but the theory in itself was amoral.

Technological Innovations

The increase in technology and its demand for skills has precipitated several social changes. It has, for example, alleviated much manual labor, made many jobs available to women, reduced the workweek, provided more leisure time, and promoted greater equality between the sexes. Through big business, it has promoted urbanization, separated the functions of work and home for most people, and provided anonymity. The increased mobility it has inspired has lessened the home's influence on adolescents' sexual standards and has allowed for greater diversity of heterosexual contacts for adults and adolescents.

The Mass Media

There is little question that the media have had a profound effect on sexual behaviors and attitudes. Its impact on recent history may have been initiated by the Life picture story "The Birth of a Baby" in 1938. A national poll indicated that 40 percent of the general public had seen the article, some 60 percent of whom considered it a good method of educating the public about childbirth and the mother's care (Erskine, 1968). Studies of sexual behavior, especially the two Kinsey reports (Kinsey et al., 1948, 1953), and numerous Gallup polls also contributed to change by providing public exposure of changing attitudes toward sexual issues.

However, motion pictures, television, and literature have precipitated the greatest change. Since World War II, openness in sexual matters has become increasingly pronounced in these media. Public pornography has also become a central aspect of our society. It dominates the movie theaters, newsstands, and nightclubs and is considered *avant-garde* in many circles.

Bensman (1970) has stated some of the behavioral effects of these changes as follows:

> At the level of personal behavior the demand is for a sexual freedom, pragmatic in character, which in its most advanced form allows for the organized and advertised orgy, nude bathing, the advertising for temporary sexual partners (at times of both sexes), the switching of partners either spontaneously or according to predetermined rules, and the public acceptance of all varieties of sexual experimentation both in public and in private, but always with public recognition [Bensman, 1970, p. 407].

The Implications of Family Planning

It was not until 1954, when two New England doctors discovered the birth-control pill, that the 2000-year-old search to remove the chances of pregnancy from sexual intercourse became a scientific reality. By 1967, 6 million American women were taking The Pill. This highly reliable form of birth control, along with other types of contraceptive devices, has tremendously reduced the number of unwanted births and provided men and women with simple alternatives to pregnancy or abstinence (see Figure 12.1). In addition to the number of women using contraceptives, some 2 million married couples have chosen surgical intervention for birth control. The male vasectomy in particular has become an increasingly popular operation, since it has become less involved and less expensive.

Abortion laws have become so liberalized that, in 1972, for every seven live births there were four aborted ones. Although there are religious and special-interest groups that oppose contraception and abortion, it appears that both alternatives to childbirth are becoming increasingly prominent in our society. As well as allowing men and women greater sexual freedom, these alternatives may very well serve the best interests of population control in the next few decades.

Changes in Marriage

Today's youths, when anticipating sexuality and marriage, build their expectations around a new concept of sexual spontaneity and a state of liberation from Victorianism, the Protestant ethic, and religious and legal repression. They engage in trial marriages, companionate marriages, serial marriages, homosexual marriages, communal marriages, and nonmarital sexual liaisons. Today's adolescents are not convinced that traditional marriages are necessarily the best or that they appropriately fit their more liberal sexual concepts. Furthermore, these new living arrangements are advocated as legitimate public forms of sexual behavior, not bound by traditional stigma or condemnation.

However, one should not overgeneralize here, for in fact these demands for greater sexual liberties and for nontraditional marital arrangements come most often from the college adolescent and from the upper-middle-class or upper-class adolescent, a large percentage of whom bridge both categories. Research by Reiss (1967) revealed that the most permissive group of adolescents he studied were those whose fathers were professional men. Reiss offers this finding as significant, for it has traditionally been thought that the lower a person is on the social ladder the more permissive he tends to be. On the contrary, according to Ferdinand, "the typical lower-upper-class or upper-middle-class young man pursues sexual experience with all the ingenuity and intensity that his father displays in pursuing professional recognition and advancement" (1969, p. 42).

Social Changes

Much social change that is occurring in U.S. society is the result of the contemporary bombardment of sexual stimuli, mentioned earlier

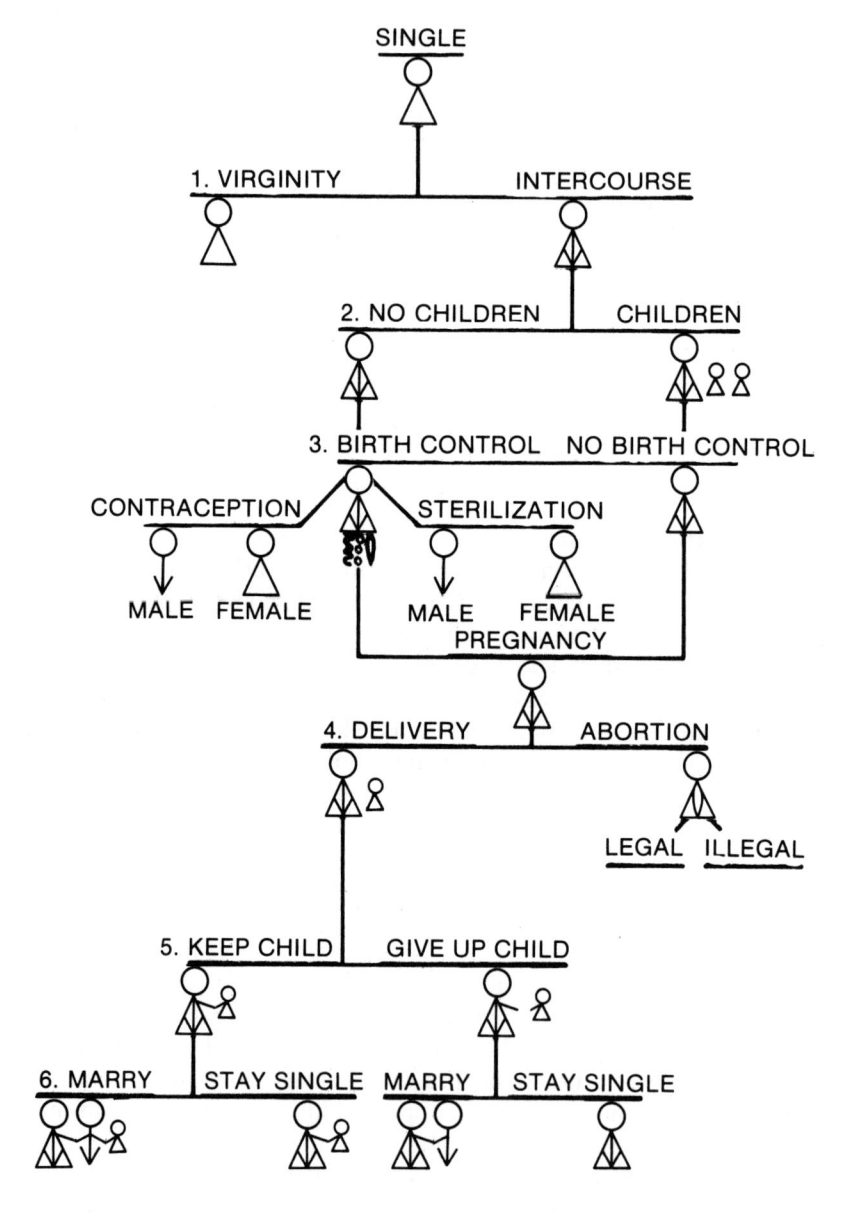

FIGURE 12.1. A model for sexual decision making. From "Sexual Decision Making: The Crux of the Adolescent Problem" by A. M. Juhasz. In R. E. Grinder (Ed.), *Studies in Adolescence* (3rd ed.). Copyright 1975 by Macmillan, Inc. Reprinted by permission.

in connection with the growth of the mass media. Motion pictures and television present sex as a product for consumption, in a way that implies that sex has no consequences. The lack of realism surrounding this "take it and leave it" approach encourages indulgence but does little to enlighten people on their true sexual nature. A good example is a *New Yorker* cartoon in which a 13-year-old girl is inquiring about an X-rated movie advertised on the billboard of the local theater. The theater attendant's response is that it is about the sex life of a little girl her age, but that she will have to bring her parents in order to see it.

Sex novels, magazines like *Playboy, Oui,* and *Viva,* pornocomics, and hard-core pornography are well within the adolescent's grasp and interest. These sources are replete with suggestions to teen-age boys and girls on how to score, how to go "all the way," how to bring out "the real you," and so on. In short, the media—in one form or another—are probably the greatest promoters of adolescent sexual involvement in the United States. Their persuasiveness may exceed even that of the peer group, and they possess no conscience.

In analyzing social reasons for changes in sexual behavior, one observes that the traditional controls have given way to the new sexual impetus. For example, parental control over adolescent sexual behaviors appears to have declined. Today's parents are not necessarily more indifferent, however. Rather, so many feel that their authority has been usurped by peers and the media that they consequently feel ineffective in discussing sexual matters. Certainly, research evidence demonstrates that strong parent-adolescent relationships have a pronounced effect on adolescent sexual behavior (Schofield, 1965). Perhaps this perceived ineffectiveness on the parents' part is the crucial variable.

Another social-change factor is lack of community pressure to conform to traditional codes, especially within the densely populated areas of the cities. In the larger cities, for example, it is now less demeaning for an unmarried woman to have a baby, partly because of the anonymity the city affords and partly because people have come to tolerate this occurrence. Numerous teen-agers have a car; to many, it is a prerequisite for dating. More adolescents are leaving home and moving into apartments. Many colleges and universities have coeducational dormitories, unlimited visiting privileges, and mixed sunbathing decks. Social services, some of which are free, are now available to people who need contraceptives, abortion, or venereal-disease treatment.

Lessening of parental and community control, combined with a reduction in fear of pregnancy, has thus led to more premarital permissiveness in both sexes. Let's explore adolescent attitudes and behaviors regarding three well-known sexual customs: dating, petting, and sexual intercourse.

DATING

Grinder (1966) compiled a comprehensive list of reasons for dating from the interpretations of sociologists, the replies of several adolescents who were asked about dating, and the advice columns of various newspapers and teen-age magazines. He limited the concept of dating to situations in which the partners constituted a heterosexual pair, were unmarried, and were unchaperoned. Four categories emerged from his analysis:

1. *Sexual gratification.* Dating offers sanctioned opportunities for physical contact with members of the opposite sex.
2. *Independence assertion.* Dating provides a means to achieve independence from adults and the accepted standards of society. Dating may also serve as a means for deviating from one's religious practices, political beliefs, parental restriction or curfew, and so forth.
3. *Status seeking.* Dating offers opportunities for associating with prestigious members of the opposite sex.
4. *Participative eagerness.* Dating sometimes appeals to adolescents because they can avoid loneliness, boredom, anxiety, work responsibilities, or activities with parents or same-sex peers.

In our society, dating has been considered a vehicle for integrating young people into heterosexual relationships. Douvan and Adelson (1966) report that most girls have begun this process by age 14 and most boys by age 15. Although these ages are normative, there is a tremendous amount of variation in the age at which adolescents begin to date. Broderick (Broderick & Rowe, 1968), for example, citing research he had done on dating, found that in one rural community 95 percent of the youths did not have their first date until after puberty, whereas in another community less than 100 miles away over 50 percent of the boys and girls had dated at least once by age 12. Even considering such variation, most adolescents are single-dating by 15 or 16 (Broderick, 1966; Dunphy, 1963).

Although dating is instrumental in helping adolescents develop social and interpersonal skills with the opposite sex, and although opportunity for a variety of dates is present in our social system, from the very beginning adolescents tend to limit their dating to only a few partners. It is natural to continue dating someone if you have a good time. Physical attractiveness has been found to be a primary influence in the frequency of dating a particular person (Byrne, Ervine, & Lambeth, 1970; Walster, Aronso, Abrahams, & Rottmann, 1966). Frequency of dating is also directly related to "steady" dating (Lowrie, 1956, 1961; Schepp, 1960). Inasmuch as dating carries some social prestige, represents an "in" with

Being together is very important to adolescents. They often feel a closeness in a heterosexual relationship that they do not feel elsewhere.

one's peers, and provides ego-strength and security to the individual, there is a strong tendency to maintain a relationship over a period of time. The potentially deleterious effect of limited dating is that it restricts the development of social skills.

"Going steady" means different things to different couples. One study (Schneider, 1966) of high school juniors and seniors currently going steady found that, although 75 percent felt that their relationships involved a commitment not to date others, the remainder felt no such absolute restriction. Seventy-five percent felt that they were "in love," but 25 percent did not. Forty percent had an informal commitment to get married, another 40 percent had thought seriously about marriage but had made no commitment, and 20 percent had never considered it seriously. As we might expect, the longer a couple had gone steady the more likely they were to have considered marriage seriously. Of those who had gone steady only two months, only three percent had announced their intention to marry, but of those who had been going together for a year or more, 50 percent had done so.

Level of intimacy also varies among steadily dating couples. A series of studies by Reiss (1967) showed that there is a general agreement

(75 percent to 89 percent) among young people in various parts of the country that it is all right for couples who are in love to pet. A study by Christensen and Carpenter (1962), however, shows that this agreement does vary from one part of the country to another. For example, students in Utah, where the Mormon influence is very strong, are considerably more conservative than students in Indiana; but in most parts of the country petting is the approved level of intimacy for steady couples. Also, it is not surprising to note that, if one looks at the actual behavior rather than at the abstract approval or disapproval of petting, between 70 percent and 85 percent of all steady couples do in fact pet (Bell & Blumberg, 1959; Reiss, 1967; Sorensen, 1973).

The percentage who go on to sexual intercourse is much smaller. About 20 percent of boys in one sample (Reiss, 1967) reported having sexual relations with their steady partners, although only about four percent of the girls in another sample reported this degree of intimacy. Since the boys and the girls studied came from two different samples, the discrepancy in reported intimacy is probably real and not the result of a reporting differential between the sexes. Nevertheless, males are generally more frank in their reporting of intimacy (Carns, 1973). In general, the overall level of intimacy among steady couples can be summarized as follows: roughly 20 percent limit themselves to necking (kissing and hugging), 60 percent go on to petting at the most intimate level, and 20 percent experience sexual intercourse (Reiss, 1967).

Steadiness of dating is related to the seriousness of the relationship. Seriousness is related to the amount of physical contact and emotional involvement present. The greater the feeling for each other, and the more enduring the relationship, the more likely youths are to engage in some form of premarital heterosexual involvement.

PETTING

There is little doubt that petting is a highly prevalent form of premarital heterosexual play, because two young people who are physically attracted to each other have strong biological urges to have body contact. Faced with a choice among having no "heavy" physical involvement, heavy physical involvement (petting), or sexual intercourse, many adolescents choose petting as a compromise position, being unable to consistently avoid body contact and having some reluctance to "go all the way." Martinson (1968) found, in his Minnesota sample, that adolescents would involve themselves in deep kissing, body fondling, petting to orgasm, simulated intercourse, and mutual masturbation as forms of physical enjoyment and release without becoming engaged in the act of intercourse.

Kinsey was the first to report the incidence of premarital petting in the general population. His 1953 study of female sexual behavior recorded the pattern of petting to orgasm among teen-agers as follows:

Before 1920	15 percent
During 1920s	30 percent
During 1930s	34 percent
During 1940s	43 percent

Among college-bound females in the 1940s, the incidence of petting to orgasm was 52 percent. Even so, the Kinsey data reveal a lesser degree of premarital involvement than do studies conducted in the 1960s and 1970s. Robinson, King, and Balswick (1972) compared the amount of premarital petting among college students in 1965 and college students in 1970. Data from their study are summarized in Table 12.1. As you can see, the number of males involved in petting did not change over the five-year span, although heavy petting became an increasingly preferred form of sexual expression. Female involvement in petting did increase, however; in 1970, 98.7 percent indicating some petting behavior. There was a strong increase in heavy petting; 59.7 percent of the 1970 sample indicated such involvement, compared with 34.3 percent in 1965 (Robinson, King, Dudley, & Clune, 1968, 1972).

TABLE 12.1. Petting behavior for 1965 and 1970 college students.

Percentages	Males	Females
No petting		
1965	1.6 (n= 3)	8.7 (n=10)
1970	2.2 (n= 3)	1.3 (n= 2)
Percentage difference	+.6	−7.4
Percentages	Males	Females
Light petting		
1965	11.6 (n=15)	32.2 (n=37)
1970	8.9 (n=12)	19.5 (n=30)
Percentage difference	−2.7	−12.7
Percentages	Males	Females
Medium petting		
1965	14.7 (n=19)	24.3 (n=28)
1970	9.6 (n= 3)	19.5 (n=30)
Percentage difference	−5.1	−4.8
Percentages	Males	Females
Heavy petting		
1965	71.3 (n= 92)	34.3 (n=40)
1970	79.3 (n=107)	59.7 (n=92)
Percentage difference	+8	+25.4

From "The Premarital Sexual Revolution among College Females" by I. E. Robinson, K. King, and J. O. Balswick, *Family Coordinator,* 1972, *21,* 190. Copyright 1972 by National Council on Family Relations. Reprinted by permission.

Studies by Packard (1968) and Luckey and Nass (1969) showed that 61 percent of junior and senior college women had had heavy petting experience. Nevertheless, among the five countries sampled in these studies, the U.S. college women were the most conservative. (The other countries were Norway, Canada, England, and Germany.) In the 1969 sample, 57 percent of the U.S. women had experienced heavy petting in high school. The Packard study suggested that there is considerable equality in rates of heavy petting for college men and women, although the men start somewhat younger.

For college women, engaging in heavy petting is strongly related to permissiveness of standards for coitus, to dating status, and to perception of the coital experience of female friends. Among those women who considered sexual intercourse acceptable when a person is in love, who were engaged in a highly involved dating relationship, and who thought that at least several of their female friends had had sexual intercourse, only six percent had not engaged in heavy petting, and only 21 percent had not engaged in coitus. Among college women at the opposite extreme (who did not approve of premarital coitus when in love, were not dating anyone special, and thought that almost all of their female friends were still virgins), only 21 percent had engaged in heavy petting, and all were still virgins. Therefore, a very striking relationship existed among personal judgment of acceptable behavior, engagement in a love relationship, and perception of others' sexual experience. This does not imply that the majority of women's decisions to engage in heavy petting or coitus were the deliberate result of following their personal standards. Rather, in many cases, the woman was uncertain or ambivalent about the sexual activity until she had had some experience with it in a particular relationship.

In reference to heavy petting, Packard's (1968) probability sample showed that 28 percent of the women had had experience with three or more partners, 55 percent had engaged in heavy petting with someone they did not love, and almost 25 percent had petted heavily with two or more partners they did not love. Therefore, very intimate petting is not restricted exclusively to loved ones or those to whom one is seriously committed, and apparently the experience of heavy petting has become acceptable to a substantial majority of college women.

PREMARITAL SEX: ATTITUDES

Reiss (1960, 1967) considered the adolescent's sexual standards to be more significant than his or her sexual behaviors. In his research, he grouped these standards on a continuum between *abstinence* and *permis-*

siveness. He found an increasing movement toward permissiveness and toward a "transitional double standard." These trends have led to (1) a decline in the incidence of premarital sex when there is no affection involved and (2) an increase in premarital sex when affection is involved. What Reiss calls the transitional double standard allows greater female permissiveness, although it still demands that the female be in love in order to engage in intercourse—a demand not made of the male. Reiss found that 86 percent of men and women who accepted premarital coitus claimed to be in love (1967). Although petting-with-affection relationships are still preferred by youth to coitus (Glass, 1972; Martinson, 1968; Reiss, 1967), it is clear that *premarital coitus with affection* is more accepted than ever before in our society (Bell & Chaskes, 1970; Christensen & Gregg, 1970; Freedman, 1965; Pope & Knudsen, 1965; Reiss, 1971; Smigel & Seiden, 1968).

Physicians' attitudes toward men's premarital intercourse

Some 880 physicians were asked to state their response to the statement: "I believe that premarital intercourse by males is acceptable...."

By specialty, 89 percent of the psychiatrists in the sample thought premarital intercourse was acceptable either often or always. This was much higher than any other specialization category. Others in the study who favored premarital intercourse were internists, 55 percent; obstetricians and gynecologists, 45 percent; surgeons, 40 percent; and general practitioners, 36 percent.*

*From "Physicians' Attitudes toward Premarital and Extramarital Intercourse" by I. B. Pauly and S. G. Goldstein, *Medical Aspects of Human Sexuality*, 1971, 5(1).

Robinson, King, and Balswick were interested in assessing changes in male and female attitudes toward premarital intercourse between 1965 and 1970. In both studies (1968, 1972), the authors asked questions relating to attitudes toward the sexual behavior of both sexes. Comparisons of the 1970 results with those of 1965 can be seen in Table 12.2. A radical change in attitudes is evidenced over the five-year interval. Although both males and females seemed to have accepted the idea that sexual intercourse is not immoral, the most radical change, again, was among the female respondents. Whereas in 1967, 70 percent of the females felt that premarital intercourse was immoral, only 34 percent of the females thought so in 1970—a shift in more than one-third of these respondents.

TABLE 12.2. Percentage of 1965 and 1970 college students strongly agreeing with certain statements regarding the morality of premarital sexual relationships.

Statement	Males	Females
1. I feel that premarital sexual intercourse is immoral.		
1965	33 ($n=129$)	70 ($n=115$)
1970	14 ($n=137$)	34 ($n=158$)
Percentage difference	−19	−36
2. A man who has had sexual intercourse with a great many women is immoral.		
1965	35 ($n=127$)	56 ($n=114$)
1970	15 ($n=137$)	22 ($n=157$)
Percentage difference	−20	−34
3. A woman who has had sexual intercourse with a great many men is immoral.		
1965	42 ($n=118$)	91 ($n=114$)
1970	33 ($n=137$)	54 ($n=157$)
Percentage difference	−9	−37
4. A man who has had sexual intercourse with a great many women is sinful.		
1965	41 ($n=128$)	50 ($n=114$)
1970	24 ($n=136$)	26 ($n=156$)
Percentage difference	−17	−24
5. A woman who has had sexual intercourse with a great many men is sinful.		
1965	58 ($n=137$)	70 ($n=113$)
1970	32 ($n=136$)	47 ($n=157$)
Percentage difference	−26	−23

From "The Premarital Sexual Revolution among College Females" by I. E. Robinson, K. King, and J. O. Balswick, *Family Coordinator,* 1972, *21,* 191. Copyright 1972 by National Council on Family Relations. Reprinted by permission.

PREMARITAL SEX: BEHAVIORS

Now let's examine some data on premarital sexual behavior. Kinsey (1948) found that 54.7 percent of the general male population had experienced heterosexual coitus by age 15. He also found that the highest incidence of premarital relations (70.5 percent) occurred during the teens. As age increased, so did the proportion of males who had visited prostitutes; but, in those 15 or under, fewer than one percent had visited prostitutes (Kinsey, 1948). Kinsey found that, in males, the incidence of premarital coitus decreased with increasing amount of education. Ninety-eight percent of those educated through the grade-school level had had coital experience before marriage, 84 percent of those who had gone through high school, and 67 percent of those who had gone through college (Kinsey, 1948).

For the female population, Kinsey (1953) found that nearly 50 percent of the total female population had experienced premarital coitus before marriage, although only 17 percent of the total population had experienced orgasm during premarital relations. "The females who were married at earlier ages had premarital coitus when they were younger; the females who married at later ages had not begun coitus until much later, for most a year or two preceding the marriage, and usually with their fiancé" (Kinsey, 1953, p. 286). Kinsey (1953) found that, in females, 30 percent of those educated through the grade-school level had coital experience before marriage, 47 percent of those who had gone through high school, and more than 60 percent of those who had gone through college. The basic difference here between male and female behavior can probably be attributed to the fact that a female is more reluctant to perform intercourse unless a note of permanence or a promise of marriage has been indicated by the male. Obviously, more promises occur among people in college.

In studying 100 males and 100 females, Eastman (1972) found that 55 percent of the men and 49 percent of the women reported having experienced sexual intercourse. Ages 18 and 19 were the most likely years for first coital experience; 50 percent of the nonvirgin males and 40 percent of the nonvirgin females had experienced first sexual intercourse during those years (see Table 12.3). These findings are comparable to Sorenson's (1973), who found that 59 percent of the boys and 45 percent of the girls in his study had experienced intercourse.

TABLE 12.3. Age at first intercourse.

Age	Men Number	Men Percent	Women Number	Women Percent
15 and under	5	9.3	1	2.3
16–17	20	37.0	9	20.9
18–19	28	51.8	17	39.5
20–21	0	0.0	14	32.6
22 and older	1	1.8	2	4.6
Total	54	99.9%	43	99.9%

From "First Intercourse" by W. F. Eastman, *Sexual Behavior*, 1972, 2(3), 25. Reprinted by permission.

In general, men have their first intercourse at a younger age than women. Almost 50 percent of the men and 25 percent of the women in Eastman's study were under 18 at the time, although only nine percent of the men had sexual intercourse before age 15, a figure that agrees with Kinsey's data (1948). Sixty-eight percent of the men and 30 percent of the women reported having intercourse before entering college. In contrast to these teen-age experiences, 37 percent of the females, as opposed to only two percent of the males, had first intercourse after age 20 (Eastman, 1972; Sorenson, 1973).

Robinson and his associates (Robinson et al., 1968), as well as Freedman (1965), found that actual rates of sexual behavior had not changed from those reported by Kinsey. Yet, a great change had occurred in *attitudes* and in the public expression of those attitudes. Some researchers (for example, Packard, 1968) have indicated their belief that the sexual revolution we have been discussing has happened in all sections of the country, but that the South is more conservative in this realm. Packard's study found the Midwest to be even more conservative than the South. Kinsey, on the other hand, felt that there was little variation in attitudes and behaviors among sections of the nation. Kinsey (1948, 1953) also found, however, that premarital relations occurred with greater frequency in urban areas than in rural areas. Looking, then, at their data from 1965 (Table 12.4), which revealed no apparent change from the Kinsey data, and then at their 1970 data, these authors found themselves agreeing with Kinsey and with Bell and Chaskes (1970), who studied the changes occurring between 1958 and 1968.

Between 1965 and 1970, as Table 12.4 indicates, behavioral patterns of premarital intercourse clearly changed. Rather surprisingly, the change that occurred was not an across-the-board phenomenon but was apparently concentrated in the behavior of females. In both 1965 and 1970, 65 percent of male college students had had sexual intercourse—approximately the same percentage Kinsey found. It appears that male college students' sexual behavior has remained relatively constant since the late 1940s, but that there has been a dramatic change in female college students' behavior. In 1965, it was found that the female students of the sample university had not changed their sexual behavior from that of the same type of sample population used by Kinsey in 1953. However, whereas, in 1965, 28.7 percent of the college females had had sexual intercourse, by 1970, 37.3 percent had had such experience. The implications of this 9.4-percent change will be discussed below.

PERMISSIVENESS

It is clear from our discussion that American youth engage in much premarital sexual activity, especially during late adolescence. Survey results vary, but the incidence of premarital sexual intercourse among youth is somewhere between 50 and 70 percent. The changes described in the preceding sections probably do not represent the sexual revolution in America that some have suggested. America is changing in many ways: philosophically, politically, technologically, socially, and behaviorally. Sexual expression may be more varied in America today, but so are many other social phenomena. With the changing nature of

TABLE 12.4. Percentage of 1965 and 1970 college students having premarital intercourse.

Percentages	Males	Females
1965	65.1 ($n=$ 84)	28.7 ($n=$ 33)
1970	65.0 ($n=136$)	37.3 ($n=158$)
Percentage difference	−.1	+9.4

From "The Premarital Sexual Revolution among College Females" by I. E. Robinson, K. King, and J. O. Balswick, *Family Coordinator*, 1972, 21, 190. Copyright 1972 by National Council on Family Relations. Reprinted by permission.

sexual expression has come a concomitant desire to develop a new moral attitude toward human sexuality—a practical code of sexual behavior. This new attitude has been evidenced somewhat by the weakening of the double standard, inferred from an increase in cross-sex identification and from a greater incidence of female permissiveness (Bell, 1966; Reiss, 1966).

Adolescent promiscuity

The term "promiscuity" is defined in the dictionary as an "indiscriminate mingling." As applied to sexual behavior among adolescents, it is often also invested with more pejorative meanings. Those who hold premarital relations to be morally wrong may regard any sexually active teenager as "promiscuous" regardless of other factors. In addition, while the young male who has many sexual partners is often described as merely "sowing his wild oats," the adolescent female who behaves in this manner is frequently labeled as being "promiscuous." Indeed we can say that the word promiscuity is in itself often promiscuously used to intone social and sexist judgments rather than simply to convey a pattern of behavior.*

*From "Adolescent Promiscuity" by A. D. Hoffman, *Medical Aspects of Human Sexuality*, May 1974, p. 63.

Further evidence of the formation of a new standard of human sexuality is a new attitude prevalent implying that sexual intercourse is related to love rather than marriage (Blaine, 1968). This attitude is demonstrated by a practice of discriminating sexual permissiveness. It is difficult to know exactly how youth apply the prerequisite of having some affection for or being in love with their sexual partner. Nevertheless, research studies show that the greater the level of emotional involvement, the more positive the attitude toward and the greater the participation in premarital sex.

An analysis of this type of sexual permissiveness was undertaken by Kaats and Davis (1970). The researchers studied 319 women and 239 men who were freshmen and sophomores in college to determine their standard of permissiveness. The results are shown in Table 12.5. As you can see, the greatest permissiveness was found among those youths who were engaged to be married, and the least permissiveness was found among those who stated that they had "little affection" for their sexual partner.

Reiss (1960, 1961, 1966, 1967, 1970) feels that the incidence of premarital sex is exaggerated, and that any observable increase in sexual behavior is not due to a sexual revolution or to moral decay. Rather, he believes that the sources of the new American permissiveness are access

TABLE 12.5. Standards of permissiveness for male and female sexual behavior as expressed by college men and women.*

	Standards for men		Standards for women	
	Initial	Follow-up	Initial	Follow-up
College men expressing permissiveness by type of activity:				
Petting	5.19	5.14	5.07	4.97
Sexual intercourse	4.32	4.48	4.21	4.04
Permissiveness by type of relationship:				
Not particularly affectionate	4.45	4.55	4.20	4.06
Strongly affectionate	5.12	5.20	5.01	5.09
In love	5.32	5.39	5.32	5.23
Engaged	5.36	5.37	5.35	5.30
Total standards	5.06	5.13	5.03	4.92
College women expressing permissiveness by type of activity:				
Petting	4.83	4.83	4.45	4.49
Sexual intercourse	3.71	3.75	2.99	2.97
Permissiveness by type of relationship:				
Not particularly affectionate	3.88	3.85	3.20	2.92
Strongly affectionate	4.80	4.75	4.36	4.40
In love	5.15	5.21	4.93	4.36
Engaged	5.21	5.09	5.05	5.11
Total standards	4.77	4.72	4.36	4.40

*Based on 1–6 scale where 6 = highly permissive. Items read, "I believe ____ is permissible before marriage when the people are ____."

From "The Dynamics of Sexual Behavior of College Students" by G. R. Kaats and K. E. Davis, Journal of Marriage and the Family, 1970, 32, 393. Copyright 1970 by National Council on Family Relations. Reprinted by permission.

to contraception, new ways to combat venereal infection, and—quite as important—an intellectual philosophy about the desirability of sex accompanying affection. "Respectable" college-educated people have integrated this new philosophy with their generally liberal attitudes about the family, politics, and religion. This change represents a new and lasting support for sexual permissiveness, since it is based on a positive philosophy rather than on one of hedonism, despair, or desperation (1960).

In fact, Reiss found that, although youths do not always maintain consistency, for the most part their sexual behavior and sexual attitudes agree. Table 12.6 reports some of his findings among unmarried white college juniors and seniors. Among these students, action did not always follow belief, but in the great majority of cases belief and action did coincide. For example, 64 percent of those who considered coitus acceptable were actually having coitus; and only seven percent of those who accepted nothing beyond petting, and four percent of those who accepted nothing beyond kissing, were having coitus.

TABLE 12.6. Sexual standards and actual behavior.

Current standard	Most extreme current behavior			Number of respondents
	Kissing	Petting	Coitus	
Kissing	64%	32%	4%	25
Petting	15%	78%	7%	139
Coitus	5%	31%	64%	84

From *The Social Context of Premarital Sexual Permissiveness* by I. L. Reiss. Copyright 1967 by Holt, Rinehart and Winston, Inc. Reprinted by permission.

Young people receive both peer pressure and peer support for much premarital permissiveness. Reiss (1971) postulates that the increase in premarital sexual permissiveness arises primarily from peer support for males and from male persuasion for females. Furthermore, today's youths show an increasing degree of tolerance for others' sexual relationships (Reiss, 1967; Schofield, 1965).

Reiss (1967) summarizes the findings of several of his studies with the following points:

1. The less sexually permissive a group is, traditionally, the greater the likelihood that new social forces will cause its members to become more permissive.

    Traditionally high-permissive groups, such as Negro men, were the least likely to have their sexual standards changed by social forces like church attendance or romantic love. Traditionally low-

permissive groups, such as white females, showed the greatest sensitivity to these social forces.
2. The more liberal the group, the more likely that social forces will help maintain high sexual permissiveness.

There was diverse support for this proposition. Students, upper-class females in liberal settings, and urban dwellers have by and large accepted more permissiveness than have those in more conservative settings.

Indeed, liberalism in general seems to be yet another cause of the new permissiveness in America. For instance, a group that is traditionally low-permissive regarding sex (such as the upper class), but that is liberal in such fields as religion and politics, would be very likely to shift toward greater premarital permissiveness.

3. According to their ties to marital and family institutions, people will differ in their sensitivity to social forces that affect permissiveness. This proposition emphasizes male-female differences in courting. Women have a stronger attachment to and investment in marriage, childbearing, and family ties. This stronger attachment affects their courtship roles. Therefore, there are fundamental male-female differences in acceptance of permissiveness, in line with differences in courtship role.

The studies indicated that romantic love led more women than men to become permissive. Having a steady date affected women predominately, and exclusiveness—that is, a one-male relationship—was linked with permissiveness. Early dating, and its link with permissiveness, varied by race, but it was far more commonly linked with permissiveness in men than in women. The number of steadies, and the number of times in love, was associated with permissiveness for females but was curvilinear for males—that is, a man with no steadies, or a number of steadies, tended to be more permissive than a man who had gone steady only once.

Such male-female differences, however, are significant only for whites. Among Negroes, male-female patterns in these areas are quite similar.

4. The higher the overall level of permissiveness in a group, the greater the extent of equalitarianism within abstinence and double-standard subgroups.

Permissiveness is a measure not only of what a person will accept for himself and his own sex, but of what behavior he is willing to allow the opposite sex. *Nonequalitarianism in abstinence* means that petting is acceptable for men, but only kissing is acceptable for women. *Equalitarianism within the double standard* means that intercourse is acceptable for women when in love, for men anytime.

The *nonequalitarian double standard* considers all unmarried women's coitus wrong. In a generally high-permissive group (men), those who accept abstinence or the double standard will be more equalitarian than will their counterparts in low-permissive groups.

5. The potential for permissiveness derived from parents' values is a key determinant of what direction change in a person's premarital sexual standards and behavior may take.

   What distinguishes an individual's sexual behavior is not the starting point—white college-educated females, for instance, almost always start with kissing only—but how far, how fast, and in what direction the individual is willing to go. The fact is that almost all sexual behavior is eventually repeated and thus comes to be accepted. And a person's basic values encourage or discourage his willingness to try something new and possibly guilt-producing. Therefore, these basic values—derived, in large part, from parental teaching, direct or implicit—are keys to permissiveness.

6. A youth tends to see permissiveness as a continuous scale, with his parents' standards at the low point, his peers' at the high point, and his own somewhere between but closer to his peers—and closest to those he considers his most intimate friends.

   The findings indicate that those who consider their standards closer to parents' than to peers' are less permissive than the others. The most permissive within one group generally reported the greatest distance from parents and the greatest similarity to peers and friends. This tendency does not contradict the previous proposition, since parents are on the continuum and exert enough influence so that their children don't go all the way to the opposite end. But it does indicate that parents are associated with relatively low permissiveness, that peers are associated with relatively high permissiveness, and that the respondents felt closer to the latter.

7. Greater responsibility for other members of the family, and less participation in courtship, are both associated with low permissiveness. The only child, it was found, had the most permissive attitudes. Older children, generally, were less permissive than their younger brothers and sisters. The older children usually have greater responsibility for the young siblings; children without siblings have no such responsibilities at all.

   The findings also showed that, as the number of children increased, the parents' permissiveness decreased. Here again, apparently, parental responsibility grew, and the decline in permissiveness supports the proposition above.

   On the other hand, as a young person gets more caught up in courtship, he is progressively freed from parental domination. He has less responsibility for others, and he becomes more permissive. The fact that students are more sexually liberal than many other groups must be due partly to their involvement in courtship and partly to their distance from the family.

A generational clash of some sort is therefore almost inevitable. When children reach their late teens or early 20s, they also reach the peak of their permissiveness; their parents, at the same time, reach the nadir of theirs (Reiss, 1967).

SEX-INFORMATION SOURCES

Research on sources and accuracy of sex information has been going on since the mid-1930s. Ramsey (1943), studying preadolescents, found that both parents and school function only as minor sex-information sources. Over half of the information obtained by his respondents came from peers. Studies by Bell (1938) among both white and black youths found that most of their information came from peers. He found that 78 percent of the white males and 47 percent of the white females, and 91 percent of the black males and 69 percent of the black females, sought out peers for sex information.

I have attempted to see if any shift in sources of sex information has occurred among adolescents within the last three decades. Three studies to be reported here provide data indicating some information-source shift. The studies were done in 1967 (Thornburg, 1970b), 1970 (Thornburg, 1972), and 1973 (reported herein). The research topics considered in these studies were abortion, contraception, ejaculation, homosexuality, intercourse, masturbation, menstruation, origin of babies, petting, prostitution, seminal emissions, and venereal disease. The 1973 study included abortion, whereas the two earlier studies did not.

The tabulated data on first source of sex information for the 88 college females who constituted the 1967 study (Thornburg, 1970b) are found in Table 12.7. Analysis of the data indicates that, with the exception of origin of babies and menstruation, the parents' role in these women's sex information was quite limited. Schools provided additional sex information (12.2 percent), but, even so, they were quite limited in the knowledge they disseminated. Other sex-education sources clearly played a minimal role. It is demonstrated rather conclusively, however, that peers (38.2 percent) and literature (16.7 percent) tended to be the basic sources of pertinent information for these young women.

The 1970 study (Thornburg, 1972) involved a much larger sample, 191 men and women from Arizona and 190 men and women from Ok-

TABLE 12.7. First sex-information source.

	Contraception	Ejaculation	Homosexual activity	Intercourse	Masturbation	Menstruation	Nocturnal emissions	Origin of babies	Petting	Prostitution	Venereal disease	Percentage
Mother	11	9	4	27	7	43	8	54	7	5	8	18.9
Father	1	2	1	0	0	0	1	1	0	2	0	.9
Both parents	3	1	0	6	1	5	0	13	3	5	2	4.0
Female companions	37	26	44	31	24	15	37	12	49	45	18	34.9
Male companions	0	7	2	4	5	0	2	1	7	3	1	3.3
School	8	7	7	4	12	10	15	2	6	6	40	12.2
Literature	22	18	26	7	25	12	12	4	7	14	15	16.7
Physician or minister	2	0	0	3	1	0	0	1	3	0	0	1.0
Street talk	2	3	3	2	1	2	2	0	6	3	1	2.6
Unanswered	2	15	1	4	12	1	11	0	0	5	3	5.5

From "Age and First Sources of Sex Information as Reported by 88 College Women" by H. D. Thornburg, *Journal of School Health*, 1970, 40(3), 156. Reprinted by permission.

lahoma. As you can see by looking at Table 12.8, the results—taken three years later, with two distinct geographical differences—are virtually the same as those of the 1967 (1970) study. Again, peers emerged as the primary information source (37.9 percent) and literature as the second most common source (20.6 percent). The combined parental contribution was 21.1 percent—highly similar to the earlier study—and the majority of parental information dealt with the areas of origin of babies and menstruation. Again, the schools were a somewhat limited source, contributing only 14.8 percent of the information.

TABLE 12.8. A comparative analysis of initial sex-information sources.

	Arizona N = 191	Oklahoma N = 190	Total	%
Mother	382	406	788	19.3
Father	23	20	43	1.8
Peers	688	829	1517	37.9
Literature	461	360	821	20.6
Schools	377	213	590	14.8
Minister	20	13	33	.8
Physician	12	9	21	.5
Street talk/experience	62	107	169	4.3
Unanswered	76	133	209	—
Totals	2101	2090	4191	100.0

From "A Comparative Study of Sex-Information Sources" by H. D. Thornburg, *Journal of School Health*, 1972, 42(2), 88. Reprinted by permission.

The 1973 study involved 392 males and 566 females from 12 different major universities in the United States. The results from this study indicate rather conclusively that most information about sex comes from peers. This finding ran true in all of the geographical areas involved in the study. The total peer contribution was 37.8 percent of all information. This figure compares favorably with those from the two previous studies, which found, respectively, that peers contributed 38.2 percent (Thornburg, 1970b) and 37.9 percent (Thornburg, 1972) of the information. My three studies report a smaller proportion of information from peers than do previously reported studies, and it is important to note that all studies (Angelino & Mech, 1955; Bell, 1938; Lee, 1952; Ramsey, 1943) reveal peers to be the primary contributor.

Evidence suggests that, more recently, peer influence has been partially supplanted by literature. In the 1973 sample, 20.9 percent of all information came from peers, 19.5 percent from schools, and 13.4 percent from the mother. As you can see in Table 12.9, adolescents gain somewhat significant amounts of information from literature; abortion is the topic most frequently learned about from this source.

TABLE 12.9. Initial sex-information sources.

Source	Male n=392	Female n=566	Total n=958
Mother	5.6	18.7	13.4
Father	4.1	.7	2.1
Peers	45.7	32.4	37.8
School	18.3	20.4	19.5
Literature	16.7	23.8	20.9
Physician	.6	.6	.6
Minister	1.0	.6	.7
Experiences	8.0	2.8	5.0

A somewhat distorted statistic is the percentage of 13.4 for information given by the mother. In actuality, the mother's contribution is quite low if one excludes the topics of menstruation (43.2 percent) and the origin of babies (44.6 percent). These two topics account for 58 percent of the total information contributed by the mother, a figure highly comparable to the 52 percent found in the 1970 (Thornburg, 1972) study. Other studies, by Ramsey (1943) and Angelino and Mech (1955), reported that information on origin of babies and menstruation accounted for 47.5 percent and 48 percent, respectively, of the mother's information output.

Boys and girls are likely to seek out different sources to learn about sex. In Table 12.9, there were two decisive differences between the sexes: girls were more dependent on their mothers for information, and boys were more dependent on peers. In addition, girls were slightly more dependent on the schools, boys on experience. For these four information sources, effects of sex were apparently more significant than effects of geographical region; no particular effects were found for the latter.

Another consideration in the 1973 study was the degree of accuracy or correctness of information, as summarized in Table 12.10. The students were asked to score the accuracy of their information as highly accurate, accurate, distorted, or highly distorted. The combined accuracy for the 12 concepts was 75.2 percent. This percentage is a positive finding, considering that most information came from peers and that other studies report a much lower combined percentage of accuracy. The greatest accuracy was found on the topics of abortion (88 percent), menstruation (85 percent), and venereal disease (83 percent). This is an interesting finding, since the students gained the abortion information primarily from literature and the schools, menstruation information from their mothers, and venereal-disease information from the schools and literature—showing not only that significant contributions are being made by sources other than peers but also that such information is highly accurate.

Two sexual concepts fell within the 60-percent accuracy range—intercourse (65 percent) and masturbation (66 percent). In addition, 59-

TABLE 12.10. Accuracy of sex information by sex. Figures indicate percentages.

Topic	Highly accurate Male	Highly accurate Female	Highly accurate Total	Accurate Male	Accurate Female	Accurate Total	Distorted Male	Distorted Female	Distorted Total	Highly distorted Male	Highly distorted Female	Highly distorted Total
Abortion	31.8	38.3	35.7	53.3	51.9	52.5	13.9	8.9	10.8	1.0	.9	1.0
Contraception	25.2	28.2	27.0	45.9	55.0	51.3	25.5	15.9	19.8	3.4	.9	1.9
Ejaculation	30.9	27.5	28.8	43.2	47.4	45.6	23.2	21.0	21.8	3.2	2.4	2.7
Homosexuality	14.6	16.3	15.6	42.4	43.7	43.2	34.3	34.2	34.3	8.7	5.8	6.9
Intercourse	25.9	26.9	26.5	36.4	39.8	38.4	30.0	25.8	27.5	7.8	7.6	7.7
Masturbation	28.0	20.4	23.4	37.8	45.8	42.5	29.1	28.8	28.9	5.2	5.1	5.1
Menstruation	28.1	58.7	46.4	43.5	35.3	38.6	21.1	5.7	11.9	7.3	.4	3.1
Origin of babies	30.6	38.4	35.3	41.3	41.5	41.4	21.5	15.9	18.1	6.7	4.3	5.2
Petting	31.3	27.2	28.9	44.6	48.7	47.1	19.4	21.3	20.5	4.2	2.8	3.4
Prostitution	24.3	21.2	22.5	46.2	53.2	50.3	26.5	23.1	24.4	3.0	2.6	2.8
Seminal emissions	26.1	25.4	25.7	46.5	54.4	51.1	22.8	18.3	20.2	4.0	2.0	2.8
Venereal disease	39.4	42.0	41.0	38.9	43.6	41.7	16.6	12.4	14.1	5.2	2.0	3.3

Male n=392; Female n=566; Total n=958

318

percent accuracy was reported for homosexuality. In each case, peers were the decisive contributors. Nevertheless, these accuracy percentages are quite high, indicating that the level of peer information is apparently more accurate than it was in the past. The fact that studies by Elias and Gebhard (1969) and Schwartz (1969) report somewhat higher incidences of distorted information than does my study may be partly due to the difference in samples. Whereas Elias and Gebhard sampled the general population and Schwartz lower-class boys, my sample was taken from college youth.

There were some differences by sex as to the accuracy of information received, with girls generally gaining the most accurate information. The concepts they clearly understood more accurately were menstruation, abortion, origin of babies, and contraception. Boys indicated gaining more accurate information on petting and masturbation. In the other areas, there were only slight differences.

Table 12.11 gives a breakdown of the amount of peer information received in each of the twelve areas. In two of the behavioral areas, petting and intercourse, it is evident that peer input is quite high. Information on homosexuality and prostitution comes from peers in such high percentages partly because these topics have negative societal connotations. Smaller percentages of peer information were found in the areas of abortion and venereal disease, where the schools and literature made greater contributions (Thornburg, 1974b).

TABLE 12.11. Peer contributions to sex information.

Concept	Percent
Abortion	18.6
Contraception	41.7
Ejaculation	43.3
Homosexuality	52.0
Intercourse	54.5
Masturbation	45.9
Menstruation	21.8
Origin of babies	26.2
Petting	55.7
Prostitution	50.0
Seminal emissions	26.3
Venereal disease	17.5
Total	37.8

It is interesting to examine the schools' contribution to sex information by comparing the 1967, 1970, and 1973 studies. Table 12.12, from the 1973 study, indicates a somewhat accelerated attempt by the schools to provide sex information. The students in this sample showed effects from the sex-education movement of the late 1960s, which un-

TABLE 12.12. School contributions to information about sexuality.

Topic	1967 n=88	1970 n=381	1973 n=958
Abortion	—	—	28.8
Contraception	9.1	10.0	20.9
Ejaculation	8.0	17.3	18.2
Homosexuality	8.0	10.5	13.1
Intercourse	4.6	9.5	9.6
Masturbation	13.6	15.2	13.5
Menstruation	11.4	12.1	21.2
Origin of babies	2.3	12.1	14.1
Petting	6.8	7.4	7.2
Prostitution	6.8	5.8	6.4
Seminal emissions	17.1	19.2	23.2
Venereal disease	45.5	42.8	48.3
Total	12.2	14.8	19.5

doubtedly contributed to the increased role of the school. It can also be observed that the students in the 1973 study stated that 30 percent of their information on abortion came from the schools. Because this topic was not included in the 1967 and 1970 studies, it too contributed to the larger percentage of school information reported in the most recent study.

The single most significant contribution made by the schools in all three studies was in teaching about venereal disease—providing 45.5 percent of that information in 1967, 42.8 percent in 1970, and 48.3 percent in 1973. As to information about petting and intercourse, two sexual issues of great concern to the adolescent, schools are very limited contributors. On petting, the school as an information source provided only 7 percent in each study. On intercourse, the percentages in the three studies fell at 4.5, 9.5, and 9.6, respectively.

Certainly, more reliable sex information is needed. Shifts from peer sources of information to parental, school, and literature sources increase the potential for accuracy. Youth often pay an unfortunate price for being thrust into sexual behaviors with limited or inaccurate information. At the same time, we cannot disregard the social impact of the peer group and the mass media, both of which tend to make sexuality appear attractive and exciting to adolescents. Increased availability, credibility, and reliability of sex information should enhance the adolescent's understanding of and responsibility toward his sexual behavior.

SHOULD THERE BE SEX EDUCATION IN THE SCHOOLS?

In 1965, a Gallup poll found that 69 percent of the American public favored sex education in the public schools. In 1969, another Gal-

> *Sexual insults by teen-age boys*
>
> Question:
>
> *Why do teenage boys constantly hurl sexual insults at each other? In jest they derogate each other's penis size, their mothers' sexual habits, accuse each other of masturbation, and everything else. There must be some significant dynamic behind this banter, and I'd very much appreciate some insight.*
>
> Answer:
>
> There are probably three underlying motives in such behavior. First, such conversation is commonplace among boys who are seeking approval among their peers. The tendency is to go with the trend of conversation. Because there is an increasing interest in talking about sex it becomes a typical form of conversation. For the most part it is done in jest, although there are occasions for some boys to become highly offended. Even with the need for peer acceptance, this may be the most shallow reason for such behavior.
>
> More basic to this behavior may be the anxiety such boys express in comparing themselves sexually to their peers. Often boys find their variance of growth to be disturbing, especially if they are comparatively underdeveloped. Research indicates that many of our youth are unfamiliar with the normal biological sequences through which they must grow. We need to educate our youth in the areas of physiological development. If they could accept the fact that rates vary, frustration and anxiety over deviating from the norm could be reduced.
>
> Underlying peer acceptance and anxiety reduction may be the search for ego identity. Erikson strongly points to the definition of one's sex role, which includes the acceptance of self sexually, as being instrumental in the search for identity. Ego support can often come through trying to enhance one's self while putting someone else down. Derogatory remarks then may have strong motives, although on the surface they appear harmless or senseless. Perhaps we can give adolescent boys emotional support through pointing out the naturalness of their growth as well as their social acceptability to others.*
>
> *From H. D. Thornburg, *Medical Aspects of Human Sexuality*, January 1973.

lup poll set the figure at 71 percent (Johnson & Schutt, 1966; "Sex Education," 1969). In 1968, a study of school administrators revealed that 56 percent favored sex education (Thornburg, 1968a). A 1970 study among pediatricians found 95 percent in favor of sex education in the schools (Feingold, 1971). However, although one can find general support for integrating sex education into the school's curriculum, resistance to the idea appears to be equally strong. Without question, school programs are needed to augment those facts or notions about human sexuality that children and adolescents learn elsewhere. Perhaps the strongest reason for teaching sex education in the schools, however, is the *appalling failure on the part of our culture as a whole to handle sex in a healthy manner and on the part of the great majority of families to give their children sound basic information regarding their sexuality.*

AA (Acronyms Anonymous): Resistance to Sex Education

AVERT	(Association of Volunteers for Educational Responsibility in Texas)
MOTOREDE	(Movement to Restore Decency)
PAUSE	(Parents Against Unauthorized Sex Education)
POPE	(Parents for Orthodox Parochial Education)
POSSE	(Parents Opposed to Sex and Sensitivity Training)
MOMS	(Mothers for Moral Stability)
SOS	(Sanity on Sex)
PURE	(Parents United for Responsible Education)

What do the organizations above have in common other than their flair for acronyms? They are all parental groups formed in 1968 and 1969 to oppose sex education in the schools. They were in fact highly successful in their attack on the programs, persuading legislators to join them in their efforts to ban them. By the end of 1969, over 95 percent of the sex-education programs in the public schools had been abandoned, and 37 states had passed laws restricting or eliminating courses dealing with sex education.

The anti-sex-education forces gained strength from some physicians and psychiatrists, fundamental religionists, anti-Communist groups, and the right-wing politicians. The groups claimed that the schools were usurping parental authority, teaching permissive morals to adolescents, exposing students to undesirable sex graphics, and, in general, filling their children's heads full of ideas. The potential danger in such reactions is twofold. First, our children and youth are constantly exposed to sexual stimuli such as those suggested here outside the school. Who is going to help them sort it out into a reasonable, normal attitudinal system? Second, although some modifications in attitude toward sexuality seem to be in progress, our culture still maintains firm allegiance to prohibitive sexual codes. Although there are exceptions, most parents feel inept and embarrassed in any effort to deal openly with their adolescents about sex, especially if it entails anything more than telling them what not to do.

One of the primary criticisms from professionals in medicine and psychiatry is that early sex education interferes with the latency (prepubertal) period, causing the preadolescent to focus prematurely on sex. The following quotes are from physicians or psychiatrists, although obviously they should not be construed to be representative reactions of these professions to sex education.

It is overwhelming, disturbing, upsetting, and exciting and very likely to lead to sex difficulties later in life....

Anyone who would deliberately arouse the child's curiosity or stimulate his unready mind to troubled sex preoccupations ought to have a millstone tied around his neck and be cast into the sea....

From ages nine to twelve the normal child is in an "asexual stage" with "a real aversion" to new information about sex. Sex education in those years upsets the psychic balance and is "just as real a seduction" as an encounter with a child molester—and worse ... because the seducer is his teacher, a parent substitute ["Sex Education," 1969, p. 27].

Elsewhere (Thornburg, 1973a), I have stated that there is a stage of *social puberty* that precedes the physiological puberty generally experienced between the ages of 12 and 14. Social puberty may be defined in this sense as the direct involvement in some manner with individuals of the opposite sex prior to the development of a physiological basis for such interaction. Social puberty may very well be encouraged by the highly suggestive social stimuli that confront youngsters in their daily environment. The exposure of the preadolescent to different sexual behaviors is quite common through television, motion pictures, literature, music, and advertising. Sex is generally presented by these media as a commodity, in an enticing, get-involved way, and the true nature of sexual involvement and its consequences (either positive or negative) are rarely realistically

---

Popular music and sex

Because youths often use music as an aspect of their courtship activities, its lyrics often implicitly or explicitly deal with sex and love....

Today's audiences for popular music can so readily identify with it because it is performed by young people for other young people. Many of its composers and impresarie are young....

Rock is the first music in history which has been by and for youth. Mass media have been saying for some years that rock musicians are the key spokesmen for their generation. The claim has been made so frequently that young and old accept and believe it....

The lubricity of much rock music has been enhanced by the widely publicized sexual adventures of some of its leading exponents....

Because so many of the rock superstars look and sound genderless, they can play and sing material which has latent or manifest sexual content and still be minimally threatening to their fans....

So many lyrics are shouted, to the accompaniment of very loud music, that the theme gets an extra dimension of social acceptability. If it does not need to be whispered, it is presumably legitimate....*

*From "Popular Music and Sex" by C. Winick, *Medical Aspects of Human Sexuality*, 1970, 4(10), 148–157.

presented. The preadolescent, as well as the adolescent, is encouraged to show interest in sex behaviorally with little regard to concomitant emotional involvement. In order to help the adolescent integrate sexuality into his total self, perspective must be given to him by competent adults.

Suggestions for Sex-Education Programs

There is general consensus that formal sex education should originate in the school and that it should probably begin by the preadolescent years (Thornburg, 1974d). However, literature on what should be included in a sex-education program is sparse.

There are apparently two schools of thought regarding sex education in the schools. One holds that sex education should be integrated into the total curriculum rather than taught as a separate subject. The second viewpoint emphasizes the need for a discrete program that will give adolescents information, a sense of direction, and control in integrating sexuality into their lives. Supporting the second viewpoint, I am concerned here with the objectives involved in a sex-education program.

It is conceivable that, without proper objectives and direction, a sex-education program could do as much harm as good to students. Therefore, five primary objectives are listed below, along with supporting statements suggesting their integrative function for sex education in its physiological and psychological dimensions.

1. Give students the sound factual information they need for their development as healthy, well-adjusted adolescents.

    Students should become familiar with common sexual terms such as masturbation, intercourse, seminal emissions, ejaculation, and menstruation, thus gaining knowledge of biological and developmental terms and an awareness of the changing but normal biological maturation processes. A better biological understanding of the body will also provide a basis for understanding the physiological dimensions of sexual behavior.

2. Explore emotional problems confronting adolescents.

    Most sexual behavior is determined by the adolescent's reactions to parental, teacher, and community pressure. He becomes concerned about the acceptable ways in which he may function socially and sexually. Since he shapes his emotional life around various problems he encounters when interacting with adult models, perhaps most important to the adolescent's proper emotional development is an awareness of parental opinion on sexual behavior.

3. Explore physical problems adolescents must face.

    The adolescent is aware of his general personal attractiveness and its subsequent effect on his sexual life. Many adolescents have physical or mental limitations that may alter their sexual roles. These limitations are often considered not as problems but rather as personal issues that will somehow be automatically resolved.

4. Help students develop a sense of personal moral responsibility based on the standards of the community in which they live.

Defining this objective becomes a rather comprehensive task. How do adolescents feel about traditional moral and sexual codes? How do they feel about changing moral and sexual codes? From whom within the community do they receive the sense of direction they seek? Involved in the answers to these questions are the adolescent's reactions to the various pressures of his peer group. His reactions to the diversified moral and sexual behavior patterns of adults should also be considered. The adolescent's reaction to billboards, advertising, television, magazines, movies, and other media is a never-ending and constantly confusing process, but it is also a behavioral pattern that satisfies his personal needs and provides him the all-important integrative function of coming to terms with his culture.

5. Help students develop simultaneous psychological and physical readiness for moral and sexual action.

The importance of making young people psychologically aware as well as physiologically aware of their capabilities cannot be overemphasized. It is important to develop a sense of self-responsibility for behavior. The adolescent cannot do this simply through becoming aware of his physical readiness for sexual behavior. Rather, he needs to understand his sexual drive and its manifest behavior from a viewpoint that encompasses mental, emotional, psychological, and moral dimensions. He can be taught the ability to assess cause-and-effect relationships in his personal actions and thus develop an awareness of his responsibility to others and to society.

The adolescents of our society need to develop a healthier definition of their sexual roles in a culture increasingly preoccupied with sex. However, our society cannot in fairness expect our youth to develop such a definition while interacting with an adult society that has yet to resolve this issue for itself.

There are some good reasons why young people so frequently violate the social norms of the adult community. Other youth are the crowd with whom the adolescent lives each day. To be excluded from this group or to become disenchanted with it is such an emotionally excruciating experience that he intuitively fights against it. The adolescent also finds it easier to bend and stretch adult expectations than those of his peers.

Many adults are oblivious to the influences on the formation of permanent attitudes in the adolescent mind. Even young people themselves vary tremendously in their personal principles and beliefs. Yet the basic task is to come to terms with one's culture; self-understanding comes as a result of internalizing all social forces and influences and finding perspective in the midst of them. Of vast importance to this quest is an understanding of one's sex role. Much of the adolescent's unrest stems from a lack of basic and proper information on sexuality. Data presented earlier in this chapter indicate that the adolescent is most likely to go to peers for sex information. It is possible to help our adolescents form better attitudes by systematically giving them accurate information about human sexuality, a task within the reach of the schools.

The Role of the Administrator

The school administrator's particular responsibility is to evaluate the need for sex education in his or her school or district. It is erroneous to think that a district needs a program in sex education simply because other districts have them. Instead, the administrator has to discern and demonstrate the need within his own school or district and then, sensitive to the biological and psychological dimension of concern to his students, outline the program's objectives in accordance with the principles discussed in the preceding section.

Several problems immediately arise. To implement any program, an administrator must consider time limitations, staff qualifications, and the availability of instructional materials. When a number of Arizona administrators were queried about these limitations, they foresaw serious problems in setting up a sex-education program. Finding time to teach the subjects was of vital concern to 56 percent of the administrators. Of even greater concern, however, was the question of the staff's ability to teach this area. A lack of personnel qualified in this subject area was indicated by 84 percent of the administrators, and 66 percent felt a definite lack of appropriate instructional materials. These percentages explain why many districts are hesitant to include sex education in their curricula (Thornburg, 1968a).

The common problems of time, staff, and instructional materials are inherent in the organizational structure of the public-school system. Compounding them is the controversial nature of sex education. Whether it is the school's right or responsibility to teach subjects that heretofore have been considered the responsibility of the home is questionable, and administrators must consider whether community need, interest, and attitude justify incorporating sex education into the school curriculum. Opinion will vary tremendously. To pinpoint the general community feeling, to identify conflicting opinions within the community, and to resolve such conflicts seem a monumental task.

Schuck (1972) analyzed the attitudes reported by 242 Arizona educators on several sex-education topics. The strongest approval was given to concepts that were psychologically or biologically bound rather than behaviorally bound (see Table 12.13). In 1968, I asked Arizona school administrators to estimate their communities' attitudes toward sex education. They were asked to rate as encouraging or discouraging the attitudes of the PTA, civic groups, churches, school boards, school faculties, and school administrators of their communities. All community opinions were viewed as generally encouraging. Fifty-four percent of the total response of the various groups supported the inclusion of sex education in the schools. An additional 38 percent of the groups' responses represented either neutrality or no response. The administrators felt that only 8 percent of the members of these groups were not favorably disposed toward sex education. Strong support was indicated by PTAs and school faculties. Even considering the problems of time, staff, and instructional materials, 65 percent of the school administrators themselves were highly favorable to sex education in the schools (Thornburg, 1968a).

TABLE 12.13. Responses on subject content for sex education by rank order of approval.

Content topic	% Approval	Mean
Venereal disease	93	1.43
Menstruation	93	1.50
Conception	93	1.57
Divorce	81	1.85
Illegitimacy	77	1.97
Menopause	78	2.02
Male and female sex roles	74	2.07
Contraception	73	2.10
Masturbation	68	2.27
Abortion	70	2.28
Homosexuality	67	2.33
Venereal-disease prophylaxis	56	2.54
Impotency and frigidity	57	2.57
Sexual behavior with marriage	56	2.58
Premarital sexual intercourse between couples	56	2.70
Premarital sexual intercourse between nonengaged couples	54	2.73
Sexual deviations and perversions	50	2.75
Premarital petting	51	2.79
Teenage sexual slang	44	3.02
Pornography and erotic literature	33	3.39
Oral-genital sexual contact	23	3.50
Sexual techniques	15	4.00

From "Attitudes of Arizona Educators toward Specific Content Areas in Sex Education" by R. F. Schuck, *Journal of School Health*, 1972, 42(2), 122. Reprinted by permission.

A trend that emerged from this study was that individuals involved with the schools, and individuals within the school community generally, have an encouraging attitude toward sex education in the Arizona schools.

Regardless of the approach used to incorporate sex education in the school, communication is vital. School personnel to whom the responsibility has been delegated should develop a schedule for implementing the sex-education program. This schedule should include in-service training for teachers to inform them of what is to be taught, how it relates to the total school curriculum, and what each teacher's involvement in the program is. In some communities, it would also be advantageous to offer adult-education classes to help interested individuals in the community better understand the concepts being taught to the students. Teacher and community understanding of the program will greatly strengthen it (Taylor & Gonring, 1974).

Venereal-Disease Education

In Schuck's study (1972) of administrator attitudes, discussed above, 93 percent favored venereal-disease education in the schools. Baker and Farber (1970) surveyed 380 boys and 264 girls and found that all girls and all but five boys favored such education in the schools. Studies (Thornburg, 1970b, 1972, 1975a) show that over half of the information youths receive on venereal disease is learned at school.

It is gratifying that these surveys all point to positive attitudes toward venereal-disease education, especially since the prevalence of syphilis and gonorrhea is increasing. Rates have increased alarmingly during the last 20 years. Table 12.14 gives comparative rates for infectious venereal diseases in 1956 and 1965. Computing the rates per

TABLE 12.14. Cases of infectious venereal disease reported in the United States in 1956 and 1965.

Age	Infectious syphilis 1956	1965	Gonorrhea 1956	1965
0 to 9 years	11	36	1,222	1,724
10 to 14 years	75	245	2,425	2,801
15 to 19 years	1,093	4,039	44,264	66,947
Total, 0–19 years	1,179	4,320	47,911	71,472
20 to 24 years	1,778	6,575	74,755	114,945
Over 24 years	3,438	12,443	102,017	138,508
Total for all ages	6,395	23,338	224,683	324,925

Source: U.S. Public Health Service and American Social Health Association.

100,000 population, in 1962, 142.8 people were infected out of 100,000; in 1965, 173.6; and in 1969, 154.9. It was estimated that over 2 million people were infected with venereal disease in 1972.

A new hotline

Statistics show that the U.S. gonorrhea epidemic continued to worsen in 1973. Yet, officials at the U.S. Center for Disease Control, in Atlanta, say that there are no plans to copy an apparently successful public education campaign conducted in Sweden, where the venereal disease has been curbed. According to statistics, an estimated 2.8 million American men and women contracted gonorrhea in 1973, with an incidence rate per 100,000 people almost twice the Swedish figure. But the Swedish public education effort, which encourages self-examination for early VD detection and the promotion of condoms for VD prevention, "would be morally unacceptable in the United States," according to Center for Disease Control education consultant William Schwartz. "No U.S. campaign could flaunt the sexual revolution in the public's face," says Schwartz. He adds that VD treatment information is available from a toll-free nationwide "hotline," Operation Venus. "Venus" is providing information to some 3000 callers a month. The hotline number: 800-523-1885.

Certain facts aggravate the venereal-disease problem. In its early and infectious stages, syphilis is not traumatic, medically speaking, and overt symptoms may be present only for a very short period. Many diseased individuals experience no visible signs and therefore do not visit a physician. Gonorrhea in women is frequently difficult to detect, since over 80 percent of females with gonorrhea are asymptomatic. Since these patients are unaware of their disease, they unknowingly infect sex partners. In Los Angeles County it is estimated that about 45,000 women, on any given day of the week, have gonorrhea unknowingly and are infecting other people (Smartt & Lighter, 1971). Another unfortunate characteristic of the venereal diseases is that, after a person has had them and has been effectively treated, he can catch them again, because no immunity develops to prevent reinfection.

One of the misfortunes of the movement against sex-education programs, described earlier, was that many schools that had been instructing students on venereal disease were pressured to abandon that part of their program as well. Many schools provide no education in this area, and many reserve it for the junior or senior years in high school. Baker and Farber (1972) found considerable interest in the topic among students of junior high school age. My investigations (Thornburg, 1970c, 1975) show that approximately two-thirds of our youths first find out about venereal disease between ages 14 and 16.

Bell (1971) has argued cogently that most sexual behavior has moral or legal overtones. One would hope that, with our society's emerging sexual diversification and new morality, a better preparedness for the emotional nature of the experience will also emerge. Sex is shrouded with antithetical meanings, diverse interpretations, and moral stigmas. Our paradoxical attitudes toward sexuality make it an effective means of social control. The combination of social control and social enticement that sexuality presents to adolescents is a real dilemma.

Whether the schools should be the primary transmitters of sexual knowledge and attitudes remains debatable. To insist that the home or the church assume the responsibility probably is not in the best interests of our youths. Still, everyone must consider ways to sort out the bombardment of sexual stimuli to which adolescents are subjected in order to help them emerge with some practical code of sexual behavior. Our adolescents are thinking, feeling, behaving organisms, and they need help in coming to grips with their sexuality in a complex and often contradictory society.

Adolescent Delinquency 13

Essentially, delinquency is the normative conflict between an adolescent and his or her society. It occurs when, for any reason, the adolescent acts in a socially deviant way. Delinquency may be a solitary act or a gang behavior; it may be spontaneous or well planned, against individuals or against institutions. Legally, an adolescent is viewed as delinquent if he or she commits an act that violates the law and if the violation comes to the attention of the police or the courts. Psychologically, a person is viewed as delinquent if he or she has emotional or personality problems that precipitate antisocial behavior. Many sociologists see the delinquent primarily as a product of his environment. In each case, the delinquent is considered behaviorally deviant, because he acts contrary to the norms of society.

Gibbens and Ahrenfeldt (1966) are among those researchers who feel that delinquency is culturally bound. They distinguish three distinct historical stages of culture in which a society exists and deals with delinquency. The first stage is the tribal culture, which has little delinquency. In this setting, juvenile behavior is defined in terms of adult behavior, and the norms of the community control most delinquency; therefore, little allowance is made for age differences. The second cultural stage emerged when separate juvenile laws came into existence. This stage began in the United States and Europe as a corollary to urbanization. The adolescent is now treated as distinctly different from the adult regarding crimes and delinquent acts. In most states, this distinction is maintained until the person reaches 16 or 18 years of age. This stage is representative of the position still maintained by most law-enforcement agencies and correctional institutions. Nevertheless, the United States is entering the third cultural stage, which Gibbens and Ahrenfeldt described as the "preventive approach." The definition of delinquency becomes more ambiguous during this stage. Emphasis is placed on the psychological and social factors that contribute to delinquency.

Social control is an accepted aspect of life. Delinquency is a social problem, since it represents deviance from social controls. Lemert (1964) believes that social controls lead to deviance and suggests that a study of such controls may help us understand the nature of deviance. The prevention of delinquency has drawn the interest of professionals from several different disciplines. Because of their diversified interests, the definition of delinquency has become more ambiguous. The emerging definition holds that delinquency is not necessarily symptomatic of some individual personality defect, psychic or otherwise. The label "delinquency" may be used to describe behavior that, because it is condemned by the dominant society, brings about official action, but that may be otherwise defined as culturally normative behavior within the social class, ethnic group, or other subgroup to which the delinquent belongs. As the adolescent interacts with the larger community he may demonstrate behaviors that are socially unacceptable, although he may be encouraged and reinforced for such behavior by his subgroup. Generational conflict arises when adults of the larger society view antisocial adolescent behavior as a problem. In any event, social action, such as the improvement of economic and educational opportunities and the development of community-action programs, must be taken to prevent delinquency.

INCIDENCE OF DELINQUENCY

In the United States, about three percent of the youths between 10 and 17 years of age annually find their way into the juvenile courts, and between 10 and 15 percent of all children and adolescents become involved with the law before becoming legal adults (at 18 or 21). Delinquency has been on the increase in the United States since the end of World War II. The *Uniform Crime Reports* published by the Federal Bureau of Investigation placed the incidence of delinquency in 1970 at about 1.16 million cases per 105 million children and adolescents. Figure 13.1 shows the increase in delinquency longitudinally and relative to population growth.

The police maintain two types of statistics based on arrests. The first is a count of the number of persons taken into custody for a particular crime. The unit of count is singular—the *person*. The second is a record of the offenses discovered by the arrest. The unit of count may be singular or multiple—the *offense*. For example, if an adolescent was arrested for breaking and entering, and it was discovered that he also had stolen a car, the number of offenses would be two.

In 1967, persons under 18 years of age were represented in 49 percent of the arrests recorded in the FBI Crime Index, as indicated in Table 13.1. The arrest rates between 1960 and 1967 for persons under 18 increased 59 percent. Since the age group from 10 to 17 constitutes only about 15 percent of the population, the arrests within this age group are disproportionately high. The number of serious crimes discovered by arrests in 1967 for persons under 18 was 33 percent, a figure that remained the same between 1960 and 1967. Since serious juvenile offenses are increasing and the discovery rate is maintaining itself, it may be concluded that additional effort is being made by law-enforcement agencies to apprehend juvenile offenders. Even though by 1980 there will be a

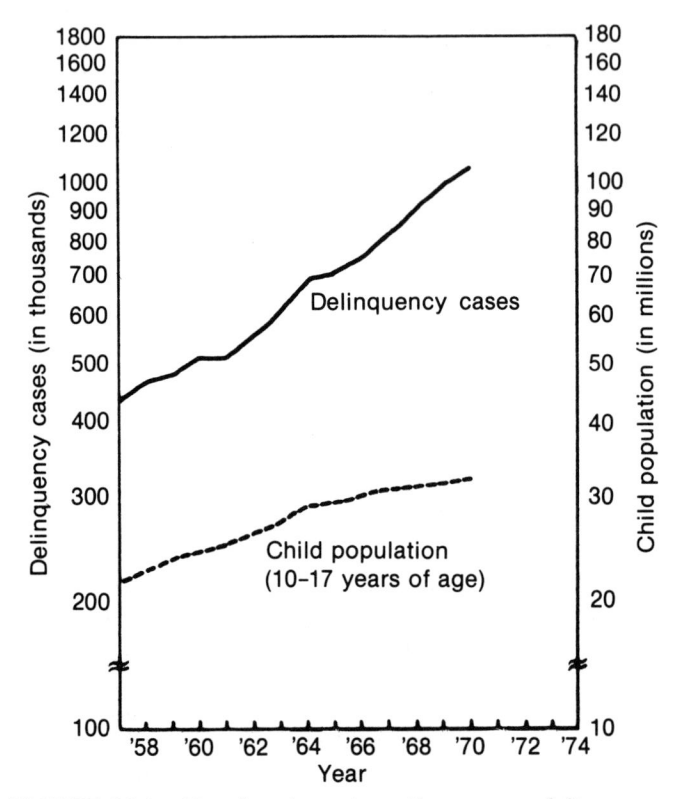

FIGURE 13.1. Trend in juvenile-court delinquency cases and child population 10–17 years of age, 1957–1970 (semilogarithmic scale). (From *Juvenile Court Statistics 1970.* National Center for Social Statistics, U.S. Department of Health, Education, & Welfare.)

significant reduction in the number of adolescents in the United States, it is not likely that a reduction in delinquency rates will be achieved, since delinquency incidence is increasing too rapidly.

The last few years have also seen less disparity between the sexes in delinquency rates, since the incidence of delinquency among females has increased more rapidly than among males. For some time, the proportion of male delinquency to female delinquency has been four or five to one (Gold, 1970). The ratio is now thought to be three to one, and the trend toward less difference is continuing. Juvenile court statistics (1972) reported that girls' cases, nationally, increased twice as much (10 percent) as boys' cases (5 percent) between 1969 and 1970. Between 1965 and 1970, female delinquency increased 78 percent, compared with a 44-percent increase in male delinquency. Between 1960 and 1970, arrests of girls between 10 and 17 years of age increased by 276 percent for violent crimes and by 255 percent for property crimes. Corresponding percentage increases for boys were 159 percent and 75 percent, respectively.

OFFICIAL TREATMENT OF DELINQUENTS

Nearly half of the juvenile offenders taken into custody in 1967 were released with no official police action being taken (see Table 13.2). Some of the reasons for not turning over an offender to the court are (1) failure of the victim to cooperate in the prosecution, (2) release of the arrested person with a warning, (3) insufficient evidence to support a formal charge, and (4) police determination that the arrested person did not commit the offense.

Table 13.2 shows that 48.4 percent of the juvenile offenders in 1967 were referred to juvenile court. This percentage is based on a national sample of 502 juvenile courts. On the basis of these reports it was estimated that 697,000 delinquency cases were handled in the courts in 1967.

In the decision whether to dismiss an offender or refer him or her to juvenile court, the attitude of the arresting officer toward the alleged offender seems to be a crucial variable. Briar and Piliavin (1966) concluded from their research that such decisions made by the police depend to a great extent on "cues which emerge from the interaction between the officer and the youth, cues from which an officer assessed the youth's character" (1966, p. 449). They also contended that the officers in their study exercised wide discretion in the handling of juveniles, and that certain types of individuals were more apt than others to be arrested. Specifically, the way a youth dresses, his race, and his attitude toward the apprehending officer influence decisions.

Goldman's study (1963) of the police's handling of delinquents in four communities, and the variation in their processing juvenile offenders, throws some light on the question of discretion, as well as on that of labeling. Utilizing statistical data from the four counties under study, Goldman found significant differences in the manner in which juveniles were handled. The author then interviewed 90 police officers in an effort to understand the disparity. He found that (1) the concept of juvenile delinquency is to some extent determined by the policeman in selectively reporting juvenile offenders to the court, and that (2) research has shown that the police base their reporting partly on the act of the offender, but also on their idiosyncratic interpretation of this act and on the degree of pressure applied by the community on the police. Goldman also names a

TABLE 13.1. Total arrests of persons under 15, under 18, under 21, and under 25 years of age, 1967 (4,566 agencies; 1967 estimated population 145,927,000).

Offense charged	Grand total, all ages	Number of persons arrested					Percentage				
		Under 15	Under 18	Under 21	Under 25	Under 15	Under 18	Under 21	Under 25
Total	5,518,420	527,141	1,339,578	2,015,338	2,613,887	9.6	24.3	36.5	47.4
Criminal homicide:									
Murder and nonnegligent manslaughter	9,145	137	830	1,948	3,415	1.5	9.1	21.3	37.3
Manslaughter by negligence	3,022	30	246	761	1,295	1.0	8.1	25.2	42.9
Forcible rape	12,659	475	2,515	5,418	8,133	3.8	19.9	42.9	64.2
Robbery	59,789	6,885	18,889	32,305	43,776	11.5	31.6	54.0	73.2
Aggravated assault	107,192	6,559	18,359	31,654	47,520	6.1	17.1	29.5	44.3
Burglary—breaking or entering	239,461	62,510	128,169	169,265	196,538	26.1	53.5	70.7	82.1
Larceny-theft	447,299	134,216	246,057	306,615	344,807	30.0	55.0	68.5	77.1
Auto theft	118,233	19,902	73,080	94,297	104,860	16.8	61.8	79.8	88.7
Subtotal for above offenses	996,800	230,714	488,145	642,263	750,344	23.1	49.0	64.4	75.3
Other assaults	229,928	14,837	37,849	65,822	101,073	6.5	16.5	28.6	44.0
Arson	8,058	3,768	5,236	5,953	6,495	46.8	65.0	73.9	80.6
Forgery and counterfeiting	33,462	806	3,918	9,783	16,572	2.4	11.7	29.2	49.5
Fraud	58,192	643	2,444	8,012	18,534	1.1	4.2	13.8	31.8
Embezzlement	6,073	53	256	810	1,863	.9	4.2	13.3	30.7
Stolen property—buying, receiving, possessing	28,620	3,542	9,901	15,247	19,502	12.4	34.6	53.3	68.1
Vandalism	109,299	54,782	83,571	93,053	98,357	50.1	76.5	85.1	90.0
Weapons—carrying, possessing, etc.	71,684	3,738	12,967	23,984	36,111	5.2	18.1	33.5	50.4
Prostitution and commercialized vice	39,744	97	848	6,729	21,017	.2	2.1	16.9	52.9
Sex offenses (except forcible rape and prostitution)	53,541	4,959	13,075	19,924	27,391	9.3	24.4	37.2	51.2

TABLE 13.1 (continued)

Offense charged	Grand total, all ages	Number of persons arrested					Percentage				
		Under 15	Under 18	Under 21	Under 25	Under 15	Under 18	Under 21	Under 25
Narcotic drug laws	101,079	2,812	21,405	49,071	69,565	2.8	21.2	48.5	68.8
Gambling	84,772	343	2,143	5,735	12,865	.4	2.5	6.8	15.2
Offenses against family and children	56,137	264	860	6,435	15,829	.5	1.5	11.5	28.2
Driving under the influence	281,152	57	2,846	17,807	48,975	*	1.0	6.3	17.4
Liquor laws	209,741	4,924	63,587	154,897	169,228	2.3	30.3	73.9	80.7
Drunkenness	1,517,809	3,509	34,621	109,655	225,654	.2	2.3	7.2	14.9
Disorderly conduct	550,469	38,078	110,004	201,169	282,074	6.9	20.0	36.5	51.2
Vagrancy	106,747	1,646	9,777	28,155	41,455	1.5	9.2	26.4	38.8
All other offenses (except traffic)	654,915	76,082	189,921	282,299	364,765	11.6	29.0	43.1	55.7
Suspicion	95,794	5,674	21,800	44,131	61,814	5.9	22.8	46.1	64.5
Curfew and loitering law violations	94,872	23,794	94,872	94,872	94,872	25.1	100.0	100.0	100.0
Runaways	129,532	52,019	129,532	129,532	129,532	40.2	100.0	100.0	100.0

*Less than one-tenth of 1 percent.
From *Uniform Crime Reports*, 1967, p. 123.

TABLE 13.2. Police disposition of juvenile offenders taken into custody in 1967, in percentages.

Disposition	Percentage
Handled within department and released	46.2
Referred to juvenile court jurisdiction	48.4
Referred to welfare agency	1.6
Referred to other police agency	2.2
Referred to criminal or adult court	1.5
Total	99.9

Based on data contained in *Uniform Crime Reports*, 1967.

number of other considerations that enter into the official handling of juveniles, including the philosophy or ideology of the department, its idea of what delinquency is, and the effect of public and community norms.

Goldman cautions against applying his findings to police departments in general; nevertheless, his findings offer some insight into the law-enforcement system. By way of criticism, it should be noted that this study did not focus on field observations, a fact that makes it difficult to ascertain the number of cases in which police made contact with a youth

---

M. H. Langley suggests that juvenile courts may actually make delinquents of some adolescents by interpreting the law too literally. He summarizes:

1. As many as 70% of the known criminal law violations are never attributed to a perpetrator. That is, the FBI statistics, which provide us with most of our national figures on crime and delinquency, represent the arrests for only 30% of the crimes known to the police.
2. A national study indicates that only about half the victims of law violations make reports to the police. Hence, our fears about the amount of crime in our society appear to be based on only half of all the allegedly criminal acts which occur.
3. The indices of delinquent behavior occurrence are typically based upon police arrest figures and not on court dispositional figures. These indices are a more accurate reflection of police enforcement behavior then they are of youths' illegal behavior.
4. Because, in part, of the wording of state juvenile court laws, youths are more susceptible to being arrested, taken into custody, and judged delinquent (found guilty) than are adults [Langley, 1972, p. 279].*

*From "Juvenile Court: Making of a Delinquent" by M. H. Langley, *Law and Society Review*, 1972, 7(2), 279. Copyright 1972 by The Law and Society Association. Reprinted by permission.

and took no action. However, it should also be noted that in the communities under study the police had the power, after making an arrest, to release the juvenile. Thus a parallel can be drawn between this finding and Briar and Piliavin's study (1966), which reported that an officer had the discretion to make or not make an arrest.

The methodology employed by Goldman represents an empirical approach to the study of institutions. One cannot completely rule out the element of subjectivity in conducting interviews; however, the researcher, recognizing the problem, did attempt to "control" the interviews by utilizing a checklist. In discussing his study, Goldman notes:

> It must be borne in mind that in this study several variables were artificially isolated. In reality, no one factor has been shown to operate in the determination of which offenders are officially reported to the court by the police. There is an interrelationship between the variables which cannot be expressed in statistical terms. . . . At times the task of the policeman may be akin to that of solving a problem containing a number of variables. At other times, *one* of the considerations . . . such as political pressure . . . may force the decision of the police officer in a given direction [Goldman, 1963, p. 132].

THE ROOTS OF DELINQUENCY

Although the data reported up to this point record the incidence of delinquency in people between the ages of 10 and 19, there is evidence that the roots of delinquency may lie within the family, thus predisposing a person to delinquent tendencies in childhood. Significant longitudinal research has been done by Glueck and Glueck (1950, 1968) on this subject. Using a matched sample of 500 delinquent and 500 nondelinquent boys, the Gluecks studied them to determine initial causative factors in delinquency and to ascertain patterns of persistence in delinquent or criminal behaviors over a 20-year period. Table 13.3, from Glueck and Glueck's initial report (1950), shows the ages at which delinquent behavior began in the subjects they studied.

Preadolescence has been defined as ages 9 to 13 (Thornburg, 1974d). According to that definition, it is easy to see that almost all delinquents began engaging in antisocial behavior either before or during preadolescence. Specifically, 48.4 percent of adolescent delinquents engaged in delinquent behavior before age 8 and 49.8 percent before age 14. Only 1.8 percent initiated delinquent behavior after 13 years of age. Furthermore, the average age of first court appearance was 12.4 years, and of first conviction, 12.5 years. Over 28 percent of the boys appeared in court before they were 11.

It is not enough to simply establish the fact that most delin-

TABLE 13.3. Age at onset of misbehavior of 500 juvenile delinquents.

	Delinquents	
Age	Number	Percent
Under 5 years	20	4.0
5–7 years	222	44.4
8–10 years	196	39.2
11–13 years	53	10.6
14–16 years	9	1.8
Total	500	100.0

Median = 8.35 years. Standard deviation = ±2.39 years.

From *Unraveling Juvenile Delinquency* by S. Glueck and E. Glueck. Copyright 1950 by Harvard University Press. Reprinted by permission.

quency begins prior to adolescence. One must look for its causes as well. Most delinquency can be explained in terms of the person's sociocultural environment, especially in cases dealing with the culturally disadvantaged delinquent. Unquestionably, distinct social disadvantages precipitate delinquent behavior when a youth becomes frustrated by the discrepancy between his lower-class goals, ambitions, and values and the middle-class goals to which he is constantly exposed (Kvaraceus & Ulrich, 1959). However, although this explanation may hold true for many lower-class delinquents, it is not a satisfactory explanation for the rising incidence of middle-class delinquency. Further, Glueck and Glueck (1968) found that the nondelinquents in their study had environments and social settings comparable to those of the delinquents. Such evidence demands an examination of other factors that may be delinquency sources.

The cause of delinquency is the "totality of conditions sufficient to produce it" (Glueck & Glueck, 1968, p. 172). This statement, of course, implies that several causes contribute to delinquent behaviors, although the causes of delinquency found in one adolescent are not necessarily the same in another. Defiance, which was found to account for the acts of 50 percent of the delinquents studied by Glueck and Glueck, obviously could not be an explanation for delinquency in the 50 percent in which no such trait was evidenced.

Glueck and Glueck did find different family characteristics in delinquents and nondelinquents. Some of these characteristics are indicated in Table 13.4. The authors considered parents' physical and mental disabilities to be strong influences on delinquent behavior. The psychological home environment is somewhat affected by the high de-

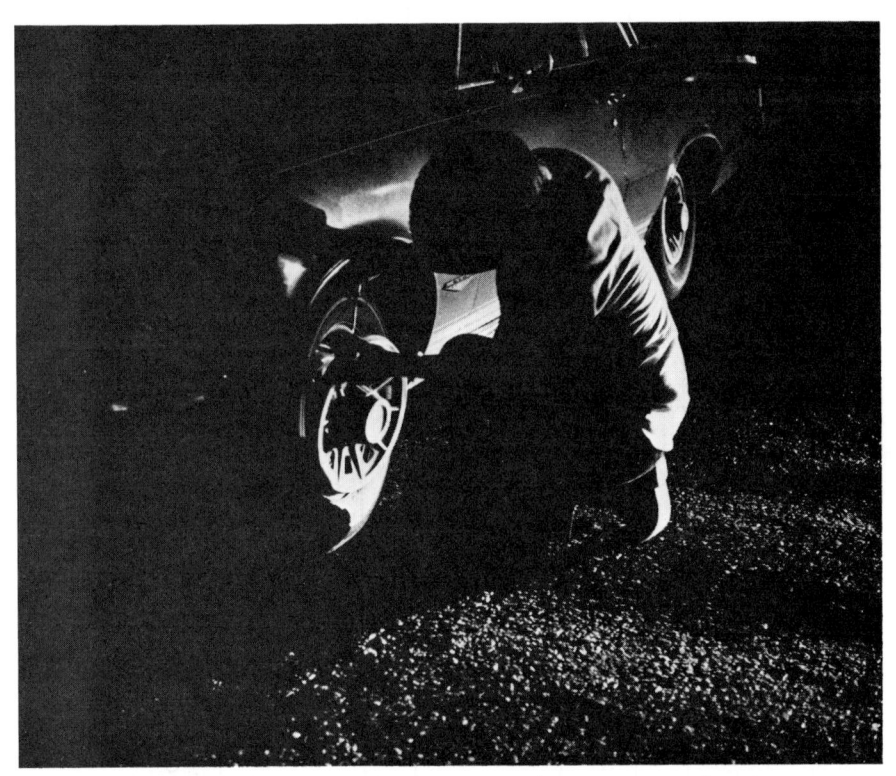

Antisocial behavior results sometimes from poor socialization, other times from a lack of meaningful things to do. In either case it is nonacceptable, sometimes criminal, behavior.

grees of emotional disturbance, drunkenness, and criminality often found in delinquents' mothers and fathers. The fact that 45 percent of the mothers and 66 percent of the fathers of the delinquent boys were themselves involved in delinquent behaviors must be regarded as a strong determinant of delinquency potential in their children. Glueck and Glueck believe that the nature of family interaction in the early years of the delinquent's life is a primary causative factor in delinquency. They provided a clear and concise analysis of factors related to delinquency:

> In emphasizing that our findings tend to confirm the view that delinquency involves both the biological make-up of the individual offender and his immediate forbears, and the family drama in which he and his parents play leading roles, especially during the first few years of life, we do not mean to ignore certain ideas which have been stressed by some sociologists. For example, we have in the past noted the influence of culture conflict in stimulating violation of social norms in some cases. Again, we recognize the special influences that are involved in the recent rise of delinquency in middle-class and upper-class regions. But such

TABLE 13.4. History of serious physical ailments, mental retardation, emotional disturbances, drunkenness, and criminality of father and mother.

Mother

Condition	Delinquents Number	Delinquents Percent	Nondelinquents Number	Nondelinquents Percent	Difference Percent	p
Serious physical ailments	243	48.6	165	33.0	15.6	<.01
Mental retardation	164	32.8	45	9.0	23.8	<.01
Emotional disturbances	201	40.2	88	17.6	22.6	<.01
Drunkenness	115	23.0	35	7.0	16.0	<.01
Criminality	224	44.8	75	15.0	29.8	<.01

Father

Condition	Delinquents Number	Delinquents Percent	Nondelinquents Number	Nondelinquents Percent	Difference Percent	p
Serious physical ailments	198	39.6	143	28.6	11.0	<.01
Mental retardation	92	18.4	28	5.6	12.8	<.01
Emotional disturbances	220	44.0	90	18.0	26.0	<.01
Drunkenness	314	62.8	195	39.0	23.8	<.01
Criminality	331	66.2	160	32.0	34.2	<.01

Note: The numbers in this table represent *minimal* incidence; percentages are based on totals of 500.
From *Unraveling Juvenile Delinquency* by S. Glueck and E. Glueck. Copyright 1950 by Harvard University Press. Reprinted by permission.

influences—rapid social mobility, conflicts in values and standards, weakening of middle-class and upper-class value systems so that they no longer guide behavior as much as in the past—are two, three, or more stages removed from the immediately and intimately operative ones. For, as previously pointed out, the influences of the culture, and of exposure to another, are *selective*. Individuals react differently to the impact of cultural standards. That is why such general etiologic theories as the "delinquent subculture," or the working-class or middle-class subculture, or the "interstitial area," or the slum or "ghetto," or the process of "differential association" and other nondiscriminative, all-embracing general theories, do not adequately account for the operative facts in etiology.

Despite the many unwholesome and antisocial features of our culture—its excessive materialism, its stress on "success," its recent overwhelming assaults on values by various mass-communication media, its encouragement of the spread of "literature" of pornography and violence, the weakening hold of the church and formal religion—the majority of people are, in normal times, relatively law-abiding. In the research of which the present study is an extension (*Unraveling Juvenile Delinquency*), we had no difficulty in finding 500 nondelinquent boys living in underprivileged and high-delinquency areas of Greater Boston.

In other words, antisocial aspects of culture are only *potential* or *possible* causes of delinquency. Persons of varied innate natures and differing early parent-child relationships respond in different ways to those elements of the culture which they wish, or are impelled, to *introject*, some of them transforming such cultural elements into antisocial motives. Environment can play no role in conduct unless and until it is, as it were, emotionally absorbed, becoming a part of the motivating force for or against the taboos and demands of the prevailing culture, its values, and its norms. For this reason it is indispensable to study individuals as well as broad social dynamics. Whatever future research may yet disclose about the causes of delinquency in the affluent segment of our society, as regards delinquency among the underprivileged, the emphases suggested by our analyses in the present and in prior works are supported by the facts [Glueck & Glueck, 1968, pp. 172–173].*

THE DELINQUENT SUBCULTURE

Delinquent youths are said to constitute a subculture. The adolescent subculture in general is a tolerated form of variation from the parent culture, but delinquent youths represent an intolerable variation. Cloward and Ohlin (1960) described three types of delinquent subcultures:

1. *Criminal*. This group is devoted to theft, extortion, and other illegal means of securing an income; some criminal delinquents may graduate to the ranks of organized or professional crime.

*From *Delinquents and Nondelinquents in Perspective* by S. Glueck and E. Glueck. Copyright 1968 by Harvard University Press. Reprinted by permission.

2. *Conflict.* The participation in acts of violence becomes an important means of securing status.
3. *Retreatist.* This group is the most enigmatic; the consumption of drugs is an expression of group solidarity, and addiction is prevalent.

Cloward and Ohlin are really talking about three different groups that emerge from lower-class culture—specifically, slum areas. Criminal subcultures are thought to occur in somewhat stable slum neighborhoods in which a criminal hierarchy exists. The authors argue that, for many youths in this type of neighborhood, the desire to move up in the neighborhood criminal hierarchy motivates them to conform to delinquent values and behavior in order to demonstrate their criminal ability. Conflict subcultures arise in disorganized slums that have no organized hierarchy for criminal development. Because these slum areas are highly disorganized and present oriented, they are limited in the opportunities they afford their residents. Cloward and Ohlin (1960) feel that this disorganization causes a breakdown in social control, which encourages deviance. Retreatist subcultures emerge as an adjustment pattern for those lower-class youths who have failed to find a position in the criminal or conflict subculture and have failed to use either legitimate or illegitimate opportunity structures.

Empey (1967) feels that Cloward and Ohlin have defined subculture too narrowly:

> They see a delinquent subculture as unique and as autonomous. Organization around a specific delinquent activity, they say, distinguishes a delinquent subculture from other subcultures. Such behaviors as truancy, drunkenness, property destruction, or theft are legally delinquent activities, but these they would not include as characteristics of a delinquent subculture unless they were the focal activities around which the dominant beliefs and roles of a group were organized [Empey, 1967, p. 36].

Lower-Class Delinquency

The work of Miller (1958) reflects his belief that delinquency is primarily the result of the urban lower-class setting. He posits the existence of a lower-class subculture that, by virtue of its long history and definitive characteristics—such as matriarchal family structures and same-sex peer groups—has a set of values or focal concerns quite different from those of the dominant middle class. The delinquency of lower-class youths is seen as action aimed at deriving positive sanction from peer-group members by exhibiting those behaviors endemic to the lower-class milieu.

Cohen (1966) presents a view comparable to Miller's. He suggests that lower-class delinquency is a collective reaction on the part of lower-class youths engendered by their inability to succeed in a middle-class-oriented status system. Frustrated in their attempts to succeed in the school system and other institutions dominated by middle-class values, they turn to each other for support. Cohen utilizes the concept of *reaction formation* to explain how these youths turn middle-class values upside down; that is, lower-class boys are frustrated by the opportunity structure and commit delinquent acts as a result.

Two other theories of lower-class delinquency are similar to Cohen's. Kvaraceus and Ulrich (1959) maintain that delinquency stems from differences between the lower-class adolescent's goals and the middle-class goals to which he is exposed. Therefore the lower-class youth seeks prestige and acceptance in norm-violating gang activity. Cloward and Ohlin (1960) have proposed a differential-opportunity theory; that is, lower-class adolescents accept most middle-class goals but are unable to pursue them because of incongruity between their aspirations and their opportunities.

Miller (1958) and Cohen (1955) theorized that lower-class delinquency is a masculine protest against a female-dominated home. There is reason to believe, however, that this once-dominant cultural phenomenon is disappearing, especially in middle-class homes, and that its disappearance is spreading downward through the lower classes via the youth subculture. It may be argued that in the United States, as the status of the sexes in many social spheres of activity has been approaching equality, there has been an increasing feminization of the general culture. Instead of females becoming more like males, males have increasingly taken on some of the roles and attributes formerly assigned to females. The point of this trend is not so much that maleness is reduced as a goal motivating young boys, but that physical aggressiveness—once the manifest feature of maleness—is being reduced to more symbolic forms and the meaning of masculinity is thus being changed. Earlier frontier mores, which placed a premium on male aggressiveness, have been replaced by other criteria for masculinity. The gun and the fist have been substantially replaced by financial ability, the capacity to manipulate others in complex organizations, and intellectual talents. Thoughtful wit, verbal skill, and even the striving after musical and artistic expression are becoming, in the dominant culture, features of male assertiveness.

It may well be that, in many lower-class communities, violence is associated with masculinity and may be not only acceptable but admired. The high rates of violent crime among lower-class males suggest that this group strongly continues to equate maleness with overt physical aggression. In the Italian slum of Boston, Gans (1962) described the families in which the men dominated and the mothers encouraged male dominance. On the other hand, lower-class boys who lack a father or other strong male figure, as is the case with many boys in black families, have the problem of finding models to imitate (see the discussion of black families in Chapter 9). Rejecting female dominance at home and at school, and the morality they associate with women, may be the means such boys use to assert their masculinity. Such assertion must be demonstrated by behavior antithetical to femininity—for example, physical aggression. Being a bad boy, Parsons (1947) has said, can become a positive goal if goodness is too closely identified with femininity.

Middle-Class Delinquency

Delinquency has traditionally been attributed to lower-class adolescents. However, recent studies show that there may be a greater incidence of delinquency among adolescents of the middle class than among those of any other class. One of the common criticisms of Miller's and Cohen's theories is that, considering greater urbanization, suburban sprawl, and the mass media, it is difficult to contend that the lower-class culture exists any longer in the pure form with which these researchers described it two decades ago. In fact, in the last 15 years, the greatest increase in the juvenile-crime rate has been seen in the suburbs (Federal Bureau of Investigation, 1972; Sebald, 1968). Furthermore, these crimes seem to be occurring among middle- and upper-middle-class boys and girls (Pine, 1966; Vaz, 1969).

By applying self-report techniques to the measurement of delinquency, recent studies have found that juvenile delinquency is becoming more evenly distributed through the socioeconomic-status levels. Nye, Short, and Olson (1967) made estimates of the extent of delinquent behavior that revealed that it is more randomly distributed among the socioeconomic strata than official records indicate. Similarly, Dentler and Monroe (1961) found no association between reported incidence of adolescent theft and low socioeconomic status. However, Reiss and Rhodes (1961) found from the self-reports of juvenile boys that delinquent deviation in the lower socioeconomic strata is more frequent and serious, regardless of the type of deviation. For example, they found that (1) career-oriented delinquents are found only among lower-class boys, (2) peer-oriented delinquency is the most common organizational form at both lower-class and middle-class levels, and (3) the typical lower-class boy is a conforming nonachiever, whereas the typical middle-class boy is a conforming achiever.

Accounting for middle-class delinquency in the United States requires an understanding of the dominant culture in which middle-class youth live. Structural changes in society over the last half century have produced opportunities for extensive adolescent peer-group participation and a mass youth culture. During the growth of this youth culture, in which the majority of middle-class teen-agers participate, both delinquent and nondelinquent patterns of behavior have emerged. Vaz (1965, 1969) contends that the bulk of middle-class delinquency occurs in the course of *customary, nondelinquent* activities and falls within the limits of adolescent group norms. Moreover, knowledge of both delinquent and nondelinquent patterns in the youth culture is widely shared among middle-class teen-agers. Therefore one need not look for a separate "delinquent subculture" in order to account for middle-class delinquency. Rather, much middle-class delinquency originates from the normal processes of group interaction. Vaz sums it up: "The motives for much middle-class delinquency are learned through sustained participation in everyday respectable adolescent activities. In this manner delinquency becomes gradually routine in the middle-class youth culture" (Vaz, 1967, p. 135).

A youth culture is not endemic to every society, but it is apt to develop under special conditions. Institutional changes in the social and economic spheres of the United States—such as migration from rural areas and the decrease in size of families—have made possible the emergence of a relatively prestigious youth culture (Elkin, 1964). The growth of unionization, which helps protect semiskilled and skilled workers from competition from new recruits, and the growth of professionalization, which makes entry into these occupations dependent upon "educational qualifications," have helped foster the almost universal consensus that children should remain in school and be kept out of the labor market (Cohen, 1966). The fact that more children have remained in school for longer periods of time has helped generate a youth culture.

The learning of delinquent behavior is insufficient to ensure its occurrence. There must be an opportunity to carry out the learned activity. That is, the structure of opportunity—the particular form of social organization—must support the actual role performance (Cloward & Ohlin, 1960). In the case of middle-class delinquency, the opportunity structure for *legitimate* behavior can provide the necessary structure for the performance of illegitimate, disapproved conduct. If the daily round of activities of middle-class adolescents includes delinquent patterns of behavior, the more a middle-class adolescent is immersed in the youth culture the more likely he is to become involved in juvenile delinquency. Some adolescents will have greater opportunities for delinquency than others. The question is: under what circumstances is the middle-class teen-ager most likely to become involved in delinquent behavior?

One condition for delinquent conduct among middle-class adolescents is access to the physical objects required for participating in the youth culture. Prominent behavior patterns among middle-class teenagers spotlight the car, alcoholic beverages and drugs, pocket money, the latest clothing styles, and so forth. Therefore, access to one or all of these objects is extremely important for participation in the middle-class adolescent culture. Indeed, it is difficult to conceive of an adolescent's becoming part of the middle-class teen-age crowd if he does not have access to some of these objects. For example, dating is a highly valued experience within the youth culture, and the possession of an automobile is a symbol of social rank; therefore, the youth who owns or has access to a car has an obvious advantage in dating. To the extent that the means of participation in teen-age activities are not equally available to all, both participation in the youth culture and involvement in juvenile delinquency will be unevenly distributed.

Pine (1966) sees a significant relationship between economic growth and the rise in delinquent behavior, an idea highly supportive of the preceding contentions. Greater economic resources and greater social mobility are influential in promoting deviant behaviors. Certainly, our history since World War II has been marked by increased affluence and increased middle-class delinquency.

Pine also believes that there has always been some delinquency in the middle-class and upper-class segments of our society and that, to a considerable extent, it has been hidden because official delinquency statistics are biased for the middle and upper classes and against the lower classes. In fact, the more recent studies by Vaz (1967, 1969), Gold (1970), and Polk (1971) all use self-report techniques in working with middle-class youths because most of this delinquency remains undetected or is ignored.

Pine cites seven pre-1960 studies that show evidence of as much middle-class as lower-class delinquency:

1. Porterfield (1946) found that 2409 northern Texas college students had committed as many delinquent offenses as their lower-class counterparts but had not been charged with them.
2. Wallerstein and Wyle (1946) found that 49 offenses punishable by at least one year in prison were commonly committed by about 2000 upper-class people surveyed in New York. In fact, 99 percent stated that they had committed at least one of these offenses.
3. Bloch and Flynn (1956) gave 340 college students a questionnaire to determine the extent of the misdemeanors and felonious acts they committed. Among these middle- and upper-middle-class youths, 91 percent admitted to some type of delinquent behaviors.
4. Clinard (1957) found, among 49 criminology students in the midwest,

that 86 percent had committed thefts and 50 percent had committed acts of vandalism.
5. Wattenberg and Balistrieri (1952) found, among 230 white boys charged with auto theft in Detroit in 1948, that they all came from good neighborhoods and had good peer relationships.
6. An investigation was conducted by Birkness and Johnson (1949) in which a group of delinquents was compared with a group of nondelinquents. Each group included 25 subjects. It was found that five times as many of the parents of delinquent children as those of the nondelinquent children were of the professional class. Almost twice as many parents of nondelinquents as parents of delinquents were classified as manual laborers.
7. Nye (1959) found no significant relationship between one's social class and the severity of delinquent behavior. Middle- and upper-class youths were involved in as much norm-violating behavior as lower-class youths.

The incidence of middle- and upper-class delinquency has been extensively investigated in recent years by Edmund Vaz and Martin Gold. Vaz investigated Canadian students, and Gold investigated students in Flint, Michigan. One of Vaz's studies (1965) among 1639 high-school-age middle-class boys was concerned with the incidence of delinquent activity and the age of the delinquent. Results of the study are summarized in Table 13.5. As you can see, the 15–19 age group was considerably more delinquent than the 13–14 age group. This pattern agrees with the finding of Glueck and Glueck (1950) that delinquent behaviors peaked between the ages of 15 and 16. Gold (1970) also found this trend. Figure 13.2 shows the proportion of boys who committed offenses between ages 13 and 16. The older boys tended to be more delinquent than the younger ones, although the differences were not so great as those Vaz found.

Vaz (1969) was also concerned with the incidence of upper-class delinquency. Because the mass youth culture cuts across social-class lines, the majority of young people are unable to escape its dominant themes, interests, and values. The world of upper-class youths is no longer all of a single weave. For an ever-increasing number of adolescents, the contemporary high school has reduced social-class distinctions. Once a youth enters high school, he or she becomes quickly absorbed in the interests and attitudes of peers and teachers from all social strata, and peers expect enthusiastic participation in their activities.

Vaz (1969) investigated 775 boys (428 middle-class, 347 upper-class) enrolled in private and public institutions. Asking questions similar to those found in Table 13.5, Vaz found a similar pattern of incidence of delinquency, with the exception of the upper-class boys enrolled in

TABLE 13.5. Self-reported delinquent behavior of middle-class boys, by age group.

	Percent admitting commission of offense		Percent admitting commission of offense more than once or twice	
	Age		Age	
Type of offense[1]	13–14	15–19	13–14	15–19
Driven a car without a driver's license	28.6	62.3	9.1	27.9
Taken little things that did not belong to you	61.0	67.2	10.4	16.7
Skipped school without a legitimate excuse	23.6	40.8	3.9	13.6
Driven beyond the speed limit	5.8	51.2	1.3	39.7
Participated in drag-races along the highway with your friends	6.5	31.1	2.0	16.3
Engaged in a fist fight with another boy	45.8	56.0	7.1	8.7
Been feeling "high" from drinking beer, wine, or liquor	11.7	39.0	2.6	17.9
Gambled for money at cards, dice, or some other game	42.2	66.0	16.9	37.4
Remained out all night without parents' permission	19.5	25.8	5.2	9.5
Taken a car without owner's knowledge	5.2	12.5	0.7	3.1
Been placed on school probation or expelled from school	0.7	5.6	0.0	1.2
Destroyed or damaged public or private property of any kind	44.8	52.0	11.7	14.8
Taken little things of value (between $2 and $50) which did not belong to you	9.7	16.0	0.7	3.5
Tried to be intimate with a member of the opposite sex	18.2	37.8	7.8	17.6
Broken into or tried to break and enter a building with the intention of stealing	5.2	7.5	0.7	1.0
Sold, used, or tried to use drugs of some kind	1.3	1.0	0.0	0.3
Bought or tried to buy beer, wine, or liquor from a store or adult	3.3	24.8	0.7	11.7
Taken money of any amount from someone or place which did not belong to you	30.5	32.7	7.1	6.9
Taken a glass of beer, wine, or liquor at a party or elsewhere with your friends	32.5	64.8	8.4	35.2
	n=154	682[2]		

[1]Two items are omitted because they were used solely as reliability check measures.
[2]Fourteen cases of boys over 19 years are omitted.
From "Middle-Class Adolescents: Self-Reported Delinquency and Youth Culture Activities" by E. W. Vaz, *Canadian Review of Sociology and Anthropology*, 1965, 2(1), 59.

FIGURE 13.2. Proportions of boys at each age level who committed each offense.

Percent	Age: 13	14	15	16
	N: 35	77	69	77
70				drinking
60		shoplifting trespass	shoplifting drinking	
50		drinking	theft	shoplifting trespass
	trespass	entering theft	trespass	truancy theft
40	drinking		property destruction entering fraud	entering false ID or age fornication fraud

30	entering
	shoplifting
	theft
		property
		  destruction
			truancy
			false ID or age
				gang fighting
				property
				  destruction

		gang fighting
		truancy
		threatened
		  assault
			gang fighting
			threatened
			  assault
				threatened
				  assault
				stealing car
				  part or gas
				drinking

20	property
	  destruction
		fraud	fornication	concealed
				  weapon

		false ID or age	UDAA[1]
			concealed
			  weapon
			stealing car
			  part or gas
			assault
				assault
				UDAA[1]
				extortion

		fornication		

10	gang fighting
	assault
	truancy
	concealed
	  weapon
	extortion
	threatened
	  assault
		assault
		concealed
		  weapon
		armed
		  robbery
		extortion
			running away
			armed
			  robbery
			extortion
			arson
				running away
				armed
				  robbery

	stealing car
	  part or gas
	armed
	  robbery
	fornication
		stealing car
		  part or gas
		running away
		hitting parents
			hitting parents	hitting parents

0	hitting parents fraud false ID or age running away arson UDAA[1]	arson UDAA[1]		arson

[1]Unlawful driving away of an automobile.

From *Delinquent Behavior in an American City* by M. Gold. Copyright © 1970 by Wadsworth Publishing Company, Inc. Reprinted by permission of the publisher, Brooks/Cole Publishing Company, Monterey, California.

private schools, among whom delinquency tended to be higher. It is interesting to observe, in Table 13.6, that the delinquency rates among middle- and upper-class boys attending public schools are virtually the same.

Vaz believes that middle- and upper-class social status gets the delinquency that it "deserves." That is, the cardinal values and interests of these adolescents contain the seeds of delinquency. It seems to be the case for many youths that attending dances *means* late hours, dating *means* varying degrees of physical intimacy, possession of an automobile *means* speeding, "dragging," and "parking," and "hanging out" with the boys *means* roughhousing and special kinds of vandalism. Conformity and deviance among these youths very likely reflect the same set of values, interests, and attitudes. What tips the scales in favor of drinking, sexual intercourse, or "raising hell" is probably not a difference in values. Therefore, a youth's commitment to "respectable" adolescent activities engages the adolescent in daily opportunities for status gain that contain potential for delinquency. Some examples are parties, dances, sports events, motoring along the highway, hanging around the drive-in—almost any occasion when boys and girls participate jointly. These situations are not likely to be defined as delinquent in themselves, but they contain the potential for delinquent behavior.

The four levels of social status designated by Gold in his study (1970) are upper-middle, lower-middle, upper-lower, and lower-lower. In Figure 13.3, you can see that lower-class boys commit offenses significantly more often, with the exceptions of unlawful driving away of an automobile, theft of car parts or gas, shoplifting, and trespassing. Shoplifting was most common among lower-middle-class boys, and the other delinquent acts mentioned here were somewhat evenly spread across all status levels. Gold's data indicate a higher incidence of middle-class delinquency than do Vaz's (1969). Regarding his findings, Gold observes:

> These data indicate that the relationship between social status and delinquent behavior is a real one among boys but not among girls. But real as the relationship appears to be, it is slight, and official records have exaggerated it. Thus theories of delinquency grounded on this relationship are directly relevant only to boys, and their ground seems to be a narrow one. These data suggest that the relationship between social status and delinquency should be considered a clue—a scant one at that—to the causes of delinquency, and that we need to probe beyond it if we wish to identify forces which account for such delinquency. They also suggest that treatment and prevention programs aimed exclusively at lower-class targets miss a lot of heavily delinquent youngsters [Gold, 1970, pp. 76–77].

As I stated earlier, Vaz's (1967) basic assertion was that delinquency among middle-class youths is a direct by-product of active par-

TABLE 13.6. Self-reported delinquent behavior of private and public school upper- and middle-class boys.

Type of offense	Upper class Private	Upper class Public	Middle class Public	Upper class Private	Upper class Public	Middle class Public
	Percent admitting offense (15–19 years)			Percent admitting offense more than once or twice		
Taken little things of value (between $2 and $50) which did not belong to you	37.9	15.5	15.2	8.6	4.8	2.3
Remained out all night without parents' permission	42.4	27.3	25.9	11.9	11.1	8.4
Gambled for money at cards, dice, or some other game	69.5	68.8	65.4	30.5	35.8	38.8
Taken a car without owner's knowledge	10.0	13.9	11.3	1.6	3.1	3.0
Destroyed or damaged public or private property of any kind	67.8	52.3	52.3	23.8	14.6	14.7
Taken a glass of beer, wine, or liquor at a party or elsewhere with your friends	72.9	65.0	66.4	44.1	34.6	36.2
Tried to be intimate with a member of the opposite sex	49.2	39.2	38.3	15.3	18.4	17.3
Driven a car without a driver's license	59.4	63.2	61.5	30.6	28.9	27.8
Taken little things that did not belong to you	74.5	71.5	64.7	27.1	19.8	15.4
Skipped school without a legitimate excuse	57.7	41.0	41.6	17.0	12.2	14.5
Driven beyond the speed limit	69.4	57.1	48.8	59.3	42.1	38.6
Engaged in a fist fight with another boy	63.8	53.0	58.2	13.8	8.0	9.6
Been feeling "high" from drinking beer, wine, or liquor	37.2	38.9	40.4	22.0	17.8	29.4
Broken into or tried to break and enter a building with the intention of stealing	16.8	9.0	7.7	3.3	.07	1.1
Bought or tried to buy beer, wine, or liquor from a store or adult	33.9	27.1	24.5	17.0	11.4	12.6
Taken money of any amount from someone or place which did not belong to you	45.8	36.8	29.2	11.9	10.4	4.7
Been placed on school probation or expelled from school	13.6	7.3	4.7	3.5	1.0	1.1

$N = 59, 288, 428; P = .956$

From "Delinquency and the Youth Culture: Upper- and Middle-Class Boys" by E. W. Vaz. Reprinted by special permission of the *Journal of Criminal Law, Criminology and Police Science*, copyright © 1969 by Northwestern University School of Law, 60(1).

FIGURE 13.3. Proportions of white boys at four levels of social status who committed each offense.

Percent	Social status:	Upper-middle	Lower-middle	Upper-lower	Lower-lower
	N:	28	100	42	25

Percent	Upper-middle	Lower-middle	Upper-lower	Lower-lower
80				drinking
70				theft
				shoplifting
60		drinking	trespass	entering
			shoplifting	trespass
50	entering	trespass	entering	threatened assault
	shoplifting	shoplifting		truancy
40	drinking	theft	drinking	property destruction
	trespass		theft	false ID or age
30	theft	entering	truancy	fornication
		property destruction	gang fighting	stealing car part, gas
		truancy	property destruction	gang fighting
				concealed weapon
				UDAA[1]
20	property destruction	gang fighting	threatened assault	assault
	gang fighting	threatened assault	stealing car part or gas	running away
	truancy		concealed weapon	armed robbery
	fornication			striking parents
10	false ID or age	stealing car part or gas	UDAA[1]	fraud
	threatened assault	UDAA[1]	fornication	extortion
	stealing car part or gas	fornication	false ID or age assault	arson
	UDAA[1]	false ID or age	running away	
	concealed weapon	concealed weapon	extortion	
	assault	assault	armed robbery	
	extortion	armed robbery	striking parents	
	fraud	extortion	arson	
	running away	running away	fraud	
		striking parents		
		fraud		
		arson		
0	striking parents			
	arson			
	armed robbery			

[1]Unlawful driving away of an automobile.
From *Delinquent Behavior in an American City* by M. Gold. Copyright © 1970 by Wadsworth Publishing Company, Inc. Reprinted by permission of the publisher, Brooks/Cole Publishing Company, Monterey, California.

ticipation in the legitimate youth culture. From this assertion, Vaz generated two hypotheses, one of which dealt with what he described as *peer-group orientation*. He stated:

> Ordinarily adolescents are preoccupied with those of their own kind, friends and acquaintances who hold their values, share their opinions, and talk their language. Recurrent participation in peer activities tends to increase one's status in the eyes of peers, and opportunities to further social activity (dates, parties, dances, etc.) are the cherished rewards for conformity to prevailing norms. Under these conditions, to be a *loner* is a passport to pariahdom, but from our perspective the loner, the boy who is not peer-oriented, is less apt to engage in delinquency [Vaz, 1967, p. 142].

Vaz found a pattern of response among middle-class boys that was consistent with his hypothesis. The rate of deviant behavior was higher among peer-oriented boys than among non-peer-oriented boys. Polk (1971) took some exception to this hypothesis and, therefore, investigated this particular contention among 284 middle-class adolescents in the U.S. Pacific Northwest. The comparative results of the Polk and Vaz studies are found in Table 13.7. Polk's argument against Vaz's hypothesis was disproved, for data from his study *supported* Vaz's hypothesis that there was a significant relationship between peer orientation and delinquent behavior. The percentage of American adolescents with high levels of deviance was highest among those most peer oriented (63 percent) and decisively lower in the less peer-oriented groups. Examining data from

TABLE 13.7. Percentage of delinquency involvement by levels of peer orientation among middle-class boys, Canadian and Pacific County.

Level of delinquency involvement	Canadian sample[1]			Pacific County sample		
	Index of peer orientation			Index of peer orientation		
	Low	Medium	High	Low	Medium	High
Low	47	41	18	70	34	13
Medium	39	42	42	21	38	23
High	15	18	40	8	28	63
Total %	101	101	100	99	100	99
(n)	(137)	(303)	(228)	(52)	(32)	(30)

[1]Canadian data as reported by Edmund W. Vaz. Percentages have been converted from percentages of the total *n* to percentages by column *n* to show more clearly the direction of relationships. The resulting total *n*s (668 and 679) are somewhat lower than Vaz reports (682), presumably because of either rounding errors or loss of cases due to nonresponse. In any case, the difference is too small to cause interpretation error.

From "A Reassessment of Middle-Class Delinquency" by K. Polk, *Youth & Society*, 1971, 2(3), 342. Reprinted by permission of the publisher, Sage Publications, Inc.

both studies, one necessarily concludes that peer-group orientation is related to delinquent behavior.

The second hypothesis Vaz generated dealt with what he termed *youth-culture participation:*

> We have described the middle-class youth culture as predominantly social in character. We have implied that the boy who has ready access to an automobile, who dates girls, attends dances, who goes to parties, and who is regularly engaged in sports is more likely to begin drinking, drag-racing, gambling, and to become partner to sexual practices and other sophisticated forms of delinquency. The more restricted, unsociable adolescent is less apt to become so involved [Vaz, 1967, p. 143].

As with his earlier hypothesis, Vaz found support for this contention as well. Among the Canadian boys, the highest level of deviance (44 percent) was found among those most involved in youth-culture activities (see Table 13.8).

However, Polk found some data that did not support Vaz's second hypothesis so well. Among the same sample of boys that he had used before (in Michigan), Polk (1971) found that his data supported the second Vaz hypothesis to some extent but not so convincingly as it had supported the first hypothesis. His data did show, however, a steady increase in the level of deviance with more youth-culture involvement. Both Vaz's and Polk's studies concluded that deviance is highest among those who spend their time in such activities as dating, hanging around with friends, cruising in cars, and so on.

FEMALE DELINQUENCY

Male and female roles and behaviors are strongly influenced by social class as well as by general cultural expectations. Since men are expected to be aggressive, and females have traditionally been socialized to adopt a passive role, males are more likely than females to be delinquent. However, with changing sex roles and increasing involvement by females in a broader spectrum of activities, it is logical that recent statistics indicate an increase in the arrest rate of females. The economic and social roles available to women in our society tend increasingly to approximate those available to men, particularly in the urban centers and particularly among the middle class. It is no longer unusual for a woman to work outside the home, earn a higher income than her husband, play the breadwinner role, and share household activities and chores equally with her husband. An adolescent girl, brought up in such a home and identifying with her mother, tends to consider herself equal to the males in the home. Since she believes herself to be capable of doing what a boy

TABLE 13.8. Percentage of delinquency involvement by levels of participation in youth culture among middle-class boys, Canadian and Pacific County.

	Canadian sample[1]			Pacific County sample		
	Index of youth-culture participation			Index of youth-culture participation		
Level of delinquency involvement	Low	Medium	High	Low	Medium	High
Low	64	38	10	64	56	31
Medium	28	45	46	25	23	29
High	8	17	44	11	21	40
Total %	100	100	100	100	100	100
(n)	(168)	(275)	(236)	(28)	(34)	(58)

[1]Canadian data as reported by Vaz.
From "A Reassessment of Middle-Class Delinquency" by K. Polk, Youth & Society, 1971, 2(3), 343. Reprinted by permission of the publisher, Sage Publications, Inc.

does, and has every right to assert herself in such a manner, she, too, has become more susceptible to delinquency.

Table 13.9 clearly indicates that arrest rates of girls are increasing for all sorts of delinquent behavior. Furthermore, arrests of girls for burglary, larceny, and auto theft have been increasing far more rapidly than have arrests of boys for these offenses. The total number of arrests of girls under 18 for burglary increased 75.9 percent between 1960 and 1967, while the increase for boys under 18 during the same period was only 40 percent. From 1960 to 1967, the arrest rate of girls under 18 for auto theft increased by 71.4 percent, while the arrest rate for boys under 18 for that offense increased 53.1 percent. Larceny arrests of girls increased 141.4 percent, and of boys 53.5 percent, during this period.

The largest percentage increase in arrests of children under 18 from 1967 to 1969 was for alleged violations of narcotic-drug laws. Arrests of boys increased 773.5 percent, and arrests for girls increased 806.5 percent. These tremendous increases reflect several factors: an increase in the use of marijuana and dangerous drugs by youths, a toughening of law-enforcement policies, and a growing willingness on the part of police officers to arrest girls for these offenses.

Konopka (1966) feels that delinquent girls are too often treated like delinquents rather than like adolescents. In other words, Konopka feels that pubertal events bring on heightened emotions, including fear, which most adolescent girls are not prepared to cope with effectively. Their use of sex is a form of "acting out" in many cases, and as such it is a motivational deviance not found in boys. Regardless of the fairness or unfairness of our sexual standards, negative social sanctions still weigh more heavily on girls than on boys for sexual behavior.

TABLE 13.9. Total arrest trends by sex, 1960–1967 (2,392 agencies; 1967 estimated population 87,495,000).*

	Males						Females					
	Total			Under 18			Total			Under 18		
Offense charged	1960	1967	Per-cent change	1960	1967	Per-cent change	1960	1967	Per-cent change	1960	1967	Per-cent change
Total	2,736,979	2,984,505	+9.0	383,923	629,287	+63.9	330,464	412,432	−24.8	66,495	129,668	+95.0
Criminal homicide:												
Murder and nonnegligent manslaughter	3,349	4,793	+43.1	290	436	+50.3	732	937	+28.0	25	54	+116.0
Manslaughter by negligence	1,590	1,569	−1.3	125	132	+5.6	179	174	−2.8	5	13	+160.0
Forcible rape	6,499	7,951	+22.3	1,100	1,520	+38.2						
Robbery	25,550	38,542	+50.8	5,880	11,576	+96.9	1,324	2,218	+67.5	340	606	+78.2
Aggravated assault	40,136	63,018	+57.0	4,847	10,333	+113.2	6,965	10,009	+43.7	569	1,612	+183.3
Burglary—breaking or entering	107,000	136,226	+27.3	50,449	70,642	+40.0	3,691	5,839	+58.2	1,625	2,858	+75.9
Larceny-theft	148,440	201,764	+35.9	73,992	113,546	+53.5	28,793	65,193	+126.4	12,104	29,223	+141.4
Auto theft	48,922	74,253	+51.8	29,382	44,996	+53.1	1,905	3,365	+76.6	1,216	2,084	+71.4
Other assaults	104,850	128,820	+22.9	9,592	18,383	+91.6	11,258	14,915	+32.5	1,409	3,232	+129.4
Forgery and counterfeiting	16,796	17,529	+4.4	1,072	2,015	+88.0	3,199	4,786	+49.6	328	501	+52.7
Embezzlement and fraud	25,902	30,979	+19.6	601	1,413	+135.1	4,390	9,166	+108.8	141	281	+99.3
Stolen property; buying, receiving, possessing	8,263	17,376	+110.3	2,267	5,544	+144.6	761	1,414	+85.8	167	355	+112.6
Weapons; carrying, possessing, etc.	26,720	39,808	+49.0	5,757	6,889	+19.7	1,563	2,830	+81.1	152	238	+56.6
Prostitution and commercialized vice	5,574	4,526	−18.8	92	129	+40.2	14,325	21,534	+50.3	227	291	+28.2
Sex offenses (except forcible rape and prostitution)	30,796	30,103	−2.3	5,740	5,490	−4.4	5,582	3,511	−37.1	2,335	1,618	−30.7

358

TABLE 13.9 (continued)

	Males						Females					
	Total			Under 18			Total			Under 18		
Offense charged	1960	1967	Per-cent change	1960	1967	Per-cent change	1960	1967	Per-cent change	1960	1967	Per-cent change
Narcotic drug laws†	23,473	62,496	+166.2	1,353	11,819	+773.5	3,831	9,728	+153.9	230	2,085	+806.5
Gambling	94,127	56,550	−39.9	1,356	1,310	−3.4	8,639	5,550	−35.8	42	49	+16.7
Offenses against family and children	33,137	30,153	−9.0	329	315	−4.3	2,936	3,123	+6.4	140	112	−20.0
Driving under the influence	123,853	158,937	+28.3	988	1,516	+53.4	7,720	11,267	+45.9	56	65	+16.1
Liquor laws	68,365	111,610	+63.3	14,024	30,548	+117.8	11,269	14,401	+27.8	2,314	5,278	+128.1
Drunkenness	1,039,393	974,308	−6.3	10,822	19,333	+78.6	91,539	72,130	+21.2	1,134	2,162	+90.7
Disorderly conduct	299,551	257,132	−14.2	37,187	53,176	+43.0	46,841	42,680	−8.9	5,969	8,765	+46.8
Vagrancy	106,374	66,763	−37.2	7,214	5,551	−23.1	9,976	7,260	−27.2	855	752	−12.0
All other offenses (except traffic)	348,319	469,299	+34.7	119,464	212,675	+78.0	63,046	100,402	+59.3	35,112	67,434	+32.1
Suspicion (not included in totals)	77,048	42,555	−44.8	15,010	10,431	−30.5	9,456	5,167	−45.4	2,454	1,338	−45.5

*Based on comparable reports from 1,713 cities representing 70,511,000 population and 679 counties representing 16,984,000 population.
†The trend for ages under 18 for narcotic drug law violation is largely influenced by the large cities of Chicago, Los Angeles, and New York.
From *Uniform Crime Reports*, 1967, p. 119. Reprinted by permission.

A second possible factor contributing to increased female delinquency to which Konopka addresses herself is that the delinquent girl shares with all girls the problem of increasing cultural change in the position of women. Aspects of this change that Konopka believes contribute to female delinquency are:

1. No tradition of vocational training for women, though hard work for women of low economic background is traditional.
2. Stereotyped, low-paying employment for women. There is no tradition of self-help to improve working conditions because the women themselves look upon their employment as temporary. The adolescent working girl sees marriage frequently as the way out of undesirable situations.
3. Lack of opportunity. This is only partially related to economic status, as is the case of many delinquents, boys and girls alike. For girls, it is directly related to being a woman. The exceptional girl can enter various vocations; the average one is still highly confined to stereotyped women's employment.
4. Little legitimate outlet for aggressive drives. The ideal image of the girl is still "sugar and spice." She may satisfy her natural adolescent drive for adventure through activities unacceptable to society or through provision of outlets by boys. Boys still have easier access to the tools for adventure through cars, pool halls, hunting, and organized sports, etc.
5. Increased awareness and resentment of the discrepancy between the stated equality of the sexes and their actual relative positions.
6. Resentment of the discrepancy between stated values and actual adult behavior [Konopka, 1967, pp. 72–73].*

Wise (1967) investigated 589 middle-class boys and girls who were either sophomores or juniors in a New England suburban high school. She hypothesized that the incidence of delinquency was the same for boys and girls, but her data did not bear out her hypothesis; she found a much higher incidence of delinquency among boys. You can see in Table 13.10 that, with the exception of participation in sex and alcohol use, boys were decisively more delinquent. Wise's sex ratio for all delinquent behavior was 1.7 boys to 1.0 girls. Although the incidence is not equal for the sexes, it is significant that this study found that boys and girls engaged in similar types of delinquency.

The research done by Gold (1970) supports Wise's conclusions. He found that boys were more delinquent than girls. Not only did girls commit fewer delinquent acts, but a comparison of Gold's figures shows that girls were especially less delinquent than boys when seriousness of offense was considered.

*From *The Adolescent Girl in Conflict* by G. Konopka. Copyright 1966 by Prentice-Hall, Inc. Reprinted by permission.

TABLE 13.10. Proportion of general offenses committed by middle-class boys and girls.

Offense category	Number of acts committed by Boys	Girls	Total	Percentage of acts committed by Boys	Girls
Sex	196	195	391	50.1	49.9
Alcohol	334	323	657	50.8	49.2
Driving	491	318	809	60.7	39.3
Ungovernability	356	202	558	63.8	36.2
Theft	568	304	872	65.1	34.9
Vandalism	540	219	759	71.1	28.9
Assault	356	97	453	78.6	21.4
		N=589			

From "Proportion of Juvenile Delinquency among Middle-Class Girls" by N. B. Wise, in *Middle-Class Juvenile Delinquency*, edited by E. W. Vaz. Copyright © 1967 by Harper & Row, Publishers, Inc. Reprinted by permission of the publishers.

Although Gold does not say specifically that his evidence bears out the similarity in the natures of male and female delinquency, to considerable extent it does. For example, his data do not show significant sex differences in the areas of running away from home, incorrigibility, and fornication, behaviors Gold describes as being regarded as "girls'" offenses. These behaviors constituted only eight percent of the girls' delinquent acts and six percent of the boys'. Therefore, 92 percent of the girls' delinquent acts were distributed across several delinquency areas. Figure 13.4 presents the nature of female delinquent offenses as well as the proportion of girls at ages 13 through 16 who committed the offenses.

The increase in female delinquency is not a chance occurrence. It probably represents (1) a percentage of girls who want to play a more masculine role and now see the opportunity to do so; (2) a percentage of girls who are in a transitional stage—that is, somewhere between the stereotyped traditional role and the emerging more active female role; and (3) a percentage of girls who simply feel unable to live up to their role expectations in school, among peers, and at home.

GANG DELINQUENCY

One of the more horrendous portrayals of the delinquent adolescent is as a member of a gang. Collectively, gangs are thought to be menacing and brutal, often preying on unsuspecting and innocent victims. This image has been perpetuated through media portrayals of inner-city gangs. In reality, the nature of adolescent gang membership has been misunderstood and its evils exaggerated.

Miller (1957, 1966) has found that gang delinquency among

FIGURE 13.4. Proportions of girls at each age level who committed each offense.

Percent Age:	13	14	15	16
N:	40	85	60	79

Percent	Age 13	Age 14	Age 15	Age 16
60				
55				drinking
50				
45				
40			drinking	
35	drinking	drinking		truancy
30	entering	entering	shoplifting trespass	
25		shoplifting trespass		shoplifting
20	trespass		entering theft	entering
15	shoplifting truancy theft	theft		UDAA[1] fornication theft
		threatened assault	truancy	trespass
10	running away		property destruction	threatened assault property destruction running away gang fighting
5	gang fighting assault fornication property destruction threatened assault	gang fighting truancy property destruction assault fornication concealed weapon running away UDAA[1] false ID or age extortion fraud hitting parents	gang fighting running away fornication hitting parents threatened assault extortion UDAA[1] false ID or age	UDAA[1] false ID or age extortion hitting parents assault
0	extortion stealing car part, gas hitting parents false ID or age fraud—arson concealed weapon armed robbery UDAA[1]	stealing car part, gas arson armed robbery	assault stealing car part, gas fraud—arson concealed weapon armed robbery	concealed weapon stealing car part, gas fraud—arson armed robbery

[1]Unlawful driving away of an automobile.

From *Delinquent Behavior in an American City* by M. Gold. Copyright © 1970 by Wadsworth Publishing Company, Inc. Reprinted by permission of the publisher, Brooks/Cole Publishing Company, Monterey, California.

street-corner groups in lower-class communities differs from that among subcultures in which, because of a conflict between middle-class and lower-class cultures, the lower-class members deliberately violate middle-class norms. His research was an exhaustive analysis of gang activity in a slum district of Boston. He focused on violent crimes that may result from class conflict, analyzing the nature and frequency of such crimes; the race, age, and social status of the offender; and the targets of violent crimes—both persons and objects. The study led him to conclude that (1) only a small minority of gang members participated in violent crimes; (2) race had little to do with the frequency of involvement in violent crimes, but social status did; (3) violence was not a dominant activity of the gangs; and (4) violence was not motivated by sadism against the weak, the innocent, or the solitary but by the boys' need to secure and defend their honor as males—a need comparable to the motivation that undergirds war among nations. Miller states that "When men have found a solution to this problem, they will at the same time have solved the problem of violent crimes in city gangs" (Miller, 1966, p. 112).

Three types of gangs appear in neighborhoods. First is the *social* gang, comprising tough youths who come together because they find that their individual goals of a socially constructive nature can best be achieved through a gang pattern. Second is the *delinquent* gang, characterized by delinquent activity such as stealing or assault, the ultimate objective being material profit. The third gang type commonly described is the *violent* gang, whose activities center around spontaneous prestige-seeking violence, the goal being personal gratification. Whatever the motivation for formation, delinquent adolescent gangs represent, as Klein (1971) describes, a "caricature of adolescence." Whatever behaviors are seen in an individual are likely to be seen in a gang, since it is a collective body acting as one.

Around 50 years ago, Thrasher (1926) provided a definition of a gang based on his observations of 1313 actual gangs in Chicago. Essentially, it was a group of individuals that formed spontaneously and without any special attachment to existing segments of society. In effect, adolescents were an interstitial group, who remained that way until they were brought together through conflict. Perhaps a gang comprises unattached individuals coming together in search of noninstitutionalized activity that will help them pass the time. This definition implies that perhaps such adolescents are not brought together by a common goal but, perhaps, that the effect of their aggregation helps them formalize and define some goals or common activities. Gangs are extremely interesting because they are not formed to enact any prescribed roles, yet they emerge with control and power equal to those of any formal group in the society.

Yablonsky has outlined the social-interactive processes that contribute to the emergence of the three gang types previously mentioned—social, delinquent, and violent (Haskell & Yablonsky, 1970). He questions whether there is any delinquency within social gangs and suggests that delinquent gangs and violent gangs emerge from the slums due to negative sociocultural factors existing there. Yablonsky thinks that the social gang is closely associated with the larger society, drawing its membership from the most emotionally stable and socially effective youths in the community. If this is the case, Yablonsky is clearly describing a group of youths who are qualitatively different from those observed by Thrasher (1926) half a century ago.

Whereas social interaction is a primary motive for gang formation in the social gang, it is viewed as a secondary characteristic of the delinquent gang (Yablonsky, 1963). Rather, the delinquent gang is organized to carry out illegal acts. Haskell and Yablonsky describe the delinquent gang as follows:

> Prominent among the delinquent gang's activities are burglary, petty thievery, mugging, assault for profit, and other illegal acts directed at "raising bread." It is generally a tight clique, a small mobile gang that can steal and escape with minimum risk. It would lose its cohesive quality and the intimate cooperation required for success in illegal ventures if it became too large. Membership is not easily achieved and must generally be approved by all gang members.
>
> The delinquent gang has a tight primary-group structure. The members know each other and rely heavily upon each other for cooperation in their illegal enterprises. The group has some duration and lasting structure. This usually continues in action until interrupted by arrest or imprisonment. Members lost in this way are usually replaced. The leader is usually the most effective thief, the best organizer and planner of delinquent activities.
>
> Often members of these cliques also participate in the activities of violent or social gangs, but such participation is only a sideline; their basic allegiance is to the delinquent gang, with its opportunities to act out their impulses for fun and profit.
>
> With some exceptions, delinquent-gang members are emotionally stable youths. Their delinquency is more likely to result from being socialized in delinquent behavior patterns than from emotional disturbance. The emotionally disturbed delinquent is more likely to steal or assault on his own, in a bizarre way. He does not usually have the social ability required to belong to the organized delinquent gang.
>
> In summary, the delinquent gang is comprised of a cohesive group of emotionally stable youths trained into illegal patterns of behavior. Violence may be employed as a means toward the end of acquiring material and financial rewards, but it is rarely an end in itself, since the activities of the gang are profit-oriented. The delinquent gang accepts the goals of the society, but rejects the normative ways of achievement [Haskell & Yablonsky, 1970, pp. 322–323].*

*From *Crime and Delinquency* by M. L. Haskell and L. Yablonsky. Copyright 1970 by Rand McNally and Company.

Violent Gangs

Miller defines violent crimes as "legally proscribed acts whose primary object is the deliberate use of force to inflict injury on persons or objects, and, under some circumstances, the stated intention to engage in such acts" (1966, p. 96). Yablonsky (1963) believes that the violent gang is organized around the need for emotional gratification, with its organization, membership, and activities shifting according to the emotional needs of its members.

Miller's work is based on the theory contending that ganging and gang behaviors are expressions of the lower-class culture. Miller (1966) also contends that violent gangs are not so prevalent as one is led to believe—a position he has supported through his participant observation of gangs in the greater Boston area. Miller contends, first, that the lower class and the middle class possess largely independent cultural systems. That of the hard-core lower class is composed of a female-based household and a serial-monogamy mating pattern. Perhaps in thus defining the lower class Miller is actually discussing only a small and not totally representative proportion of the slum population of major cities. Miller also believes, second, that gangs form in imitation of the larger society, which is composed of a set of age-graded, same-sex peer groups. Third, Miller believes that lower-class adolescents possess a set of concerns or needs that are conducive to law-violating behavior—trouble, toughness, smartness, excitement, fate, and autonomy (1957). This third aspect of Miller's position lends itself well to diagnosing the behavior of delinquent gangs that have tendencies toward violence.

Miller's "trouble" component probably stems from the feelings of hopelessness or the "I have to fend for myself" idea common in so many lower-class areas. However, Short and Strodtbeck (1965) found that middle-class delinquents appeared to be as troubled as lower-class delinquents, as reported by self-description data.

There is little disagreement with Miller's contention that "toughness" is a primary motivational component of the lower-class gang delinquent. Among most minority groups, in slum districts and more widely dispersed areas, this trait is commonly found. To a considerable extent, toughness is a value resulting from mother-dominated homes (see the discussion of black families in Chapter 9) and father absence (Andry, 1960; McCord, McCord, & Thurber, 1962; Toby, 1967). Toughness seems to be a crucial variable in determining gang leadership, and the leader role is not readily relinquished (Sherif & Sherif, 1965; Yablonsky, 1963).

Miller's contention that gang members are psychologically normal and often the most able individuals in the area is not supported by many other researchers of delinquent gangs, although some of the discrepancy is semantic.

Miller observed some 150 street-corner gangs made up of either all males or all females of adolescent age. Miller's findings are based on the activities of seven gangs that he subjected to intensive observation. Five of the gangs were male ($n = 155$) and two female ($n = 50$). He also studied 14 gangs solely on the basis of their court records. Five of the intensive-observation gangs were white ($n = 127$) and two Negro ($n = 78$); eight of the court-record gangs were white ($n = 169$) and six Negro ($n = 124$). None of the court-record gangs was female. The research data focused on (1) *field-recorded behavior*, in which all actions and sentiments related to assault were recorded for the seven intensive-observation gangs ($n = 1600$); (2) *field-recorded crimes*, dealing with all recorded instances of illegal acts of assault and property damage engaged in by members of these seven intensive-observation gangs ($n = 228$); and (3) *court-recorded crimes*, dealing with all charges of assault or property-damage offenses recorded by court officials for members of the 14 male gangs between the ages of 7 and 27 ($n = 138$).

Assault-oriented behavior. Approximately 1600 actions and sentiments relating to assaultive behavior were recorded by field workers during the course of their intensive observation with the seven Boston gangs during a period averaging two years per gang. This number comprised about three percent of a total of about 54,000 actions and sentiments classified in some 60 behavioral areas. Assault-oriented behavior was relatively common, ranking ninth among the 60 behavioral areas. A substantial portion of this behavior, however, took the form of words rather than deeds. For example, although the total number of assault-oriented actions and sentiments was over two and one-half times greater than the number relating to theft, the actual number of "arrestable" incidents of assault was less than half the number of theft incidents. This finding agrees with others that depict the area of assaultive behavior as one characterized by considerably more smoke than fire (Miller, 1966).

Frequency of violent crime. One of the most interesting aspects of Miller's research is his assertion that violent crime is tremendously overstated and that in actuality the incidence is much lower than popular opinion suggests. In analyzing five highly violent gangs of 7- to 18-year-olds over a 12-year period, the 228 violent offenses recorded comprised 24 percent of all categories of illegal involvements (assault 17 percent, property damage 7 percent); assault was about one-half as common as theft, and property damage was about one-fourth as common as theft. The 138 court charges comprised 17 percent of all categories of charge (assault charge 11 percent, property damage 6 percent); assault charges were about one-third as common as theft, the most common charge, and property damage was about one-fifth as common. The total number of violence-oriented actions and sentiments examined in the previous section comprised a little under four percent of the gangs' total of actions and sentiments (assault-oriented behavior 3.2 percent; property-damage-oriented behavior .5 percent) (Miller, 1966). These figures indicate that violence and violent crimes did not play a dominant role in the lives of urban gangs.

Miller categorized violent crime in five ways: (1) *forms of crime directed at persons*, in which distinctions were based on age, gang membership, and number of actors and targets; (2) *forms of crime directed at objects*, in which distinctions were based on mode of inflicting damage; (3) *forms of crime directed at persons and objects*, distinctions based on official classifications; (4) *targets of crime directed at persons*, distinctions based on age, sex, race, gang membership, and collectivity; and (5) *targets of crime directed at objects*, distinctions based on the identity of the object.

Table 13.11 (column 1) shows the distribution of 11 specific forms of field-recorded assault directed at persons. In 75 percent of these incidents, participants on both sides were peers of the same sex. In 60 percent of the incidents, gang members acted in groups; in 40 percent, they acted as individuals. Fifty-one percent of the incidents involved collective engagements between same-sex peers. The most common form was the collective engagement between members of different gangs; it constituted 33 percent of all forms and was three times as common as the next most common form. Few of these engagements were full-scale massed-encounter gang fights; most were brief strike-and-fall-back forays by small guerrilla bands. Assault on male adults, the second most common form (11 percent), usually involved the threat of or use of force in connection with theft (for example, threatening a cab driver with a knife or "mugging" or attacks on policemen trying to make an arrest). Those forms of gang assault that most alarm the public were rare. No case of assault on an adult woman, by either individuals or groups, was recorded. In three of the four instances of sexual assault on a female peer, the victim was either a past or a present girlfriend of the attacker. Only three incidents involving general rioting were recorded; two were prison riots and the third was a riot on a Sunday-excursion boat.

The character of violent crimes acted on by the courts parallels that of field-recorded crimes. Table 13.12 shows the distribution of 14 categories of offense for 293 gang members during the age period from late childhood to age 27. Charges based on assault (187) were five and one-half times as common as charges based on property damage (42). About 33 percent of all assault charges involved the threat of force rather than its direct use. The most common charge was "assault and battery," which

TABLE 13.11. Forms of violent crime: Field-recorded offenses: Seven intensive-observation gangs (N=205): Incidents (N=125).

Person-directed	Number of incidents	Percentage of known forms	Object-directed	Number of incidents	Percentage of all forms
1. Collective engagement: different gangs	27	32.9	1. Damaging via body blow, other body action	10	27.0
2. Assault by individual on individual adult, same sex	9	11.0	2. Throwing of missile (stone, brick, etc.)	10	27.0
3. Two-person engagement: different gangs	6	7.3	3. Scratching, marking, defacing, object or edifice	8	21.6
4. Two-person engagement: gang member, nongang peer	6	7.3	4. Setting fire to object or edifice	4	10.8
5. Two-person engagement: intragang	5	6.1	5. Damaging via explosive	1	2.7
6. Collective assault on same sex peer, nongang member	5	6.1	6. Other	4	10.8
7. Threatened collective assault on adult	5	6.1		37	100.0
8. Assault by individual on group	4	4.9			
9. Assault by individual on female peer	4	4.9			
10. Participation in general disturbance, riot	3	3.6			
11. Collective assault on same-sex peer, member of other gang	2	2.4			
12. Other	6	7.3			
13. Form unknown	6	—			
	88	99.9			

From "Violent Crimes in City Gangs" by W. B. Miller, *Annals of the American Academy of Political and Social Sciences*, 1966, *364*, 96–112. Reprinted by permission.

TABLE 13.12. Forms of violent crime: Court-recorded offenses: 14 Male gangs (N=293): Court charges through age 27 (N=229).

Offense	Number	Percentage
1. Assault and battery: no weapon	75	32.7
2. Property damage	36	15.7
3. Affray	27	11.8
4. Theft-connected threat of force: no weapon	22	9.6
5. Possession of weapon	18	7.9
6. Assault, with weapon	18	7.9
7. Theft-connected threat of force: with weapon	11	4.8
8. Assault, threat of	8	3.5
9. Sexual assault	8	3.5
10. Arson	6	2.5
11. Property damage, threat of	—	—
12. Arson, threat of	—	—
13. Manslaughter	—	—
14. Murder	—	—
	229	100.0

From "Violent Crimes in City Gangs" by W. B. Miller, *Annals of the American Academy of Political and Social Sciences*, 1966, 364, 96–112. Reprinted by permission.

included primarily unarmed engagements such as street fighting and barroom brawls. The more serious forms of assaultive crimes were less prevalent: armed assault, eight percent; armed robbery, five percent; sexual assault, four percent (Miller, 1966).

In summarizing his research, Miller makes an important distinction between the concepts of *means violence* and *ends violence*. Violence as means involves the use of violence when other means of attaining a desired outcome have failed, as in the case of the student activism of the late 1960s. Gang members may become means violent in order to secure and defend their honor as males, to secure and defend the reputation of their local area and the honor of their women, or to show that an affront to their pride and dignity demands retaliation. The concept of violence as an end involves the use of violence simply to be violent, without any expressed purpose or objective. Adults sometimes advocate means violence, such as in war, but ends violence is never tolerated. In the adolescent, neither form of violence is accepted by adults and, unfortunately, most adults equate delinquent-gang violence with ends violence.

THE DROPOUT AND DELINQUENCY

It is difficult to know whether the high school dropout is prone to delinquency or the delinquent is prone to drop out of school. No doubt both tendencies hold true. There is much evidence indicating that the adolescent who drops out of school is unlikely to find employment, is marginal to the society, and is a potential delinquent. Characteristics of the delinquent who is a high school student are negative attitudes toward school, poor grades, behaviors requiring disciplinary action, and being over-age for his or her grade levels.

Glueck and Glueck (1968) found, in their study of 500 delinquent lower-class white boys, that 96.6 percent of them dropped out of school by age 16. This percentage, when compared with that for the 500 nondelinquents in their study, is extremely high (see Table 13.13). Only 51.9 percent of the nondelinquents dropped out of school before their seventeenth birthday. Two comparative percentages in Table 13.13 are of interest. First, the greatest dropout rate occurred among the delinquents before their sixteenth birthday. Glueck and Glueck found that, whereas 62.3 percent dropped out, only 2.5 percent of them were employed. In contrast, only 12.2 percent of the nondelinquent group dropped out of school before their sixteenth birthday, 48.1 percent went through most of high school, and 21.5 percent graduated. Only 1.6 percent of the delinquents earned a high school degree. Second, when Glueck and Glueck asked each boy why he left school, they found that 39.3 percent of the delinquents were pulled out of school to be placed in a correctional institution, but that none of the nondelinquents were expelled from school. Only 9.1 percent of the delinquents cited necessity to earn money for the family as a reason for leaving school. In contrast, this reason was given by 28.1 percent of the nondelinquents.

Ahlstrom and Havighurst (1971) surveyed 400 boys from five low-status junior high schools in Kansas City. Most of the sample was black, although there were also white and Mexican-American students in

TABLE 13.13. Age on first leaving school as determined during first follow-up investigation.

	Delinquents		Nondelinquents	
	Number	%	Number	%
Less than 16 years	273	62.3	54	12.2
16 years	150	34.3	175	39.7
17 years or over	15	3.4	212	48.1
Total	438	100.0	441	100.0
		$\chi^2=319.55$; $P<.01$		

From *Delinquents and Nondelinquents in Perspective* by S. Glueck and E. Glueck. Copyright © 1968 by Harvard University Press. Reprinted by permission.

the group. The researchers found that by seventh grade 30 percent of the group had police records, and that three percent of these had been confined for delinquency. Six years later, when most of the boys were between 17 and 19, 68 percent had police records. The average number of arrests, excluding moving traffic violations, was 5.6 per boy. Table 13.14 indicates the nature of these boys' delinquency.

Sixty-eight percent of the arrests were for "serious delinquency," which the researchers defined as acts comparable to felonies for an adult. Twenty-two percent of the arrests were for less serious behaviors, such as drinking in public, loitering, trespassing, disorderly conduct, and so on. The other ten percent of the arrests were for investigation, home and school referrals, re-arrests, resisting arrest, and parole violations. Ahlstrom and Havighurst noticed that, when arrest data were compared with local youth norms for the same period (1962–1967), arrests for serious crimes were four to five times greater for their research group than for their comparison group, the youth population of the same age in greater Kansas City. Table 13.15 gives the comparative data.

Thirty percent of the delinquent group had official police records before entering junior high school. After they reached adolescence, these percentages increased. By age 16, 73 percent had police records; by 17, 86 percent. The remaining 14 percent were arrested at ages 18 and 19. Within this study, 71 percent of the black adolescents and 60 percent of the whites had police records. The dropout rate for the students in this study was 67 percent (Ahlstrom & Havighurst, 1971).

A new type of high school dropout has emerged in our society, although the extent of his delinquent involvement is not known. The middle- and upper-middle-class adolescent may drop out of school because of his (1) dislike for the "Establishment," (2) lack of interest in working at jobs available in the society, (3) rejection of the school (typically reflected by underachievement), (4) conviction that the older generation has misrepresented the world to him, forcing him to grow up in a fraudulent society, and (5) feelings of powerlessness to effect any change in the social system. Although one must be cautious not to generalize, many of these youths are also heavy users of drugs, which for some intensify their feeling of alienation and, for others, provide them with income. At this point, middle-class dropouts constitute a substantial proportion of the total delinquent population.

PREVENTING DELINQUENCY

Today, juvenile-delinquency rates are highest in the cities, lower in the suburbs, and lowest of all in the rural areas—at least as far as

TABLE 13.14. Arrests of work-study youth* during adolescence.

Seriousness and type of arrests[1]	Number of all arrests	Percentage of all arrests	Number of boys with one or more arrests
Serious delinquency	1079	68.0	
Physically aggressive behavior toward persons or things	288	18.0	
Homicide	7		7
Robbery	115		73
Rape	23		21
Aggravated assault (includes assault with intent to kill)	60		46
Extortion	3		3
Purse snatching	14		11
Destruction of property (includes arson and vandalism)	52		49
Common assault	14		9
Behavior not aggressive toward others	749	46.0	
Larceny	237		132
Shoplifting	52		46
Burglary	242		119
Auto theft—includes riding in stolen car (18) and driving car without permission (8)	200		111
Petty theft (till tapping)	5		3
Forgery	5		5
Possession of stolen property	8		8
Other serious delinquent behavior	42	4.0	
Carrying concealed weapons	27		26
Exhibitionism	4		4
Crimes against nature (includes sodomy and other homosexual acts)	7		3
Possession of narcotics	2		2
Glue sniffing	2		2
Less serious delinquency[2]			
Public nuisances	356	22.0	
Drinking or being intoxicated in public	55		42
Causing disturbance, being disorderly, fighting in public	203		122
Loitering or vagrancy	28		25
Contributing to delinquency of minor	10		8
Trespassing	15		15
Prowling	21		15
Other—includes frequenting disorderly house (3), procuring (1), gambling (10), discharging firearms (3), sending false fire alarm (2), giving false report to police (5)	24		22

TABLE 13.14. (continued)

Seriousness and type of arrests[1]	Number of all arrests	Percentage of all arrests	Number of boys with one or more arrests
Other arrests (seriousness relative to other factors present)	162	10.0	
Investigation, interrogation	33		29
Truancy	26		22
Running away from home	28	4.0	19
Uncontrollability	15		14
Response to arrest, confinement, and parole—includes running away from institution (18), escape from police (7), resisting arrest (18), and parole violation (17)	60		55

*Work-study youth work one-half day and go to school one-half day.
[1]Seriousness ratings are based in part on Cambridge Sommerville rating criteria and in part on consultation with the Kansas City Police Department.
[2]Less serious as individual acts; in a pattern of arrests may represent serious maladjustment.
From *400 Losers* by W. M. Ahlstrom and R. J. Havighurst. Copyright 1971 Jossey-Bass, Inc. Reprinted by permission.

official police records are concerned. Regardless of the particular ethnic or racial group that happens to be living there at any given time, big-city slums produce a disproportionately large number of juvenile offenders.

Over the years, delinquency in all communities has shown a dramatic rise. This rise is partly the result of better statistical reporting systems. It also stems partly from increases in the number and proportion of the national population under 18 years of age. At present, it is predicted that one out of every six boys will end up in court for other than a traffic offense sometime before his eighteenth birthday (the upper limit of most juvenile court jurisdictions). When boys and girls are considered together, the prediction is one out of every nine. Various studies indicate that the actual rate of delinquency is much greater than that suggested by the reported figures. It is estimated that about 90 percent of all youths commit acts for which they might be brought to court if apprehended.

From the standpoint of proper analysis and prevention programming, "delinquency" is a category that includes an unfortunately large assortment of behaviors and acts, ranging from the little pranks of highly active youngsters to serious crimes. In addition, many activities are contained within the category that are not considered legal offenses for adults—truancy, incorrigibility, running away from home, insubordination, endangering one's health and morals, and numerous others. Obvi-

TABLE 13.15. Arrests of study-group boys and total Kansas City youth population.

	Arrests from age 13 through age 18			
	Study group (N=400)		Kansas City youth (N=19,649)	
Offense	Number of arrests	Percentage of sample	Number of arrests	Percentage of population
Homicide	7	1.7	53	0.3
Robbery	115	28.0	953	5.0
Rape	3	5.5	178	0.9
Aggravated assault	60	15.0	423	2.0
Burglary	242	61.0	3,128	16.0
Larceny	237	59.0	4,304	22.0
Auto theft	200	50.0	2,449	12.0

From *400 Losers* by W. M. Ahlstrom and R. J. Havighurst. Copyright 1971 Jossey-Bass, Inc. Reprinted by permission.

ously, far too much is left to the discretion of others (adults) in determining who is or is not delinquent. In fact, eight states do *not* define in their statutes what is meant by delinquent behavior. In these states, delinquency is what the courts say it is, and thus delinquency can increase or decrease according to the temper of court officials and the public at large. The remaining 42 states are subject to the same criticism, for, as we know, many delinquent acts go unreported for numerous reasons. Statistics reflect only reported acts.

Deviant behavior, like all complex behavior, involves many inter-related personal, social, and cultural variables, as well as a variety of situational and accidental conditions. Thus it follows that no single interpretation of delinquent behavior is possible. Nevertheless, it is both desirable and necessary to make certain assumptions and generalizations about the variables involved in the many adolescent behaviors society identifies as delinquent.

Since deviancy is always related in some way to the social context within which the act occurs, the particular beliefs, values, and legal descriptions characteristic of any given period become especially significant. In America, with its 50 more or less autonomous states, considerable variation exists in what constitutes delinquent behavior. Variations in the judicial process and differences in police policy, court policy, and propensity to report to authorities, as well as attitudes toward different social and racial groups, affect the available data at different times. These variations can be quite confusing when one attempts to come to grips with the problem of delinquency.

Robinson (1967) points out very forcefully the role of the police in determining who will be designated delinquent and what happens to those so labeled. "As petitioner in more than 75 percent of the cases, police decide *what* and *whose* conduct will be labeled 'delinquent' and, to a considerable extent, what will be done about it" (Robinson, 1967, p. 160). Since the police are reputed to handle more than 1 million youngsters per year, it becomes quite important to consider the procedures of our law-enforcement agencies. The manner in which these cases are handled depends upon departmental organization and policy, the individual policeman's view of his role, his empathy toward youth in general, and the varying community pressures put on the police, particularly by the news media.

The apparently higher rates of deviant behavior among lower-class groups seem to be unrelated to ethnic background. In some instances, however, police themselves acknowledge definite biases against certain groups. Robinson (1967) reports, for example, that in Garden City, Long Island, an upper-class white community, no one was labeled a delinquent during the 20 years between 1940 and 1960, because the community ruled the police. However, in a neighboring city, Freeport, all the *reported* delinquents were blacks. It has been suggested many times that the higher delinquency rates among the lower classes are a function of (1) the relative inability of the poor to buy help in defending themselves against law-enforcement agencies and (2) the relatively few opportunities open to the poor to engage in the so-called "safe" forms of deviation, such as white-collar crimes, car thefts, and the car-sex-booze syndrome of affluent youth (Shanley, 1967).

Incidence of deviance may also vary according to country and region, according to urban-rural differences, and according to neighborhood differences in urban areas. Some localities appear to have very little crime of any kind, some seem to have a great deal of one type of crime and not of another, and some have high rates of all kinds of deviance. Finally, recall that deviant behavior occurs in all areas of any given community, but that in the more affluent areas it is kept from official notice or passed off as "adolescent pranks." The recent increase in middle-class delinquency has reached such proportions that the literature insists that former assumptions about delinquency distribution must be revised. A status differential in delinquent behavior is no longer tenable. The factor of hidden delinquency looms very large when middle-class youth are involved. Although in general the statistics show that poor, disadvantaged, or dark-skinned youth are disproportionately responsible for the current statistics on delinquency, there is increasing evidence of considerable deviant behaviors in the affluent classes, particularly in terms of frequency of police contacts and seriousness of offenses, which are nearly comparable to those of the lower classes.

Each community should determine the amount, scope, and nature of its juvenile delinquency. Some sort of classification system for youthful deviance is also very helpful. For example, distinctions among aberrant, subcultural, and politically oriented behavior are extremely useful. It is one thing to deal with arson committed by a mentally deranged boy; it is something else to deal with car thefts by gangs of middle-class "joy-riding" youths; and it is something else again to deal with the demands of militant and sometimes violent young activists.

Kvaraceus (1969) maintains that current efforts to prevent delinquency, which center around legislation, financing, and law enforcement, are essential but inadequate. He discusses nine goals that must be realized for effective delinquency control and prevention. He stresses the importance of public awareness of the problem and suggests that lessons can be learned from the lives of juvenile delinquents. Some of Kvaraceus' suggestions are:

1. The public must be willing to give up delinquency. The average citizen, beset with his own problems of daily life, seldom reacts to reports of delinquency with any degree of objectivity or understanding; he often becomes emotionally involved. An informed and disinterested citizenry is a prerequisite to effective social planning. It is a rare community that can achieve this.

2. Delinquents must be better defined and differentiated. The term *juvenile delinquent* is a nontechnical and pejorative label; it refers not to a specific diagnostic category but to a potpourri of youthful offenders. Few communities bother to define delinquency or to distinguish one kind of delinquent from another. In fact, it is not yet known how many different types of offenders are to be found in the delinquency spectrum. There are no pure types, and there are many variants along the norm-violating continuum.

In planning preventive programs, the police and the courts must differentiate more thoroughly among the varieties of delinquent youth. For example, they will have to spot the emotionally disturbed or sick offender, for whom child-guidance treatment is indicated. They will have to identify the culturally determined offender, for whom the delinquent act may represent justifiable or even acceptable behavior when viewed in light of the value system of the gang or neighborhood.

3. The community attitude should be positive and not exclusive. Apart from the conscious and unconscious exploitation of delinquents, one can sense in the climate of many communities five moods or attitudes expressed by citizens who are concerned with delinquency prevention: Messianic-sentimental, punitive-retaliatory, positive-humanistic, diagnostic-therapeutic, and cultural-reconstructionist.

The Messianic sentimentalist believes that there is no such thing as a "bad boy" and clings optimistically to the notion that all will be well if the youngster can "be reached" somehow.

At the other extreme is perhaps the most popular stance taken in dealing with delinquents, the punitive-retaliatory orientation—the "hard line" or "get tough" school of thought. Today many state officials and a large segment of the citizenry, fed up with the mounting rate of serious offenses and frustrated by the ineffectiveness of "scientific approaches," revert to "sterner measures" like the night stick, the curfew, and institutional confinement.

In contrast to the punitive back-of-the-hand, the positive humanist extends a helping hand. Believing that "there are no problem children, merely children with severe problems," he looks for causes but often confuses them with cures. For example, noting the kinds of leisure-time habits that are characteristic of young offenders, the positive humanist hastens to provide more playground space, using recreation like a flit gun to eradicate the problem. In the meantime, the gang merely shifts its crap game to the lot behind the billboard.

The diagnostic-therapeutic stance assumes that the delinquent or his parents are emotionally disturbed and require the services of a clinic. True, some delinquents are sick (to estimate exactly what proportion is difficult) and need medical help within mental-health centers, but what proportion of the delinquents seen in the juvenile courts should or could receive the services of specialists needs to be studied carefully.

The cultural reconstructionist views the neighborhood or the peer group, with its value system, as "the patient" to be studied and helped. In this approach, the agency or institution—school, public housing, recreation department, church, club, Boy Scout troop, YMCA—is considered a powerful means of cultural change and renewal. In this sense, the agency is seen as both a creation and an instrument of the culture. The cultural-reconstructionist stance is perhaps the most promising and the one most neglected at the local level.

4. *Youth should be involved in the solution of youth problems.* Youth can be mined as a rich community resource, but in most communities they are a surplus commodity. Juvenile delinquency is a youth problem, and only youth can solve it. It cannot be solved by professionals working on their own. Agencies in which adults are the subject of the verb "serve" and youth are the direct object will be limited in their

attempts to prevent or control norm-violating behavior. Youth must become the subject of "serve" for only when they begin to serve themselves and the community can we expect to halt the rise in juvenile delinquency.

Generally, youths are kept powerless in adult society. They have no vote, are locked out of significant jobs, are kept dependent through prolonged education, and are unorganized. Organized power movements on college campuses and some student political groups can be viewed as youthful organizations seeking a voice in decision making. Youth must be organized into a corporate structure in order to communicate and work with other corporate structures in American society, such as schools and colleges, police, labor unions, court systems, health and welfare agencies, and churches.

Youth involvement in the containment of delinquency is based on the following assumptions:

1. Every youth needs to feel that there is a significant place for him as an adolescent in his immediate social world.
2. Every youth needs to be able to exercise his intelligence, initiative, and growing maturity in solving problems of real concern to him and to the adult world.
3. Every youth needs to be given an opportunity to learn that his own life situation is not the only one there is.
4. Youth need to be incorporated as a structure in order to communicate and deal with the corporate structures maintained by adults in our urbanized, bureaucratic, anonymous society.
5. The emergence of an adolescent subculture characterized by self-directing community participation is not likely to occur without specific and special adult leadership.

The public school is also a vital agency in the prevention and control of delinquency. The principal and superintendent can help by selecting faculty members who offer positive goals to adolescents. The teacher should be a help and not just another critic; he should be willing to listen rather than just dictate ready-made answers. Moreover, if the teacher is aware of the student's frame of reference, he or she will be able to understand and help students from different cultures and family situations. Effective, personable teachers greatly enhance teacher-student interaction.

Most adolescents who become dissatisfied with their curriculum drop out of school, and this situation compounds the delinquency problem. Personalizing the courses of study of potential dropouts can meet a wider variety of their needs and thus reduce failure and boredom. If a student cannot perform under the standard curriculum, he should be provided with alternative subject matter (Thornburg, 1974c).

The school, as the agency with the widest range of practical opportunities for contact with adolescents, must join "with all other community youth and family agencies in coordinated effort to identify, study, and treat the troublesome student" (Kvaraceus, 1966, p. 143). This community-wide approach can help the school obtain information about a student from other perspectives. The combined efforts of all agencies involved in combating delinquency can increase the value and effectiveness of the overall endeavor.

Identity Pursuits 14

Erikson's concept of ego identity provides a good construct by which to view the inner unfolding of the individual during adolescence. To Erikson, ego identity is the "accrued confidence that the inner sameness and continuity are matched by the sameness and continuity of one's meaning for others" (Erikson, 1959, p. 28). Two aspects of this definition are important to the adolescent. First, the attainment of ego identity is related to how an adolescent views himself and how he perceives that others view him. Elkind (1967) identifies two egocentric mental configurations that arise from the adolescent's struggle for ego enhancement, the "personal fable" and the "imaginary audience" (see Chapter 4). Second, the attainment of ego identity depends upon the degree to which an adolescent is able to integrate past experiences and to identify with his present role expectations.

Erikson believes that, as a result of puberty, the adolescent goes through enough physiological and emotional changes that he begins to question the continuities and regularities he relied upon in earlier developmental stages. Erikson (1968) holds that the adolescent must resolve three major issues in order to attain ego identity. First, sexual maturation and its accompanying urges must be accommodated by the ego. The adolescent experiences discontinuity between childhood teachings, which were primarily parental, and his adolescent behavioral urges, which are primarily biologically based and peer suggested. This discontinuity is becoming more severe in contemporary society, since adolescents are urged to "let go" and express themselves in any way they want. For the adolescent male, sexual outlets have traditionally been more available and sexual behavior more accepted. He has therefore had less difficulty resolving this phase of identity than the adolescent female. With changing norms, however, larger numbers of adolescent females are pursuing roles that give them greater satisfaction as individuals and enable them to be less dependent on males. New sex roles thus make this aspect of Erikson's identity resolution more complicated but, at the same time, perhaps easier. In fact, greater numbers of youths might strengthen their identity as a result of more complementary roles. The second issue the adolescent must contend with in identity resolution is the implications of his physical growth, including his appearance to others. Height, weight, body hair, sex organs, acne, early or late maturation, and attractiveness are all of concern. Third, Erikson feels that the adolescent must actively seek perspective on his functions as an adult member of society. This chapter and Chapter 15 will explore this search for perspective in some depth. Erikson (1963) has suggested that selecting and moving toward an occupational goal is the best way of achieving this perspective. Since meaningful work experiences are difficult for adolescents to find in our competitive job market, this task is the most difficult of the three to realize.

THE IDENTITY SEARCH AND THE CONTEMPORARY ADOLESCENT

Identity search among today's youth must undergo some new definition and find expression within wider perimeters. Social approval or reinforcement for acceptable behaviors helps confer ego strength. When an adolescent participates in activities that receive little societal reinforcement, the adolescent ego often seeks the support it needs from peers.

Whatever the perimeters of the adolescent's identity search, he generally undergoes the following three processes in determining what behaviors or actions clarify his identity and strengthen his ego.

1. The adolescent must define the components that go into identity resolution. These may be traditional, contemporary, or a combination of the two.
2. The adolescent must act upon the components.
3. The adolescent must then evaluate how adequately his actions satisfy his identity components, continuing to exercise options that give identity strength and gradually dropping those that do not. This selectivity process in part determines the ways in which a person will function as an adult, since ego strength must be maintained beyond adolescence.

The hypothesis of this chapter is that *due to social and technological changes, today's youth must seek identity in ways for which there is little historical precedent in our society.* Specifically, youth are seeking or have sought identity in:

1. student activism, which represents a social and political alternative;
2. drugs, which often strengthen peer-group identity and provide a means of escape from the established culture;
3. greater sexual freedom, because it allows emotional commitment at an intimate level not found in the impersonal society or in conversation with parents;
4. alienation—the passive behavioral counterpart to activism—which like activism denies established social and political goals;
5. counterculture institutions—hippie life-styles, Eastern religions, trial marriages—because they provide new types of social structures

and identities in place of traditional institutions that have been rejected—traditional religion, marriage, families, schools, and so on.

Chapters 10 and 11 dealt with the meaning of drugs for the adolescent; Chapter 12 with his expanding sexual freedom. This chapter will explore still other behaviors or philosophies the contemporary adolescent turns to in his identity search: activism, alienation, and the counterculture.

ACTIVISM

The modern student-activism movement began on February 1, 1960, when four black students from an all-black college in the South decided to request service at a segregated lunch counter. Upon being refused, they staged the first sit-in demonstration and brought into play the civil-rights component of student activism (Fishman & Solomon, 1963). This was the first of five phases of the student-activism movement. During 1960 the civil-rights struggle was expanded through the formation of the Student Nonviolent Coordinating Committee (SNCC) and through sympathy demonstrations in many predominately white northern universities (Flacks, 1967; "New Left," 1969).

The 1960 activities set the stage for the second phase of activism, the massive and extensive use of sit-ins as a means of protest. By April 1961 there had been thousands of demonstrations, and tens of thousands of demonstrators had occupied over 75 southern cities and towns. There had been 3500 demonstrators arrested, 95 percent of whom were high-school-age and college-age youths. Black protesters and their white supporters hoped that the evils of racism and segregation would be eliminated if they were pointed out through nonviolent demonstrations (Hartford, 1968). The sit-ins and nonviolent demonstrations were the primary activities of the activists from 1960 to 1964.

By May 1963, over 5000 southern eating facilities, as well as many libraries, recreation centers, and churches, had been desegregated (Fishman & Solomon, 1963). By then, several influential student organizations had formed, among which was the Students for a Democratic Society (SDS) in 1962. Such groups were to have increasing influence on student attitudes and behaviors.

During 1963 and 1964, black-power movements became dissatisfied with the progress that had been made and with the lack of social concern on the part of the masses in America. The third phase of student activism therefore came into play. Essentially, this phase differed from the preceding two in that activists had become convinced of the futility of their attempts to eliminate social and political inequities through nonviolent means and, therefore, began advocating the use of violence to achieve their moral and political ends. This phase was also characterized by the involvement of nonstudents in the struggle (Hartford, 1968). In 1964, the Free Speech Movement—a new force that was to reshape the direction of student activism—was organized on the campus of the University of California at Berkeley. After the so-called Berkeley Rebellion, student protests became common on university campuses. From the activists' viewpoint, society was as impervious to pressure (Phase Three) as it was to moral persuasion (Phase Two). "Pressure tactics had failed to stop the war in Vietnam and had failed to deal with radical oppression. The result was to move into resistance and base building for a revolution (Phase Four)" (Hartford, 1968, p. 65).

Between 1964 and 1969, activism swept over more than 200 other college and university campuses. In addition, ghetto uprisings, big-city riots, and draft resistance became common. Several student organizations designed to recruit new activists emerged. The groups were of three basic types: (1) the various black-power organizations tried to ensure more equality and less injustice for black Americans; (2) avid political groups such as Socialists, Communists, and Marxists—the "New Left"—advocated political systems contrary to the existing system of the United States; and (3) white students' organizations challenged the Establishment, conservatism, and traditionalism—in effect, the existing American life-style. All of these student activists were theoretically seeking a society, based on justice and equality, in which power lies with all people, not just a few, and in which human rights are valued over all other rights.

The Free Speech Movement

Berkeley students were strong advocates of the civil-rights movement. They had taken an active part in civil-rights demonstrations in the Berkeley and San Francisco areas, and many of them (including Mario Savio, who emerged as the Free Speech Movement's leader) participated in the 1964 Mississippi Summer Project. The FSM was ignited by a University administrative ruling banning on-campus solicitation for off-campus political action. Students in the movement felt that the ruling was aimed at civil-rights groups, especially when the ban was lifted only for the purposes of campaigning for the 1964 national election.

After the Free Speech Movement was organized on the Berkeley campus in November 1964, several researchers began to make extensive studies of the student body at that school. Somers (1965) interviewed 285 students and found that 63 percent favored the goals of the FSM and 34 percent favored its tactics. Thirty percent supported its goals but not its tactics, and only 22 percent of the students surveyed were opposed to both its goals and its tactics.

An academic profile of these students revealed that 45 percent of those who favored both FSM goals and FSM tactics had a grade average of B+ or better, whereas only 10 percent of those who supported neither its goals nor its tactics had that high a grade average (Somers, 1965).

Watts and Whittaker (1966) conducted a more systematic study of student activists on the Berkeley campus, which revealed two important patterns. First, in contrast to Somers' study, the study by Watts and Whittaker could not establish greater academic achievement on the part of FSM members as compared with that of other students. Second, Watts and Whittaker found that the parents of FSM members were more likely to have advanced academic degrees than were the parents of other students: 26 percent of the fathers and 16 percent of the mothers of the FSM members had either a Ph.D. or an M.A.—percentages significantly higher than those for the parents of the other students.

The New Left Movements

Several groups were organized during the 1960s with radical philosophies of open hostility to law and order as defined by the prevailing laws and norms of U.S. society. Their political ideologies comprise elements of Communism, Marxism, Maoism, or Castroism ("New Left," 1969).

One characteristic of all of these groups, referred to collectively as the "New Left," is inclusiveness. Keniston (1968) has stated:

> Psychologically, inclusiveness involves an effort to be open to every aspect of one's feelings, impulses and fantasies, to synthesize and integrate rather than repress or dissociate, not to reject or exclude any part of one's personality or potential. Interpersonally, inclusiveness means a capacity for involvement with, identification and collaboration with those who are superficially alien: the peasant in Vietnam, the poor in America, the nonwhite, the deprived and deformed [Keniston, 1968, p. 232].

Student Nonviolent Coordinating Committee (SNCC). This group was formed as a civil-rights organization in Atlanta in 1960. The pursuit of civil rights by nonviolent means shifted its goal in 1966 to gaining black power through violence. Its primary spokesman was Stokely Carmichael, followed by H. Rap Brown in 1967. Both men advocated "bringing the country to its knees" by whatever means were necessary ("New Left," 1969). The organization is currently inactive.

Students for a Democratic Society (SDS). Formed in 1962 among only 59 students from 11 colleges, within the decade this group became the most powerful on-campus organization, spurring sit-ins, riots, strikes, and other militant activities ("Who's in Charge," 1969). Yet the SDS did not limit its concern to colleges and universities; it took a strong stand against the draft and the U.S. military structure. It also supported oppressed workers, both black and white ("New Left," 1969).

By 1970, the SDS had about 35,000 members on 350 campuses. Most members were white, middle-class, highly idealistic, and very bright ("Who's in Charge," 1969). The SDS denounced the United States as a "capitalist, imperialist, racist state" ("New Left," 1969, p. 37). The group's aim was to effect a Marxist-Leninist revolution built on the Cuban model ("New Left," 1969; "Who's in Charge," 1969). Some factions of the SDS were quite successful in their resistance, as was seen in the Columbia University crisis of 1968 (Barton, 1968). The SDS's *Striker's Manifesto*, which was posted around the Columbia campus during the protest, advocated striking for any reason ("Rampage," 1969). Although an in-depth study (Barton, 1968) of the SDS showed that many of its causes seemed justified, most students and faculty disapproved of its tactics.

Today, the SDS is a dormant organization; student interest in activism has faded, and SDS chapters on university campuses have largely ceased to pursue activist goals.

Students' Afro-American Society. This group was organized by black students enrolled in predominately white universities. Its efforts focus primarily on demands for new curricula, more black athletic coaches and faculty, black foreign-exchange programs, and scholarships and housing for black students ("New Black Student," 1969). Members of this organization were largely responsible for the major confrontations at Cornell University and San Francisco State University in 1969 ("New Left," 1969).

Progressive Labor Party. This group was formed in 1962 by dissident Communists who had been expelled from the American Communist Party because they favored the political system of Communist China. Its members, working on many college campuses, claim to be waging a ceaseless struggle against the ruling class ("New Left," 1969).

Youth International Party. This informally organized group, more commonly known as the "Yippies," was founded in 1967. Spreading their antiestablishment ideas through the underground press, they set out to destroy the present system of government, personified as "the man." As one Yippie organizer stated, "Yippies are chipping away, blacks are chipping away, the enemy overseas is chipping away. If you keep on hitting the man from every side, punching him, laughing at him, ridiculing him, he will eventually collapse. That's what is going to happen in America" ("New Left," 1969, p. 37).

During the summer of 1969, the activism movement entered a fifth phase, which I have described as "constructive activism" (Thornburg, 1971a). The extreme militancy of student activities on university campuses caused many students to feel that resistance had gotten out of hand and was no longer accomplishing the goals upon which it was originally based. In the fall of 1969, the Vietnam Moratorium Committee was organized to launch large-scale peace demonstrations protesting the war in Vietnam. These protests, which gained much public support from adults and noncollege youths, were orderly, peaceful marches that proved that students could express discontent without becoming violent. This activity did not mark the end of student violence, but it shifted the direction of student activism toward more constructive channels, and widespread violence diminished.

The environment and the battle against pollution became of increasing concern. Students formed groups to clean up Lake Erie, to recycle many manufactured products, and to stop mutilation of the land. More active but nonviolent political involvement in crusades against poor housing and malnutrition also began to emerge.

Studies show that between 1964 and 1969 only about five percent of the total college-student enrollment was actually actively involved in base-building for a revolution and in resistant behaviors, although some 50 percent of college students were sympathetic to the goals of the activists (Barton, 1968; "Generations Apart," 1969). In an attempt to see what issues and problems were important to college students without selecting a sample that was activism oriented, I (Thornburg, 1971d) presented 2500 students from five different universities with an open-ended question: "What major issues, problems, or concerns exist within our society today?" The most frequent responses are recorded in Table 14.1." Although it is recognized that there is bias in a college sample, and one would expect concern for education to be primary, it is significant that 45.8 percent of the students mentioned education as an open-choice response. The intensity of militant student activism, and its wide coverage by the mass media, undoubtedly contributed to the 44.1-percent frequency with which the Vietnam conflict was mentioned. As can be seen in Table 14.1, personal concerns tended to rank higher than political or social concerns. This evidence suggests, at least in part, that even when student activism was at its peak many students continued to place personal aspirations and issues above the activist themes of those years. In addition, many students undoubtedly worked effectively for both personal and activist goals.

TABLE 14.1. Most frequent responses listed by 2500 college students.

40% or over		39.9 to 30.0%		29.9 to 20.0%		19.9 to 10.0%	
Education	45.8	Sexuality	36.6	Occupations	28.5		
Vietnam	44.1	Self-identity	32.4	Competition	27.5	Future	18.9
		Draft	30.4	Civil rights	27.4	Cultural norms	18.7
				Religion	23.8	Parental approval	18.1
				Activism	22.6	Drugs	16.5
				Politics	21.9	Marriage	15.8
				Economic stability	21.8	Individuality	13.4
				Social identity	21.7	Violence	13.3
				Morality	21.5	Generation gap	12.5
				Peer approval	21.1	Emancipation	10.6
				Social approval	21.0	World affairs	10.4

From *Contemporary Adolescence: Readings*, edited by H. D. Thornburg, Copyright © 1971 by Wadsworth Publishing Company, Inc. Reprinted by permission of the publisher, Brooks/Cole Publishing Company, Monterey, California.

High School Activism

Although most discussions of activism focus on college students, activism was also widespread on the junior and senior high school levels. Research by Trump and Hunt in 1969 among 1026 secondary-school principals revealed the extent of some form of activism as follows: junior high schools, 56 percent; senior high schools, 59 percent; urban schools

---

Student activism today is on different levels, on issues which affect them directly and immediately. I don't think it is at all unpopular anymore to be identified with a religious movement or organization. Quite the contrary, it is acceptable as far as the social context is concerned. I do think that there are some students who go deeply into this kind of thing and at that point there may be reaction from other students who feel they have gone off the deep end.

We see less activity on an experimental basis in drug use and abuse. I was a police officer on this campus for two and a half years and worked in the area of narcotic investigations. Several years ago there was an intense awareness on the part of the community; there was experimentation, first-time usage. We either see less of this now or know less of it. Either people are relying less on this type of euphoria or they are more sophisticated about it, less blatant.

I learned a great deal from the period of the 1960s we consider as a period of unrest. I learned both as a student and as a university administrator. But I have to be honest. I'm happier about things as they are now.*

*From "Once Again It Is Fashionable to Be Greek" by J. Johnson, *The Sooner Magazine*, May 1974. Reprinted by permission of the University of Oklahoma.

(junior high and senior high combined), 67 percent; rural schools (junior high and senior high combined), 53 percent (Trump & Hunt, 1969).

Most student activism in high schools focused on protesting school regulations, an issue markedly different from those of college activists. Dress and hair regulations headed the list of complaints (Harris, 1969; Trump & Hunt, 1969). Prohibition of smoking, censorship of school newspapers and underground newspapers, and restriction of outside resource people were additional complaints. Trump and Hunt found that 82 percent of all protests involved some action against school regulations.

Character differences between high school activism and college activism are also found in protests of a social or political nature. Only about 25 percent of the high school protests studied by Trump and Hunt involved such issues as Vietnam, the draft, and race relations. In fact, only five percent of the schools reported an SDS group on their campus (Trump & Hunt, 1969).

Richard Flacks, sociology professor at the University of California at Santa Barbara and one of the founding members of the SDS, believes that the New Left movements that emerged in the United States during the 1960s have disintegrated (1971). Of course, he does not imply that the youths of America have returned to an earlier social and political ideology. Protests occasionally occur—such as at Kent State in the spring of 1970, and less violent ones on other campuses—leaving some evidence that a new political consciousness exists, which will be expressed through protest if necessary. Students today are more anticapitalistic, disillusioned with existing social and political structures, and prone to disagree with dominant cultural values.

In 1970, Yankelovich showed that 67 percent of the college students he surveyed thought that student radicalism would continue to grow. These data were gathered in the wake of the shooting of four Kent State students by the National Guard and are considerably more supportive of activism than Yankelovich's 1971 findings, which showed that more than half of the students believed that radicalism was declining (Yankelovich, 1972). Turner (1972), studying the UCLA student body during the 1970–1971 academic year, asked 851 students whether they thought there had been too much or too little disruption of regular campus activities in the past year. "Too much" was the reply of 11.2 percent; 24.7 percent said "Somewhat too much," 38.3 percent "About right," 20.6 percent "Too little," and 5.1 percent "Much too little."

ALIENATION

The Yankelovich study seemed to get at the roots of alienation and the students' continuing search for ways to cope with a system they

> Three or four years ago, we were seeing the philosophy of do-your-own-thing—an independence on the part of the student. Students seemed to gravitate away from the structured or organized type of extracurricular activities. Interest was geared to smallness. Recently, however, there has been a definite rebirth of interest in the organized type of student activities.
>
> It's happening in fraternities and sororities. We have an increase in the number of people going through Rush. The revival of Greek interest is most noticeable on the West Coast, where, at Berkeley, 22 chapters of national fraternities have been rechartered in the last two years.
>
> Membership in Greek chapters on this campus really did not drop that much during the 1960s. In fact, it remained static. What did drop was the ratio of the number of Greeks to students enrolled. Now we are seeing an increase in that ratio. It is no longer unfashionable to be Greek; in fact it is becoming fashionable and this, of course, is the way it was prior to about 1965.
>
> I hesitate to say that we are going back to something. I really don't perceive it that way. There may be some throwbacks, but what seems to have happened is that organizations which came under attack—much of it legitimate—engaged in introspection and re-evaluation. Changes were made and the organizations today are more applicable to student needs.
>
> We see that students are now very intense about their education. Many fraternities are devoting a great deal of time to scholastic endeavors and, for the first time in history of the Greek system on this campus, we had a fraternity whose membership averaged over a 3-point grade-point average. This included the pledge class, and that is phenomenal. Many of the Greek groups have scholarship incentive programs.*
>
> *From "Once Again It Is Fashionable to Be Greek" by J. Johnson, *The Sooner Magazine*, May 1974. Reprinted by permission of the University of Oklahoma.

did not understand and found intolerable. His data seem to indicate that, by the early 1970s, only about 11 percent of American students continued identifying with the New Left. The rest of the students felt that most social and political change stood an equal chance of occurring "within the System," and they saw no need to resort to means used by students in the late 1960s. Dissatisfaction with the dominant cultural values seemed to be replaced by attraction to the counterculture rather than attraction to activism *per se* (Roszak, 1969; Zurcher, 1972). Today's youths consistently express changing values in regard to sex, marriage, religion, work, authority, and living arrangements. Viewed as a whole, the movement for change now seems to be more personally oriented than socially or politically oriented. Therefore, the swing from violent activism to counterculture activities seems to be consistent with the process of attaining a sense of identity that each adolescent must work out for himself (Erikson, 1963).

Since there are many ways in which a person can feel alienated, a multiple definition is required to totally represent the concept. The simplified definition given here emerges from the work of Bronfenbrenner (1972) and Keniston (1965, 1968, 1971). Alienation is *the perceived loss or absence of a previous desirable relationship that carries with it feelings of rejection of and by the outside world.* As a result of these feelings, the alienated individual may become a marginal or deviant person. Because his reference points are badly defined and his behaviors inappropriate, he thus perpetuates his feelings of rejection.

Bronfenbrenner (1972) believes that the roots of adolescent alienation lie in one's childhood experiences. He declares that our society has planned only in a mediocre way for maternal and child care, day care, and other services to children and families. Furthermore, he has observed increasing discrepancy in interaction between parent and child as the child grows older, in both national and cross-cultural studies. The outcome of this interaction deficit seems to be the child's greater dependence on the peer group. His research indicates that, at every single grade level from elementary through high school, children and adolescents are showing a greater dependence on their peers than they did one decade earlier (in 1962). Bronfenbrenner's research indicates that, when you compare the relative influence of parents and peers on the behavior of children, peers by far outweigh parents in every aspect of the child's behavior, especially in influencing him toward antisocial behavior.

Keniston (1965, 1968, 1971) believes that adolescents experience *developmental estrangement,* the sense of alienation that comes with the abandonment of ties to one's childhood self. The degree of estrangement is dependent upon the nature of one's childhood experiences and upon the nature of the substitutes for them that one finds as an adolescent. This concept, of course, is directly in line with Erikson's concept of ego identity; it conceives of alienation as one of the processes through which identity is found.

Dimensions of Alienation

There are several positions on what constitutes alienation. Bronfenbrenner (1972) suggests that alienation consists of (1) withdrawal, (2) hostility, and (3) reform. Generally, the alienated adolescent withdraws from the community in which he lives and its customs, values, and responsibilities. Hostility manifests itself in rejection of the social norms basic to the adolescent's environmental setting and, sometimes, in deliberate antisocial action. Finding ways to express himself that are different from the adopted ways of the society seems to be a primary goal.

Reform as discussed in the activism section of this chapter

is qualitatively different from reform as Bronfenbrenner describes it here. American adolescents are replacing traditional values with their own system. Bronfenbrenner notes that our dominant culture values science and technology in business and in maintenance of our national prestige and, at a personal level, places a premium on achievement, industriousness, emotional control, and propriety. Today's youths are rejecting scientific and business careers, ignoring technology because of its presumed impersonal nature, and concentrating their energies and aspirations in the humanities, social sciences, and education. Adolescents are becoming interested in nature and in what they regard as natural ways of living, advocating and experiencing sexual freedom, turning to the occult and to mysticism, and fortifying themselves through drugs. The able mind may now be an artist as well as a physicist, a social worker as well as a business manager, a self-styled individualist rather than a regimented conformist.

Alienation emerges in some youths as a result of a specific situation. The student-activism movement included many alienated youths, especially those who protested American involvement in Vietnam and the draft. Domestic affairs have alienated others; some adolescents have dropped out of the larger society because of racial discrimination, environmental destruction, and political corruption. These youth tend to take one specific alienating factor and generalize it to the entire society. The fact that a specific issue may bring on general alienation should not be misconstrued or overgeneralized. Although many youths who were against the Vietnam war acted out against American involvement, numerous youths who disliked the war did not do so. These youths may have found themselves alienated from the political and military philosophy of that era, but they nevertheless found viable substitutes for antisocial action within the framework of the larger society. Some such viable substitutes were involvement in politics within the existing political framework and in environmental and ecological concerns.

Whereas alienation precipitated activism in some, in others it engendered apathy. Typically, the apathetic youth looks upon himself and the world with despair and hopelessness, lacking meaningful outlets to take the place of his alienated feelings.

Gould (1969) defined alienation as a syndrome consisting of feelings of pessimism, cynicism, distrust, apathy, and emotional distance. He developed a 20-item scale, the Manifest Alienation Measure, to assess these feelings. A battery of attitude and personality measures, including the MAM, was given to a sample of 429 freshmen and sophomore college men. Analysis of Gould's data revealed a highly consistent pattern resembling this description of the alienation syndrome. Students scoring high in alienation tended to reject socially approved rules of interpersonal conduct and showed some social introversion and depression. This particular response pattern may serve a self-defeating attitude, thus in turn causing greater withdrawal in the individual, but not excluding the possibility of his acting out in a self-debasing way—such as is characteristic of much delinquent behavior.

A final manifestation of alienation is to withdraw into a private world, being neither activistic nor apathetic. This type of alienated youth seeks alternative life-styles. I believe that most youths who are part of this movement are acting out personality traits transmitted to them by their parents and other adults. The difference lies in their behavior, since these youths are in a position to exercise behavioral alternatives, whereas their parents are not. This is not to say that many adults wish they were in such a position, but that the realities of their age and place in time preclude that possibility. The problem is not so simple. It is quite possible that many adults who feel that they have failed to adequately socialize their adolescent may have in reality succeeded, although the discrepancy in the behavioral forms that these parents' socialization of their adolescent has taken may be startling indeed to the parents.

As has been mentioned, our society is constantly changing, and today's adults, like their children, have lost some of their faith in the American dream. They are experiencing widespread unease and disengagement from their value structures. Divorce, unfaithfulness, wife-swapping, drug use, and alcoholism are symptomatic of conflict responses in the adult population. Adults are reacting to the tax system, crowded cities and streets, energy shortages, political dishonesty, lawsuits, and communication delays. They are reacting to retirement villages, to the custom of committing one's parents to rest homes, to the decline of family interaction, and to numerous social, economic, and political inequities. In short, our society is experiencing multiple sources of discontent that evoke feelings of futility, anger, and bitterness, many of which are socially directed. Without question, these adult reactions serve as a model for the adolescent's attitudes and emotions. The adolescent may act in ways that he thinks will help him avoid the plight he sees his parents in. To the adolescent, "The System" is undesirable, and anything that takes its place is better than what exists; hence his search for alternatives. Some of these alternative systems are discussed later in this chapter.

The challenge that arises is not to help our youths avoid alienation but how to help them work through their feelings of alienation in order to enhance their emotional growth and understanding. There is no simple way to deal with newness. To some extent, considering the developmental and social changes society is undergoing, newness is a crucial variable. The professions have yet to discover what to do in the face of cultural, technological, economic, political, and educational disorder.

Adults must resolve their own internal conflicts, for as long as adults feel and act out distress, anger, and disparagement of the system, so will youths. Probably most adolescents would benefit from consistency and strength in their homes. Likewise, the school can help youths by providing more relevant curricula and teaching problem-solving skills. The adolescent with limited coping skills who wants to stand on his own will probably be forced to fall back on parental teachings. In some cases, however, parental teachings will still fail to help him cope with environments that his parents never encountered.

THE COUNTERCULTURE

"The individual self is the only true reality," wrote Charles Reich in *The Greening of America* (1970), which describes the new youth movement—the counterculture—and its interaction with the mainstream culture, which will in time create a new culture. Reich believes that a gradual cultural evolution is necessary and that youth are the agents for change. Today's adults, Reich says, are trapped at an institutional level (Consciousness II) that is bound by social acceptance and public concerns. (Consciousness I had trapped their parents.) A person functioning in Consciousness II believes that institutions change people, dictating their range of development and self-understanding. According to the revolutionary Consciousness III, human aspirations and consciousness emerge as primary, and institutional change will follow them.

The intense self-reflection among revolutionary youths can be interpreted as a process of transition from a self-concept based in the stability of "straight" society to one based in the individual's own phenomenological experiences. Roszak (1969) has suggested that the adherent of the counterculture divests himself of the destructive objectified self that has been defined and imposed on him by society. Roszak's view of cultural conflict may be cited:

> If the counterculture is, as I shall contend here, that healthy instinct which refuses both at a personal and political level to practice such a cold-blooded rape of our human sensibilities, then it should be clear why the conflict between young and adult in our time reaches so peculiarly and painfully deep. In an historical emergency of absolutely unprecedented proportions, we are that strange, culture-bound animal whose biological drive for survival expresses itself generationally. It is the young, arriving with eyes that can see the obvious, who must remake the lethal culture of their elders, and who must remake it in desperate haste [Roszak, 1969, p. 48].*

*From *The Making of a Counter Culture* by T. Roszak. Copyright © 1968, 1969 by Theodore Roszak. Reprinted by permission of Doubleday & Company, Inc. and Faber and Faber Ltd., London.

Reich, of course, said essentially the same thing as Roszak. Consciousness III is that stage at which the adolescent recovers the healthy, nonrestricting self-concept he had lost to Consciousness II. Stressing change in both culture and consciousness, Reich stated:

> The revolution will originate with the individual and with culture, and it will change the political structure only as its final act. It will not require violence to succeed, and it cannot be successfully resisted by violence. It is now spreading with amazing rapidity. It is both necessary and inevitable, and in time it will include not only youth, but all people in America [Reich, 1970, pp. 251–252].

The new breed of youths seek immediate gratification and are struggling with identity. They are present oriented, sensually oriented, alienated, spontaneous in affective expression, nonintellective, existentially oriented, personalistic, passive, and agonizingly self-reflective (Keniston, 1968; Reich, 1970; Roszak, 1969; Slater, 1970; Yablonsky, 1968). These characteristics are considered to be functionally adaptive for the counterculture; these youths have tended to reject the opposite characteristics, which are manifested by individuals who represent the straight society. Slater (1970) has described the polarizing of the two cultures:

> The old culture, when forced to choose, tends to give preference to property rights over personal rights, technological requirements over human needs, competition over cooperation, violence over sexuality, concentration over distribution, the producer over the consumer, means over ends, secrecy over openness, social forms over personal expression, striving over gratification, Oedipal love over communal love, and so on. The new counterculture tends to reverse all of these priorities [Slater, 1970, p. 101].

Proponents of the new counterculture movement see dissenting youths not simply as a revolutionary force but as a regenerative one. They believe that the major cultural and institutional transitions occurring today should take a direction away from their technological base, since the industrial state, while amassing wealth and affluence, has also thrust the world into states of turmoil, war, manipulation, and exploitation. Real human needs and interests have been ignored in the pursuit of organization, political power, international trade, and so on (Keniston, 1971). Since the industrial societies have been an economic success but have bred moral failure, the revolutionaries contend that a new culture (consciousness) and new values, aspirations, and life-styles are now possible and necessary. Keniston has analyzed this point as follows:

> The old industrial state was founded upon the assumption of scarcity. It was organized to reduce poverty, to increase production, to provide plen-

An assessment of the collective consequences of cultural revolution

> Consideration of the applicability of "cultural revolution" in one's own society, or of its perceived effects in another society, is generated by some roughly quantitative assessment of collective "reward or punishment." Revolution, especially in so broad a sense as cultural revolution suggests, seems to become a viable avenue of social action when it can be reckoned that the consequences of such action will be less "punishing" or more "rewarding" to some group, allegedly to the society as a whole, than are the consequences of continuing the present way of life. Conversely, the honest opposition to cultural revolution is based on the view that the society has become progressively safer and more comfortable, thus reducing the degree and extent of natural and social punishment threatening the person. Since this view credits not only fixed social elements, but also social and behavioral processes with such progress, continued evolution of present forms appears to offer more promise for human fulfillment than does the prospect of revolutionary change. The social conflict implied in these different assessments is settled at present through a power contest between the respective combatants. Scientifically, it is necessary to approximate the quantities inferred in those assessments. If historical and comparative analyses can tell us that change has occurred and that a given change has altered the degree in which certain qualities or behaviors are exhibited in a society, it is imperative to go further into the more difficult matter of quantifying degrees of change on specific indices. The quantification of such data will require far greater formula complexity than presently appears to be available. It cannot develop without continued and refined studies of the socio-educational conditions, institutions, and relationships which can provide the formula data.*
>
> *From "Thoughts on Cultural Revolution and Comparative Studies" by R. F. Lawson, *Comparative Education*, 1973, 9(3), 121.

titude. But today it has largely succeeded in this goal, and as a result a new generation has been born in affluence and freed from the repressed character structure or the scarcity culture. In an era of abundance, the niggardly, inhibited psychology of saving, scrupulosity, and repression is no longer necessary. Alienated relationships between people who view each other as commodities are no longer inevitable. The "objective consciousness" of the scientist or technician is becoming obsolete. In brief, the material successes and moral failures of corporate liberalism permit and require the emergence of a new and truly revolutionary generation with a new consciousness, a post-scarcity outlook, and a new vision of the possibilities of human liberation [Keniston, 1971, p. 11].*

*From "A Second Look at the Uncommitted" by K. Keniston, *Social Policy*, 1971, 2(2), 6–19. Copyright 1971 by K. Keniston. This and all other quotes from this source are reprinted by permission.

The Countercounterculture

In turn, a counterrevolutionary movement has appeared whose proponents contend that society and the individual can be enhanced tremendously by increasing our technological skills rather than abandoning them (Feuer, 1969; Toffler, 1970). This movement, like that of the counterculture, agrees that the society is undergoing major transformations that will plunge us into a postindustrial *technetronic* society (Brezesinska, 1960; Galbraith, 1967; Reich, 1970). However, this movement feels more positive about this prediction, declaring that the new society will be more rationalized and precise than the existing one. Some of its characteristics will be high productivity, automation, increased leisure time, better social planning, greater opportunities for individual expression, rapid social change, greater education among its leaders, and more rational administration of government (Keniston, 1971).

In contrast to those who decry the social ills that have resulted from technology, the counterrevolutionary force hopes for an even more complex society consisting of massive organizations, global communications, and a highly technical approach to the solution of human problems. In essence, today we are in transition from the industrialized society as we have known it in the twentieth century to the technetronic society that will dominate the future. The dissatisfaction and social disturbance evidenced since the mid-1960s are to some extent a reaction protest by those who may see their skills and values become obsolete in the emerging culture.

Whether one advocates the counterculture or the countercounterculture, it is clear that today's youth are set on making marked social changes, convinced that the need for such changes does exist and persuaded that there is no better time than now to realize them. Some of the most cogent writing on the two revolutionary trends has been done by Keniston. His comparative analysis of the two positions outlined above is presented here because of its clarity and convincingness.

> We should first acknowledge that each of the theories has highly persuasive points. Those who view the new opposition as historically counterrevolutionary are correct in underlining the increasing importance of technology, complex social organizations, and education in the most industrialized nations. They have pointed accurately to the new role of a highly educated and technologically trained elite. And they seem to help us explain why youthful dissenters are virtually absent among potential engineers, computer specialists, and business administrators, but drawn disproportionately from the ranks of social scientists and humanists.
>
> Above all, however, the opponents of the youthful opposition are accurate in their criticism of that opposition. They rightly argue that the counterculture almost completely neglects the institutional side of mod-

ern life. Thus the call for liberation, for the expansion of consciousness, and for the expression of impulse has not been matched by the creation, or even by the definition, of institutions through which these purposes could be achieved and sustained in anything like a modern technological society. Furthermore, in its cultural wing, the new opposition has often been callous toward continuing injustice, oppression, and poverty in America and abroad. In its political wing, the counterculture has been vulnerable to despair, to apocalyptic but transient fantasies of instant revolution, to superficial Marxism, and to a romance with violence. Finally, the youthful opposition as a whole has never adequately confronted or understood its own derivative relationship to the dominant society. Perhaps as a result, it has too often been a caricature rather than a critique of the consumption-oriented, manipulative, technocratic, violent, electronic society it nominally opposes. In pointing to the weakness of the counterculture, its critics seem to me largely correct.

Yet there is a deep plausibility, as well, in the theory that the youthful opposition is, in historical terms, a revolutionary movement. In particular, the "revolutionary" theorists accurately capture the growing feeling of frustration and the increasing sense of the exhaustion of the old order that obsesses growing numbers of the educated young in industrialized nations. Furthermore, they correctly recognize the irony in the fact that the most prosperous and educated societies in world history have generated the most massive youthful opposition in world history. And in seeking to explain this unexpected opposition, the revolutionary theory understands well its relationship to the "systemic" failings of corporate liberalism—its failure to include large minorities in the general prosperity; its exploitative or destructive relationship to the developing nations; its use of advanced technology to manipulate the citizens in whose interest it allegedly governs; its neglect of basic human needs, values and aspirations in a social calculus that sees men and women as merely "inputs" or "outputs" in complex organizations.

The strengths of each theory, however, are largely negative; in essence, each is at its best in pointing to the flaws of the culture of the social system defended by the other. But judged for its positive contribution, each theory tends to have parallel weaknesses; each disregards the facts at odds with its own central thesis. In order to do this, each operates at a different level of analysis; the counterrevolutionary theory at the level of social institutions, the revolutionary theory at the level of culture. As a consequence, each theory neglects precisely what the other theory correctly stresses.

The counterrevolutionary theory of the new opposition starts from an analysis of social institutions, modes of production, and the formal organization of human roles and relationships. Despite its emphasis upon the psychopathology of the new rebels, it is fundamentally a sociological theory of institutional changes and technological transformations. It stresses the importance of applied science, the growth of new educational institutions, and the power of the new elite that dominates the "knowledge industry." In defining the future, it emphasizes the further development of rational-bureaucratic institutions and the revolutionary impact of new electronic technology upon social organization, communication, and knowledge. But it tends to forget consciousness and culture, treating ideas, symbols, values, ideologies, aspirations, fantasies, and dreams largely as reflections of technological, economic, and social forces [Keniston, 1971, pp. 12–13].

The Hippie Subculture

"Turn on, tune in, and drop out," recommended Timothy Leary in 1964. The movement that came to be labeled "hippie" appealed to thousands of youths, who joined a diversified movement with one common attribute—the passive rejection of the values of the dominant culture. The movement corresponded with the new sexual freedom, widespread use of drugs, and activism. Hippie groups tended to exercise freely their increased liberties with sex and drugs, but saw themselves playing a more passive than activist role.

Freedom and *expression* became the ideological backbone of the hippie movement. Freedom meant that these individuals wanted to be free to do whatever they wanted, whenever they wanted, and wherever they wanted. Since they were passive and withdrawn from the mainstream, it was assumed that this freedom would not abuse others. By expression, the hippies meant giving full symbolic and bodily attention to feelings. This philosophy was typically expressed through nudity, sexual relations, and drug use. They sought pleasure and sensuousness. Their uninhibited, impulsive nature brought them back to what they saw as the basics of life, living close to one another and to nature.

Yablonsky (1968) presented a classification scheme for hippies. He described six hippie types, only two of whom he contended were "real," the other four were "plastic." Briefly, Yablonsky's groupings are:

1. *High priests*: The high priests are truly committed hippies who, through drugs, have come to a level of awareness wherein they understand man's basic godlike nature. They hold a pantheistic view of the world, promote the love ethic, and advocate nonviolence. The priests are, in a sense, missionaries to the Establishment world, promulgating the attitudes of love and trust.
2. *Novitiates*: This is the second type of truly committed hippie. They are highly enthusiastic about being different from the Establishment, although they are qualitatively different from the high priests in two ways. First, they have not gained the inner peace characteristic of the priests. Second, they are still conscious of the law, such as that against illegal drug use, whereas the priest has no fear of the law.
3. *Teeny-boppers*: This is one of the plastic hippie groups. These are teen-agers who are not ideologically committed to being hip, but who are attracted by the music, drugs, and self-indulgence they see when they associate with hippies.

4. *Drug addicts:* This second plastic category is youths who are commonly addicted to heroin or barbiturates or habituated to amphetamines. They use the instability and freedom of the hippie life to maintain their self-destructive habits.
5. *The emotionally disturbed:* This category is used by Yablonsky to describe those adolescents who benefit from the tolerance and acceptance of their peers to keep out of trouble with the law or the psychiatric community. Their disturbance is usually severe.
6. *Unidentifiables:* For lack of a better name, Yablonsky lumps into this category various small segments of the population who occasionally cannot be easily differentiated from hippies. Examples are motorcycle groups such as the Hell's Angels, tourists, social scientists, and refugee criminals.

The hippie counterculture was only one of the initial youth movements. It helped establish trends that were adopted by masses of adolescents who made no pretense of being hippies, ideologically or behaviorally. For example, the hippie movement emphasized drugs, sex, rock music, unisexual clothing, and long hair, which might not otherwise have become so popular so soon. These behaviors and styles are now characteristic of youths in general today. Another factor that made the hippie movement so attractive was that, in reality, all of its activities are not antiestablishment or contrary to commonly accepted social values; in a sense, hippie groups were a mirror image of society (Weakland, 1969). At the same time, they accentuated the traditional polarity between society and youth explored earlier in this book. Youths, for example, like and advocate the use of marijuana. Most adults do not. The hippie ideology is as inflexible and staunch in its position as is the Establishment. The plastic-hippie image may be the most appealing to most adolescents, since they generally like to identify with some but not all aspects of this subculture. This may be one of the reasons why true hippies are found in rural areas or isolated communes, whereas plastic hippies predominate in metropolitan areas.

Music

Rock music occupies much of many youths' time; its sounds dominate most radio stations and concerts. Its attraction for counterculture youths lies in part in its encouragement to flaunt the forbidden. The music speaks of sex, drugs, love, and social ills. Rock lyrics generally encourage the listener to think for himself, declaring that freedom is his choice, and that it is not only acceptable but "the thing" to drop out of an impersonal society resistant to change.

Many individual artists are idolized, and often made culture heroes, by adolescents. Furthermore, because their message is hip, their philosophies popular, and their antiestablishment themes realistic, they are exonerated by their followers from any guilt or personal failures. The deaths of Jimi Hendrix and Janis Joplin were considered tragedies, because these artists were not simply musicians who overdosed on drugs but champions who expounded the truth with their lives, freeing youths from the enslavements of society.

There is little question that the counterculture has been perpetuated to a great extent by its music. In 1969 and 1970, 1.124 billion dollars' worth of records were sold. Popular music is a mass art (Denisoff & Levine, 1972). A study done by Denisoff and Levine in Los Angeles among 919 individuals indicated strong preferences for rock and folk music. In this instance, the rock category accounted for the largest number of records produced by individuals or groups. The folk category was represented by traditional artists and interpreters such as Joan Baez, Pete Seeger, and John Denver. "Folk-rock" was included in the folk category. Table 14.2 indicates the number and percentage of individuals preferring each of six musical categories. The study showed that folk music was preferred by 29 percent of the sample 17 to 29 years of age. Rock was preferred by 21 percent. Therefore, 50 percent of all preferred music fell into one of these two categories (Denisoff & Levine, 1972). One may speculate that the percentages would be equal, or perhaps higher, in the 12-to-17 age range, since jazz and classical music seem to have less appeal for early and middle adolescents than for the age range studied.

Counterculture Protest

As was mentioned earlier in this chapter, the Vietnam conflict and the draft caused massive violent resistance during the 1960s and early 1970s. Youths hoped that, through protest, they could spread their message to the nation. This protest was not always inconsistent with other aspects of the counterculture. One dominant theme of the counterculture is resistance to organizations, predesigned roles, and subservient obedience. Youth of the counterculture saw the war and their role as military persons as clear violations of these ideologies. Consciousness III finds any war incomprehensible and a natural undesirable outcome of functioning at the Consciousness-II level (Reich, 1970). The counterculture movement also makes an assertive effort to bring man into harmony with himself and nature. Aggression, whatever its form, is the polar opposite of inner peace. The anti-war protesters felt that it is no longer necessary for our country to resort to aggression to get what it wants—to remain in a

TABLE 14.2. Age and musical preference.

	17–19	20–22	23–25	26–28	29 and over	Total
Folk	20(.24)	104(.36)	58(.30)	29(.25)	25(.18)	236(.29)
Motown	19(.23)	34(.12)	29(.15)	17(.15)	22(.16)	121(.15)
Rock	32(.39)	74(.26)	40(.21)	20(.17)	6(.04)	172(.21)
Jazz	3(.04)	25(.09)	18(.09)	14(.12)	19(.14)	79(.10)
Class	4(.05)	27(.09)	30(.15)	23(.20)	44(.32)	128(.16)
Other	5(.06)	26(.09)	20(.10)	12(.10)	22(.16)	85(.10)
Total	83(1.01)	290(1.01)	195	115(.99)	138	821

$\chi^2 = 102.774$ [a] $D.F. = .20$ $\phi^2 = .125$

[a]Significant at the .01 level.

From "Youth and Popular Music: A Test of the Taste Culture Hypothesis" by R. S. Denisoff and M. H. Levine, *Youth and Society*, 1972, 4(2), 248. Copyright 1972 by Sage Publications, Inc. Reprinted by permission of the publisher, Sage Publications, Inc.

national adolescent stage in which we, the conquerers, use the world for our conquest.

Naturalism and Supernaturalism

During the 1960s and 1970s, "awareness workshops" have emerged, usually on university campuses, where a participant can express ultimate individuality. One of the aims of this movement is to allow the natural self to emerge in an uninhibited, expressive way. Another aspect of the movement—what has been called "supernaturalism"—is mysticism, a search for experiences that transcend rational thought (Cross & Pruyn, 1973). These two purposes, of course, stand in direct contrast to those of the dominant culture.

Experiencing is vital to the counterculture. It is not considered so necessary to have a learning base, or to be able to conceptualize one's behavior, as it is to give one's affective state free rein to do as it wishes without fear of the lack of rational or objective criteria. The new popularity of Eastern religions and Jesus movements demonstrates this hunger for experience. The extent of people's search for self-awareness and mystical involvement can be seen in the following list of participant activities available during a two-day Community Awareness Workshop held in Tucson, Arizona, in the fall of 1973:

Hatha Yoga
Zen Meditation
Kundalini Yoga
Transcendental Meditation
Kirtan and Chanting

Eastern and Organic Music
Tai Chi
Autogenic Training
Transactional Analysis
Arica Gym and Breathing Exercises
Sufism Discussion
Candle Meditation
Acupuncture
Sensory Awareness
Psychodrama
Guided Fantasy Journey
Directed Daydream
Actualism
Reincarnation and Death
Meditation and Gestalt

Cross and Pruyn (1973) believe that the dominant culture has legitimized a mode of thinking that is overly analytical, reductionistic, logical, and rigid. In contrast, the counterculture is flexible enough to accept new modes of construing reality without being bound by the dominant culture:

> To date, it has evolved several modes, all of which tend to be experiential rather than conceptual; holistic rather than reductionistic, multilinear rather than linear; and immediate rather than goal oriented. Since it is the less powerful of the two cultures, the counterculture cannot lay claim to the legitimizing symbol of "rational" for its modes of construction [Cross & Pruyn, 1973, p. 364].

There is little question that supernaturalism and, to a lesser extent, naturalism are part of the life philosophy of youths who identify with the counterculture.

Communes

The hippie movement placed much stress on communal living, an alternative living style that is diametrically opposed to the institutions of marriage and the nuclear family typical of the larger society. Some couples living in the communal group are married; others are not. Although one cannot conclusively state that marital partnerships, even within communal groups, do not serve communal interests, there are some indications that such grouped couples do not get along well. Constantine and Constantine (1970a, b) found that married communal-living units that exceeded six adults tend to break up during the first year, primarily because the state of flux demanded by the communal setting did not lend itself to group stability.

Communes are aggregates of individuals who seek isolated living, often in rural settings, and small-group membership, which satisfies their strivings for individuality, freedom, autonomy, and honesty. The communal arrangement itself involves the sharing of work and property, close interaction within its membership, and some common way of making a living. Their compulsion to get "back to nature" has caused many communes to specialize in arts and crafts, making their services available to all segments of society.

Some communes have been formed in cities, but most are rural, although often close enough to the cities to sell their goods. In some areas, such as North Beach in San Francisco, Sunset Strip in Hollywood, Canyon Road in Santa Fe, or Old Town in Chicago, they cater primarily to tourists. In Arizona, where the weather is an obvious benefit, communal groups grow flowers and sell them on the street to passersby.

Commitment is a key concept in communal living. It is accomplished through communal ownership of property, cooperative labor, and a high degree of intimacy. Being of one accord is essential, and it marks a way of life quite different from that of the typical American family. If an individual member is unable to align himself behaviorally to the commune's ideology, he or she usually leaves voluntarily. Group meetings and therapy sessions are conducted frequently in hopes of alleviating the conflicts that do arise.

It was stated at the beginning of this chapter that forming an identity is the most difficult but most important task that an adolescent must accomplish during his or her high school and college years. One of the primary ways of accomplishing this task is through experiencing diverse social roles and integrating them into the self. Erikson (1963) pointed out that identity diffusion—the failure to achieve identity—results in the adolescent's inability to commit himself to physical intimacy, to a decision on occupational choice, to energetic competition, or to psychosocial self-definition. This chapter has attempted to show some of the alternatives being explored by today's youths in search of ego-identity status.

Crisis is one major form of self-encounter in the identity search. Crisis refers to the process of decision making; as Erikson describes it, one is occupational, the other ideological. The counterculture movement represents attempts to deal with both of these aspects of crisis. Commitment is another major identity-search encounter. It refers to the personal investment an adolescent is willing to make in the alternatives he selects. One of the positive aspects of communal living is the commitment it requires, helping the individual who makes the commitment resolve identity conflict. The lack of commitment may work against successful task completion (Barnett, 1971), since individuals lacking commitment are likely to achieve poorly under stressful conditions.

Marcia and Friedman (1970) have found that adolescents suffering from identity diffusion are highly vulnerable to manipulation of their self-esteem. Bunt (1971) has found that, in order to avoid identity diffusion, an adolescent must develop a realistic self-concept and a realistic perception of how others view him. Bunt contends that, for the adolescent to develop this perception, there must be an accepting, understanding, democratic relationship between the adolescent and his parents and other significant adults in his life.

One's personal sense of worth, and the exercise of one's self-worth in relation to others, determine to considerable extent one's identity strengths. If traditional means of expression are no longer valid for today's adolescents, they will seek alternatives. In so doing, they may succeed in resolving their inner conflict and restoring equilibrium between the ego and its manifestations. Youths who are experimenting with life-style and behavioral alternatives need guidance, perhaps through nontraditional methods as well as traditional ones, since the process of sorting out new experiences is crucial to their ego-identity resolution.

Aspirations and Self-Realizations 15

Most of the adolescent identity struggle is thought to be centered around *life issues*, those individual choices relevant to one's ongoing, everyday functioning. Examples of life issues are decisions about education, competition, occupations, marriage, economic stability, and religion (Thornburg, 1969d, 1971d). Tied to the resolution of these issues are occupational attainment, level of education, and the ability to make money. This chapter will discuss adolescents' aspirations, their varying opportunities to realize these aspirations, and the relationship between their attempts to realize their aspirations and their struggle for identity.

Numerous studies have sought to determine the typical individual's life goals and the factors that influence his or her choices. These studies usually try to ascertain the individual's aspirational level, in terms of either education or occupation. The adolescent's aspirational level is often idealistic, since it refers to the post-high-school occupational or educational goal the adolescent would like to achieve were there no constraints on his intellectual ability, financial resources, and opportunities. As opposed to *aspirations*, the literature uses the term *expectations* to connote the level of a post-high-school occupational or educational goal the adolescent actually intends to achieve, having assessed his intellect, finances, and opportunities. An adolescent's expectations are thought to be more realistic than his aspirations.

Merton (1957) hypothesizes that the proportion of adolescents with high aspirations does not vary significantly with social status. On the other hand, many writers, such as Hollingshead (1949) and Kuvlesky (Kuvlesky, Wright, & Juarez, 1971), believe that the desire to "get ahead" does vary with social status. Hollingshead believes that upper- and middle-class youths have a more dominant success orientation than lower-class youths. Accepting this contention, Bell (1963) suggests four distinct components of aspirational level, summarized below.

1. Direct aspirational stimulus
   a. Social-class position of parents (Hollingshead, 1949)
   b. Parents' aspirational urges (Bordua, 1960; Simpson, 1962)
   c. Social status of an individual's close peers (Simpson, 1962)
   d. Social-class competition within one's school (Wilson, 1959)
2. Susceptibility to direct stimulus
   a. Individual's socioemotional adjustment (Turner, 1962)
3. Desire to excel
   a. Need for achievement (Rosen, 1956)
   b. Downward social mobility of parents (Lipset & Bendix, 1962)

4. Perceived likelihood of success
   a. Intelligence (IQ) (Sewell, Haller, & Straus, 1957)
   b. Early school performance (Kahl, 1951)
   c. Talent in sports, personality (Kahl, 1951)

THE WORLD OF WORK

Psychoanalytic theory holds that the need for occupational participation has its roots in Erikson's industry-versus-inferiority stage, the age period corresponding to the time the child is in elementary school. The child urgently seeks to win social approval through being an achiever and through cooperative efforts with other children in planning and carrying out activities, each of which is accomplished through being industrious in school. During the latency period, the child's psychosexual urges diminish in intensity, and the child can concentrate his energies in learning and adopting the skills of his society, an active goal that allows him to become socialized to his culture.

Erikson (1968) has stated that, sooner or later, children of this age become "dissatisfied and disgruntled without a sense of being able to make things and make them well and even perfect; it is this that I have called the sense of industry" (Erikson, 1968, p. 123). The child begins to move away from his focus on the family in order to master the technology required to live in the adult world. His new environment is the school, and his new developmental task is to become a productive person. The child is now confronted with the necessity of distinguishing between play and work, and he must also begin to deal with authority figures who are not members of his family. The idea of someday becoming a worker and economic provider now takes root. School may be thought of as a precursor to adult work, providing appropriate models. The child is required to become increasingly productive, to be serious, to meet prescribed standards, and to turn out the required amount of work at fixed levels of quantity and quality.

There is some evidence from the studies of Ginzberg (Ginzberg, Ginsburg, Axelrad, & Herman, 1951) and Super (Super & Overstreet, 1960) that work conceptualized as an actual career or occupation has no particular meaning for the child until he approaches the beginning of preadolescence (9 to 11). Before the age of 11, vocational aspirations primarily take the form of fantasy, involving such choices as being a nurse, doctor, astronaut, or fireman. These choices are more emotional than practical, made in the context of the child's world rather than in the actual world in which the adolescent will eventually function.

Although Ginzberg's *fantasy period* coincides with the child's elementary-school years, the term does not imply that this age span is vocationally meaningless or empty. Indeed, the attitudes and response patterns developed during the early school years are important determinants of the child's subsequent attitudes and response patterns. Thus a child's habitual response patterns to authority and achievement become self-fulfilling. The school experience will be both gratifying and frustrating. It will provide occasions for success and failure. Parents may play supportive, punitive, or indifferent roles, as may the child's peers, to whom he becomes increasingly attracted (Thornburg, 1973c). By the time the child becomes an adolescent and begins thinking seriously about work, many of his cognitive and affective components are thus already well defined. It is possible that the behaviors Ginzberg describes as characteristic of *tentative* and *realistic* periods, described below, serve more to clarify and consolidate early tendencies than to generate new ones or change existing ones.

Between the ages of 11 and 17 (*tentative* period), the individual's aspirations gradually shift toward reality. At this point, interests play a vital role. On the basis of his interest, the adolescent begins to consider his aptitudes, education, personal values, and goals. If his initial interest is in a vocational area that he cannot pursue, he modifies his choice to one more harmonious with his abilities and limitations. During the *realistic* period (beyond 17), the adolescent assesses his aspirational level, his motivation, and the requirements of the job he wants, and then pursues his objective through educational and vocational planning.

Selecting and preparing for a vocation that will provide economic independence are quite difficult. Our highly industrialized and technological society has prolonged the period of adolescence. At the same time, since many skilled and semiskilled jobs once held by adolescents have been eliminated by automation, the number of meaningful work experiences available to adolescents is meager. Those jobs that are available are usually routine and of little usefulness to the worker's career development.

Kuvlesky and Bealer (1966) equate occupational choices with aspirations. They have singled out several factors that contribute to the development of adolescent aspirational levels: social class of parents, aspirational urges of parents, socioemotional adjustment of the adolescent, social status of peers, school performance, and need for achievement.

Needs often affect a person's aspirations. Needs may be perceived consciously, or they may appear only as vague interests that draw a person in certain directions; in either case, they influence choices. Needs and values often change. A person frequently experiences a shift in needs or values and subsequently makes an occupational change in order to accommodate them.

Economic factors also affect occupational choice. High income usually is not a major factor; most adolescents prefer a modest but secure income. Immediate and potential earnings do, however, affect the extent to which a contemplated occupation can be expected to meet a person's economic needs.

Another major influence on career choice is education, which provides an awareness of occupational opportunities. Today, one in every three adolescents attends college. Of this group, one out of three graduates. Realistically, therefore, employment opportunities for the college graduate involve only one out of every six adolescents in the United States. Most educational pursuits are spurred by either parental or peer influences. Studies indicate that a student's level of educational aspiration is highly related to his father's educational and occupational levels (Alexander & Campbell, 1964; Rehberg & Westby, 1967).

"In February 1963, there were 6.7 million out-of-school persons 16 to 21 years old who were not college graduates. About 45 percent of this group dropped out before completing high school, 48 completed high school, and 7 percent completed 1 to 3 years of college" (Perrella & Bogan, 1964, p. 1260). Thus a large percentage of those who graduate from high school have no intention of furthering their education. A study by Little (1967) assessed the relationship between adolescent plans and action. The results are shown in Table 15.1.

It is important to make adolescents aware of the changing work world. Since the early 1900s, the number of professional jobs has doubled and jobs in unskilled occupations have virtually disappeared. Wolfbein's study (1964) shows that only five percent of today's jobs require an unskilled worker. Moreover, many jobs that were once considered masculine, and that therefore excluded women, are now available to either sex depending on individual qualifications. Adolescents must also be prepared for the increasing trend toward occupational mobility, which usually results from job obsolescence or from the worker's desire for economic improvement. Rapid technological change may require the re-

TABLE 15.1. Educational plans and their fulfillment.

	Plan	Action	Difference
To attend college	1584 (37.8%)	1792 (42.9%)	+208
To attend vocational school	363 (8.7%)	66 (15.9%)	+303
To get no further schooling	2239 (53.5%)	1728 (41.2%)	−511
Total	N=4186 (100.0%)	N=4186 (100.0%)	N=0

From "The Occupations of Non-College Youth" by J. K. Little, *American Educational Research Journal*, 1967, 4, 147-154. Copyright 1967 by the American Educational Research Association. Reprinted by permission.

training of thousands of workers in the next few years, and the adolescent who has acquired transferable work skills will be prepared to adapt to new jobs.

Generally, a person is oriented toward a number of goal areas simultaneously: he desires an occupation, a residence, an education, an income, and probably many other goal objects. Furthermore, he characteristically desires a particular type of occupation, a specified range of income, a certain level of education, and so on. These goals may or may not be perceived by the individual as directly inter-related; consequently, his goal-specifications may or may not be logically consistent. Nevertheless, because the individual does visualize himself in future statuses, he can and usually does have relatively specific aspirations for each goal area. With reference to occupation, there is evidence that adolescents can indicate relatively specific goals (Stephenson, 1957).

The imbalance between the growth rates of the adult male civilian labor force and the number of college graduates among them has been especially pronounced. Over the 13 years between 1958 and 1971, the male-labor-force increase averaged only .6 percent per year, whereas its component of men with at least four years of college grew at the average annual rate of 3.8 percent, or about six times as rapidly. The corresponding disparity among adult working women has been much smaller—a ratio of 2.5 percent to 4.8 percent.

According to the projections, this disparity in growth rates will continue in the future. Between the early 1970s and 1990, the adult male civilian labor force is estimated to increase at an average annual rate of 1.6 percent, with the holders of college degrees increasing at an average rate of 4 percent. The corresponding increases during that period for the adult female civilian labor force are estimated at 1.9 and 5 percent per year. It is apparent that one of the major challenges to the U.S. economy, both during the current decade and in the 1980s, will be the continued absorption of this rapidly growing supply of well-educated workers (Johnston, 1973).

The corresponding prospective decline in the number of less well-educated workers is equally dramatic. In the late 1950s, over one-third of the adult civilian labor force—19.3 million workers—had completed eight years or less of formal education. By the early 1970s, this group had been reduced to about 12.5 million, or less than one-fifth of the entire labor force. It is projected to decrease to about one-eighth of the labor force by 1980 and to about one-sixteenth by 1990. This continuing drop in the number of less well-educated adult workers implies an average annual rate of decline of 3.9 percent throughout the 1958–1990 period. The projected changes (Johnston, 1973) are:

1. Workers with four years of college or more: from 9.6 million to 14.3 million by 1980 and to 21.8 million by 1990, increasing from 14.6 percent to 23.8 percent of the civilian labor force
2. Workers with one to three years of college: from 7.9 million to 10.8 million by 1980 and to 15 million by 1990, increasing from 12 percent to 16.4 percent of the labor force
3. Workers with four years of high school: from 24.6 million to 31.4 million by 1980 and to 37.7 million by 1990, from 37.5 percent to 41.2 percent of the labor force
4. Workers with one to three years of high school: from 11.1 million to 11.7 million by 1980 and to 11.4 million by 1990, from 16.9 percent to 12.5 percent of the labor force
5. Workers with eight years of elementary school or less: from 12.5 million to 9.1 million by 1980 and to 5.6 million by 1990, from 19 percent to 6.1 percent of the labor force

ADOLESCENT WORK OPPORTUNITIES

In 1971 there were 15 million U.S. youths 16 to 19 years of age, 71 percent of whom were in school (Rosenfeld & Gover, 1972). At the same time, unemployment rates for this age group steadily increased, due in part to a reduction in unskilled and semiskilled jobs and in part to affluence. Teen-age employment during the 1960s was heaviest in the classifications of common laborers, farm laborers, private household workers, operatives, and service workers. Throughout the 1960s, the employment of teen-agers increased about 85 percent, compared with an 18-percent increase in the labor force for all workers. In addition, more teen-agers than adult workers moved into clerical and sales work.

The increase in school-enrollment rates from 1961 to 1971 was greatest for the groups that had the lowest proportions at the start of the decade—18- and 19-year-olds, blacks, and women. Among blacks, for example, only 60 percent were in school in 1961, compared with about 70 percent in 1971.

Along with the increase in school enrollment, the proportion who remained in school long enough to graduate from high school also increased. Of out-of-school teen-age workers, 68 percent had at least a high school education in October 1971, compared with 58 percent in 1963 (the earliest year for which comparable data are available for teen-agers). More than half of the teen-age labor force was enrolled in school. Seven million were working or looking for work; of these, 4 million, or 56 percent, were in school.

Labor-force-participation rates (that is, the percentage of the population working or looking for work) increased sharply among students since 1965, but they remained virtually unchanged among teenagers no longer in school. The proportion of teen-age students who combined school with work hovered at about 37 percent in the last few years, compared with under 30 percent in the early 1960s. The increase in the labor-force-participation rate reflects a number of factors: the greatest increase in enrollment was among 18- and 19-year-olds, who are more likely than younger students to work; the cost of tuition and other school-related expenses rose; and the number of available jobs increased (Rosenfeld & Gover, 1972).

Because many students want part-time or short-term jobs that fit in with their school schedules, they are a labor force that shows a great deal of flux between employment and unemployment. Since older teenagers are preferred by many employers, unemployment rates tend to be appreciably lower for 18- and 19-year-olds than for 16- and 17-year-olds, among both students and nonstudents. In addition, some jobs that are closed by law to younger teen-agers are open to 18- and 19-year-olds. Students are more likely than nonstudents to be working in service occupations, in which part-time and temporary jobs are available, but it is the younger teen-agers in both groups who are more likely to be doing so. On the other hand, nonstudents are more likely than students to be employed in clerical jobs, although in their case it is the older adolescents, both students and nonstudents, who are more likely to be hired.

High School and College Graduates

Of the 3 million adolescents who graduated from high school in 1972, only 49 percent went on to college—the lowest percentage since 1964 (Young, 1973). Of the high school graduates who did not go on to college, 1.2 million were either working or looking for work by October 1972. About 1 million more teen-agers were in the labor force in October 1972 than in October 1971. Only a small percentage of this increase was among students in school. Almost all of the increase was among nonstudent youths, who constituted 14 million out of a total 20 million in the younger labor force. The actual unemployment rate for out-of-school youths in October 1972 was 14.7 percent (Young, 1973). Growth in the out-of-school labor force resulted from such factors as a decline in inductions into the armed services and a higher labor-force-participation rate for women (Michelotti, 1973). Much of the rise in the number of persons not in school occurred among those 18 to 21, reflecting to some extent a decrease in the proportion attending college (Young, 1973).

Most 1972 high school graduates who did not go to college had

Sometimes aspirations are clarified through school activities. This young girl has found that she likes working with ceramics.

entered the labor force by early fall. In October 1972, more than 90 percent of the men and 75 percent of the women were working or looking for work. Like those who went on to college or who went to college but dropped out, these young people ranged in age from 16 to 24; the great majority were under 20.

The labor-force-participation rate for men did not change significantly during 1972. Since a lower proportion went on to college, more were in the labor force. Most took blue-collar jobs, as is typical of young men entering the full-time labor force. Among women graduates as well, the number in the labor force increased, although the participation rate was not significantly different from that of 1971. Labor-force participation was higher for single women graduates than for married women graduates, no doubt because of the latter women's domestic responsibilities and the limits on their employment imposed by their need to live in an area mutually convenient for husband and wife. Over half of the women who were employed held white-collar jobs, primarily as clerical workers.

About one-third of all graduates not in college and not in the labor force were in special schools, such as trade schools or business colleges. There has been a downward trend in the enrollment of high school graduates in special schools since 1962, when more than half of the graduates not in college and not in the labor force attended special schools. This trend may reflect the increasing opportunity for technical training in two-year colleges, whose students are counted as enrolled in "regular" school. Also, the development of company-sponsored "in-house" training programs provides people with some incentive to seek employment with business concerns that offer such programs, rather than to remain outside the labor force while obtaining training at a special school at their own expense (Young, 1973).

Dropouts

An estimated 730,000 persons 16 to 24 years old left elementary or high school during the year ending in October 1972. An over-the-year increase of about 70,000 in the number quitting school brought the total back to the same level as in October 1970.

Among these dropouts, the labor-force-participation rate for men (82 percent) was substantially lower than that for out-of-school graduates (91 percent); and the rates for both single and married women dropouts were much lower than for graduates. Unemployment rates for recent white dropouts were considerably higher than for recent white graduates. Among black youths, unemployment rates were about the same for high school graduates as for dropouts, and these rates have been consistently higher than for whites.

Many of the factors that may influence young persons to leave school—such as poor academic skills, discontent with programs offered, health problems, or trouble with authorities—are also likely to be a hindrance to employment. Their relative youth and inexperience also tend to be obstacles.

ADOLESCENT WORK MOTIVES

Among the mass of statistics available on adolescent-employment trends, it is important not to lose sight of the fact that the adolescent's developmental nature and the influences of his environment are strong contributors to his occupational *involvement* as well as to his educational and occupational *aspirations*. Hammond (1971) holds the view that a high school student's part-time job is directly related to the process of his development, contributing to his understanding of work and the clarification of his aspirations.

The high unemployment rate for teen-agers (averaging 14.7 percent) has raised the question of whether teen-age attitudes toward work or unrealistic expectations about work are a contributing factor. Information from a recent nationwide survey (Perrella, 1972) refutes this contention. The survey data show clearly that young workers are strongly work oriented and fairly knowledgeable about the kinds of work and rates of pay available to them. Wage expectations of unemployed and potential labor-force participants were pretty much in line with the wages they later earned, indicating that they had a good knowledge of the going wage rates for people in their age group. The proportion of unemployed youths who turned down jobs was relatively small, and their reasons for doing so were not inconsistent with reasonable criteria for meeting their individual needs and special circumstances, such as their student status—which limits their working hours and location—and their efforts to find the kinds of work for which they were best fitted.

Among the young women surveyed, regardless of school status, the two dominant occupational groups were clerical and service. Among students, a larger proportion were in the service jobs than in clerical jobs; among those not in school, more were in clerical jobs. Since 1960, the proportion of female students in service occupations has remained relatively stable; a decrease in private-household work has been offset by a rise in other service occupations. In clerical jobs, the proportion of female students has risen somewhat, whereas the proportion has declined for women not in school. Among the latter, the proportion in service occupations (excluding private-household work) has doubled since 1960 (Perrella, 1972).

The nature of teen-age employment reflects the fact that most jobs are low-paying; in most cases youths are unable to make enough money to be self-supporting. Statistics indicated (Rosenfeld & Gover, 1972) that, among students during 1970, only 36.9 percent of men and 27 percent of women 16 to 21 worked at full-time jobs. In addition, about 25 percent held a job for less than 13 weeks, a factor that no doubt reflects summer employment for students.

The earnings of adolescents 16 to 21 who were students are shown in Table 15.2. More than 70 percent of the employed students had part-time jobs during 1970, compared with fewer than half of those not in school. On the other hand, fewer than 5 percent of those in school held full-time jobs for 27 weeks or more, compared with about 30 percent of the employed teen-agers not in school.

Median earnings of teen-age male students during 1970 were higher than those for female students, and earnings of those 16 and 17 years old were lower than earnings of those 18 and 19 (see Table 15.2). The lower earnings for women and for the 16- and 17-year-olds reflect

Part-time employment gives adolescents a preview of adult work and shows them that they have earning power.

fewer weeks of work and more part-time work. Also, to some extent, the hourly earnings of the younger students may be less than those of the older ones, and the earnings for the girls may be lower than those for the boys, because of the difference in the types of jobs they held.

Hammond (1971) researched 240 male and 181 female high school students who were employed part time, with the intentions of dispelling the myth that kids work just to have money to spend on cars or on one another and of showing that the teen-ager's work was tied to a complex of values. The students were asked any reasons that were important to them personally for having a part-time job, whether they were actually employed or not. Table 15.3 shows the data from the 240 males who completed the questionnaire.

Almost all of the boys listed the need for money for current personal expenses as a reason for having a job. They could expect to be more free of parental control if they could spend their own earnings. But approximately three-fourths considered the job important for maintaining a savings account, and more than two-thirds desired to obtain money to

TABLE 15.2. Earnings in 1970 of students 16 to 21 years old in March 1971, by age and sex.

Age in March 1971 and sex	Total with earnings	Under $500	$500 to $999	$1,000 to $1,499	$1,500 to $1,999	$2,000 to $2,999	$3,000 and over	Median earnings 1970
Both sexes								
16 to 21 years old, total	100.0	45.7	25.6	12.3	6.4	5.6	4.1	$ 584
Men								
16 to 21 years old	100.0	38.9	26.8	14.3	8.0	7.4	4.7	707
16 to 19 years	100.0	44.1	27.0	12.8	6.7	6.3	3.1	609
16 and 17 years	100.0	57.0	26.0	8.9	3.9	2.9	1.4	439
18 and 19 years	100.0	27.6	28.4	17.8	10.3	10.6	5.3	894
20 and 21 years	100.0	17.5	25.8	20.4	13.4	11.9	11.0	1,162
Women								
16 to 21 years old	100.0	54.5	24.0	10.2	4.4	3.4	3.4	459
16 to 19 years	100.0	60.3	22.2	8.4	3.4	2.8	2.8	415
16 and 17 years	100.0	73.1	17.0	5.3	2.0	1.2	1.4	341
18 and 19 years	100.0	44.9	28.6	12.2	5.2	4.8	4.3	589
20 and 21 years	100.0	31.2	31.3	17.4	8.1	5.8	6.1	799

From "Employment of School-Age Youth" by C. Rosenfeld and K. R. Gover, Monthly Labor Review, 1972, 95(8), 30. Reprinted by permission.

TABLE 15.3. Reasons for part-time employment checked by male respondents.

Reason	Number checking	Percent checking	Rank
Training and experience in a vocation	46	19.2	9
Help support family	39	16.2	10
Money for future education	165	68.7	3
Money for current expenses	226	94.2	1
Enjoyable activity	90	37.5	6
Family-owned business	17	7.1	11
Savings account	178	74.2	2
Learning to get along in adult world of work	91	37.9	5
Something to fill time	66	27.5	8
Education not related to future vocation	69	28.7	7
Cost of buying and operating automobile	144	60.0	4
Total responding	240		

From "Part Time Employment" by W. Hammond, *National Association of Secondary School Principals Bulletin,* 1971, 55(357), 67. Reprinted by permission.

pay for future education. In general, the boys appeared interested in part-time employment because it would help give them financial independence in the future as well as in the present. They wanted to work in order to obtain those things that have real value to them.

Table 15.4 shows how the 181 female respondents viewed their reasons for desiring part-time employment. As among the boys, both the employed and the nonemployed tended to give similar reasons for want-

TABLE 15.4. Reasons for part-time employment checked by female respondents.

Reason	Number checking	Percent checking	Rank
Training and experience in a vocation	69	38.1	6
Help support family	35	19.3	10
Money for future education	120	66.3	3
Money for current expenses	161	89.0	1
Enjoyable activity	80	44.2	5
Family-owned business	14	7.7	11
Savings account	137	75.7	2
Learning to get along in adult world of work	115	63.5	4
Something to fill time	39	21.5	9
Education not related to future vocation	53	29.3	8
Cost of buying and operating automobile	61	33.7	7
Total responding	181		

From "Part Time Employment" by W. Hammond, *National Association of Secondary School Principals Bulletin,* 1971, 55(357), 67. Reprinted by permission.

ing to work. In general, the girls appeared to be even more mindful of planning for the future than their male classmates. Although most of the girls, like the boys, expected earnings to help defray current expenses, three-fourths of them were interested in a savings account (in some instances to enable them to marry or to travel), and two-thirds saw the job as a means to a future education. Perhaps most significantly, three out of five regarded the job as a way of learning to get along in the adult world. But only one-third of them, in contrast to the boys, attached any importance to buying a car while in high school.

When asked to identify the single most important reason for having a job, 38.5 percent of the respondents of both sexes listed current personal expenses. However, another 30 percent of each sex listed either future education or savings, with the boys favoring education and the girls favoring savings. As the prime reason for employment, cars were listed by only 17 of the 240 boys and by just two of the 181 girls.

Occupational Values

Thompson (1966) assessed the occupational values of 2287 freshmen in ten California high schools, following up on 1970 of them during their sophomore year. His study was designed to test Super and Overstreet's (1960) hypothesis that the ninth grader is in a vocational-exploration stage, in which he determines what features of a vocation will help him gain personal satisfaction.

The results of Thompson's study are summarized in Table 15.5. When the data were organized by sex, some differences were found in rating occupational values. Since there was so little difference between the responses of freshmen and sophomores, only those of the sophomores are tabled. Girls placed significantly less emphasis than boys on the importance of a job in which the respondent would be a leader or the boss, high pay was involved, and recognition was possible. In contrast, boys placed significantly less importance than girls on a job that would permit an expression of one's own ideas and in which one could help other people. No differences were found between the sexes in the importance placed on the remaining four values: having an interesting job, having security, gaining esteem, and having independence.

Relationships were found between certain occupational values and certain sociopsychological factors. For example, the importance that a student placed on leadership in one's occupation was related to the socioeconomic level of the student's family, as measured by the father's occupation. Students whose fathers had high-prestige vocations placed significantly more importance on a job in which one could be a leader than did students whose fathers were manual laborers or in the skilled

TABLE 15.5. Comparison of occupational values held important by sophomore high school students.

Occupational value	Men n=895	Women n=893
Having an interesting job	836	854
Opportunity to express own ideas	802	829
Having security	787	765
Helping other people	670	808
Being recognized	587	530
Gaining esteem	563	526
Obtaining a high salary	517	332
Having independence	470	444
Being a leader	369	206
Being a boss	248	69

Rated value as important

From "Occupational Values of High School Students" by O. E. Thompson, *The Personnel and Guidance Journal*, 1966, 44, 852. Copyright 1966 American Personnel and Guidance Association. Reprinted by permission.

trades. This finding was also reflected in the occupations the students thought they might pursue: those choosing a high-status vocation placed more importance on being a leader than did those choosing a vocation in the low-white-collar or blue-collar classifications. Leadership in one's vocation was significantly more important to students in the college-preparatory curriculum and to high-achieving students.

Job security seemed to be more important to students whose fathers were in the low-prestige occupations than to those whose fathers were in the professions, and students who chose occupations in the low-prestige areas were more security-conscious than those choosing the professions. Rural students also placed higher importance on security. Students whose mothers worked outside the home deemed security exceedingly important. Security was less vital to college-preparatory students, high-achieving students, and high-IQ students than to other students (Thompson, 1966).

DeRoche (1969) conducted a study somewhat similar to Thompson's. He studied the job values of 613 senior boys and 831 senior girls. He found that boys valued leadership, security, and profit to a greater extent than girls, whereas girls valued social service more than boys. These findings compare favorably not only with Thompson's findings (1961, 1966) but also with the research done by Singer and Stefflre (1954).

Super and Overstreet's (1960) hypothesis that ninth graders are ready to consider their vocational aspirations seems to be borne out in these studies. Thompson's finding (1966) that freshmen had definite ideas on what was important to them continued to hold true in over 75 percent of the students one year later. Furthermore, the values Thompson found to be most dominant were also found to be dominant among the seniors in DeRoche's study (1969). These studies do not necessarily lead one to conclude that adolescents entering high school are ready to make a specific vocational choice, but they do clearly indicate that this domain of the individual's life has become increasingly important. Even so, our high schools are so specialized that most students in the ninth grade are already being thrown into college-preparatory classes or urged to pursue vocational interests.

WORK OPPORTUNITIES FOR DISADVANTAGED YOUTH

Several research studies indicate that white youths have higher aspirational levels than black, Mexican-American, and other minority youths (Gottlieb, 1964; Kuvlesky & Upham, 1967; Kuvlesky, Wright, & Juarez, 1971; Nunalee & Drabick, 1965; Sprey, 1962). On the other hand, studies tend to show an inverse relationship between parental occupational status and adolescent aspirations (Forslund & Malry, 1970; Keig, 1969). In other words, as one moves down the social-class hierarchy, an increasing proportion of adolescents tend to believe that they will enter an occupation with a higher prestige level than that of their father.

Interviewing black high school youths, Keig (1969) indicated that most favored professional and managerial occupations, although their parents were primarily employed as laborers, household workers, and cooks. Later follow-up interviews, however, found most of these aspiring youths working in jobs similar to those of their parents or those traditionally open to blacks. Most youths felt that they lacked the educational qualifications required for better jobs. This finding was supported by Goldman's research (1970), which found black and Puerto Rican youths to be limited to low job-income levels, with 86 percent of those he interviewed making less than $3000 a year at full-time employment.

The problem of employment for culturally disadvantaged youths is severe. By the end of 1970, the black labor force had shrunk somewhat despite population growth. In the 16-to-19 age group, for instance, the black male labor force slumped 12 percentage points during 1970. The percentage of eligible blacks in this group working or seeking work had dropped to 40.5 percent from 48.4 percent for 1969 (Leggett & Cervinka, 1972).

The employment status of black high school graduates as of October 1972 revealed that 34.5 percent of them were unemployed, compared with only 12.2 percent for their white counterparts. Among that year's black high school dropouts, 36.3 percent were unemployed, as were 23.7 percent of the white high school dropouts. In comparison, the unemployment rate for dropout students of Spanish origin was 15.8 percent (Young, 1973).

Table 15.6 compares the occupational status of white, black, and Spanish-origin youths from 16 to 24 years of age. Data for both high school graduates and dropouts are included. It is apparent that white youths are employed by a higher percentage in the category that includes professional and technical workers. Employment of youths of Spanish origin was distributed among the various occupations and industries in proportions about equal to those of their white and black contemporaries of equal educational attainment. However, a much smaller proportion of Spanish-origin graduates than white graduates were in professional and technical occupations, and a somewhat higher proportion of Spanish-origin graduates worked as operatives. Among the dropouts, lower proportions of Spanish-origin youths than of whites were clerical workers or craftsmen, whereas the proportion who were farmworkers was double that of white dropouts.

There were also some differences in occupational distribution between the black and Spanish-origin minority groups. More black than Spanish-origin graduates were in service occupations. Among dropouts, a lower proportion of youths of Spanish origin were in clerical occupations, probably in part because of their language problem. About one-fifth of both Spanish-origin and black dropouts worked in laborer occupations; but the majority of the Spanish-origin laborers worked on farms, whereas eight out of ten of the black laborers worked in construction and other nonagricultural industries. Although 84 percent of the Spanish-origin population of all ages lived in metropolitan areas in 1970, many whose home base was in an urban area spent much of the year working in rural areas as migrant farmworkers (Ryscavage & Mellor, 1973).

There were no significant differences between graduates of Spanish origin and white graduates in the distribution of employment by industry. However, graduates of Spanish origin were somewhat less likely to work in manufacturing industries than black graduates, especially in the durable-goods sector. On the other hand, a larger proportion of Spanish-origin graduates than of black graduates were in wholesale and retail trade.

Among dropouts, twice as many Spanish-origin youths worked in agriculture as either blacks or whites, reflecting the large proportion working in farm occupations. However, a much smaller proportion of the dropouts of Spanish origin worked in the construction industry, reflecting the lower percentage who were craftsmen or nonfarm laborers. Dropouts of Spanish origin were as likely as white dropouts, but less likely than blacks, to be employed in service industries (Ryscavage & Mellor, 1973; Young, 1973).

WORK ALTERNATIVES

In our society, the individual worker—with the exception of the unionized laborer, whose work life is protected by the collective group—has very little control over his working situation. For semiskilled or unskilled laborers, the poorly educated, some minority workers, and some women workers, the idea of representation within one's occupation is especially remote. In each case, if an adolescent or adult worker sees himself as a pawn always at the mercy of a superior, alienation is likely to occur, the meaning of his work likely to get lost, and the personal satisfaction of doing work well sure to become clouded. But to remedy this situation seems an impossible task.

The occupational orientations of the young person today are not the traditional orientations of the adult worker. He is not so likely to view work as a privilege and subservience as an inevitable consequence of employment. Consistent with the values he has learned from the counterculture, he is often interested in putting aside racist and sexist attitudes and practices. He is not interested in manipulation and oppression, or even in competition in the traditional sense. He is interested in meaningful work experiences, in maintaining good interpersonal relationships with his fellow workers, in leadership opportunities, and in having some say in his occupational behavior. In fact, many of today's youth are interested in changing the nature of existing occupations as well as in effecting general societal change, which will in turn affect work demands and occupational roles.

EDUCATIONAL ASPIRATIONS

The proportion of high school graduates enrolling in college soon after graduation has dropped sharply since the peak reached in 1968—55 percent (see Table 15.7). The decline has been concentrated among male graduates; the proportion going on to college in the same year of graduation from high school fell sharply between 1968 and 1972, from 63 to 53 percent. Among women going on to college, the drop was less severe— from 49 to 46 percent over this period. Despite the decrease in total

TABLE 15.6. Occupation and industry of employed high school graduates and dropouts, age 16 to 24 years, by race or national origin, October 1972 (percent distribution).

Occupation and major industry group	Graduates[1]			Dropouts		
	All whites	Spanish origin[2]	Negro and other races	All whites	Spanish origin	Negro and other races
Total employed: Number (thousands)	8,941	361	1,026	1,999	313	440
Occupation						
Total	100.0	100.0	100.0	100.0	100.0	100.0
White collar	51.7	45.2	41.0	13.1	7.7	11.1
Professional and technical workers	12.1	3.9	6.6	1.1	.6	.7
Managers and administrators, except farm	4.6	3.6	1.7	2.0	1.0	.5
Salesworkers	6.2	5.8	3.0	2.9	3.2	2.7
Clerical workers	28.8	31.9	29.6	7.1	2.9	7.3
Blue collar	35.4	41.8	40.5	65.8	59.7	58.9
Craftsmen and kindred workers	11.8	9.4	7.3	15.4	7.3	6.8
Operatives, except transport	13.6	19.4	20.7	31.5	37.4	25.2
Transport equipment operatives	3.1	3.0	3.4	5.4	5.7	8.6
Laborers, except farm	6.9	10.0	9.2	13.6	9.3	18.2
Service	10.7	10.8	17.1	15.3	19.8	25.5
Private household workers	.7	1.4	1.3	2.4	2.9	2.3
Other service workers	10.0	9.4	15.8	12.9	16.9	23.2
Farmworkers	2.2	2.2	1.4	5.9	12.8	4.5
Industry						
Total	100.0	100.0	100.0	100.0	100.0	100.0

TABLE 15.6 (continued)

Occupation and major industry group	Graduates[1]			Dropouts		
	All whites	Spanish origin[2]	Negro and other races	All whites	Spanish origin	Negro and other races
Agriculture	2.6	2.8	1.5	7.1	14.0	5.5
Nonagricultural industries	97.4	97.2	98.5	92.9	86.0	94.5
Wage and salary workers	95.3	96.7	97.4	89.2	83.4	93.2
Mining	.7	.8	.4	.6	—	.2
Construction	6.8	6.6	5.6	13.6	4.5	10.2
Manufacturing	23.0	21.9	28.9	36.6	38.2	31.4
Durable goods	13.9	10.5	16.1	19.0	21.0	17.5
Nondurable goods	9.1	11.4	12.8	17.5	17.2	13.9
Transportation and public utilities	6.4	5.8	6.1	3.3	3.5	4.3
Wholesale and retail trade	22.7	24.7	16.9	20.6	19.1	17.8
Service	32.6	30.5	33.3	14.1	18.2	27.6
Private household	.8	1.4	1.5	2.4	3.5	3.0
Other services	31.8	29.1	30.8	11.7	14.6	24.6
Public administration	3.1	6.4	6.3	.6	—	1.6
Self-employed and unpaid family workers	2.1	.6	1.2	3.7	2.5	1.4

[1] Includes persons in the age group with 1 or more years of college.
[2] These were persons who identified themselves as Mexican-American, Chicano, Mexican (Mexicano), Puerto Rican, Cuban, or of "other Spanish origin." About 97 percent were white and were also included in data published for "all whites."

From "The High School Class of 1972" by A. M. Young, *Monthly Labor Review*, 1973, 96(6), 31. Reprinted by permission.

enrollment rates, however, the actual number going on to college—about 1.5 million—has changed little over these four years, because population increases compensated for the drop in enrollment rates (Young, 1973).

The decrease in college enrollment has been entirely among white graduates, whose rate fell from 57 percent in 1968 to 49 percent in 1972, a level about equal to that of ten years earlier. On the other hand, the proportion of black high school graduates of 1972 who went on to college (48 percent) was about the same as that for 1968 but substantially higher than that of ten years earlier (34 percent). As a result of these converging trends, there was no significant difference in the proportions of white and black graduates of 1972 enrolled in college in October. However, larger proportions of black youth drop out of junior high or high school; in October 1972, 21 percent of all blacks 16 to 24 had done so, compared with 14 percent of whites (Young, 1973).

It is difficult to explain this recent decrease in the percentage of high school graduates going on to college. However, if one considers the fact that between 1965 and 1971 over half of all high school graduates went to college, it appears that the decline may simply represent a return to normal rates. Another factor may be that, as the counterculture emerged in the mid-1960s, commitments to conventional routes to success were weakened. This phenomenon was due in part to a breakdown in the concept of delayed gratification among youths, to the increasing number of youths who took time out for work or travel between high school and college, and to a growing belief that years in college are no longer crucial to later employment, in light of the increase in unemployment in recent years among new college graduates (Perrella, 1972).

Nevertheless, projected labor statistics make clear that the trend toward more high school and college education will make the job market more available to youths. By 1990, four out of five workers are projected to have completed at least four years of high school; just over 60 percent of these workers will be 65 and over, and nearly 90 percent will be 25 to 34. A somewhat wider range is evident in the 1990 projection for those with at least four years of college: they are expected to make up over 20 percent of the labor force, ranging from about 16 percent among those 65 and over to nearly 30 percent among those 25 to 34 (see Table 15.8). It is also expected that the differences between working male and female high school graduates will narrow somewhat over the projection period. The percentage of high school graduates is projected to increase somewhat faster among working men than among working women, but the projection is reversed for college graduates; except for workers 55 and over, the percentage of women with college degrees is expected to rise somewhat faster than that of men. By 1990, the gap between educational levels for the sexes will be considerably smaller than it is today (Johnston, 1973).

TABLE 15.7. Proportion of high school graduates enrolled in college in October of the year of graduation, 1962–1972 (percentages).

Year of graduation	All persons	Men	Women	White	Negro and other races
1962	49	55	43	51	34
1963	45	52	39	46	38
1964	48	57	41	49	39
1965	51	57	45	52	43
1966	50	59	43	52	32
1967	52	58	47	53	42
1968	55	63	49	57	46
1969	54	60	47	55	37
1970	52	55	49	52	48
1971	53	58	50	54	47
1972	49	53	46	49	48

From "The High School Class of 1972" by A. M. Young, *Monthly Labor Review*, 1973, 96(6), 31. Reprinted by permission.

The existing gap between the number of college graduates 25 to 34 years of age (20.1 percent) and the number over 65 (12.4 percent) in the labor force is 7.7 percent. By 1990, due to the greater numbers of high school graduates, with approximately half going on to college, the gap will widen to 13.3 percentage points. It is anticipated that 29.7 percent of the labor force will be between 25 and 34, and that 16.4 percent will be over 65 (Johnston, 1973).

Projections also reveal that a highly significant proportion of college graduates will have pursued some form of graduate education. Among the nearly 16.4 million college graduates projected to be in the labor force in 1980, about 6.7 million (41 percent) are expected to have completed at least one year of graduate work. By 1990, the projected number of workers with at least five years of college education rises to 10.7 million, or 45 percent of the college graduates in the labor force. The corresponding proportions among working men are 46 percent in 1980 and 50 percent in 1990; among working women, they are 31 percent in 1980 and 34 percent in 1990. Here also, the disparity between the younger and older workers is pronounced. By 1980, 10.7 percent of the workers 25 to 34 are estimated to have completed at least five years of college, compared with 6.8 percent of the workers 65 and over; by 1990, the corresponding projections are 14.4 and 8.4 percent, respectively (Johnston, 1973).

There is considerable evidence that college pursuits are tied to occupational goals, especially in studies comparing urban and rural youths. Several studies (Berdie & Hood, 1964; Gregory & Lionberger,

TABLE 15.8. Civilian labor force 16 years old and over, by sex and years of school completed, 1950, 1960, and 1970 censuses, projected to 1980 and 1990.

		\multicolumn{5}{c}{Years of school completed}
Sex and year	Total	8 or less[1]	9 to 11	12	13 to 15	16 or more
Both sexes						
1950 census	57,141	23,671	11,222	13,593	4,545	4,110
1960 census	67,545	20,832	15,016	18,623	6,855	6,219
1970 census	80,393	14,431	17,157	28,168	10,556	10,081
Projected 1980	99,809	10,002	17,262	40,302	15,844	16,399
Projected 1990	110,576	6,139	15,683	44,771	19,960	24,023
Men						
1950 census	41,051	18,607	8,049	8,584	2,950	2,861
1960 census	45,339	15,315	10,044	11,161	4,373	4,446
1970 census	49,634	10,034	10,688	15,647	6,424	6,841
Projected 1980	60,630	6,933	10,301	22,568	9,895	10,933
Projected 1990	66,947	4,316	8,955	25,468	12,615	15,593
Women						
1950 census	16,090	5,064	3,173	5,009	1,595	1,249
1960 census	22,206	5,517	4,972	7,462	2,482	1,773
1970 census	30,759	4,397	6,469	12,521	4,132	3,240
Projected 1980	39,179	3,069	6,961	17,734	5,949	5,466
Projected 1990	43,629	1,823	6,728	19,303	7,345	8,430
	\multicolumn{5}{c}{*Average annual percentage change*}	
Both sexes						
1950–60	1.7	−1.3	2.9	3.1	4.1	4.1
1960–70	1.7	−3.7	1.3	4.1	4.3	4.8
1970–80	2.2	−3.7	.1	3.6	4.1	4.9
1980–90	1.0	−4.9	−1.0	1.0	2.3	3.8
Men						
1950–60	1.0	−1.9	2.2	2.6	3.9	4.4
1960–70	.9	−4.2	.6	3.4	3.8	4.3
1970–80	2.0	−3.7	−.4	3.7	4.3	4.7
1980–90	1.0	−4.7	−1.4	1.2	2.4	3.6
Women						
1950–60	3.2	.8	4.5	4.0	4.4	3.5
1960–70	3.2	−2.3	2.6	5.2	5.1	6.0
1970–80	2.4	−3.6	.7	3.5	3.6	5.2
1980–90	1.1	−5.2	−.3	.8	2.1	4.3

[1]Includes persons reporting no formal education.
From "Education of Workers: Projections to 1990" by D. F. Johnston, *Monthly Labor Review*, 1973, 96(11), 24. Reprinted by permission.

1968; Lindstrom, 1965) show that from 50 to 70 percent of urban youths aspire to go to college, with another 15 to 20 percent undecided. In contrast, only about 33 percent of the adolescents living in rural areas have college plans (Berdie & Hood, 1964; Gregory & Lionberger, 1968; Lionberger & Gregory, 1965; Lindstrom, 1965; Youmans, 1965). These statistics align themselves consistently with those for occupational aspirations. Youths in small towns, large cities, and metropolitan areas tend to look for occupational status within their larger communities. Although there is considerable migration from rural to urban areas, about 40 percent stay in rural settings (Rieger, 1972). Several studies (Andrews & Sardo, 1965; Blau & Duncan, 1967; Leuthold, Farmer, & Badenhop, 1967; Rieger, 1972) show that, soon after high school graduation, young people migrate from their rural communities into urban areas, thus obtaining higher subsequent educational and occupational status than nonmigrant youths.

WOMEN'S ASPIRATIONS

In the context of the changing sex, educational, and occupational roles of women today, it is important to consider the concomitant changes in their aspirations. Angrist's (1972) five occupational orienta-

Most adolescents think actively about the future. The problem of how to prepare for adulthood often raises more questions than it answers.

tions of college women are discussed here because they clearly demonstrate women's changing aspirations and some of the dilemmas that arise as a consequence.

1. The *careerists*, or consistent career aspirers, are oriented toward combining career with family roles in adult life. The careerist majors in a humanities field and, unlike the other student types, she alone chooses a male-dominated occupation. She does not value an occupation for being secure or high-paying, or because it involves helping others. She is influenced by her mother's example as an educated woman who works and participates actively in the community. Yet she does not try to fit her parents' notions about success. She shuns sororities during college. She views domesticity and child care as matters in which other adults can assist or replace her when necessary.
2. The *noncareerists*, or consistent noncareer aspirers, are oriented primarily to family roles and then to some work and leisure pursuits. The noncareerist's goal is to center her life totally on family, and she is concerned with selecting a mate. She becomes engaged to a boyfriend in her senior year. Her occupational choice represents a practical means to achieve security if she ever needs to work.
3. The *converts* to career aspirations begin college without career orientation but move toward career interests by their sophomore, junior, or senior years. The convert is noteworthy mainly because she slowly emerges as a competent student and develops career interests in the process. She is willing to delay marriage and, after marriage, to make flexible work arrangements.
4. The *defectors* from career aspirations are career oriented as freshmen and even thereafter, but they shift to a noncareer orientation by their senior year. The defector is most likely a home economics major, unlikely to be in physical or social sciences. Her father has at least a bachelor's degree. She changes majors often but ends up choosing a teaching program, for example, which leads her to work suitable for a woman. It also matches her parents' expectations and does not require an advanced degree. She is a poor student, not eager to finish college. She wants to marry young and to focus her energies on home and children.
5. The *shifters* are inconsistent or changeable women whose life-style aspirations vary from year to year, lacking clear-cut direction toward or away from career orientation. The shifter is a social science major and a top student. She savors both people and ideas, but she is confused about her goals. Her ideas of husband and wife responsibilities are traditional and remain so after she graduates.

ADOLESCENT MARRIAGE

Many studies have noted that youthful marriages are characterized by more disillusionment and greater risks of failure than later marriages. Research in this area (Burchinal, 1960; Burgess & Cottrell, 1939) has shown that self-assessed marital-happiness ratings, made at various points after marriage, become more positive as the age at the time of marriage increases. Inselberg (1961, 1962) investigated typical problem areas in high school marriages and the degree of marital satisfaction expressed by the spouses. She compared the marital characteristics and problems of young married couples with the problems of those who married between 21 and 26 years of age. Her findings offer a dismal picture of marital satisfaction in the younger group. In the areas of economic, social, and personal adjustment, the younger couples expressed a significantly greater magnitude of problems than did their older counterparts—a pattern partly due to their incomplete resolution of identity.

De Lissovoy (1973) studied in detail 48 married high school couples over a three-year period to assess their attitudes toward the different roles and expectations they encountered in marriage. The general findings of de Lissovoy's research were:

1. *Ages at marriage:* the mean age of husbands was 17.1; of wives, 16.5.
2. *Educational attainment:* 41 wives and 35 husbands dropped out of school before graduating.
3. *Pregnancy:* 46 wives were expecting a child prior to the marriage.
4. *Motivation for marriage:* pregnancy appeared to be the chief motivating factor.
5. *Previous dating patterns:* both husbands and wives had limited dating experience.
6. *Status orientation:* the predominant pattern was that of the rural working class.

Because 46 of the 48 women were teen-agers and were pregnant before marriage, de Lissovoy was especially interested in their maternal attitudes. Their attitudes toward child rearing were measured by means of semistructured interviews. A total of 31 mothers whose firstborn was at least 24 months old were interviewed. Seventeen had one child, and 14 had two; of the mothers with one child, eight were pregnant, and three of the mothers with two children were pregnant.

The questionnaire used was based on that utilized by Sears and his associates (Sears, Maccoby, & Levin, 1957). The intent of this part of de Lissovoy's investigation was to assess the maternal-attitude variables and child-rearing practices of very young mothers. Of the questions in the interview schedule, 22 were designed to determine the degree of maternal *acceptance* and 16 the degree of maternal *control*. The ratings for maternal acceptance were generally low. The ratings for maternal control suggest that the mothers were just over the midpoint toward the high-control end of the scale.

The investigator's clinical impressions lead him to conclude that these young mothers, with a few notable exceptions, were impatient and intolerant with their children. A similar conclusion had been reached by Sears and his associates (1957) in the analysis of the younger mothers in their investigation: "the younger mothers did in fact tend to be somewhat more severe in their treatment of young children . . . younger mothers appeared to be more irritable, in that they were quick to punish. . ." (Sears et al., 1957, p. 437).

Adolescents who get married are, in reality, in several binds. First, they usually do not have the wherewithal to maintain themselves independent of their families. Because they are still trying to resolve personal-identity conflicts, they typically use each other for ego support, commonly through physical attractiveness and sexual interaction. If de Lissovoy's research is descriptive of typical teen-age marriages, then family responsibilities begin affecting the marriage in its earliest months. Finally, for most of these youths, school is interrupted—generally voluntarily, sometimes involuntarily. The combination of new responsibilities makes it difficult for them to continue maintaining earlier adolescent patterns of behavior.

Fortunately, the laws governing the status of married students in public high school have loosened up. Federal regulations state:

> *Right to attend.* School boards cannot legally suspend a married student from the public schools on the basis of marriage alone; however, they can legally suspend a married student temporarily if they can show that the suspension is necessary for the orderly operation of the school. School board policies that exclude married students from the public schools on the basis of marriage alone will be held invalid by the courts. School boards cannot legally suspend or expel married students from the public schools because they have committed immoral acts unless the school boards can show that the married students are of an immoral character. The fact that a recently married girl gives birth to a child which was conceived out of wedlock is insufficient evidence for legally suspending her from the public schools. Married students are to be treated the same as the unmarried students insofar as the right to attend the public schools is concerned [Brown, 1972, pp. 321–322].

Actual school practices in regard to student marriage were researched by Brown (1972) among 759 Texas high schools. His findings are reported in Table 15.9. As can be seen, there are very few incidents in which a married student was kept from attending school, although 7.6

TABLE 15.9. Types of verbal and written policies in effect on married students in 475 participating school districts.

Content of policy	Responding schools	%
1. Married students are allowed part-time attendance in the regular day school. Each case is considered by the board of education.	160	33.6
2. Married students are allowed to attend regular day school but are not allowed to participate in cocurricular activities.	398	83.8
3. Married students are allowed part-time attendance in the regular day school. Each case is considered by the board of education.	8	1.7
4. Married students must make application to the board of education through an authorized member of the administration to remain in the regular day school.	6	1.3
5. Each case will be judged on its own merits.	36	7.6
6. A special committee is appointed and makes a recommendation to the board. If the student is allowed to remain in the day school, there are no restrictions based solely upon his married status placed upon him.	4	0.8
7. Pregnancy brings immediate expulsion.	36	7.6
8. If both students are enrolled, one must withdraw, the choice being theirs.	3	0.6
9. Married students must make application through an authorized member of the administration. If the student is allowed to remain in the regular day school, his cocurricular activities are subject to regulation by either the board or by the administrative staff.	50	10.6
10. All married students are suspended from school for a prescribed period of time immediately after marriage.	7	1.5
11. Failure to report marriage immediately after marriage shall constitute justification for immediate suspension.	16	3.4

From "Married Students in Public High Schools: A Texas Study" by B. B. Brown, *Family Coordinator*, 1972, 21(3), 323. Copyright 1972 by National Council on Family Relations. Reprinted by permission.

percent of the schools' responses indicated that pregnancy brought about immediate expulsion. However, it appears that married students are discriminated against within the school itself, since, for example, 83.8 percent of the schools prohibited married-student participation in coeducational ativities.

Adolescents' Aspirations for Marriage

Kuvlesky and Obordo (1972), Kuvlesky and Upham (1967), Thomas (1972), and Thomas and Jacob (1970) have studied the marital aspirations and expectations of high school students. Kuvlesky and Obordo (1972) show that most girls prefer to get married in their early

20s, and that the white girls they studied indicated stronger preference for early marriage than did the black girls. Thomas' (1972) study included both boys and girls. She found the same trends among female students as did Kuvlesky and Obordo, and a similar trend among white males, but a trend toward marriage after 25 for the majority of the black males in her study.

Both research studies were also interested in desires for work outside the home after marriage, both for oneself and for one's spouse. Table 15.10, adapted from Thomas' study (1972), indicates these adolescents' aspirations (idealistic) and their expectations (realistic). White boys did not want their wives to work (54 percent), and 40 percent believed that they would not have to. Girls were much less inclined to stay at home. Although 17 percent expressed no desire to work, only 11 percent felt that they actually would not have to. Considerably fewer black males expected their wives to stay at home (19 percent), although black female expectations for staying at home (22 percent) were much higher than those of the white females (11 percent). The results of the Kuvlesky and Obordo (1972) study were almost identical.

As you can see in Table 15.10, males, whether black or white, were less inclined to want their wives to work once children were born. This pattern undoubtedly reflects some traditional values. In contrast, females, whether white or black, were more inclined than their husbands to think about their working, although they too indicated a preference for staying at home far more often than is actually the case among women in America today. However, Gump (1972) found that only 25 percent of the college women she studied felt that a woman could gain personal fulfillment by staying in the home.

CHANGING LIFE-STYLES

Since life-styles in our society are changing, it is necessary to prepare today's youths for them. An adolescent's occupational, educational, and marital aspirations must be understood in light of the contemporary sociocultural milieu. The identity strivings of youths will be better realized in preparing for and implementing life goals if youths' emotional awareness is aligned with reasonable expectations.

Adolescents need some insight into the art of expressing one's individuality while at the same time bringing satisfaction to the family or community as a whole. Some of the insights and abilities they must acquire are:

1. Freedom to choose a mutually acceptable life-style within a marriage may be an important indicator of happiness in that relationship. The

TABLE 15.10. Boys' and girls' aspirations and expectations for spouse or self, respectively, to work outside the home after marriage (percentages).

	Aspirations				Expectations			
	Whites		Negroes		Whites		Negroes	
Conditions for working	Boys (N=97)	Girls (N=83)	Boys (N=77)	Girls (N=72)	Boys (N=96)	Girls (N=83)	Boys (N=76)	Girls (N=69)
Not at all	54	17	26	11	40	11	19	22
Part-time until child	29	14	36	20	37	19	42	24
Full-time until child	13	59	23	26	15	42	17	16
Part-time after child	4	4	11	28	8	19	18	25
Full-time after child	0	6	4	15	0	9	4	13
Total	100	100	100	100	100	100	100	100
No information	7	5	7	5	8	5	8	8

From "A Comparison of Teenage Boys' and Girls' Orientations towards Marriage and Procreation" by Katheryn Ann Thomas, paper presented at the annual meeting of the Association of Southern Agricultural Workers, Jacksonville, Florida, February 1971. Reprinted by permission.

freedom to choose alternative patterns of behavior in role relationships within the family is a potential strength.
2. The ability to live with multiple social possibilities, rather than according to custom, suggests qualities of adaptability and flexibility that indicate both individual and family strength.
3. Increasing opportunities for the self-actualization of family members, and the corresponding movement away from power relationships, can be regarded as a family strength.
4. The ability to communicate ideas, needs, and frustrations may enable each family or group member to deal with his frustrations in a responsible and socially acceptable manner.
5. Adolescents are socialized by both male and female adults, and they should be acquainted with the nonfamily roles of both.

Throughout adolescence, the individual attempts to clarify his value structure, which serves as his guide to behavior. The more a person can internalize a workable social, moral, and ethical philosophy, the more definitive his behavior will be in relation to long-range goals. This value structure starts forming during childhood, through social-psychological training by the family. During adolescence, the person's values are tested further through experiences, primarily those outside the home (Thornburg, 1973c). It is during this time that the youth finds out how close his values are to his parents' and how much functional value autonomy he has. Through considering the often contrasting values of his parents, peers, religion, society, and school, a value structure emerges that serves as his reference point for functioning (Thornburg, 1970a).

In the identity-seeking process, a person typically asks himself who, what, and where he is. Disillusionment with today's mass society has caused youths to examine its appropriateness to their particular lifestyle, a factor that has contributed to the emergence of various counter-culture activities.

Although the adolescent himself often cannot perceive them, his experiences have important long-term effects. In addition, adolescence today is a lengthening period, making emergence into adulthood more difficult. The defining experiences that occur during adolescence are sometimes highly satisfying, sometimes stressful. If the adolescent is given some guidance so that he knows what is expected of him, he can focus better on his task of identity resolution and thus evolve into a functioning adult.

References

Aberle, D. F., & Naegele, K. D. Middle-class fathers' occupational role and attitudes toward children. *American Journal of Orthopsychiatry*, 1952, 22(2), 366–378.

Acrylic glue component poses hazard. *Journal of the American Medical Association*, 1972, 222(9), 1115–1116.

Adams, A. A. Identifying socially maladjusted schoolchildren. *Genetic Psychology Monographs*, 1960, 61, 3–36.

Adams, P. L. Late sexual maturation in girls. *Medical Aspects of Human Sexuality*, 1972, 6(3), 50–75.

Adelson, J. What generation gap? *New York Times Magazine*, January 18, 1970, pp. 10–11; 34–36.

Adler, N. Kicks, drugs, and politics. *Psychoanalytic Review*, 1970, 57, 432–441.

Ahlstrom, W. M., & Havighurst, R. J. *400 losers*. San Francisco: Jossey-Bass, 1971.

Alexander, C. N., Jr., & Campbell, E. Q. Peer influences on adolescent educational aspirations and attainments. *American Sociological Review*, 1964, 29, 568–575.

Alexander, C. N., Jr., & Campbell, E. Q. Peer influences on adolescent drinking behaviors. *Quarterly Journal of Studies on Alcohol*, 1967, 28(3), 444–453.

Alexander, W. M., & Hines, V. Z. *Independent study in secondary schools*. Cooperative Research Project No. 2969. Gainesville: University of Florida, 1966.

Alissi, A. S. Concepts of adolescence. *Adolescence*, 1972, 7(28), 491–510.

Alschuler, A., & Irons, R. B. Motivating adolescents' achievements. *Urban Education*, 1973, 7(4), 323–340.

Anderson, J. G., & Evans, F. B. Family socialization and educational achievement in two cultures: Mexican-American and Anglo-American. Paper read at the American Educational Research Association Meeting, New Orleans, February 1973.

Anderson, N. H. Information integration theory applied to attitudes about U.S. presidents. *Journal of Educational Psychology*, 1973, 64(1), 1–8.

Andrews, W. H., & Sardo, J. Migration and migrants from Sedgwick County, Colorado. Ft. Collins: Colorado Experimental Station, Technical Bulletin No. 82, 1965.

Andry, R. G. *Delinquency and parental pathology*. Springfield, Ill.: Charles C Thomas, 1960.

Angel, W. Gaposis: The new social disease. *Vital Speeches*, 1968, pp. 671–672.

Angelino, H., Dollins, J., & Mech, E. V. Trends in the fears and worries of schoolchildren as related to socio-economic status and age. *Journal of Genetic Psychology*, 1956, 89, 263–276.

Angelino, H., & Mech, E. V. Fears and worries concerning physical changes: A preliminary survey of 32 females. *Journal of Psychology*, 1955, 39, 195–198. (a)

Angelino, H., & Mech, E. V. Some "first" sources of sex information as reported by 67 college women. *Journal of Psychology*, 1955, *39*, 321–324. (b)

Angelino, H., & Shedd, C. Shifts in content of fears and worries relative to chronological age. *Proceedings of the Oklahoma Academy of Sciences*, 1953, *34*, 180–186.

Angrist, S. S. Variations in women's adult aspirations during college. *Journal of Marriage and the Family*, 1972, *34*, 465–467.

Anspach, K. Clothing selection and the mobility concept. *Journal of Home Economics*, 1961, *53*, 428–430.

Aronfreed, J. *Conduct and conscience.* New York: Academic Press, 1968.

Asayama, S. Comparison of sexual development of American and Japanese adolescents. *Psychologia*, 1957, *1*, 129–131.

Ausubel, D. P. *Theory and problems of adolescent development.* New York: Grune & Stratton, 1954.

Ausubel, D. P., & Ausubel, P. Cognitive development in adolescence. *American Educational Research Journal*, 1966, *3*, 403–413.

Bachman, J. G. *Youth in transition* (Vol. 2). Ann Arbor, Mich.: Institute for Social Research, 1970.

Backman, E. L., & Finlay, D. J. Student protest: A cross-national study. *Youth and Society*, 1973, *5*(1), 3–46.

Baden, M. M. Narcotic abuse. *New York State Journal of Medicine*, 1972, *72*(7), 834–840.

Baker, C. B., & Farber, E. M. A program for venereal disease education in secondary schools. *California Journal for Instructional Improvement*, 1970, *13*(1), 3–10.

Baldwin, A. L. *Theories of child development.* New York: Wiley, 1968.

Bandura, A. The story decade: Fact or fiction? *Psychology in the Schools*, 1964, *1*, 224–231.

Bandura, A. *Principles of behavior modification.* New York: Holt, Rinehart and Winston, 1969.

Bandura, A., & Huston, A. C. Identification as a process of incidental learning. *Journal of Abnormal and Social Psychology*, 1961, *63*, 311–319.

Bandura, A., Ross, D., & Ross, S. A. Imitation of film-mediated aggressive models. *Journal of Abnormal and Social Psychology*, 1963, *66*, 3–11.

Barnett, J. Dependency conflicts in the young adult. *Psychoanalytic Review*, 1971, *58*, 111–125.

Barton, A. H. *The Columbia crisis: Campus, Vietnam, and the ghetto.* New York: Columbia University Bureau of Applied Social Research, 1968.

Barty, N., Bethell, B., & Bellward, G. Drug abuse education: A practical approach for elementary school. *Education Canada*, 1973, *13*(1), 10–13.

Bates, W., & Crowther, B. *Drugs: Causes, circumstances, and effects of their use.* Morristown, N.J.: General Learning Press, 1973.

Baur, E. J. Student peer groups and academic development. *College Student Survey*, 1967, *1*, 22–31.

Beiser, M. Poverty, social disintegration, and personality. *Journal of Social Issues*, 1965, *21*, 56–78.

Bell, G. D. Processes in the formation of adolescent aspirations. *Social Forces*, 1963, pp. 179–186.

Bell, H. M. *Youth tell their story.* Washington, D.C.: American Council on Education, 1938.

Bell, R. R. Parent-child conflict in sexual values. *Journal of Social Issues*, 1966, *22*, 34–44.

Bell, R. R. Swinging. *Sexual Behavior*, 1971, *1*, 72–79.

Bell, R. R., & Blumberg, L. Courtship intimacy and religious background. *Marriage and Family Living*, 1959, *21*, 356–360.

Bell, R. R., & Blumberg, L. Courtship stages and intimacy attitudes. *Family Life Coordinator*, 1960, *8*, 60–63.

Bell, R. R., & Chaskes, J. B. Premarital sexual experiences among coeds, 1958 and 1968. *Journal of Marriage and the Family*, 1970, *32*, 81–84.

Beller, E. K. Theories of adolescent development. In J. F. Adams (Ed.), *Understanding adolescence* (2nd ed.). Pp. 102–133. Boston: Allyn & Bacon, 1973.

Benedict, R. *Patterns of culture*. New York: New American Library, 1950.

Benedict, R. Continuities and discontinuities in cultural conditioning. In W. Martin & C. Stendler (Eds.), *Readings in child development*. Pp. 142–148. New York: Harcourt, Brace, 1954.

Bengtson, V. L. The generation gap: A review and typology of social-psychological perspectives. *Youth and Society*, 1970, *2*(1), 7–32.

Bensman, J. The sexual revolution and cultural styles: A reactionary point of view. *Psychoanalytic Review*, 1970, *57*(3), 405–431.

Berdie, R. F., & Hood, A. B. Personal values and attitudes as determinants of post-high-school plans. *Personnel and Guidance Journal*, 1964, *42*, 754–759.

Berk, L. E., Rose, M. H., & Stewart, D. Attitudes of English and American children toward their school experience. *Journal of Educational Psychology*, 1970, *61*, 33–40.

Bernard, H. W. *Human development in western culture* (3rd ed.). Boston: Allyn & Bacon, 1970.

Bernard, J. Teen-age culture: An overview. *Annals of the American Academy of Political and Social Sciences*, 1961, *338*, 1–12.

Bettelheim, B. The problem of generations. In E. Erikson (Ed.), *The challenge of youth*. Pp. 76–109. New York: Anchor, 1965.

Bijou, S. W., & Baer, D. M. *Child development*. New York: Appleton-Century-Crofts, 1961.

Biller, H. B. Father absence and the personality development of the male child. *Developmental Psychology*, 1970, *2*, 181–201.

Birkness, V., & Johnson, H. C. Comparative study of delinquent and nondelinquent adolescents. *Journal of Educational Research*, 1949, pp. 561–572.

Blaine, G. B. Sex among teenagers. *Medical Aspects of Human Sexuality*, 1968, *2*, 6–13.

Blau, P. M., & Duncan, O. D. *The American occupational structure*. New York: Wiley, 1967.

Bloch, H. A., & Flynn, F. T. *Delinquency: The juvenile offender in America today*. New York: Random House, 1956.

Block, J., Haan, N., & Smith, M. B. Socialization correlates of student activism. *Journal of Social Issues*, 1970, *26*, 25–38.

Bloom, B. S. *The stability and change of human characteristics*. New York: Wiley, 1964.

Blos, P. *On adolescence: A psychoanalytic interpretation*. New York: Free Press, 1961.

Blum, R. H. *Students and drugs*. San Francisco: Jossey-Bass, 1969.

Bordua, D. J. Educational aspirations and parental stress on college. *Social Forces*, 1960, *38*, 262–269.

Bowerman, C. E., & Elder, G. H., Jr. The adolescent and his family. Unpublished manuscript, 1962.
Bowerman, C. E. & Elder, G. H., Jr. Variations in adolescent perception of family power structure. *American Sociological Review*, 1964, 29, 551–567.
Bowerman, C. E., & Kinch, J. W. Changes in family and peer orientation of children between the fourth and tenth grades. *Social Forces*, 1959, 37, 206–211.
Braham, M. Peer group deterrents to intellectual development during adolescence. *Educational Theory*, 1965, 15, 248–258.
Brecher, E. M. *Licit and illicit drugs.* Boston: Little, Brown, 1972.
Brezezinska, Z. The attitude of today's youth toward life. *Psychologia Wychowawcza*, 1960, 3, 150–160.
Briar, S., & Piliavin, I. Delinquency, situational inducements, and commitments to conformity. *Social Problems*, 1965, 13(1), 35–45.
Briar, S., & Piliavin, I. Police encounters with juveniles. In R. Giallombardo (Ed.), *Juvenile delinquency: A book of readings.* Pp. 442–341. New York: Wiley, 1966.
Brim, O. G. Socialization through the life cycle. In O. G. Brim & S. Wheeler (Eds.), *Socialization after childhood: Two essays.* Pp. 3–49. New York: Wiley, 1966.
Brittain, C. V. Adolescent choices and parent-peer cross pressures. *American Sociological Review*, 1963, 28, 385–391.
Brittain, C. V. An exploration of the bases of peer-compliance and parent-compliance in adolescence. *Adolescence*, 1967/68, 2, 445–458.
Brittain, C. V. A comparison of urban and rural adolescence with respect to peer versus parent compliance. *Adolescence*, 1969, 4(13), 59–68.
Broderick, C. B. Sexual behavior among preadolescents. *Journal of Social Issues*, 1966, 22, 6–21.
Broderick, C. B., & Rowe, G. P. A scale of preadolescent heterosexual development. *Journal of Marriage and the Family*, 1968, 30, 97–101.
Bronfenbrenner, U. Childhood: The roots of alienation. *National Elementary Principal*, 1972, 52(2), 22–29.
Brown, B. B. Married students in public high schools: A Texas study. *Family Coordinator*, 1972, 21(3), 321–324.
Brozovsky, M., & Winkler, E. Glue-sniffing in children and adolescents. *New York State Journal of Medicine*, August 1, 1965, pp. 1984–1989.
Bruner, J. S. *Toward a theory of instruction.* New York: Norton, 1966.
Bryan, A. H., & Greenberg, B. G. Methodology in the study of physical measurements of schoolchildren. *Human Biology*, 1952, 24, 117–144.
Bunt, M. E. Ego identity: Its relationship to the discrepancy between how an adolescent views himself and how he perceives that others view him. *Psychology*, 1971, 8, 14–24.
Burchinal, L. J. Research on young marriage: Implications for family life education. *Family Life Coordinator*, 1960, 9, 6–24.
Burchinal, L. J. Characteristics of adolescents from unbroken, broken, and reconstituted families. *Journal of Marriage and the Family*, 1964, 26, 44–51.
Burgess, E. W., & Cottrell, L. S. *Predicting success or failure in marriage.* Englewood Cliffs, N. J.: Prentice-Hall, 1939.
Burlingame, W. V. *An investigation of the correlates of adherence to the adolescent peer culture.* Unpublished doctoral dissertation, University of Washington, 1967.

Byrne, D., Ervine, C. R., & Lamberth, J. Continuity between the experimental study of attraction and real-life computer dating. *Journal of Personality and Social Psychology*, 1970, 16, 157–165.

Calden, G., Lundy, R. M., & Schlafer, R. J. Sex differences in body concepts. *Journal of Consulting Psychology*, 1959, 23(4), 378.

Campbell, E. Q. Adolescent socialization. In D. A. Goslin (Ed.), *Handbook of socialization theory and research*. Pp. 827–835. Chicago: Rand McNally, 1969.

Carry, R. W. Youth breaks the rules. Research Resume No. 38. *Proceedings of the 20th Annual State Conference on Educational Research*, Burlingame, Calif., 1968.

Cartwright, A., Martin, F. M., & Thompson, J. G. Distribution of development of smoking habits. *Lancet*, 1959, 2, 726.

Cawelti, G. Youth assess the American high school. *PTA Magazine*, 1968, 62, 16–19.

Chapel, J. L., & Taylor, D. W. Drugs for kicks. *Crime and Delinquency*, 1970, 16(1), 1–35.

Chickering, S. B. How we got that way. *American Scholar*, 1967, 36, 602–607.

Christensen, H. T., & Carpenter, G. R. Value-behavior discrepancies regarding pre-marital coitus in three western cultures. *American Sociological Review*, 1962, 27, 66–75.

Christensen, H. T., & Gregg, C. F. Changing sex norms in America and Scandinavia. *Journal of Marriage and the Family*, 1970, 32, 616–627.

Cicoure, A. V., & Kitsuse, J. I. *The educational decision-makers*. Indianapolis: Bobbs-Merrill, 1963.

Clark, W. H., & Funkhouser, G. R. Physicians and researchers disagree on psychedelic drugs. *Psychology Today*, 1970, 3(11), 48–50.

Clausen, J. A. Family structure, socialization, and personality. In L. W. Hoffman & M. L. Hoffman (Eds.), *Review of child development research* (Vol. 2). New York: Russell Sage, 1966.

Clinard, M. B. *Sociology of deviant behavior*. New York: Holt, Rinehart and Winston, 1957.

Cloward, R. A., & Ohlin, L. E. *Delinquency and opportunity: A theory of delinquent gangs*. Glencoe, Ill.: Free Press, 1960.

Cohen, A. K. *Delinquent boys: The culture of the gang*. Glencoe, Ill.: Free Press, 1955.

Cohen, A. K. *Deviance and control*. Englewood Cliffs, N.J.: Prentice-Hall, 1966.

Cole, L., & Hall, I. N. *Psychology of adolescence* (6th ed.). New York: Holt, Rinehart and Winston, 1970.

Coleman, J. S. The adolescent subculture and academic achievement. *American Journal of Sociology*, 1960, 65, 337–347.

Coleman, J. S. *The adolescent society*. New York: Free Press, 1961.

Coleman, J. S. *The adolescent and the schools*. New York: Basic Books, 1965.

Coleman, J. S., Mood, A. M., Campbell, E. Q., et al. *Equality in educational opportunity*. Washington, D. C.: U. S. Government Printing Office, 1966.

Committee on Alcoholism and Drug Dependence. Recovery from drug dependence. *Journal of the American Medical Association*, 1970, 214(3), 579.

Conger, J. J. A world they never knew: The family and social change. In J. Kagan and R. Coles (Eds.), *Twelve to sixteen: Early adolescence*. Pp. 197–230. New York: Norton, 1972.

Conger, J. J. *Adolescence and youth*. New York: Harper & Row, 1973.

Constantine, L., & Constantine, J. How to make group marriage. *Modern Utopian,* 1970, *4,* 33–37. (a)
Constantine, L., & Constantine, J. Where is marriage going? *The Futurist,* 1970, *3,* 44–45. (b)
Contamination brings vitamin tablet recall. *Journal of the American Medical Association,* 1972, *221*(13), 16.
Corboz, R. J. Psychological aspects of retarded puberty. *Adolescence,* 1966, *1*(2), 141–143.
Croake, J. W. Adolescent fears. *Adolescence,* 1967, *2*(8), 459–468.
Croake, J. W., & Knox, F. H. A second look at adolescent fears. *Adolescence,* 1971, *6*(23), 279–284.
Cross, H. J., & Davis, G. L. College students' adjustment and frequency of marijuana use. *Journal of Counseling Psychology,* 1972, *19*(1), 65–67.
Cross, H. J., & Pruyn, E. L. Youth and the counterculture. In J. Adams (Ed.), *Understanding adolescence.* Pp. 339–374. Boston: Allyn & Bacon, 1973.
Crowther, B., & Baumer, T. L. The use of drugs by secondary school students in the greater Egypt region. In Huper & Associates (Eds.), *Drug abuse in middle America: Problems and proposals.* Pp. 7–24. Report submitted to the Illinois Law Enforcement Commission, 1971.
Daniel, W. *The adolescent patient.* St. Louis: C. V. Mosby, 1970.
Darwin, C. *The origin of species.* London: J. J. Murray, 1859.
Darwin, C. *The descent of man.* London: J. J. Murray, 1871.
Davids, A. *The influence of personality on auditory apperception and memory.* Unpublished doctoral dissertation, Harvard University, 1953.
Davis, A. Socialization and adolescent personality. In *Adolescence: Yearbook of the National Society for the Study of Education,* 43(Pt. 1), 198–210. Chicago: University of Chicago Press, 1944.
Davis, K. The sociology of parent-youth conflict. *American Sociological Review,* 1940, *5*(4), 523–534.
Davis, K. Adolescence and the social structure. *Annals of the American Academy of Political and Social Science,* 1944, *236,* 8–16.
Davis, K. B. *Factors in the sex life of twenty-two hundred women.* New York: Harper & Row, 1929.
de Lissovoy, V. Child care by adolescent parents. *Children Today,* 1973, *2*(4), 22–25.
de Lissovoy, V. High school marriages: A longitudinal study. *Journal of Marriage and the Family,* 1973, *35*(2), 245–255.
Denhardt, R. B., & Allen, H. D. Youth response to cultural incongruities. *Youth and Society,* 1971, *3*(2), 237–255.
Denisoff, R. S., & Levine, M. H. Youth and popular music: A test of the taste culture hypothesis. *Youth and Society,* 1972, *4*(2), 237–255.
Dentler, R., & Monroe, L. J. Early adolescent theft. *American Sociological Review,* 1961, pp. 733–743.
Dependence on cannabis (marijuana). *Journal of the American Medical Association,* 1967, *202,* 47–50.
Derbyshire, R. L. Adolescent identity crisis in urban Mexican-Americans in East Los Angeles. In E. B. Brady (Ed.), *Minority group adolescents in the United States.* Pp. 73–110. Baltimore: Williams & Wilkins, 1968.
DeRoche, E. F. Occupational values of public and private high school seniors. *Catholic Educational Review,* 1969, *66*(3), 838–843.
Deutsch, H. *The psychology of women* (Vol. 1). New York: Grune & Stratton, 1944.

Dishotsky, N. I., Loughman, W. D., Mogar, R. E., & Lipscomb, W. R. LSD and genetic damage. *Science,* 1971, *172*(3982), 431–440.
Dodson, D. Education and the powerless. In A. H. Passow (Ed.), *Education of the disadvantaged.* New York: Holt, Rinehart and Winston, 1967.
Douvan, E., & Adelson, J. *The adolescent experience.* New York: Wiley, 1966.
Drugs on campus: A remarkable increase. *U.S. News and World Report,* February 1, 1971, pp. 26–27.
Duncan, O. D., et al. Peer influences on aspirations: A reinterpretation. *American Journal of Sociology,* 1968, *74,* 119–137.
Dunphy, D. C. The social structure of urban adolescent peer groups. *Sociometry,* 1963, *26,* 230–246.
Dwyer, J., & Mayer, J. Psychological effects of variations in physical appearance during adolescence. *Adolescence,* 1969, *3,* 353–380.
Eastman, W. F. First intercourse. *Sexual Behavior,* 1972, *2*(3), 22–27.
Eddy, N. B., Halbach, H., Isbell, H., & Seevers, M. H. Drug dependence: Its significance and characteristics. *Bulletin of the World Health Organization,* 1965, *32,* 721–733.
Edson, L. Schools attack the smoking problem. *American Education,* 1973, *9*(1), 10–14.
Eichorn, D. H. Biological correlates of behavior. In H. W. Stevenson (Ed.), *Child psychology: 62nd yearbook of the National Society for the Study of Education.* Pp. 4–61. University of Chicago Press, 1963.
Eidsmore, R. M. High school athletes are brighter. *School Activities,* 1963, *35,* 75–77.
Eisenman, R., & Platt, J. J. Underachievement and creativity in high school students. *Psychology,* 1972, *7,* 52–55.
Eisenstadt, S. N. *From generation to generation.* New York: Free Press, 1956.
Elder, G. H., Jr. Structural variations in the child rearing relationship. *Sociometry,* 1962, *25*(3), 241–262.
Elder, G. H. Jr. Socialization and ascent in a racial minority. *Youth and Society,* 1972, *2*(1), 74–110.
Elias, J., & Gebhard, P. Sexuality and sexual learning in childhood. *Phi Delta Kappan,* 1969, *50,* 401–406.
Elkin, F. Socialization and the presentation of self. *Marriage and Family Living,* 1958, *20,* 320–325.
Elkin, F. *The family in Canada.* Ottawa: Canadian Conference on the Family, 1964.
Elkind, D. Conceptual orientation shifts in children and adolescents. *Child Development,* 1966, *37,* 493–498.
Elkind, D. Egocentrism in adolescence. *Child Development,* 1967, *38,* 1025–1034.
Elkind, D. *A sympathetic understanding of the child six to sixteen.* Boston: Allyn & Bacon, 1971.
Ellis, R. A., & Lane, C. Structural supports for upward mobility. *American Sociological Review,* 1963, *36,* 743–756.
Empey, L. T. Delinquency theory and recent research. *Journal of Research in Crime and Delinquency,* 1967, *4,* 28–42.
Entwisle, D. R., & Greenberger, E. Adolescents' views of women's work role. *American Journal of Orthopsychiatry,* 1972, *42*(4), 648–656.
Epperson, D. C. A reassessment of indices of parental influence in the adolescent society. *American Sociological Review,* 1964, *29,* 93–96.
Erikson, E. H. *Childhood and society.* New York: W. W. Norton, 1950.

Erikson, E. H. Identity and the life cycle: Selected papers. *Psychological Issues Monograph Series*, I, No. 1. New York: International Universities Press, 1959.

Erikson, E. H. *Childhood and society* (2nd ed). New York: W. W. Norton, 1963.

Erikson, E. H. Youth: Fidelity and diversity. In E. H. Erikson (Ed.), *The challenge of youth*. New York: Anchor, 1965.

Erikson, E. H. Memorandum on youth. *Daedalus*, 1967, 96(3), 860–870.

Erikson, E. H. *Identity: Youth and crisis*. New York: W. W. Norton, 1968.

Erskine, H. G. What polling shows about sexual attitudes in the United States. *Medical Aspects of Human Sexuality*, 1968, 2(5), 54–62.

Essig, M., & Morgan, D. H. Adjustment of adolescent daughters of employed mothers to family life. *Journal of Educational Psychology*, 1945, 37, 219–233.

Excluded Student: Report III. U. S. Commission on Civil Rights. Washington, D.C.: U. S. Government Printing Office, 1972.

Fantini, M. Alternatives within public schools. *Phi Delta Kappan*, 1973, 54(7), 444–449.

Faust, M. S. Developmental maturity as a determinant in prestige of adolescent girls. *Child Development*, 1960, 31, 173–184.

FDA endorses proposal that intake of Saccharin should be limited. *Journal of the American Medical Association*, 1971, 217(4), 412; 417.

Federal agency lifts ban on sale of aerosol glue. *Journal of the American Medical Association*, 1974, 228(1), 16–17.

Federal Bureau of Investigation, U. S. Department of Justice. *Uniform Crime Reports*. Washington, D. C.: U. S. Government Printing Office, 1967.

Federal Bureau of Investigation, U. S. Department of Justice. *Uniform Crime Reports, 1960–1972*. U. S. Government Printing Office, 1972.

Feigelson, N. *The underground revolution*. New York: Funk & Wagnalls, 1970.

Feingold, M. Should there be sex education in the schools? *Medical Aspects of Human Sexuality*, 1971, 5(1), 11–47.

Felker, D. W. Relationship between the self-concept, body build, and perception of father's interest in sports in boys. *Research Quarterly*, 1968, 39, 413–517.

Ferdinand, T. N. Sex behavior and the American class structure: A mosaic. *Medical Aspects of Human Sexuality*, 1969, 3(1), 34–46.

Ferdon, N. M. Chromosomal abnormalities and antisocial behavior. *Journal of Genetic Psychology*, 1971, 118, 281–292.

Ferguson, G. A. On transfer and the abilities of man. *Canadian Journal of Psychology*, 1956, 10, 121–131.

Ferguson, L. R. *Personality development*. Monterey, Calif.: Brooks/Cole, 1970.

Festinger, L. *Theory of cognitive dissonance*. New York: Harper & Row, 1957.

Feuer, L. *The conflict of generations*. New York: Basic Books, 1969.

Fink, P. J. Dealing with sexual pressures of the unmarried. *Medical Aspects of Human Sexuality*, 1970, 4(3), 42–53.

Fisher, S. Sex differences in body perception. *Psychological Monographs*, 1964, 78(14).

Fishman, J. R., & Solomon, F. Youth and social action: 1. Perspectives on the student sit-in movement. *American Journal of Orthopsychiatry*, 1963, 33(5), 872–882.

Fitt, A. B. An experimental study of children's attitudes toward school. *British Journal of Educational Psychology*, 1956, 26, 25–30.

Fitzsimmons, S. J., Cheever, J., Leonard, E., & Macunovich, D. School failures: Now and tomorrow. *Developmental Psychology*, 1969, *1*, 134–146.

Flacks, R. The liberated generation: An exploration of the roots of student protest. *Journal of Social Issues*, 1967, *23*, 52–75.

Flacks, R. The New Left and American politics after ten years. *Journal of Social Issues*, 1971, *27*(1), 21–34.

Floyd, H. H., Jr., & South, D. R. Dilemma of youth: The choice of parents or peers as a frame of reference for behavior. *Journal of Marriage and the Family*, 1972, *34*(4), 627–634.

Ford, T. Social factors affecting academic performance: Further evidence. *School Review*, 1957, *55*, 415–422.

Forney, R. B., & Hughes, F. W. *Combined effects of alcohol on other drugs*. Springfield, Ill.: Charles C Thomas, 1968.

Forslund, M. A., & Malry, L. Social class and relative level of occupational aspiration: Implications for delinquency and education. *National Association of Secondary School Principals Bulletin*, 1970, *54*(349), 106–115.

Fort, J. Youth: How to produce drop-ins rather than drop-outs. Research Resume No. 38. Pp. 53–64. *Proceedings of the 20th Annual State Conference on Educational Research*, Burlingame, Calif., 1968.

Fort, J. *The pleasure seekers: The drug crisis, youth and society*. New York: Grove Press, 1969.

Frazier, A., & Lisonbee, L. K. Adolescent concerns with physique. *School Review*, 1950, *58*, 397–405.

Freedman, M. B. The sexual behavior of American college women. *Merrill-Palmer Quarterly*, 1965.

Freud, S. The dissolution of the Oedipus complex. *Complete Psychological Works of Sigmund Freud, Standard Edition*, 1924, *19*, 173–179.

Freydinger, J. E., Fishel, S. S., & Golding, L. A. Steroid effects on college athletes. Paper presented at the National Conference on the Medical Aspects of Sports, San Diego, Calif., 1973.

Friedenberg, E. Z. The generation gap. *Annals of the American Academy of Political and Social Science*, 1969, *382*, 32–42.

Friedman, H. L. The mother-daughter relationship: Its potential in treatment of young unwed mothers. *Social Casework*, 1966, *48*(8), 502–506.

Friesen, D. Academic-athletic-popularity syndrome in the Canadian high school society (1967). *Adolescence*, 1968, *3*(9), 39–52.

Frisch, R. E., & Revelle, R. Variations in body weights and the age of the adolescent growth spurt among Latin American and Asian populations in relation to calorie supplies. *Human Biology*, 1969, *41*, 185–212.

Frisch, R. E., & Revelle, R. Height and weight at menarche and a hypothesis of critical body weights and adolescent events. *Science*, 1970, *169*(3943), 397–398.

Frye, V. H., & Dietz, S. C. Attitudes of high school students toward traditional views of women workers. *Journal of the Student Personnel Association for Teacher Education*, 1973, *11*(3), 102–108.

Fuchs, V. R. Women's earnings: Recent trends and long-run prospects. *Monthly Labor Review*, 1974, *97*(5), 23–26.

Gagné, R. M. *Essentials of learning for instruction*. Hinsdale, Ill.: Dryden, 1974.

Galbraith, J. K. *The new industrial state*. Boston: Houghton Mifflin, 1967.

Gallemore, J. L., & Wilson, W. P. Adolescent maladjustment or affective disorder? *American Journal of Psychiatry*, 1972, *129*(5), 120–124.

Gallup, G. H. The fifth annual Gallup poll of public attitudes toward education. *Phi Delta Kappan,* 1973, *55*(1), 38–50.

Gallup, G. H., & Davis, J. V., III. Gallup poll. *Tucson Daily Citizen,* May 26, 1969, p. 41.

Gans, H. J. *The urban villagers.* New York: Free Press, 1962.

Garai, J. E. Sex differences in mental health. *Genetic Psychology Monographs,* 1970, *81,* 123–142.

Generations apart. New York: Columbia Broadcasting System, 1969.

Gergen, M. K., Gergen, K. L., & Morse, S. J. Correlates of marijuana use among college students. *Journal of Applied Social Psychology,* 1972, *2*(1), 1–16.

Gerzon, M. *The whole world is watching.* New York: Paperback Library, 1970.

Gesell, A., Ilg, F. L., & Ames, L. B. *Youth: The years from ten to sixteen.* New York: Harper & Row, 1956.

Gibbens, T. C. N., & Ahrenfeldt, R. H. *Cultural factors in delinquency.* London: Lippincott, 1966.

Ginsburg, H., & Opper, S. *Piaget's theory of intellectual development.* Englewood Cliffs, N. J.: Prentice-Hall, 1969.

Ginzberg, E., Ginsburg, S. W., Axelrad, S., & Herma, J. L. *Occupational choice: An approach to a general theory.* New York: Columbia University Press, 1951.

Glass, J. C. Premarital sexual standards among church youth leaders: An exploratory study. *Journal for the Scientific Study of Religion,* 1972, *11*(4), 361–367.

Glueck, S., & Glueck, E. *Unraveling juvenile delinquency.* Cambridge, Mass.: Harvard University Press, 1950.

Glueck, S., & Glueck, E. *Delinquents and nondelinquents in perspective.* Cambridge, Mass.: Harvard University Press, 1968.

Gold, M. *Delinquent behavior in an American city.* Belmont, Calif.: Brooks/Cole, 1970.

Gold, M., & Douvan, E. *Adolescent development: Readings in research and theory.* Boston: Allyn & Bacon, 1969.

Goldberg, M. M. A qualification of the marginal man theory. *American Sociological Review,* 1941, *6,* 52–58.

Goldman, I. Characteristics of jobs held by economically disadvantaged youth. *American Journal of Orthopsychiatry,* 1970, *40*(1), 97–105.

Goldman, N. *The differential selection of juvenile offenders for court appearance.* New York: National Council on Crime and Delinquency, 1963.

Goode, W. J. *After divorce.* New York: Free Press, 1956.

Gordon, C. Social characteristics of early adolescence. In J. Kagan & R. Coles (Eds.), *Twelve to sixteen: Early adolescence.* Pp. 25–54. New York: W. W. Norton, 1972.

Gordon, I. *Human development: From birth through adolescence.* New York: Harper & Row, 1962.

Gorman, B. W. Change in the secondary school: Why and how. *Phi Delta Kappan,* 1972, *53,* 565–568.

Gossett, J. T., Lewis, J. M., & Phillips, V. A. Extent and prevalence of illicit drug use as reported by 56,745 students. *Journal of the American Medical Association,* 1971, *216,* 1464.

Gottlieb, D. Teaching and students: The views of Negro and white teachers. *Sociology of Education,* 1964, *37,* 345–353.

Gottlieb, D., & Hodgkins, B. College student subculture: Their structures and

characteristics in relation to student attitude change. *School Review,* 1963, *71,* 377–385.
Gottlieb, D., & Ramsey, C. *The American adolescent.* Homewood, Ill.: Dorsey Press, 1964.
Gould, L. J. Conformity and marginality—two faces of alienation. *Journal of Social Issues,* 1969, *25*(2), 39–63.
Gregory, C. L., & Lionberger, H. F. *Occupational and educational plans of male high school seniors.* College of Agriculture Research Bulletin No. 937. Columbia: University of Missouri Press, 1968.
Grimes, J. W., & Allinsmith, W. Compulsivity, anxiety and school achievement. *Merrill-Palmer Quarterly,* 1961, *7,* 247–269.
Grinder, R. E. Relations of social dating attractions to academic orientation and peer relations. *Journal of Educational Psychology,* 1966, *57,* 27–34.
Grinder, R. E. Distinctiveness and thrust in the American youth culture. *Journal of Social Issues,* 1969, *25*(2), 7–20.
Grinder, R. E. *Adolescence.* New York: Wiley, 1973.
Grinder, R. E., & Schmitt, S. S. Coeds and contraceptive information. *Journal of Marriage and the Family,* 1966, *28,* 471–479.
Guilford, J. P. Three faces of intellect. *American Psychologist,* 1959, *14,* 469–479.
Guilford, J. P. Intelligence: 1965 model. *American Psychologist,* 1966, *21,* 20–26.
Gump, J. P. Sex-role attitudes and psychological well-being. *Journal of Social Issues,* 1972, *28*(2), 79–92.
Gusfield, J. The structural context of college drinking. In G. L. Maddox (Ed.), *The domesticated drug: Drinking among collegians.* New Haven, Conn.: College and University Press, 1970.
Haan, N., Smith, M. B., & Block, J. Moral reasoning of young adults: Political-social behavior, family background, and personality correlates. *Journal of Personality and Social Psychology,* 1968, *10,* 183–201.
Haeckel, E. *Evolution of man.* London: Routledge & Kegan Paul, 1879.
Hall, C. S., & Lindzey, G. *Theories of personality.* New York: Wiley, 1957.
Hall, G. S. *Adolescence* (Vols. 1, 2). New York: Appleton, 1904.
Hall, G. S. Evolution and psychology. In American Association for the Advancement of Science (Eds.), *Fifty years of Darwinism.* New York: Henry Holt, 1909.
Haller, A. O., & Butterworth, C. E. Peer influence on levels of occupational and educational aspirations. *Social Forces,* 1960, *38,* 289–295.
Hammond, W. Part-time employment. *National Association of Secondary School Principals Bulletin,* 1971, *55* (357), 67.
Haring, D. G. Racial differences and human resemblances. In M. L. Barron (Ed.), *American minorities.* Pp. 33–39. New York: Knopf, 1957.
Harris, L. The *Life* poll. *Life,* May 16, 1969, *66*(19), 22–23.
Harris, L. Change, yes—upheaval, no. *Life,* January 8, 1971, *70*(1), 22–27.
Harsch, C. M., & Schrickel, H. G. *Personality development and assessment.* New York: Ronald Press, 1950.
Hartford, B. Student liberation: Perspective of a political activist. Research Resume No. 38. *Proceedings of the 20th Annual State Conference on Educational Research.* Burlingame, Calif., 1968.
Hartley, M. C., & Hoy, W. K. Openness of school climate and alienation of high school students. *California Journal of Educational Research,* 1972, *23*(1), 17–24.
Hartshorne, H., & May, M. A. *Studies in deceit.* New York: Macmillan, 1928.

Haskell, M. L., & Yablonsky, L. *Crime and delinquency.* Chicago: Rand McNally, 1970.

Hassan, I. N. *The body image and personality correlates of body type stereotypes.* Unpublished doctoral dissertation, Indiana University, 1967.

Havighurst, R. L. *Developmental tasks and education.* New York: McKay, 1952.

Havighurst, R. L. The middle school child in contemporary society. *Theory into Practice,* 1968, 7(3), 120–122.

Havighurst, R. L. Minority subcultures and the law of effect. *American Psychologist,* 1970, 25(4), 313–322.

Havighurst, R. L. *Developmental tasks and education* (3rd ed.). New York: McKay, 1972.

Havighurst, R. L., Graham, R. A., & Eberly, D. American youth in the mid-seventies. *National Association of Secondary School Principals Bulletin,* 1972, 56(357), 1–13.

Havighurst, R. J., & Neugarten, B. L. *Society and education* (3rd ed.). Boston: Allyn & Bacon, 1967.

Hawkes, G. R., Burchinal, L. G., & Gardner, B. Measurement of preadolescents' views of family control of behavior. *Child Development,* 1957, 28, 387–392.

Heald, F. P., Daugela, M., & Brunschyber, P. Physiology of adolescence. *New England Journal of Medicine,* 1963, 268, 192–198; 243–252; 299–307; 361–366.

Hellenbrand, S. C. Client value orientation: Implications for diagnosis. *Social Casework,* 1961, 42, 163–169.

Heller, C. S. *Mexican-American youth: Forgotten youth at the crossroads.* New York: Random House, 1966.

Herriott, R. E. Some social determinants of educational aspiration. *Harvard Educational Review,* 1963, 33, 157–177.

Herzog, E., Sudia, C. E., & Harwood, J. H. Drug use among the young: As teenagers see it. *Children,* 1970, 17(6), 206–212.

Hess, E. H. Imprinting. *Science,* 1959, 130, 133–141.

Hetherington, E. M. A developmental study of the effects of the dominant parent on sex-role preference, identification, and imitation in children. *Journal of Personality and Social Psychology,* 1965, 2, 188–194.

Heyman, F. Methadone maintenance as law and order. *Society,* 1972, 9(8), 15–25.

High school students look at their world. *Ohio Schools,* 1970 48(16), 17–20.

Hilgard, E. R., Atkinson, R. C., & Atkinson, R. L. *Introduction to psychology* (5th ed.). New York: Harcourt Brace Jovanovich, 1971.

Hoffman, M. L., & Hoffman, L. W. (Eds.). *Review of child development research* (Vol. 1). New York: Russell Sage, 1964.

Hoffman, M. L., & Saltzstein, H. D. Parent discipline and the child's moral development. *Journal of Personality and Social Psychology,* 1967, 5, 45–57.

Hollingshead, A. B. *Elmtown's youth.* New York: Wiley, 1949.

Hollingshead, A. B. *Two-factor index of social position.* New Haven, Conn.: Privately printed, 1957.

Hollister, W. G. Preparing the minds of the future. *National Association of Secondary School Principals Bulletin,* 1966, 50, 30–50.

Hollister, W. G. Why adolescents drink and use drugs. *PTA Magazine,* 1969, 63, 2–5.

Holm, J. M. Employment and women: Cinderella is dead! *Journal of the National Association of Women Deans and Counselors,* 1970, 34(1), 6–13.

Horn, D. Behavioral aspects of cigarette smoking. *Journal of Chronic Diseases,* 1963, 16, 383.

Horn, D., Courts, F. A., Taylor, R. M., & Solomon, E. S. Cigarette smoking among high school students. *Journal of Public Health,* 1959, 49, 1497–1511.

Horrocks, J. E. *The psychology of adolescence* (3rd ed.). Boston: Houghton Mifflin, 1969.

Howard, E. R. Developing student responsibility for learning. *National Association of Seconday School Principals Bulletin,* 1966, 50, 235–246.

Hoy, W. K. Dimensions of student alienation and characteristics of public high schools. *Interchange,* 1972, 3(4), 38–52.

Hurlock, E. B. *Adolescent development* (4th ed.). New York: McGraw-Hill, 1973.

Illegitimacy: Data and findings for prevention, treatment, and policy formation. New York: National Council on Illegitimacy, 1965.

Inhelder, B., & Piaget, J. *The growth of logical thinking from childhood to adolescence* (A. Parsons & S. Seagrin, trans.) New York: Basic Books, 1958.

Inselberg, R. M. Social and psychological factors associated with high school marriages. *Journal of Home Economics,* 1961, 53, 766–772.

Inselberg, R. M. Marital problems and satisfaction in high school marriages. *Marriage and Family Living,* 1962, 24, 74–77.

Jackson, R. M., & Cosca, L. R. Methods and results of an every-child program for the early identification of developmental deficits. *Psychology in the Schools,* 1973, 10, 421–426.

Jacobson, C. B., & Stubbs, M. V. L. Clinical and reproductive dangers inherent in use of hallucinogenic agents. *Proceedings of the American Association of Clinical Scientists,* Washington, D.C., 1968.

Jensen, A. R. How much can we boost IQ and scholastic achievement? *Harvard Educational Review,* 1969, 39, 1–123.

Jersild, A. T., & Tasch, R. J. *Children's interests and what they suggest for education.* New York: Teachers College, 1949.

Jessor, R., Collins, M. I., & Jessor, S. L. On becoming a drinker: Social-psychological aspects of an adolescent transition. *Annals of the New York Academy of Sciences,* 1972, 197, 199–213.

Jessor, R., Graves, T. D., Hanson, R. C., & Jessor, S. L. *Society, personality and deviant behavior: A study of a tri-ethnic community.* New York: Holt, Rinehart and Winston, 1968.

Johnson, F. K., & Westman, J. C. The teenager and drug abuse. *Journal of School Health,* 1968, 38, 646–654.

Johnson, M. The adolescent intellect. *Educational Leadership,* 1965, 22, 200–204.

Johnson, W., & Schutt, M. Sex education attitudes of school administrators and school board members. *Journal of School Health,* 1966, 36, 66–67.

Johnston, D. F. Education of workers: Projections to 1990. *Monthly Labor Review,* 1973, 96(11), 23–30.

Johnston, L. Drug use among nation's youth explored in study: Many drugs rejected, marijuana attitudes divided. *Institute for Social Research Newsletter,* 1972, 1(14), 4–5.

Jones, K. L., Shainberg, L. W., & Byer, C. O. *Drugs and alcohol* (2nd ed.). New York: Harper & Row, 1973.

Jones, M. C. The later careers of boys who were early- or late-maturing. *Child Development,* 1957, 28, 113–128.

Jones, M. C., & Bayley, N. Physical maturing among boys as related to behavior. *Journal of Educational Psychology*, 1950, *41*, 129–148.

Juvenile Court Statistics, 1970. Washington, D. C.: National Center for Social Statistics, U. S. Department of Health, Education & Welfare, 1970.

Kaats, G. R., & Davis, K. E. The dynamics of sexual behavior of college students. *Journal of Marriage and the Family*, 1970, *32*(3), 390–399.

Kagan, J. The concept of identification. *Psychological Review*, 1958, *65*, 296–305.

Kahl, J. *Adolescent ambition.* Unpublished doctoral dissertation, Harvard University, 1951.

Kahl, J. A. Educational and occupational aspirations of "common man" boys. *Harvard Educational Review*, 1953, *23*, 186–203.

Kandel, D., & Lesser, G. S. Parent-adolescent relationships and adolescent independence in the United States and Denmark. *Journal of Marriage and the Family*, 1969, *31*(2), 348–358.

Kandel, D. B., & Lesser, G. S. Parental and peer influences on educational plans of adolescents. *American Sociological Review*, 1969, *34*(2), 213–223.

Kaplan, R. *Drug abuse: Perspectives on drugs.* Dubuque, Iowa: W. C. Brown, 1970.

Kardiner, A., & Ovesey, L. *Mark of oppression.* New York: World, 1962.

Kardiner, A., & Ovesey, L. Psychodynamic inventory of the Negro personality. In T. Weaver (Ed.), *To see ourselves.* Pp. 76–83. Glenview, Ill.: Scott, Foresman, 1973.

Katz, I. The socialization of academic motivation in minority group children. In D. LeVine (Ed.), *Nebraska symposium on motivation.* Pp. 133–191. Lincoln: University of Nebraska Press, 1967.

Keele, R. L. A comparison of the effectiveness of remediation of non-readers by trained Mexican-American aides and certified teachers. Paper read at the American Educational Research Association Meeting, New Orleans, February 1973.

Keig, N. G. The occupational aspirations and labor force experience of Negro youth. *American Journal of Economics and Sociology*, 1969, *28*(2), 113–130.

Keislar, E. R. Experimental development of "like" and "dislike" of others among adolescent girls. *Child Development*, 1961, *32*, 59–69.

Keniston, K. *The uncommitted.* New York: Harcourt Brace Jovanovich, 1965.

Keniston, K. *Young radicals: Notes on committed youth.* New York: Harcourt Brace Jovanovich, 1968.

Keniston, K. A second look at the uncommitted. *Social Policy*, 1971, *2*(2), 6–19.

Kestenberg, J. S. Phases of adolescence, Part I: Antecedents of adolescent organizations in childhood. *Journal of Child Psychiatry*, 1967, *6*(3), 426–463. (a)

Kestenberg, J. S. Phases of adolescence, Part II: Prepuberty diffusion and reintegration. *Journal of Child Psychiatry*, 1967, *6*(4), 557–614. (b)

Kestenberg, J. S. Phases of adolescence, Part III: Puberty growth, differentiation, and consolidation. *Journal of Child Psychiatry*, 1968, *7*(1), 108–151.

Kingston, A. J., & Gentry, H. W. Discipline problems and practices in the secondary schools of a Southern state. *National Association of Secondary Schools Principals Bulletin*, 1961, *45*, 34–44.

Kinsey, A. C., Pomeroy, W. B., & Martin, C. E. *Sexual behavior in the human male.* Philadelphia: Saunders, 1948.

Kinsey, A. C., Pomeroy, W. B., & Martin, C. E. *Sexual behavior in the human female.* Philadelphia: Saunders, 1953.

Klein, M. *Street gangs and street workers.* Englewood Cliffs, N. J.: Prentice-Hall, 1971.

Knafle, J. D. The relationship of behavior ratings to grades earned by female high school students. *Journal of Educational Research*, 1972, 66(3), 106–110.
Kohlberg, L. Development of moral character and moral ideology. In M. L. Hoffman & L. W. Hoffman (Eds.), *Review of child development research* (Vol. 1). Pp. 383–441. New York: Russell Sage, 1964.
Kohlberg, L. Indoctrination versus relativity in value education. *Zygon*, 1971, 6(4), 285–310.
Kohlberg, L., & Kramer, R. Continuities and discontinuities in childhood and adult moral development. *Human Development*, 1969, 12, 93–120.
Komarovsky, M. Functional analysis of sex roles. *American Sociological Review*, 1950, 15, 508–516.
Konopka, G. *The adolescent girl in conflict*. Englewood Cliffs, N. J.: Prentice-Hall, 1966.
Konopka, G. Requirements for healthy development of adolescent youth. *Adolescence*, 1973, 8(31), 291–316.
Kowitz, G. T. An analysis of underachievement. In M. Kornich (Ed.), *Underachievement*. Pp. 464–473. Springfield, Ill.: Charles C Thomas, 1965.
Kraft, A. A class for academic underachievers in high school. *Adolescence*, 1969, 4(15), 295–318.
Krauss, I. Sources of educational aspirations among working-class youth. *American Sociological Development*, 1964, 29, 867–879.
Kuo, Z. Y. Studies on the basic factors in animal fighting: VII. Interspecies coexistence in mammals. *Journal of Genetic Psychology*, 1960, 97, 211–225.
Kurtz, R. M. Sex differences and variations in body attitudes. *Journal of Consulting and Clinical Psychology*, 1969, 33, 625–629.
Kuvlesky, W. P., & Bealer, R. C. A clarification of the concept "occupational choice." *Rural Sociology*, 1966, 31, 265–276.
Kuvlesky, W. P., & Obordo, A. S. A racial comparison of teenage girls' projections for marriage and procreation. *Journal of Marriage and the Family*, 1972, pp. 77–84.
Kuvlesky, W. P. & Thomas, K. A. Social ambitions of Negro boys and girls from a metropolitan ghetto. *Journal of Vocational Behavior*, 1971, 1(2), 177–187.
Kuvlesky, W. P., & Upham, W. K. Social ambitions of teen-age boys living in an economically depressed area of the South: A racial comparison. Paper read at the Southern Sociological Society Meeting, Atlanta, 1967.
Kuvlesky, W. P., Wright, D. E., & Juarez, R. Z. Status projections and ethnicity: A comparison of Mexican American, Negro, and Anglo youth. *Journal of Vocational Behavior*, 1971, 1(2), 137–151.
Kvaraceus, W. C. *Anxious youth: Dynamics of delinquency*. Columbus, Ohio: Merrill, 1966.
Kvaraceus, W. C. Delinquency prevention: Legislation, financing, and law enforcement are not enough. *Crime and Delinquency*, 1969, 15, 463–470.
Kvaraceus, W. C., & Ulrich, W. E. *Delinquent behavior: Principles and practices*. Washington, D.C.: National Education Association, 1959.
Landis, J. T. The trauma of children when parents divorce. *Marriage and Family Living*, 1960, 22, 7–13.
Larson, L. E. The influence of parents and peers during adolescence: The situation hypothesis revisited. *Journal of Marriage and the Family*, 1972, 34, 66–75.
Larson, L. E. System and subsystem perception of family roles. *Journal of Marriage and the Family*, 1974, 36, 123–138.
Larson, W. R., & Myerhoff, B. G. Primary and formal family organization and

adolescent socialization. *Sociology and Social Research,* 1965, *50,* 63–71.

Late onset asthma linked to aspirin sensitivity. *Journal of the American Medical Association,* 1972, *221*(3), 244.

Latham, A. J. The relationship between puberal status and leadership in junior high school boys. *Journal of Genetic Psychology,* 1951, *78,* 185–194.

Lee, M. R. Background factors related to sex information and attitudes. *Journal of Educational Psychology,* 1952, *43,* 467–485.

Leggett, J. C., & Cervinka, C. Countdown: Labor statistics revisited. *Society,* 1972, *10*(1), 99–103.

Leidy, T. R., & Starry, A. R. The American adolescent—a bewildering amalgam. *National Education Association Journal,* 1967, pp. 8–12.

Lemert, E. M. Social structure, social control, and deviation. In M. Clinard (Ed.), *Anomie and deviant behavior.* New York: Free Press, 1964.

Lennard, H. L., Epstein, L. J., & Rosenthal, M. S. The methadone illusion. *Science,* 1972, *176,* 881–884.

Lerman, P. Gangs, networks, and subcultural delinquency. *American Journal of Sociology,* 1967, *73,* 63–72.

Lerner, R. M., Schroeder, C., Rewitzer, M., & Weinstock, A. Attitudes of high school students and their parents toward contemporary issues. *Psychological Reports,* 1972, *31,* 255–258.

Leuthold, F. O., Farmer, C. M., & Badenhop, M. B. *Migration of young adults from a low-income rural county.* Tennessee Farm and Home Science Progress Report No. 63. Knoxville: Tennessee Agricultural Experiment Station, 1967.

Lever, M. F., & Upham, W. K. *Poverty among nonwhite families in Texas and the nation: A comparative analysis.* College Station: Texas A & M University, Texas Agricultural Experimental Station, 1968.

Levin, T. New myths about drug programs. *Social Policy,* 1971, *2*(3), 30–33.

Levitt, E. E., & Edwards, J. A. A multivariate study of correlative factors in youthful cigarette smoking. *Developmental Psychology,* 1970, *2,* 5–11.

Levy, L. Drug use on campus: Prevalence and social characteristics of collegiate drug users on campuses of the University of Illinois. *Drug Forum,* 1973, *2*(2), 141–171.

Lewin, K. *Resolving social conflict.* New York: Harper & Row, 1941.

Lewis, D. C. Drug education. *National Association of Secondary School Principals Bulletin,* 1969, *53*(341), 87–98.

Lewis, D. C. How the schools can prevent drug abuse. *National Association of Secondary School Principals Bulletin,* 1970, *54*(346), 43–51.

Lewis, D. C. Drug education and prevention. In H. D. Thornburg (Ed.), *Contemporary adolescence: Readings* (2nd ed.). Monterey, Calif.: Brooks/Cole, 1975.

Lewis, L. S. The value of college to different subcultures. *School Review,* 1966, *77,* 32–40.

Lindstrom, D. E. Educational needs of rural youth. *Journal of Cooperative Extension,* 1965, *3,* 33–41.

Linner, B. What does equality between the sexes imply? *American Journal of Orthopsychiatry,* 1971, *41*(5), 747–756.

Lionberger, H. F., & Gregory, C. L. *Occupational and college choices of farm and non-farm male high school seniors in Missouri.* Columbia: University of Missouri, Department of Rural Sociology, 1965.

Lipset, S. M., & Bendix, R. *Social mobility in an industrial society.* Berkeley: University of California Press, 1962.

Liquor hurts livers, regardless of diet. *Journal of the American Medical Association,* 1974, *228*(4), 447.

Little, J. K. The occupations of non-college youth. *American Educational Research Journal,* 1967, *4*, 147–154.

Litwin, G. H., & Stringer, R. A. *Motivation and organizational climate.* Cambridge, Mass.: Harvard Graduate School of Business Administration, Division of Research, 1968.

Long, D., Elkind, D., & Spilka, B. The child's conception of prayer. *Journal of the Scientific Study of Religion,* 1967, *6*, 101–109.

Looft, W. R. Egocentrism and social interaction in adolescence. *Adolescence,* 1971, *6*(24), 487–494.

Loree, M. R. *Psychology of education* (2nd ed.). New York: Ronald Press, 1970.

Loughman, W. Leukocytes of humans exposed to LSD—Lack of chromosomal damage. *Science,* 1967, *158*, 508.

Lowrie, S. H. Factors involved in the frequency of dating. *Marriage and Family Living,* 1956, *18*, 46–51.

Lowry, T. P. First coitus. *Medical Aspects of Human Sexuality,* 1969, *3*(5), 91–97.

Luckey, E. B., & Nass, G. D. A comparison of sexual attitudes and behavior in an international sample. *Journal of Marriage and the Family,* 1969, *31*, 364–379.

Ludwig, A. M., & Levine, J. Patterns of hallucinogenic drug abuse. *Journal of the American Medical Association,* 1965, *191*(2), 92–96.

MacIver, R. M., & Page, C. H. *Society: An introductory analysis.* New York: Rinehart, 1949.

Maddox, G. L. *The domesticated drug: Drinking among collegians.* New Haven, Conn.: Yale University Press, 1970.

Malinowski, B. *Sex and repression in savage society.* New York: Harcourt, Brace, 1927.

Malinowski, B. *Argonauts of the Western Pacific.* New York: Dutton, 1961. (Originally published, 1922.)

Mannheim, K. *Essays on the sociology of knowledge.* London: Routledge & Kegan Paul, 1952.

Manuel, H. T. *Spanish-speaking children of the Southwest—their education and welfare.* Austin: University of Texas Press, 1965.

Marcia, J. E., & Friedman, M. L. Ego identity status in college women. *Journal of Personality,* 1970, *38*, 249–263.

Martinson, F. M. Sexual knowledge, values, and behavior patterns of adolescents. *Child Welfare,* 1968, *47*, 405–410.

Maslow, A. H. A theory of human motivation. *Psychological Review,* 1943, *50*, 370–396.

Mausner, B., & Mischler, J. B. Cigarette smoking among junior high school students. *Journal of Special Education,* 1967, *1*, 61–66.

McCandless, B. R. *Adolescents: Behavior and development.* Hinsdale, Ill.: Dryden, 1970.

McClelland, D. C. *The achieving society.* Princeton, N.J.: Van Nostrand Reinhold, 1961.

McClelland, D. C., & Alschuler, A. E. *The achievement motivation development project.* Final Report, U.S. Office of Education, Project 7-1231. U.S. Government Printing Office, 1971.

McCord, J., McCord, W., & Thurber, E. Some effects of paternal absence on male children. *Journal of Abnormal and Social Psychology*, 1962, 64(5), 361–369.

McCord, J., McCord, W., & Thurber, E. Effects of maternal employment on lower-class boys. *Journal of Abnormal and Social Psychology*, 1963, 67, 177–182.

McDill, E. L., & Coleman, J. Family and peer influences in college plans of high school students. *Sociology of Education*, 1965, 38, 112–126.

McKennell, A. C. Smoking motivation factors. *British Journal of Social and Clinical Psychology*, 1970, 9, 8–22.

McNeil, E. B. *Human socialization*. Monterey, Calif.: Brooks/Cole, 1969.

Mead, M. *Coming of age in Samoa*. New York: Mentor, 1928.

Mead, M. *Growing up in New Guinea*. New York: New American Library, 1935.

Mead, M. *From the South Seas: Studies of adolescence and sex in primitive societies*. New York: Morrow, 1939.

Mead, M. *Culture and commitment: A study of the generation gap*. New York: Basic Books, 1970.

Mead, M. Future family. *Transaction*, 1971, 8(11), 50–53.

Medical group favors milder marijuana laws. *Journal of the American Medical Association*, 1974, 227(3), 262.

Meissner, W. W. Parental interaction of the adolescent boy. *Journal of Genetic Psychology*, 1965, 107, 225–233.

Meredith, H. V. The rhythm of physical growth: A study of eighteen anthropometric measurements. *University of Iowa Studies in Child Welfare*, 1939, 11(3), 128.

Meredith, H. V. A synopsis of pubertal changes in youth. *Journal of School Health*, 1967, 37, 171–176.

Merton, R. K. *Social theory and social structure*. New York: Free Press, 1957.

Michelotti, K. Young workers: In school and out. *Monthly Labor Review*, 1973, 96(11), 11–15.

Miller, W. B. Lower class culture as a generating milieu of gang delinquency. *Journal of Social Issues*, 1957, 14, 5–19.

Miller, W. B. Violent crimes in city gangs. *Annals of the American Academy of Political and Social Science*, 1966, 364, 96–112.

Modern medicine poll on sociomedical issues: Abortion-homosexual practices-marijuana. *Modern Medicine*, 1969, 37(22), 18–25.

Moore, B. M., & Holtzman, W. H. *Tomorrow's parents*. Austin, Texas: Hogg Foundation for Mental Health, 1965.

Morrow, W. R., & Wilson, R. C. Family relations of bright high-achieving and under-achieving high school boys. *Child Development*, 1961, 32, 501–510.

Mowrer, O. H. *Learning theory and personality dynamics* (2nd ed.). New York: Ronald Press, 1960.

Murdock, G. P. *Social structure*. New York: Macmillan, 1949.

Musgrove, F. The social needs and satisfactions of some young people: Part 1—At home, in youth clubs, and at work. *British Journal of Educational Psychology*, 1966, 36, 61–71.

Mussen, P. H., Conger, J. J., & Kagan, J. *Child development and personality* (3rd ed.). New York: Harper & Row, 1974.

Mussen, P. H., & Jones, M. C. Self-conceptions, motivations, and interpersonal attitudes of late- and early-maturing boys. *Child Development*, 1957, 28, 242–256.

Mussen, P. H., & Rutherford, E. Parent-child relations and parental personality in relation to young children's sex role preferences. *Child Development,* 1963, *34,* 589–607.

Muuss, R. E. Jean Piaget's cognitive theory of adolescent development. *Adolescence,* 1967, *2*(7), 285–310.

Muuss, R. E. *Theories of adolescence* (3rd ed.). New York: Random House, 1975.

Myerhoff, B. G., & Larson, W. R. Primary and formal aspects of family organization: Group consensus, problem perception, and adolescent success. *Journal of Marriage and the Family,* 1965, *29,* 213–217.

Nader, R. Lo, the poor Indian. *The New Republic,* March 30, 1968, *158,* 14–15.

Nelson, D. D. A study of personality adjustment among adolescent children with working and non-working mothers. *Journal of Educational Research,* 1971, *64*(7), 328–330.

Nelson, R. A., & Gastineau, C. F. Exceptional nutritional needs of the athlete. Paper read at the Annual Conference on the Medical Aspects of Sports, San Diego, Calif., 1973.

New black student. *Sooner Magazine,* 1969, *41*(4), 8–11.

"New Left" in action. *U. S. News and World Report,* May 19, 1969, *66*(20), 35–37.

Norman, R. D. The interpersonal values of achieving and nonachieving gifted children. *Journal of Psychology,* 1966, *64,* 49–57.

Nowlis, H. H. *Drugs on the college campus.* New York: Anchor, 1969.

Nye, F. I. Adolescent-parent adjustment: Age, sex sibling number, broken homes, and employed mothers as variables. *Marriage and Family Living,* 1952, *14,* 327–332.

Nye, F. I. Child adjustment in broken and unhappy unbroken homes. *Marriage and Family Living,* 1957, *19,* 356–361.

Nye, F. I. *Family relationships and delinquent behavior.* New York: Wiley, 1959.

Nye, F. I., Short, J. F., Jr., & Olson, V. J. Socioeconomic status and delinquent behavior. *American Journal of Sociology,* 1958, *63,* 318–329.

O'Connell, W. E. The adaptive functions of wit and humor. *Journal of Abnormal and Social Psychology,* 1960, *61,* 263–270.

Ostermeier, A. L. Adolescent behavior as manifested in clothing. *Bulletin of the State University College, Buffalo,* 1967, *3,* 1–9.

Packard, V. *The status seekers.* New York: Pocket Books, 1961.

Packard, V. *Sexual wilderness.* New York: Pocket Books, 1968.

Parsons, T. *The structure of social action.* Glencoe, Ill.: Free Press, 1947.

Patella, V. M. *A study of the validity of language usage as an indicator of ethnic identification.* Unpublished master's thesis, Texas A & M University, 1971.

Pearce, J. The role of education in combating drug abuse. *Journal of School Health,* 1971, *41,* 83–87.

Perrella, V. C. Working teenagers. *Children Today,* 1972, *1*(3), 14–17.

Perrella, V. C., & Bogan, F. A. Out-of-school youth, February 1963. *Monthly Labor Review,* 1964, *87,* 1260–1268.

Peterson, D. R., Becker, W. C., Hellmer, L. A., Shoemaker, D. J., & Quay, H. C. Parental attitudes and child adjustment. In N. S. Endler, L. R. Boulter, & H. Osser (Eds.), *Contemporary issues in developmental psychology.* Pp. 590–598. New York: Holt, Rinehart and Winston, 1968.

Petras, J. W. *Sexuality in society.* Boston: Allyn & Bacon, 1973.

Petrich, B., & Chadderdon, H. Family beliefs of junior high school pupils. *Family Coordinator,* 1969, *18*(4), 374–378.

Phillips, J. L., Jr. *The origins of intellect: Piaget's theory.* San Francisco: Freeman, 1969.

Piaget, J. *The moral judgment of the child.* Glencoe, Ill.: Free Press, 1948.

Piaget, J. *The psychology of intelligence* (trans. M. Percy & D. E. Berlyne). London: Routledge & Kegan Paul, 1950.

Piaget, J. *The origins of intelligence in children* (trans. M. Cook). New York: International Press, 1952.

Piaget, J. *The child's conception of physical causality* (trans. M. Gabain). Totowa, N. J.: Littlefield, Adams, 1960.

Piaget, J. A theory of development. In D. L. Sills (Ed.), *International encyclopedia of the social sciences,* 1966.

Pickle, D. E. Periodontal disease: Part II—Prognosis. *Journal of the American Dental Hygienists' Association,* 1967, 41(2), 77–80.

Pine, G. U. The affluent delinquent. *Phi Delta Kappan,* 1966, 48(4), 138–143.

Polk, K. A reassessment of middle-class delinquency. *Youth and Society,* 1971, 2(3), 333–354.

Pollock, M. J. Changing the role of women. *American Journal of Orthopsychiatry,* 1971, 41(5), 716–724.

Pop drugs: The high as a way of life. *Time,* 1969, 94(13), 68–78.

Pope, H., & Knudsen, D. D. Premarital sexual norms: The family and social change. *Journal of Marriage and the Family,* 1965, 27(3), 314–323.

Porterfield, A. L. *Youth in trouble.* Fort Worth, Texas: Leo Potishman Foundation, 1946.

Propper, M. M., & Clark, E. T. Alienation: Another dimension of underachievement. *The Journal of Psychology,* 1970, 75, 13–18.

Rallings, E. M. Problems of communication in family living. *Family Coordinator,* 1969, 18, 289–291.

Rampage at Fair Harbor. *Life,* 1969, 66(16), 24–35.

Ramsey, C. V. Sex information of younger boys. *American Journal of Orthopsychiatry,* 1943, 13, 347–352.

Rehberg, R. A. Behavioral and attitudinal consequences of high school interscholastic sports: A speculative consideration. *Adolescence,* 1969, 4(13), 69–88.

Rehberg, R. A., & Shafer, W. E. Participation in interscholastic athletics and college expectations. *American Journal of Sociology,* 1968, 73(6), 732–740.

Rehberg, R. A. & Westby, D. L. Parental encouragement, occupation, education and family size: Artificial or independent determinants of adolescent educational expectations? *Social Forces,* 1967, 45, 362–374.

Reich, C. A. *The greening of America.* New York: Random House, 1970.

Reiss, A. J., & Rhodes, A. L. The distribution of juvenile delinquency in the social class structure. *American Sociological Review,* 1961, 26, 720–732.

Reiss, I. L. *Premarital sexual standards in America.* New York: Free Press, 1960.

Reiss, I. L. Standards of sexual behavior. In A. Ellis & A. Abarbanel (Eds.), *Encyclopedia of sex.* New York: Hawthorne, 1961.

Reiss, I. L. The sexual renaissance: A summary and analysis. *Journal of Social Issues,* 1966, 22, 126.

Reiss, I. L. *The social context of premarital sexual permissiveness.* New York: Holt, Rinehart and Winston, 1967.

Reiss, I. L. The influence of contraceptive knowledge on premarital sexuality. *Medical Aspects of Human Sexuality,* 1970, 4(2), 71–86. (a)

Reiss, I. L. Premarital sex as deviant behavior: An application of current approaches to deviance. *American Sociological Review*, 1970, 35(1), 78–87. (b)

Reiss, I. L. *The family system in America.* New York: Holt, Rinehart and Winston, 1971.

Reynolds, E. L., & Wines, J. V. Individual differences in physical changes associated with adolescence in girls. *American Journal of Diseases of Children*, 1948, 75, 329–350.

Richards, L. G., Joffe, M. H., Smith, J. P., & Spratto, G. R. *Layman's guide to pharmacology, physiology, psychology, and sociology of LSD.* Washington, D.C.: U.S. Government Printing Office, 1969.

Rieger, J. H. Geographic mobility and the occupational attainment of rural youth: A longitudinal evaluation. *Rural Sociology*, 1972, 37(2), 189–207.

Rigsby, L. C., & McDill, E. L. Adolescent peer influence processes: Conceptualization and measurement. *Social Science Research*, 1972, 1, 305–321.

Robeck, M. C. Comparison of red Indian and white American children on language functioning. Paper read at the Annual Meeting of the California Educational Research Association, San Diego, Calif., 1971.

Robinson, D. Scraps from a teacher's notebook. *Phi Delta Kappan*, 1967, 49, 160.

Robinson, I. E., King, K., & Balswick, J. O. The premarital sexual revolution among college females. *Family Coordinator*, 1972, 21, 189–194.

Robinson, I. E., King, K., Dudley, C. J., & Clune, F. J. Change in sexual behavior and attitudes of college students. *Family Coordinator*, 1968, 17, 119–123.

Rogers, D. *Adolescence: A psychological perspective.* Monterey, Calif.: Brooks/Cole, 1972. (a)

Rogers, D. *The psychology of adolescence* (2nd ed.). New York: Appleton-Century-Crofts, 1972. (b)

Rogers, E. Group influence on student drinking behavior. In G. L. Maddox (Ed.), *The domesticated drug: Drinking among collegians.* New Haven, Conn.: College and University Press, 1970.

Rose, P. I. *They and we: Racial and ethnic relations in the United States.* New York: Random House, 1964.

Rosen, B. C. Conflicting group membership: A study of parent-peer group cross-pressures. *American Sociological Review*, 1955, 20, 155–161.

Rosen, B. C. The achievement syndrome: A psychocultural dimension of social stratification. *American Sociological Review*, 1956, 21, 203–211.

Rosen, B. C. Socialization and achievement motivation in Brazil. *American Sociological Review*, 1962, 27, 612–624.

Rosen, B. C. Family structure and value transmission. *Merrill-Palmer Quarterly*, 1964, 10, 59–76.

Rosenfeld, C., & Gover, K. R. Employment of school-age youth. *Monthly Labor Review*, 1972, 95, 26–30.

Rosenmayr, L. Introduction: New theoretical approaches to the sociological study of young people. *International Social Science Journal*, 1972, 24(2), 216–256.

Ross, D. *G. Stanley Hall.* Chicago: University of Chicago Press, 1972.

Roszak, T. *The making of a counter culture: Reflections on the technocratic society and its youthful opposition.* New York: Anchor Books, 1969.

Rothman, J. Minority group status, mental health, and intergroup relations: An appraisal of Kurt Lewin's thesis. *Journal of Intergroup Relations*, 1962, 3, 299–310.

Rotter, J. B., & Rafferty, J. *Manual for the Rotter Incomplete Sentences Blank, College Form*. New York: Psychological Corporation, 1950.

Rouman, J. Schoolchildren's problems as related to parental factors. *Journal of Educational Psychology*, 1956, 50, 105–112.

Roy, P. Adolescent roles: Rural-urban differentials. *Marriage and Family Living*, 1961, 23, 340–349.

Russell, D. G., & Sarason, I. G. Test anxiety, sex, and experimental conditions in relation to anagram solution. *Journal of Personality and Social Psychology*, 1965, 1, 493–496.

Ryan, M. S. *Clothing: A study in human behavior*. New York: Holt, Rinehart and Winston, 1966.

Ryscavage, P. M., & Mellor, E. F. The economic situation of Spanish Americans. *Monthly Labor Review*, 1973, 96(4), 3–7.

Salber, E. J., & McMahon, B. Cigarette smoking among high school students related to social class and parental smoking habits. *American Journal of Public Health*, 1961, 51, 1780–1789.

Sampson, E. E. Status congruence and cognitive consistency. *Sociometry*, 1963, 26, 146–162.

Sanford, R. N., Adkins, N. M., Miller, R. B., Cobb, E. A., et al. Physique, personality, and scholarship: A cooperative study of schoolchildren. *Monograph of Social Research and Child Development*, 1943, 8(1).

San Mateo Department of Public Health and Welfare. *Surveillance of student drug use, San Mateo County, California, 1973*. San Mateo, Calif., 1973.

Sasidhorn, N. Youth problems in Thailand. *Youth and Society*, 1970, 1(4), 380–391.

Sauber, M., & Rubinstein, E. *Experiences of the unwed mother as a parent*. New York: Community Council of Greater New York, 1965.

Scammon, R., & Wattenberg, B. J. *The real majority*. New York: Coward-McCann, 1970.

Schab, F. Adolescence in the south: A comparison of white and Negro attitudes about home, school, religion and morality. *Adolescence*, 1968, 3(9), 33–38.

Schab, F. Cheating in high schools: Differences between the sexes. *Journal of the National Association of Women Deans and Counselors*, 1969, 33(1), 39–42.

Schab, F. Honor and dishonor in the secondary schools of three cultures. *Adolescence*, 1971, 6(22), 145–154.

Schaffer, H. R., & Emerson, P. E. The development of social attachments in infancy. *Society for Research in Child Development Monographs*, 1964, 29(3), Series No. 94.

Schaimberg, L. Some sociocultural factors in adolescent-parent conflict. A cross-cultural comparison of selected cultures. *Adolescence*, 1969, 4, 333–360.

Scharf, J. *The effects of anxiety, stress instructions, and difficulty on verbal problem solving behavior*. Unpublished doctoral dissertation, New York University, 1964.

Scheinfeld, A. *Heredity in humans* (Rev. ed.). Philadelphia: Lippincott, 1971.

Schepp, G. J. Survey of going steady and other dating practices. *American Catholic Sociological Review*, 1960, 20, 238–250.

Schilder, P. The image and appearance of the human body. In *Studies of the construction energies of the psyche*. London: Routledge & Kegan Paul, 1935.

Schneider, A. J. *Measurement of courtship progress of high school upperclassmen currently going steady.* Unpublished doctoral dissertation, Pennsylvania State University, 1966.

Schofield, M. *The sexual behavior of young people.* Boston: Little, Brown, 1965.

Schonfeld, W. A. Body-image disturbances in adolescents with inappropriate sexual development. *American Journal of Orthopsychiatry,* 1964, *34,* 493–502.

Schrag, P. The schools of Appalachia. In D. Gottlieb & H. L. Heinsohn (Eds.), *America's other youth: Growing up poor.* Pp. 117–122. New York: Prentice-Hall, 1971.

Schuck, R. F. Attitudes of Arizona educators toward specific content areas in sex education. *Journal of School Health,* 1972, *42,* 122–125.

Schwartz, M. S. Report of sex information knowledge of 87 lower class ninth grade boys. *Family Coordinator,* 1969, *18,* 361–371.

Scott, J. P. Critical periods in the development of social behavior in puppies. *Psychosomatic Medicine,* 1958, *20,* 42–54.

Sears, P. S. Child-rearing factors related to playing of sex-typed roles. *American Psychologist,* 1953, *8,* 431.

Sears, R. R., Maccoby, E. R., & Levin, H. *Patterns of child rearing.* Evanston, Ill.: Row, Peterson, 1957.

Sebald, H. *Adolescence: A sociological analysis.* New York: Appleton-Century-Crofts, 1968.

Seeley, J. Youth in revolt. In *Britannica book of the year.* Pp. 313–315. Chicago: University of Chicago Press, 1969.

Sewell, W. H., Haller, A., & Straus, M. Social status and educational occupational aspirations. *American Sociological Review,* 1957, *22,* 67–73.

Sewell, W. H., & Shah, V. P. Social class, parental encouragement, and educational aspirations. *American Journal of Sociology,* 1968, *73,* 559–572.

Sex education, doctors, and the backlash. *Medical World News,* 1969, *10*(40), 25–28D.

Shafer, R. P. (Chmn.). *Marijuana: A signal of misunderstanding.* New York: Signet, 1972.

Shanley, B. C., Zail, S. S., & Joubert, S. M. *Lancet,* 1968, *1,* 70.

Shanley, B. C., Zail, S. S., & Joubert, S. M. *British Journal of Hoematology,* 1969, *17,* 389.

Shanley, F. J. Middle-class delinquency as a social problem. *Sociology and Social Research,* 1967, *51,* 185–198.

Sheldon, W. H. *The varieties of human physique.* New York: Harper & Row, 1940.

Sheldon, W. H. *The varieties of temperament.* New York: Harper & Row, 1942.

Sherif, C. W., & Sherif, M. Seeking thrills with the "in" crowd. *PTA Magazine,* 1966, *60,* 5–6.

Sherif, M., & Sherif, C. W. *Reference groups: Exploration into conformity and deviation of adolescents.* New York: Harper & Row, 1964.

Sherif, M., & Sherif, C. W. *Problems of youth: Transition to adulthood in a changing world.* Chicago: Aldine, 1965.

Short, J. F., Jr., & Strodtbeck, F. L. *Group processes and gang delinquency.* Chicago: University of Chicago Press, 1965.

Shuttleworth, F. K. Sexual maturation and the physical growth of girls ages 6 to 19. *Society for Research in Child Development Monographs,* 1937, *2*(5), 291.

Shuttleworth, F. K. The physical and mental growth of girls and boys ages 6 to 19 in relation to age at maximum growth. *Society for Research in Child Development Monographs*, 1944, 9(1), 291.
Sieg, A. Why adolescence occurs. *Adolescence*, 1971, 6(23), 337–348.
Silberman, C. E. *Crisis in the classroom: The remaking of American education*. New York: Random House, 1970.
Simon, H. A. *The science of the artificial*. Cambridge, Mass.: M.I.T. Press, 1969.
Simpson, R. L. Parental influence, anticipatory socialization, and social mobility. *American Sociological Review*, 1962, 27, 517–522.
Singer, S. L., & Stefflre, B. Sex differences in job values and desires. *Personnel and Guidance Journal*, 1954, 22, 483–484.
Skolnick, J. H. Religious affiliation and drinking behavior. *Quarterly Journal of Studies on Alcohol*, 1958, 19, 452–470.
Slater, P. *The pursuit of loneliness: American culture at the breaking point*. Boston: Beacon Press, 1970.
Slater, P. E. Parental behavior and the personality of the child. *Journal of Genetic Psychology*, 1962, 101, 53–68.
Slocum, W. L. *Agricultural sociology: A study of sociological aspects of American farm life*. New York: Harper & Row, 1962.
Slocum, W. L., & Stone, C. L. Family culture patterns and delinquent-type behavior. *Marriage and Family Living*, 1963, 25, 202–208.
Smart, R. G., Fejer, D., & White, J. *The extent of drug use in metropolitan Toronto schools: A study of changes from 1968 to 1970*. Toronto: Addiction Research Foundation, 1970.
Smartt, W. H., & Lighter, A. G. The gonorrhea epidemic and its control. *Medical Aspects of Human Sexuality*, 1971, 5(1), 96–115.
Smigel, E. O., & Seiden, R. The decline and fall of the double standard. *Annals of the American Academy of Political and Social Science*, 1968, 376, 6–17.
Smith, C. E. *Child development*. Dubuque, Iowa: W. C. Brown, 1966.
Smith, D. D. The trip there and back. *Emergency Medicine*, 1969, 1, 26–41.
Smith, M. E. Report to parents of students in Castro Valley Unified School District. In D. F. Berg (Ed.), *Illicit use of dangerous drugs in the United States: A compilation of studies, surveys, and polls*. Drug Sciences Division, Bureau of Narcotics and Dangerous Drugs. Washington, D.C.: U.S. Government Printing Office, 1970.
Snyder, C. R. *Alcohol and the Jews*. Glencoe, Ill.: Free Press, 1958.
Snyder, E. E. High school athletes and their coaches: Educational plans and advice. *Sociology of Education*, 1972, 45, 313–325.
Snyder, E. E. High school student perceptions of prestige criteria. *Adolescence*, 1972, 6(25), 129–136.
Solomon, T. *A pilot study among East Village "hippies."* Monograph No. 35. New York: Associated YM-YMHAs of Greater New York, 1968.
Somers, R. H. The mainsprings of the rebellion: A survey of Berkeley students in November, 1964. In S. M. Lipset & S. S. Wolin (Eds.), *The Berkeley student revolt*. Pp. 530–537. New York: Anchor, 1965.
Sorensen, R. C. *Adolescent sexuality in contemporary America*. New York: World, 1973.
Southam, A. L., & Gonzaga, F. P. Systemic changes during the menstrual cycle. *American Journal of Obstetrics and Gynecology*, 1965, 91, 142–165.
Spanish-speaking Americans: Their manpower problems and opportunities. *Manpower Report of the President*, 1973, pp. 85–112.

Spaulding, R. L. What teacher attributes bring out the best in gifted children? *Gifted Child Quarterly*, 1963, 7, 150–156.
Spaulding, R. L. Achievement, creativity, and self-concept correlates of teacher-pupil transactions in elementary schools. In C. B. Stendler (Ed.), *Readings in child behavior and development*. Pp. 313–318. New York: Harcourt Brace Jovanovich, 1964.
Spearman, C. *The abilities of man*. New York: Macmillan, 1927.
Spearman, C., & Jones, L. W. *Human ability*. London: Macmillan, 1950.
Spielberger, C. D. The effects of anxiety on complex learning and academic achievement. In C. D. Spielberger (Ed.), *Anxiety and behavior*. Pp. 361–398. New York: Academic Press, 1966.
Spranger, E. *Types of men* (trans. P.J.W. Pigoros). Halle-Saale, Germany: Max Niemeyer, 1928.
Spranger, E. *Psychologie des Jugendalters* (24th ed.). Heidelberg, Germany: Quelle & Meyer, 1955.
Spreitzer, E., & Pugh, M. Interscholastic athletics and educational expectations. *Sociology of Education*, 1973, 46, 171–182.
Sprey, J. Sex differences in occupational choice patterns among Negro adolescents. *Social Problems*, 1962, 10, 11–22.
Staffieri, J. R. A study of social stereotype of body image in children. *Journal of Personality and Social Psychology*, 1967, 7, 101–104.
Staffieri, J. R. Body build and behavioral expectancies in young females. *Developmental Psychology*, 1972, 6, 125–127.
Stahmann, R. F., Hanson, G. R., & Whittlesey, R. R. Parent and student perceptions of influences on college choice. *National Association of College Admissions Counselors Journal*, 1973, 16(2), 21–22.
Stark, E. Up from the underground: Notes on youth culture. In S. D. Feldman & G. W. Thielbar (Eds.), *Life styles: Diversity in American society*. Pp. 265–272. Boston: Little, Brown, 1972.
Stephenson, R. M. Realism of vocational choice: A critique and an example. *Personnel and Guidance Journal*, 1957, 35, 482–488.
Stevic, R., & Uhlig, G. Occupational aspirations of selected Appalachian youth. *Personnel and Guidance Journal*, 1967, 45, 435–439.
Stolz, H. R., & Stolz, L. M. Adolescence related to somatic variation. In *Adolescence: 43rd yearbook of the National Committee for the Study of Education*. Pp. 80–99. Chicago: University of Chicago Press, 1944.
Stone, C. L. Family recreation: A family dilemma. *Family Life Coordinator*, 1963, 12, 85–87.
Stonequist, E. *The marginal men: A study in personality and culture conflict*. New York: Scribner, 1937.
Strack, A. E. Drug use and abuse among youth. *Journal of Health, Physical Education, and Recreation*, 1968, 39, 26–28; 55–57.
Straus, M. A. Conjugal power structure and adolescent personality. *Marriage and Family Living*, 1962, 24, 17–25.
Strodtbeck, F. L. Family interaction, values, and achievement. In D. C. McClelland et al., *Talent and society*. New York: Van Nostrand, 1958.
Suchman, E. A. The "hang-loose" ethic and the spirit of drug use. *Journal of Health and Social Behavior*, 1968, 9, 146–155.
Sundby, P. *Alcoholism and mortality*. Oslo, Norway: Universitetsforlaget, 1967.
Super, D. E., & Overstreet, P. L. *The vocational maturity of ninth-grade boys*. New York: Columbia University Bureau of Publications, 1960.

Talbot, N. B., et al. *Functional endocrinology from birth through adolescence.* Cambridge, Mass.: Harvard University Press, 1952.

Tanner, J. M. *Education and physical growth.* London: University of London Press, 1961.

Tanner, J. M. *Growth at adolescence* (2nd ed.). Oxford: Blackwell Scientific Publications, 1962.

Taylor, J., & Gonring, R. W. Venereal disease campaign in Colorado—A model for community action. *Health Services Reports,* 1974, 89(1), 47–52.

Tenenbaum, S. Uncontrolled expressions of children's attitudes toward school. *Elementary School Journal,* 1940, 40, 670–678.

Terman, L. M., et al. *Psychological factors in marital happiness.* New York: McGraw-Hill, 1938.

Terry, C. E., & Pellens, M. *The opium problem.* Camden, N.J.: Haddon Craftsmen, 1928.

Thomas, E. C., & Yamamoto, K. Minority children and their school-related perceptions. *Journal of Experimental Education,* 1971, 40, 89–96.

Thomas, K. A. A comparison of teenage boys' and girls' orientations towards marriage and procreation. Paper presented at the Southwestern Sociological Association Meeting, New Orleans, 1972.

Thomas, K. A., & Jacob, N. L. A longitudinal analysis of change in occupational and educational orientations of east Texas boys: A racial comparison. Paper presented at the Rural Sociological Society Meeting, Washington, D. C., 1970.

Thomes, M. M. Children with absent fathers. *Journal of Marriage and the Family,* 1968, 30(1), 89–96.

Thompson, D. C. Development of attitudes in respect to discrimination. *American Journal of Orthopsychiatry,* 1962, 41, 687–693.

Thompson, G. G., & Gardner, E. F. Adolescents: Perceptions of happy, successful living. *Journal of Genetic Psychology,* 1969, 115, 107–120.

Thompson, O. E. What is the high school student of today like? *Journal of Secondary Education,* 1961, 36, 210–219.

Thompson, O. E. Occupational values of high school students. *Personnel and Guidance Journal,* 1966, 34, 850–853.

Thornburg, H. D. Administering a sex education program. *Arizona Teacher,* 1968, 57(2), 18–19; 24. (a)

Thornburg, H. D. Sex education, Part II: The student. *Arizona Teacher,* 1968, 57(1), 11; 27–28. (b)

Thornburg, H. D. Sex education: A teaching approach. *Arizona Teacher,* 1968, 56(5), 12–13. (c)

Thornburg, H. D. Evaluating the sex education program. *Arizona Teacher,* 1969, 57(3), 18–20. (a)

Thornburg, H. D. *Sex education in the public schools.* Phoenix: Arizona Education Association, 1969. (b)

Thornburg, H. D. The statistics of dissent. *Arizona Teacher,* 1969, 57(4), 10–11. (c)

Thornburg, H. D. Student assessment of contemporary issues. *College Student Survey,* 1969, 3, 1–5; 22. (d)

Thornburg, H. D. Adolescence: A re-interpretation. *Adolescence,* 1970, 5(20), 463–484. (a)

Thornburg, H. D. Age and first sources of sex information as reported by 88 college women. *Journal of School Health,* 1970, 40(3), 156–158. (b)

Thornburg, H. D. Learning and maturation in middle school age youth. *Clearing House*, 1970, *45*, 150–155. (c)
Thornburg, H. D. *Contemporary adolescence: Readings.* Monterey, Calif.: Brooks/Cole, 1971. (a)
Thornburg, H. D. An investigation of attitudes among potential dropouts from minority groups during their freshman year in high school. Final Report, U. S. Office of Education, Bureau of Research, Contract No. OEC-9-71-0002(057). Washington, D. C.: U. S. Government Printing Office, 1971. (b)
Thornburg, H. D. Peers: Three distinct groups. *Adolescence*, 1971, *6*(21), 59–76. (c)
Thornburg, H. D. Student assessment of contemporary issues. In H. D. Thornburg (Ed.), *Contemporary adolescence: Readings.* Pp. 330–335. Monterey, Calif.: Brooks/Cole, 1971. (d)
Thornburg, H. D. A comparative study of sex information sources. *Journal of School Health*, 1972, *52*(2), 88–91.
Thornburg, H. D. *Adolescent development.* Dubuque, Iowa: W. C. Brown, 1973. (a)
Thornburg, H. D. The adolescent and drugs. *Journal of School Health*, 1973, *43*(1), 40–44. (b)
Thornburg, H. D. Behavior and values: Consistency or inconsistency. *Adolescence*, 1973, *8*(32), 513–520. (c)
Thornburg, H. D. *Child development.* Dubuque, Iowa: W. C. Brown, 1973. (d)
Thornburg, H. D. *School learning and instruction.* Monterey, Calif.: Brooks/Cole, 1973. (e)
Thornburg, H. D. Educating the preadolescent about sex. *Family Coordinator*, 1974, *23*(1), 35–40. (a)
Thornburg, H. D. Evaluation of selected measurement strategies in adolescent research. Paper read at the annual meeting of the Southwestern Psychological Association, El Paso, Texas, 1974. (b)
Thornburg, H. D. An investigation of a dropout program among Arizona's minority youth. *Education*, 1974, *94*(3), 249–265. (c)
Thornburg, H. D. *Preadolescent development: Readings.* Tucson: University of Arizona Press, 1974. (d)
Thornburg, H. D. Sources in adolescence of initial sex information. Paper read at the annual meeting of the Southwestern Psychological Association, El Paso, Texas, 1974. (e)
Thornburg, H. D. Adolescent sources of initial sex information. *Pediatric Annals*, 1975, in press. (a)
Thornburg, H. D. *Contemporary adolescence: Readings* (2nd ed.). Monterey, Calif.: Brooks/Cole, 1975. (b)
Thornburg, H. D. Attitudinal determinants in holding dropouts in school. *Journal of Educational Research*, 1975, *68*(5), 181–185. (c)
Thornburg, H. D., & Grinder, R. E. Children of Aztlán: The Mexican-American experience. In *Adolescence and early adulthood in the American seventies.* Chicago: National Society for the Study of Education Yearbook, 1975.
Thrasher, F. M. *The gang (1313 Chicago gangs).* Chicago: University of Chicago Press, 1926.
Toby, J. Affluence and adolescent crime. In The President's Commission on Law Enforcement and Administration of Justice (Eds.), *Task force report:*

Juvenile delinquency and youth crime. Pp. 132–145. Washington, D. C.: U.S. Government Printing Office, 1967.

Toffler, A. *Future shock.* New York: Random House, 1970.

Trends. U. S. Department of Health, Education and Welfare. Washington, D. C.: U. S. Government Printing Office, 1961.

Triandis, H. C. *Attitude and attitude change.* New York: Wiley, 1971.

Trump, J. L., & Hunt, J. The nature and extent of student activism. *National Association of Secondary School Principals Bulletin,* 1969, *53,* 150–158.

Turner, R. H. Some family determinants of ambition. *Sociology and Social Research,* 1962, *46,* 397–411.

Turner, R. H. Campus peace: Harmony or uneasy truce? *Sociology and Social Research,* 1972, *57*(1), 5–21.

Two doctors warn against the abuse of amphetamines. *U. S. News and World Report,* 1969, *57*(26), 24–25.

Ulibarri, H. The bicultural myth and the education of the Mexican American. *Journal of Comparative Cultures,* 1972, *1,* 83–95.

Ullmann, L. P., & Krasner, L. *Case studies in behavior modification.* New York: Holt, Rinehart and Winston, 1965.

U. S. Commission on Civil Rights. *Racial isolation in the public schools* (Vol. 1). Washington, D. C.: U. S. Government Printing Office, 1967.

U. S. Commission on Civil Rights. *The excluded student, Report III.* Washington, D.C.: U.S. Government Printing Office, 1972.

U.S. Department of Labor, Wage and Labor Standards Administration. Women's Bureau. *Fact sheet on the earnings gap.* Washington, D.C.: U.S. Government Printing Office, 1970.

Vaz, E. W. Middle-class adolescents: Self-reported delinquency and youth culture activities. *Canadian Review of Sociology and Anthropology,* 1965, *2,* 52–70.

Vaz, E. W. (Ed.). *Middle-class juvenile delinquency.* New York: Harper & Row, 1967.

Vaz, E. W. Delinquency and the youth culture: Upper- and middle-class boys. *Journal of Criminal Law, Criminology, and Police Science,* 1969, *60*(1), 33–46.

Vernon, W. M. *Motivating children: Behavior modification in the classroom.* New York: Holt, Rinehart and Winston, 1972.

Vogl, A. J. Influencing kids against drugs: What works? *Medical Economics,* April 20, 1970.

Wallerstein, J. S., & Wyle, G. J. Our law-abiding lawbreakers. *Probation,* 1946, pp. 107–112.

Walsh, R. Intergenerational transmission of sexual standards. Paper presented at the annual meeting of the American Sociological Association, Washington, D. C., 1970.

Walster, E. The effect of self-esteem on romantic liking. *Journal of Experimental Social Psychology,* 1965, *1,* 184–197.

Walster, E., Aronso, V., Abrahams, D., & Rottmann, L. Importance of physical attractiveness in dating behavior. *Journal of Personality and Social Psychology,* 1966, *4,* 508–516.

Wattenberg, W. W., & Balistrieri, J. Automobile theft: A favored group delinquency. *American Journal of Sociology,* 1952, pp. 575–579.

Watts, W., & Whittaker, D. Free speech advocates at Berkeley. *Journal of Applied Behavioral Sciences,* 1966, *2,* 41–62.

Weakland, J. H. Hippies: What the scene means. In R. H. Blum & Associates (Eds.), *Society and drugs*. San Francisco: Jossey-Bass, 1969.
Weiner, I. B. *Psychological disturbances in adolescence*. New York: Wiley, 1970.
Weinstock, A., & Lerner, R. M. Attitudes of late adolescents and their parents toward contemporary issues. *Psychological Reports*, 1972, *30*, 239–244.
Weissman, R. Teens and drugs: Monkey on our backs. *Arizona Teacher*, 1969, *57*, 10–13.
Westley, W. A., & Elkin, F. The protective environment and adolescent socialization. *Social Forces*, 1956, *35*, 243–249.
Who's in charge—IV. The students. *Sooner Magazine*, 1969, *41*(5), 10–13.
Wilkins, L. *The diagnosis and treatment of endocrine disorders in childhood and adolescence*. Springfield, Ill.: Charles C Thomas, 1965.
Williams, A. Psychological needs and social drinking among college students. *Quarterly Journal of Studies on Alcohol*, 1968, *29*, 355–363.
Williams, A. College problem drinkers: A personality profile. In G. Maddox (Ed.), *The domesticated drug: Drinking among collegians*. New Haven, Conn.: College and University Press, 1970.
Willmott, P. *Adolescent boys of East London*. London: Routledge & Kegan Paul, 1966.
Wilson, A. B. Residential segregation of social classes and aspirations of high school boys. *American Sociological Review*, 1959, *24*, 836–845.
Winter, G. D. Physical changes during adolescence. In G. D. Winter & E. M. Nuss (Eds.), *The young adult*. Chicago: Scott, Foresman, 1969.
Wirth, L. The problems of minority groups. In R. Linton (Ed.), *The science of man in the world crisis*. New York: Columbia University Press, 1945.
Wise, N. B. Juvenile delinquency among middle-class girls. In E. W. Vaz (Ed.), *Middle-Class juvenile delinquency*. Pp. 179–187. New York: Harper & Row, 1967.
Wolfbein, S. L. Labor Trends, manpower, and automation. In H. Borow (Ed.), *Man in a world at work*. Boston: Houghton Mifflin, 1964.
Wolff, O. H. Obesity in childhood. *Triangle*, 1966, *7*, 234–239.
Xenia. *Ohio Schools*, 1972, *50*(7), 11–13.
Yablonsky, L. *The violent gang*. New York: Macmillan, 1963.
Yablonsky, L. *The hippie trip*. New York: Pegasus, 1968.
Yamamoto, K., Thomas, E. C., & Karns, E. A. School-related attitudes of middle-school-age students.
Yancy, W. S., Nader, P. R., & Burnham, K. L. Drug use and attitudes of high school students. *Pediatrics*, 1972, *50*(5), 739–745.
Yankelovich, D. *The changing values on campus*. New York: Pocket Books, 1972.
Yarrow, M. R. Maternal employment and child rearing. *Children*, 1961, *8*, 223–228.
Yarrow, M. R., Scott, P., Deleeuw, L., & Heinig, C. Childrearing in families of working and non-working mothers. *Sociometry*, 1962, *25*, 122–140.
Youmans, G. E. Occupational expectations of twelfth grade Michigan boys. *Journal of Experimental Education*, 1965, *24*, 259–271.
Young, A. M. The high school class of 1972. *Monthly Labor Review*, 1973, *96*(6), 26–32.
Zeller, W. *Konstitutionen and Entwicklung*. Göttingen, Germany: Psychologische Rundschau, 1952.
Zimbardo, P., & Formica, R. Emotional comparison and self-esteem as determinants of affiliation. *Journal of Personality*, 1963, *31*, 141–162.

Zuk, G. H. The influence of social context on impulse and control tendencies in preadolescents. *Genetic Psychology Monographs,* 1956, *54,* 117–166.
Zurcher, L. A., Jr. The poor and the hip: Some manifestations of cultural lead. *Social Science Quarterly,* 1972, *53*(2), 357–376.
Zygulski, K. Sociological approaches to the culture of youth. *International Social Science Journal,* 1972, *24*(2), 366–376.

Author Index

Aberele, D. F., 146
Abrahams, D., 300
Adams, A. A., 188
Adams, P. L., 44, 45
Adelson, J., 97, 113, 114–115, 124, 132, 139, 147, 172, 193, 300
Adkins, N. M., 52
Adler, N., 242
Ahlstrom, W. M., 205–207, 370–374
Ahrenfeldt, R. H., 332
Alexander, C. N., 196–197, 212, 255, 411
Alexander, W. M., 212
Alissi, A. S., 19, 20
Allen, H. D., 220
Allinsmith, W., 192
Alschuler, A. E., 204
Ames, L. B., 448
Anderson, J. G., 236
Anderson, N. H., 57
Andrews, W. H., 431
Andry, R. G., 365
Angel, W., 168, 169
Angelino, H., 9, 49, 55, 56, 316, 317
Angrist, S. S., 431–432
Anspach, K., 153
Aronfreed, J., 91, 116
Aronso, V., 300
Asayama, S., 38
Atkinson, R. C., 52
Atkinson, R. L., 52
Ausubel, D. P., 62, 69, 144, 176
Ausubel, P., 62, 69, 176
Axelrad, S., 409

Bachman, J. G., 193
Backman, E. L., 221
Baden, M. M., 242, 279
Baer, D. M., 88
Baker, C. B., 328
Baldwin, A. L., 25
Balistrieri, J., 349
Balswick, J. O., 303, 305–306, 309
Bandura, A., 88, 89, 90, 146
Barnett, J., 406

Barton, A. H., 387
Barty, N., 287
Bates, W., 251
Baumer, T. L., 251
Baur, E. J., 165
Bayley, N., 44
Bealer, R. C., 410
Becker, W. C., 124
Beiser, M., 237
Bell, G. D., 194, 408–409
Bell, H. M., 314, 316
Bell, R. R., 172, 302, 305, 308, 309, 330
Beller, E. K., 20, 33
Bellward, G., 287
Bemis, S. E., 129
Bendix, R., 408
Benedict, R., 29–30
Bengston, V. L., 168–173
Bensman, J., 296
Berdie, R. F., 429, 430
Berk, L. E., 187, 188
Bernard, H. W., 220
Bernard, J., 154
Bethell, B., 287
Bettelheim, B., 171
Bijou, S. W., 88
Biller, H. B., 139
Birkness, V., 349
Blaine, G. B., 309
Blau, P. M., 147
Bloch, H. A., 348
Block, J., 171
Bloom, B. S., 80
Blos, P., 26
Blum, R. H., 251, 281, 282
Blumberg, L., 302
Bogan, F. A., 411
Bordua, D. J., 146, 408
Bowerman, C. E., 111, 115, 147, 151
Braham, M., 71
Brecher, E. M., 248–249, 286
Brezesinska, Z., 398
Briar, S., 335, 339
Brim, O. G., 199
Brittain, C. V., 148–149, 150

469

Broderick, C. B., 300
Bronfenbrenner, U., 392–393
Brown, B. B., 434–435
Brown, H. R., 386
Brozovsky, M., 267
Bruner, J. S., 177
Brunschyber, P., 40
Bryan, A. H., 37
Bunt, M. E., 406
Burchinal, L. J., 87, 137–139, 433
Burgess, E. W., 433
Burlingame, W. V., 144
Burnham, K. L., 251–252, 280, 282, 285
Butterworth, C. E., 147
Byer, C. O., 245–246
Byrne, D., 300

Calden, G., 53
Campbell, E. Q., 83, 146, 172, 196–197, 201, 255, 411
Carmichael, S., 386
Carns, D. E., 302
Carpenter, G. R., 302
Carry, R. W., 165
Cartwright, A., 257
Cawelti, G., 180, 191–192, 214
Cervinka, C., 423
Chadderdon, H., 93
Chapel, J. L., 257, 267
Chaskes, J. B., 305, 308
Cheever, J., 205
Chickering, S. B., 168–169
Christensen, H. T., 302, 305
Clark, W. H., 203, 273
Clausen, J. A., 86, 226
Clinard, M. B., 348–349
Cloward, R. A., 159, 343–344, 345, 347
Clune, F. J., 303
Cobb, E. A., 52
Cohen, A. K., 159, 344, 347
Cole, L., 108
Coleman, J. S., 71, 83, 147, 148–149, 155, 158–159, 178–179, 198, 201, 214
Coles, R., 174
Collins, M. L., 253
Conger, J. J., 18, 88, 172–174, 186, 198
Constantine, J., 404–405
Constantine, L., 404–405
Cosca, L. R., 236
Cottrell, L. S., 433
Courts, F. A., 257

Croake, J. W., 49, 55–56
Cross, H. J., 272, 403–404
Crowther, B., 251

Dachler, H. P., 76
Daniel, W., 44
Darley, C. F., 261
Darwin, C., 18, 19
Daugela, M., 40
Davis, A., 173, 203
Davis, G. L., 272
Davis, J. V., 190–191
Davis, K., 32–33, 82–83, 170, 171, 173, 221
Davis, K. E., 310
DeLeeuw, L., 132
DeLissovoy, V., 141–142, 433
Denhart, R. B., 220
Denisoff, R. S., 402–403
Dentler, R., 346
Derbyshire, R. L., 232
DeRoche, E. F., 422–423
Deutsch, N., 27
Dietz, S. C., 134–135
Dishotsky, N. I., 277
Dollins, J., 49
Douvan, E., 97, 113, 114–115, 116, 124, 132, 139, 147, 172, 193, 300
Dudley, C. J., 303
Duncan, O. D., 147
Dunphy, D. C., 7, 97, 144–146, 300
Dwyer, J., 51

Eastman, W. F., 307
Eberly, D., 108–109
Edson, L., 255–256
Edwards, J. A., 94
Eichorn, D. H., 43
Eidsmore, R. M., 201
Eisenman, R., 203
Eisenstadt, S. N., 152
Elder, G. H., 82, 83, 111, 119, 151, 156–157, 158
Elias, J., 319
Elkin, F., 115, 347
Elkind, D., 71–73, 88, 94, 95, 97, 382
Ellis, R. A., 147
Emerson, P. E., 88
Empey, L. T., 344
Entwistle, D. R., 133
Epperson, D. C., 148–149
Epstein, L. J., 280

Erikson, E. H., 27–29, 34, 55, 58, 102, 110, 382, 391, 405, 409
Erskine, H. F., 296
Ervine, C. R., 300
Essig, M., 132
Evans, F. B., 236

Fantini, M., 210–211
Farber, E. M., 328
Faust, M. S., 42
Feigelson, N., 172
Feingold, M., 321
Fejer, D., 282
Felker, D. W., 53
Ferdon, N. M., 46–47
Ferguson, G. A., 62
Ferguson, L. R., 24
Festinger, L., 57, 99
Feuer, L., 172, 398
Fink, P. J., 10
Finlay, D., 221
Fishel, S. S., 248
Fisher, S., 51
Fishman, J. R., 384
Fitt, A. B., 188
Fitzsimmons, S. J., 205
Flacks, R., 384, 390
Floyd, H. H., 148, 150–151
Flynn, F. T., 348
Ford, T., 204
Formica, R., 55
Forney, R. B., 262–263
Forsuland, M. A., 423
Fort, J., 172, 273
Frazier, A., 49, 50
Freedman, M. B., 305, 308
Freud, S., 23–27, 28, 34, 90, 294–295
Freydinger, J. E., 248
Friedenberg, E. Z., 122, 169, 171
Friedman, H. L., 140, 406
Friesen, D., 71, 180–181, 214
Frisch, R. E., 37, 40, 44
Frye, V. H., 134–135
Fuchs, V. R., 127
Funkhouser, G. R., 273

Gage, N. L., 76
Gagné, R. M., 177
Galbraith, J. K., 398
Gallemore, J. L., 56
Gallup, G. H., 173, 190–191
Gans, H. J., 345

Garai, J. E., 60
Gardner, B., 59, 87
Gastineau, C. F., 248
Gebhard, P., 319
Gentry, H. W., 191–192
Gergen, K. L., 272
Gergen, M. K., 272
Gerzon, M., 172
Gesell, A., 22–23, 24
Gibbens, T. C. N., 332
Ginsburg, H., 67
Ginsburg, S. W., 409
Ginzberg, E., 409–410
Glass, J. C., 305
Glueck, E., 132, 339–343, 349, 370
Glueck, S., 132, 339–343, 349, 370
Gold, M., 114–115, 116, 334, 348, 349, 351, 352, 354, 360–362
Goldberg, M. M., 223
Golding, L. A., 248
Goldman, I., 423
Goldman, N., 335, 338–339
Goldstein, S. G., 305
Gonring, R. W., 328
Gonzaga, F. P., 40
Goode, W. J., 136
Gordon, C., 86
Gordon, I., 7, 102
Gorman, B. W., 211–212
Gossett, J. T., 282
Gottlieb, D., 165, 423
Gould, L. J., 393–394
Gover, K. R., 413, 414, 417, 419
Graham, R. A., 108–109
Graves, T. D., 151, 153
Greenberg, B. G., 37
Greenberger, E., 133
Gregg, C. F., 305
Gregory, C. L., 429, 430
Grimes, J. W., 192
Grinder, R. E., 26, 47, 144–145, 205, 298, 300
Guilford, J. P., 74–75
Gump, J. P., 436
Gusfield, J., 253–254

Haan, N., 100–101, 171
Haeckel, E., 19
Hall, C. S., 52
Hall, G. S., 18–22, 23, 25, 31, 32, 53, 60
Hall, I. N., 108
Haller, A. O., 147, 409

Author Index

Hammond, W., 416–418, 420
Hanson, G. R., 251, 253
Hanson, R. C., 194
Haring, D. G., 219
Harris, L., 173, 190–191
Harsch, C. M., 29
Hartford, B., 384–385
Hartley, M. C., 183
Hartshorne, H., 188
Harwood, J. H., 257
Haskell, M. L., 364
Hassan, I. N., 52
Havighurst, R. L., 5–11, 49, 51, 83, 108–109, 159, 205–207, 222, 226, 370–374
Hawkes, G. R., 87
Heald, F. P., 40
Hedges, J. N., 129
Heinig, C., 132
Hellenbrand, S. C., 238–239
Heller, C. S., 233
Hellmer, L. A., 124
Herma, J. L., 409
Hernstein, R., 76
Herriott, R. E., 147
Herzog, E., 257
Hess, E. H., 87
Hetherington, E. M., 139
Heyman, F., 280
Hilgard, E. R., 52
Hines, V. Z., 212
Hodgkins, B., 165
Hoffman, A. D., 309
Hoffman, L. W., 146
Hoffman, M. L., 116–117, 124
Hofman, A., 274
Hollingshead, A. B., 80, 82, 408
Hollister, W. J., 12, 270
Holm, J. M., 125, 126, 128, 130
Holtzman, W. H., 119, 124
Hood, A. B., 429, 430
Horn, D., 257
Horrocks, J. E., 25, 56, 122–123
Howard, E. R., 214
Hoy, W. K., 183
Hughes, R. B., 262, 263
Humpreys, L. G., 76
Hunt, J., 389–390
Hurlock, E. B., 47, 59, 155
Huston, A. C., 89

Ilg, F. L., 448

Inhelder, B., 67, 70–71
Inselberg, R. M., 433
Iron, R. B., 439

Jackson, R. M., 236
Jacob, N. L., 435
Jacobson, C. B., 278
Jensen, A. R., 76–78
Jersild, A. T., 188
Jessor, R., 251, 253
Jessor, S. L., 251, 253
Joffe, M. H., 274
Johnson, F. K., 260, 273, 274
Johnson, H. C., 349
Johnson, J., 389, 391
Johnson, M., 241
Johnson, W., 321
Johnston, D. F., 412–413, 429–430
Jones, K. L., 245–246
Jones, L. W., 63
Jones, M. C., 43–44
Joubert, S. M., 375
Juarez, R. Z., 408, 423
Juhasz, A. M., 298

Kaats, G. R., 310
Kagan, J., 18, 88, 90, 174
Kahl, J., 147, 409
Kandel, D., 119–121, 147, 149, 197, 198–199
Kaplan, R., 267
Kardiner, A., 223–226
Karns, E. A., 188
Katz, I., 82, 83
Keele, R. L., 236
Keig, N. G., 423
Keislar, E. R., 58
Keniston, K., 171, 173, 386, 392, 396–397, 398–400
Kestenberg, J. S., 37–39
Kinch, J. W., 147, 151
King, K., 303, 305–306, 309
Kingston, A. J., 191–192
Kinsey, A. C., 43, 169, 170, 294, 296, 303, 306–308
Klein, M., 363
Knafle, J. D., 192–193
Knox, F. H., 55–56
Knudsen, D. D., 305
Kohlberg, L., 84, 91–93, 95, 97–98, 100–101, 116
Komorovsky, M., 150

Konopka, G., 240, 357, 360
Kopell, B. S., 261
Kowitz, G., 204
Kraft, A., 202
Kramer, R., 453
Krasner, L., 242
Krauss, I., 147
Kuo, Z. Y., 87
Kurtz, R. M., 51
Kuvlesky, W. P., 408, 410, 423, 435–436
Kvaraceus, W. C., 340, 376–379

Lacy, C. L., 206
Lamarck, J., 17, 18, 19
Lambreth, J., 300
Landis, J. T., 136
Lane, C., 147
Langley, M. H., 338
Larson, L. E., 148, 149–150
Larson, W. R., 123–124
Latham, A. J., 43
Lawson, R. F., 397
Leary, T., 14
Lee, M. R., 316
Leggett, J. C., 423
Leidy, T. R., 186–187, 214
Lemert, E. M., 332
Lennard, H. L., 280
Leonard, E., 205
Lerman, P., 144
Lerner, R. M., 53, 169
Lesser, G. D., 119–121, 147, 149, 197, 198–199
Lever, M. F., 226, 237
Levin, H., 433
Levin, T., 288–289
Levine, M. H., 277, 402–403
Levitt, E. E., 94
Levy, L., 251, 257, 259, 262, 263, 275, 280
Lewin, K., 223
Lewis, D. C., 287, 290
Lewis, J. M., 282
Lewis, L. S., 165–167
Lighter, A. G., 329
Lindstrom, D. E., 430
Lindzey, G., 52
Linner, B., 126
Lionberger, H. F., 429, 430
Lipscomb, W. R., 277
Lipset, S. M., 408

Lisonbee, L. K., 49, 50
Little, J. K., 411
Litwin, G. H., 204
Locke, J., 17, 18
Long, D., 73
Looft, W. R., 73–74, 176
Loree, M. R., 54
Loughman, W. D., 277
Lowrie, S. H., 300
Luckey, E. B., 304
Ludwig, A. M., 277
Lundy, R. M., 53

Maccoby, E. R., 433
MacIver, R. M., 219
Macunovich, D., 205
Maddox, G. L., 251–254
Malinowski, B., 26
Malry, L., 423
Mannheim, K., 170
Manuel, H. T., 234
Marcia, J. E., 406
Martin, C. E., 294
Martin, F. M., 257, 294
Martinson, F. M., 302, 305
Maslow, A. H., 177
Mausner, B., 257
May, M., 188
Mayer, J., 51
McCandless, B. R., 42
McClelland, D. C., 194, 204
McCord, J., 132, 365
McCord, W., 132, 365
McDill, E. L., 147, 197–198
McKennell, A. C., 256
McMahon, B., 257
McNeil, E. B., 80–81
Mead, M., 21, 29–31, 109, 126, 169, 171
Mech, E. V., 9, 49, 316, 317
Meissner, W. J., 118–119
Mellor, E. F., 424–425
Meredith, H. V., 37
Merton, R. K., 408
Miller, R. B., 52
Miller, W. B., 159, 344, 363–369
Mischler, J. B., 257
Mogar, R. E., 277
Monroe, L. J., 346
Mood, A. M., 83, 201
Moore, B. M., 119
Morgan, D. H., 20, 21, 132
Morrow, W. R., 194, 195

Morse, S. J., 272
Mowrer, O. H., 89
Munan, L., 48
Murphy, P., 261
Murphy, P. L., 261
Musgrove, F., 147
Mussen, P. H., 18, 43, 88, 89
Muuss, R. E., 18, 23, 28, 31, 67, 68–69
Myerhoff, B. G., 123–124, 147

Nader, P. R., 229–230, 251–252, 280, 282, 285
Naegele, K. D., 146
Nass, G. D., 304
Nelson, D. D., 248
Nelson, R. A., 133
Neugarten, B., 226
Norman, R. D., 194
Nowlis, H. H., 272
Nuss, E. M., 39
Nye, F. I., 133, 136, 346, 348

Obordo, A. S., 435, 436
O'Connell, W. E., 59
Ohlin, L. E., 159, 343–344, 345, 347
Olson, V. J., 346
Opper, S., 67
Ostermeier, A. L., 153
Overstreet, P. L., 409, 421, 422
Ovesey, L., 223–226

Packard, V., 155, 304, 308
Page, C. H., 219
Parsons, T., 346
Patella, V. M., 232–233
Pauly, I. B., 305
Pearce, J., 288
Pellens, M., 279
Perrella, V. C., 411, 417, 428
Peterson, D. R., 124
Petras, J. W., 295
Petrich, B., 93
Phillips, J. L., 70
Phillips, V. A., 282
Piaget, J., 63–71, 78, 91, 93, 116
Pickle, D. E., 45
Piliavin, I., 335, 339
Pine, G., 346, 348
Platt, J. J., 203
Polk, K. A., 348, 355–357
Pollock, M. J., 128
Pomeroy, W. B., 294

Pope, H., 305
Popoff, D., 284
Porterfield, A. L., 348
Propper, M. M., 203
Pruyn, E. L., 403–404
Pugh, M., 199

Quay, H. C., 124

Rafferty, J., 272
Rallings, E. M., 122
Ramsey, C., 423
Ramsey, C. V., 314, 316, 317
Rehberg, R. A., 147, 199, 201, 411
Reich, C. A., 395–396, 398, 402
Reiss, A. J., 346
Reiss, I. L., 10, 169–170, 171, 297, 301–302, 304–305, 309, 310–314
Revelle, R., 37, 40, 44
Rewitzer, M., 53, 169
Reynolds, E. L., 37
Rhodes, A. L., 346
Richards, L. G., 274, 275, 277–278, 286
Rieger, J. H., 431
Rigsby, L. C., 197–198
Robeck, M. C., 231–232
Robinson, D., 375
Robinson, I. E., 303, 305–306, 308–309
Rogers, D. R., 42–43, 44, 125, 253
Rose, M. H., 187
Rose, P. I., 223, 227
Rosen, B., 111, 147, 408
Rosenfeld, C., 413, 414, 417, 419
Rosenmayr, L., 55, 221
Rosenthal, M. S., 280
Ross, D., 89
Ross, D. G., 18, 19
Ross, S. A., 89
Roszak, T., 172, 391, 395–396
Roth, W. T., 261
Rothman, J., 223
Rotter, J. B., 272
Rottmann, L., 300
Rouman, J., 132
Rousseau, J. J., 17, 19
Rowe, G. P., 300
Roy, P., 132
Rubenstein, E., 140
Russell, D. G., 55
Rutherford, E., 89
Ryan, M. S., 153
Ryscavage, P. M., 424, 425

Author Index 475

Salber, E. J., 257
Saltzstein, H. D., 117, 124
Sampson, E. E., 201
Sanford, N., 52
Sasidhorn, N., 221
Sauber, M., 140
Savio, M., 385
Scammon, R., 172
Scarr-Salapatek, S., 76
Schab, F., 188–190, 238
Schaffer, R. J., 88
Schaimberg, L., 122
Scharf, J., 56
Scheinfeld, A., 40
Schepp, G. J., 300
Schilder, P., 51
Schmitt, S. S., 300
Schneider, A. J., 301
Schofield, M., 299
Schonfeld, W. A., 49, 51
Schrag, P., 228
Schrickel, H. G., 29
Schroeder, C., 53, 169
Schuck, R. F., 327, 328
Schwartz, M. S., 319
Scott, J. P., 87
Scott, P., 132
Sears, P. S., 88
Sears, R. R., 433–434
Sebald, H., 107, 346
Seeley, J., 171
Seiden, R., 10, 169–170, 305
Sewell, W. H., 147, 409
Shafer, R. P., 250, 279
Shafer, W. E., 199
Shah, V. P., 147
Shainberg, L. W., 245–246
Shanley, B. C., 375
Shedd, C., 55
Sheldon, W. H., 52
Sherif, C. W., 96, 159–161, 365
Sherif, M., 96, 159–161, 365
Shockley, W., 76
Shoemaker, D. J., 124
Short, J. F., 159, 161, 346
Shuttleworth, F. K., 37
Sieg, A., 30
Silberman, C. E., 186
Simon, H. A., 13
Simpson, R. L., 147, 408
Singer, S. L., 422
Slater, P., 94, 396

Slocum, W. L., 147
Smart, R. G., 282
Smartt, W. H., 329
Smigel, E. O., 10, 169–170, 305
Smith, C. E., 88
Smith, D. D., 260, 274, 282, 284–286
Smith, J. P., 274
Smith, M. B., 171
Snyder, C. R., 254
Snyder, E. E., 180, 199–201
Solomon, E. S., 257
Solomon, F., 384
Somers, R. H., 385–386
Sorensen, R. C., 302, 307
South, D. R., 148, 150–151
Southam, A. L., 40
Spaulding, R. L., 193
Spearman, C., 63
Spielberger, C. D., 56
Spilka, B., 73
Spranger, E., 31
Spratto, G. R., 274
Spreitzer, E., 199
Sprey, J., 423
Staffieri, J. R., 53
Stahmann, R. F., 194–195
Starry, A. R., 186–187, 214
Stefflre, B., 422
Stephenson, R. M., 412
Sternlieb, J. J., 48
Stevic, R., 228–229
Stewart, D., 187
Stolz, H. R., 41
Stolz, L. M., 41
Stone, C. L., 121–122, 147
Stonequist, E., 223
Strack, A. E., 260, 268, 275
Straus, M. A., 147, 409
Stringer, R. A., 204
Strodtbeck, F. L., 159, 161, 201
Stubbs, M. V. L., 278
Suchman, E. A., 251, 275, 281–282
Sudia, C. E., 257
Sundby, P., 262
Super, D. E., 409, 421, 422

Talbot, N. B., 38, 40
Tanner, J. M., 37, 38, 40, 41–42, 43
Tasch, R. J., 188
Taylor, D. W., 257, 267
Taylor, J., 328
Taylor, R. M., 257

Tenenbaum, S., 188
Terman, L. M., 62–63, 170, 294
Terry, C. E., 279
Thomas, E. C., 188
Thomas, K. A., 435–437
Thomes, M. M., 136–137
Thompson, D. C., 239
Thompson, G. G., 59
Thompson, J. G., 257
Thompson, O. E., 421–423
Thornburg, H. D., 5, 7, 11, 18, 25, 27, 28, 31–32, 40, 54, 57, 65, 73, 85, 89, 94, 95, 99, 100, 108, 115, 148, 152, 157, 159, 174, 176, 192, 198, 205, 206–209, 230, 233, 234, 250, 314–321, 323, 324–326, 328, 330, 339, 379, 388–389, 408, 410, 438
Thrasher, F. M., 363, 364
Thurber, E., 132
Tinklenberg, J. R., 261
Toby, J., 365
Todd, D. M., 12
Toffler, A., 398
Triandis, H. C., 219
Trickett, E. J., 12
Trump, J. L., 389–390
Turner, R. H., 390, 408

Uhlig, G., 228–229
Ulibarri, H., 234
Ullmann, L. P., 242
Ulrich, W. E., 340
Upham, W. K., 226, 237, 423, 435

Vaz, E. W., 346–347, 348, 349–350, 352–353, 355–357, 361
Vernon, W. M., 88
Vogl, A. J., 288

Wallerstein, J. S., 348
Walsh, R., 172
Walster, E., 300
Wattenberg, B. J., 172
Wattenberg, W. W., 349

Watts, W., 386
Weakland, J. H., 401
Weiner, I. B., 262
Weinstock, A., 53, 169
Weismann, R., 286
Westby, D. L., 147, 411
Westley, W. A., 115
Westman, J. C., 260, 273, 274
White, J., 282
Whittaker, D., 386
Whittlesey, R. R., 194–195
Wilkins, L., 37, 38
Williams, A., 254–255
Willmott, P., 4
Wilson, A. B., 56, 408
Wilson, R. C., 194, 195
Wines, J. V., 37
Winick, C., 323
Winkler, E., 267
Winter, G. D., 39
Wirth, L., 219
Wise, N. B., 360–361
Wolfbein, S. L., 411
Wolff, O. H., 45
Wright, D. E., 408, 423
Wyle, G. J., 348

Yablonsky, L., 172, 361, 363, 364, 365, 396, 400–401
Yamamoto, K., 188
Yancy, W. S., 251–252, 273, 280, 281–282, 285
Yankelovich, D., 390–391
Yarrow, M. R., 132
Youmans, G. E., 430
Young, A. M., 414–416, 424–429

Zail, S. S., 375
Zeller, W., 37
Zimbardo, P., 55
Zuk, G. H., 60
Zurcher, L. A., 218, 391
Zygulski, K., 222

Subject Index

Activism, 384–390
   constructive, 388–389
   Free Speech Movement, 385–386
   high school, 389–390
   New Left, 386–388
Adolescent egocentrism, 72–74
   imaginary audience, 72–73
   personal fable, 72–73
Alienation, 183, 390–395
Attitudes:
   defined, 53–54
   toward home, 118–123
   toward school, 181–188
Authoritarianism, 33, 111, 119–121, 124, 142
Automation, 108
Autonomy, 111–118
   behavioral, 113–114
   emotional, 114–115, 116
   value, 115–118

Behavioral subculture, 152–157
   clothes, 153
   meeting places, 156–157
   money, 153–155
   physical appearance, 153
   speech, 152–153
   status objects, 155–156, 158, 164
Body types:
   ectomorph, 52–53
   endomorph, 52–53
   mesomorph, 52–53

Cheating, 188–190
Class inclusion, 68
Cognitive dissonance, 57–58, 99–100
Competition, 96, 146, 162
Conformity, 96–97, 146
Conservation, 67–68
Counterculture, 220, 395–406
   communes, 404–406
   countercounterculture, 398–400
   hippies, 400–401
   music, 401–403

Counterculture *(continued)*
   naturalism, 403–404
   protest, 402–403
Crossculture, 220–222
Culture, 218–220
   pluralism, 222–226
Curriculum options, 207–212

Dating, 300–302
Decentering, 66–67, 176
Delinquency, 335–339
   and dropouts, 369–371
   and the family, 340–342
   female, 356–361
   in gangs, 361–369
   incidence of, 159, 333–335, 339–340, 350–351, 353–355, 357–359, 361–362, 368–374
   and the law, 335, 338–339
   lower-class, 159, 160–161, 344–346
   middle-class, 159, 346–356
   as self-reported, 350–351, 353–355
   and sex role, 345
   and social class, 344–346
   and subcultures, 343–356
   upper-class, 349, 352
Delinquency prevention, 371, 373–379
Developmental norms, 22–23
Developmental stages, 4–5
Developmental tasks, 4–12
Developmental theories:
   anthropological, 29–31
   biological, 22–23
   evolution, 18
   Greek philosophies, 16–17
   predeterminism, 17
   preformationism, 17
   psychoanalytic, 23–29
   psychological, 31–32
   recapitulation, 18–22
   sociological, 32–34
Discrimination:
   toward minorities, 222–226
   sex, 126–127
Divorce, 110, 136–137

Drug abuse, 242–244, 258–259
Drug classifications:
    alcohol, 243, 249–255, 263, 282, 283, 284–285
    amphetamines, 244, 248, 259–262, 263, 282, 283, 284–285
    barbiturates, 244, 247, 257–259, 263, 282, 283, 284–285
    marijuana, 243, 248–249, 263, 267–274, 282, 283, 284–285
    narcotics, 243, 244, 248, 263, 278–281
    nicotine, 255, 257, 263, 283
    psychedelics, 243, 244, 263, 282, 284–285
    solvents, 266–267, 282, 285
Drug dependence, 244–245, 270–271
    addiction, 245, 246, 279–280
    habituation, 244–245, 246, 279–280
Drug education, 286–291
Drugs:
    and authority, 255
    defined, 242
    laws, 249, 262–263, 279
    multiple use, 281
    and parents, 246, 253
    and peers, 253
    and religious affiliation, 254
    and social development, 249
    and society, 245–249
Drug use, 243, 248, 250–252, 256, 258–259, 267, 268, 270–272, 273, 279, 281–286
Drug users:
    compulsive, 285–286
    experimental, 285
    recreational, 285
    ritualistic, 286

Educational aspirations, 193–204
    coaches' influence, 199–202
    parents' influence, 194–195, 198–199
    peers' influence, 196–199
Ego, 24, 26
Emancipation, 96
Emotional manifestations:
    anxiety, 56–57
    fear, 55–56
    guilt, 57–58
    happiness, 58–59
    love and affection, 58–59

Emotional skills, 59–60
Employment:
    rates of, 108–110
    women, 110

Family socialization, 5, 9–10, 84, 87–90, 96–97, 111
Family structures, 107–111, 119–122
    authoritarian, 111, 119–121, 124, 142
    autocratic, 111
    democratic, 111, 119–121
    equalitarian, 111
    ignoring, 111
    laissez-faire, 111
    one-parent, 135–139, 142
    permissive, 111, 124

Generation gap, 107, 167–174
    gap-is-an-illusion position, 169–171, 173
    great-gap position, 168–169, 173
    selective-continuity position, 171–173
Growth variables:
    accidents, 47–48
    anxiety, 49–52
    chromosome aberrations, 47
    fatigue, 45
    nutritional deficiency, 44
    obesity, 44–45, 48
    poor health, 45–46
    skin blemishes, 47
Guilt, 84, 98–99

Hallucinogens, 274–278
    central effects, 275–278
    chromosome damage, 277–278
    perceptual effects, 276–277
    use of, 243, 244, 263, 282, 284–285
Heterosexuality, 97, 146, 158
High school dropouts, 159, 205–207
Human development, 2–4
    growth, 2–3
    maturation, 3

Identification, 87–88, 89–90, 118, 144–146
Identity, 382–383
Imitation, 88–89
Imprinting, 87
Individuality, 110
Industrialization, 125

Intellectual development, 63–71
Intellectual mechanisms:
  accommodation, 64–65
  adaptation, 64–65
  assimilation, 64–65
  organization, 64
  schema, 64–65
Intellectual stages:
  concrete operations, 65, 66–69
  formal operations, 65, 69–75
  preoperational, 65–66
  sensorimotor, 65
Intellectual theory:
  mental ability, 76–78
  multifactor, 74–76
  single-factor, 62–63
  two-factor, 63
Intelligence, defined, 62–63

Marijuana:
  attitudes toward, 273–274
  long-term effects, 270–273
  short-term effects, 269–270
  use of, 243, 248–249, 263, 267–274, 282, 283, 284–285
Marriage, adolescent, 5, 10–11, 433–436
Masturbation, 38–39
Mexican-American youth:
  dropouts, 235–236
  education, 234–236
  family, 232–234
Minority youth:
  Appalachian whites, 228–229
  blacks, 222, 223–226, 236–240
  Indians, 222, 229–232
  Mexican Americans, 222, 232–236
  migrants, 229
  Puerto Rican, 222, 227–228
Modeling, 88–89, 120
Moral development:
  instrumental relativist, 92, 95
  interpersonal concordance, 92
  law and order, 92, 97, 101
  punishment and obedience, 92, 93
  social-contract legalistic, 92–93, 97–98, 101
  universal ethical principle, 93, 98

Narcotics, 278–281
  codeine, 279
  heroin, 279–281

Narcotics *(continued)*
  methadone, 280
  morphine, 278–279
  opium, 278–279
  use of, 243, 244, 248, 263, 278–281

Occupations:
  aspirations, 8, 10–11, 408, 410–412, 416
  attainment, 32, 431–432
  and education, 415–416, 426–431
  rates of, 411–416
  sex-typing, 128–130, 429
  skilled, 426–427
  and social class, 423–425
  and values, 419–423
Oedipus complex, 25–27
Ontogeny, 18–19

Parental roles, 123–131
  father, 124–125
  mother, 125–135
Peer groups:
  college youth, 157, 161–167
  high school youths, 157–161
  noncollege youths, 157, 161–165
Peers:
  versus parents, 146–151
  subculture, 147–149, 151–167
Petting, 302–304, 310–311
Phylogeny, 18–19
Physical development, 5, 9–10
  early-maturing boys, 43
  early-maturing girls, 41–43
  late-maturing boys, 43–44
  late-maturing girls, 43
  morphological age, 36
  secondary sex characteristics, 36
  skeletal growth, 36
Pluralism, 222–226
Postpuberty, 40
Prepuberty, 36–39
Problem solving, 72, 176–177
Psychosexual stages:
  adulthood, 28
  anal, 24–25
  genital, 27
  latency, 26
  maturity, 28
  oral, 24–25
  phallic, 25–26
  young adulthood, 28–29

Puberty, 39–40
Puberty rites, 30–31

Rebellion, 55
Religion, 162
Reproduction, 32–33
Reversibility, 67–68

School:
  and academics, 177–181
  adolescent attitudes toward, 181–188
  dropouts' attitudes toward, 205–207
  parents' attitudes toward, 190–191
  and socialization, 177–181
  student participation in, 184–186
  teachers' attitudes toward, 191–192
Sex education, 320–330
  attitudes toward, 321–322, 326–327
  guidelines for, 324–326
  parents, 322
  schools, 320–324
  society, 321–323
Sex-information sources, 314–320
  experience, 315–317
  literature, 315–317
  minister, 315–317
  parents, 315–317
  peers, 315–317
  physician, 315–317
  schools, 315–317, 319–320
Sexual attitudes, 304–306
Sexual behaviors:
  abortion, 163, 297, 299, 318–319
  attitudes on, 304–306
  and contraception, 296–297, 298
  and education, 313, 315–317, 319–320
  extramarital, 163, 170
  and family, 312–313
  homosexuality, 163, 318–319
  incidence of, 301–304, 306–311

Sexual behaviors *(continued)*
  masturbation, 38–39, 318–319
  media's effect on, 296
  petting, 302–304, 310–311, 318–319
  premarital, 163, 170, 304–314
  and society, 297–299
  and technology, 295–296
  and venereal disease, 318–320, 328–330
Sexual evolution, 294–295
Sexual revolution, 304–311
Socialization:
  and culture, 80–82
  developmental, 84–103
  by parents, 87–90, 96–97
  by peers, 96–97
  primary, 87–88, 94
Socialization stages:
  acquisition, 85, 86–93
  confirmation, 85, 93–95
  identity, 85, 102–103
  integration, 85, 100–102
  maturation, 85, 95–100
Social roles, 5, 7–8, 11–12
Sturm und Drang, 21, 25, 31
Subculture, 218–220
  ethnic group, 219
  minority, 219
  race, 219
  social class, 219–220

Underachievement, 202–204
Unwed mothers, 139–142

Values:
  culture, 33–34
  learning of, 93–95, 116–118, 124, 161–165
Virginity, 37

Working mothers, 130–135
  attitudes toward, 133–135
  effects on children, 132–133